# THE
# CAMBRIDGE
# ECONOMIC HISTORY

GENERAL EDITORS: M. POSTAN, Professor Emeritus of Economic
History in the University of Cambridge, and H. J. HABAKKUK,
Chichele Professor of Economic History in the University of
Oxford

VOLUME IV

# THE
# CAMBRIDGE
# ECONOMIC HISTORY
# OF EUROPE

## VOLUME IV

## THE ECONOMY OF EXPANDING EUROPE IN THE SIXTEENTH AND SEVENTEENTH CENTURIES

EDITED BY

### E. E. RICH

*Vere Harmsworth Professor of Imperial and
Naval History in the University of Cambridge, and
Master of St Catharine's College*

AND

### C. H. WILSON

*Professor of Modern History in the
University of Cambridge, and
Fellow of Jesus College*

CAMBRIDGE
AT THE UNIVERSITY PRESS
1967

PUBLISHED BY
THE SYNDICS OF THE CAMBRIDGE UNIVERSITY PRESS

Bentley House, 200 Euston Road, London, N.W.1
American Branch: 32 East 57th Street, New York, N.Y. 10022

©

CAMBRIDGE UNIVERSITY PRESS

1967

Printed in Great Britain by
Spottiswoode, Ballantyne & Co. Ltd.
London and Colchester

# CONTENTS

## CHAPTER I

## The Population of Europe
## from the Black Death to the Eve of the Vital Revolution

By KARL F. HELLEINER, Professor of Economic History, University of Toronto

## CHAPTER II

## Scientific Method and the Progress of Techniques

By A. RUPERT HALL, Professor of the History of Science and Technology, Imperial College, London

## CHAPTER VI

## Colonial Settlement and Its Labour Problems

By E. E. RICH, Professor of Imperial and Naval History, University of Cambridge, and Master of St Catharine's College

## CHAPTER VII

## Prices in Europe from 1450 to 1750

By F. P. BRAUDEL, Directeur du Centre de Recherches Historiques, Professeur au Collège de France and F. SPOONER, Professor of Economic History, University of Durham

## CHAPTER VIII

### Trade, Society and the State *page 487*

By C. H. WILSON, Professor of Modern History, University of Cambridge

## BIBLIOGRAPHIES

# ILLUSTRATIONS

*page*

# PREFACE

Since this volume and its successor were planned, in 1948, to set out the economic history of the wider world which was brought together in a new sense by the geographical discoveries of the fifteenth and sixteenth centuries, interest in these problems has become noticeably broader and more active. To some extent the spread of interest derives from that quickening of historical and economic study which accompanies political development, part of the intellectual apparatus of emergent nationalism. Interest has been focused on indigenous societies and economies, and on their reactions to European traders, missionaries, settlers and administrators. New studies have called for a review of much which had previously been accepted, and have stimulated fresh enquiry into many aspects of European history, so that European studies also have received a fresh impetus, and the motivation, machinery, and achievements of European expansion have been more closely studied and subjected to different and more cogent criticism. Discussion must now be formulated, not against the simple theory that trade follows the flag, but in terms which take account of the concepts of a dual society, of under-developed territories, dependent economies, primary producers, terms of trade, capital formation, protected markets, bulk purchasing and colonial nationalism. The *pacte coloniale* has become highly complicated.

Much of the modern approach to the problems of imperialism is ideological; and much is legalistic and constitutional. As national fulfilment is achieved, however, emphasis becomes increasingly economic. This must inevitably happen as external investment dries up or is squeezed out, compassion withdraws and the emergent countries are left to balance their economies, produce for their domestic markets at prices which can be afforded, and produce for world markets at prices and in quantities which attract consumers but which still allow necessary external purchases to be made. The new states, whether as recipients of aid or as managers of viable and independent economies, are parts of a world trade-system; as were the colonies from which they have emerged. The situation is vitally different from that of the old colonial, mercantilist system with its Navigation Acts and Sugar Duties, its *pacte coloniale* and its *exclusif* policy in trade, finance and shipping. Different too from the Dual Mandate System with its comparatively simple prescription of making the resources of tropical territories available for the civilized world and of making the resources of the civilized world available to tropical peoples. For there was necessarily inherent in the mandatory approach something of an element of European priority, at least in assessing and controlling the situation; and that priority has disappeared as a basic assumption, to reappear only as an economic necessity.

The fact that the emergent and under-developed territories must live within the context of a world-economy is less exciting than the fact that they must themselves decide how to do so, and must implement their own decisions. But not less significant. Their independence of status and freedom of action are new things, signs of a new era. Their economic involvement is a continuing result of the series of events which brought Europeans by maritime routes to their territories, and of the purposes and concepts which lay behind those events. For western Europe and the other continents of the world—Africa, America, Asia and, ultimately, Australia—were brought into new, closer and more continuous econo- mic relations by the changes which stemmed from the movement of expansion which began with the Portuguese voyages of discovery in the second half of the fifteenth century. A new world-economy was then created, an economy in which Lisbon and the *Casa da Contratación* con- trolled the spice trade of the world and directed the fleets of spice-ships to their entrepot at Goa and then to the anchorages of the Tagus. Portuguese administrative and financial techniques proved inadequate for such lucrative burdens, the Dutch proved their capacity as interlopers (a word, significantly, of Dutch origin), and the 'great rich purses of the Antwerpians, subjects of the King of Spain, ingrossed them all into their own hands, yea oftentimes gave money for them before hand, making thereof a plaine Monopoly'. The complaint is that of the secretary of the Merchant Adventurers of England, who would gladly have created such a monopoly for themselves; what is a matter of fact, not of opinion, is that the spice trade under Dutch control formed an invaluable adjunct to their trade to the Baltic and to north-western Europe. The new and expanded trade in spices and eastern produce was geared into a trade- system which spread throughout Europe and, indeed, across the Atlantic.

Before the Portuguese lost their control they had fashioned a pattern of trade in which the vital harbours of East Africa were incorporated, and in which negro slaves from the west African coast were given an essential role in the advance of colonial settlement, from the Atlantic islands to Brazil and the mainland of America. The sugar trade had bound together the continents of Europe, Africa and America, and shipping was the essential link. Already too, before Portuguese predominance had been clearly thrown off, the plunder of the Inca and Aztec kingdoms, anticipating the great revenues from the silver mines, had begun to flow into the Spanish treasury, and the Habsburg kings were discovering that the great European bankers upon whom their ability to acquire the imperial title, and their subsequent ability to maintain it, rested were beginning to be more attracted by Castilian control of the specie which was upsetting the currency system of Europe than by the hereditary revenues of the Spanish monarchy.

By the end of the sixteenth century not only were the agricultural economies of the spice islands, the domestic industries of large parts of India, the Arab trading-economy of the Indian Ocean and of the western Pacific, the native societies of West Africa and the way of life in the Caribbean islands and in the vast areas of the two vice-royalties of Spanish America, all deeply affected by the impact of Europeans; Europe itself was in a process of radical re-organization for which the new, sea-borne, regular and comparatively easy access to the new worlds of Africa, Asia and America was largely responsible. It is of course true that access to the trade of Africa and of Asia had been available earlier, although America was previously unknown and indeed remained unacceptable as a separate land-mass for many years after its discovery. The 'silk-route' across Asia had brought the produce of China to Rome, the medieval grocer traded in *kolonialwaren*, and the great impulse to explore the seas in the fifteenth century was as much motivated by a desire to turn an existing and lucrative trade (the source of much of the wealth of Venice, Genoa and Pisa) into new channels, as by eagerness to establish new trades. It is equally true that the process of change is not yet complete, and that large areas of the world still live in isolation from the economic currents of the rest of the world. But when all the reservations have been made, it remains that the economy of the world was brought into a new and lasting coherence by the Discoveries, and by the way in which the Discoveries were exploited.

In allocating two volumes to the problem of the creation and nature of this world-economy, the editors hope that they may be able to set out objective accounts of the situation in Europe which led to the desire for overseas trade and settlement, the motives which derived in large part from that situation, and the past experience and accepted ideas and institutions which the Europeans brought to the problem of satisfying their requirements by securing control of non-European commodities, lands and even peoples.

The approach is, perhaps, uncompromisingly European. This is due to the conviction that the world-economy which resulted *was* European in incentive, in organization, and in its pre-occupations. The results on non-European societies were certainly as noteworthy as those in Europe, sometimes immediate and overwhelming, as in the virtual elimination of the society of the Carib Indians in the West Indies or the overthrow of the Mexican and Peruvian kingdoms by the Spanish conquistadors. But the reactions upon non-European societies were normally more insidious and slow to gain recognition. It was the French in the late nineteenth century who described the process as that of a *tache d'huile*, a creeping penetration of European ideas and influences reminiscent of the spread of a drop of oil on a piece of blotting-paper. Shattering, stimulating, or merely insidious, the results for non-European societies are in any case a separable story (if not essentially separate), to be told from a different point of view and by the use of different techniques and different kinds of evidence. First, even from the non-European point of view, it is essential to get the European aspects in perspective. For it is clear that the Europeans were the active creators of the new bonds. It was Europe which sought out the New World, not the New World which discovered Europe, Europeans who controlled the exchanges which were established, who came to trade or to settle according to their needs; not Asiatics, American Indians or Indonesians, who imposed their own prescriptions upon their contacts with the Europeans.

In approaching these problems from a European stand-point, moreover, we cannot easily overlook the fact that it was a Europe in a state of ferment, of challenge to existing institutions and concepts, which brought the New World within its orbit; in its turn, access by new, regular and comparatively reliable routes to the New World played a significant part in shaping the changes which were taking place in Europe. To divide these two aspects of a study of the problem is difficult and to some extent improper, and the editors have not set out to attempt it. They have, however, tried to deal with the European contributions to the situation in the first volume devoted to this issue—with population, currency, labour shortages, scientific achievements, agricultural developments, and commercial organization. In the second volume the results in developing social classes, trade techniques, and above all in economic precepts, will come under review. There is neither chronological sequence between the two volumes nor logical distinction between them. They should stand together, setting out different aspects which in the end should be considered together; and much of the allocation to one volume or the other has been the result of the simple difficulties in getting the chapters written by specified times!

Although within these two volumes no chronological division has been attempted, it is nevertheless necessary to emphasize that in such a study chronology is all-important. The danger is not so much that facts will be related in their wrong sequence—for a badly-constructed narrative will eventually fall apart by itself—but that events and movements will be considered out of the context of contemporary developments in other fields. It is, for example, difficult to overstate the consequences which stemmed from the fact that the New World was opened up before the eyes of a Europe in which the omnicompetence of the nation-state was a new but generally-accepted doctrine. The nation-state was certainly not a novelty in the fifteenth century; in its concepts and claims, its loyalties and animosities, its legal and economic dogmas, it had been long a-growing. But in its conjunction with reformed and national churches it took on a new authority and purpose; and as national statesmen, beating together the ideas and the administrative machinery for a national economy, appreciated the potential wealth to be derived from the overseas territories which were being revealed, they incorporated such territories into their theories and into their practice.

The results were even more startling than those which derive from a comparable situation—the way in which the exploration of outer space has coincided with an era in which capitalist and communist ideologies confront each other, each dominated by a single great world power. For the economic advantages of the New World were immediately apparent (though not easily developed) and overseas possessions fell easily and naturally into the contexts of a self-contained national economy which seemed so essential to the European statesmen of the fifteenth and sixteenth—and indeed subsequent—centuries.

At the first challenges, European reactions were gravely affected by the dominant position of the Iberian states; and not only was the strength of the Habsburg monarchy in Europe accepted as deriving largely from its overseas possessions, but the opposition to that monarchy and to the world order for which it stood was embittered by fears, ambitions and animosities, which were directly traceable to the New World. 'And entringe into the consideracion of the way how this Phillippe may be abased, I meane firste to begynne with the west Indies', wrote Richard Hakluyt, adding, with a pungency which lost little in the phrasing, 'If you touche him in the Indies, you touche the apple of his eye, for take away his treasure, which is *nervus belli*, and which he hath almoste oute of his west Indies, his olde bandes of souldiers will soone be dissolved, his purposes defeated, his power and strengthe diminished, his pride abated, and his tyranie utterly suppressed.'

The increasing hostility between England and Spain, developing from the point at which Phillip had supported Elizabeth's claims to the throne against Mary Queen of Scots at the Treaty of Cateau Cambrésis to the preparations for the Armada and Drake's raid on Cadiz, owed much to overseas rivalries. For the *larrecins sans fin* of the Devonshire seamen in the Channel, and Drake's fabulous round-the-world plundering voyage, were in large part traceable to the Spanish attack on the English ships at San Juan d'Ulloa and to Hawkins's attempt, naif perhaps but not improbable in itself, to supply the Spanish planters with the West African slaves which they required.

In this there can be no question of sole causation, nor any serious possibility of estimating the relative importance of the various factors involved. But it must be accepted that the mood in which the Europeans approached the newly-discovered world, and organized production and trade there, was all-important. These Europeans were in any case the volatile elements in the populations of their states. Sometimes inspired by inordinate greed, sometimes by missionary fervour, sometimes by simple personal assertiveness, they were always affected deeply by the national rivalries of their Europe and by the theories implicit in those rivalries; more, in fact, by the theories than by the realities, especially in economic affairs. For while the day-to-day life of Europe was changing slowly, and was affected at first but little (often at fourth or fifth hand, or even more remotely) by the flow of produce, the creation of wealth, and the market for labour which the New World offered, the nation-states which increasingly controlled men's lives and dominated their thoughts directed their efforts unremittingly to the bullion which was the first scintillating product of overseas dominion.

The dynamic of the bullion-flow was the more compulsive because of the dogma, easily justifiable in any age and most especially so in an age of mercenary soldiers, that 'bullion is the sinews of war'. That dogma in turn led to preoccupation with a balance of trade, and so to efforts to regulate the trade which developed with colonies in such a way as to redress national trade-balances and to leave the increments from shipping, finance and maritime insurance, in the balance-sheets of the mother country.

The colonial world, in short, fitted well into the mercantile system. It was only a question of time until the Old Colonial System emerged, in the shape of the Navigation Acts, from the opposition of Cromwellian England to the Dutch and their prosperity. The maritime and colonial wars of the eighteenth century were only in part the outcome of colonial and trade rivalries, the clash of hostile colonial systems. There was in them a notable element of purely personal rivalry—the rivalries of such men as Dongan and de la Barre, of Clive and Dupleix, of Washington and Montcalm—and much of competition for trade between Hudson's Bay Company, Ohio Company, and Compagnie du Nord; or between East India Company and Compagnie des Indes Orientales; or the Dutch East and West India Companies. There was much, too, of an increasingly irreconcileable hostility between Bourbon sun-kings and Stuart and Guelph rulers of the seas, a hostility in which overseas territories and overseas trade assumed steadily growing importance.

European rivalries for the wealth, and for the strategic strength, of New World possessions have gone through many phases; but both the constitutional relationships and the economic development of overseas territories have throughout been conditioned by the fact that they came to hand in a period when a national economy and its balances were a heavy preoccupation. From time to time emphasis has changed, and the devices by which the ends have been sought have varied greatly, as has the social class which has manipulated those devices. But the outcome has always been the same; the ends of the earth have been brought together, and the urge to keep them together has been perpetuated because at the formative time the mould of a controlled national economy was clamped on both east and west.

That European interests should predominate in this relationship—to such an extent that, even when political control has been removed, economic dependence remains a lasting heritage—was in part due to the purposefulness and competence of the Europeans who made the contacts, in part to the ambitions and organization of the European states. Much, however, was the result of economic circumstances. Whatever the motives with which the Europeans set out on their quests, what they most often found were vast, fertile, and comparatively empty spaces whose most obvious function was to produce the raw materials required by European industry. Preoccupation with spices, and then with bullion, had first to be played out, though neither has ever been completely abandoned. Then tobacco had to find its proper level in the ranking of consumer-goods in the European market, and furs for felting and sugar for common consumption proved the most desirable raw materials which the New World produced in bulk for the consumption of the Old World.

This outcome was disappointing, for there had been great hopes of pitch, rosin, tar, hemp, straight-grained timber for spars and standing rigging—all the secondary materials for naval equipment hitherto derived from a highly vulnerable trade with the Baltic. The unbelieveable wealth of the Grand Banks of Newfoundland—soles above a yard long, and especially a 'great abundance of that kinde of fish which the Savages call baccaloes [cod]', wrote a contemporary of John Cabot— indeed led to such a development in shipping that the crossing of the Atlantic became almost a commonplace. By 1578 it was reported that, taking one year with another, between thirty and fifty English ships annually found their way to the Grand Banks, the Spaniards sent about a hundred for cod, and for whaling twenty or thirty Biscayan ships totalling up to five or six thousand tons. The Portuguese cod-fleet numbered about fifty sail, up to 3,000 tons; and though the French habitually sent about 150 ships they were not normally above forty tons each, a total of about 7,000 tons or less. Fishing on the Grand Banks was clearly a very considerable enterprise, of great economic significance in itself, and entailing ramifications in the salt-making industry, in ship-building, and in the domestic habits of thousands of European consumers. It was also a notable nursery for seamen, and was accorded a unique place in the politico-economic writings of the day. But the fishing industry did not satisfy the desire of the European nations for actual munitions of war; nor did any other contact with the overseas world until in the middle years of the seventeenth century the Indian mainland began to produce saltpetre in satisfying quantities; and that was a manufactured product rather than a natural staple.

These disappointments and delays notwithstanding, the European powers were sufficiently impressed with the vast potential wealth of the newly-discovered lands to make great efforts to comprehend them under the control of their own national economies. The ultimate outcome was that they fought each other (in peace and in war) for sole control—which came to mean sole possession—of the most attractive areas, and then treated such areas as satellites to themselves. That the Europeans, operating at considerable distances, almost in isolation, from their own countries and the sources of their strength, should have been able to impose their pattern of life and trade upon the rest of the world was an essential condition for the outcome—that the world-economy which was then created should be cast in a European mould, governed by Christian and western European concepts and dogmas. It was, ultimately, dominated and administered by western European men, a fact which in itself goes far to explain the predominance of the western European outlook.

The ultimate predominance of European interests is easily assumed, especially by European historians; but it is in itself one of the most astonishing and far-reaching phenomena of world-history. Important as the outlook and purpose of the Europeans may have been in bringing about this result, much must be attributed to the simple accident of chronology. For the penetration of the secrets of the oceans was part of a general enlargement of the European horizon. The Europeans who opened up the New World had modified their ships, had improved their knowledge both of the theory and of the practice of navigation, and had entered upon a technological revolution which enabled them to supply goods to the overseas markets which they discovered and to use raw materials in ever-increasing quantities. All of these changes had their place in creating the movement to join together the forum of Europe and the assets of overseas territories, to make expansion possible, desirable and even necessary.

But trade is, in natural conditions, a transaction for the mutual advantage of both buyer and seller. There must be temporary advantages for one side or the other; and the hope of achieving a position of power which can be exploited so as to secure extreme profits is an enduring element in most trades. These are the commonplaces of any trading system, and the technological advantages of the sixteenth-century Europeans, combined with their adventurous outlook, would go far to explain why they secured immediate predominance. But the long-term subservience to the markets of Europe in which colonial economies were maintained was the result not only of economic conditions but also of the military power exercised by the white races at the moment of impact and during the period of consolidation. Cortes set forth to conquer the great Montezuma and the kingdom of Mexico with only 600 men. Their fire-power was only fifteen muskets and seven small cannon which used stones as shot. Indian auxiliaries and later reinforcements played their parts in the final conquest of Mexico, but Cortes won his first swift victories with only his original strength. Examples could easily be multiplied—the victory of the handful of Puritan settlers over the Indian hordes in the battle for the Pannunky corn-field; the dispersal of the victorious Mohawks by Samuel de Champlain and his solitary white companion; or the defeat of the Arab fleet at the siege of Ormuz by the English ships which the Shah of Persia had forced into his alliance. The story runs through the conquest of India, down to the Ashanti and Zulu wars, and up to modern times by way of Omdurman, the Maori Wars and the Burma wars. On many occasions the Europeans were helped, as were Cortez and de Champlain at the start of the story, by allies from among the native peoples; often the outcome was to support by European arms a native regime which would meet the requirements of the victorious Europeans. But these are only variations upon a theme—the theme that European arms were, and were confidently expected to be, triumphant. This was no reflection on the courage, the devotion, the horsemanship or the skill at arms, of the non-European. Yet it was in part a result of the military skill which the Europeans had acquired in a period of constant warfare and of life-long professional soldiering; in part it was due to the terrifying, and increasingly lethal, use of gunpowder and to the selfconfidence which its users derived from their technical superiority.

Gunpowder alone, however, was not responsible for the amazing self-confidence of the fifteenth- and sixteenth-century Europeans. Great as are the literary and artistic triumphs of the period, and enduring and magnificent as are the palaces, cathedrals and colleges which were then built, they rose in a Europe of which agriculture was unquestionably the major industry, and in which agriculture was based upon an ignorant and oppressed peasantry while city life was dominated by oligarchic guilds and councils from whom the new industries were seeking refuge in the country districts. Powerful nobles could be, and often were, masters of great wealth and of great culture; but few indeed were the great nobles who ventured overseas. Predominantly the adventurers

were of middle-class professional origin (professional courtiers sometimes), men of active minds and habits but coming from a social and
domestic scene which ought to have left them awestruck at the culture
and sophistication of some of the societies upon which they burst. For
not only were the Europeans, at best, vigorous but coarse; they came
from a continent in which, the dynamic of the nation-state notwithstanding, the monarchs disputed their precarious thrones with each other and
with ever-encroaching rivals.

To set the European position in proportion to the wealth and power
of the kingdoms of the East it is best, perhaps, to look appraisingly at the
record of Sir Thomas Roe's mission to the Great Moghul, in 1615, on
behalf of the English East India Company. Undoubtedly an able man,
well-educated and acting as the official ambassador of a monarch who
could not be overlooked in Europe (however much he might be personally despised) Roe spent almost three years at the Moghul's court in an
effort to secure a treaty of trade and alliance. He achieved much more
than the previous emissary, William Edwards, who had merely found
the emperor a ready recipient of English novelties; but Roe failed to
secure a treaty although he managed to get reliable terms for English
trading establishments. His failure was partly due to the conviction that
trade was not a matter worthy the attention of the Moghul; but it was
also explained to Roe that there seemed little point in a treaty between a
monarch so wealthy and powerful as the Moghul and the ruler of so
small and poverty-stricken a kingdom as England. The point was well
made, for there could be no denying the discrepancies between the two
rulers.

Yet Thomas Roe, and indeed all Europeans, approached the mighty
kings of the East always as equals, normally as superiors, never as
suppliants. Instructed by a chamberlain that he must approach Sultan
Purveis (the Moghul's second son, ruler at Barampore), touching the
ground with his head, and with his hat off, Roe replied that he 'came in
honour to see the Prince, and was free from the custom of servants';
he demanded equal status with the ambassador of the king of Persia and
of the Great Turk, and when he appeared before the Great Moghul
himself he stipulated beforehand that he should be free to behave according to English customs 'so that I would perform them punctually'.

Roe was an admirable envoy, and he secured treatment such as had
never before been accorded to any European. His achievement was great,
and his narrative most revealing. But he was not alone in his self-confidence, nor were the English the only nation to feel so assertive. The
atmosphere of Roe's Journal is the commonplace of the period and of the
century and a half of which Thomas Roe was the heir. It was the self-
confidence of a military man, bred to the wars; and gunpowder must

have its place in explaining it, still more in explaining why it was
accepted by monarchs who could so easily have resented it and whose
cultural standards often equalled anything which Europe could show.
But there was no hint in Roe's mission at any time that failure to achieve
his objects would be followed by military intervention. To the Indian
princes any such suggestion would certainly have been laughable; and,
indeed, Roe himself was convinced that military action must always rob
overseas trade of its profits, that the Portuguese had 'never made an
advantage of the East Indies since they defended them' and that the
Dutch, who had sought plantations by the sword, had found 'that their
dead pays consumed all their gain'. It is indeed true that he also proclaimed that the English East India Company's efforts merely to trade
in India could never bring the real wealth of India within the British
grasp since that wealth was not allowed to remain in the hands of India's
vast population of potential consumers but was concentrated in the hands
of the nobles and rulers by a cruel system of taxation, rent charges and
service-dues. Avid though such eastern potentates might be for western
luxuries, they had only one necessity which they required from Europe
—firearms. To gain access to the real wealth of India, therefore, Roe
maintained that the East India Company must share in the profits of
ruling by taking a part in that process, by selling military support to the
rulers. This was certainly not a new policy when Roe expounded it,
but when systematically adopted it proved to be fraught with the
gravest consequences for India and was the basis of the links which
bound India to the heels of the British economy more closely and
enduringly than any mere trading nexus could possibly have done.

Such developments, however, were not yet matter of fact at the time
of Roe's embassy. His assurance, and the Indian acceptance of that
assurance, were of course in part due to personal qualities. But they also
represent something of more general significance. The seventeenth
century was still being carried forward on the tide of self-confidence, still
animated by the spirit of enquiry which had led the men of the fifteenth
century to turn their backs upon the land-masses known to them and to
sail boldly into uncharted seas. Of the seventeenth century itself—'an
age of immense energy'—it has been said that 'there is far too much life
in the period to compress it into a formula'. The generalization applies
equally to all the centuries during which the pattern of European
relations with the overseas world was set; and the pattern was set in
a form dominated by European needs, European values, European
personalities.

The nation-state, and military prestige, counted for much. Equally
important were the economic techniques for outfitting and financing
the *voyages de longue course*, for insuring against the hazards involved,

and for dispersing among many participants both the risks and the profits. But the financing of world trade demands not only an ability to underwrite an expedition but the confidence and the courage to use the techniques which are available; and knowledge of world markets and of world supplies to make the trade profitable. A further point of chronological significance is therefore the fact that comparatively easy and continuous access to overseas markets became available to European merchants at a time when they, as persons and often as king-makers, were acceptable and when their 'feat of merchandise' was dogmatically defensible in a sense which was new.

Usury laws and the formal ecclesiastical notions of price were certainly not abandoned in Europe in the fifteenth century, nor were the techniques of partnerships, insurances and loans so simple as to have freed merchants completely from all inhibitions. Much has been written about the possible connections between the Protestant ethic and the rise of capitalism, with no inescapable conclusiveness either from the point of view of logic or of chronology. For it is certain that there was as much avarice abroad before the Reformation as after it, and that there were great merchants, and merchants companies, working with the same techniques and within the same conventions, in the fourteenth century as in the sixteenth. Individual studies of fourteenth-century merchants are few, but when they emerge they are of convincing stature. There were such men as John Cannynge of Bristol, who played a substantial part in financing Edward IV's campaign for the English throne and who set to sea his own fleet of men-of-war, or Sir Edward Shaw, goldsmith and mayor of London, who also did much to finance Edward IV, who personally presented the crown to Richard III, and who then played a prominent part under Henry VII. Richard Whittington, thrice lord mayor of London, mayor of the Staple of Westminster continuously from 1405 to 1422, is an earlier and notorious example of the purposeful, experienced and wealthy merchants who were there, ready to share the adventure with the kings and the admirals, when the wider horizons of the New World were opened up to them. Sometimes, like Jean Ango and the *armateurs* of the Britanny ports, or the Society of Merchant Venturers of Bristol, they led and organized the advance. But whether they led their sovereigns or were led by them, the European merchants were capitalists in a sense which was alien to the peoples of the New World and of the East even when those peoples were already engaged in merchandising.

For the most part the Europeans sought, and found, producers of primary staples, mostly of agricultural origin. In the formative period they were essentially 'Adventurers' in the full historical meaning of that word; they ventured forth with cargoes of European goods, not knowing where, or to whom, they would sell them—in distinction from merchants who knew their customers and their market before they set out. Their trade was, therefore, almost of necessity based on barter; and so it remained long after the routes and the habits of trade had become established. In a barter trade, even more than in a trade based on currency, the differences between European and non-European notions of value and of capital became apparent. For whereas to the European merchant, whatever his religion, the merchant's function was to buy cheap and to sell dear, and his stock in trade was a capital which must be exploited and increased regardless of its value in use, the non-European (as such and until he had adopted European notions) worked to different scales of value.

The situation varied from one society to another. At the extreme, where Europeans met North American Indians and bartered their furs from them, the Indians continued for many years to regard the process as a simple gift-exchange, in which unwanted and superfluous goods changed hands without any sense of value, and with very little attention even to quantity. For them, ironware of any kind, even down to a single needle, had great attractions while their furs could be got in almost any quantity in a normal year. The same basic approach to trade with Europeans was to be found in West Africa, in South America, and in large parts of Indonesia. Even when trading habits had become fixed, and certain sections of the population had developed a function and a place in society by trading with Europeans, there remained widespread economic concepts and habits which differentiated them sharply from their European counterparts. Their motives were significantly different, and to their surprise the Europeans found that supplies of native produce dried up before the market was satisfied and that increases in price did not stimulate production but rather curtailed it since the non-European was then more easily able to satisfy his immediate wants. They found, too, that the point at which those wants were satisfied lay much nearer to the surface and that there was comparatively little interest in long-term acquisitiveness on the European pattern. In so far as they could find a desire to accumulate, it was motivated perhaps by simple covetousness, perhaps by an urge to display; perhaps it might lead to the accumulation of a hoard, but seldom was gain sought as a capital, a means for financing further and yet further gains. There was little of that *appetitus divitiarum infinitus* which was accepted as the constant spur by the European.

So the fur-traders, even when they recognized that they were dealing with groups of professional Indian traders, knew no means as late as the mid-eighteenth century to prevail on them to bring their maximum catch to market. In the same way the Dutch in Indonesia could find no economic incentive to stimulate the production of spices for the European market. They had to resort to warfare, to peddling supplies of arms, to the exaction of 'contingencies' and forced deliveries from the native rulers whom they maintained in authority. Much the same thing happened in West Africa, where the support of Europeans became a considerable element in the balance of strength between the local chiefs, while in North America the Dutch, the French and the English, likewise were forced, each in their different ways, to secure the loyalty of native allies not only to support them in their struggles with each other but also in their efforts to control and to maximize the fur trade. The goods supplied were indeed such as to alter the native way of life radically, to make the Indians of North America abandon bows and arrows and become dependent upon regular shipments of firearms and of gunpowder. But even with dependence on European supplies the native society remained, by European standards, 'improvident'. A high proportion of the annual income was devoted to immediate consumption and to social display, very little went to saving or to any kind of capital accumulation.

Standard features of such trade were that luxuries, firearms, fineries and drink, soon became, and remained for centuries, staple articles of European export; and that native requirements were quickly and cheaply satisfied in the absence of a native profit-motive or (if something of a profit-motive emerged) without a capital-accumulation motive. In consequence, various forms of compulsion were exploited, and this in its turn added to the authority of European demands. Normally some form of military intervention was a necessary element in such a process; the result, according to circumstances, might be the assumption of direct rule by the Europeans, or indirect rule in which the Europeans supported a native ruler (as Roe had advocated in India). Sometimes the outcome was a debtor-creditor relationship which exploited immediate desires, for drink or finery, or arms, and stimulated production in order to pay off the debt so incurred.

From such generalizations it must not be assumed that always the knowledgeable and avaricious European merchant exploited, and erected a system for the long-term exploitation of, the simple and uncontaminated native peoples with whom he came in contact. Endless examples could be given, especially from the Indian mainland, of skilled entrepreneurs who organized and maintained a closely-integrated productive system (whether of muslins or of saltpetre), who knew all the ramifications of credit-finance and to whose 'country-trade' the European merchants were little more than accessories. Great fortunes, a numerous trading class, and an economy which penetrated throughout the life of India, developed in this way; and all were native in origin and control, pre-European in background. The less articulate native trading system in West Africa likewise reveals that European traders merely provided an outlet for a native organization. It was not the European but the African or the Arab who captured the slaves, procured the gold dust, the ivory or the red peppers, and brought them to the coast.

In stressing that, from the start of sea-borne contacts, the Europeans have traded at an advantage, it is important to accept that they did not always derive that advantage from the fact that they were dealing with primitive peoples. They appear to have enjoyed equal privileges when they faced sophisticated traders; and the world-economy which developed has been so centred upon Europe and European needs that political domination has normally ensued, as the only sure means of safeguarding those needs. Only slowly and reluctantly have the economic identities and necessities of the overseas territories been accepted as in their own right. For centuries, pending the date when white settlers would formulate and vindicate a challenge to metropolitan interests which would later be taken up by indigenous peoples, the luxury-demands of Europe maintained precedence over the necessity-demands of native producers. It is difficult to make a dispassionate appraisal of the resultant antithesis of 'developed' and 'under-developed' territories, especially in a period when the values of such a system are under vociferous dispute. But at least it must be accepted that, whatever the moral or racial considerations involved in such a system may be, they would in themselves have been of little importance if the economic attraction to the Europeans had not been sufficient, and the economic competence of the Europeans adequate, to make the system work. The outcome was, in any case, indisputable; the needs of Europe predominated over the needs of the native societies—with the notable exceptions of Japan and, in a different way, of China.

Neither habits of thought, nor analysis of motives, nor even relative cultural developments and command of resources, completely explain this significantly one-sided development. Initially the Europeans hoped to find their way to areas in which a thriving, numerous and industrious native population would provide goods for the European markets, and that desire persisted well into the eighteenth century and was then responsible for much of the enthusiasm for the various South Sea projects which enlivened and distorted the expansionist movements of that century. But, like the French in their advance into Africa yet a century later, the Europeans were constantly discovering comparatively empty and under-populated lands—*terres sans peuple*. Their problem was therefore not only to devise means to stimulate production from such existing and potentially competent societies as they found, but also to organize production for themselves where a competent native society could not be found, or could not be coerced. The means of production were then taken into European hands—land, minerals, and labour.

European control of labour frequently involved the mobilization of a body of alien labourers and its transportation to, and maintenance on, land which lacked this essential element in production. It was not until the nineteenth century that this process began to be reversed and, having hitherto taken labour to the sites of raw materials, European powers began to bring the raw materials to the centres of their population. Even with a modern transport system, this is a method which has definite limitations, and even in the nineteenth century the earlier and simpler solution was widely used, with marked success. This was the period of Chinese coolie labour, the period when the indentured Indian took over from the negro slave in the West Indies and when he created fresh wealth, and fresh difficulties, in Ceylon, Malaya, East, Central and South Africa.

The natural difficulties faced by the Europeans as they made their impact on new territories were in any case considerable; they were greatly increased by inter-European rivalries which led to demarcations of land without regard for either natural features or for native societies. It was, for example, a purely European diplomatic decision which cut off the comparatively well-populated districts of Ruanda and Urundi from the rest of the former German East Africa and left Tanganyika a territory marked by serious shortage of labour. Likewise it was a European decision which cut off the vast area of West Africa under French domination from its only good natural harbour, in the British British colony of the Gambia. There have indeed been occasions when European influence has created a unity, and ultimately something of a viable economy, which did not previously exist—as in Nigeria, or India, Malaya, or South and (for a time) Central Africa. But such examples must be set against those in which European influence split or overthrew a native society and overrode the natural geographic and economic unity of an area. Decision upon the merits or demerits of such action cannot begin to be objective until some attempt has been made to discover why, at such distances from the sources of their strength, the Europeans managed to gain and to retain the initiative. The more the cry is raised that a valid native society and economy were overthrown (or undermined) the more need is there to understand how such a situation could be brought about.

To emphasize that European control of the opportunities presented by the Discoveries was all-important is not to accept a value-judgment that, because the Europeans made their interests dominant, therefore it was right that they should do so. By no means all that succeeds is defensible; nor is all that is defensible inevitable. Each case must be taken on its merits, social, economic, perhaps national or racial; and much that is hypothetical must enter into any judgment since any verdict must rest upon an assumption as to what might have happened if events had followed a different course. Justification or recrimination apart, an understanding of the reasons why power lay where it did, and why certain assumptions were accepted by the power-holders, must lead far along the road towards an objective understanding of the whole problem.

In so far as an attempt to set out the motives and the conditions of the Europeans explains why power lay with them, the purpose of this volume and of its successor is served; and in so far as a review of the historical circumstances fails to explain that situation, it should lead to consideration of other factors, not historical only in that they are not temporary but are permanent. There do indeed seem to have been certain 'natural laws' at work to swing the balance in favour of the Europeans; at least, certain 'economic laws'. The laws of economics, if indeed they exist, are far from simple, and he would be a rash historian who attempted to set them out, or even to adduce them from historical examples. But there remains something elementary and acceptable in such maxims as that 'the difference between buying and selling is ten per cent'—not that any importance should be attached to the actual percentage. The dogma rests not upon the immediate conditions which will cause variations in the percentage but upon the general assumption that the buyer will buy because he foresees a use or a future profit, whereas the seller sells because he has a redundancy; he has little use for his own articles but has need for some of the commodities offered in exchange. The contrast of positions goes further than this, for the willing buyer is seldom a compulsive buyer; he can hold off, or turn to an alternative product, or to an alternative source of supply. The initiative lies with him. The seller has far less freedom of action; he is committed to a sale, and is to that extent at a disadvantage. Seldom has he an alternative purchaser, or an alternative use for his wares, available.

In so far as Europeans had undergone considerable hardships and had met considerable expenses before they made their trading encounters, committing capital and enterprise to voyages from which they would not willingly return empty-handed, they forfeited their position of vantage as buyers. In so far, too, as they carried European goods for barter, and often found them unacceptable (as Aurungzeb found English woollens) they placed themselves at an open disadvantage. But in dealing with peoples who entered upon trade largely for immediate gratification and for social consequence, they found that a reasonable selection of European goods could be given almost overwhelming importance. The luxuries which they brought acquired great status-value and were given marked preferences for their ability to give immediate pleasure—

especially as European competence in distilling spirits gave them a preference over native brewed drinks.

So, for a variety of not entirely logical, or indeed explicable, reasons, European goods acquired and retained a value in trade which more than compensated for the disadvantages under which the European might well have laboured as a trader who had come far to market and who was forced to trade by barter. Although his goods were often of little value in use, and of still less intrinsic worth, and were normally quickly and completely consumed in use, the possibility that he might withhold, or might be interrupted in, his trade threatened disaster. For the non-European societies with which he traded, one after the other, accepted the position of dependent economies.

The implications of dependence become clear when, in the middle years of the eighteenth century, a series of colonial wars emphasized the need for continuous access to the controlled markets of Europe, the close connection between command of the seas and colonial power, and the vulnerability of any colonial society which was not secure in its communications. Then British ability to cut off the Dutch East Indian empire from the markets of Europe brought the economy of the islands to the chaotic state in which Raffles found it. Many other circumstances contributed to the Dutch predicament besides the fact that the East Indies under Daendels were in a state of siege; but they all emphasized the general character of Dutch colonial society as a dependent economy— dependent to the extent that supplies for European consumers took precedence over maintenance of a market in which European goods could be disposed of.

The Dutch East Indian empire is perhaps an exceptional case, in which the close connection between trade and rule must be taken into account. But the interdependence of the system which had developed, with Europe and European interests in a position of overwhelming predominance, may be judged from the extent to which the grand naval strategy of the Revolutionary and Napoleonic Wars turned (as the strategy of the War of American Independence had also turned) round the problems of maintaining communications between the colonies and their markets. The West Indies, the colonies *par excellence* of this period and system, utterly dependent economically, then became the eccentric cockpit of Europe. When any kind of dispute arose, thither the powers repaired, as to a cockpit—as Bryan Edwards, the historian of the British West Indies, noted.

The dependence of colonial producers upon their European markets and upon the merchants who supplied them was without doubt in part due to the preponderance in military and governmental matters of the Europeans, as well as to their greater assertiveness in trade. But it was also

in part due to the inherent nature of colonial trade itself. For whether
Europeans migrated in person and set to work to develop there sources of
overseas territories, or whether they merely traded as adjuncts to a
predominantly native system of production, the new trade to Europe
which developed after the Discoveries, as distinct from the medieval
luxury trades which were diverted by the Discoveries, was almost certain to be a trade in bulk supplies of agricultural surpluses or of other
primary produce. The relationship was ideally supposed to be that
between town and country, a description which somehow seems to
embody a sense of mutual dependence, mutual support, and equal
status. The description is in fact more acceptable in its express simple
terms than in such implied meanings. For to the extent that excess
population, or fears of excess population, motivated European expansion
the movement was one away from areas in which land was dear and
labour was cheap and towards areas in which land was cheap (in plentiful supply) and labour dear (in short supply). Accent on land, and on
agricultural products, was therefore inevitable; and the economic
machinery which lay behind much emigration further emphasized this.
For the normal support for emigrants came either from aristocratic con-
cessionaries who took up their monarch's claims to territory on condition that they achieved settlement, or from chartered companies in
which the stockholders were anxious for early shipments of vendible
commodities—which could only be got from exploitation of the
obvious agricultural possibilities. If the colonists were not to remain 'as
banished men' but were to receive their annual shipments of supplies
and reinforcements, they had to meet the 'adventurers'' reasonable
hopes of profit, and this they did with cargoes of potash and logwood,
fool-gold and spices, fish and hemp, tobacco and furs, and ultimately of
sugar. Few of them fulfilled the expectations of their supporters, and
many a settlement bought its own territory at easy terms (as did the
Pilgrim Fathers, the French of Canada and the Dutch of Manhattan).
Whether they paid their way or whether they failed, they were almost
without exception tied to the soil. So were the native cultivators when
the European came as manager, director and exploiter, rather than as
practising agriculturist.

Tied to export staples, since these were the commodities which
Europe required, the overseas territories began to suffer from what
appears to be an economic law, as gloomy in its implications as any
which Malthus or Ricardo uttered. This was the law of the Terms of
Trade, a law for which little compulsion and less reason can be vouched
but which declares empirically that, as a matter of historical fact and of
practical contemporary experience, the terms of trade simply do worsen
steadily against primary products. This means that over a period more

and more primary products, especially agricultural products, must be given in exchange for the same quantity of manufactured or processed goods. The chief reason which has been urged, in an attempt to explain this phenomenon, is that as men achieve a more advanced economic state, with greater capacity for expenditure, they can afford to spend a greater portion of their earnings on luxuries and a lesser portion on necessities. They still satisfy their basic needs, but at the cost of a smaller proportion of their individual or national incomes. In consequence the demand for luxuries rises in proportion to the demand for necessities, and the value in exchange of the luxuries also rises; and the terms of trade harden against primary produce. Then, as the primary producers find their situation worsening, the only remedy which they can apply to recover their purchasing power is to increase production and to put more of their commodities on the market. This only ends in a further weakening of the price per unit and may well end by driving supply higher than demand and inducing sellers' competition and a buyers' market. It also brings the producer in danger of Diminishing Returns since rapid increases in agricultural production can normally be achieved only by cultivating marginal lands, often at the cost of increased distance from the market and of greater expenses for transport.

The primary producer is driven to these straits because it is difficult, slow, and often impossible to change production from one agricultural staple to another—a matter requiring three or four years at the least, during which period the market trend may well have altered. In contrast, the manufacturer can change with comparative ease from one production to another. At least capital, even when heavily committed by investment in plant, can be transferred more easily in industry than in agriculture, and urban labour is more mobile and more versatile than agricultural labour. The manufacturer, moreover, can not only turn to alternative products when the market goes against him, he also enjoys the advantage of diminishing costs per unit when the market runs in his favour and he can make and sell increased quantities of his product.

In one way or another, then, the consumers and manufacturers of the western world have enjoyed advantages in trade which have perpetuated the initial superiority which they acquired in the fifteenth and sixteenth centuries; so much so that the terms *Colonial Economy*, *Dependent Economy*, and *Underdeveloped Economy*, have become almost synonymous though each is capable of an exact and distinct meaning. Lack of that capital which western men have so conspicuously and successfully exploited during the period of modern history is accepted as the hallmark of all three, and the consequent subordination of the economic and social life of overseas territories assumes so much importance that the end of colonialism as a constitutional status is now widely accepted as of

only limited value unless subservience to western economic domination
can also be ended.

This volume and its successor are not intended as works of economic
analysis, which would explain and discuss the reasons for the peculiar
shape taken by the world-economy which developed in the fifteenth and
sixteenth centuries. Ultimately, without doubt, it is essential that this
work of analysis and explanation should be accomplished. But first a start
must be made by setting out as objectively as possible a substantial narrative of what happened; and for this the proper starting-point would
seem, at least for European historians with their natural background of
knowledge and understanding, to be a narrative of the economic situation in Europe. Problems of population, of scientific knowledge,
ignorance and curiosity, financial ability, national power and national
ambition, and the overwhelming obsession with precious metals as the
only secure basis for national solvency, must all be considered as formative influences. So should the acceptance by the Europeans of the need to
organize an adequate labour-force, and the expedients adopted for that
purpose. In dealing with most of these aspects of the problem it is a
question whether the European situation, over the period, should be
treated initially as a cause of the later development, or should be kept for
later consideration since it was in its turn greatly affected by the impact
of non-European supplies and opportunities. On the whole, there
seemed reason for including in the opening volume chapters on the
aspects of the changing economy and outlook of Europe which are here
included. The problems of agriculture seemed less essentially formative;
for while in general terms it is true that agriculture was the major
industry of Europe and that any study of the European economic and
social structure must be based on the agricultural situation, yet it is
difficult to establish any direct relationship between the agricultural
situation and either the urge to seek fresh territories, or the attitudes towards the exploitation of the opportunities given by them. Equally, it
was not until the nineteenth century, and the development of a steam-
transport system both on land and at sea, that agriculture in Europe was
noticeably affected by overseas production. The diets and the working-
power, as well as the survival-rate, both of the European population
and of overseas peoples, were nevertheless early affected by the way in
which Europeans transferred seed about the world. So a chapter on this
fascinating subject has been included in this volume, and a chapter on
European agriculture during this period has been deferred to the next
volume.

But neither the arrangement of chapters nor the priority allotted to
one consideration over another can be entirely logical or entirely
defensible. Within the range of the two volumes devoted to the problems

of the old colonial economic system the order of treatment has necessarily been affected by the inherent difficulties of planning and editing. Much will have been achieved if the chapters prove interesting and satisfying in themselves and if, when the two volumes together are available, they form a factual historical base from which enquiries into the nature of the world-economy can be launched.

E. E. R.

# CHAPTER I

# The Population of Europe from the Black Death to the Eve of the Vital Revolution[1]

## I. *Introduction*

Among historians—as distinguished from administrators and writers on political arithmetic, both of whom were concerned with the present rather than the past—interest in demographic data was slow in arising. As late as 1764 Voltaire found it necessary to admonish his fellow-historians to pay more attention to questions of population. 'On exige', he wrote in his programmatic article 'Histoire' (*Dictionnaire philosophique*), 'des historiens modernes plus de détails, ... des dates précises, ...plus d'attention à la population.'

Few modern historians, presumably, will demur at Voltaire's injunction; but most of us would protest that, in the field of population at least, his demand for '*détails*' and '*dates précises*' is difficult to meet. Indeed, the historian who undertakes to trace the demographic development of Europe in the early modern period has more than once occasion to recall Professor Sée's emphatic disclaimer, 'Nous n'en savons rien et nous n'en pouvons rien savoir.'

Even if he does not fully subscribe to this declaration the historian of early modern population cannot fail to recognize that his task is formidable. Admittedly, the period to be covered is no longer innocent of statistical inquisitiveness. What seems to be the oldest reference to a count of 'hearths' (*focaticum*) dates from 1092; and Italian cities, no less precocious in this respect than in so many others, are known occasionally to have collected quasi-demographic intelligence as early as the twelfth and thirteenth centuries. On the eve of the modern era enumerations of one sort or another had long since ceased to be a novel feature of public administration, though it was only in sixteenth-century Italy (in Venice, on the island of Sicily, and a little later in Tuscany) that census-like data would be gathered as a matter of routine. To the Italian author Luigi Guicciardini, writing in 1560, frequent population counts apparently were such a familiar practice of statecraft that he expressed his astonishment about the failure of the city government of Antwerp and the

[1] The typescript of this chapter was completed in the autumn of 1955.

territorial authorities of the Low Countries to conduct such enumerations, '*nisi urgente necessitate*'.

But while fiscal, military, religious, and, on occasion, genuinely demographic interests produced, from an early date, such documents as enumerations of 'hearths', muster returns, lists of 'people that receyve the Blessed Communyon', and, towards the end of the period more and more frequently, even something like real censuses, these sources as a rule fail to provide the historian of population with the kind and the mass of quantitative information that become available to him in the nineteenth and twentieth centuries. There is no lack of figures; but almost all of them require careful scrutiny and some processing before they can be used. Most of those data have strictly local significance and do not lend themselves to spatial generalization. Very few of them form time-series. Some of the figures are even seriously misleading and may have to be discarded altogether. Another group of fairly ancient sources, the parish registers of baptisms, marriages, and burials, could, if analysed systematically, indeed yield much more reliable and detailed demographic information than tax registers and the like. However, their exploitation is an exceedingly wearisome business, and has, for this reason, not yet progressed very far.

Thus the demographic history of that 'proto-statistical' age requires that quantitative information be supplemented by circumstantial evidence, as well as by the recorded opinions of contemporaries. But the use, albeit cautious use, of contemporary estimates based on judgment and symptomatic evidence rather than on actual counts calls for some justification. The modern student of social development, accustomed to scientific methods of weighing, measuring, and counting, instinctively distrusts assertions about mass phenomena that are not firmly grounded on numerical evidence. This suspicion is not unfounded.[1] Man's inability to appraise large aggregates, a defect that becomes especially glaring whenever his emotions or interests come into play, has often been demonstrated; and people in the olden days were notoriously bad at estimating large magnitudes. However, scepticism must not be carried too far. Man's capacity to appraise quantities in terms of 'more' or 'less', 'large' or 'small', 'growing' or 'declining'—as distinguished from his ability to guess at absolute numbers or rates of change—was probably not much less developed in the sixteenth and seventeenth

---

[1] It must be realized that, prior to the eighteenth century, only few people had access to the results obtained in official enumerations, since in most countries population data, so far from being published, were treated as secrets of state by mercantilist governments. See Roger Mols S.J., *Introduction à la démographie historique des villes d'Europe* (Louvain, 1954), I, 197 f. As late as 1780 a Swiss clergyman and amateur demographer, J. H. Waser, who had been rash enough to publish the results of his calculations of the population of the city and canton of Zürich, was charged with high treason and executed (*ibid.*, pp. 124 f.).

centuries than it is now. It would seem that competent contemporary witnesses were not often mistaken in their appraisal of short-run trends. (Opinions about the secular trend are frequently influenced by preconceived notions.) Indeed, it can be argued that the specious finality of figures whose defectiveness remains unrecognized, or for that matter a faulty analysis of otherwise trustworthy magnitudes, can become sources of grosser errors than 'impressionistic' appraisals of a situation by well-informed observers. Historians have, perhaps, been unduly impressed by the failure of Dr Price and others to realize that England's population in the second half of the eighteenth century was on the increase. If such qualified students, so the argument runs, could be misled about the demographic trend, how are we to put any trust in more casual observations, unsupported by quantitative evidence? However, it should be emphasized that those men who maintained that England's eighteenth-century population was declining based their opinions *not* on symptomatic evidence, but on—faulty—calculations. Indeed, they must have deliberately discarded whatever symptomatic evidence to the contrary may have come their way, just because their figures seemed to support a different conclusion. We would argue, then, that in default of trustworthy statistics, or together with fragmentary or otherwise defective numerical intelligence, the records of contemporary opinion on population trends should not be summarily dismissed as unreliable. On occasion contemporary observers may indeed have been carried away by their feelings, and become guilty of exaggeration. But they are not likely to have erred very widely in their general view of a situation. They cannot often have mistaken prosperity for misery, progress for decline, demographic growth for depopulation.

For the rest, the student of early demographic history should not expect too much of sophisticated statistical techniques. Certainly, to maintain that one can 'find truth more easily from rough statistics roughly handled than from rough statistics carefully handled' is a logically improper position. But, as the late Professor Greenwood reminds us, the belief 'that, given a sufficiently refined method of investigation, truth can be elicited from *any* data, however inaccurate or biased' is equally untenable. Yet most of our earlier sources are inaccurate and biased, sometimes grossly so.

We are not speaking here of data which can easily be recognized as worthless (or nearly so). No demographer surely will be tempted to press too hard the numbers of able-bodied men returned by the county of Cambridgeshire in the years 1569, 1573, 1577, and 1588—a neat 1,000 in each case. Nor will he attach much weight to the *fouages* of Languedoc, where the 'hearth' is known to have become a unit of purely fiscal significance. But even when one can be reasonably certain that figures were not conventional, but based on actual counts, there is ample room for doubt as to their accuracy or their meaning. As indicated above, hearth censuses and the like were undertaken, almost invariably, with a view to securing fiscal or military information, purposes which tended to vitiate results from the very beginning. Assessment commissioners and recruiting officers, even if they are honest and conscientious, are not the best of enumerators. They meet with distrust and local opposition. Faced with the prospects of new taxes or conscription, people resort to individual or collective evasion. In regions of isolated hamlets and widely scattered farmsteads concealment was, of course, particularly easy. Nor was it at all likely that, even in cases where instructions called for separate returns of the poor, very strenuous efforts would have been made to ascertain the exact number of households that were not expected to contribute anything towards the impost. Society's flotsam and jetsam, the gypsies, tinkers, jugglers, beggars, and other vagrants, probably were never counted at all. Establishments and groups that were taxed separately, or enjoyed exemption from regular taxation—the households of noblemen and clergymen, monasteries, the Jewish communities, military garrisons, the inmates of hospitals, workhouses and gaols—posed special problems of enumeration; yet our sources do not always reveal the manner in which they were handled.

Nor are these the only sources of uncertainty. Before 'hearth' censuses can be utilized for demographic purposes it becomes necessary in each case to ascertain, if possible, the exact nature of the units counted: did such terms as '*feux*', '*foyers*', '*fuochi*', '*haardsteden*', etc. refer to physical hearths, to households, or to houses? Unfortunately, one cannot always be sure. Yet an answer to this question would be a prerequisite to, though it would not in itself suffice for, the solution of another and more fundamental problem, namely that of the coefficient or multiplier. What, in any given case, was the average number of heads per house (or household)? And if, as seems likely, this question admits of an answer only within an uncomfortably wide margin of error, is it not advisable to ponder a further point: to what extent is it possible at all to proceed from a demography of households or habitations towards demography proper?

Obviously, there exists a certain correspondence between the number of houses (or households) and the number of individuals in any given city or territory; but that correlation need not be a very close one, at any rate not in the short run. An epidemic might seriously reduce the number of people without causing any immediate change in the number of families, let alone of dwellings. Warfare, on the other hand, can be very destructive of habitations, but need not result in any great loss of life among the civilian population. Again, an increase in marital fertility or a reduction in infant and child mortality would lead to population growth, but this would not be reflected in a larger number of 'hearths' until twenty or thirty years later. Nor can successive enumerations of urban dwellings or households be relied upon to reveal temporary demographic gains or losses resulting from the ebb and flow of migration, in response to economic opportunity, of unmarried workers: people of this sort would take up lodgings in existing houses.

Still, major and permanent demographic changes may be expected to reveal themselves in the trend-values of habitation, if not instantaneously at any rate in the long run. It follows that the utilization of hearth-counts and similar sources, while it does not permit the historian to form more than tentative ideas about absolute magnitudes, does enable him, as a rule, to trace the secular demographic dynamics of past societies. From the viewpoint of economic history the limitations imposed on us by the nature of our sources, though regrettable, are not decisive. To be sure, some aspects of demographic statics, for instance the size and average distance apart of urban communities, or regional population densities at a given time, are of considerable interest to the economic historian, if they can be ascertained. But his main concern is with the reciprocal impact of demographic and economic *changes*. To an understanding of these causal relationships the history of populations in the proto-statistical age can make a contribution, even though its data may be fragmentary and for the most part mere approximations.

## II. *The Black Death and its Aftermath*

The appearance in Europe of the Black Death in the years 1347–51 —probably the greatest single event in the demographic history of the Middle Ages after the plague of Justinian—had such lasting effects that it must find a place even in an account that deals with Europe's population in post-medieval times. For the plague, once it had been introduced, did not disappear from Europe until about 350 years after its first outbreak. In endemic or epidemic form it continued to exercise a profound influence both on the long-term average and on short-run fluctuations of the death-rate. The fact that in some, perhaps in most, European countries the density of population on the morrow of the medieval period was still below that of 1300 or 1340 testifies to the secular consequences of that demographic catastrophe in the fourteenth century.

The number of victims claimed by that pandemic will forever remain unknown. Not even the crude death-rate of the first plague years can be ascertained; only its order of magnitude may be estimated with some confidence. The most promising starting point for any such conjecture are the results obtained by Professor Josiah Cox Russell from a careful statistical analysis of English sources. His calculations suggest that the epidemic wave of 1348–50 caused an initial loss of life of about 20 per cent. However, it might be well to pause before generalizing from English experience. For fourteenth-century England was much less urbanized and generally less densely settled than France, or Italy, or the western parts of the Holy Roman Empire; and one may presume the chances of contagion to have been substantially higher in the crowded villages, towns, and cities of the European heartland.

*Prima facie* evidence would seem to bear out this expectation. Suffice it to adduce three pieces of information about death rates in widely different territories. The author of a will written at Viterbo on the last day of 1348 puts the death toll in the Tuscan parts of the papal states as high as two-thirds. A South-Tyrolian chronicler asserts that in his parts only one-sixth of the population survived the pestilential visitation. Another contemporary source, a charter for the collegiate church of St Peter in Coimbra (Portugal), states that three-tenths of the city's inhabitants were killed off by the plague. These and similar estimates of panic-stricken witnesses, it is true, must not be pressed too hard. Still, a good deal of much better-substantiated intelligence also points to an incidence of mortality well in excess of 20 per cent.

One must not forget, however, that even some of our best sources of information need to be handled cautiously. For instance, the monstrous mortality among the inmates of some continental monasteries can be matched by English experience. But such figures have to be discounted rather heavily because of the non-representative nature of the samples. Data obtained for the incidence of plague mortality among the members of various city councils, ranging from 27 per cent in Reval (Tallinn) to as high as 60 per cent or even 75 per cent in Bremen and Montpellier, suffer from the same statistical bias: aldermen—the word itself testifies to the fact—were, as a rule, elderly people. A similar bias operates when-ever tax rolls or *terriers* are made the basis of computation: heads of households also constitute an over-aged group. Moreover, information indicating a decline in the number of taxpayers or manorial tenants in a given community is not easily interpreted. Vacancies such as are revealed by mid-fourteenth-century assessment records at Saint-Flour (Haute-Auvergne), the town of Albi (Languedoc), and in Pongau (Salzburg), amounting to 40 per cent and upwards, may indeed have been caused by a high incidence of mortality in those places and regions; but they may also have been due, at least partially, to post-plague emigration.

However, there do exist a few contemporary sources not subject to the same qualifications. We have that unique parish register of Givry in Burgundy, which permits a comparison between the annual number of deaths in the decade and a half prior to the Black Death, and that in 1348. We also possess a remarkably detailed count of plague victims in 1350 in the city of Bremen. Both these documents suggest a death toll of no less than 40 or 50 per cent. Data obtained for some other towns and cities on the European continent (e.g. Siena, Florence, Palermo, Hamburg), though less well substantiated than those for Givry and Bremen, also point to a very high incidence of mortality, sometimes well in excess of one-half of the total population.

The evidence submitted so far is reasonably consistent, and would seem to confirm the impression that plague mortality in continental Europe was indeed substantially higher than 20 per cent, the figure computed for England by Professor Russell. But a few isolated pieces of quantitative information are obviously insufficient for general conclusions. For one thing, most of our figures refer to urban or semi-urban populations; average mortality in the countryside may well have been considerably lower. However, one should not be too dogmatic about this point either. The ravages of the Black Death in rural Scandinavia and in the sparsely settled mountain regions of Salzburg seem to have been at least as frightful as those inflicted upon the inhabitants of neighbouring cities; and a curious document from Languedoc affirms in so many words that the plague sought its victims chiefly among rural folk, 'potissime cultorum et agricolarum'. Furthermore, there are strong indications that Pasteurella pestis was capable of behaving in a surprisingly erratic fashion. Within the same region the percentage of plague victims seems to have varied widely from place to place.

Such discrepancies may have been due, in some cases, to the coexistence of two different forms of plague, the bubonic and the pneumonic. (A third variant, septicaemic plague, is rare.) The former requires for its diffusion an insect carrier, the flea;[1] yet it appears to spread much more readily than the latter, which, though highly infectious in its primary form, is transmitted only from person to person by coughing and sneezing. Pneumonic plague, on the other hand, is a much more deadly disease; it is almost invariably fatal, while bubonic plague gives the patient a chance to recover. The prevalence in different districts of the one or the other variant might suffice to account for the breadth of regional variations in the death-rate.

However, this hypothesis can hardly explain why certain places and

---

[1] While the human flea (Pullex irritans) seems to be a less important vector of plague nowadays than a certain species of rat flea (Xenopsylla cheopis)—see L. Fabian Hirst, The Conquest of Plague (Oxford, 1953), pp. 236 ff.—it may have played a more significant part in medieval and early modern Europe as an agent of infection. See Ernst Rodenwaldt, 'Pest in Venedig 1575–1577. Ein Beitrag zur Frage der Infektkette bei den Pestepidemien West-Europas', Sitzungsbericht der Heidelberger Akademie der Wissenschaften, Mathematisch-naturwissenschaftliche Klasse, Jahrg. 1952, 2. Abhandlung, 218 ff.

areas should have remained nearly or altogether free from infection. Of course, it is quite conceivable that the plague passed by a few remote districts or habitations, whose isolation would protect them against epidemics. This may have been the case with a French seigniory in the Forez region (west of Lyons), whose *terrier*, compiled less than five years after the first attack of the pestilence, lists only one single vacant holding in a total of more than 300. But we have at least one report according to which one of the foremost commercial and industrial centres of medieval Italy, the city of Milan, together with a few other, though much smaller, towns in Lombardy (e.g. Parma and Valletidone, near Piacenza), remained miraculously free from the plague in 1348, or were touched only lightly. Until recently claims of this sort would receive scant credence. It appeared exceedingly unlikely that a pandemic which is known to have raged from Portugal to Poland, and from Sicily to Sweden should have allowed any significant pockets to go scot-free. However, new evidence submitted by Professor Hans van Werveke and other scholars suggests that such was indeed the case.[1] It now appears likely that a sizeable section of the southern Low Countries, including such populous and much-frequented cities as Louvain and Ghent—the latter, with its 50,000 to 60,000 inhabitants was the largest city after Paris in cismontane Europe—remained virtually untouched by the Black Death. The city of Ypres, while it did not escape the visitation altogether, seems to have suffered only moderately. Professor van Werveke's arguments may be supported by the fact that some Belgian municipalities, if they did not actually experience a population increase after the middle of the fourteenth century, seem to have at least anticipated an upward movement in a not too distant future. How else can one account for the fact that the burghers of Louvain should have decided, in 1357, to begin the construction of a new city wall which, when finished, enclosed an area three times the previous size? That same year saw the start of work on greatly enlarged lines of urban fortifications at Brussels and Namur. The town of Tirlemont in Brabant, a few years later, also undertook an extension of its ramparts.

In view of the surprising spottiness of the plague map, and keeping in mind the order of magnitude of vital losses sustained by European cities during some of the worst epidemics of the sixteenth and seventeenth centuries, one hesitates to raise the estimate of Europe's population-loss

---

[1] Van Werveke's views have been criticized, but only partly invalidated, by P. Rogghé, 'De Zwarte Dood in de Zuidelijke Nederlanden', *Revue Belge de Philologie et d'Histoire* (1952), xxx, 834, 837. Other instances of striking local variations of the death-rate are cited for the Bordelais by Robert Boutruche, *La crise d'une société: Seigneurs et paysans du Bordelais pendant la Guerre de Cent Ans* (Paris, 1947), p. 199, and for Salzburg by Herbert Klein, 'Das Grosse Sterben von 1348/49 und seine Auswirkung auf die Besiedlung der Ostalpenländer', *Mitteilungen der Gesellschaft für Salzburger Landeskunde* (1960), c, 91 ff.

in 1347–51 much above the figure of 25 per cent, suggested more than a hundred years ago by J. F. C. Hecker in his pioneer work on the Black Death of the fourteenth century.

But while the initial impact of the great pestilence appears to have been somewhat milder than was assumed at one time, its demographic aftermath was probably more serious than is generally realized. To be sure, the recuperative powers of the social organism became operative at once. As the church registers of Givry and other sources demonstrate, there was the usual spate of weddings upon cessation of the epidemic. Widows and widowers were finding themselves new helpmates, and—still more important for boosting the birthrate—young people were getting married earlier than was customary, when they found themselves unexpectedly in possession of an inheritance which made it possible and perhaps even indispensable for them to start a family, e.g. upon taking over a craftshop or an agricultural holding. Contemporary references to an abnormal fecundity of women after the plague must of course be discounted;[1] but observations of this sort are not without value for the historian: they reflect, even if they naïvely misinterpret, some palpable evidence of speedy demographic recovery.

In this connection attention should be drawn once more to civic undertakings which, if they were not actually necessitated by overcrowding, must at least have been motivated by expectations of further population growth. There is the case of the French town of Rodez (Aquitaine), whose consuls, referring to the reconstruction on an extended scale of its walls, stated explicitly that the work had been decided upon 'cum loca ipsa fuissent ampliora et municipibus et incolis aucmentata'. These words were written in 1358, only a decade or so after the cessation of the pestilence. It is, of course, conceivable that Rodez, like those Flemish and Brabantine towns mentioned earlier, had been spared by the Black Death. But what about Paris and Basle? They are known to have been hit rather hard by the epidemic; yet by 1359 and 1361 both these cities are busy enlarging their ancient ramparts. It might be objected that their actions may have been inspired by military rather than demographic considerations. Indeed we know that in some

---

[1] Or do those observations contain a kernel of truth after all? If, as seems likely, the average length of the lactation period is, in the absence of birth control, directly related to what French demographers call *les intervalles intergénésiques* (i.e. the intervals between births), epidemics would, other things being equal, indeed have been followed by brief periods of slightly increased birth rates. For both widespread illness among nursing mothers and higher infant mortality would result in a shortening of the average duration of lactation, and thus cause the averages of the intervals between births to diminish temporarily. The operation of yet another chain of physiological causation tended to produce the same effect. Since disease often leads to abortion, and miscarriage is known to increase the probability of rapid conception, there must have occurred a slight shortening of the *intervalles intergénésiques* after epidemics.

cases city walls were extended, not with a view to creating space for new houses, but in order to provide protection for already existing suburbs, or else for the purpose of including within the fortifications open land on which some food or livestock could be raised during a siege. But even if such had been the primary objective of the authorities in question, the fact that they decided to start work on new walls at that very moment nevertheless betrays a modicum of optimism about the demographic situation. For, although operations of this kind usually proceeded at a leisurely pace and did not therefore require a very large labour force at any given time, the city fathers must at least have been confident that they would be able to hire the necessary hands at reasonable wage rates in the foreseeable future. The decision taken by a number of German cities soon after the plague of 1348–9 to start work on large cathedrals, though probably inspired by religious rather than demographic motives, must have been supported by similar expectations. Apparently labour shortages and high wages were regarded as merely temporary dislocations, soon to be overcome by immigration and natural increase. As a matter of fact, English evidence suggests a slight check on wages in the thirteen-fifties. All in all, there seem to have been elements of hopefulness in the demographic picture as it presented itself to people in the first decade after the Black Death.

But whatever instantaneous recovery there may have been in the years following the catastrophe was fated to be shortlived. For the plague, though it had spent some of its pandemic power in the first attack, returned with great vehemence in 1360–1, and many times thereafter. In these subsequent outbreaks the disease is known to have visited with particular fury age-classes that had not been exposed to previous attacks, as well as social groups and regions which it had formerly spared or touched only lightly. Such, for instance, seems to have been the fate of Milan in 1361 and of the Southern Netherlands in 1400–1. Having once made its appearance in a given area, the pestilence would linger on for many decades, lying dormant in one place and flaring up in another; and while it is true that some of these later outbreaks were only local or regional, and on the whole somewhat less severe than the first visitation, the harvest of death must have been heavy throughout the second half of the fourteenth and the better part of the fifteenth century, since epidemic sickness was frequently aggravated by dearth and even famine. Crowd diseases, if not actually engendered by food shortages—malnutrition, by lowering people's resistance, caused endemic infections to spread—were often accompanied or followed by subsistence crises, as agricultural operations were delayed or restricted by lack of manpower, and trade and transport suffered from dislocation during epidemic outbreaks. Between epidemics, the death-rate may indeed have tended to fall below normal, seeing that many weak, sickly, and elderly people, who would have died before very long anyway, must have succumbed to the infection, thus leaving a population with a higher mean expectation of life. But there is some evidence that any such tendency was at least partly offset by other factors. Persons who had contracted the plague and survived, while they undoubtedly acquired a high degree of immunity against this particular disease, may have remained permanently enfeebled, and susceptible to other maladies, so that their life expectancy would be diminished.

Nor apparently was the birth-rate in this period high enough to outweigh the potent forces of death; for the age distribution in the last quarter of the fourteenth century was unfavourable to reproduction. While the plague of 1347–51 seems to have been particularly fatal to people past middle age—at any rate in England—some of the subsequent epidemics, especially that of 1360–1, appear to have affected chiefly the young. An English source speaks of that second outbreak as the '*mortalité des enfauntz*', and the same age-specific mortality is reported from Provence and Poland. The creation of 'hollow' age-classes among the young must have had a depressing effect on the birth-rate in the following decades. Other factors which must have influenced the birth-rate adversely are directly related to the physiological effects of serious illness on fertility. It is more than likely that the number of conceptions was sharply reduced during each of the numerous spells of epidemic sickness,[1] and many a pregnancy must have terminated prematurely as a result of the woman's febrile condition.

It is exceedingly unlikely that in these circumstances *sustained* demographic recovery would occur at all quickly. On the contrary, all the available evidence suggests that the initial loss of life, so far from being compensated by natural growth, was followed in most countries of Europe by a further drastic and prolonged decline of population after 1360 and 1370. Even in those regions where the recuperative powers of the race appear to have operated somewhat more successfully, growth was often thwarted decisively in the course of the fifteenth century.

Without displaying in detail all the quantitative information assembled by Karl Julius Beloch and others, we may state that Italy, a country which seems to have suffered as grievously as other parts of Europe from recurrent plagues in the later Middle Ages, was slow to recover from the Black Death. True, certain rural districts in Lombardy and Emilia, judging from the appearance in those parts of a host of new hamlets in

---

[1] Apart from physiological factors, the belief that sexual incontinence weakened man's organism, and made it more susceptible to contagion may have acted as a deterrent to intercourse.

the fifteenth century, seem to have achieved demographic gains. So did some urban communities that were favoured by special circumstances; Padua, for instance, just about doubled her population between 1430 and 1490. But in other regions, and above all in most of the *cities* for which there are figures, the population, if it did not actually decline, appears to have remained stationary. The annual mean of baptisms in the city of Siena, for instance, was approximately the same at the end of the fifteenth century as it had been in the 1380's. Parma is reported to have lost about half its population between 1395 and 1421, but seems to have rallied again before the end of the fifteenth century. The city of Bologna, which numbered 40,000–50,000 inhabitants in 1371, may have gained a few thousands by 1496, but the population of its *contado* does not seem to have increased between 1396 and 1495. Pavia was not even able to hold its own: the city, having declined from 20,000 to 16,000 between 1250 and 1480, lost another 5,000 people in the course of a violent epidemic in 1485. Rough estimates of the number of Sicilian hearths in 1277 and 1501 respectively would suggest that the island was no more densely settled at the end of the Middle Ages than in the thirteenth century. In the kingdom of Naples the sum total of 'taxed hearths' (*fuochi tassati*), having remained about stationary between 1448 and 1475, is reported to have declined from 232,000 to 215,000 in the following decade, probably in consequence of a severe epidemic which decimated the population in the years 1477–9.

Circumstantial evidence agrees well with these data. The recrudescence of domestic slavery in the cities of late medieval Italy—in Florence importation of pagan slaves was authorized in 1366—betokens a chronic labour shortage which was undoubtedly occasioned by the Black Death and its aftermath.

The demographic history of medieval Spain is still largely *terra incognita*. Two isolated figures, offered for what they are worth, show a very sharp decline—from 1,347 in 1248 to 616 in 1495—in the number of hearths in the city of Huesca (Aragon). A similar, if much less drastic, downward trend is revealed by two fourteenth-century records of Catalonia. They indicate that the number of *fochs* (hearths) in the city of Barcelona, no doubt already depleted by the Black Death, diminished from 7,651 to 7,295 between 1359 and 1378, while the province as a whole experienced a drop from about 81,000 to about 78,000 hearths during that same period.[1]

Demographic recovery seems to have set in about the middle of the fifteenth century, at any rate in some parts. Thus in Aragon the number of hearths increased from 42,683 to 50,391 between 1429 and 1495; and

---

[1] Some oblique references to late-medieval *Wüstungen* (cf. p. 14) in New Castile are discussed below, p. 28.

the movement of prices in Valencia and Navarre also suggests population growth in that period. However, the demographic record of late-medieval Spain, sketchy as it is, is not without its discrepancies. The shrinkage of Barcelona appears to have continued in the second half of the fifteenth century: by 1515 only 6,432 *fochs* were counted in the Catalan city.

Of Portugal's population in the later Middle Ages little is known beyond the fact that, having sustained heavy losses from the Black Death in 1348, it was further reduced by a disastrous earthquake in 1355, as well as by a succession of epidemics.

As far as England is concerned, there can be little doubt that the trend of population was still sharply downward in the sixties and seventies of the fourteenth century; and though the rate of decline appears to have diminished substantially during the last quarter of the century, the population by 1400 may have shrunk to little more than half its size in 1348, or, if Professor Russell's estimate be accepted, to something like 2·1 millions. After the turn of the century this secular decline seems to have stopped; indeed, if the evidence of cultivated areas and that of wages can be relied upon accurately to reflect demographic trends, the second and third decades of the fifteenth century must have been years of slight recovery. But the late 1430's—years of plague and subsistence crises throughout Western and Central Europe—brought severe food shortages and renewed epidemic outbreaks; and in the following two decades rising wages both in the industrial and the agrarian sectors of the economy once again indicate a growing scarcity of labour. All in all there is little to suggest any sustained population increase in England before 1450 or even 1470.

In France, a country ravaged by the Hundred Years War, the Jacquerie, the internecine struggles of the Burgundian and Armagnac factions, and the depredations of the ubiquitous *routier*, conditions must have been even less favourable for demographic recovery. Vivid descriptions by contemporary observers of the country's utter desolation in the fifteenth century—their echo rings in the lines spoken by the duke of Burgundy in Shakespeare's *Henry V*—cannot be dismissed as rhetorical exaggerations. These plaintive accounts as well as numerous specific statements about local distress, contained in petitions for tax relief, are substantially confirmed by the quantitative evidence which modern historians have distilled from unimpeachable documentary sources. We know for instance that the population of Toulouse, which numbered more than 30,000 souls in 1335 and about 26,000 in 1385, fell to about 20,000 by 1450. Other sources testify to large numbers of vacant peasant holdings and a corresponding drop in seigniorial revenues. The downward trend of the rents which the abbey of Saint-Germain-des-Prés found it possible to charge its tenants is perhaps the most eloquent instance of a universal phenomenon. Though rental payments are a function of more than one variable, their persistent and drastic decline from an average of 84 *deniers* per *arpent* in the period from 1360–1400 to 56 *deniers* in 1422–61, and 31 *deniers* in 1461–83 would seem to provide *prima facie* evidence of a continuous drop in population.[1] Its outward manifestations—derelict ploughland and vineyards, tumbledown houses and deserted villages—were of course most spectacular in regions which had borne the brunt of conquest and reconquest. Not every province can have suffered as badly as Normandy, where 221 parishes are found to have lost 40 per cent of their members between the thirteenth and the end of the fifteenth century. But even districts that were not directly exposed to devastation can be shown to have undergone progressive depopulation throughout the second half of the fourteenth and the first half of the fifteenth century. Such, for instance, was the case in the sub-alpine district of Oisans (south of Grenoble), where the number of homesteads, after an initial decline of 46 per cent in the period from 1339 to 1428, diminished by another 24 per cent between 1428 and 1446, and once again by 22 per cent in the years 1446–50. How much of this accelerated drop was due to internal migration towards depopulated areas it is impossible to tell. All we know is that such movements (as well as immigration from Spain, Italy and the Empire) did take place on a considerable scale, in some cases as early as the latter part of the fourteenth century, but more frequently after the end of the Hundred Years War. The Bordelais was still receiving immigrants from other parts of France in the early years of the sixteenth century.

'*Wüstungen*'—i.e. the recession of settlements, often enough culminating in the disappearance of entire villages ('*Ortswüstungen*'), and almost invariably accompanied by a more or less drastic shrinkage of the cultivated area ('*Flurwüstungen*')—are also the most striking symptoms of a secular decline of population during late-medieval times in Germany and in Scandinavia. Almost without exception that shrinking process, which in some areas becomes noticeable even before the middle of the fourteenth century, continues long after the Black Death. Indeed, in quite a few cases (Brandenburg, Denmark, Norway) it appears to have gained considerable momentum only after 1370—further proof that in most countries the trend of population was still downward in the last decades of the fourteenth and the first half of the fifteenth century. In the colonial areas of eastern Germany the process of shrinkage did not

---

[1] If these rents were measured in weights of silver they would be seen to have fallen even more steeply, since the intrinsic value of the *livre tournois* was gradually lowered to about 50% of its original standard between 1343 and 1500. See E. Perroy, 'Wage Labour in France in the Later Middle Ages', *Economic History Review*, 2nd ser., VIII, 233.

come to a halt before 1500. As late as 1525, 24 per cent of 332 villages belonging to the bishopric of Ermland were totally deserted. Of their 10,944 *hufen* 5,163 (or 47 per cent) were still vacant at that time.

Farms and fields were not abandoned at random, however. In Germany as elsewhere[1] it was chiefly marginal lands whose cultivation was given up, often soils that had been won for the plough only in fairly recent times. Moreover, recession of settlement was a selective process with regard to the size of holdings. The percentage of small holdings abandoned in the course of the later Middle Ages appears to have been much higher than that of full-sized farms.

To some extent rural depopulation may have been the result of migrations from the countryside to the towns. After every major epidemic, urban communities, despairing of their ability to replenish their ranks by natural increase alone, would liberalize their immigration policies. Admittance to the craft guilds and acquisition of the franchise were made easier for a while. In several cases guilds, or at any rate compulsory guild membership, were abolished altogether by central or municipal authorities. But even though German towns and cities invariably received substantial numbers of newcomers in post-plague years, the great majority of them seem to have been barely able to hold their own demographically. There were exceptions, no doubt; it is difficult to believe that such thriving communities as Augsburg or Nürnberg should not have increased their populations in the fifteenth century. But almost all the available figures (Frankfurt-am-Main, Ulm, Lübeck, Butzbach, Mühlhausen) suggest demographic stagnation and even some retrogression. It has been estimated that Germany's urban population, already drastically reduced by the Black Death and the epidemic outbreaks in the 1360's, declined by another 15 or 20 per cent from 1370 to 1470.

The demographic histories of Germany's neighbours to the south-west and north-west, Switzerland and the Low Countries, are relatively well documented for the later Middle Ages. What is more, many of the available sources have been published and carefully analysed. These materials—the visitation reports of the bishoprics of Lausanne and Geneva, the tax records of the cities of Zürich and Basle with their dependent territories, the censuses of Freiburg-im-Üchtland and those of Ypres, the long series of reliable hearth counts in the Duchies of Brabant and Hainault, together with various supplementary sources—confirm the views advanced on the previous pages. Indeed, Switzerland and the Low Countries conform remarkably well to most of the other European countries in giving no evidence of sustained population

---

[1] For England see Maurice Beresford, *The Lost Villages of England* (London, 1954), esp. chaps. VI and VII.

growth for a hundred years or more after the Black Death; rather the demographic trend was downward, at any rate during part of the fifteenth century. (Our knowledge of the fourteenth century is too fragmentary, and the evidence too conflicting, to permit generalization.)

In nearly every case where decline becomes observable, specific historical circumstances can be cited which may have produced that result. The decrease in the number of 'hearths' in the western half of Switzerland, revealed by the visitation reports of the bishoprics of Lausanne (1416 and 1453) and Geneva (1411 and 1481) can be attributed to the disintegration of the Savoyard state, the Burgundian Wars, and to other military struggles. The population of the city of Zürich, which had fluctuated between about 5,000 and about 6,500 inhabitants during the preceding ninety years, tumbled to less than 4,000 after 1440 and did not regain its former strength before the second quarter of the sixteenth century. It is generally assumed that the so-called Old Zürich War was responsible for that decline. The year 1440 also marks a turning-point in the demographic history of Basle. This city had enjoyed a state of high economic prosperity during the first four decades of the fifteenth century. By 1429 its population had reached nearly 10,000, only to receive a further boost after 1431, when the meeting of the great Church Council brought a large influx of temporary residents. But in 1440 the city-state of Basle became involved in hostilities which culminated, in 1444, in the disastrous St Jakob's War; and in 1449 the Council disbanded. In these circumstances the evidence of the poll-tax lists of 1454 does not come as a surprise: they reveal a sharp drop in numbers, to something like 8,000; and as in Zürich, it was not until after the turn of the century that the loss was made up. Like Basle, the city of Freiburg-im-Üchtland was favoured by economic circumstances in the first decades of the fifteenth century. Its population had risen from 3,000 to over 5,000 between 1379 and 1444. After this date, however, there is nothing to indicate further growth. The disturbances referred to above seem to have crippled Freiburg no less than other Swiss towns and territories.

Turning from the alpine regions to the north-western plains of Europe the student of late-medieval populations does not become aware of any striking change in the demographic scene. To be sure, the Low Countries were, of course, on the whole much more densely settled than mountainous Switzerland. The Duchy of Brabant, covering an area of some 10,000 square kilometres, was inhabited, in 1374, by 300,000 to 400,000 people, while western Switzerland (the country between Lake Geneva and the Aare river), an area of about 8,500 square kilometres, numbered only about 140,000 to 145,000 inhabitants at the beginning of the fifteenth century. The mean density of population in Brabant, then, was just about twice that of western Switzerland (35 as against 17 persons per square kilometre). But the demographic trends were about the same in both countries.

The best and also the most spectacular instance of secular population shrinkage in the Low Countries is furnished by Ypres. A city which may have numbered 30,000–40,000 inhabitants about the year 1300, and whose burghers would proudly compare their community with Paris, Rome, and Constantinople, is found to have been reduced to only slightly more than 10,700 souls by 1412; and her decline continued, albeit at a slower rate, throughout the fifteenth century. But Ypres's may have been a special case. The hapless city is known to have undergone a long siege in 1382, during which she was forced to put the torch to her suburbs. What is more, Ypres suffered from a progressive decay of her woollen manufacture. This adverse development, which was no doubt mainly responsible for the spectacular decline of her population, had no parallel in the other two big cities of Flanders; for Ghent and Bruges managed to prevent the rise of a competing rural cloth industry, while Ypres, less successful in that respect than her rivals, had to watch an exodus of her main trades to the countryside. Thus the loss of population sustained by Ypres may well have been compensated, or perhaps even more than compensated, by demographic growth in the villages of southwestern Flanders.

How misleading it could be to form hasty generalizations on the basis of isolated urban evidence may be demonstrated by a brief reference to Antwerp, whose meteoric rise in the fifteenth century contrasts so sharply with the decay of Ypres in that same period. While Ypres's population declined from 9,400 in 1437 to 7,600 in 1491, that of the Brabantine city, judging from the number of its dwellings, increased by leaps and bounds: 3,440 'hearths' were counted at Antwerp in 1437, and 6,586 in 1496.[1] However, Antwerp's demographic development in the fifteenth century was even less typical than that of Ypres. The general picture of the Low Countries which emerges from a scrutiny of the Brabantine hearth censuses and similar sources is certainly not one of growth, but of secular standstill or decline. True, there is some evidence of demographic gains in certain parts of Brabant between 1374 and 1437; but during the remainder of the fifteenth century the trend was downward. In the Duchy of Hainault the total of rural hearths counted in 1468–9 was lower than the number returned in 1365; and this decline continued in the following decade. Similar, if much less complete and reliable, enumerations conducted in the Counties of Flanders and

---

[1] Both these figures refer to *inhabited* houses, inclusive of suburban habitations; though the sources usually speak of enumerations of 'hearths', the practice followed both in Brabant and Flanders (and probably also in Hainault and Holland) was to count the houses in the different communities.

Holland in the second half of the fifteenth century also indicate a highly vulnerable condition of the social organism.

### Table 1. *Duchy of Brabant*

| Year | Number of inhabited houses | Percentage change over preceding year for which information is available | Annual percentage change in each interval |
|---|---|---|---|
| 1437–38 | 92,738 | | |
| 1464 | 91,957 | −0·8 | −0·03 |
| 1473* | 85,527 | −7·0 | −0·78 |
| 1480 | 86,483 | +1·1 | +0·16 |
| 1496 | 75,343 | −12·9 | −0·81 |

* The year given in Cuvelier's edition (1472) is erroneous. See Jules Vannérus, 'Dénombrements luxembourgeois du quinzième siècle (1472–1482)', *Bulletin de la Commission Royale d'Histoire* (*Académie Royale de Belgique*), CVI, 241, fn. 1.
SOURCE: Joseph Cuvelier, *Les dénombrements de foyers en Brabant* (*XIVe–XVIe siècle*) (Brussels, 1912).

### Table 2. *County of Flanders* (*Three Châtellenies*)

| Year | Number of houses | Percentage change over preceding year for which information is available | Annual percentage change in each interval |
|---|---|---|---|
| 1469 | 9,447 | | |
| Before 1477* | 11,572 | +22·5 | +3·2 |
| 1485 | 8,321 | −28·1 | −3·1 |

* Based on information given in 1485.
SOURCE: J. de Smet, 'Les dénombrements des foyers en Flandres en 1469', *Bulletin de la Commission Royale d'Histoire* (*Académie Royale de Belgique*), XCIX, 105 ff.

### Table 3. *County of Holland* (*Rural Communities*)

| Year | Number of 'hearths' | Percentage change over preceding year for which information is available | Annual percentage change in interval |
|---|---|---|---|
| 1477 | 23,713 | | |
| 1494 | 19,011 | −19·8 | −1·2 |

SOURCE: Quoted by Carlo Cipolla, Jean Dhont, M. M. Postan, and Philippe Wolff, *IXe Congrès International des Sciences Historiques*, I: Rapports (Paris, 1950), 62.

There can be little doubt that these sharp fluctuations in the figures of houses exaggerate, perhaps grossly so, the magnitude of demographic changes. It should be remembered that the majority of rural and suburban dwellings were yet mere hovels, flimsy structures, which were easily wiped out in times of war and quickly rebuilt after the return of peace. (Habitations behind the shelter of city walls usually escaped destruction from hostile bands, but every so often many of them were razed to the ground by great accidental conflagrations. However, such local catastrophes, while they could and did affect individual returns, were hardly of any significance for the totals.) What these figures reflect, then, are the varying conditions of security and socio-economic prosperity. But is it likely that adverse circumstances of a general nature, which caused the number of houses to remain virtually stationary over long periods, as well as grave calamities, which on at least two occasions caused that number to decline sharply within a few years, would not have seriously interfered with population growth? No matter how heavily one wishes to discount the symptomatic evidence of habitation records, the conclusion seems inescapable that the general late-medieval pattern of secular demographic stagnation was repeated in the Low Countries.

As in the cases of France and Switzerland, it is possible to name specific historical events which may be held accountable for what must have been —unless the evidence of hearth counts is entirely misleading—phases of population decline in the fifteenth-century Low Countries. The pronounced downward trend in the duchy of Brabant during the 1480's, for instance, was undoubtedly occasioned by the grave disorders which followed upon the death of Mary of Burgundy in 1482. The drastic decline in the number of hearths in Flanders between 1477 and 1485 is explicitly attributed by one contemporary source to the war between Maximilian of Austria and Louis XI of France.

However, even though he may be quite successful in his search for proximate causes of regional population decline or stagnation, the demographic historian must remain vaguely dissatisfied with these explanations. The observed patterns are too consistent in time and space not to invite speculations about more general forces which, acting in the same direction as those specific factors, may have helped to check population growth in the later Middle Ages. One of the universal and long-run influences—and this the most powerful one—which must have had a depressing effect on demographic trends in that period has been mentioned already: the high mortality engendered by the prevalence of endemic and epidemic plague and other diseases. But then, the sixteenth century was not exactly a healthy period either (nor, for that matter, a very peaceful one); yet, as will be seen presently, it managed to achieve a remarkable rate of population increase in most European countries. Indeed, it is only by contrasting the demographic depression of the late-medieval with the lusty growth of the following period that the phenomenon in question can be viewed in its proper perspective. For this reason, before an attempt is made to form hypotheses about the causes of that secular standstill the evidence for the subsequent upswing will be presented in some detail.

## III. *Demographic Recovery and Advance*

The optimistic notion, propounded by David Hume and accepted as true by many later writers on population, that societies invariably recover from the ravages of even the severest epidemics within a generation or two, while it conforms to the experience of the eighteenth century, is not supported by the evidence of demographic trends in late-medieval Europe. On the whole, as has been demonstrated, sustained recovery—as distinguished from brief and uncertain spells of advance—was long delayed. Yet when it did set in it was apparently decisive, and in very many cases its momentum tended to carry the population quickly back to and even beyond the level attained in the first half of the fourteenth century.

However, enumerations in this crucial period are still, for the most part, widely and irregularly spaced; and while they may leave little doubt that a demographic upswing was under way, they fail to show for how long the process had been going on. Thus, in the absence of time-series, it is rarely possible to ascertain with any accuracy the turning point for a given territory. Typically, the secular upward movement seems to have started soon after 1450; though as late as the last quarter of the fifteenth century, as has been seen above, recovery was retarded in certain regions, and even reversed temporarily by specific factors. However, after 1500 evidence of sustained demographic growth becomes overwhelming in all countries. Indeed, quite apart from the spectacular metropolitan development of the early modern period—a phenomenon to be discussed later—uncommonly high rates of territorial population increase are indicated wherever censuses of 'souls' or 'hearths', or similar sources provide some basis for computation. Tables 4–13 give some instances from different parts of Europe.

These data—a mere sample taken from a much larger body of quantitative information—are of unequal value. It is probable, indeed it is almost certain, that some at least of these steeply rising figures reflect, not so much phenomenal rates of growth, as mounting fiscal pressure or substantial improvements in the methods of enumeration. Certainly, no demographic historian will accept at their face value data like those

Table 4. *Kingdom of Naples (without the city of Naples)*

| Year | Number of taxed hearths | Percentage change over the preceding year for which information is available | Annual percentage change in each interval |
|------|------|------|------|
| 1487 | 215,127 | | |
| 1501 | 254,380 | +18·2 | +1·3 |
| 1505 | 254,823 | +0·0 | +0·0 |
| 1507 | 267,324 | +4·9 | +2·5 |
| 1510 | 263,510 | −1·4* | −0·48 |
| 1514 | 261,377 | −0·82* | −0·20 |
| 1518 | 262,345 | +0·37 | +0·09 |
| 1532 | 315,990 | +20·4 | +1·5 |
| 1535 | 343,849 | +8·8 | +2·9 |
| 1541 | 335,395 | −2·5* | −0·40 |
| 1545 | 422,080 | +19·9 | +5·0 |
| 1553 | 425,837 | +0·89 | +0·11 |
| 1559 | 470,589 | +10·5 | +1·8 |
| 1561 | 481,345 | +2·3 | +1·1 |
| 1562 | 482,301 | +0·19 | +0·19 |
| 1565 | 485,522 | +0·67 | +0·22 |
| 1573 | 487,378 | +0·38 | +0·05 |
| 1595 | 540,090 | +10·8 | +0·49 |

* Decline in the second and at the beginning of the fifth decade seems to be attributable to expulsions of the Jews which occurred in 1510 and again about 1540.
SOURCE: Giuseppe Coniglio, *Il regno di Napoli al tempo di Carlo V* (Naples, 1951), 152.

Table 5. *Sicily (without Palermo and Messina, and exclusive of the clergy and indigent people)*

| Year | Number of hearths | Number of inhabitants | Percentage change over the preceding year for which information is available (inhabitants) | Annual percentage change in each interval (inhabitants) |
|------|------|------|------|------|
| 1501 | 123,662* | 502,761* | | |
| 1548 | 152,989 | 671,560 | +36·3* | +0·77 |
| 1570 | 196,089 | 788,362 | +14·8 | +0·67 |
| 1583 | 194,268 | 801,401 | +1·6 | +0·01 |
| 1607 | 203,400 | 831,944 | +3·7 | +0·01 |

* The census of 1501, unlike the following enumerations, included the island of Malta, which at that time numbered approximately 10,000 people. The percentage increase between 1501 and 1548 has been computed on the assumption that Sicily proper had 492,761 inhabitants in 1501.
SOURCE: Karl Julius Beloch, *Bevölkerungsgeschichte Italiens*, I, 117.

### Table 6. *Sardinia*

| Year | Number of hearths | Percentage change over the preceding year for which information is available | Annual percentage change in the interval |
|---|---|---|---|
| 1485 | 26,263 | | |
| 1603 | 66,669 | +153·9 | +1·3 |

SOURCE: Francesco Corridore, *Storia documentata della popolazione di Sardegna (1479–1901)*, 2nd ed. (Turin, 1902), 87 and 91.

### Table 7. *Spain (Castile)*

| Year | Number of heads of families (*vecinos*) | Percentage change over the preceding year for which information is available | Annual percentage change in the interval |
|---|---|---|---|
| 1541 | 1,179,303* | | |
| 1594 | 1,340,320 | +13·7 | +0·27 |

\* A substantially lower figure (889,440) is quoted by Fernand Braudel, *La Méditerranée et le Monde Méditerranéen à l'époque de Philippe II* (Paris, 1949), 355.

SOURCE: Albert Girard, 'Le chiffre de la population de l'Espagne dans les temps modernes', *Revue d'Histoire Moderne*, III (1928), 426.

### Table 8. *Spain (Navarre)*

| Year | Number of heads of families (*vecinos*) |
|---|---|
| 1553 | 30,833 (clergy omitted) |
| 1587 | 41,901 (clergy included) |

SOURCE: Albert Girard, *op. cit.*, p. 433.

### Table 9. *Spain (Aragon)*

| Year | Number of heads of families (*vecinos*) | Percentage change over the preceding year for which information is available | Annual percentage change in the interval |
|---|---|---|---|
| 1495 | 50,391 | | |
| 1603 | 70,984 | +40·9 | +0·4 |

SOURCE: Albert Girard, *op. cit.*, p. 432.

Table 10. *Portugal*

| Year | Number of hearths | Percentage change over the preceding year for which information is available |
|------|-------------------|------------------------------------------------------------------------------|
| *temp.* Alphonso V (*regnabat* 1448–81) 1527–32 | 252,261 278,468 | +10·4 |

SOURCE: J. T. Montalvão Machado, 'A população portuguesa através da História, *Jornal do Médico*, XVI (1950), 473–6.

Table 11. *Duchy of Brabant*

| Year | Number of hearths | Percentage change over the preceding year for which information is available | Annual percentage change in the interval |
|------|-------------------|------------------------------------------------------------------------------|------------------------------------------|
| 1496 1526 | 75,343 97,013 | +28·8 | +0·96 |

SOURCE: Joseph Cuvelier, *Les dénombrements de foyers en Brabant (XIVe–XVIe siècle)*.

Table 12. *Duchy of Hainault (Rural communities)*

| Year | Number of hearths | Percentage change over the preceding year for which information is available | Annual percentage change in the interval |
|------|-------------------|------------------------------------------------------------------------------|------------------------------------------|
| 1468–9 1540–1 | 29,212 34,286 | +17·4 | +0·24 |

SOURCE: M.-A. Arnould, 'De tellingen van de haardsteden in Henegouwen (XIV–XVIe eeuw)', *Statistisch Bulletin*, XXXVII/4 (Brussels, 1951), 601.

found in the Neapolitan materials suggesting annual increments in the number of 'hearths' of 2·6 per cent over a period of twenty-seven years (1518–45). Growth rates of this order of magnitude are characteristic of early colonial development, but are not likely to be achieved in an old country. Even in cases where the rate of increase which may be inferred from our data is less spectacular, an element of exaggeration may conceivably be present. But while individual figures may be suspect, the overall picture which emerges from a synopsis of sixteenth-century sources is perfectly clear in its outlines: all the evidence, statistical and

Table 13. *Territory of Zürich (without the city of Zürich)**

| Year | Estimated number of inhabitants | Percentage change over the preceding year for which information is available (mean) | Annual percentage change in each interval |
|------|-------------------------------|----------------------------------------------------------------------------------|-------------------------------------------|
| 1467 | 26,700–28,900 | | |
| 1529 | 48,100–58,790 | +92·3 | +1·4 |
| 1585 | 69,975–85,525 | +45·5 | +0·81 |
| 1649–50 | 90,000 | +15·8 | +0·24 |

\* The area of the territory (*Landschaft*) over which the city of Zürich exercized sovereign rights since the first half of the fifteenth century was only slightly smaller than that of the present canton of Zürich.

SOURCE: Werner Schnyder, *Die Bevölkerung der Stadt und Landschaft Zürich vom 14.–17. Jahrhundert* (Schweizer Studien zur Geschichtswissenschaft, XIV/1), 108.

other, points to a pronounced secular upswing of Europe's population.

The long-run trends of wage-rates and prices in various countries of Europe lend further support to this view. Recent investigations[1] have shown that in many European regions real wages of urban producers as well as the quantity of foodstuffs obtainable in exchange for a physical unit of industrial products declined sharply in the last quarter of the fifteenth, and throughout the sixteenth century. The conclusion to be drawn from this and related evidence seems inescapable: one has to assume that, in the period under review, the pressure of population on its land resources was mounting.

In sixteenth-century Germany, for example, symptoms of demographic expansion seem to have been so strong and numerous that quite a few contemporary writers felt constrained to comment on the phenomenon. As early as 1483 the author of an Erfurt chronicle was struck by the evidence of population growth, and tried to account for it by the fact that 'within these twenty years there has not been any real pestilence; and seldom is there a couple but they have eight, nine, or ten children'. A few decades later Aventinus, the Bavarian humanist and court historiographer, also remarked on the great generative power of his nation: it looked to him as if people in Germany grew on trees! Similar observations, though expressed in a much gloomier vein, are found in the preface to Sebastian Franck's *Germaniae Chronicon* (Augs-

[1] See E. H. Phelps Brown and Sheila V. Hopkins, 'Wage-rates and Prices: Evidence for Population Pressure in the Sixteenth Century', *Economica*, new ser., XXIV (1957), 290–306; Ingrid Hammarström, 'The "Price Revolution" of the Sixteenth Century: Some Swedish Evidence', *Scandinavian Economic History Review*, V (1957), 118–54, esp. 136 ff.; E. H. Phelps Brown and Sheila V. Hopkins, 'Builders' Wage-rates, Prices and Population: Some Further Evidence', *Economica*, new ser., XXVI (1959), 18–38.

burg, 1538). Speaking more specifically of Swabia and Bavaria, the author writes:

These lands give enough folk to the rest of the world; yet is there such an abundance [of people] that landed property and rents for dwellings be become so very dear that they can hardly go any higher. I hold that, unless God ordains war, and a mortality intervenes, we must once again as of old be mustered out, by lot or otherwise, and make to seek foreign lands, and depart, like the gypsies. . . . Now, an hundred thousand peasants, it is said, have perished in the rebellion [of 1525], yet there is no lack of men; rather all villages are so full with people that noone is admitted. The whole of Germany is teeming with children.

Another South-German chronicle of the sixteenth century, the so-called *Zimmerische Chronik*, also uses emphatic language to describe the growing pressure of population on land. 'In our times,' it says, 'the people in Swabia as well as in all the other countries are greatly augmented and increased, whereby the land has been opened up more than within the memory of men; and hardly a nook, even in the bleakest woods and on the highest mountains, is left uncleared and uninhabited.' After this general reference to clearing operations, the author proceeds to report in detail on the progress of settlement in the county of Zimmern during recent times: how droves of people had been coming down from the crowded Allgäu, where they could no longer support themselves; how they had asked and been given permission to start clearings; and how these colonists had won back for the plough lands that had long since been abandoned and reverted to bush, as well as made inroads on ancient forests. 'And it passes belief how greatly these [new] villages have increased in inhabitants and dwellings within a few years, as is evident nowadays.'

Lest it be thought that this was an isolated case of demographic expansion let us emphasize at once that similar instances of systematic reoccupation of anciently deserted land, and renewed clearing activities, are met with in many other parts of sixteenth-century Germany, especially in the east. One of the best-documented cases of demographic recovery and advance in western Germany comes from the Principality of Osnabrück. The population of this territory is estimated to have increased by 84 per cent between 1500 and 1604. For the neighbouring Sauerland an average annual increment of about four per thousand over the period from 1576 to 1618 has been calculated. Comparable and even higher rates of growth are found elsewhere, for instance in Hesse and in the Tyrol.

Clearings and resettlement, however vigorously pursued, were not sufficient in the long run to maintain the previous ratio of full-sized farms in an agrarian society that was growing by leaps and bounds. Indeed, among the strongest indications of secular demographic growth in sixteenth-century Germany is the disproportionate increase in the number of small holdings, not only in East-Elbia, where the rise of the *Gutsherrschaft* involved the gradual elimination of the old manorial tenantry and the creation of numerous tiny cottage-holdings, but also in regions where development was in the direction of peasant-ownership. In some areas, where *morcellement* proceeded so far that the economic viability of the fragments became questionable, territorial legislation attempted—not always successfully—to stop the process.[1] At the same time efforts were made by some princes to provide for the surplus population of the countryside in other ways. The Saxon Elector August I (1553–86) is known for his systematic purchases of large estates, which he ordered to be split up into peasant holdings. Similar agrarian policies were pursued elsewhere in Central Germany.[2]

However, fragmentation of farms and domains, while it may have led to a more intensive utilization of the soil, and thus provided a modicum of relief for population pressure, was neither a complete nor a permanent solution to the problems created by rapid demographic expansion. The surplus population of the countryside had to find additional outlets. What other opportunities presented themselves? The cities and towns undoubtedly continued to absorb fair numbers of rural folk, and the spreading domestic system of manufacture also provided alternative employment. Moreover, in the last years of the fifteenth and the first decades of the sixteenth century streams of migrants are known to have converged on the booming mining areas of Saxony, Bohemia, and the Tyrol. But perhaps the most significant development—apart from the clearing operations referred to above— was the resumption, after 1500, of the old German movement eastwards.[3] The number of people involved in these younger migrations (including the religiously-motivated migrations of the Hutterites, the Dutch Mennonites, and other sectarian groups) may not have been very much smaller than the number of those who had taken part in the great colonial enterprises of the twelfth and thirteenth centuries.

Nor was Germany the only country whose economy was called upon to adjust itself to rapid population growth. Switzerland, whose demographic development in the late fifteenth and the sixteenth centuries has already been illustrated with some partial figures, may be cited as another example of a region where population increase provided a fresh stimulus

[1] See Friedrich Lütge, *Die mitteldeutsche Grundherrschaft und ihre Auflösung*, 2nd ed. (Stuttgart, 1957), 67 ff.

[2] *Ibid.*, pp. 32 f.

[3] See Walter Kuhn, *Geschichte der deutschen Ostsiedlung in der Neuzeit*. I (Cologne-Graz, 1955).

to the progress of settlement in this period. The Swiss population, estimated at 600,000–650,000 about 1450, may have risen to 800,000 or 850,000 by the third decade of the sixteenth century. About that time the War of Religion seems to have acted as a temporary check; but when peace was concluded in 1531 the upward movement was resumed, carrying the population towards the million mark by 1600.

This secular growth, though not inordinate by any means, could be supported only by a determined economic effort. It became necessary for the Swiss to draw upon land resources which until then had not been used intensively, possibly not at all. Some of the sparsely-settled mountain districts of Western Switzerland, such as the Jura and the Vaud, began to fill up fairly rapidly. But this shift of the margin of cultivation apparently was not sufficient to provide for the growing numbers. At this juncture—about the end of the fifteenth century—the Swiss hit upon an ingenious, if morally dubious, method of relieving population pressure, namely organized military emigration. 'Reislaufen', enlistment in foreign armies that is, though perhaps more widely practised by the Swiss than by people of other nations, was not a Swiss monopoly in early modern Europe; nor was it exactly a novelty. But what had previously been, and elsewhere continued to be, a matter of individual enterprise developed into a public institution in Switzerland, where cantonal and federal authorities, under a system of 'capitulations' would supply foreign powers with mercenaries. The numbers of men involved in this traffic cannot be ascertained with any accuracy; but they were substantial. The Crown of France, the chief customer of Switzerland, is said to have been supplied with 700,000 men between 1474 and 1792. It has been estimated that 50,000 to 60,000 Swiss soldiers were serving foreign princes at any given time in the first half of the eighteenth century. A conservative estimate puts the vital losses—all the more serious since they were confined to one sex!—sustained by Switzerland from *Reislaufen* at 50,000–100,000 for the fifteenth, 250,000–300,000 for both the sixteenth and the seventeenth, and 300,000–350,000 for the eighteenth century.

The individual data assembled in Tables 7–9 (p. 22) to illustrate the upward movement of population in sixteenth-century Spain are of questionable validity, and, in the case of Navarre, not even strictly comparable; but the trend which they exhibit is unmistakable. It is, moreover, corroborated by the results of an inquiry into the state of the country carried out in the 1570's on the orders of Philip II. Even though only the materials concerning the provinces of Madrid and Toledo have been published so far, the available evidence is so strong and unambiguous that the demographic development of all the central regions of Spain may confidently be inferred from it.

The great majority of towns and villages stated in so many words that they had never been more populous; and quite a few reported specifically that the number of their houses or households (*vecinos*) had increased within memory. Where figures are given the rate of growth appears to have been substantial. In some cases the number of families is found to have multiplied much faster than the number of dwellings—a sure sign of rapid demographic expansion. Only very few places, almost all of them of insignificant size, admit decline. At the same time, references to vanished villages and church ruins in the vicinity are not rare; but they are couched in what may be described as legendary language, leaving no doubt that these *Wüstungen* must have occurred in the distant past.

When trying to elicit information about the causes of local growth (or decline) the commissioners charged with this inquiry were less successful. Not surprisingly, the answers to this question usually remain rather vague: the healthy condition of the people (or, conversely, the prevalence of disease) is most often given as the reason for the reported population changes. Local immigration or a high marriage frequency are also mentioned among the causes of growth. One answer, interestingly enough, attributes the local increase of population to clearing operations (*rompimiento de los campos e terminos de la villa*).

The demographic record of sixteenth-century New Castile which has just been presented would not seem to lend much weight to the view, advanced by some Spanish scholars, that the fifteenth and sixteenth centuries witnessed a shift in relative population densities from the central to the peripheral regions of Spain. This is not to minimize the progress achieved by such provinces as Navarre, Aragon (see Tables 8 and 9, p. 22), or Galicia. Indeed, the last, whose early demographic history has recently been made the subject of a special study, exhibits some of the characteristic features of an over-populated region. A seemingly inordinate rate of growth in the century after 1480 or 1490 before long created conditions which forced this province into attempts to rid itself of part of its surplus population through large-scale emigration, including enlistment of thousands of able-bodied men as mercenaries. Towards the end of the sixteenth century seasonal migration of labour also was resorted to. Yet this overflow apparently did little to relieve overcrowding. The number of *vecinos*, so far from diminishing, showed an increase from 121,603 to 125,718 between 1557 and 1594. Not even the great famines which struck the country in a curiously periodic sequence (1563, 1573–4, 1583, 1597, 1618–20, 1628–30) seem to have stemmed the rising demographic tide, although they were usually followed by severe and prolonged epidemic outbreaks. Public authorities, intensely preoccupied with the symptoms, if not with the causes, of growing economic distress, were helpless. Almsgiving and the appointment of commissions for the banishment of vagabonds were, of course, no cure for population pressure.

Difficulties created or aggravated by excessive population growth, and more or less enlightened attempts to overcome them are met with almost everywhere in late fifteenth- and sixteenth-century Europe. Adjustment to the changing demographic situation did not come easily to a social economy whose land resources were limited, and whose technology, though not stationary, was advancing only slowly; and one of the most intractable problems of the age was the rise of a sub-proletarian class. There was hardly a country but was plagued by hordes of 'masterless men', unemployed and unemployable, who hoodwinked, pestered, or terrorized the traveller on the highway, the countryman in the fields and on the farm, and the residents of boroughs and cities. Of course, thieving, roguery, mendicancy and vagrancy were neither altogether new, nor for that matter purely demographic phenomena: for instance, as early as 1383, at a time when there could hardly have been any question of 'surplus population', the English Parliament found it necessary to make statutory provisions against vagrants, who were 'running in the country more abundantly than they were wont in times past' (7 Richard II, c. v). But there can be no doubt that the problem of the 'sturdy beggar' assumed a character of unprecedented urgency in this era. It is significant that one of the most thoughtful writers of the Renaissance devoted a special treatise to the problem of pauperism, and that his book met with general interest: Luis Vives' *De subventione pauperum* was published at Bruges in 1526, and presently translated into German, French, Spanish, Italian, and English. The popularity of the picaresque novel in sixteenth-century Spain and France and of the cony-catching stories in Elizabethan England points in the same direction: the rogue looms large in fact as well as in fiction.

It is generally assumed that in England the proliferation in town and country of beggars and vagrants was occasioned by the enclosure move-ment. But this view, which merely echoes one of the favourite argu-ments of contemporary opponents of the great transformation, should not be accepted without a pinch of salt. The agrarian revolution of the late fifteenth and the sixteenth centuries must indeed have caused serious socio-economic dislocations. But the 'putting down of houses of husbandry' (as well as the dismissal of feudal retainers) may have merely intensified growing pains produced in the first instance by a process of rapid demographic expansion which seems to have carried the popula-tion of the realm within two or three generations from its low level in the first half of the fifteenth century back to or near the level attained before the Black Death. If the rise of a native *Lumpenproletariat* (as distinguished from those strange incorrigible wayfarers, the gypsies, who happened to make their appearance in England about this same time) was a source of grave concern to the English public and their rulers, they might have derived some small comfort from the knowledge that many other countries were beset by the same troubles. Henry VII's 'Acte against Vacabounds and Beggers' of 1495, and Elizabeth's 'Acte for the Punishment of Vacabondes, and for Releif of the Poore and Impotent' of 1572—to name only two of a large number of Tudor enactments and proclamations of this nature—have their parallel in scores of similar ordinances issued by other princes throughout the sixteenth century, e.g. by the dukes of Burgundy for Brabant, or by the Habsburg emperors for their Austrian territories. Among the upper ranks of society land-hunger may have been responsible for the spate of litigation about landed property in sixteenth-century England and elsewhere. Population pressure caused not only vagabonds but also lawyers to multiply.

In these circumstances it is not surprising that an undercurrent of Malthusian anxiety should be discernible in the writings of many a contemporary. 'The people are increassid and grounde for plowes dothe wante, corne and all other victuall is scante', wrote an Englishman in 1576. 'People woulde laboure yf they knew wher one; the husbande man woulde be glade to have grounde to set his plowe to worke yf he knew wher.' Sebastian Franck's wistful remarks on the demographic state of Germany in the 1530's have been quoted already. Some years previously (1518) another German, Ulrich von Hutten, had advocated war against the Turks on the ground that it would relieve the country of its excess population. The celebrated humanist exclaims:

There is a dearth of provisions and Germany is overcrowded [*populosissima*] in this age. What we all ought to have wished for—a foreign war, whereby we could relieve ourselves of that multitude—has providentially come to pass; it is providential, I say, that war against the Turks should have become both warranted and necessary. . . . Many are suffering want, many are going hungry; everywhere in cities, towns, and villages idle soldiers are roaming at will.[1]

What may have been a bold novel suggestion at the beginning of the sixteenth century—recourse to war as an effective remedy for population pressure—a hundred years later apparently was a widely accepted maxim of statecraft. 'And herupon', an English author, writing in 1609, assures his readers, 'many statesmen haue thought nothing more profitable for populous common-wealths, then to haue foreigne and externe warres, to the ende that thereby the superfluous braunches might be cut

---

[1] 'Ad principes Germanos ut bellum in Turcas concorditer suscipiant exhortatoria, *Vlrichi Hvtteni . . . Opera* (ed. Eduard Böcking), v, 101.

off.'[1] Perhaps the most outstanding representative of these views was Sir Walter Raleigh. In his *Discourse of War* he says 'When any country is overlaid by the multitude which live upon it, there is a natural necessity compelling it to disburden itself, and lay the load upon others, by right or wrong. . . . Wherefore the war that is grounded on general, remediless necessity may be termed the general and remediless, or necessary war.'

However, by that time another and perhaps more promising outlet for the surplus population was opening up on the transatlantic shores, and Englishmen in late Elizabethan and Stuart times came to think more and more of colonization as a means of demographic relief. Indeed, the congested condition of the country became one of the most telling arguments used by promoters of colonial ventures in this period. 'Truthe it is', wrote one of them,[2] 'that throughe our longe peace and seldome sickness wee are growen more populous than ever heretofore; so that now there are of every arte and science so many, that they can hardly lyve one by another, nay rather they are readie to eate upp one another.'

The evidential value of this and similar utterances in a Malthusian vein is not seriously impaired by the fact that many of the writers who voiced fear of over-population—no less than the opponents of the enclosures, who stressed the danger of depopulation—were engaged in special pleading. These champions of colonial schemes and emigration may have been inclined to draw exaggerated conclusions from observations that were in all likelihood intrinsically valid.

Unfortunately, in the case of England it is not easy to verify or correct contemporary statements about demographic trends by confronting them with quantitative evidence; for what few figures have come down from the sixteenth and early seventeenth centuries are anything but reliable. Neither the chantry surveys of 1545, nor the muster rolls of the Elizabethan period, nor the figure of 2,065,498 communicants and recusants upwards of sixteen years, certified to the Privy Council by the bishops in 1603, inspire much confidence. Perhaps the best materials are still J. Rickman's estimates of the population of England and Wales in 1570 and 1600. Though far from unexceptionable, both as regards his data and his method of computation, these estimates by the nineteenth-century statistician have at least this advantage, that they are mutually comparable, being based on the same process of averaging baptisms burials, and marriages. Used in this way—not as absolute magnitudes, but as rough indices of a trend—Rickman's figures leave no doubt that the population of England and Wales was increasing at a fair, if not spectacular, rate in Elizabethan times (see Table 14). In the early and

---

[1] Robert Gray, *A Good Speed to Virginia* (1609), The Epistle Dedicatorie, quoted by Klaus E. Knorr, *British Colonial Theories, 1570–1850* (Toronto, 1944), 43.

[2] Richard Hakluyt, *A particular Discourse concerning Westerne discoveries*, 36 f.

middle decades of the sixteenth century the speed of growth probably had been even more pronounced.

The demographic history of sixteenth-century France is even more scantily documented than that of Tudor England, and the historian must resign himself to the fact that he can do no more than trace its barest outlines. When the Hundred Years War lost momentum in the 1440's, and eventually came to an end in 1453, the French people got a first chance to rebuild their wrecked economy. But the hapless country was not yet fully at peace; throughout the reign of Louis XI (1461–83)

Table 14. *England and Wales*

| Year | Estimated number of inhabitants | Percentage change over the preceding year for which information is available | Annual percentage change in the interval |
|------|---------------------------------|------------------------------------------------------------------------------|-------------------------------------------|
| 1570 | 4,123,708 | | |
| 1600 | 4,811,718 | +16·7 | +0·56 |

SOURCE: J. Rickman, 'Estimated Population of England and Wales, 1570–1750', *Great Britain: Population Enumeration Abstract (1843)*, XXII, 37.

struggles against domestic and foreign foes continued almost without interruption, and during the first generation following the expulsion of the English re-settlement of devastated regions seems to have proceeded but slowly. There is nothing to suggest that demographic recovery made headway any more quickly; as a matter of fact, there was famine and widespread sickness in Louis's closing years, probably wiping out whatever small gains the French population may have been able to achieve in the preceding decades.

Soon afterwards, however, a pronounced secular upswing must have set in. For only a long period of demographic growth can have restored the population density of an utterly prostrate country to such a point that a foreign observer, in 1561, should have been struck by evidence of demographic saturation. France, the ambassador of the Republic of Venice reported to his government, 'is heavily populated . . .; every place has as many inhabitants as it can well have.' If he had chosen to, the Venetian could have supported his statement by a good deal of circumstantial evidence. In many parishes, churches which had become too small for their congregations had to be enlarged or rebuilt in this period. Cities like Paris and Tours were beginning to suffer from housing shortage. The population of Lyons is reported to have increased by 50 per cent. The impression that by the middle of the sixteenth century or a little earlier the French nation had recovered from the vital losses suffered in the period from 1350 to 1450 is confirmed by what is known —admittedly not very much—about the results of a hearth census, apparently held in the 1560's. A comparison of these results with the ones obtained in 1328, though beset with many grave uncertainties, seems to indicate that the average density of the French population was just about the same after the middle of the sixteenth century as it had been 250 years earlier—something like 35–40 persons per square kilometre.

It is not certain, however, that this level was maintained after the outbreak of the French Wars of Religion in 1562. More than thirty years of continual domestic strife accompanied by foreign intervention could not but inflict heavy losses on the population. A contemporary, writing in 1581, estimated the number of casualties up to that time at more than three-quarters of a million. But this figure is hardly an adequate index of the combined action of all the positive and preventive checks in that period of profound upheaval. The fate of Vienne, though perhaps not altogether typical, was by no means unparalleled, and may serve to illustrate the ravages of the Wars of Religion. Captured and recaptured no less than twenty times, pillaged in turn by Huguenots, Catholics, and forces of the League, visited by plagues in 1563–4, 1567 and 1584, the city was a mass of ruins and half deserted when it finally submitted to Henry IV in 1595.

The figures presented in Tables 4–6 (pp. 21–22) are illustrative of a general demographic upward movement in sixteenth-century Italy. But while the broad picture which those data portray is undoubtedly correct, the trend was not quite as uniform as they might lead us to assume. It is only by consulting the political and military history of the country that we can hope to gain an adequate idea of its demographic development.

The second half of the fifteenth century had been a period of relative peace for Italy, and some regional population growth, as has been noted above, appears to have set in earlier than in other countries of Europe. However, with the invasion of the peninsula by Charles VIII of France, in 1494, Italy entered upon a phase of profound disturbances. For more than a generation the country was prey to a ruthless soldiery. Native and foreign armies forgathered on Italian soil to fight the battles of their masters, leaving in their wake devastation and disease. Lombardy in particular, having been the scene of some of the fiercest fighting in the 1520's, and having, moreover, been visited in 1524 and 1528 by epidemics of extraordinary violence, suffered acutely. A letter of 1529, addressed to King Henry VIII by two of his envoys, paints a picture of utter desolation.

It is, Sire, [the ambassadors wrote] the most pitie to see this contree, as we suppose, that ever was in Christyndom; in some places nother horsmete nor mans mete to be found, the goodly townes destroyed and desolate. Betwexte

Verceilles [i.e. Vercelli] ... and Pavye [Pavia], the space of 50 miles, the moost goodly contree for corne and vynes that may be seen, is so desolate, in all that weye we sawe [not] oon man or woman laborers in the fylde, nor yett creatour stering, but in great villaiges five or six myserable personnes; sawyng in all this waye we sawe thre women in oon place, gathering of grapis yett upon the vynes [the time was December!], for there are nother vynes orderyd and kepte, nor corne sawed in all that weye, nor personnes to gather the grapes that growith uppon the vynes, but the vynes growith wyld. ... In this mydde waye is a town ... is all destroyed and in maner desolate. Pavye is in lyke maner, and great pitie; the chyldryn kryeng abowt the streates for bred, and ye dying for hungre. They seye that all the hole peuple of that contrey and dyvers other places in Italya, as the Pope also shewyd us, with many other, with warre, famine, and pestilence are utterly deadde and goone; so that there is no hope many yeres that Italya shalbe any thing well restored, for wante of people.[1]

Fortunately, this pessimistic prognosis was not borne out. As early as the middle of the sixteenth century even those parts of the country which had had to bear the brunt of the military campaigns, or had at any rate suffered grievously from the war-begotten epidemics of the 1520's, were well on the way to demographic recovery. Though little is known about the countryside,[2] the remarkable resilience of many of the urban communities of northern Italy may be regarded as *prima facie* evidence of a general upswing. The city of Pavia, whose population had been reduced to scarcely more than 5,000 souls by 1529, thirteen years later numbered about 11,000. The population of Verona, having declined from 47,000 to 27,000 between 1501 and 1529, by 1557 had regained its former strength. Mantua, too, went through a thirty years' period of rapid demographic recovery after 1529. Florence, decimated by the plague of 1527 and the siege of 1530, was slow to rally. Her population, having shrunk from an estimated 72,000 in 1510 to about 60,000 in 1531, remained on this lower level for the next thirty years. However, soon afterwards demographic recovery must have set in; for the decennial average of baptisms performed in the city of Florence in 1591–1600 (3,016) was significantly higher than the corresponding figure for the decade 1491–1500 (2,523). The city of Brescia, which had been sacked in 1512, was not doing so well; but Modena's population grew from 15,500 to 18,000 between 1539 and 1581, while that of Milan increased by 40 per

---

[1] *State Papers Published under the Authority of Her Majesty's Commission*, vol. VII: King Henry the Eighth, part v—continued (1849), 226.

[2] We do have a few striking instances of rural growth, e.g. in the duchy of Milan and in the neighbourhood of Rovigo. In this latter region the draining of marshes was accompanied by a trebling of population between 1548 and 1603. Other instances of rapid demographic recovery after 1535, incidental to a phenomenally high birth rate, are cited by Carlo M. Cipolla, 'Per la storia della popolazione lombarda nel secolo XVI', *Studi in Onore di Gino Luzzatto*, II (Milan, 1950), 144–55.

cent in the fifty years after 1542. The number of Como's inhabitants rose from 8,000 in 1553 to 12,000 in 1592, that of Bergamo's from 18,000 in 1548 to 24,000 in 1596. The population of Pavia, during this same period, appears to have more than doubled.

The demographic gains achieved by the last-named cities in the second half of the century are all the more remarkable since in 1575-7 northern Italy had once again been struck by an epidemic outbreak of uncommon violence, which caused the population of Venice to tumble from about 170,000 to only a little over 120,000, while the city of Padua lost one-third of its inhabitants. Pavia, to be sure, seems to have escaped with only minor losses, but neighbouring Milan counted more than 17,000 victims. Before this catastrophe the urban population of northern Italy may have exceeded by an appreciable margin the level attained at the beginning of the sixteenth century; by 1600 it was certainly not lower, and probably once more considerably higher than in 1500.

Those cities and regions of Italy that were exposed only briefly or not at all to the military upheavals of the early sixteenth century may not have entirely escaped the indirect effects of warfare—disease and economic dislocation; nevertheless they seem to have achieved very substantial rates of growth even during the troublous decades after 1494. Of this the demographic records of the Kingdom of Naples and of Sicily as tabulated above (Tables 4 and 5, p. 21) provide the most striking, though not the only, illustrations. Other instances of rapid population increase in the first half of the sixteenth century are furnished by Venice and Siena. The former city grew from an estimated 115,000 inhabitants in 1509 to 130,000 in 1540, and 160,000 in 1555. In Siena the decennial averages of baptisms, having remained stationary from the 1380's to the end of the fifteenth century, began to rise steeply after 1500; and this new level, higher than the previous one by one-third or more, was maintained until the mid-fifties, when the city succumbed to siege and conquest.

Disasters like the one just mentioned, or, to cite a better known instance, the sack of Rome in 1527, which introduce discontinuities into local demographic trends, tend to blur, but cannot really obscure, the main features of Italy's development in this period. The total picture shows life triumphant in the face of adversity. It is only in the latter years of the sixteenth century that the secular trend of demographic growth appears to level out in some parts of the country, and in a few even turns negative—presumably a manifestation of pressure of population on land and incipient economic stagnation (see below, p. 51).

The population history of the Low Countries in the sixteenth century bears some resemblance to that of northern Italy: in both regions the demographic development was decisively influenced by the course of political and military events. Only the sequence of quiescence and commotion was different in the two countries. For Italy the time of troubles was the first, for the Netherlands it was the last, third of the sixteenth century.

After a period of severe hardships in the 1480's, during which the number of houses in the southern Low Countries (Flanders, Hainault, and Brabant) and in the county of Holland can be shown to have declined sharply (see Tables 1–3, p. 18), recovery set in shortly before the turn of the century (see Tables 11 and 12, p. 23). By about 1520 at the latest the losses were made good. But so far from levelling off, demographic growth appears to have continued for another half century, the most spectacular instance being that of the city of Antwerp. Owing to immigration her population, inclusive of some 10,000 suburban residents, had risen to about 100,000 by 1568. The number of houses inside and outside the walls was about 13,500 at that time, as compared with 6,586 and 8,479 inhabited dwellings counted in 1496 and 1526 respectively. That the rest of the country should have increased at anything like this rate is altogether unlikely; but if the development of the duchy of Hainault was at all typical, the demographic gains achieved during the first seven decades of the sixteenth century must have been sizeable.

The turn of the tide came in 1567 with the arrival of Alva and the outbreak of insurrection in the Netherlands. Measured with the yardstick of demography, the loss of population directly attributable to the activities of Alva's Council of Blood was insignificant. The number of persons executed by the Spaniards in the years 1568–73, so far from reaching 18,000 (a figure derived from the statements of horror-stricken contemporaries), probably did not exceed 7,000. In a country of approximately three million inhabitants any minor epidemic might have carried off as many victims or more. More serious perhaps, as far as manpower was concerned, was the exodus from the Low Countries of many thousands of refugees. To be sure, emigration was counterbalanced, quantitatively, by the influx of large numbers of foreign mercenaries; but disreputable soldiers of fortune were poor substitutes for the skilled artisans and wealthy merchants who were fleeing the country. Nor was organized prostitution—Alva's army was accompanied by two thousand Italian harlots—a substitute for family life, even if the relative merits of the two institutions be judged purely on the ground of quantitative demography.

Meanwhile losses of life and property must have mounted as confused and savage fighting between the forces of the Crown of Spain and those of the prince of Orange and his successors dragged on year after year. Death made little distinction between soldiers and non-combatants.

When a besieged city was starved into surrender or taken by storm, the conquerors would vent their rage on garrison and citizens alike. Typhus and other crowd-diseases also sought their victims indiscriminately among soldiers and civilians. Abbreviating desperately we may state that, except during the first period of the struggle, the southern Netherlands suffered much more heavily than the provinces in the north. Among the latter, Holland and Zeeland in particular, well entrenched behind strong lines of defence, came to enjoy virtual freedom from devastation and slaughter after 1576.

Figures to illustrate the demographic development of the southern Low Countries in this period are hard to come by; but such data as have come to light, though fragmentary, fully confirm what a knowledge of the country's sorry plight would lead one to expect. Thus we find, starting in the south-west, that in the city of Ath, the third largest urban community in the duchy of Hainault, the number of chimneys counted for purposes of taxation diminished by 59 per cent between 1553 and 1594. At Avesne, a smaller town in the same province, the drop was equally drastic. In one of the rural districts of neighbouring Flanders, the *châtellenie* of Audenarde, the trend was roughly the same: with 27 out of 32 parishes reporting, the number of households declined from 4,372 in 1557 to 2,520 in 1600—a drop of more than 42 per cent. However, in this particular instance decline cannot have set in much before 1576, since in this year the number of able-bodied men reported by twenty-six parishes was still substantially higher than the number returned in 1558.[1] In the duchy of Brabant the best-known and most striking case of depopulation is that of Antwerp. This great metropolis lost more than half its inhabitants between 1568 and 1589, chiefly as a result of mass-emigration after 1585, when religious oppression and grave economic disorders combined to make life in the city intolerable.

Many of these migrants turned to the northern provinces, whose citizens, having by this time gained *de facto* independence from their Spanish overlords, were in a position to offer a haven to their Protestant co-religionists. Thus, while the cities of Flanders and Brabant emptied themselves, those of Holland expanded by leaps and bounds. Leiden's population jumped from 12,144 in 1581 to 44,475 in 1622. Amsterdam, having doubled its area in three successive extensions between 1585 and 1611, counted 105,000 inhabitants by 1622. 'God', wrote an Englishman of the Dutch about the turn of the sixteenth century, 'hath so blessed the frute of theyr labours that all the towns for the moste parte, as Amsterdam, Rotterdam, Enchusen, Briell, Midleborowe, and, in fine, ye moste towns of ye Lowe Countries are growne as greate againe as they

---

[1] The paradox may resolve itself when it is recalled that in the years 1557–8 Flanders had been the scene of heavy fighting and had, moreover, been struck by famine and plague.

have beene (the new towne as greate as ye olde) as is daily to be sene.'

However, growth was not confined to urban centres, nor was Holland's demographic advance in the sixteenth century due primarily to immigration: natural increase undoubtedly accounted for most of her secular gain. Its order of magnitude may be judged by holding the total of 'hearths' counted in 1514 (45,857) against the result of a census of persons, held in the year 1622, in Holland and West-Friesland (671,675).[1] Although such a comparison can be only rough, it suggests that the population of Holland proper must at least have doubled in the course of the sixteenth century.

If information about demographic developments in the heartland of Europe is at best fragmentary, the history of population in Europe's peripheral areas during this period is even less easy to elucidate in its details. We do know that both Norway and Denmark experienced a secular upswing in the sixteenth century; though as far as the former is concerned, it was not before 1600 that the heavy loss of population which this country had sustained after the middle of the fourteenth century appears to have been made good. (At that time Norway may have numbered about 400,000 and Denmark, within her pre-war boundaries, about 570,000 inhabitants.) The population of Sweden is generally believed to have increased very substantially during the prosperous reign of Gustavus I (1523–60). However, in the following decades the realm, torn by domestic strife and exhausted by foreign wars, can hardly have achieved significant demographic gains, the less so since it, like many other European countries, was struck by a series of disastrous crop failures in the 1590's. For Finland, at that time a Swedish dependency, we have the results of two hearth counts (1557: 33,046; 1589: 31,570) which would seem to indicate a more or less stationary population. Whether Finnish immigration into the forest areas of central Sweden, whose beginnings date from the last years of the sixteenth century, was indicative of population pressure cannot be decided.

Poland, perhaps because some of her southern regions appear not to have been affected by the Black Death, seems to have overcome the demographic crisis of the late-medieval period more quickly than most of the western countries. The fact that a native movement of forest-clearing got under way as early as the fifteenth, and persisted in the sixteenth, century (see vol. 1, p. 396) must be regarded as symptomatic of renewed population pressure in eastern Europe; and the quantitative information at our disposal lends weight to the argument. To be sure, our statistics leave much to be desired. The population total for 1578 of the three most important provinces of the kingdom, as calculated

[1] Of this total Holland proper (*Zuiderkwartier*) accounted for 505,185 persons.

by Adolf Pawiński (2,118,000) and Egon Vielrose (3,200,000) respectively is highly conjectural. Moreover, there do not exist any previous data with which these figures can be compared, except an equally hypothetical total for 1340, calculated variously at 453,000 (Mitkowski), 658,000 (Kula), 842,000 (Ladenberger), or 1,240,000 (Vielrose) inhabitants. Nevertheless, a pronounced secular upswing in the fifteenth and sixteenth centuries can hardly be called in question, though the actual rate of increase may have been somewhat lower than these figures would suggest.

By far the greatest part of the Balkan Peninsula was in the hands of the Ottoman Power during the sixteenth century, and until recently the prospects of demographic information coming to light for this territory must have appeared rather dim to western scholars. However, the Turks were better administrators than they are generally given credit for; and a census of households, undertaken in the early years of Suleiman the Magnificent, has enabled Professor Ömer Lûtfi Barkan of the University of Istanbul to attempt a calculation of the population of the Balkan countries in the third decade of the sixteenth century. It appears that the territory to the south of the rivers Save and Danube, exclusive of the city of Constantinople, contained a little more than one million households, about 80 per cent of which were Christian, 20 per cent Moslem, and less than one-half of one per cent Jewish. Using a co-efficient of five, and adding an estimated 400,000 so as to account for Constantinople, Professor Barkan arrives at a population figure of approximately 5·6 millions.

More important, however, than a necessarily conjectural notion of absolute demographic magnitudes would be the trend of population in the European provinces of sixteenth-century Turkey. For this purpose, too, Turkish sources have yielded important information. It can be shown that the urban population of the Balkans was increasing at a substantial rate. The number of households in such towns as Sofia and Skoplje more than doubled between the third and the eighth decade of the sixteenth century. Nikopol, Mostar, Adrianople, and Athens did not grow quite that fast, but Sarajevo quadrupled its population in this period. Salonica, having received more than 2,600 Jewish families after their expulsion from Spain in 1492, by 1529 counted almost 5,000 households, an increase of 3,000 over the number reported for 1478. Thereafter the population of Salonica seems to have become stationary.

While we have no quantitative information concerning the rural population of the Balkans in this period, there can be little doubt that it, too, was growing. The Turkish authorities, anxious to consolidate their rule in the conquered provinces, had long encouraged immigration, and even resorted to deportation, of Moslems from Anatolia to the

Balkan countries; and while it is known that there also occurred some forcible displacement of Christians, the balance of demographic gains and losses from these migrations was almost certainly in favour of the west.

Though by far the greatest part of the Balkan Peninsula had fallen under Turkish rule by the beginning of the sixteenth century, the Venetians managed to retain footholds on the Dalmatian coast, in the Ionian Islands, in Crete, and, until 1540, in Morea; and the archives of the Republic have yielded valuable material for the history of population in these areas. On the whole, the fate of these outposts was not a happy one. Venice was at war with the Porte in 1537–40 and again in 1570–3, and the vicissitudes to which the Balkan possessions of the Republic were exposed are reflected in their demographic trends. To take one of the most drastic cases first: the island of Corfu, whose population numbered 37,000 in 1499, saw some 15,000–18,000 of its rural inhabitants abducted into slavery by the Turks in 1537; by 1576, after the second Turkish war, only 17,500 people were left on the island; of these 7,500 lived in the capital. Two other Ionian islands, Cephalonia and Ithaca, lost one-quarter of their inhabitants between 1569 and 1572. The Venetian possessions on the mainland of Dalmatia and the islands off-shore also suffered severely: their population declined by about one-third between 1559 and 1576. It would, of course, be entirely unwarranted to draw conclusions from these highly vulnerable outposts as to conditions in other parts of the Balkans. Indeed, as has been shown, the population of south-eastern Europe was on the increase in the sixteenth century. For Turkish rule, whatever its shortcomings, must be credited with at least one achievement: the Ottoman Empire succeeded in eliminating the scourge of war for the majority of its subjects over long stretches of time.

# IV. *A Century of Reverses*

In the year 1604 many an anxious eye was turned towards a strange new star, blazing forth in ominous brightness. Was it a portent, presaging an era of wars, famines, and pestilence? In due course men were to learn that the warning of the 'Sidereal Messenger' for once had not been a mockery: the signature of the seventeenth century was indeed one of violence and disorder. Its plight is reflected in the demographic record.

To convey an adequate idea of the afflictions brought upon themselves by the nations of Europe and their rulers in this epoch would require an account of its confused political and military history. Nothing of the sort can be attempted here; only a few of the major events will be touched upon. Except for a new flare-up of violence in the restless Baltic area and in Russia the beginnings of the century were not inauspicious. Henry IV had restored religious peace to France; in 1604 the protracted war between England and Spain was terminated; the Empire, after 1606, was enjoying a breathing spell in its perennial struggle with the Turks, while its two main denominational blocs, though poised uneasily, were yet reluctant to plunge into war; and in 1609 a twelve years' truce was arranged between Spain and the United Provinces. However, if the God of War appeared to hold his hand in the first two decades, he certainly assumed direction of man's affairs during the remainder of the seventeenth century, and more particularly in the period from 1620 to 1660.

The Thirty Years War (1618–48), though interlocked with practically every major conflict on the contemporary European scene, was first and foremost a fratricidal struggle within the Empire. That its demographic consequences for many parts of Germany and for the central regions of Bohemia were disastrous has never been in doubt; but it is only on the basis of a critical synopsis of innumerable local studies, undertaken by Professor Günther Franz, that a clear picture of the total impact of the catastrophe begins to emerge. It appears that Germany by the end of the war had lost no less than 40 per cent of her pre-war population.[1] Battle casualties and civilian victims of atrocities committed by the brutalized soldiery can have made up only a small portion of the death toll. The most powerful agents of destruction, both among soldiers and non-combatants, were hunger and disease. Congestion, filth, and malnutrition bred epidemics in military hospitals and encampments as well as in towns and cities crowded with fugitives from the harassed countryside. From these foci, and in the wake of marching troops, infections such as dysentery, typhus, plague (chiefly in the years 1624–30 and 1634–9), and, towards the end of the war, smallpox, spread from place to place. As the main theatres of military operations shifted back and forth across the length and breadth of the Empire, disease, devastation, and famine descended.

Although there was hardly a region in Central Europe but at one time or another suffered grievous losses of population, the demographic situation at the end of the Thirty Years War varied widely from district

---

[1] Professor Franz's thesis, it is fair to state, has not gone unchallenged. However, the view that Germany suffered very serious population losses in the Thirty Years War cannot be dismissed lightly. It is supported by new evidence of a declining trend in the price of cereals after the middle of the seventeenth century, as well as of a noticeable recession of grain-growing in favour of sheep-breeding in Central, East, and South Germany. See Friedrich-Karl Riemann, *Ackerbau und Viehhaltung im vorindustriellen Deutschland* (Beihefte zum Jahrbuch der Albertus-Universität zu Königsberg, III) Kitzingen/Main, 1953.

to district (see Fig. 1), the degree of depopulation depending largely on the time, duration, and scope of military operations in the different territories. Thus, to mention only a few extreme cases, the Palatinate and Württemberg in the south, Thuringia in Central Germany, and

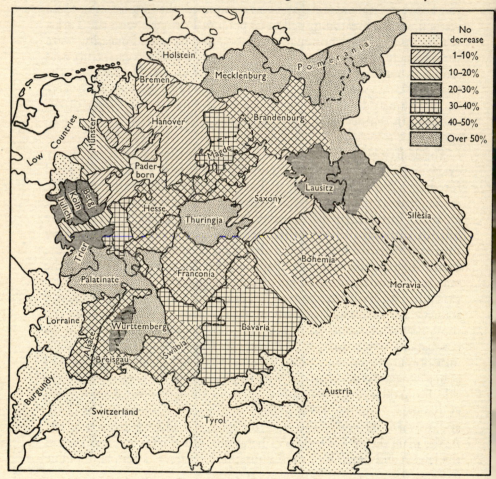

Fig. 1. Population decrease in the Holy Roman Empire during the Thirty Years War. (After G. Franz.)

Mecklenburg and Pomerania in the north-east, appear to have lost more than 50 per cent of their inhabitants between 1618 and 1648. Lower Saxony, on the other hand, by the end of the war had had time to recover almost completely from the ravages she had suffered during the early phases of the conflict.

Regional demographic recovery was to a certain extent a matter of internal migration. There had been a great deal of population movement even during the war: not only temporary displacement—peasants taking to the woods, or seeking safety behind the walls of a neighbouring city—but also genuine migration, as fugitives who had seen their homes go up in flames tried to re-establish themselves in regions that had escaped devastation. Other migratory currents were induced by religious persecution. Thus, to cite only one instance, large numbers of Lutheran exiles from Austria in the decades after 1625 had found new homes in Franconia and other Protestant territories. After the return of peace the main stream of migrants was directed towards badly-depopulated regions. Swiss settlers had a considerable share in the economic and demographic rehabilitation of such territories as the Palatinate, Alsace, and Brandenburg.

Internal migration, by reducing regional differences in relative population density that had been caused, or become accentuated, by the war, incidentally created conditions favourable to natural increase, which was, of course, the chief agent of demographic recovery. There is some evidence to suggest that post-war fertility was high. An Italian who visited Germany soon after the war observed that the number of men capable of bearing arms was low, but that there were plenty of children around. Even so, and notwithstanding the fact that the plague disappeared from Central Europe about 1700, a drastically depopulated territory such as Württemberg did not regain its former demographic strength before 1730. In other German regions, especially in the north-eastern parts of the country and in Silesia, the heavy population losses of the Thirty Years War resulted in the spread of the *Gutsherrschaft*, as aristocratic landowners appropriated many vacant peasant holdings and added them to their estates, which were farmed for profit with the help of semi-servile smallholders. Though perhaps deplorable from a social point of view, this development did not necessarily retard demographic recovery. The existence of a numerous rural proletariat in such Prussian provinces as East Prussia, Kurmark, Neumark, or in Pomerania did not prevent their populations from doubling, or more than doubling, in the following century.

The demographic catastrophe which befell the German people in the decades after 1618 had no parallel in other countries, even though many of them also passed through periods of adversity in the first half of the seventeenth century. Switzerland was swept by a pestilential wave of great violence in 1610–11. In the city of Basle, for which we have uncommonly good figures, more than half of its 12,000 inhabitants sickened, and nearly one-third died of this plague, while the small town of Winterthur lost almost half its population. A new outbreak in 1615–16, though considerably weaker, is known to have carried off about one-eighth of the population of Geneva. In 1629–31 the country again suffered heavy losses, as a terrible epidemic of plague spilled over from Italy in the wake of the Mantuan War of Succession. That disease is no respecter of frontiers was demonstrated once more in the second half of the fourth decade, when war-begotten plague invaded Switzerland from neighbouring Germany.

In view of this gloomy epidemiological record it is rather surprising that the country should have been able to hold its own demographically in the first half of the seventeenth century. Yet such apparently was the case, at any rate in the Cantons of Berne and Zürich. In the former, the number of 'hearths' counted in 1653 was 60 per cent higher than in 1558–9. The population of the Zürich *Landschaft*, estimated at 70,000–85,000 in 1585, seems to have risen to about 90,000 by 1650. Even though some of the increase in both these cases is likely to have occurred in the decades before 1610, the impact of the subsequent epidemics on the rural population cannot have been quite as heavy as some of the urban figures might lead one to assume. In any case, the country was spared the worst ravages of war. Only Graubünden and the adjacent Valtelline, one of the strategic areas of seventeenth-century Europe, saw a good deal of campaigning and troop movements, and suffered grievously. But the rest of the Swiss Confederacy, with the exception of some frontier districts, escaped serious harm.

The contrast between war-torn Germany and tranquil Switzerland was striking indeed. 'The country', wrote a contemporary German author, 'appeared to me so strange compared with other German lands, as if I had come to Brazil or China. There I saw the people going about their business in peace; the stables were filled with livestock, the farm yards teeming with chickens, geese and ducks. Nobody stood in fear of the foe, nobody dreaded pillage, nobody was afraid of losing his property, his limbs, or his life.'[1]

The second half of the seventeenth century was an uneventful period in the history of the Swiss people. While a goodly number of their sons still went abroad to fight the battles of foreign monarchs, the country successfully avoided embroilment in international conflicts. As for epidemics, there was one other outbreak of plague, in 1667–8; but it remained localized, and was, moreover, the last of these dreadful visitations.

In these circumstances population growth, which must have been interrupted in the first half of the century, was resumed. It is estimated that by 1700 the country numbered 1·2 million inhabitants, about 200,000 more than in 1600—and this despite the fact that in the course of the

[1] Hans Jacob Christoph von Grimmelshausen, *Der abenteuerliche Simplicissimus* (1669), bk. v, chap. 1.

seventeenth century some 300,000 Swiss had left home, the majority of them mercenaries and the rest colonists who helped to resettle some of the depopulated regions of Germany.

The political and military factors which had begun to shape the demographic pattern of the Low Countries in the last decades of the sixteenth century remained operative after 1600. The Twelve Years Truce (see above, p. 41) was too brief a respite for recovery to make much headway; and when it expired, in 1621, the Spanish Netherlands once again became a battle-ground, while the United Provinces managed, as they had done before, to keep the enemy out. In the circumstances demographic developments in the south and in the north continued to diverge. The difference was summed up tersely by a Spanish envoy. 'I have come on to Amsterdam where I now am', reported the Abbé Scaglia in 1627, 'and find all the towns as full of people as those held by Spain are empty.'

When these words were written the end of the fighting was not yet in sight: two more decades were to elapse before the Southern Netherlands were able to settle down to peaceful pursuits. By this time the country lay prostrate, and even half a generation after the cessation of hostilities reconstruction had barely set in. This is how the Estates of Brabant described the state of their province as late as 1663.

Through the long troubles and wars the country of Brabant—both the walled towns, big and small, and the liberties and villages of the countryside—have changed greatly; they are depopulated, ruined, and spoiled. The houses in many places are burned, thrown down, and derelict; the land is neglected, nay completely waste in many spots—a dwelling place for the birds of the heavens.

The quantitative evidence at our disposal does nothing to detract from these statements. The results of two censuses held in Brabant in 1693 and 1709 reveal that the duchy (within its then existing borders) numbered only slightly more inhabitants (373,000) at the turn of the seventeenth century than must be assumed to have lived in the same territory in 1526 (363,000). Keeping in mind that, under the somewhat more favourable circumstances prevailing in the second half of the seventeenth century, demographic recovery must have made some strides, one is forced to conclude that the population losses suffered during the Eighty Years War (1568–1648) wiped out all the gains achieved during the relatively peaceful and prosperous period from 1526 to 1568.

Though we have no global data for Flanders the figures available for the *châtellenie* of Audenarde show convincingly that the demographic development in this part of the Spanish Netherlands was remarkably similar to that of Brabant. The pre-war number of households in twenty-seven parishes, having tumbled from 4,372 to 2,520 between 1557 and 1600, was barely reached again by 1698, when 4,385 *ménages* were counted. Another set of figures, illustrating population trends in the district of Veurne-Ambacht (West Flanders), also indicates the operation of strong depressive forces in the seventeenth century. Demographic conditions in the Prince-Bishopric of Liège, where industrialization proceeded apace after the middle of the seventeenth century, may have differed favourably from those in neighbouring regions; but we have no figures to prove it.[1]

As usual, it was the countryside and the smaller towns rather than the cities that suffered most from depopulation in wartime. The latter, as a rule, were well defended and supplied, and for these reasons proved attractive to country dwellers as places of refuge in times of peril. Such influx probably accounts for the fact that Ghent, so far from declining, achieved considerable demographic gains during the troubled first half of the seventeenth century. The same apparently was true of Malines and Liège. The population of Antwerp, too, after its precipitous drop in the 1570's and 1580's, resumed a steady, if not spectacular, growth which continued throughout the seventeenth century.

The enthusiastic and often envious testimony of contemporaries to the populousness of the Dutch Republic leaves little doubt about the favourable demographic evolution of the United Provinces in this period, though unfortunately it cannot be illustrated by any global figures. In a century when statesmen and writers were much concerned with promoting population increase the Dutch were held up as a model, 'a brave people, rich, and full of Cities . . .; they swarm with people as Bee-hives with Bees' (Anonymous, *England's Great Happiness*. London, 1677).

In Holland, the most advanced of the Seven Provinces, urbanization had indeed gone very far, as early as the beginning of the seventeenth century. In 1622 fully 60 per cent of the population were townsfolk; and of these the great majority—three-quarters, to be exact—lived in ten cities of more than 10,000 inhabitants. Among these there were at least two—Leiden and Haarlem, with 45,000 and 40,000 inhabitants respectively—which by contemporary standards must be classified as very large, and one veritable giant, Amsterdam, with 105,000 inhabitants. Even Italians, natives of the most highly urbanized country of early modern Europe, were strongly impressed with Holland's precocious development. Nowhere else, wrote the Venetian ambassador

---

[1] We do know that in 1790 as many as 83,224 inhabitants were counted in Liège (*cité* and suburbs).

Trevisano in 1619, were so many flourishing cities to be found in such a narrow compass. Had he but known that a hundred years later all these Dutch cities would be more populous still! Haarlem and Amsterdam, for instance, having both undertaken extensions in 1610–11, found it imperative once more to enlarge their areas, in 1671–2 and 1658 respectively. Amsterdam's population by 1700 cannot have fallen far short of 200,000. Rotterdam, where about 20,000 inhabitants were counted in 1622, by the middle of the following century was estimated to number 56,000.[1] The population of Leiden, though decimated three times by violent epidemics, increased from 45,000 to approximately 70,000 between 1622 and 1685, but declined sharply in the following decades with the collapse of the boom in the city's textile industry.

Although the secular development of seventeenth-century Holland was undoubtedly more favourable than that of her neighbours, her demographic history was not altogether free of temporary setbacks. The Dutch, for all their reputed cleanliness, were no more immune to plague than other people, major outbreaks being reported for the years 1623–5, 1635–7, 1654–5, and 1663–4.[2] The bitter struggles against the French, especially in 1672, when the greater part of the Republic was overrun by the enemy and the defenders had to resort to the desperate measure of cutting their dams, must also have caused serious reverses. However, it would appear from all accounts that recovery was always speedy. 'If a plague come, they [sc. the cities of Holland] are fill'd up presently . . .; they do all this by inviting all the World to come and live among them' (Anonymous, *England's Great Happiness*. London, 1677). Indeed, Holland's astonishing urban growth in the first half of the seventeenth century seems to have been due, in no small measure, to an uncommonly liberal immigration policy. If most Dutch cities were prepared to open their doors wide to fellow-Netherlanders and foreign co-religionists, others like Amsterdam welcomed even Portuguese Jews and *Marranos*.

While the Dutch were the envy of Europe because of their increasing numbers, seventeenth-century Spain became proverbial as a state whose population was declining. Her enemies gleefully took notice, while her natives worriedly complained, of the country's depopulation. However, early Spanish data being what they are, it is exceedingly difficult to ascertain how serious it was, and when exactly it occurred. Indeed, the statistical evidence bearing on these questions is so ambiguous that it was possible for a level-headed student of demographic history such as

---

[1] This contemporary estimate, even though it may have erred on the high side, is still worth quoting: it cannot have been wildly wrong.

[2] It will be observed that three of these four epidemics coincided with, or preceded, great pestilential outbreaks in London.

Karl Julius Beloch to advance the view that there was no decline at all in this period. With this opinion not many historians will concur; it is known that almost all the manufacturing cities of Castile suffered a catastrophic decline in population between the censuses of 1594 and 1694; Valladolid, Toledo and Segovia, for example, lost more than half of their inhabitants. However, it should be admitted that population trends varied from province to province. If the figures presented in Tables 15–19 mean anything at all there must have occurred a sharp drop in numbers, at any rate during the first half of the seventeenth century, in the kingdoms of Castile, Aragon, and Valencia, while the population of Navarre remained about stationary and that of Catalonia (including the city of Barcelona) increased appreciably in the course of the seventeenth century. On balance, Spain may have lost about a quarter of its inhabitants between 1600 and 1700.

Even the most cursory study of Spanish history will suggest ample reasons why the country should have found it difficult to maintain, let alone raise, its level of population in the period under review. The seventeenth century is known to have opened with an epidemic whose disastrous demographic effects were reflected in a sharp upswing of

### Table 15. *Spain (Castile)*

| Year | Number of heads of families (*vecinos*) | Percentage change over the preceding year for which information is available | Annual percentage change in each interval |
|------|------|------|------|
| 1591 | 1,340,320 | · | |
| 1646 | 807,903 | −39·7 | −0·72 |
| 1723 | 965,610 | +19·5 | +0·25 |

SOURCE: Albert Girard, 'Le chiffre de la population de l'Espagne dans les temps modernes', *Revue d'Histoire Moderne*, III (1928), 429.

### Table 16. *Spain (Aragon)*

| Year | Number of heads of families (*vecinos*) | Percentage change over the preceding year for which information is available | Annual percentage change in the interval |
|------|------|------|------|
| 1603 | 70,984 | | |
| 1650 | 22,688 | −68·0 | −1·4 |

SOURCE: Albert Girard, *op. cit.*, p. 432.

### Table 17. *Spain (Valencia)*

| Year | Number of houses | Percentage change over the preceding year for which information is available | Annual percentage change in the interval |
|------|------------------|---------------------------------------------|------------------------------------------|
| 1609 | 97,372 | | |
| 1714 | 76,524 | −21·4 | −0·20 |

SOURCE: Albert Girard, *op. cit.*, p. 433.

### Table 18. *Spain (Navarre)*

| Year | Number of heads of families (*vecinos*) | Percentage change over the preceding year for which information is available | Annual percentage change in the interval |
|------|------------------|---------------------------------------------|------------------------------------------|
| 1587 | 41,901 | | |
| 1678 | 43,184 | +3·1 | +0·03 |

SOURCE: Albert Girard, *op. cit.*, pp. 433 ff.

### Table 19. *Spain (Catalonia)*

| Year | Number of heads of families (*vecinos*) | Percentage change over the preceding year for which information is available | Annual percentage change in the interval |
|------|------------------|---------------------------------------------|------------------------------------------|
| 1553 | 65,394 | | |
| 1717 | 124,032 | +89·7 | +0·55 |

SOURCE: Albert Girard, *op. cit.*, p. 433.

money wages, as well as real wages, in the following decade. The expulsion of the 275,000 *Moriscos* in 1609, even if exaggerated notions of its *economic* effects be discounted, further weakened the demographic strength of the nation, while the number of Irish refugees arriving in Spain in the course of the seventeenth century was hardly large enough to offset these losses. Emigration to the colonies, though sometimes mentioned by contemporaries as a cause of depopulation, was of no great significance quantitatively. More important, no doubt, was the loss of manpower caused by warfare: not so much by the numerous campaigns in distant lands, which, while conducted under Spanish colours, were largely fought with the help of foreign mercenaries, but by the long and sanguinary conflict with Portugal (1640–68). Of the *modus operandi* of still another factor which has often been cited as one of the main causes of Spanish depopulation one cannot be equally certain. Enough is known about the economics of a declining population to warrant the query whether Spain's economic decadence in the seventeenth century was not, perhaps, as much a consequence as it was a cause of her demographic recession. Contemporaries apparently were inclined to think so. It was lack of capital and manpower ('la falta de haciendas y de las personas'), a member of the Spanish Council of State declared in 1624, that was at the root of the country's economic troubles.

What little is known about the secular rhythm of demographic growth and decline in Portugal suggests that development there was similar to that of Spain. An earlier phase of growth (see Table 10) seems to have been cut short before the end of the sixteenth century. For the disastrous war of 1578–80, accompanied as it was by epidemics and famine, must have reduced numbers drastically. Nor apparently did the following decades bring any decisive recovery: the number of men of military age returned in 1636 was only slightly higher than the corresponding figure obtained in 1580. The long struggle for liberation from the Spanish yoke after 1640 may have caused further losses. However, towards the end of the seventeenth century, at the onset of a long period of economic prosperity, Portugal appears to have entered upon another phase of sustained demographic expansion, sufficiently vigorous to carry her population towards the two-million level by 1732.

The secular demographic trend of seventeenth-century Italy was dominated by the effects of two of the worst epidemics in the country's history: the plagues of 1630–1 and 1656–7 were largely responsible for the fact that most Italian cities and territories by 1700 were no more, and some appreciably less, populous than they had been a hundred years earlier. This is not to imply that the population of Italy, but for these catastrophes, would have continued to expand at a rate comparable to that achieved in many parts of the country during periods of quiescence in the preceding century. The secular stagnation of the Italian economy in the period under review would probably have militated against demographic expansion in any case.

As a matter of fact, there were definite indications, as early as the last decade of the sixteenth and the first years of the seventeenth century, that growth was slowing down here and there, for instance in Sicily (see Table 5, p. 21) and in the cities of Florence and Pavia, or that it was even turning negative, as was the case with Venice (1586: 149,000 inhabitants; 1624: 142,000 inhabitants), Bologna (both city and diocese), Ferrara, and

Siena. Our evidence of incipient demographic stagnation, it will be noted, is based not only on urban instances (which might be explained in terms of local economic distress exercising an adverse influence on the flow of immigration from the countryside), but also on territorial data.

The supposition that the population of Italy—at any rate in some districts—was beginning to press on its resources of land is, perhaps, not a far-fetched one. It can be supported by reference to the Sicilian famines of 1590–1 and 1607–8, and the demographic recession in the city and diocese of Bologna mentioned above. It probably was no accident that this latter region, having been spared by the great plague in the 1570's, should have been struck especially hard by the famine which visited all Italy in 1590–1. One may also see some significance in the fact that it was in those very years of widespread dearth that an Italian author, Giovanni Botero, developed a theory expounding the natural limitations of population increase: his *Della ragione di Stato* was first published in 1589. However, there is of course no telling when and in what form Malthusian checks would have begun to operate in full force had not the plagues of 1630 and 1656 wiped out a large part of the Italian population.

It can be stated with confidence that the first of these epidemics carried off rather more than a third of the urban,[1] and probably not much less than a third of the rural and small-town inhabitants[2] of Piedmont, Lombardy, Venetia, and Emilia. Tuscany was affected, too, but seems to have got off a little more lightly. Twenty-six years later it was the turn chiefly of those regions that had escaped the earlier visitation: central and southern Italy, Liguria, and the island of Sardinia. Once again, mortality in the cities was appalling. Naples, Benevento, Salerno, and Genoa each lost about half of their inhabitants. The city of Rome, thanks, perhaps, to a strict quarantine imposed by the Papal Commissioner of Health, was fortunate enough to escape with a loss of only 10 per cent of its population. The impact of the plague on the provinces of the kingdom of Naples varied widely from district to district. The average loss (including the city of Naples) may have amounted to about one-eighth of the inhabitants. The total of victims in the papal states of central Italy probably remained below 10 per cent of the pre-plague population. Sicily, if it was touched at all by this epidemic, cannot have suffered much. Sardinia, too, escaped with minor losses, only to be hit by a terrible famine in 1680, which reduced the population of the island from 300,000 (census of 1678) to 230,000 (census of 1688).

[1] Losses ranged from 22% in Bologna to as high as 60% in Cremona and Verona. The fortress-city of Mantua, having gone through a siege and a sack, lost about 70% of her population.

[2] In the province of Verona losses amounted to one-half, in the States of the House of Este (Modena and Reggio) to 20–30% of the pre-plague population.

It would be tedious to retrace the road to recovery in the various regions of Italy step by step. Suffice it to say that the demographic resilience of the country was barely high enough to neutralize the effects of the two great epidemics before the end of the century. Most of the big cities (Naples, Venice, Milan, Genoa, Palermo, Messina) and some of the smaller ones (e.g. Pavia) had fewer inhabitants in 1700 than they had had a hundred years before. The population of the country as a whole by the end of the seventeenth century seems to have been more or less the same as in 1600. Even Sicily, notwithstanding the fact that the island, except for a relatively mild outbreak of plague in 1624, had been free from major epidemics, achieved only an insignificant increment in this period (1607: 1,100,000 inhabitants; 1713: 1,121,000 inhabitants).

The spectre of plague loomed as large in seventeenth-century England as it did in contemporary Italy. True, even the worst English epidemics in this period seem to have been somewhat less lethal than the two Italian outbreaks; but then their frequency was much greater. London was struck in 1603, 1625, 1636–7, and 1665—not to mention a long sickly season in the 1640's, which produced a higher total of deaths from plague than the preceding epidemic of 1636–7. Since the population of London in any of these years can only be roughly guessed at, it is impossible to say with any certainty what proportion of its inhabitants fell victim to these various epidemics. It would seem, though, that plague casualties and deaths from other causes did not exceed 25 per cent in 1603 and 1625, and 30 per cent in 1665. (The flare-up of 1636–7 was relatively mild.) However, the total number of plague deaths between 1600 and 1665—upwards of 170,000—was not much lower, and possibly a little higher, than the total population of London 'within the Bills of Mortality' in the latter years of Queen Elizabeth.

If Rickman's figures could be trusted to reflect accurately the trend, if

Table 20. *England and Wales*

| Year | Estimated number of inhabitants | Percentage change over the preceding year for which information is available | Annual percentage change in each interval |
|------|-------------------------------|------------------------------------------------------------------------------|-------------------------------------------|
| 1600 | 4,811,718 | | |
| 1630 | 5,600,517 | +16·4 | +0·55 |
| 1670 | 5,773,646 | +3·1 | +0·08 |
| 1700 | 6,045,008 | +4·7 | +0·15 |

SOURCE: J. Rickman, 'Estimated Population of England and Wales, 1570–1750', *Great Britain: Population Enumeration Abstract* (1843), XXII, 36 f.

not the actual numbers,[1] of population in seventeenth-centuryEngland and Wales, one would have to conclude that the impact of plague on the country as a whole was much weaker than that produced by the Italian epidemics of the period. On the face of it such a discrepancy might seem to be not unlikely. After all, England was much less urbanized than Italy: apart from the 'Great Wen', there were only four cities with more than 10,000 inhabitants—Norwich, Bristol, York, and Exeter. Might it not be presumed that in a country like this crowd-diseases tended to be much less severe? However the evidence at our disposal does not bear out such an optimistic assumption. It is known that even small provincial towns, such as Chester, Shrewsbury, Colchester, Hull, Newcastle upon Tyne, and others, were often hit as hard as, and sometimes far harder than, the capital: at Newcastle, for instance, more than 5,000 persons died of plague from 7 May to 31 December 1636, while Colchester lost about as many inhabitants during an epidemic in 1665–6. These figures betoken monstrous death rates. Still, there remains the evidence, presented in Table 20, of moderate secular growth; but such figures may well require correction. That the population of England and Wales was somewhat larger at the end of the seventeenth century than it had been at the beginning, few would deny. Even the order of magnitude of the secular percentage increase suggested by Rickman's data (25 per cent) looks reasonable enough.[2] The virtual standstill in the period from 1630 to 1670 also conforms to expectations; for, with the exception of a few bountiful harvests in the mid-fifties and in the latter half of the seventh decade, this period was one of chronic dearth. What is, perhaps, a little more doubtful is whether the secular increment was really achieved, mainly if not wholly, in the first thirty years of the seventeenth century (as Rickman's figures would indicate), or whether it was not rather the last third of the century that produced most of the demographic advance;[3] the plagues of 1603 and 1625 and the severe economic depressions of the 1620's would hardly have been conducive to population growth.

To be sure, the English birth-rate may have been somewhat lower in

[1] Rickman's figures undoubtedly are much too high. Even Gregory King's estimate of the population of England and Wales in 1688 (5·5 millions) may have to be subjected to a slight downward revision. See D. V. Glass, 'Gregory King's Estimate of the Population of England and Wales, 1695', *Population Studies*, III (1949–50), 338 ff., esp. 358.

[2] For the period from 1570 to 1670 Rickman's figures suggest an average increment of four-tenths of 1% per annum. This appears to be have been exactly the rate of growth achieved by twelve Worcestershire parishes between 1563 and 1665. See D. E. C. Eversley, "A Survey of Population in an Area of Worcestershire from 1660–1850 on the Basis of Parish Records', *Population Studies*, X (1956–57), 253–79.

[3] Though it would be hazardous to generalize from the population figures of a single county the estimates given for Derbyshire by R. Morden (*Description of England, 1704*, p. 33, quoted by J. D. Chambers, *The Vale of Trent 1670–1800*, p. 39) deserve to be quoted in support of our view: '1676 . . . 68,000, 1704 . . . 127,000.

the period from 1670 to 1740 than it had been in the seventy years from 1560 to 1630. Moreover, the 'seven ill years' at the end of the century (1692–9)—a time of very high food prices and endemic 'fevers'—seem to have caused a noticeable, if only temporary, rise of the death rate, at least in some provincial towns and country parishes. But over the whole period, from 1670 to 1700, the virtual disappearance of the plague from England—the great epidemic of 1665–6 (followed by a delayed outbreak at Peterborough, in 1667) was the last—should have brought about a significant reduction of mortality.

This is not to overlook the fact that smallpox, which had already become an alarming disease in the first half of the seventeenth century, was turning into a powerful killer after the Restoration: 30,000 deaths from smallpox were recorded in the London Bills of Mortality during the two decades from 1670 to 1689, accounting for 7 per cent of deaths from all causes. Nor are we unmindful of the prevalence throughout this period of 'malignant fevers' (probably typhus in the majority of cases), 'consumption and tissick' (pulmonary tuberculosis), 'griping in the guts' (probably infantile diarrhoea in the majority of cases), and other crowd diseases which continued to exact a heavy toll of life, especially among the poorer classes of the metropolis. But when all is said, the complete cessation of plague epidemics after 1666 and a secular upswing in England's economy must have brought a modicum of relief. An average annual increment over the last third of the seventeenth century of something like one-half of 1 per cent—a rate of growth which, as will be seen, corresponds closely to that achieved by England's population in the period from 1700 to 1750—would seem to be well within the realm of possibility.

Demographic trends in seventeenth-century Scotland, judging from the country's epidemiological record, cannot have diverged very widely from those of England. However, the peaks of pestilential seasons in Scotland—1606 and 1647–8—do not seem to have coincided with major outbreaks of plague south of the border: and the Scots were delivered from this ancient scourge twenty years sooner than their English neighbours. For the rest, the people of Scotland suffered as badly as the English, or worse, from all sorts of 'sore fluxes and strange fevers' during that period of dearth and famine, the 1690's, which were years of acute distress and abnormally high mortality in most countries of Europe.

Ireland, after a stormy decade at the beginning of the seventeenth century, got a chance to recuperate demographically during the thirty years of relative peace and prosperity which preceded the Rebellion of 1641. However, the next ten years of turmoil, culminating, in the late forties, in famine and epidemics of plague and smallpox, must have left the country in a state of demographic exhaustion. The estimates of

William Petty, who, in 1672 and 1687, put the population of Ireland at only 1·1 million and 1·3 million respectively, may indeed have been too low; but they indicate that a qualified contemporary observer still looked upon the country as sadly depopulated a generation after the catastrophe. Indeed, to William Petty the situation must have appeared so grave as to warrant even desperate measures for promoting demographic recovery. To what lengths he was prepared to go in his schemes for raising Irish fertility may be gathered from his memorandum 'On Marriages',[1] in which he advocated a radical, if only temporary, liberalization of sexual relations. However, over the next one hundred years peace and the potato patch were to provide less drastic yet more effectual remedies for depopulation.

It is to be expected that upon completion of an ambitious research project aiming at systematic analysis of a large number of French parish registers the main lines of the demographic history of early modern France will emerge more clearly than they can be discerned at present. Unfortunately, these explorations are only in their beginning, and for the time being any statement about the trends of French population in the seventeenth century must be regarded as more or less conjectural.

If, as the late Ferdinand Lot once suggested, the French Wars of Religion equalled or surpassed in ferocity even the Hundred Years War, the settlement brought about by Henry IV in the last years of the sixteenth century must have marked a turning point in the country's demographic history. Indeed, there is some scattered evidence that the first three decades of the seventeenth century, though by no means entirely tranquil, did produce an upswing of the secular trend. In the absence of devastating epidemics and major subsistence crises, the French population seems to have grown quite rapidly. However, the years from 1628 to 1638, with famines and violent plagues raging at various times in many parts of the country, must have brought serious reverses, if not everywhere, at any rate in the Midi, but also in Poitou, and the valley of the Loire. Lorraine, Alsace and Burgundy, having been drawn into the vortex of the Thirty Years War, may have suffered even heavier losses than other regions, especially in 1636-7, when invasion by a hostile army was followed by plague and famine.

Another grave demographic crisis developed about the middle of the century, during the troubles of the Fronde. Hunger and disease, the usual concomitants of man-made chaos, on this occasion were aggravated by adverse seasons: we know that the years 1646-52 produced very poor crops, not only in France, but in many other parts of Europe. The parish records examined so far clearly show the magnitude of this crisis: in

---

[1] *The Petty Papers*, ed. by the Marquis of Lansdowne, II (London, 1927), 50 f.

one of the villages of the Beauvaisis more than one-third of the population perished.

Ten years later, in 1660–2, famine strikes again; and once again dearth and shortages in France, though possibly more pronounced than elsewhere, are part of a general pattern, with grain selling at famine or near-famine prices in England, the Low Countries, and Germany. Passing over two minor subsistence crises in 1674–5 and 1679, we reach what may have been the most disastrous episode in the demographic history of seventeenth-century France, the great famine of 1693–4. The hardships and horrors created by this catastrophe, especially among the rural poor, have often been described, and contemporaries have left us estimates of population losses. Thus, as early as January 1694, 4,000 of the 25,000 or 26,000 inhabitants of the city of Rheims were reported to have died within the past six months—there was still half a year to go until the next harvest! In the south, especially in Armagnac, conditions were, if anything, even more appalling. According to a statement made by the archbishop of Auch, the population of his diocese in 1694 was only a quarter of what it had been three years before; deaths from disease, and migration, accounted for the losses. A report submitted by the *Intendant* at Montauban confirms this picture of desolation. 'The sterility of the previous years', he wrote in 1695, 'has carried off one-half or two-thirds of the population of [these] parishes, so that in many places there are not enough people left to cultivate the soil. . . . It is worst in Armagnac, and it may be necessary to bring in colonists from neighbouring provinces to repopulate that region.' Even if, as these last words clearly imply, things were not equally bad in all parts of the kingdom, samples of local population losses collected from regions as far apart as Normandy, the Beauvaisis, the Blois district, and the Lyonnais leave no doubt that the demographic crisis was a general one.

In view of this latest catastrophe, and keeping in mind that the country appears to have lost some 175,000 Protestant citizens by emigration during the last decades of the seventeenth century, one can hardly assume that France was any more densely settled in 1700 than she had been fifty or seventy years earlier. To be sure, with more than nineteen million inhabitants—the grand total of the figures returned by the *Intendants* at the end of the seventeenth century—the kingdom probably was somewhat more populous than under Louis XIII; but the increase was due neither to natural growth nor to net gains from migration, but solely to territorial acquisitions under the Treaties of Westphalia (1648), the Pyrenees (1659), Aix-la-Chapelle (1668), and Nijmegen (1678). From a demographic point of view, the seventeenth century cannot be described as the *Grand Siècle* of French history.

Swedish population increase, apparently very slight during the period 1560–1630, seems to have accelerated somewhat in the following two generations, which yielded an estimated increment of about 25 per cent. However, even this moderate gain in numbers may have involved a substantial lowering of the standard of living.[1] After 1695 growth ceased altogether and was not resumed before 1720. The population of Finland, after a spell of vigorous growth from the middle of the seventeenth century to the early 1690's, suffered an even greater setback in consequence of a disastrous famine which struck the country in 1696–7. Denmark had been afflicted by a similar demographic catastrophe in the 1650's.

The demographic history of seventeenth-century Poland, like that of her western neighbour, was marked by serious reverses. Developments were dominated by the calamitous effects on life and property of the wars and Cossack revolts which engulfed the entire country after 1648. Egon Vielrose has estimated that the population of the kingdom declined from 3,200,000 to 2,250,000 between 1578 and 1662. Samples collected by other Polish scholars for various regions moreover show drastic declines in the number of baptisms during the decades 1650–60, 1670–80, and 1710–20. Generalizing from these statistics one may conclude that the depopulation of the Polish countryside and the small towns after 1648 was about as great as that incurred by Germany in the first half of the century, during the Thirty Years War.

Information about developments in the Balkans, though scanty, suffices to establish the fact that there, too, the rising demographic trend of the sixteenth century was followed by stagnation or decline. 'Between 1600 and 1700', a recent student of the Balkan economy has told his readers, 'the cities of Constantinople, Adrianople, Sarejevo, Skoplje, Novi Pazar, Belgrad, and Banja Luka experience a loss of population.... In the seventeenth century, long stretches of fertile country in the Balkans lie untilled, numerous lowlands villages have disappeared.'[2] Even in that distant corner of the European continent, powerful forces making for secular demographic contraction must have been operative in this period; but we do not know enough to identify them. The only thing one may be reasonably certain about is that population pressure on land was not one of them: the appearance of deserted fields and villages precludes an explanation on Malthusian grounds.

The same may be said of Hungary. Subsequent to the establishment, in 1541, of Turkish rule over the central and southern lowlands, a process

[1] See Eli F. Heckscher, *An Economic History of Sweden* (Harvard Economic Studies, xcv), Cambridge, Mass., 1954, 116. More recent studies of Swedish food budgets, while they suggest certain modifications, do not call for any drastic revision of the views advanced by Heckscher.

[2] Traian Stoianovich, 'Land Tenure and Related Sectors of the Balkan Economy, 1600–1800', *The Journal of Economic History*, xiii (1953), 399 and 402.

of depopulation is known to have set in, the extent of which can hardly be overestimated. When the Habsburgs reconquered the country after 1683 they recovered a virtual desert, albeit a potentially fertile one. Thus by 1700 a 'new country' was opening up in Europe once again, beckoning to immigrants who were willing to start a new life under a strange sky. And once again they came: young peasants from the congested villages of south-western Germany and Lorraine, singing melancholy farewell songs as their barges floated down the Danube into the distant country to the east, which they vaguely referred to as '*Griechenland*'. Serbian families came, some 30,000 of them, under their own patriarch, fleeing before the Turks across the lower Danube; hardworking Slovak colonists, descending into the fertile plains from the highlands in the north-west; Wallachs, crossing the mountains of Transylvania; and the ubiquitous Greek and Jew, coming from nowhere into what was to be known as the 'Hungarian Canaan'. However, the history of this last 'frontier' movement on a grand scale in Central Europe, if it were to be treated in greater detail, would find its proper place in the following section of this chapter: it forms one of the aspects—at once symptom and ancillary cause—of the demographic upswing of the eighteenth century.

## V. *On the Eve of the Vital Revolution*[1]

The historian's understanding of past situations benefits greatly from the fact that he, unlike any contemporary observer, knows a good deal about subsequent development. It is only in retrospect, if at all, that germinal forces, unnoticed or underestimated at the time, can be seen in their true significance. However, hindsight also has its dangers. Reading history backwards we are easily misled into postulating *specific* 'antecedents' and 'early phases' of phenomena which seem to require a long period of gestation; and we are almost inclined to distrust our records, if they fail to confirm our expectations.

It is well to be on guard against this temptation when trying to appraise the general character of the closing years of the seventeenth, and the early decades of the eighteenth century. Certainly, as far as the demographic situation of this period is concerned, there was little if anything to herald the impending changes. Man was still very much at the mercy of the elements. As late as the 1690's, as we have seen, a succession of poor and indifferent harvests created severe subsistence-crises in almost

---

[1] A shortened version of this section was published in the *Canadian Journal of Economics and Political Science*, XXIII, 1–9, under the title 'The Vital Revolution Reconsidered'.

all countries of Europe. So far from growing, the population declined here and there, as dearth and starvation stalked through the lands from Castile to Finland, and from Scotland to Austria. In 1698, after a serious crop failure, certain regional death rates in Sweden are known to have risen to 9 and 16 per cent respectively. In one Finnish province, Tavastland, no less than one-third of the inhabitants must be assumed to have perished during the famine of 1696–7.[1] Parts of France, as has been shown above, had suffered comparable losses in 1693–4. An enumeration held in the duchy of Brabant in 1709 did not reveal any gain in numbers over those ascertained in 1693. The Kurmark, in 1728, counted slightly fewer inhabitants than forty years earlier. The population of the city of Milan shrank from 125,000 to 110,000 between 1688 and 1710. In England and Scotland, the 'seven ill years', if they did not cause a diminution, must have checked, or at least retarded, the growth of population. Nor was this the last visitation of the kind. The excessively cold and long winter of 1708–9, followed as it was by widespread crop failures, again caused intense misery and high mortality among the poorer classes, especially in France, where this season was long remembered as '*le Grand Hiver*'. In England, the scarcity did not reach famine proportions, and its demographic effects do not seem to have been drastic; still, the price of corn did rise very high in 1709–10, and the London Bills of Mortality record an unusual incidence of fatal cases of 'fever'.

Meanwhile Europe had once more entered upon a phase of universal belligerency. While the campaigns of the War of the Spanish Succession (1701–14) were fought in the west, the nations of the north-east were engaged in an even longer and fiercer conflict, the Great Northern War (1699–1721).

Historians have tended to minimize the *direct* demographic effects of warfare; and in general this view of things is probably correct. However, the Great Northern War appears to have been an uncommonly sanguinary affair. This may be inferred from Finnish population data from the middle of the eighteenth century, which reveal a highly abnormal sex distribution in all the older age groups. At that time, there was an excess of females over males in the groups born between 1676 and 1695, ranging from 21 per cent to as high as 68 per cent. The conclusion to be drawn is that a significant proportion of the men who were of military age during the period of hostilities perished in the war. The effects of these losses on the reproductive power of the nations involved need no emphasis.

Nevertheless, the number of military casualties, if it could be as-

[1] See Eino Jutikkala, 'The Great Finnish Famine in 1696–7', *Scandinavian Economic History Review*, III (1955), 48–63.

certained, would undoubtedly again be dwarfed by the heavy losses
inflicted upon the civilian population by war-time epidemics. While the
theatres of operations in the west (e.g. Bavaria in 1703–4) experienced the
usual flare-up of typhus, north-eastern Europe was once again invaded
by plague. Though virtually extinct in the west, plague was still endemic
in the eastern parts of the continent. As early as 1708 the infection appears
to have spread through Poland into Silesia; and in the next few years,
undoubtedly in connection with military movements, but probably
also fomented by the food crisis of 1709–10, it invaded Brandenburg-
Prussia, the Baltic countries and Scandinavia. In the city of Danzig and
its suburbs 32,600 persons—between one-third and one-half of the
population—are reported to have died of plague during the epidemic of
1709; Copenhagen is said to have lost 21,000 persons, about a third of its
inhabitants, in 1710–11. Other cities of north-eastern Europe, such as
Königsberg (with 8,500 deaths, approximately one-fifth of the population), Riga, Stockholm, Karlskrona, Upsala, and Helsinki also suffered
grievously. Nor was it only the large urban centres that were afflicted.
As Süssmilch's figures for (East) Prussia and Lithuania indicate, mortality
was heavy throughout the Baltic littoral in 1709 and 1710. In East Prussia
nearly 11,000 vacant farms are said to have been counted after the
plague.

Progressing relentlessly towards the west, the infection reached
north-western Germany in 1712, and Austria, Bohemia, and Bavaria
in 1713. However, by this time the epidemic, while still murderous in
some places—the city of Prague, if our source can be trusted, counted
about 37,000 deaths in 1713—seems to have exhausted its powers.
Before it was able to penetrate into Italy and the west of Europe the
plague ceased abruptly.

To people in western Europe it must have seemed as if their countries
had acquired some sort of immunity against plague; and events in the
following years, though very upsetting at first, could not but confirm
them in their optimism. In May 1720, a ship coming from a plague-
infested port in Syria brought the deadly disease to Marseilles. There
followed a furious outbreak, killing about 40,000 of the city's 90,000
inhabitants. Within a few weeks after its first appearance the epidemic
was sweeping through Provence; and while in some places the losses
were relatively light, in others, especially the more populous towns and
cities, the death toll was appalling. Aix-en-Provence, Martigues, and
Saint-Remy are reported to have lost about one-third, Toulon, Auriol,
and Berre about one-half, and Arles and La Vallette about three-fourths
of their inhabitants.

The news of this catastrophe caused grave anxiety throughout
Europe. Authorities everywhere hastily decreed quarantine and other

precautionary measures—the Pope had six of Rome's sixteen gates walled up so as to facilitate the inspection of incoming freight and travellers. In England—such is the tangled skein of historical causation— the scare produced an unexpected boom in the textile trades, as people stopped buying French manufactures and transferred their demand to English goods. However, the fears proved unfounded. Inexplicably, the plague failed to spread beyond the borders of Provence and a few adjoining districts of Languedoc; and by August 1721 it was all over.

The sequence of crises which, often reinforcing one another, had afflicted many nations of Europe during the 1690's and the early years of the eighteenth century was followed by a period which appears considerably more auspicious by comparison. The 1720's and 1730's, on the whole, were years of adequate and even abundant harvests in most European regions. Endemic diseases no doubt continued to exact a heavy toll of life, while an occasional flare-up of smallpox, typhus, dysentry or malignant influenza, would send death-rates up momentarily, sometimes, for instance in 1727–30 in various parts of England, to a point where they exceeded the birth-rates. However, there were no more epidemics of plague, except that limited outbreak in Provence. Fighting was tapering off: the Spanish succession was settled by treaty in 1714, and Austria's conflict with Turkey ended in 1718. The Northern War was in its last phase, and terminated in 1721. The stage was set for demographic recovery and advance.

At this point in his narrative the historian of population, for the first time, finds himself in a position to support his conclusions with tolerably reliable data arranged in time-series; though in the beginning it is only for a very limited territory—Finland and ten counties of Sweden—that this kind of information becomes available. In both these countries the death-rate remained remarkably constant and low for a period of about fifteen years following the end of the Northern War, the average being 21·2 per mille for Sweden[1] and 20·8 per mille for Finland in 1721–35.

For no subsequent period during the rest of the century did the death-rate remain at so low a level, and in spite of wide fluctuations in the death-rate in later years it was very rare for the rate to fall again to the low level of 1721–35, and in no year did it fall below that earlier level. Not until the 1830's in Sweden and the 1870's in Finland did the death-rate fall to a comparably low figure (H. Gille).

[1] This figure, which is based on slightly defective contemporary compilations from the church registers, would have to be raised to 23·9 per mille, if the corrections suggested by a regional investigation were to be applied to the whole kingdom. See Bertil Boëthius, 'New Light on Eighteenth-Century Sweden', *Scandinavian Economic History Review*, II (1953), 151, fn. 2.

To some small extent, this uncommonly low death-rate can be explained by viewing it as a function of the birth-rate. Since infant mortality formed a very important component of total mortality in the eighteenth century, a low birth-rate would tend to reduce the death-rate. As a matter of fact, in consequence of the highly unfavourable age and sex distribution referred to above, the birth-rate *was* relatively low in this period, both in Sweden and in Finland. However, since the death-rate was substantially lower still—despite local crop failures in 1725–7—the population of the two countries was growing rapidly. In Finland the average annual increase was 14·3 per thousand in 1722–8, and 16·7 per thousand in 1729–36. In the ten Swedish counties for which information is available, natural growth, if somewhat slower, was also quite impressive: the annual average was 9·7 per thousand in 1722–8, and 7·8 per thousand in 1729–36.

However, the time had not yet arrived when European societies would be capable of weathering adversity well enough to produce an excess of births over deaths year after year and decade after decade. In Sweden, for instance, natural increase turned negative momentarily as late as 1809–10. To be sure, the secular demographic trend was rising in all the Scandinavian countries after 1720. Subsistence crises and epidemics in this period were very much milder than those of the preceding century; yet the gravest of them—for instance those of 1737–43, 1771–3, and 1788–90—were still sufficiently powerful to slow down population growth, and even reverse it temporarily. In no case, however, were the losses caused by hunger and disease crippling. Finland by 1745–6 had already overcome the demographic effects of the bad years after 1736. The net losses suffered by Sweden and Norway in 1772–3 (71,000 and 17,000 respectively) did not amount to more than 2·3 and 3·5 per cent of their populations, and were also made good within three or four years.

Demographic developments in eighteenth-century Scandinavia were in many respects typical of what was happening elsewhere in Europe at that time. Though the rates of growth varied widely from country to country, population was on the increase everywhere from about 1740 onwards, and in most cases at an accelerated pace after the middle of the century. This general trend is clearly illustrated by the figures presented in Tables 21–35—whatever the reservations one may have in accepting at their face value some of these enumerations or estimates.

Once more, none of the figures presented in these tables, with the exception of some of the Scandinavian data, should be pressed very hard.[1]

---

[1] The sources of some serious errors which have vitiated most, if not all, estimates of English population growth in the eighteenth century have been pointed out by J. T. Krause, 'Changes in English Fertility and Mortality, 1781–1850', *Economic History Review*, 2nd ser., XI (August 1958), 52–70.

## Table 21. *Sweden*

| Year | Number of inhabitants | Percentage change over the preceding year for which information is available | Annual percentage change in each interval |
|------|------|------|------|
| 1721 | (1,462,000) | | |
| 1735 | (1,703,000) | +16·5 | +1·2 |
| 1750 | 1,781,000 | +4·6 | +0·30 |
| 1775 | 2,021,000 | +13·5 | +0·54 |
| 1800 | 2,347,000 | +16·2 | +0·65 |

SOURCE: H. Gille, 'The Demographic History of the Northern European Countries in the Eighteenth Century', *Population Studies*, III (1949–50), 19. Figures in brackets are estimates. In the light of recent investigations (see above, p. 61, fn. 1) they may have to be scaled down somewhat.

## Table 22. *Finland*

| Year | Number of inhabitants | Percentage change over the preceding year for which information is available | Annual percentage change in each interval |
|------|------|------|------|
| 1721 | (289,000) | | |
| 1735 | (360,000) | +24·6 | +1·8 |
| 1750 | 422,000 | +17·2 | +1·1 |
| 1775 | 610,000 | +44·6 | +1·8 |
| 1800 | 833,000 | +34·1 | +1·4 |

SOURCE: H. Gille, *op. cit.*, p. 19. Figures in brackets are estimates.

## Table 23. *Norway*

| Year | Number of inhabitants | Percentage change over the preceding year for which information is available | Annual percentage change in each interval |
|------|------|------|------|
| 1735 | (569,000) | | |
| 1750 | (591,000) | +3·87 | +0·26 |
| 1775 | (718,000) | +21·5 | +0·86 |
| 1800 | 883,000 | +23·0 | +0·92 |

SOURCE: H. Gille, *op. cit.*, p. 19. Figures in brackets are estimates.

Table 24. *Denmark*

| Year | Number of inhabitants | Percentage change over the preceding year for which information is available | Annual percentage change in each interval |
|------|------------------------|------------------------------------------------------------------------------|-------------------------------------------|
| 1735 | (777,000) | | |
| 1750 | (806,000) | +3·75 | +0·25 |
| 1775 | (843,000) | +4·59 | +0·18 |
| 1800 | 926,000 | +9·85 | +0·39 |

SOURCE: H. Gille, *op. cit.*, p. 19. Figures in brackets are estimates.

Table 25. *Sicily (including Palermo and Messina)*

| Year | Number of inhabitants | Percentage change over the preceding year for which information is available | Annual percentage change in each interval |
|------|------------------------|------------------------------------------------------------------------------|-------------------------------------------|
| 1713 | (1,143,000) | | |
| 1747 | (1,319,000) | +15·4 | +0·46 |
| 1798 | 1,660,000 | +25·9 | +0·50 |

SOURCE: Karl Julius Beloch, *Bevölkerungsgeschichte Italiens*, I, 152. Figures in brackets are estimates.

Table 26. *Papal States*

| Year | Number of inhabitants | Percentage change over the preceding year for which information is available | Annual percentage change in each interval |
|------|------------------------|------------------------------------------------------------------------------|-------------------------------------------|
| 1701 | 1,969,000 | | |
| 1736 | 2,064,000 | +4·8 | +0·14 |
| 1769 | 2,204,000 | +6·8 | +0·21 |
| 1782 | 2,400,000 | +8·9 | +0·68 |

SOURCE: Karl Julius Beloch, *op. cit.*, II, 122. The figures are totals, based partly on enumerations, partly on estimates of territorial populations.

### Table 27. *Tuscany*

| Year | Number of inhabitants | Percentage change over the preceding year for which information is available | Annual percentage change in each interval |
|------|------|------|------|
| *c.* 1700 | (950,000) | | |
| *c.* 1750 | 1,079,000 | +13·5 | +0·27 |
| *c.* 1800 | 1,188,000 | +10·0 | +0·20 |

SOURCE: Karl Julius Beloch, *op. cit.*, II, 237. The figures are totals, based partly on enumerations, partly on estimates of territorial populations.

### Table 28. *Spain*

| Year | Number of inhabitants | Percentage change over the preceding year for which information is available | Annual percentage change in each interval |
|------|------|------|------|
| 1723 | (6,100,000) | | |
| 1747 | 7,380,000 | +20·0 | +0·87 |
| 1756 | 8,000,000 | +8·40 | +0·93 |
| 1768 | 9,310,000 | +16·4 | +1·36 |
| 1787 | 10,410,000 | +11·8 | +0·62 |

SOURCE: Albert Girard, 'Le chiffre de la population de l'Espagne dans les temps modernes', *Revue de l'Histoire Moderne*, IV (1929), 6. The first of these data is no more than a rough estimate based on enumerations of *vecinos*. The whole series probably exaggerates the rate of growth.

### Table 29. *Portugal*

| Year | Number of inhabitants | Percentage change over the preceding year for which information is available | Annual percentage change in the interval |
|------|------|------|------|
| 1732 | (1,743,000) | | |
| 1801 | 2,932,000 | +68·2 | +0·99 |

SOURCE: J. T. Montalvão Machado, *loc. cit.*, pp. 475 f. The figure in brackets, a contemporary estimate, may be somewhat too low, and therefore the percentage increase given above somewhat exaggerated.

## Table 30. *Duchy of Brabant*

| Year | Number of inhabitants | Percentage change over the preceding year for which information is available | Annual percentage change in the interval |
|---|---|---|---|
| 1709 | 373,000 | | |
| 1755 | 445,000 | +19·3 | +0·42 |
| 1784 | 618,000 | +38·9 | +1·34 |

SOURCE: A. Cosemans, *De Bevolking van Brabant in de XVIIde en XVIIIde Eeuw* (Brussels, 1939), 187 f. and 224. The figures are estimates based on enumerations.

## Table 31. *Switzerland*

| Year | Number of inhabitants | Percentage change over the preceding year for which information is available | Annual percentage change in the intervals |
|---|---|---|---|
| 1700 | 1,200,000 | | |
| 1789 | 1,700,000 | +41·7 | +0·43 |

SOURCE: W. Bickel, *Bevölkerungsgeschichte der Schweiz seit dem Ausgang des Mittelalters* (Zürich, 1947), 49 ff. Both figures are estimates, but the second is based on an (incomplete) enumeration.

## Table 32. *Germany* (*some Prussian provinces*)

| Year | Number of inhabitants | Percentage change over the preceding year for which information is available | Annual percentage change in each interval |
|---|---|---|---|
| 1740 | 2,257,000 | | |
| 1748 | 2,314,000 | +2·53 | +0·32 |
| 1752 | 2,497,000 | +7·91 | +1·98 |
| 1778 | 3,487,000 | +39·6 | +1·52 |
| 1790 | 3,911,000 | +12·2 | +1·01 |

SOURCE: V. Inama-Sternegg and Häpke, 'Bevölkerungswesen: Die Bevölkerung des Mittelalters und der neueren Zeit', *Handwörterbuch der Staatswissenschaften*, 4th ed., II (Jena, 1924), 672.

## Table 33. *England and Wales**

| Year | Estimated number of inhabitants | Percentage change over the preceding year for which information is available | Annual percentage change in each interval |
|------|------|------|------|
| 1700 | 5,200,000 | | |
| 1750 | 6,500,000 | +25 | +0·50 |
| 1800 | 9,600,000 | +47·7 | +0·95 |

* All three figures are estimates; that for 1700 is based on Gregory King's estimate for 1688 as tentatively revised by D. V. Glass (see above, p. 53, fn. 1), that for 1800 on the census figures of 1801 as tentatively revised by J. T. Krause (see below, p. 62, fn. 1).

## Table 34. *Ireland*

| Year | Estimated number of inhabitants | Percentage change over the preceding year for which information is available | Annual percentage change in each interval |
|------|------|------|------|
| 1712 | 2,791,000 | | |
| 1718 | 2,894,000 | +3·69 | +0·62 |
| 1725 | 3,042,000 | +5·11 | +0·73 |
| 1732 | 3,018,000 | −0·80 | −0·01 |
| 1754 | 3,191,000 | +5·73 | +0·26 |
| 1767 | 3,480,000 | +9·06 | +0·70 |
| 1772 | 3,584,000 | +2·99 | +0·60 |
| 1777 | 3,740,000 | +4·35 | +0·87 |
| 1781 | 4,048,000 | +8·24 | +2·06 |
| 1785 | 4,019,000 | −0·72 | −0·02 |
| 1788 | 4,389,000 | +9·21 | +3·06 |
| 1791 | 4,753,000 | +8·29 | +2·76 |

SOURCE: K. H. Connell, *The Population of Ireland, 1750–1845* (Oxford, 1950), 25. The figures are estimates, based on revised estimates of the number of houses.

## Table 35. *France**

| Year | Number of inhabitants | Percentage change over the preceding year for which information is available | Annual percentage change in each interval |
|------|------|------|------|
| c. 1700 | 21,000,000 | | |
| c. 1715 | 18,000,000 | −14·3 | −0·95 |
| c. 1770 | 24,000,000 | +33·3 | +0·61 |
| c. 1789 | 26,000,000 | +8·3 | +0·44 |

* These figures are estimates offered by E. Levasseur, *La population française*, I (Paris, 1889), 206, 213 and 216 f. They refer to France without Alsace-Lorraine.

Yet even if they be used for no purpose other than that of demonstrating the universal character of the demographic upswing in the eighteenth century, their heuristic value remains very great indeed; for it is only by taking cognizance of the universality of this phenomenon that we can hope to understand its causal mechanism.

## VI. *Some Causal Factors of Secular Dynamics*

It has been suspected for some time that the society which was struck down by the Black Death about the middle of the fourteenth century had already passed from an epoch of secular economic and demographic advance into one of incipient stagnation. The growth of population in the preceding centuries, it seems, had created a precarious situation, as the number of under-sized holdings increased, and settlement penetrated into regions of inferior soil and inclement climate. Moreover, the progress of clearing had led to a continuous shrinkage of the area which maintained the animal population indispensable to medieval husbandry. The result was either over-stocking, which must have caused the pastures to deteriorate quickly and produced conditions favourable to epizootics, or else deliberate curtailment of livestock production, which was tantamount to depriving the fields of manure, and man of some of his sources of protein. The stage, apparently, was set for the activation of some of Malthus's 'positive checks'. The great European famine of 1315–17 may have been a first harbinger of disaster.

When the Black Death and other severe epidemics drastically reduced the population of Europe in the second half of the fourteenth century, the margin of cultivation, which had been pushed dangerously near, and even beyond, the line of rapidly diminishing returns, receded. Productivity increased, as cereal production concentrated on the better lands, and by 1370 grain prices started a secular downward movement. The crudely Malthusian *modus operandi* would have permitted the population to resume growth, all the more so since the new demographic situation should have made it very much easier than previously for young people of the lower orders to establish families. An abundance of vacancies enabled landless labourers to acquire holdings at reasonable rents; and the prevailing labour shortage, in conjunction with the fall in the price of grain, resulted in an upward trend of real wages in town and country. Yet, as demonstrated above, population long failed to respond to these favourable conditions.

The frequency and severity of late-medieval epidemics as well as grave disorders in the political and social spheres tended, no doubt, both to raise the level of mortality and to lower the birth-rate. In addition to these adverse factors, however, the very improvements in the economic position of the lower classes may have militated against speedy demographic recovery. It is to be assumed on *a priori* grounds, and there is some evidence to support this view,[1] that those improvements led to an upward revision of the living standard, involving a partial shift from a cereal to a meat standard of consumption. This change in consumers' preference is reflected in the movement of relative prices of animal products and grain, which must have intensified that *Wüstung* process referred to earlier, one aspect of which was a partial 'decerealization' of Europe in favour of animal husbandry.[2] However, given a certain level of agrarian technology, five or six times as much land is required for the raising of one calory of animal food as is needed for the production of one calory of vegetable food. It follows that whatever relief from pressure of population on land was afforded by the initial demographic slump must have been partly offset by that change in the pattern of consumption and production. This hypothesis helps to explain an otherwise rather puzzling fact, namely that the later Middle Ages should have suffered scarcely less than previous centuries from dearth and famine,[3] even though man's *per capita* supply of fertile land was undoubtedly much higher in this period.[4] These subsistence-crises invariably engendered epidemic outbreaks, and may thus have been among the chief factors responsible for the high mortality of late-medieval times.

One further corollary of the tentative views advanced in the foregoing paragraph should be noted. It is arguable that the relative prosperity enjoyed by the lower orders of late-medieval society, so far from promoting early marriages and high marital fertility, may have produced

[1] See Wilhelm Abel, 'Wüstungen und Preisfall im spätmittelalterlichen Europa', *Jahrbücher für Nationalökonomie und Statistik*, CLXV (1953), 380–427 esp. 398 ff., and J. C. Drummond and Anne Wilbraham, *The Englishman's Food* (London, 1940), 52.

[2] In the special circumstances of sixteenth-century England some conversion of plough-land into pasture continued even after demographic recovery had set in. However, it was widely recognized that the recession of arable farming had been brought about, in the first instance, 'by decaye or lacke of people, so that corne and other victuall grewe to be so good cheape that they dyd suffer their plowes to decaye and their grounde lye waste.' *Tudor Economic Documents* (ed. R. H. Tawney and Eileen Power), I, 74.

[3] A secular deterioration of the late-medieval climate may also have played a part. See G. Richter, 'Klimaschwankungen und Wüstungsvorgänge im Mittelalter', *Petermanns geographische Mitteilungen*, XCVI (1952), 249 ff.

[4] The paradox was commented upon by a contemporary observer, the Florentine chronicler Matteo Villani. 'Men thought,' he wrote, 'that by reason of the diminished numbers of mankind there should be abundance of all produce of the land; yet, on the contrary ... everything came to unwonted scarcity and remained long thus; nay, in certain countries, ... there were grievous and unwonted famines.' Though couched in moralizing language, the explanation offered by the author substantially agrees with the one suggested above, namely a drastic rise in the standard of consumption. '[Men] dissolutely abandoned themselves to the sin of gluttony, with feasts and taverns and delight of delicate viands.' Quoted by G. G. Coulton, *The Black Death* (London, 1929), 67 f.

the opposite effects. For man is determined, as a rule, fiercely to defend any conspicuous improvement in his socio-economic position—be it the result of individual upgrading, or of a rise in the general level of real earnings. The son of a labourer turned leaseholder or customary tenant was not likely to be allowed to jeopardize the newly acquired status of his family by a hasty marriage. A farm hand or journeyman, accustomed to meat dishes, would not calmly face a return to porridge and rye bread, which encumbrance with a large family would entail. Medieval figures, being what they are, do not, of course, permit us to offer anything like conclusive proof of this contention. But there exists at least one source which clearly demonstrates that a surprisingly large portion of the grown-up population of a late-medieval city was indeed reluctant, or unable, to get married. An analysis of the Zürich tax registers of 1467 indicates that only slightly more than 50 per cent of the taxpayers had spouses; about 44 per cent were single, and the rest were widowed. It cannot be affirmed that this state of affairs was typical;[1] but the well-known role of organized prostitution in late-medieval town life suggests that it was.[2] Pre-marital intercourse with women other than prostitutes probably played an important part, too; and there is strong evidence— though it dates only from the middle of the sixteenth century—that in such relations *coitus interruptus* was freely resorted to.[3] This practice not only tended to keep the rate of illegitimate births relatively low, but, if it was carried over into married life, would have had a depressing effect on marital fertility. However, on this latter point our sources are silent. It is not before the second half of the seventeenth century that we have any positive indication of birth control *within* marriage.

But even without recourse to contraceptive practices (all of which were frowned upon severely by the Church) the size of a man's family could be kept low: a young fellow espousing a middle-aged woman need not be afraid of getting too many children. We cannot offer any quantitative evidence to show that such judicious selection of marriage partners, jocularly alluded to in many an old story and in a well-known German folk song,[4] was more common in the later Middle Ages than at other

[1] J. Krause's calculations ('The Medieval Household: Large or Small?,' *Economic History Review*, 2nd ser., IX, 1957, 431) suggested that in 1377 about 66% of England's male poll-tax population (though only 59% of the *total* male adult population) were married. However, these percentages were probably above the medieval average.

[2] According to Martin Luther ('Vom ehelichen Leben', 1522, *D. Martin Luthers Werke, Kritische Gesamtausgabe*, x/2, 302), many a poor man refrains from matrimony, because he cannot see how to provide for a family. 'This is the chief obstacle to married life, and the cause of all whoredom.'

[3] See *Zimmerische Chronik* (ed. Karl August Barack), 2nd rev. ed. (Freiburg i.B. and Tübingen, 1881–2), II, 425, and IV, 10.

[4] '*Als ich ein jung Geselle war, nahm ich ein steinalt Weib*' ('When I was a young lad, I took an old, old wife').

times. But in this age of growing guild exclusiveness marrying the widow of a master craftsman was often the only way for an ambitious journeyman to gain economic independence.

Still another form of family limitation—infanticide—had long been proscribed both by Church and state. But though this heinous practice had been greatly reduced in Christian society, it had not disappeared entirely. English figures for the fourteenth and fifteenth centuries show an unmistakable deficiency in the number of female children, both among the more prosperous landholding groups and in servile families. This anomalous sex ratio makes one suspect that some tampering with human life may have occurred. It need not be assumed, however, that a significant number of female babies were killed at birth. Humans are exceedingly vulnerable creatures during the first weeks and months of life, and neglect on the part of their mothers or nurses—not necessarily and always conscious neglect—will result in death as surely as deliberate infanticide.

The rise of the secular demographic trend in some European countries after the middle of the fifteenth century, and its pronounced upswing in all of them during the better part of the sixteenth century, are not easily accounted for. Contemporaries speculating on the causes of the phenomenon would point to the absence of war and pestilence; and to the extent that their diagnosis applied to local or regional conditions, especially in the initial phase of population growth, it may well have been correct. Italy, during the forty years preceding the French invasion (1454–94), was virtually at peace. To some other countries the latter half of the fifteenth century afforded at least a modicum of relief from the calamities of war. France saw the Hundred Years War come to an end in 1453; and this same year brought the conclusion of an equally savage, if much shorter, conflict in south-western Germany. In the north-east, the Peace of Thorn (1466) put a stop to thirteen years of ferocious fighting between Poland and the Teutonic Knights. A generation earlier, the victory of the moderate Hussites over the extremists, and their temporary reconciliation with the Catholics, had led to a cessation of those furious mutual raids which had long inflicted intolerable hardships on Bohemia and its adjacent territories.

But if some regions enjoyed a respite from slaughter and devastation in the last decades of the medieval period, others, like the Burgundian state and its neighbours, were still in the throes of violence during most of that time. In the south-east, too, there was a good deal of unrest, culminating in the conquest of Austria by King Matthias Corvinus of Hungary (1477–85). England did not emerge from her dynastic quarrels before 1485.

As to the sixteenth century, it is hardly necessary to dwell upon its bellicose and sanguinary character. The secular struggle for European hegemony between the houses of Habsburg and Valois at one time or another engulfed regions as far apart as the Kingdom of Naples and the Netherlands. The bloody Peasants' Rebellion in Germany (1524–6) is reliably estimated to have resulted in the death of 100,000 men. There were the Wars of Religion in Switzerland (1529–31) and France (1562–95) already referred to, as well as a similar armed conflict in Germany (1547–55). There was the revolt of the Netherlands against their Spanish masters (1567 ff.) and the Seven Years Nordic War (1563–70). There was the relentless defensive struggle along the south-eastern frontier of the Empire against the Ottoman Power.

Amidst all these trials and tribulations the population of Europe was growing; not, it is true, without major regional setbacks at times, but at a secular rate sufficient to yield substantial increments in all countries over the demographic level of 1450. Is there any indication that famine and disease relaxed their grip on mankind in this epoch? Of course, for lack of comprehensive and reliable histories of subsistence-crises and epidemics it is almost impossible to compare the aggregate weight of the afflictions of one period with that of another. The demographic impact of such calamities is a function, amongst other things, of their frequency, duration, scope, and severity; and of all this not enough is known.

On balance—if one is rash enough to draw up a tentative balance sheet of collective disasters in the face of all these uncertainties—there may indeed have occurred a slight weakening of some, at least, of the positive checks, not only in that relatively peaceful period from 1453 to 1494, but also for some time thereafter. This statement must come as a surprise in view of what has just been said about the temporal and spatial extent of hostilities in the sixteenth century. War, pestilence, and famine very frequently form a syndrome, the former begetting and perpetuating the other two evils. Is it at all likely that disease and hunger diminished in an age of almost ubiquitous and interminable warfare?

A cursory examination of the epidemiological record of the period under review seems to vindicate these doubts. If anything, standards of sanitation seem to have gone from bad to worse, as new diseases are found to have made their appearance (or, possibly, old ones to have changed their character) in this age. We hear of outbreaks of a mysterious 'sweating sickness' in England (1485, 1508, 1517, 1529, 1551), and on the continent (1529). Syphilis, another new scourge of mankind, within a few years after 1494 was carried through the length and breadth of Europe by soldiers and camp followers returning from the Italian campaigns. Typhus, while it may have existed before, yet seems to have become a major epidemic disease only in the sixteenth century. A louse-borne infection, it must have found excellent conditions for its spread among the filthy inmates of crowded military tents and barracks. It is known to have flared up repeatedly in various theatres of war in the course of the sixteenth century, one of the worst outbreaks being that of 1566. It occurred among the Imperial troops sent against the Turk, whence this disease came to be called the 'Hungarian sickness' by contemporary writers.

But when all is said, the demographic effects of these evils should not be overrated. With the exception of typhus, a dreadful malady indeed, whose killing power may at times have equalled that of plague, these 'new' diseases were not very destructive of human life. If the 'English Sweat' received a good deal of attention from terrified observers, this was due to its novelty, to the dramatic suddenness with which this strange disease attacked its victims, and perhaps also to the fact that it seemed to show a tendency to strike members of the well-to-do classes rather than the poor. However, mortality incidental to the sweating sickness apparently was not very high. The epidemics, except for one outbreak, remained confined to England; and in any case nothing more is heard of this illness after 1551. Syphilis at the time of its explosive spread, after 1494, had all the marks of an exceedingly virulent and malignant infection. But within a generation it appears to have changed its nature, turning into the kind of insidious malady for which it has been known ever since: a disease likely to shorten the lives of its victims (and to reduce their procreative faculty), but not lethal in the short run. Another disease, fated to play a deleterious role in the seventeenth and eighteenth centuries—smallpox—apparently did not yet loom large among the great epidemic scourges of this period. For the rest, it is necessary to emphasize that differential diagnosis was, and long continued to be, in a rudimentary state. Except in cases where his sources clearly comment on the appearance of buboes or of carbuncles and dark spots on the skin of the patient it is seldom possible for the modern epidemiologist to identify with any certainty from the descriptions given by contemporaries a crowd-disease of earlier times.

Even so, it is safe to say that in the period under review and for some time to come plague retained its rank as the worst killer of all. This being the case, it would be all the more significant to find indications that its power was waning, or the resistance of the population increasing. If it could be shown that outbreaks of plague were, on the whole, milder, shorter, or less numerous than in the preceding century, this would provide us with an important clue to the causes underlying the demographic upswing after 1450. Let it be said once more that, with the information available at present, no definite statement about these matters can be offered. On the face of it, the epidemiological record certainly does not indicate any spectacular weakening of the plague. If anything, we hear more about pestilential outbreaks in this period than before; but the fact that documentation for post-medieval times is generally more abundant probably accounts for that. As a matter of fact, there is some evidence to suggest that mortality incidental to plague may have declined, not to any striking extent, but perhaps sufficiently to cause a slight secular downward trend of the general death-rate in the century after 1450 or 1470. What seems to have happened is that the plague, formerly known swiftly to overrun whole countries had, for the time being, turned into a more localized disease. 'Plague', writes Dr Charles Creighton, the noted historian of epidemics in Britain, 'henceforth [i.e. after the middle of the fifteenth century] is seldom universal; it becomes more and more a disease of the towns, and when it does occur in the country, it is for the most part at some few limited spots.' This impression is confirmed by the statement of a competent contemporary observer. 'They have some little plague in England well nigh every year', the Venetian ambassador in London reported in 1554, 'for which they are not accustomed to make sanitary provisions, *as it does not usually make great progress.*' A German writer of the earlier part of the sixteenth century, Paul Lang, the author of the Naumburg Chronicle, also comments on the sporadic and endemic character of the plague. 'It is remarkable and astonishing', he writes, 'that the plague should never wholly cease, but that it should appear every year here and there, making its way from one place to another, from one country to another. Having subsided at one time, it returns within a few years by a circuitous route.'[1] In Sweden, no general outbreak of plague seems to have occurred between 1495 and 1565.

To suggest that the epidemic power of plague was somewhat diminished (or man's resistance strengthened) is not to imply that the local visitations of the sixteenth century were trifling matters. Indeed, in the second half of the sixteenth century outbreaks were becoming more violent again. If it was possible for the city of London, its Liberties, and its Out-parishes to lose, *from plague alone*, more than 20,000 inhabitants in a single year (1563), and 15,000 in another (1593); if in a relatively small city like Norwich more than 4,800 deaths were recorded during a plague season (20 August 1578, to 19 February 1579), the plague germ cannot have lost much of its lethal strength. Moreover, after 1560, a year which appears to have marked a turning point in climatic history, too, there occurred once again a number of severe epidemics of a non-localized nature. The years 1563–6 witnessed a veritable pandemic, with numerous outbreaks recorded in England, Sweden, Germany, Switzer-

[1] Paulus Langius, *Chronica Numburgensis Ecclesiae* in Johann Burchard Mencken, *Scriptores rerum Germanicarum, praecipue Saxonicarum,* II (Leipzig, 1728), 88.

land, Savoy, France, and Spain. The plague of 1575–7, though more limited in scope, was not a local affair either. Having flared up in Sicily and in the South Tyrol, the infection was speedily carried into northern Italy, where it played havoc among the inhabitants of Venice and Milan, as well as of many smaller cities and towns. Similar outbreaks of a territorial, rather than local, character occurred in Switzerland and France in the 1580's and in Spain in 1599–1600.

If the epidemiological record of the latter part of the fifteenth and the sixteenth centuries does not seem to warrant any too positive inference as to the trend of mortality, neither does the information relating to dearth and famine. This field of historical inquiry, more than many others, still requires a great deal of spade work. Preoccupied with problems of the 'long run', economic historians hitherto have paid singularly little attention to what they regard as ephemeral events, such as subsistence crises. Moreover, and this may have been another reason for neglect, the evidence available for earlier centuries—a few series of grain prices and widely scattered, if numerous, references to food shortages in contemporary chronicles and administrative records—is too fragmentary and heterogeneous to admit of formal statistical treatment. In any case, the historian who might wish to compare the incidence of dearth and famine in successive periods would be confronted with the intractable problem of how to discount the bias introduced by the growing volume of his source-material.

Thus we cannot even assert with any confidence that the frequency of subsistence crises was sensibly diminished in the period under review. Local and regional scarcities, due to warfare or elemental disorders, certainly were still common enough. In a marginal area, like the semi-arid high plateau of Castile, markedly poor harvests and high grain-prices occurred about once in every decade. But even in countries with a more temperate climate grave food shortages were not rare. If, as happened not infrequently, large sections of Europe were simultane-ously afflicted by inclement seasons, the ensuing crop deficiencies were all the more a serious matter, since regional shortages could not be relieved by shipments from neighbouring countries. This is not the place to draw up an exhaustive chronology of these major calamities, but a few may be listed.

The years 1481–2 brought poor harvests in England, France, the Low Countries, Germany, and Bohemia, causing the English wheat price to rise to about twice the long-term average. Twenty years later, in 1501–2, England and Germany were again suffering from dearth, and in France, too, the price of wheat was well above normal. The late twenties and early thirties of the sixteenth century saw a series of bad harvests all over Europe: 1527 was a year of dire scarcity in England, followed by four more years of high wheat prices. About the same time (1529–31), Germany was struck by crop failures. Spain, too, was in dire straits, with high wheat prices prevailing in Old and New Castile, as well as Valencia, in 1529–31. Of the deplorable conditions in war-torn Italy during the late twenties we have spoken earlier. Only France seems to have done a little better in this period of universal adversity, with only one year of severe dearth (1531) recorded. Another season of widespread distress was 1556–7, with famines or famine-prices reported for England, the Netherlands, north-western Germany, Denmark, parts of France (Burgundy and the Rhone basin), Italy, and Spain.[1]

As the sixteenth century draws to its close the frequency and severity of food shortages seem to increase, not only in the Mediterranean world, where Professor Braudel has found striking symptoms of a *crise de blé*, but also in other parts of Europe. (England's Poor Laws of 1597 and 1601 were meant to cope with the distress engendered by this very period of general dearth.) In order to account for this phenomenon it is hardly necessary to have recourse to hypotheses—not easily verifiable in any case—about a secular deterioration of the climate; though the influence of strictly exogenous factors of a long-run nature should not, perhaps, be disregarded altogether.[2] It may be sufficient to call to mind that the population of Europe had grown appreciably for a hundred years or more. Presumably, the European economy, by the second half of the sixteenth century, was again approaching a state of temporary demographic satiety, similar to that which it had reached once before, early in the fourteenth century, and from which it had first been relieved by the Great Famine of 1315–17.

However, not one of the subsistence crises of the sixteenth century—if we may hazard a comparison which, for lack of a proper yardstick, must needs remain tentative—seems to have equalled that catastrophe in severity; and only one—the famine of 1556–7—approached it in scope. Man's defence against hunger, though still woefully inadequate, had become stronger in the meantime. By the sixteenth century the policy of municipal grain storage, previously practised only by wealthier and more far-sighted city governments, had become universal; even territorial princes were beginning to experiment with emergency food stores.[3] And while it cannot be denied that in times of threatening short-

[1] See Astrid Friis, 'An Inquiry into the Relations between Economic and Financial Factors in the Sixteenth and Seventeenth Centuries. I: The Two Crises in the Netherlands in 1557', *Scandinavian Economic History Review*, I/2 (1953), esp. 199 ff.

[2] See Gustaf Utterström, 'Climatic Fluctuations and Population Problems in Early Modern History', *Scandinavian Economic History Review*, III (1955), 3–47.

[3] In Sicily, royal granaries (*orrea imperialia*) existed as early as the first half of the thirteenth century. But their function was a different one. The Crown required storage facilities in its capacity as the largest grain exporter of the kingdom. See Adolf Schaube, *Handelsgeschichte der romanischen Völker des Mittelmeergebiets* (Munich and Berlin, 1906), 505.

age large-scale purchases on public account may have aggravated an incipient panic, the aggregate quantity of bread corn permanently kept in hundreds of municipal and other public granaries throughout the country must have been large enough to act as a strong physical as well as psychological buffer during periods of adversity.

Another factor, and not the least important one, which must have tended both to mitigate the physical impact of subsistence crises and to discourage speculative hoarding, was the growing likelihood of timely relief. In the period under review, countries stricken by crop failure came to rely increasingly on grain-shipments from the vast storehouses of Dutch merchants—Amsterdam, early in the seventeenth century, was said to be 'never without seven hundred thousand quarters of corn'—or on direct imports from surplus areas distant enough not to be affected by particular military operations or regional vagaries of the weather. Even though it was only places with easy access to navigable water that could draw on foreign food supplies to any significant extent—land transport of bulky low-priced goods being still a slow, uncertain, and unprofitable business—it did make some difference to a country as a whole, if at least its coastal cities received shipments from abroad in an emergency. Such, we are told, was the case at the height of the English famine in 1527, when 'the merchants of the Steelyard brought from Danzig such store of wheat and rye, that it was better cheap at London than in any other part of the Realm'. The history of a crisis in Tuscany, in 1540, provides a similar instance of relief afforded by the timely arrival in the harbour of Leghorn of a grain fleet from the Levant.

Of course, by the sixteenth century inter-regional sea-borne trade in victuals already had a long history behind it. The Low Countries, for instance, had received grain imports from the southern Baltic as early as the thirteenth century; and England and Spain, too, had drawn on this source of supply in emergencies from an early time. What may be claimed, however, is that now, owing to a more elaborate marketing mechanism, and above all to a greatly increased volume of disposable surpluses in East-Elbia, Poland and Estonia, areas of permanent or temporary grain deficits could be provisioned from abroad more amply and with greater regularity than in previous times. By the middle of the sixteenth century the amount of grain exported annually through the port of Danzig was from six to ten times greater than the average shipped in the years 1490–2. Towards the end of the sixteenth century Dutch, German and English vessels are found unloading cargoes of Baltic grain even in Mediterranean ports.[1] Agricultural progress making

---

[1] These imports may have been necessitated by the apparent failure, in the last quarter of the sixteenth century, of the previous main source of grain supplies for the western Mediterranean, the Near East, to produce exportable surpluses.

for higher average yields per acre, as well as the resumption of clearing and draining operations in western Europe, must also have had a share in reducing the severity of subsistence crises in the sixteenth century. Nor was it only the supply of cereals that was improving. Two or three important new sources of animal food had opened up to European man in this period: the rich fishing banks from Cape Cod to Labrador were yielding increasing quantities of valuable protein, while the Hungarian and Wallachian plains as well as the Danish lowlands had for some time past become breeding-grounds of vast numbers of oxen for export to Austria, Germany, and Holland.

In trying to assess the demographic significance of all these improvements, the historian may be in danger of attaching too much weight to the rather discouraging record of subsistence crises commented upon earlier. In point of fact, the percentage of people who starved to death was never very large, not even in times of dire shortages. Rather men died—if they did die—of 'fevers' and 'fluxes' engendered by improper or contaminated food which they were compelled to consume in times of dearth, or of other infections which their emaciated bodies were too weak to ward off. For the rest, it may be presumed that at all times as many, or more, people had their lives shortened through chronic malnutrition than perished from acute want of food. It is arguable, then, that the improvement in the general level of nutrition, however modest, brought about by the favourable factors listed above was more important than the gloomy record of famines would lead one to suspect.

Whether the demographic upswing of the late fifteenth and the sixteenth centuries was due solely to a decline in mortality, or whether it owed something to a rise in fertility, is a question which for lack of quantitative information cannot be answered with any confidence. Occasional references in contemporary sources to the strong generative power of mankind, inspired though they may have been by observations of a growing abundance of children, are not necessarily indicative of a rising trend in fertility. Teeming nurseries may bear witness as much to low infant mortality as to high fertility. But there was one major institutional change which, in Protestant countries, must indeed have tended to raise the gross reproduction rate in the sixteenth century: the abolition of celibacy among the secular clergy, and the dissolution of monasteries and nunneries. Though it is not possible to measure the demographic effects of this augmentation of the parental stock it may be asserted that they were not negligible. It was not merely a matter of the birth-rate: the sons and daughters of the parsonage and the manse, born as they were into moderately well-to-do and tolerably enlightened families, had a better than average chance of surviving infancy and childhood, and becoming parents in their turn. It is no accident that the seventeenth-century champions of pro-natalist policies in Catholic countries should have frowned upon clerical celibacy, and demanded restrictions on recruitment for monastic establishments.

A factor which, on Malthusian grounds, might be expected to have had a depressing effect on fertility was the sustained fall in the level of real wages incidental to population pressure and the secular inflation of the sixteenth century. (We assume, perhaps somewhat rashly, that regularity of employment did not change greatly.) Might not the lower orders of society have been induced to practise a higher degree of 'prudence' as the price of foodstuffs rose and the purchasing power of their customary money-incomes declined from decade to decade? A Flemish proverb, current since the sixteenth century, told the poor in so many words that large families were the root of their distress.

> Luttel goets ende vile kynder
> Dit brengt den meneghen in groten hynder.[1]

Yet there is no indication that the warning was heeded. Indeed, some of the demographic resilience of the sixteenth century, which contrasts so strikingly with the marasmus of late-medieval times, can perhaps be explained on the assumption that there occurred a certain weakening of the 'prudential restraints' among the wage-earning classes, if not among their betters. The progressive decay of the old guild system and the rise of an industrial organization which availed itself largely of semi-skilled labour, and accorded its workers much greater freedom in the ordering of their private lives, must have tended to raise the proportion of married people and to lower the average age at marriage.[2] Though earnings were low and employment unsteady, young people may have decided all the more readily upon setting up home together, since nothing was to be gained by waiting. Children would be born, no doubt, but most of them would die in infancy, and the family burden at any given time would not be insupportable.

It is not surprising that efforts of mercantilist governments to retain and acquire 'treasure' should have become frantic in an age which saw the vital silver imports from the New World diminish at an alarming rate. Is it to be wondered at that statesmen in this same period—the seventeenth century—should have felt a like concern about the other

---

[1] Little property and many children
Brings many a man into great difficulties.

[2] An English statute of 1555 complained about the evils of 'over-hasty marriages and over-soon setting up of householdes by the young folke of the city, be they never so young and unskilled.' R. H. Tawney, *The Agrarian Problem in the Sixteenth Century* (London, 1912), 104, n. 3.

source of national wealth and power, population; seeing that it, too, threatened to decline, as sanguinary wars, famines, and a succession of great epidemics took their heavy toll of life in almost all countries of Europe?

Fears of depopulation were not unfounded in an age whose survival rates may have been significantly lower than those of the preceding century. They certainly were lower among members of ruling families, a social group, be it noted, that was not normally exposed to the hazards of war, was undoubtedly better fed and housed than ordinary people, and probably also in a better position to protect itself against contagion and infection. It has been shown that, in the seventeenth century, of one hundred children born alive into ruling families only 61·7 survived their fifteenth year, as against 70·1 in the sixteenth century.[1] Also, in this same privileged class, of one hundred males alive at the age of fifteen only 41·6 of those born between 1580 and 1679 reached the age of fifty, as against 44·6 of those born between 1480 and 1579. These data are in keeping with earlier observations on Danish materials which suggest that mortality among adult aristocrats of both sexes was significantly higher in the decades from 1630 to 1679 than it had been from 1530 to 1579, notwithstanding the adverse effects in this latter period of the Seven Years Nordic War.[2]

Yet another set of figures, showing a decrease in the average age at death of some hundreds of upper-class and professional Englishmen born in the seventeenth century as compared with that of a similar group born in the sixteenth century, might lend further support to the view that the mortality of the seventeenth century compared unfavourably with that of the preceding century. However, since it is doubtful whether changes in the mean age at death can be used to diagnose mortality trends,[3] these data should not be pressed.

It is conceivable that variations in the demographic trend values of early modern Europe were in some way related to a secular rhythm of economic activity. Business fluctuations no doubt influenced both mortality and fertility in the short run: a severe slump spelt hunger and

[1] The corresponding figure obtained from a sample of the rural population of northern France in the years 1657–76 was 58. See Pierre Goubert, 'En Beauvaisis: problèmes démographiques du XVIIe siècle', *Annales: Économies, Sociétés, Civilisations*, VII (1952), 454.

[2] See Harald Westergaard, *Die Lehre von der Mortalität und Morbilität*, 2nd ed. (Jena, 1901), 277.—The remarkable increase in the mean expectation of life at birth in the city of Geneva —from about 23 years in the period 1561–1600 to about 27·5 years in the period 1601–1700 —observed by Louis Henry, *Anciennes familles genevoises. Étude démographique: XVIe–XXe siècle* (Paris, 1956), 157, may well have been exceptional, and due to the relatively favourable conditions of life in seventeenth-century Switzerland noted above (p. 44).

[3] See René Baehrel, 'La mortalité sous l'ancien régime', *Annales: Économies, Sociétés, Civilisations*, XII (1957), 85 ff.

deferred marriages to many individuals in that growing sector of the population which depended for its livelihood on wage-work. (This was, of course, particularly true of situations in which industrial employment contracted as a result of poor harvests, which are known to have caused the effective demand for manufactured goods to decline at the very time when bread was dear.) If this be granted, it is tempting to see more than a fortuitous parallel between the high frequency and severity of trade-depressions and the apparent slackening of population growth in many countries during the last decades of the sixteenth and the better part of the seventeenth century.[1] However, too little is known about either phenomenon to warrant positive inferences. In any case, wars and epidemics seem to have been much more potent factors of demographic dynamics in the period under review.

The causal connection between warfare and increased mortality, stressed more than once in the preceding pages, need not again be given special emphasis here. Instead, a less obvious chain of causation will be considered in this context. Were there any other reasons why the severity and frequency of epidemics should have increased so noticeably in the century after 1560? This *crescendo* of crowd-diseases—plague above all, but also dysentry, typhus, and after 1600 more and more prominent, smallpox—roughly coincided, and was almost certainly linked up, with another phenomenon, namely the headlong growth and multiplication of large cities.

A new urban 'species' was emerging in this epoch; or rather a species which until then had been exceedingly rare was becoming more common. It is not generally realized that apart from Constantinople, that unique relic of the ancient world, no more than four or five European cities—Paris, Naples, Genoa, Venice and, possibly Milan—had reached, and only the first of these may have appreciably exceeded, a population figure of 100,000 on the eve of the modern era. Only a handful—Florence, Bologna, Seville, Córdoba, Granada, Lisbon, and Ghent—are known, or may be assumed, to have numbered 50,000 or a little more. Upwards of a dozen other 'large' cities of late-medieval times, among them Verona, Palermo, Rome, Messina, London, Barcelona, Cologne, Antwerp, and Brussels, possibly also Vienna and Prague, ranged from 30,000 to 50,000 inhabitants. Outside of Italy, Spain, and the Low Countries, even relatively important centres of international trade and

[1] See E. J. Hobsbawm, 'The General Crisis of the European Economy in the 17th Century', *Past and Present*, no. 5 (May 1954), 33–53, and no. 6 (November 1954), 44–65. It is noteworthy that the colonial world, too, was suffering from demographic recession and economic malaise in this period. See Woodrow Borah, *New Spain's Century of Depression* (Publications in Ibero-Americana, No. 35), Berkeley and Los Angeles, 1951, and the review of this study by Pierre Chaunu in *The Journal of Economic History*, XVI (1956), 421 ff.

industry, such as Toulouse, Strasbourg, Lübeck, Nürnberg, Augsburg, Danzig, and Ulm, barely reached, or did not exceed by much, a population of 20,000.

Within the next 100 or 150 years, this picture changed profoundly. Antwerp, as has been seen, touched the 100,000 mark as early as 1568; and while in this particular case expansion was followed by precipitous decline, the city nevertheless remained in the 50,000–65,000 class throughout the seventeenth century. Amsterdam, having passed the 100,000 point a few years before 1622, continued to grow to about 200,000 by the end of the century. Venice, already a large city in late-medieval times, reached a maximum of about 170,000 by 1568; and though the community was struck by disastrous epidemics in 1575 and 1630, its population never fell below 100,000 and was back at 140,000 by 1700. The city of Milan also had substantially more than 100,000 inhabitants in the late sixteenth and early seventeenth centuries. Naples (with suburbs), another giant, was nearing 300,000 early in the seventeenth century; even after the violent plague of 1656 her population must still have numbered upwards of 150,000 (1688: 188,000). Rome, a city of only secondary rank, demographically, in the later Middle Ages, had moved up to 100,000 before the end of the sixteenth century; so had Palermo and Seville. Messina (with its *casali*) and Lisbon reached this size, if only temporarily, about 1600.

Paris was larger than any of these great cities, with the possible exception of Naples. The French capital, to quote a Venetian ambassador writing in the first half of the sixteenth century, was

'a very large, beautiful, rich and populous city; alone, in my opinion, is it fit to compare with Venice; indeed, it is much more populous, and has many more shops and much more trade. . . . Paris is, in truth, beyond my powers of description, and I can best end by saying that no city in Europe is as large or as fine.'

He had been told, the ambassador added, that Paris numbered 700,000 people. This estimate appeared to him excessive; but he was inclined to think that the city did have 300,000–400,000 inhabitants. As a matter of fact, even this figure was probably too high by at least 100,000 for that period; however, it is almost certain that Paris (with suburbs) reached and surpassed this level some time in the seventeenth century.

We are equally at sea if we try to estimate the population of London in the sixteenth and seventeenth centuries, the uncertainty being related, in part, to our inability to account for the inhabitants of districts which formed part of the city in a topographical, but not in an administrative sense. It is almost certain, however, that Greater London—City, Liberties, Out-parishes, and Westminster—had passed the 100,000 level about the middle of the sixteenth, and was nearing, if it had not yet exceeded, 200,000 in the first years of the seventeenth century. James I was not mistaken when he proudly asserted that 'our Citie of London is become the greatest or next the greatest citie of the Christian World' (Royal Proclamation of 16 July 1615). On the eve of the Great Plague (1665) the population of London (in the sense defined) cannot have fallen far short of half a million.

In addition to the cities listed so far, a number of others edged the 100,000 mark in the period under review. Lyons may have come close to this level before the end of the seventeenth century. Madrid, having been made the capital and chief royal residence in 1561, was growing rapidly, and by 1700 also seems to have approached 100,000. Vienna, too, profited from its position as the imperial residence: by the end of the seventeenth century the city and its suburbs, with nearly 100,000 inhabitants, had become the most populous German city. Marseilles— if the figure unearthed by Professor Braudel can be trusted—may have numbered over 80,000 people as early as 1583; though almost certainly less populous in 1666, the city (suburbs probably included) is known to have come near the 80,000 mark by the end of the seventeenth century. Valencia had more than 12,000 houses, or about 70,000 inhabitants, in 1609; Granada was just about as large. Genoa had over 70,000, Hamburg and Danzig about 60,000 inhabitants in the 1640's.

This mushroom growth, in the century from 1550 to 1650, of large and very large urban centres was not only a significant demographic phenomenon in itself; it was also a causal factor. For the multiplication of these vast agglomerations of people exercised a profound influence on mortality, and thus on the general course of demographic history, in this period.

It needs little imagination to realize that the emergence of these large human anthills created a host of problems—food, water, and fuel supply, sewage and garbage disposal, housing, paving, etc.—problems which a society with scanty resources of capital and technological skill, and a good deal of callousness, was ill-equipped to solve. As a consequence of over-crowding, filth, contaminated water, and, occasionally, food shortages, urban mortality was high even in 'normal' years, and catastrophic during those frequent epidemic seasons to which reference has been made in a previous section; and though fertility was high too, the long-term average of deaths was significantly higher than that of births in most of the large cities for which we have data. Only a permanent stream of rural immigrants made it possible for these cities to maintain, let alone increase, their populations in the long run.

However, it was not only in this way that the large urban centres acted as a drain on the human resources of the country; they also tended to deplete its manpower in their capacity as foci of epidemics. The process of dissemination was usually started by the flight to the country of well-to-do households upon the onset of an epidemic; but sooner or later some spreading of crowd-diseases from metropolitan areas would have occurred in any case. Though it is rarely possible to trace the direction and progress of an epidemic wave with any certainty, there is much to suggest that large cities were the starting-points of more than one such wave. In the second half of the sixteenth and in the seventeenth century, the impact of a major London epidemic would be felt as far away as northern Germany after two or three years.[1]

Yet this same period which witnessed an unprecedented concentration of human beings in large cities, creating conditions favourable to epidemic outbreaks, paradoxically enough saw the beginnings of a development that was to end with the complete extinction of plague in western and central Europe soon after 1700. The disappearance of this disease, which for 300 years and more had been the greatest single agent of death, is still much of a mystery. To explain it in terms of a gradual weakening of the plague germ or a growing immunity of the population will not do. Some of the last outbreaks, e.g. the Italian and the English epidemics of 1656–7 and 1665–6 respectively, are known to have been fully as virulent as any of the preceding ones. The growing efficacy of quarantine in the Mediterranean ports and the establishment, early in the eighteenth century, of a *cordon sanitaire* all along the Austrian-Turkish border, must have helped somewhat to shield western Europe from incursions of the plague, which in Turkey continued to rage unabated. However, the importance of these sanitary precautions should not be overrated. Isolation, if it could be made effective at all, would guard a city or a country against human plague-carriers and their ectoparasites, but was powerless against a much more dangerous agent of infection, namely the flea-infested rat. Indeed, the bubonic plague, as is now known, is first and foremost a rodent epizootic; it is only when fleas, having fed on diseased rats, attack human beings that an epidemic gets under way.[2]

The recognition of this chief chain of infection (rat→flea→man) may incidentally provide us with a clue for the understanding of the cause (or causes) that led to the extinction of plague in Europe. Investigations have shown conclusively that it is one particular species of rodents, the black

---

[1] London in turn seems to have received infections from urbanized Holland on several occasions in the seventeenth century. See above, p. 47, fn. 2.

[2] This may, however, not always have been so. If, as Professor Ernst Rodenwaldt (see p. 7, fn. 1) is inclined to think, the human flea is an effective carrier of the plague germ in the temperate zone, plague epidemics in medieval and early modern Europe need not invariably have been preceded by outbreaks among the rats; rather sometimes the chain of infection could have been from man to man through the intermediary of *Pullex irritans*.

rat (*Mus rattus*), which is mainly responsible for the spread of major epidemics of plague. It breeds in human homes and ships, and thrives best on cereals, the chief food of man; but above all, it is the favourite host of *Xenopsylla cheopis*, which is the plague flea *par excellence*. However, this highly domesticated rat must have found its habitat less and less congenial, as brick walls began to be built more frequently in place of timber-framed walls, as shingled or tiled roofs gradually supplanted thatched roofs, and as domestic grain-storage became a thing of the past in the cities. To the extent that the human flea had a share in the propagation of plague the gradual disappearance of wooden structures and pig-sties from the cities of Europe, by depriving *Pullex irritans* of some of its favourite breeding-grounds, must have tended further to reduce the likelihood of pestilential outbreaks. Yet more important, possibly, than any of these changes may have been the fact that, some time after 1600, a relative newcomer of Asiatic origin began to appear on the scene, the brown or wander rat (*Mus norvegicus*), which began to challenge, and in the end almost completely ousted, the older species. This revolution in the animal kingdom must have gone far to break the lethal link between rat and man. For although the brown rat is quite as susceptible to plague as the black, its chief parasite is not *Xenopsylla cheopis*, but another flea, *Nosopsyllus fasciatus*, which is a much less efficient vector of the plague bacillus, and has, furthermore, little or no appetite for human blood. Experience gathered in England during the early decades of our century has shown, moreover, that plague among colonies of brown rats has a tendency to self-extinction.

The cessation of plague epidemics in Europe meant that one of the factors which had kept the secular average of the death rate so appallingly high in late-medieval and early modern times became inoperative. However, the improvement was not at all spectacular in the short run. The two decades centring about the year 1700, as has been shown above, produced formidable demographic crises in many European countries. By and large it was not until two generations after the disappearance of plague from the various regions of Europe that their populations show definite signs of a permanent excess of births over deaths. This is not to deny the existence of a causal connection between the extinction of plague and the Vital Revolution. Indeed the latter, in one of its aspects, was merely the manifestation of the cumulative effects of population growth in the absence of catastrophic reversals.

The trend of natality in the seventeenth century is very difficult to ascertain. Not even the crude birth-rate, a notoriously imperfect tool for measuring fertility, can be calculated with any accuracy, except in a few isolated cases. All that can be said with confidence is that the reproductive power of populations producing annually some thirty to forty births per thousand is still very high by present standards. Fluctuations and regional variations in the birth-rate, it must be assumed, were due mainly to temporal changes or local differences in the marital condition of the populations concerned, perhaps also to changes in age-distribution, produced by age-specific epidemics in the past.

However, there are reasons for believing that marital fertility was not entirely uncontrolled in the period under review. (Attempts to avoid the consequences of pre-marital or extra-marital intercourse, by means of infanticide, abortion, or contraception, seem to have been fairly common at all times—and not only in 'Popish Countries', where, according to John Graunt, 'unlawfull Copulations beget Conceptions but ... frustrate them by procured Abortions or secret Murthers.')[1] It would be absurd to deny that the contraceptive effects of *coitus interruptus* were generally known; and moralists found it necessary to utter grave warnings against these and similar practices designed to frustrate the first and foremost purpose of married love, the procreation of children.[2] 'Toutes les actions du mariage', wrote St Francis de Sales early in the seventeenth century, 'qui ne sont pas conformes à celle qui est ordonnée pour la production des enfants sont vicieuses et damnables.' The Spanish Jesuit Thomas Sanchez (1550–1610), writing in Latin for fellow-theologians, could afford to be even more specific; and his doctrines were repeated in a treatise by a German casuist, published in 1645. More or less unequivocal references to birth control within marriage are also found both in the sermon and the erotic literatures of early eighteenth-century Germany.[3]

Motives for reducing the number of pregnancies were not lacking. As early as 1656 the Abbé de Pure protested against what he called '*l'hydropisie amoureuse*' to which women are condemned;[4] and a goodly number of letters written in 1671 and 1672 by Madame de Sévigné echo the same sentiments. When apprised by her daughter that she was once again expecting a child the old lady is exasperated. 'Mais vous êtes grosse

[1] John Graunt, *Natural and Political Observations made upon the Bills of Mortality*, ed. Walter F. Willcox (Baltimore, 1939), 60 (First edition 1662). Criminal codes of sixteenth- and seventeenth-century Germany invariably contain clauses dealing with infanticide.

[2] See André Venard and Philippe Ariès, 'Deux contributions à l'histoire des pratiques contraceptives', *Population*, IX (1954), 683–92. However, as has been shown above (p. 170), the sin of Onan had not been rediscovered recently. Whether Walter Raleigh's reference to 'artificial sterility' (in his *History of the World*, bk. I, chap. VIII, sect. IV) implied *coitus interruptus* or other methods of birth control (abortifacient potions?) must remain undecided.

[3] E.g. Abraham a Sancta Clara, 'Abrahamisches Gehab dich wohl', *Sämmtliche Werke*, XI (Passau, 1837), 289 and 456 (First, posthumous edition 1729); and Johann Gottfried Schnabel, *Der im Irrgarten der Liebe herumtaumelnde Cavalier* (ed. Paul Ernst: Munich, 1907), 288 f. and 474 ff. (First edition 1746).

[4] See Philippe Ariès, *Histoire des populations françaises et de leurs attitudes devant la vie depuis le XVIIIe siècle* (Paris, 1948), 508.

jusqu'au menton', she exclaims; 'Je n'aime point cette grosseur excessive.' And then, turning to her son-in-law, whom she obviously
regards as the chief culprit. 'Il paroît bien que vous ne savez ce que c'est
que d'accoucher. Mais écoutez, voici une nouvelle que j'ai à vous dire:
c'est que si après ce garcon-ci, vous ne lui donnez quelque repos, je
croirai que vous ne l'aimez point. . . . Pensez-vous que je vous l'aie
donnée pour la tuer, pour détruire sa santé, sa beauté, sa jeunesse ?' This
philippic seems to have had the desired effect; and Madame de Sévigné
now is profuse in her protestations of delight and gratitude. 'Je suis
ravie, ma bonne', she tells her daughter, 'que vous ne soyez point grosse;
j'en aime M. de Grignan [her son-in-law] de tout mon coeur.'

If among aristocratic families considerations of health and beauty
were the main deterrents against too frequent pregnancies, social and
economic motives seem to have begun to influence middle-class behaviour in these matters. The comedy Le Franc-bourgeois, performed in
1709, contained the following lines.

> Il faut de temps en temps se sevrer de plaisir
> Et ne faire d'enfants que ceux qu'on peut nourrir.

One naturally hesitates to draw too many inferences from a few
isolated passages; but we have additional indications that, as early as
the middle of the seventeenth century, and probably even before that,
counsels of prudence were acted upon here and there, if not under
ordinary circumstances, at any rate in times of acute distress. Evidence is
accumulating that people—and not only Frenchmen—resorted to one
form of family limitation or another during periods of adversity. A
French economist who in his capacity as a local official must have had
ample opportunity to observe the *mores* of the ordinary citizen, in a
treatise on grain written about the year 1700, is quite specific on this
point. 'An extreme necessity', Sieur de Boisguilbert exclaims,

not only dries up all the tenderness of nature, but even outrages nature on
pressing occasions. . . . Since necessity knows no laws, she transgresses even
the most sacred [laws] in proportion to the excess in which she is found. Let
one not to be at all astonished, then, at what is advanced, namely, that extreme
poverty causes the diminution of families to be regarded as a blessing, and that
this situation carries with it the means of procuring [the diminution].[1]

---

[1] Pierre le Pesant Boisguilbert, *Traité de la nature, culture, commerce et interest des grains*,
367–8; quoted by Hazel van Dyke Roberts, *Boisguilbert: Economist of the Reign of Louis XIV*
(New York, 1935), 176. An eighteenth-century English demographer, Thomas Short,
also comments on the effect of crises on reproduction, but simply argues that 'times of
Poverty, Sickness, Famine, or Plague are . . . great Enemies to Sensuality.' Quoted by
R. R. Kuczynski, 'British Demographers' Opinions on Fertility, 1660–1760', *Political
Arithmetic: A Symposium of Population Studies*, ed. Lancelot Hogben (London, 1938), 298,
fn. 2.

This was not mere rhetoric; statistical evidence tends to show that the great subsistence crises of seventeenth-century France were accompanied by a decline of conceptions apparently altogether disproportionate to the drop in total population. Such, for instance, was the case during the terrible years from 1649 to 1652 in a number of parishes in the Beauvais region, and again, in this same district as well as in other parts of the country, during the famines of 1661–2 and 1693–4.[1] A recent analysis of data obtained from the Principality of Liège has disclosed the same striking correlation between famine and the rate of conceptions.[2]

The magnitude of this phenomenon is such that it is doubtful whether it can be fully explained on physiological grounds, or by reference to the undeniable decline in the marriage rate during the years of crisis. Rather it may be assumed that this 'baisse brutale des conceptions', to use the phrase of M. Meuvret, was due, in part, to deliberate restriction. (Infanticide may also have played some role in reducing the number of registered baptisms. But is it likely that people should have had recourse to this particularly repulsive form of family limitation after the crisis had passed?)

Nor are these French and Belgian cases isolated instances. It appears that the number of baptisms recorded in the city of Venice during the calendar year 1631 was down by 45 per cent from the average of the preceding thirty years. The reason for this decline was a severe plague which was raging at the time. Yet the magnitude of the drop is altogether surprising.[3] For by March 1631, the latest time at which children born in 1631 can have been conceived, the city had lost only about 28,000 persons since the start of the epidemic in August 1630, or about 20 per cent of its population. True, during epidemics baptisms were often postponed; but since the plague had ceased before the end of 1631 many, if not all, of these delayed baptisms (including some of infants born in 1630) must have been performed and recorded that year. Still, a certain number of infants may have died, from plague or from lack of care in a household disorganized by sickness, before they could be carried to church to be baptized. Also, one has to take account of miscarriages brought on by illness of expectant mothers,[4] as well as of other physio-

[1] See Pierre Goubert, loc. cit., p. 461, and 'Une richesse historique en cours d'exploitation: les registres paroissiaux', Annales: Économies, Sociétés, Civilisations, IX (1954), 92 f. See also J. Canard, 'Les mouvements de population à Saint-Romains d'Urfé de 1612 à 1946', Bulletin de la Diana, XXIV (1945), 121, and Abel Chatelain, 'Notes sur la population d'un village bugiste: Belmont (XVIIe s.–XXe s.)' Revue de Géographie de Lyon, XXVIII (1953), 113 ff.

[2] J. Ruwet, 'Crises démographiques: Problèmes économiques ou crises morales?', Population, IX (1954) 451–76.

[3] Instances of a drastic drop in the number of births during crises are also known in the city of Genoa, in 1591–2 and 1626–7 (see Giuseppe Felloni, 'Per la storia della popolazione di Genova nei secoli XVI e XVII', Archivio Storico Italiano, CX (1952), 263 ff.), and elsewhere. But it is rarely possible to subject the available figures to any close analysis.

[4] John Graunt, discussing the disproportionate decline of weekly baptisms during the

logical and psychological circumstances liable to reduce conceptions (or births) during an epidemic. But when all is said there remains a strong presumption that one of the reasons for that wholly disproportionate decline in the number of baptisms was birth control.

One further instance may be cited. A census taken in Iceland in 1703, after several years of terrible hardships, reveals a curious age distribution, resembling that found in many European countries during the 1930's: the proportion of persons in the youngest age groups is substantially lower than in some of the older brackets. This may have been partly due to under-enumeration of very small children, partly to abnormally high infant morality, and postponement of marriages during the crisis; but it is conceivable that infanticide, induced abortions, and contraception were also responsible for this anomalous age distribution.

As for England, samples collected by Dr Thomas Short suggest a remarkable decline in the ratio of baptisms to marriages after the middle of the seventeenth century (3·44 in the period 1670–1740 as against 4·06 in the period 1560–1630). Whether these figures can be trusted, and if so, whether the drop was caused by a change in the marital conditions, or by a certain amount of birth control, are questions which cannot be decided.

A growing readiness of people to cheat nature, and thus to intensify the demographic consequences of periods of distress, if recognized, may well have added to the worries of seventeenth-century statesmen about depopulation, and may have inspired some of the pro-natalist policies of this age. But was it recognized? The taboos surrounding sexual activities in Christian society did not encourage open discussion of such matters. It was not before the eighteenth century that men like Moheau began to speak more or less freely of 'those baneful secrets, unknown to all living creatures except man, [which] have already penetrated to the country-side'.[1]

Surveying the course of demographic history over the last 500 years in the various countries of Europe, one becomes dimly aware of some rough synchronism. In certain periods, seemingly unrelated, or at any rate not closely related, events appear to form congruent patterns of adversity which are found to have produced a downward trend of population over wide areas, while at other times conditions seem to have been sufficiently favourable to permit an increase of people almost every-where. As far as short-run oscillations are concerned, this synchronism is perhaps not surprising. It may be explained on the ground that epidemics, and even wars, have a tendency to spread, and that climatic

initial phase of the London plague of 1603, concluded that the reduction of births was mainly due to miscarriages. See R. R. Kuczynski, *loc. cit.*, p. 289.

[1] Moheau, *Recherches et considérations sur la population de la France* (ed. René Gonnard, Paris, 1912), 258 (First edition: 1778).

disturbances are often extensive enough to cause simultaneous crop-failures in many countries. However, the parallelism of secular trends is not so easily accounted for. Even such a relatively recent phenomenon as the universal demographic upswing in eighteenth-century Europe still awaits an adequate explanation.

Some of the theories advanced by students of the earlier phases of the Vital Revolution are not entirely convincing. The vaunted advances in medical knowledge and skill to which the reduction of mortality in this period has been partly attributed can hardly have exercised much influence on life-expectancy in, let us say, Finland or Portugal, or even in the rural districts and city slums of western Europe. It is safe to say that the great majority of the people received no medical attention at all, and that those who did might have been better off without the radical purgings and bleedings administered even by the more enlightened practitioners of the art of healing. Jacques Casanova's flippant remark that 'more people perish at the hands of doctors than are cured by them'[1] probably was not wide of the mark. Though there had been some progress in medical theory, eighteenth-century therapy was not much different from that inflicted upon Molière's *malade imaginaire* a hundred years earlier. The barbarous methods of eighteenth-century medicine partly account for the amazing success of homoeopathy. This form of treatment, with its infinitesimal doses, amounted to doing nothing at all. Yet many a patient who had gone from bad to worse under the hands of orthodox practitioners recovered quickly when treated homoeo-pathically—not in response to that absurd therapy, but because he had escaped the harmful ministrations of orthodox medicine.

It is not always realized how little doctors could do to cure any of the major ills that flesh is heir to, before the coming of aseptic surgery and the discoveries of salvarsan, insulin, and the antibiotics. That the powers of the medical profession were strictly limited was frankly admitted by William Cullen, the leading British physician of the eighteenth century. 'We know nothing of the nature of contagion', he declared, 'that can lead us to any measures for removing or correcting it. We know only its effects.'[2] Therapy, therefore, could not, as a rule, directly attack the agents which carried the disease, but had to be content with moderating the symptoms. To be sure, a few drugs of potential efficacy, such as mercury, digitalis, ipecacuanha root, and cinchona bark, were already known in the eighteenth century; yet they were by no means always used correctly. In any case, not many of these last-named

---

[1] *The Memoirs of Jacques Casanova*, ed. Madeleine Boyd, Modern Library (New York, 1929), 7. A similar view was expressed by Goethe in *Faust*, Part I, verses 695–9.

[2] Quoted by Lester S. King, *The Medical World of the Eighteenth Century* (Chicago, 1958), 142.

remedies can be regarded as life-saving, and it is almost certain that their use cannot have had any appreciable effect on the national death-rate.

As to preventive medicine, the profession was equally helpless. To be sure, inoculation, a crude method of immunization against smallpox, had been introduced to western Europe early in the eighteenth century; but its practice remained limited, and its value was, moreover, doubtful. For the treatment was risky; and while it may have helped individuals to overcome the disease more easily than if they had caught an infection at random, the inoculated person did go through an attack of real smallpox, and was therefore a source of danger to his family and attendants and, indirectly, to the community at large. Opponents of inoculation claimed that the incidence of smallpox was actually higher at the end of the eighteenth century than it had been before this practice was introduced.[1] The discovery of vaccination came too late to have any effect on mortality in the eighteenth century: Edward Jenner's famous essay on the cowpox appeared only in 1798.

Nor did eighteenth-century medicine have any effective means of protecting people against such infections as puerperal fever or typhus. This being the case it seems doubtful whether the establishment of a few new maternity and other hospitals in the period under review can properly be listed among the factors which contributed to the decline of mortality. The statement heard in early nineteenth-century Ireland, that a poor man attacked by fever was as likely to recover under a hedge as in a fever hospital, was hardly a paradox. What beneficial effects such institutions may have had were almost certainly more than counterbalanced by the dissemination among their inmates of all sorts of dangerous germs. Eighteenth-century hospitals were unspeakably overcrowded. It was not uncommon for two or even three patients to have to share one bed.[2] In these circumstances the hospitals' reputation of being gateways to death was not undeserved.

Another development which is usually mentioned among the factors held responsible for the fall of the death-rate in eighteenth-century Europe—advances in sanitation—also requires reconsideration. That there were some improvements in public water-supply and sewerage should not be denied. However, what progress there was affected only urban populations, and may, moreover, have been offset, at any rate in Britain, by the growth of appallingly unsanitary slums in the new

[1] See Lester S. King, *loc. cit.*, p. 320 ff.
[2] The number of hospital beds was woefully insufficient everywhere. Brussels, for instance, a city of 70,000 inhabitants, in 1776 had only one hospital with 77 beds. Antwerp and Ghent, about the same time, had 96 and 69 hospital beds respectively for their 50,000 people. See Paul Bonenfant, *Le problème du paupérisme en Belgique à la fin de l'ancien régime* (Académie royale de Belgique, Classe des lettres et des sciences morales et politiques, Mémoires, 2nd ser., XXXV, 1934).

industrial centres. Yet even if it be granted that on balance sanitation was improving, the effects on total mortality should not be overrated. Cleaner water and proper sewers, while they must have been instrumental in reducing the incidence of such diseases as typhoid and dysentry, could not prevent the spread of such equally potent killers as typhus, smallpox, diphtheria, or tuberculosis. Some of these could have been checked by a higher degree of personal cleanliness, better housing, and adequate nutrition. But do we have any evidence of such improvements on a *general* scale? Other factors, such as the gradual draining of the fens in East Anglia, which may have been responsible for the disappearance of 'ague' from England,[1] or the drastic drop, after 1751, in the amount of spirits consumed by the English, must indeed have had very wholesome effects on regional morbidity and mortality; but any such local reductions of the death-rate cannot, of course, be held accountable for the universal growth of population in eighteenth-century Europe. It is this larger phenomenon which requires an explanation.

Most students of the history of population seem to agree that a significant reduction in mortality was the primary cause of the demographic upswing; and, though the statistical evidence is inconclusive, we see no decisive reason why this proposition should be challenged. Indeed, it can be shown that, when mortality is high (as it still was in the eighteenth century), a decline in the death-rate is inherently a more powerful causative factor of population growth than a rise in the birth-rate.[2] We should argue, however, that it was the peaks rather than the plateau that were lowered. In other words, it was not so much a reduction of mortality in 'normal' years that produced the secular downward trend of the death rate, but an unmistakable abatement of the 'great crises'. The disappearance of plague above all, but also a very sensible mitigation of subsistence crises,[3] brought about not only by progress in agriculture but also by improved marketing and transport techniques, seem to have been chiefly responsible for the increase in life expectancy.

Not that dearth and epidemics had become things of the past: for instance, the late thirties and early forties, afflicted as they were by pandemics of influenza and typhus as well as by widespread crop failures (in 1740–1), were times of acute distress in most countries of Europe; and so were the early seventies of the eighteenth century. However,

[1] Assuming, that is, that the 'ague' of earlier English records was malaria, an identification which is disputed by some epidemiologists.

[2] See Thomas McKeown and R. G. Brown, 'Medical Evidence Relating to English Population Changes in the Eighteenth Century', *Population Studies*, IX (1955), 119–41, esp. 127 ff.

[3] This phenomenon did not escape the attention of contemporaries. 'It can scarcely be doubted', wrote Malthus in his *Second Essay* (7th ed., Everyman's Library, II, 261), 'that, taking Europe throughout, fewer famines and fewer diseases arising from want have prevailed in the last century than in those which preceded it.'

while death rates greatly increased in such periods, and momentarily exceeded the birth-rates, mortality no longer assumed *catastrophic* proportions. Even death-rates of 69 and 112 per mille, such as were recorded in 1742 in Norway and the Swedish province of Värmland respectively, are still a far cry from those experienced by some regions of Europe in times of adversity half a century earlier. As M. Goubert put it, 'Après 1741, un monde démographique semble défunt: les mortalités s'attenuent jusqu'à disparaître.' (The fact that subsistence crises, unlike those of previous centuries, could no longer raise the spectre of plague had of course a great deal to do with this attenuation.)

Since famines and epidemics are known to have been particularly hard on the very young, it is safe to conclude that the general abatement of crises must have had disproportionately beneficial effects on infant mortality; and the fact that a higher percentage of the population survived into the reproductive age could not fail to exercise a favourable influence on the birth-rate. One further corollary should be noted. As has been shown above (pp. 87 ff.), severe crises invariably caused not only a jump in the death-rate, but also a drastic drop in the number of conceptions and live births. It follows that the substantial mitigation of crises which becomes obvious in the course of the eighteenth century must also have tended somewhat to raise the secular average of the birth-rate.

Keeping in mind these favourable conditions, one is somewhat surprised to discover that—as far as our very fragmentary information permits us to judge—there are no striking instances of a secular rise in the birth-rate anywhere in eighteenth-century Europe, with the possible exception of Ireland. Indeed, Swedish, Finnish, and Norwegian data, as well as some indirect French evidence, suggest a slight decline of the birth-rate after the middle of the century, brought about, perhaps, not only by a falling marriage-rate, but also by declining fertility. M. Bourgeois-Pichat assumes that in France the gross reproduction rate, having remained more or less stationary at 2·50 during the first half of the century, fell to 2·35 by 1771–5, and to 2·00 by 1801–5. The spread of contraceptive practices, referred to above (pp. 86 ff.) may have been chiefly responsible for this drop. Nor was it only the French who resorted to birth control: a demographic analysis of the Scandinavian data suggests that in the northern countries, too, family limitation may have been of some importance in this period;[1] and students of local condi-

[1] See H. Gille, 'The Demographic History of the Northern European Countries in the Eighteenth Century', *Population Studies*, III (1949–50), 39 and 53, and Gustaf Utterström, 'Some Population Problems in Pre-Industrial Sweden', *The Scandinavian Economic History Review*, II (1954), 159. As in France, the negative correlation between crops and the number of conceptions was remarkably close in eighteenth-century Scandinavia. E.g., in eastern Sweden the number of births dropped by about 50% following the crop failures of 1771–2.

tions in eighteenth-century Switzerland have come to the same conclusion.[1] German evidence pointing in this direction has been quoted
earlier. As for England, Boswell's London Diary and other sources
reveal that the 'fast set' of the metropolis was well acquainted with the
'sheath', though its purpose seems to have been chiefly a prophylactic
one.

However, the conclusion that European man was about to assume
effective control over his generative faculty would be wholly unwarranted. In this, just as in the fields of preventive and curative
medicine, he was only taking a few faltering steps on that long road which
was to lead from the realm of necessity to one of relative freedom.

# VII. *Conclusions*

If the secular trends of population have been at all correctly presented
in the foregoing pages, some of the current views of demographic
history will have to be modified. The opinion, still widely held, that
before the Vital Revolution Europe's population, though subject to
violent short-run fluctuations, remained stationary over long periods,
or was growing only imperceptibly, is no longer tenable. There is
sufficient evidence to indicate that these oscillations were superimposed
on clearly recognizable 'long waves'.[2] It has been shown that the decisive
secular upswing of the High Middle Ages, having been cut short
by a succession of catastrophes in the fourteenth century, was followed
by a hundred years of demographic decline and depression. This period
in turn gave way to one which, in the face of much adversity, once again
achieved very substantial rates of secular growth in most countries
of Europe, only to be succeeded by another century of reverses and
stagnation.

What the exact rates of growth during those two upswings of the
cycle were, it is impossible to ascertain. But their order of magnitude
can be estimated with some confidence, and there can be no doubt that
it was comparable to that observed in the early phases of the Vital
Revolution. In this sense the demographic development of the eighteenth
century was not unique. What was unprecedented about it was the
fact that the secular upward movement started from a higher level,
and that it was able to maintain, and for some time even to increase, its
momentum. Unlike that of previous epochs, growth in the eighteenth

[1] See Alice Denzler, *Die Bevölkerungsbewegung der Stadt Winterthur von der Mitte des
16. bis zum Ende des 18. Jahrhunderts* (Winterthur, 1940), 18, and Louis Henry, 'Anciennes
familles genevoises', *Population*, XI/2 (1956), 334–8.

[2] So as to guard against a possible misunderstanding it should be emphasized that this
term does not imply the existence of a wave-generating mechanism.

and nineteenth centuries was not terminated and reversed by catastrophe. When increase did eventually slow down, this was due to personal decisions of millions of human beings, not to Acts of God.

However, it would be vainglorious for European man to claim that the partial victory over the forces of death which enabled the Vital Revolution to run its course was altogether of his own making. To insist on the co-operation of strictly exogenous factors is not to belittle man's achievements in the fields of agricultural and industrial production, transport, and marketing. Without these advances, and equally impressive accomplishments in the theory and practice of hygiene and therapy, demographic growth would have been arrested very soon by the inexorable operation of Malthusian forces. However, when all is said, that ecological revolution among rodents which we believe to have been largely responsible for the disappearance of plague from Europe should also be given its due: not merely in the sense that it helped to eliminate the greatest single agent of mortality, but in the sense that perhaps only a society freed from the fear as well as from the material and spiritual consequences of sudden death was able to achieve that high rate of intellectual and technical progress without which population growth could not have been sustained. The historian can only subscribe to the wistful words of Albert Camus. 'Personne ne sera jamais libre tant qu'il y aura des fléaux.'

# CHAPTER II

# Scientific Method and the Progress of Techniques

## I. *From Medieval to Modern*

Criticism has left little unchallenged of the once popular view that scientific and technological progress was conspicuously lacking from the Middle Ages. On the contrary it is now clear that the period after the twelfth century was one of rapid and fairly continuous development, surmounting even the great demographic and economic crisis of the Black Death. Intellectually, the rise of the universities furnished centres for the study of natural science based largely (but not exclusively)on the works of the ancient Greeks. Technologically, the employment of power derived from water and wind, the adoption of textile machinery and a more efficient metallurgy (vol. II, pp. 408–13, 458–69), together with the spread of more recent inventions such as the mechanical clock, the compass, and gunpowder gave promise of a new era in production, trade, and warfare. It may indeed be argued that it was still necessary to clear away most of the doctrines of late medieval science and medicine in order that modern ideas and methods should take their place, and to revolutionize the practices of the medieval craftsman in order that they should support a modern society. Nevertheless, in each case what had been achieved by the end of the fifteenth century was as superior to the standards prevailing in Charlemagne's time, as it was in turn inferior to the science and technology of the nineteenth century. Without this intermediate stage neither the scientific revolution of the seventeenth century, nor the industrial revolution of the eighteenth, could have occurred.

Recognition of this fact determines our initial perspective. For it would clearly be as misleading to attribute all fundamental changes in science and technology to the unprecedented originality of the modern mind, as to seek their origin solely in the deterministic play of economic factors. In science and technology as in economic life there was no moment of sharp and violent transition; it was rather the case that changes happened gradually as new processes or ideas proved their worth; certain tendencies of the Middle Ages expanded, while others declined.

Although the phenomenon of new invention must often be considered, since it was an outstanding attribute of western European science and technology during the early modern period, even this rarely worked in such a way as to produce abrupt changes in thought or economic life. One basic aspect of the progressive differentiation between the characteristics of the medieval and modern worlds underlines the whole argument of this chapter. This concerns the relationship existing between the philosopher and the artisan, or in modern terms the scientist and technologist. It has often been too readily assumed that in the Middle Ages the hiatus between their respective functions was largely responsible for both sterility in science and crudity in techniques. It follows, on this view, that appreciation of the strong links and community of interest between these functions in modern times effected a double improvement. Science ceased to be speculative in proportion as technology became more worthy of serious study. Thus it has become a contemporary truism that technological proficiency demands the encouragement of 'pure' science, and is the essential requirement for efficient production. The danger of this view is that it may be supposed to signify that technology has always advanced only in so far as it is directed by science, and science only in so far as it is stimulated by technical needs.

It was certainly not so in the past. In the Middle Ages and the Renaissance the relationship between the study of Nature and the control of Nature for human purposes was acknowledged in only a few limited instances, such as the usefulness of knowledge of the properties of herbs in curing disease. The relationship was not ignored through sheer obtuseness, but because conditions deprived it of any real value. The forms of scientific study then cultivated, and the confused processes of traditional craftsmanship, had so little in common that no profit could result from closer liaison between their respective exponents. Only very rarely, as with the application of astronomical doctrines to oceanic navigation in the fifteenth century, was there a prospect of scientific procedures being useful, or on the other hand of practical needs suggesting a problem which the natural philosopher could well attempt to solve. And though it was not until the seventeenth century that the systematic description of trade processes was begun, much of our knowledge of technology in medieval and early modern times is in fact derived from accounts of contemporary crafts written by men of learning. That such writers, in spite of their interest in these matters, were able to do no more than give a barely intelligible rendering of the craftsman's methods suggests the extent of the gap between thinking and doing.

Thus a long series of independent changes, and whole stages of development, were required both in science and in technology before the one could genuinely reflect upon the other. The scientist had to learn the importance of examining facts rigorously, of the experimental method, of restraint in the formulation of general theories. Only when there was a solid, detailed and experimental foundation to mechanics, physics and chemistry could these sciences throw light on technical methods. Similarly, a certain level of economic and technical organization must be attained before the opportunity to apply science exists. The growth of large-scale production; the demand for power, more elaborate machines, and more complex chemical processes; the effects of competition and the search for national self-sufficiency, all these must operate to create the need for the scientific analysis and direction of techniques. Throughout the period now under consideration the independent evolution of science and of technology was taking place, until towards its close the experimental scientist was at last able, in a few respects, to give the lead to industrial invention. In the late eighteenth century the effective liaison of science and technology begins; but until this time the internal problems, the internal development, of each are far more significant than any occasional interaction between them.

There is another major difference between the intellectual and economic traditions that produced Leonardo da Vinci, and those that produced James Watt. The progress of medieval civilization, in its scientific and technological aspects particularly, owed much more to assimilation of knowledge from without than to native European invention. The prerequisite for the revival of science in the West was the availability in Latin of the scientific works written in antiquity. These were obtained partly direct from the Greek, rather more commonly through the medium of Arabic translation. With the writings of the ancients those of Islamic philosophers, mathematicians and physicians stood in almost equal authority. Again, many of the great technical innovations of medieval Europe—the windmill, the compass and rudder, printing, the manufacture of gunpowder, paper, silk, and tin-glazed pottery—were also importations from Islam or Byzantium. Some of these arts had a longer history of transmission from the remote civilizations of China and India. Almost until the beginning of the modern period Europe had been a technically backward region whose chief advantage was its ability to adopt and improve its borrowings from more advanced societies. The use of water-power, early for the milling of corn and later in branches of the textile industries, is a notable contrary example. The efficient water-powered corn-mill was a Roman invention. The operation of hammers, stamps, bellows and so forth by means of tappets on the shaft of a vertical water-wheel seems to have been devised in medieval Europe, though it was known in other parts of the world.

With the sixteenth century the situation was reversed. Diffusion from without became much less significant than diffusion within Europe, from those regions with the highest traditions of technical proficiency and greatest fertility of invention to those less advanced. Those areas, like Italy, which had benefited in the past from their proximity to the routes by which exotic products and foreign techniques flowed into Europe, yielded their superiority to others with ampler natural resources or sharper stimuli to invention. And by the early seventeenth century Western Europe had attained a scientific and technological ascendancy over the rest of the world; an ascendancy to be measured not only by the quality of its scientific literature and the scale of its production but by the gradual retreat of the Islamic Empire, the intervention of European merchants in Far Eastern trade, and the success of their colonial ventures among the numerically larger and long civilized populations of India and China. The political and economic factors bearing on this ascendancy of the West cannot be discussed here, but the importance of its superiority in shipbuilding and navigation, in land and naval warfare, is sufficiently obvious.

The economic dominance of modern Europe, reaching its peak in the nineteenth century, was founded upon technological progress and thus on the transition from the phase of assimilation to that of invention which took place towards the close of the Middle Ages. Eastern colonialism, for example, flourished in proportion as goods took the place of bullion as the European export. For this progress the major credit must be assigned to the long line of empirical inventors and entrepreneurs extending from the almost unknown pioneers of the fifteenth century to the familiar figures of the industrial revolution. How was it possible for European technology to be so transformed? The social and economic incentives are discussed elsewhere: here it is relevant to emphasize one factor. In a favourable economic situation, ambitions to increase private profits and national grandeur seemed capable of realization through the use of machinery, reduction of human labour, and increase in size of the unit of production. This was understood intuitively, if not explicitly, in the seventeenth century. At the same time, there was an increasing tendency to consider such technical improvements as attainable only by means of a systematic exploitation of patient enquiry and resourcefulness. Scientists and entrepreneurs alike tended to regard forwarding technical progress as a worthy task. Though technology owed little directly to science before the nineteenth century, and their objects and methods show few parallels in detail, nevertheless the spirit of discovery among scientists tended to re-appear among a different class of men as the spirit of invention. The steps of industrial advance were to be surmounted by careful study and experiment, rather than by occasional flashes of splendid inspiration.

## II. *The Sixteenth Century*

Industry and agriculture remained in the last phases of a series of changes, both technical and organizational, which had deeply affected the economic life of Europe since the fourteenth century. Economically, the slow working-out of processes already in being, such as the price-rise (in part a remote consequence of fifteenth-century improvements in shipbuilding and navigation), the growth of total and especially urban populations, and the weakening in some regions of guilds and villeinage, was far more important than any technological innovation, with one exception to be mentioned later. The sixteenth century was rich in technical invention, now for the first time recorded in printed books, but generally inventors followed traditional lines and met with little success. Leonardo da Vinci offers a well-known instance of this; and he, like others, was able to draw little help or inspiration from contemporary science.

The diffusion of techniques from the core to the periphery of European civilization remained an important feature of the century. In printing and engraving, in textile-making, pottery, shipbuilding and the metal trades the production of the north attained equality with or surpassed that of the south. The introduction of the cast iron industry into England early, and into Sweden late, in the sixteenth century was one marked agent in transferring the balance of power to the north. By the end of Elizabeth's reign the English iron industry was struggling against political restraints on its export trade and had contributed materially to the country's maritime strength. Typical also were the English attempts, made with less success, to introduce from Germany the mining of ores of copper and zinc, as well as the smelting and working of copper and brass. In Central America the Spanish colonists greatly enlarged the yield of precious metals by the use of European techniques, particularly after the opening of Potosi (1545), where the new method of extracting silver by amalgamating the crushed ore with mercury was developed.[1] Perhaps the most striking evidence of the effect of the diffusion of techniques on a national economy is to be seen in the United Provinces. While the Dutch relied enormously on their fishing and their carrying-trade (which, for the Indies, adopted Iberian techniques of navigation), their agriculture was increasingly dependent on drainage engineering. Their luxury products—books, tin-glazed pottery (Delft-ware), fine metal-work—enjoyed a considerable sale abroad. Thus to the political and

[1] The silver amalgamation process was described by Biringuccio (1540) but not applied in European metallurgy till two centuries later.

geographical advantages of the northern seaboard of Europe was added by diffusion rather than by local invention a notable degree of technological progress.

This diffusion was certainly assisted by the appearance of a new technical literature, though it is difficult to assess its effects in detail. Many of the books were specifically written for craftsmen, and some won extensive popularity. Those on husbandry continued a medieval tradition—farmers' calendars and the like—and are of slight interest here. Little was published on textiles and shipbuilding: their turn was to come in the next century. Most interesting are the long series of works on the chemical or pyrotechnical arts, beginning with Brunschwig's *Liber de Arte distillandi* (1500). Distillation was already the basis of minor industries and the increase of its importance is signified by numerous further publications in all languages. In Germany also were published the *Bergbuchlein* (1505) and *Probierbuchlein* (c. 1510), practical handbooks on mining and the working of precious metals. These subjects were greatly developed in three classical treatises—the *Pirotechnia* of Biringuccio (1540), the *De re metallica* of Agricola (1556) and the *Treatise on Ores and Assaying* of Lazarus Ercker (1576). Biringuccio's book in addition gives much information on the extraction and working of non-precious metals (especially on the art of the bronze-founder), the manufacture of glass, of cannon and of gunpowder. Agricola gives a very complete picture of the varied techniques used in the south German mining region. He describes and illustrates in detail the great machines driven by animal- or water-power for raising the spoil, draining, and ventilating the mines; the works for preparing mineral acids and other reagents; the crushers, washers, furnaces, melting- and refining-shops of the metal workers; and many ancillary processes of manufacture.

Without attempting a complete catalogue of the technological writings of the sixteenth century, it is obvious that the printing press vastly accelerated the process by which both the established methods of a localized industry and the new techniques of a successful invention could be made generally available. Naturally the luxury trades demanding the highest skills—and no doubt furnishing the highest profits— were those most frequently dealt with, as in the works of Palissy on pottery, Cellini on metalwork, and Neri on glass (1612), for there was as yet little point in describing the universal methods of spinning, weaving, or shipbuilding. The large specialized industries, such as silk weaving in Italy, were probably able for some time to maintain a policy of secrecy with regard to their methods. Yet beside such books as were, perhaps, of more interest to the connoisseur than to the artisan must be set the long series of practical treatises on artillery and fortification, others dealing with the control of rivers and artificial drainage, and the extensive material on cartography and navigation which will be mentioned later.

Among writers who strove to transform, rather than codify, the best technological practices of their time the impulse to mechanization is very evident. In Leonardo, for example, though his inventions were probably entirely lacking in influence, it is possible to see not only what problems of technology presented themselves to a man of the Renaissance equipped with a degree of scientific and mechanical insight amounting to genius, but the solutions by which he proposed to overcome them. They tend strongly towards the use of natural power, and the substitution for manual skill of machines suitable for mass-production. The principle that machines are ultimately cheaper than men was well understood in Italy and extensively applied, in the silk industry for example and in the arsenal at Venice. Leonardo's designs show an advanced technique for replacing the operations of the hand-worker by the movements of machine parts—wheels, levers, cams, screws, and so on—a technique steadily gaining usefulness throughout the modern period. It reappears strikingly in the *Theatra machinarum* of Ramelli, Besson, and Zonca.[1] Such books illustrate, no doubt more in hope than reality, the powered mechanization of textile manufacture, timber-working, screw-cutting, water-lifting, grinding, crushing, and boring operations. Mechanical skill of a more fanciful kind is also evident among the 'natural magicians' (of whom Giambaptista della Porta is the best known) who devised automata and other marvels, drawing in part upon the recovered tradition of Hero of Alexandria. As with Leonardo, all such new inventions trespass upon the unpractical and the trivial, and the ambition promoting them was not new (military 'tanks', paddle-boats, automatic spinning equipment, and many other innovations were already described in the fourteenth century) but they indicate, with greater confidence than in the past, a new path which economic opportunity might explore.

Even a cursory survey of these books on industrial technology, describing both established practices and new inventions of varying degrees of usefulness, may arouse surprise that the general improvement of techniques, especially by use of the power-driven machine, did not proceed more rapidly. The mechanical spirit of the eighteenth-century industrial revolution may have been anticipated in the sixteenth, but there were good technological as well as economic reasons for its frustration. Often the 'secrets' of manufacture were valueless. Vaunted recipes for dyeing cloth, tanning leather, hardening metals or improving the yield of crops were simply based on superstition and error.

---

[1] A. Ramelli, 'Le diverse et artificiose machine', 1588; J. Besson, 'Theatre des instrumens mathematiques et mechaniques', 1579; V. Zonca, 'Novo Teatro di Machine et Edificii', 1607.

Hence traditional practices continued undisturbed, sometimes (as in tanning) down to recent times. Elaborate machines often proved unworkable, or at least capable of offering little economic profit—and the sixteenth century was a period of a decline in real wages. Strong prejudices and interests stood in the way of innovation. As earlier and later, craftsmen were ready to voice their fear of technological unemployment, and the mercantilist state was sometimes sensitive to their complaints. Such fears compelled William Lee, the inventor of the knitting-frame (1589), to set up at Rouen under the patronage of Henri IV when he was denied encouragement at home. After the death of the French king the new industry almost collapsed, and only slowly gained ground in face of the hostility of the hand-knitters. It was doubtless true, as inventors perennially lamented, that men with capital were reluctant to invest in untried novelties. Considering the uncertainty of patent protection, the unskilfulness of workmen and the absence of criteria for distinguishing useful from fanciful inventions, their hesitancy is understandable.

As for the mechanization of production, here two technical factors operated. The first concerns power, the second materials. The only prime movers available to the technicians of the sixteenth century, and before the time of Newcomen, were men, animals, wind and water. Men and animals were expensive to support and the maximum power available from a single installation was restricted. Wind- and water-driven machines were more costly in capital, but running costs were low; hence they were very desirable where continuous working was needed, as in pumping. The unit of attainable power, about 5–20 h.p., was also somewhat higher. For these reasons there was a tendency to exploit natural power as freely as possible, but the tendency was limited by the difficulty of obtaining it where it was most needed, in towns and ports. The high cost of machinery rendered it uneconomic where the power required was small, or needed only intermittently. The machine could only justify itself where a communal effort and large capital expenditure were called for in any case (as in land-drainage), where the demand was heavy and continuous (as with the water-supply of towns), or where for other reasons the industrial unit had become of considerable size (like the iron-foundry). The size of the industrial unit being governed at least as much by economic as by technological considerations, it follows that the limitations on the use of natural power were technical only in certain cases. One of them was the draining of mines. Even a 20 h.p. water-wheel, coupled to very inefficient pumps, was soon overloaded and the difficulties involved in multiplying the system are easily imagined. The same is true of the water-supply of towns, a problem of increasing importance which could be adequately solved on the small scale but not when urban populations ran into some hundreds of thousands.

Thus there was a scale-effect usually adverse to the engineer; the comparative inflexibility of his natural-power engines made them too feeble for the great problems, and too large for the small manufacturer. A different scale-effect applies to the machines themselves and indeed to every kind of engineering construction, including shipbuilding. The problem here was to build, at a practical cost, machines, bridges or ships having a useful economic capacity and sufficient strength to endure for a reasonable period. It turns partly upon the techniques available for working the materials, and even more upon the characteristics of the materials themselves. Stone and brick are heavy to transport, are laborious to work, and have a low tensile strength. Wood is often difficult to procure in sufficient dimensions, has poor resistance to decay and wear, and again bends or breaks under moderate strains. The metals are much more perfect constructional materials. Their qualities of hardness and toughness can be widely varied, so that metal parts can be made to resist wear. Metals have high tensile strength, and some methods of working them, such as casting, are very economical. The difficulty was to obtain metals, especially iron and steel, cheaply and in adequate quantity. This was a secular impediment to technical progress, first relieved by the invention of the blast-furnace in the fifteenth century, and then by the metallurgical innovations of the eighteenth.

The results are easily enumerated. Roads and bridges were poor; factory-buildings with broad, lofty spans costly to erect. (In England, after the Dissolution of the Monasteries, the possibility of seizing their buildings for the textile industry was not overlooked.) Large ships, whose hulls had to be almost solidly constructed of timber, were uneconomic on account of the low ratio between their capacity and displacement. Machinery of all kinds, and much else required for industrial purposes—pipes, vats, trolleys and rails, even boilers—was made of wood, frequently requiring renewal, and extremely clumsy. For strength the framing and moving parts were made of massive timbers; frictional wear was rapid; and the accuracy of the working parts was much less in wood than in metal. Many of the ideas for mechanization rendered impracticable by the wood-using technology of the sixteenth century became attainable when the age of iron was beginning 200 years later.

There were already signs, however, that the reign of wood as the prime material for human ingenuity was closing. For domestic (and some industrial) purposes it was being replaced by glass, pottery and metal—bronze, pewter, and cast iron. Cast iron was not yet of direct value as a constructional material, partly because it was brittle, partly because sufficiently large castings could not be made. Most of the cast iron coming from the blast-furnace was laboriously worked by repeated hammering and heating into wrought iron, of which the consumption rose steadily. Wooden pins gave place in construction to iron bolts, screws and nails; wooden bearings to iron ones. Two trades working in iron, those of the locksmith and the clockmaker, are particularly interesting as leading the way towards higher levels of engineering skill. Both were descended from the blacksmith. By specialised improvement of tools and dexterity they rose to a different order of precision and neatness, producing the elaborate table-clocks, watches and chest-locks of the age. No other product of the time could compare with these in mastery of hammer, chisel, file and drill, which was later to be applied to more fundamental purposes.

Of greatest economic importance was the replacement of wood as a fuel by coal, though this development was largely confined to England and northern France. The use of coal was not new, and it spread simply because wood was scarce. Growth of population and a gradual rise in the standard of living increased the pressure on fuel supplies, not only for domestic heating and metalworking but for such purposes as salt-panning, brick-making, brewing, dyeing, and glass-making; a pressure increased by the parallel extension of agriculture into woodland and waste. In particular regions where smelting flourished (the Weald, the Forest of Dean, Cornwall) the shortage of fuel became acute; the ship-building yards were similarly forced to range further for suitable stands of timber. Its price rose far more than the average. Northumberland coal was a cheap substitute fuel, despite the sea-carriage to Lynn and the fen rivers, to the Thames and London, to the coasts of southern England and northern France. It could be readily applied to the heating of vats and boilers and to other operations, such as brick-burning and smith's work, where its harmful constitutents, of which sulphur was the chief, were not troublesome. The use of coal in furnaces and ovens where the raw material was easily contaminated by combustion-products was less easy; in glass-making it was achieved by enclosing the 'metal' in covered pots and re-designing the furnaces. Clearly it would have been very desirable to use coal for smelting, particularly of iron (where the consumption of fuel by weight was several times greater than the yield of metal) but the secret continued to evade seventeenth-century inventors, despite many hopeful patents, which included the 'charking' of the fuel. Even after Abraham Darby's success (1709), Swedish iron, charcoal-smelted from a pure ore, remained superior to the cheaper English iron smelted with pit-coal.

The consequences of this change of fuel have been called 'the early English industrial revolution'. In economic terms the appellation is not unjust, for English industries could hardly have developed otherwise.

The cheapening of heat-treatment had many ramifications, since the multiplication of operations it allowed (for example, roastings, washings, solutions, crystallizations) tended towards the improvement of the product and inevitably, if economy was secured, expansion of markets and enlargement of the units of production followed. The use of coal favoured capitalistic development—not least in the mines from which it came. But at the same time it must be remembered that the simple substitution of one fuel for another often had only a minor effect on technological methods—indeed, it was only where existing techniques could be easily modified that coal could be used at all.

Hitherto the craftsman and the entrepreneur have occupied the centre of the picture; skilful, inventive and ambitious, their endeavours were ruled by tradition and undirected empiricism. They neither knew nor desired theoretical insight into their problems. Their books were practical ones. Nevertheless, the background of science was beginning to envelop their activities. The fringes of science and technology were beginning to overlap to a more useful purpose.

Yet the Renaissance, and the return to classicism, had little effect in equipping the natural philosopher to play a less narrowly speculative part in society. The two great achievements of sixteenth-century science, the new astronomy of Copernicus and the new anatomy perfected by Vesalius, belong equally to the realm of pure knowledge. They were of no immediate use, though they were to give rise to things of use in the future. In the more practical departments of science—mechanics, physics, chemistry—no new principles emerged to redirect technological practice; on the contrary, as the next section will show, the reverse influence was rather more important.

The history of medicine furnishes striking examples of the inadequacy of scientific learning to cope with the problems arising from social and economic developments. Physicians and surgeons were faced with many fresh demands upon their skill, to which at first they responded only by more dogmatic confidence in the doctrines of the ancients. The growth of towns crowded the citizens more thickly upon each other. Insanitary suburbs sprang up, streams and wells were defiled, hygienic regulations ignored. Conditions highly favourable to the spread of plague, typhus, cholera and smallpox were created. Possibly also the food of the townsman was less abundant than that of the country-dweller, and certainly it was less wholesome because food had to be carried over longer distances. Decline of corporate regulation allowed evil tendencies to flourish unchecked.

Warfare in the sixteenth and seventeenth centuries also made clear the poverty of contemporary medical resources. The fate of major campaigns was as likely to be decided by the outbreak of disease, as by the fortunes of battle. This happened to Lautrec's siege of Naples in 1528. Since larger armies were recruited, and fighting extended into the winter months, there was greater likelihood both of epidemic disease and of a collapse of the military organization. More destructive cannon were introduced, the troops were armed with handguns, and large civilian populations were involved in the horrors of war. Death outright was far less common than death from disease, or the infection of crudely treated wounds.

The seaman was scarcely more fortunate than the soldier. One new disease, scurvy, is dismally associated with the history of maritime expansion. There is no certain identification of it in all the history of seafaring before the Portuguese circumnavigation of Africa, no doubt because ships were rarely deprived of fresh food. Whole populations must have suffered in the Middle Ages from milder manifestations of vitamin deficiency, but the extreme and highly mortal scurvy that became a terrible commonplace of ocean voyages was something new. It was a direct consequence of the need for the navigator to seek the steady winds of the high seas. Vasco da Gama could never have reached India had he not stood out from the land into the trade-winds. He remained at sea for one period of four months, and most of his crew perished; Columbus, on the other hand, preserved a healthy crew through a voyage of a mere five weeks' duration. As English and Dutch vessels attempted similar voyages they suffered a similar affliction. Since food and water soon corrupted on these long voyages, it was natural that the occurrence of scurvy should be attributed to the badness of the diet, rather than to its lack of fruit and vegetables. Hardly less fatal to mariner and adventurer were such tropical diseases as yellow fever and cholera, so that the land proved little more healthful than the sea.

One new disease seemed to have irrupted from nowhere. Syphilis was first described at the end of the fifteenth century; it was said to have been carried into Italy by the army of Charles VIII. A flood of tracts greeted this new medical wonder, which in a generation spread through all ranks of society to become a usual feature of medical practice. The disease was popularly supposed to have been brought from the Indies by Columbus's men—a theory still favoured though never proved. It was often treated with wood *guaiacum*, a New World remedy presumably furnished by providence for a New World scourge.

The physician's resources against disease were still mainly traditional. His knowledge of its manifestations, causes and treatment, derived from Hippocrates and Galen, his pharmacology from the *Materia medica* of Dioscorides. Though there were hospitals—perhaps no worse organized and staffed than those of medieval cities—there were no facilities for research into old or new medical problems. These the individual physician or surgeon had to tackle as best he might, single-handed. Nevertheless, there were several ways in which the sixteenth-century medical man was in a stronger position than his predecessors. He was probably more widely read, for the printing-press had made the classical texts, and the new works of the Renaissance, freely available. The iconoclastic school of Paracelsus (c. 1493–1541) introduced medicaments prepared by chemical art; many of these drugs were valueless, some were harmful, like vitriol and arsenic, but others were strikingly successful, as was mercury in the treatment of syphilis. There was some improvement of medical teaching through the more rational outlook shown by Jean Fernel (1497–1558) and others. Anatomy, rendered an exact discipline in the hands of Vesalius (1514–64), enlightened the work of a new generation of surgeons. The career of Ambroise Paré (1510–90), who won great esteem despite his many departures from established practices, illustrates the surgeon's slow rise in professional learning and social standing, in which the apothecary also shared. And if the physician was hampered by prejudice—as in his excessive reliance on the virtues of phlebotomy and purgation—there were benevolent elements in his tradition. The notion that disease was caused by bad food and bad air was mistaken, but the measures of reformers who strove to raise hygienic standards were obviously beneficial.

Yet it may be doubted whether the medical profession was holding its own against social trends which were increasing the hazards of life for large numbers of people. The fact that the individual sufferer had perhaps a marginally higher chance of survival under medical attendance counts for little when the chance of becoming ill was greatly increased. There were two reasons for the weakness of society's medical defences. The first, of course, was pure ignorance. There was almost no rational physiology, the organisms causing disease were totally unknown, and the arsenal of pharmacology and surgery was pitifully feeble. Secondly, the powerlessness, incompetence or apathy of public administration ensured the neglect of plain principles that were frequently and forcefully enunciated—principles in many cases embalmed in unobserved regulations. Failure to enforce ordinances providing for the cleanliness of streets and the sound quality of foodstuffs; failure to organize proper supplies for armies, ships and prisons, or to appoint competent medical services; in short the almost complete deafness of authority (in practice) to the claims of preventive medicine except in times of epidemic crisis, were of great detriment to public health. For throughout these three centuries there were in all parts of Europe medical reformers, like the numerous neglected technical inventors, who demanded the enforcement of the commonsense hygienic principles supported even by the imperfect knowledge of their times. The long surrender to scurvy—

though the specific action against it of fresh fruit and vegetables was noted already in the sixteenth century—is a clear example of the way in which professional obtuseness could combine with official nonchalance to inhibit a medical advance.

Another aspect of the interest of governments and men of science in the development of sea-transport is navigation, in the more precise sense of the word. Here the sixteenth century was more successful, for its mathematics was a great deal more sound than its medicine. That there was an audience eager to learn the recondite art of numbers is evident from the steady appearance of elementary manuals, and the growing class of mathematical teachers, who naturally attended chiefly to practical topics. In all major languages books on elementary computation were published, the examples often relating to questions of trade, exchanges and mercantile accounts; the medieval merchant had been more at ease with mechanical devices like the abacus. The first English work of this kind is Archbishop Tunstall's *De arte supputandi* (1522);[1] many earlier works on commercial arithmetic had been written, especially in Italy, from the time of Leonardo of Pisa (*c.* 1170–*c.* 1250) onwards. They established the use of 'Arabic' in place of Roman numerals for the common purposes of life. More ambitious works, in the second half of the sixteenth century, entered upon the mysteries of algebra and geometry.

An understanding of geometry is the essential foundation of the arts of navigation, cartography and surveying. Learning from Jewish-Arabic masters (whose knowledge derived indirectly from the Greek mathematicians) the Portuguese in the fifteenth century had worked out a combination of astronomical and cartographical techniques which made possible first the coastal exploration of Africa and then the long voyage to the Indies. This new scientific navigation depended on the use of astrolabe or fore-staff, compass and log-line to establish position in terms of latitude and longitude. The preparation of maps using the same co-ordinates spread to Italy and the rest of Europe. Ocean navigation was an art totally different from the old skill in pilotage, soundings, marks and tides. It was futile to attempt to share in the profits of the ocean voyage without the attendant skills.

The ideas and methods of scientific navigation were diffused first by practical sailors, men like Columbus and the Cabots; but men of learning such as the mathematicians and astronomers Martin Behaim, Gemma Frisius and John Dee were soon at work upon the inevitable difficulties. These were both practical and theoretical. The practical problems included the devising of astronomical instruments suitable for use at sea; the measurement of distance travelled; and the simplification of charts,

---

[1] Followed by the anonymous *Introduction for to lerne to recken with the Pen* (1537), and the works of Robert Recorde (*c.* 1510–58).

tables, and sailing-directions. The theoretical problems, with which the mathematicians were mainly concerned, were more intractable. The most doubtful point in sixteenth- and seventeenth-century navigation was the fixing of longitude by dead reckoning, and the recognition of marks whose position was supposed (often falsely) to be accurately charted. The principles of fixing longitude, by the measurement of time or by the method of lunar distances, were well known, but all attempts to render them practicable failed. The magnetic compass was hardly less puzzling. The displacement of magnetic north from true north was commonly recognized; compass-makers, however, fixed the needle to the card so as to indicate (presumed) true north at the place of manufacture. Thus compasses from Germany and Portugal failed to agree, and no compass indicated true north in distant waters. The mistaken belief (held by Sebastian Cabot and Jean Rotz, among many others) that there was a simple relationship concealed in the deviation of magnetic north from true in all parts of the world, by which a ship's position could be ascertained, was only tardily relinquished. Much research into geomagnetism, stemming from that pioneer classic William Gilbert's *De magnete* (1600), was needed before the genuine extent of the compass's usefulness to the mariner could be appreciated. Further, since the navigator derived his latitude from altitudes of the sun and stars (always chiefly the former) he required accurate astronomical tables and simple procedures for reducing his observations. (It should be noted here that the Copernican reform of astronomical theory had negligible results in improving the accuracy of such tables.) Plotting star-positions was an important part of the astronomer's work from the time of Tycho Brahe (1546–1601) onwards, with which the foundation of the Observatories of Paris (1666) and Greenwich (1675) was closely linked.

Mere determination of a ship's position was of little value unless it could be plotted on a reliable chart, on which the proper course could be laid off. Upon the cosmographers—Peter Apian (1492–1552), Sebastian Münster (1489–1552) and especially Abraham Ortelius (1527–98)—who based their maps on critical appraisal of explorer's reports, there reposed a heavy responsibility. To the seaman the value of cartographical information depends greatly on the type of projection used to display it; here the major step was Mercator's projection (1569).[1] In the sixteenth century this new science of navigation became truly international, the result of co-operation between mathematicians and navigators in all parts of Europe. There was correspondingly a large publication of works, both original and derivatory, dealing with geography and cartography, navigation and seamanship. One of the most influential in

[1] The mathematical theory of this projection was first expounded by Edward Wright in 1599.

the latter group was Martin Cortes' *Breve Compendio de la Sphera y de la Arte de Navegar* (1551), from which many subsequent writers borrowed. It was translated into English by Richard Eden in 1561.

In the early history of scientific survey—topography as distinct from cartography—many of the same names reappear, since the scientific problems were much the same as in navigation. The methods of measuring heights and distances by trigonometrical operations were taught by countless authors. For trigonometrical operations the precise measurement of angles in the horizontal and vertical planes was essential, thus stimulating the invention of many new instruments, among them the first crude form of theodolite (Waldseemüller, 1512; Digges, 1571). Surveying instruments, together with many others used in applied geometry, were largely described in the first general manuals, such as Oronce Finé's *De re et praxi geometrica* (1556), Münster's *Rudimenta mathematica* (1551) and Gallucci's *Della fabrica et uso de diverse stromenti* (1597). A more direct method of survey was offered by use of the chain and plane-table, the popular method of the professional estate-surveyor. The practical uses of scientific survey and levelling were many and important. Besides undertaking the first adequate regional maps (a task well under way by 1600) the surveyor prepared maps of estates and towns, and plans for drainage schemes, harbour-works and canalization projects. His art was much in demand for military purposes too, especially in connection with the increasingly geometrical development of fortification. Many books revealing the significance of mathematics to the military commander were published, deriving largely from the pioneer works of Machiavelli (*Dell'Arte della Guerra*, 1521) and Tartaglia (*La Nova Scientia*, 1537).

From all this it may be judged that the impact of science upon technology, and hence upon the economic life of Europe, was as yet marginal. The greater scholarship of the medical profession had little effect upon the death-rate and the occurrence of epidemic disease; renewed activity in physics, mechanics and chemistry barely touched the workers in the primary productive industries—agriculture, textiles, building, mining and metal-working. Even the more glowing colour of mathematical proficiency adorning navigational and military science is barely visible in the history of European commerce and war. The scientist had indeed small chance of teaching the practical man his business, and from the many laments upon the obtuse ignorance of the artisan, seaman and gunner, it appears that practical men were not ready to learn. The academic loftiness of much scientific activity, tenacious still of ancient ideas and mingled with strong elements of superstition and mysticism—for alchemy and astrology maintained and even strengthened their claims to privileged attention—was a serious obstruction to the efforts of pioneers who sought to find in mathematics, physical science or medicine the key to the improvement of useful arts. The uncertainty of scientific opinion, the multiplicity of conflicting recommendations and the practical failure of so many confident proposals were testimonies to the limitations of science when its usefulness was tested, and grounds for the practical man's scepticism of its value. Nevertheless, the claim that learning was an agent in the advance of material civilization had been asserted, and was not wholly lacking in apposite illustrations.

## III. *The Age of Bacon, Galileo and Descartes, 1600—1640*

'The true and lawful goal of the sciences is none other than this', wrote Francis Bacon, 'that human life be endowed with new discoveries and powers.'[1] This striking phrase, though it should not be taken as epitomizing Bacon's attitude towards scientific research, is symptomatic of a major trend in seventeenth-century thought on the scientist's function. With varying degrees of emphasis the same opinion was expressed by Bacon's contemporaries and successors. It was not new. The virtue of cultivating science for its potential utility to society had been urged in the Middle Ages, most clearly by Roger Bacon. Then, however, and even in early modern times, the usefulness of science was rarely visualized as residing in the intelligent perfection of the ordinary processes of farming and manufacture. It was rather hoped that science would confer on man dominion over the supposedly mysterious forces of nature and so make him a natural and lawful magician—not merely a superior technician. Thus the claim that science is of use had been, and sometimes still was, most clearly illustrated by the supposed usefulness of the pseudo-sciences. One of the great achievements of the seventeenth century was the separation of this claim—then becoming increasingly suspect—from the belief that there is an inevitable conjunction between natural science and the common arts of mankind. The scientist's orderly theoretical and experimental study of the processes of nature was rather to be conceived as strictly parallel to the craftsman's fragmentary exploitation of some of them. The laws of nature, if they could be discovered by science, must hold equally in the laboratory and the workshop. When they were known the tradesman's practice could be best advanced by careful observance of them.

There was another side of this view of the relations of science and technology. If it fell to the scientist to acquire that complete view of the

[1] *Novum Organum*, bk 1, lxxxi.

natural world, organic and inorganic, which would vastly increase man's power of control over his environment, it was nevertheless recognized that in the then imperfect state of scientific knowledge the practical experience of the artisan gave in many ways a more intimate acquaintance with nature. The engineer and metal-worker were daily proving the value of techniques which the philosopher could not explain, encountering new phenomena of which he had remained ignorant, and making useful innovations to which he contributed nothing. Thus it seemed to Bacon, instancing the inventions of the compass, gunpowder and printing, that in past centuries learning had contributed nothing to material civilization; all utilitarian advances had been the work of unlettered, undirected artisans. As Galileo put it, speaking of the skilled workmen in the arsenal at Venice,

Conference with them has often helped me in the investigation of certain effects including not only those which are striking, but also others which are recondite and almost incredible. At times also I have been put to confusion and driven to despair of ever explaining something for which I could not account, but which my senses told me to be true.[1]

Following the Baconian tradition, the same arguments are stated at length by Boyle in his *Usefulness of Experimental Natural Philosophy* (1663, 1671). In general they implied that craft skill had an interest not narrowly limited to those whose livelihoods depended on it, but was an important branch of human knowledge. Such was the attitude of the compilers of the Royal Society's histories of trades, as it was of the editors of the *Encyclopédie*.

Yet one must be cautious in reviewing the effect of this double-edged attack on the academic seclusion of science, for it would be mistaken to conclude either that the rapid progress of science in the seventeenth century was wholly due to a diversion from abstract to practical problems, or that the industrial revolution was simply the product of applied science. Science became experimental, but not by trying to solve technological problems; indeed, to simple minds the spectacle of the philosopher vindicating his proclamations of utility by studies of the weight of the air and the anatomy of the louse was a subject for comedy. The method of modern science had its first great triumphs in handling questions far removed from common needs, seeming to belie the assertions of those who had sought to quicken public interest in the 'new and experimental philosophy' by exaggerating its immediate usefulness.

For though, in the battle with Aristotelian orthodoxy, it was advan-

[1] *Dialogues concerning two New Sciences* (trans. H. Crew and A. de Salvio, New York, 1914), 1. The speech is put in the mouth of Sagredo.

tageous to declare that a science of real things, founded on solid experiments and impeccable mathematical reasoning, was bound to be a fertile source of useful knowledge, in contrast to the empty learning of the schools, the step from theory to practice often proved more troublesome than had been imagined. Even such a work as Galileo's *Discorsi e dimostrazione intorno a due nuove scienze* (1638) is misleading in this respect. The first of Galileo's new sciences treats of the strength of materials, a study which today forms an important branch of engineering. Galileo's discussion is wonderful pioneer work, but it is very incomplete and sometimes wrong. It was of negligible value to the practical architect, and indeed the subject, despite a succession of brilliant mathematical analyses, remained almost entirely divorced from engineering practice until the nineteenth century. Again, Galileo's contributions to the second new science, dynamics, are quite fundamental. But he thought that it was a straightforward step from the principles which he correctly enunciated for the first time to such a matter-of-fact task as the calculation of the ranges of artillery. Mathematically, granting certain assumptions, he was correct; but the gunners who attempted to follow Galileo's procedures went astray, for the assumptions were vitiated by practical conditions. In many other instances the endeavour to profit from a new scientific principle was frustrated not by any inadequacy in the principle itself, but by failure to solve the incidental problems. In solving these, as in the case of the marine chronometer, the practical inventors of the eighteenth century played their invaluable part.

Moreover, if there was in mechanics a relationship between theory and practice recognized since at least the time of Archimedes, it was very different with other branches of science in which notable advances were made during the first half of the seventeenth century. William Gilbert, for example, in his *De Magnete* (1600) was not primarily concerned with the problems arising from the use of the compass in navigation which had aroused so much interest in the preceding century. He makes an eloquent plea for the experimental method; he devotes great labour to the factual elucidation of the properties of magnetic bodies, including the Earth itself; and he develops the first geomagnetic theory. But it is quite obvious that he approaches his task as a natural philosopher, for the discovery of magnetism as a grand cosmic principle (by which Gilbert justifies his adhesion to the Copernican theory) forms the climax of the work. However, he did believe that latitude could be determined from the inclination of a dipping-needle, and hoped that this discovery would prove useful to seamen. The almost contemporary, and even more celebrated, discoveries of Harvey and Kepler were yet further removed from the busy world. The theory of the circulation of the blood was the first major onslaught upon the Galenic physiology, but it did not immediately check the influence of Galen's writings in the medical schools. The further development of Harvey's experimental and observational methods in medical science was long delayed. Keplerian astronomy, with its strange notion of attractions between celestial bodies and new mathematical formulations for their motions, was so little valued, until it was approved by Newton's system of universal gravitation, that it had no effect upon those parts of astronomical science which were related to practical needs. Nor is there any indication that Kepler ever dreamed it would have such an effect; on the contrary, his outlook is altogether mathematical, philosophical, and mystical. His ambition was to reveal the harmony of God's design in the heavens, not to enslave them further to human purposes.

Even when, therefore, the new generation of natural philosophers who did not scruple to soil their hands with the charcoal and lute of the chemical laboratory, to grind their own telescope lenses, and to collect notes on remarkable technological feats[1] thought that they had embarked upon some investigation of public utility, they were often mistaken. And they were conscious that their interests were intellectual rather than truly practical; whatever they might think of the ultimate usefulness of science to mankind, they were more usually led to tackle a particular problem because it stimulated curiosity than because its solution might bring some material good. Frequently the problems, as in astronomy, anatomy, embryology, and optics are directly in the medieval tradition, though now handled in a very different fashion from the scholastic. Religion was now taken to give its blessing to intellectual curiosity, so that it was as commonly urged that scientific knowledge stimulated a proper veneration for the Creator of nature, as that it might be useful. As Boyle said,

we can never praise and admire [God] for those works which we think it pernicious or dangerous to consider . . . our admiration always rises here, in proportion to our knowledge; because the farther we contemplate, the more signs we discover of the author's perfection: and even our utmost scrutiny can give us but a faint veneration of his omniscience.[2]

Scientific learning therefore was a religious virtue.

The empirical trend of seventeenth-century science was never overwhelming; the desires for philosophical systems and universal theories were still strong enough to influence the scientific movement. Bacon revealed a leaning towards atomistic philosophy, and the later English

[1] As did, for example, the four contemporary Englishmen John Evelyn (*Diary*), John Ray (*Observations topographical* . . ., 1673), John Locke (*Travels in France* . . ., 1953), and Edward Browne (*Travels* . . ., 1685).
[2] *Usefulnesse of Philosophy.*

empiricists who followed the Great Instauration all favoured 'mechanical' (corpuscularian) hypotheses. Galileo prosecuted the mathematical method of Archimedes, but he too was an atomist. Descartes especially was confident that he had discovered the fundamental principles from which a complete system of philosophy—moral, ethical and scientific—must unfold. Though he admitted that one 'might proceed so far in philosophy as to arrive, by its means, at the knowledge of the arts that are useful to life', it was more significant for him that 'to live without philosophizing is in truth the same as keeping the eyes closed without attempting to open them; and the pleasure of seeing all that sight discloses is not to be compared with the perfection afforded by the discoveries of philosophy'.[1] Despite his *Dubiae etiam pro falsis habenda* and other rules of reasoning, despite his great contributions to mathematics and optics, Descartes' pleasure in philosophizing rendered his most comprehensive book a volume of ingenious, well-knit, and unverified speculation, *un beau roman de physique* as Huygens later called it. The grand system of the universe with its three species of particulate matter, its laws of motion and celestial vortices, which Descartes described in the *Principia Philosophiae* (1644), he regarded as adequate after the elaboration of outstanding details to embrace all the different branches of science. Yet because of the very magnitude of his imagination the authority of Descartes for his time was more complete than that of any contemporary. None of his immediate successors escaped the Cartesian touch, while in France (and to a less extent in other continental states) he was regarded as the master of modern scientific achievement down to the middle of the eighteenth century. The hope that there was some single omnipotent key to the treasury of nature, some primary methodological discovery or technique of thinking with whose aid patient industry alone would suffice to give complete knowledge of, and power over, the natural world was fondly cherished by many of the great scientific reformers, by Bacon and Descartes, perhaps even by Newton. This vision of Universal Truth just over the horizon (which was itself one of the factors in the picture of the technological Golden Age soon to come) was a luxury that the tedious development of applied science could hardly afford, though it was a stimulus to pure research.

Remembering therefore the long delay before its major fruits won acceptance (twenty years for Galileo, thirty for Harvey, forty for Kepler), and the inevitably protracted descent from the level of the natural philosopher and mathematician to that of the ordinary practical man, it is not surprising that the new science of the first half of the

---

[1] *Les Principes de la Philosophie, Oeuvres*, ed. Ch. Adams and P. Tannery, IX (Paris, 1904), 3.

seventeenth century left untouched the technological problems inherited from the sixteenth. The activities of a few inventive men, like Cornelius Drebbel with his design for a submarine boat, in a half-world between science and craft not fully belonging to either, provide no more than marginalia to a magnificent theme. To give it substance much was required, really effective scientific organization, patronage, the interest of men of wealth, and a far wider accumulation of facts. In the later seventeenth century conditions became more suitable, and the endeavour towards an applied science more hopeful.

# IV. *The Scientific Societies*

The foundations of several modern branches of science were securely laid by 1650, by Gilbert in magnetism and electricity, by Kepler in astronomy, by Harvey in physiology, by Galileo in dynamics. To this period also belong the first real textbooks on chemistry, beginning with Jean Beguin's *Tyrocinium Chymicum* (1610), and the first steps towards systematic arrangement and description of plant and animal species. Some of the most important scientific instruments emerge in a clear light—the telescope, microscope, barometer, thermometer. Modern mathematics was born in the period between Viète (*d.* 1603) and Descartes (*d.* 1650). So much individual originality, scattered through half a dozen countries and a hundred treatises, disrupted the existing traditions of science and supported the more synthetic attacks of Bacon and Descartes on the residua of scholasticism.

Yet to those living about the middle of the century the incoherence of the new scientific movement was easily apparent. The physicians, who offer the nearest approximation to a homogeneous group of scientifically educated men, were split by rifts between the Galenists and Paracelsians, the followers and critics of Harvey. The new mechanistic attitude to natural phenomena, which seemed to promise so much in physics especially, was troubled by disputes between the Gassendists, who believed in atoms, and the Cartesians who did not. Two of the greatest individual pioneers, Galileo and Kepler, had worked on such independent lines in astronomy that their ideas scarcely ever mingled. A vast number of discrete duels were being fought with success—too often between members of the same scientific party—but in spite of Bacon there was little evidence of generalship and co-operation in the struggle against Nature and authority. The important tasks of making new discoveries known to all, and searching out their public usefulness, were neglected; it was as necessary in 1660, as it was in 1831, for 'Philosophy to come forth and show herself in public'.

By this time the reforming spirit in science and medicine had reached many who were not to be important investigators, but were content to play their parts in other ways. Among them were patrons like the dukes of Florence, Habert de Montmor, Colbert and Charles II; and 'intelligencers' of science such as Marin Mersenne, Samuel Hartlib and Henry Oldenburg. Far more numerous were the dilettanti, amateurs, virtuosi, curiosi, attracted to the new philosophy for a variety of reasons —disgust with the formal and linguistic learning of the schools, the desire to alleviate human life, or sheer love of marvels. The seventeenth was the first century of the club and the learned society. As a taste first for disputations about the merits of the innovators—Copernicus, Galileo, Descartes—and then for experiments and natural history began to extend through the aristocracy and professions, regular meetings for debate and demonstration began to be held in many cities. They were more often associated with a court than with a university. The first to acquire a formal organization was the Accademia del Cimento at Florence (1657), followed by the Royal Society of London (1662) and the Académie Royale des Sciences in Paris (1665). Each owed its existence to the interest of a ruling house, and the first and last were provided with financial endowments.

The origins and early history of the Royal Society, which alone of these three had a previous informal existence as a private club, shows features which illuminate the relations of science and technology in the mid-seventeenth century. Bacon's double insistence on the sound empiricism of craft knowledge, and on the duty of science to contribute to the improvement of man's estate, had not been forgotten in England. When, after the outbreak of civil war, the government at Westminster was controlled by men of serious and Godly intent, the time seemed ripe to commend to its attention schemes designed to promote the unity of Protestant Christendom, and to develop useful knowledge for social ends. In these the prime mover was Samuel Hartlib, a German Protestant refugee, who joined to himself other emigrés such as Theodore Haak and Henry Oldenburg (who was to be Secretary of the Royal Society from 1662 to 1677), and a considerable number of serious-minded young Englishmen, of whom William Petty and Robert Boyle were to become famous. John Milton also was favourable to the ambitions of this group. Hartlib seems to have drawn his personal inspiration from Comenius rather than Bacon, but in his hopes for the foundation of a great philosophical college, and for the advancement of technology, he was at one with aspects of the Baconian tradition. He encouraged Petty and others to investigate and record craft processes, and published a number of little tracts promoting mechanical or agricultural innovations for the public good. Hartlib had no interest in theoretical science; it was Haak who encouraged the meetings of scientists at Gresham College, beginning about 1645, which fifteen years later developed into the Royal Society. At the Gresham Club, and at the Philosophical Society in Oxford to which it gave rise, there seems to have been little discussion of applied science. With the foundation of the Royal Society Baconian notions came to the fore again. Sprat argues in his *History* (1667):

*that the surest Increase remaining to be made in Manual Arts, is to be perform'd by the conduct of Experimental Philosophy.* . . . What greater *Privilege* have Men to boast of than this; that they have the Pow'r of using, directing, changing or advancing all the rest of the Creatures? This is the *Dominion* which *God* has given us over the *Works* of his Hands. . . . It is impossible for us to administer this *Power* aright, unless we prefer the Light of Men of *Knowledge*, to be a constant Overseer and Director of the *Industry* and *Works* of those that labour. . . . By this the Conceptions of Men of *Knowledge*, which are wont to soar too high, will be made to descend into the *material world*; and the flegmatick Imaginations of Men of *Trade*, which use to grovel too much on the Ground, will be exalted.[1]

To further these aims the Royal Society had, since 1660, announced its intention to encourage ingenious and enlightened tradesmen as well as philosophers and physicians; it had organized the compilation of a history of trades; it had discussed the best ways to improve specific craft processes; it had begun to collect information about the agricultural practice of different parts of the country, with a view to transplanting those that seemed best. Prominent in such activity were three or four former disciples of Hartlib; but others did not despise the utilitarian defence of science. However, at the time when Sprat wrote and printed some of its results in his *History*, the Fellows were already tiring of this Baconian programme. Before many more years passed it had been forgotten. The real history of the Royal Society is to be found in the work of its members in pure science, and in the long run its contributions to the perfection of agriculture and industry were almost negligible, for reasons already discussed. That this would happen could be predicted; what is more important is the change of attitude. By the end of the century, in William Wotton's *Reflections on Ancient and Modern Learning*, for example, the new scientific outlook is defended on purely intellectual grounds, not by the subsidiary and conjectural argument of usefulness. Science is no longer valued (and therefore misunderstood) for its social significance, and technology has been quietly abandoned to take its own course.

The obvious function of a scientific assembly in providing a forum and

[1] Thomas Sprat, *History of the Royal Society* (London, 1722), 393, 395–6.

a stimulus needs no emphasis. This led, fairly directly, to the foundation of the first scientific periodicals. Nor is it surprising that the societies should have divided into committees or sections for the joint study of the different branches of science and special problems; nor again that they should attempt projects beyond the means of a single individual, such as the French expedition to Cayenne (1672–3). It may be said too that the societies were just in their recognition of the greatest of the age, Huygens, Newton, Cassini, Ray, Roemer, Boyle. With experience it was found that the broad encouragement of common interests was a society's most useful function; and the somewhat more rigid, institutional notions of Bacon were abandoned even in London. The formal character of the society was most clearly shown when it acted as the official representative of science within the state, and its acts in this way were nearly all concerned with applied science and technology. This, as has been said, was not opposed to the views of the great pioneers. Many individuals were of course reluctant to be drawn in any way from their private pursuits, but few at this time would have made a staunch defence on abstract grounds of the necessity to preserve the absolute disinterestedness of research into nature.

In Paris, it had been foreseen from the first by Louis XIV and Colbert that the Académie des Sciences could serve as a department of scientific and industrial research. Within the terms of a managed mercantilist economy it was not difficult to conceive of the advantages flowing from a government agency whose duty it should be (besides advancing knowledge) to promote useful inventions and expose idle fancies; to survey the natural resources of the country and explore the means of rendering them useful; and generally, by helping to raise the level of technical proficiency, to increase both its exports and its independence of foreign supplies. Towards the end of the century all the possible merits of state-encouraged research were ably set forth by Leibniz in his endeavour to secure patronage for a German national scientific academy, which ultimately bore fruit in Berlin (1700). The results of a more systematic search for scientific utilities were, however, incommensurate with the ambition. The Observatories of Paris and Greenwich did magnificent work in astronomy, but they did not solve the problem of determining longitude at sea. The direction of the Parisian mathematicians to the uncertainties of ballistics and the design of the Versailles fountains produced nothing of profit. No major innovation in technology wrought its effect through the blessing of a scientific academy. Too much pressure caused the Royal Society to refuse to meddle with the craft of shipbuilding, and the temporary frustration of the less resilient Académie des Sciences. As in England and France the scientific movement flourished around the national societies, individual inclinations triumphed over communal programmes; in other scientifically advanced states, such as the Netherlands, there was never any explicit attempt to direct scientific research into utilitarian channels.

Even the endeavour to codify technological information was frustrated in both England and France. Some of the Royal Society's histories of trades were published in Sprat's *History* or the *Philosophical Transactions*, though to no apparent effect, and the Royal Society never exercised any right of approval over new inventions, such as was intended for it at one stage. No Secretary after Oldenburg was eager to push schemes of the Hartlib type. The French Académie did make an annual review of inventions: a volume of *Machines et inventions approuvées par l'Académie royale des Sciences* (since 1666) was issued in 1735. Its description of industries progressed slowly, but came to fruition at last. In the eighteenth century the work was taken over first by Réaumur and later by Duhamel du Monceau, who published between 1761 and 1788 a series of *Descriptions des Arts et Métiers faites ou approuvées par Messieurs de l'Académie Royale des Sciences*. This is an invaluable historical source for the study of the manufactures of its time; since it was published at a moment of rapid technical change, it is doubtful whether the work ever served any more useful purpose. The same interest in technology is reflected in the more famous *Encyclopédie* of Diderot and d'Alembert. Earlier encyclopaedists, like John Harris in his *Lexicon Technicum* (1704), (which has the first description of the Savery steam-pump) and Ephraim Chambers, had also compiled information on technical matters. Meanwhile individuals, a few of whom had scientific standing (like Christopher Merret, the English translator of Neri's *Art of Glass*) did much to compensate for the lack of the accounts of trades planned by the scientific societies. In England Joseph Moxon prepared descriptions of printing, building, metal-working and other trades; the Dutch naturally excelled in descriptions of the millwright's craft, as in the *Groot Volkomen Moolenboek* (1734); Jacob Leupold, a German, published between 1724 and 1735 several volumes on crafts and general mechanical engineering; shipbuilding was treated in books like Sutherland's *Shipbuilders Assistant* (1711). Although there was little in this growing technological literature suggestive of scientific insight, it was realistic, and not stuffed with fanciful novelties. Before the mid-eighteenth century it was possible to learn from books the 'secrets' of most trades, though few can have supposed any longer that these had much relation to contemporary science.

In the same way that the private researches of the Fellows of the Royal Society and the French academicians far exceed in importance the corporate efforts of their societies, it is in the personal interests of individuals that the possible technological implications of seventeenth-century science are most clear and, if anywhere, most effective. It would be difficult to name any mathematician, astronomer, or natural philosopher of that century who devoted himself consistently to matters of practical importance; but equally few would have been so obscurantist as to conceal discoveries or techniques of practical use. Until modern times the development of science furnished such discoveries only incidentally. Unless a use in everyday affairs presented itself readily to the scientist's attention, he was unlikely to trouble to search for it. Thus Newton was totally unconcerned about any technical implications of his work on celestial mechanics (though this was commented upon by others), yet he did design a novel form of navigation instrument because its curious optical principle (that later employed in Hadley's quadrant) interested him. Galileo suggested that the beat of a pendulum might be adjusted to the throb of a patient's pulse, so rendering medical observation more exact. Glauber advocated the use of spirit of salt as a substitute for lemon-juice in cooking, and nitre as an agricultural fertilizer; Boyle's work on the behaviour of substances at low pressures led him to hint that foodstuffs might be preserved in containers exhausted of air. At many points scientific experimentation would suggest a passing thought of this kind, usually fairly trivial, rarely seriously developed into a practical technique. Only chemists as a class had the application of their results constantly in mind; this was because most chemists were preoccupied with the discovery of new medical remedies. As yet few were, like Boyle, chiefly concerned to obtain through chemical experiments an insight into the structure of matter. Those members of scientific societies who were mainly remarkable for practical interests were secondary figures or dilettantes. Men like Evelyn, with his enthusiasm for sylviculture, or Petty whose energies were long bent to proving the merits of his strange twin-hulled ship, were not in any significant sense scientists, though they tried to work 'philosophically'. Some scientifically-minded virtuosi were fascinated by matters of this sort, which nevertheless were far outside the range of proper scientific analysis.

Two specific instances of the interaction between science and techniques are worth fuller discussion. The familiar problem of longitude was constantly thought to be within the grasp of science. Soon after he had discovered four satellites of Jupiter, Galileo proposed that their frequent eclipses behind the planet should be used as a means of time-comparison between a ship and some fixed point. Had accurate tables of the eclipses been available, reckoned from some determined meridian, the method would indeed have served—if a trained astronomer were at hand to make the observations with a large telescope from the unsteady deck of a ship. All astronomical solutions of the problem of measuring longitude failed to meet these difficulties. Then, about 1660, Christiaan Huygens and Robert Hooke independently applied themselves to the perfection of mechanical devices that should be both seaworthy and precise time-keepers. Hooke, having invented the balance-spring now so familiar in watches, passed on to other things; Huygens was led by his inquiry into the properties of oscillating bodies to devise the first pendulum-controlled clock.[1] With several differently designed chronometers and through lengthy trials, Huygens sought at intervals throughout his life to achieve his end, but without success. The interesting fact is that in the mechanics of horology one of the greatest of physicists was surpassed by practical clockmakers. It was they who made the pendulum clock an instrument of great precision, inventing mechanisms quite different from those of Huygens, and it was another clockmaker, John Harrison, who constructed the first effective marine chronometer, in 1761. It is true that the singular property of a pendulum, of oscillating very regularly, was discovered and investigated by scientists. Hence the pendulum clock is a scientific invention of importance. Yet it was practical craftsmen who adapted this invention so that it became a serviceable mechanism.

Other examples of invention exhibit the same pattern. In the case of the steam-engine the story is even more intriguing. The Italian mathematican Torricelli invented the mercury barometer in 1644, and was one of the first to realize that the atmosphere exerts a pressure in all directions at the Earth's surface. The 'Torricellian vacuum', the empty space above the mercury in the tube, invited experimentation, which was further facilitated by the use of the air-pump. This was rendered a useful laboratory instrument by Boyle's assistant, Hooke. Experience showed that great force was required to draw out the piston of the pump against the pressure of the atmosphere. It was again Huygens, with his alertness to everyday issues, who saw that this pressure might be made to do mechanical work. He designed a form of internal-combustion engine: the explosion of a small charge of gunpowder was to drive out the air from a cylinder, into which as the gases cooled the pressure of the atmosphere was to force a piston. His design was made known in England by Denys Papin, who proposed to improve it by substituting for the explosion of gunpowder the expansion of steam. So far all these scientific schemes were totally visionary—as impracticable as the various dreams of writers on 'secrets' who touched on steam-power. Then in 1698 Thomas Savery, who was probably connected with the Cornish tin-mines, patented a pump in which water was drawn up directly by the condensation of steam, and then expelled upwards from the pump-

[1] Such a clock had been designed earlier by Galileo—a fact known only in his immediate circle.

chamber by the admission of fresh steam. This machine worked, though inefficiently. Seven years later another craftsman, Thomas Newcomen, reverted to the idea of a separate steam-cylinder and piston, connected to the pump by an oscillating beam overhead, and the commercial history of steam-power was begun. The point here is not the obvious operation of economic factors in the early development of the engine—the relative prices of coal and tin, for instance—though economic factors are very relevant. It is that the ingenious practical man was required, as with the marine chronometer, to make a scientific concept practicable. Unless his interest was aroused, unless he could be convinced of the importance of the problem and of the merits of the scientific principle offered as a solution to it, it was unlikely that the invention ever would be worked. Scientific knowledge might offer hints, now as in the past; but great inventiveness at the craft level was necessary to put such hints into industrial effect. Craftsmanship had to come more than half way to derive any occasional advantage from science; and the attitude of the artisan to scientific work was at least as significant in the relationship as that of the scientist to the improvement of technology.

Thus it seems that planned attempts to guide scientific interest towards what were then conceived as socially useful ends failed in the seventeenth and early eighteenth centuries, whether made by scientific corporations or by the state. The scientists themselves were far more eager to follow lines of their choice; the basis of knowledge was too thin to allow its application to problems of technological detail, and the problems that were generally envisaged as fit for scientific attack were too sweeping and ill-defined. Nor were institutions, laboratories and resources available for a long research by teams of trained investigators. The task of building the structure of pure science proved far more prolonged, and the difficulty of applying what was painfully learnt to the business of brewing and baking and candlestick-making proved far more complicated, than had ever been supposed by propagandists like Francis Bacon, who expected to transform the intellectual and material worlds in a generation or two. Yet if planned campaigns brought little ransom from Nature, here and there the suggestions of individuals had already proved beneficial. Perhaps after all a policy of laissez-faire was best: let the inventor and entrepreneur struggle as best they might with such aid as science and craft experience afforded, and with such encouragement as they could derive from their profits. Striking a balance, it could hardly be said when Newton died (1727) that such public inspiration to scientific work as the last century had provided had been justified by the degree of material progress it had effected.

# V. *Scientific and Craft Discovery in the Age of Newton, 1640–1740*

The preceding discussion of the relations of science and technology unfortunately tells us little about either separately, since their relations were tangential. The narrative of history would be seriously distorted by imagining that the astronomers of the seventeenth century had no object but the improvement of navigation, or that inventors of textile machinery drew heavily on the mechanics of Galileo and Newton. The development of science was dominated by its own inner coherence. The progress of arts was hastened by the inventiveness of manufacturers and landowners spurred on by the profit motive. Both were indeed conditioned in some measure by the variable dynamics of society. It is not surprising that nations which were politically and economically aggressive were also energetic in science and technology; nor that aspects of changing religious belief should be invoked as factors influencing both scientific and commercial evolution. A world which was moving away from stereotyped forms towards freer ones, in which an individual could expect to be impelled upwards by the force of his own achievements, stimulated intellectual and materialistic enterprise alike. But in considering specific issues of importance such generalizations lose their edge. They do not help much in understanding the difference between the universe as it was seen in 1600, and in 1700; or the innovations in man's use of the machine between 1700 and 1800.

Such views can best be illustrated by considering science as the realm of ideas, technology as the realm of processes. The growing ideas of science at this time may be divided into two categories, the cosmological and the microcosmological—if for the moment the biological sciences are set aside. The principle of mechanism was dominant in each. By this it is not meant that physical science was materialistic: for those who regarded the universe as comparable to a watch, in the minute perfection of its parts and their unchanging logic of cause and effect, nevertheless welcomed the necessity for a divine watchmaker. Mechanism signified that all phenomena were explicable in terms of universal laws of nature, being produced by the rational and constant action of forces upon the particles of which gross and subtle matter were thought to be constituted. Hence, in the end, the very great and the very small levels of physics would be united in a single consistency of explanation. The physics of Galileo, of Descartes, and of Newton, different among themselves, were all agreed in this. The groundwork of cosmological ideas lay in the descriptive science of astronomy. Probably its most striking feature was the extension of the qualitative description of the solar system begun by Galileo: astronomy did not penetrate beyond this limit till the end of the eighteenth century. Besides the study of Saturn by Huygens and Cassini, of Jupiter by Roemer, and Hevelius's selenography, more traditional work on charting the stars and observing minutely the places of the Moon was continued with an accuracy that suddenly increased very swiftly, notably by Flamsteed at Greenwich. The time taken by light to traverse the Earth's orbit was observed by Roemer; later Bradley was able to account for apparent displacements of the fixed stars by knowing the approximate velocity of light.[1] Attempts to detect the Earth's motion directly in such displacements failed—the stellar parallax was still too minute to be measurable. All evidence pointed to the immensity of the stellar distances. Since there was no reason to suppose all stars at the same distance from the Sun, or that all the stars in the heavens were visible from the Earth, or that the infinite power of God was restricted in his creation, it seemed reasonable to argue that no finite limit to the extent of the Universe could be set. 'It is repugnant to my mind [wrote Descartes], or what amounts to the same thing, it implies a contradiction, that the world be finite or limited, because I cannot but conceive a space outside the boundaries of the world wherever I presuppose them. But for me this space is a true body. . . .'[2] The infinity of the Universe was an idea opposed by the earlier Copernicans, like Kepler, but by the late seventeenth century even popular expositions did not shrink from admitting that 'The distance from the Sun to the farthest Planet is nothing in comparison of the Distance from the Sun, or from the Earth, to the fixed stars; it is almost beyond Arithmetick.' Far from shuddering at the immensity of space, the new pride of imagination was to

think it very pleasant: When the Heavens were a little blue Arch, stuck with Stars, methought the Universe was too strait and close; I was almost stifled for want of Air: but now it is enlarg'd in Height and Breadth, and a thousand and a thousand Vortexes taken in, I begin to breathe with more freedom, and think the Universe to be incomparably more magnificent than it was before.[3]

Fontenelle also maintained, in a deliberately light-hearted manner, that there were inhabitants (though not Earth-men) on other planets and in these other worlds.

Within the vastness of space, however, the solar system was uniquely

[1] Bradley's reasoning (1727) makes the aberration of light the first observational witness to the revolution of the Earth about the Sun.

[2] Descartes, *Oeuvres*, ed. Ch. Adam and P. Tannery, v (1903), 345.

[3] B. le B. de Fontenelle, *Conversations with a Lady on the Plurality of Worlds* (1686; 4th ed. 1719), 122, 124.

presented to the investigation of science, whose greatest achievement
was to subject the motions of the heavenly bodies to scientific law. The
perennial problem of theoretical astronomy, since the time of Plato,
had been the discovery of the mathematical pattern in these motions: a
problem effectively solved by Kepler between 1609 and 1619. The
seventeenth century imposed on itself the disclosure of the physical
relations inherent in the structure of the universe by which these
motions were produced. In the *Philosophiae Naturalis Principia Mathematica* of Newton (1687) this too was accomplished, by applying to the
universal law of gravitation the principles of dynamical analysis, instituted half a century before by Galileo, developed by Descartes,
Huygens and others, and now further advanced by Newton himself.
The exactitude of the law was demonstrated by the precise agreement
between the mathematical theory derived from it, and the results of
astronomical observation; for the first time it was possible to predict
the complex variations in the motion of the Moon, for instance (though
later mathematicians had better success with this than Newton himself),
not by extrapolation from previous observations but from the physical
forces of gravitation by which the Sun, Earth and Moon act upon each
other. Newton's *Principia* furnished not only the outstanding proof of
the power of physical science to explain phenomena; it was the triumph
of mechanism. Though the nature of gravitation and of its association
with matter remained a mystery, it had been shown in the most decisive
and dramatic fashion that knowledge of the structure of the solar system
was sufficient to account for its manifestations—all was comprehensible
within the working-out of the laws of matter and motion. Was God still
required in physics, therefore, save as the Creator of its laws? This was
the question in dispute between Samuel Clarke and Leibniz. To the latter
it seemed that

the Machine of God's making, is so imperfect, according to [Newton and his
followers]; that he is obliged to *clean* it now and then by an extraordinary
Concourse, and even to *mend* it, as a Clockmaker mends his Work; who must
consequently be so much the more unskilful a Workman, as he is oftener
obliged to mend his Work and to set it right. According to *My* Opinion, the
*same* Force and Vigour remain always in the World, and only passes from one
part of Matter to another, agreeably to the Laws of Nature, and the beautifully
pre-established Order.[1]

In Newton's theory of gravitation the relevance of the small world of
physics to the great world of cosmology is crucial, for the force that
impels the planets in their revolutions is compounded of the forces acting

[1] *The Leibniz-Clarke correspondence*, ed. H. G. Alexander, Manchester, 1956, 11–12.
Cf. A. Koyré, *From the Closed World to the Infinite Universe* (Baltimore, 1957), 123, 236.

between the minute particles of matter. Like Galileo, Descartes and even Bacon before him, Newton was a corpuscularian and he took the chief tenets of the 'mechanical philosophy' for granted. That the properties of the 'least particles of all bodies', such as hardness, mobility, inertia, could be inferred as necessary from the existence of identical properties in whole bodies he regarded as the 'foundation of all philosophy'.[1] Since it was the ambition of the mechanical philosophy to explain all phenomena in terms of the motions, properties and combinations of particles their study was the prime object of physical science. Any explanation of a phenomenon of nature in less ultimate terms than these was therefore only partial. In the *Principia* Newton studies the gravitational force—which is, it must be stressed, for him a force attributed to the fundamental particles—very completely; in more conjectural language he suggested elsewhere (as in the *Quaeries* appended to the various editions of his *Opticks*) how other forces might be supposed to be involved in the phenomena of optics, magnetism, electricity and chemical reaction.[2] Newton's use of the mechanical philosophy is far more sophisticated than that of his predecessors, but the general framework was that which they had shaped.

With distrust of forms and qualities and what were classed as 'esoteric' explanations, the material microcosm, as the last resort of Nature's mysteries, became the centre of interest in the theories of physical science. Men had long been satisfied to think of heat as a 'form' of matter; but two such disparate exponents of the new philosophy as Bacon and Galileo agreed that heat was properly a sensation produced in the human body (or otherwise made apparent) by the motions of the small particles of matter. For them the attributes of particles were the reality underlying the superficial deceptions of the senses. Descartes had sought to explain the whole universe on the hypothesis of three different kinds of matter, each with its appropriate mechanical function. For all the new philosophers light was either a pulsation in a particulate aether, or an actual emission of particles; optical effects all resulted from the interaction of light and the particles of matter. Experimental study of the air also supported a particulate theory, which was further developed to account for the necessity of air for combustion and respiration. Boyle was the great interpreter of chemical experiments in the light of the mechanical philosophy; for him indeed the qualifications 'corpuscularian' and 'experimental' were virtually identical. Wherever natural philosophers rejected sympathies and antipathies, magic and

---

[1] *Principia*, Book III, Rule III.
[2] In a letter to Cotes (2 March 1713) Newton indicated that he 'intended to have said much more about the attraction of the small particles of bodies' in the General Scholium to Book III of the *Principia*.

mysticism, wherever they preferred mechanism to animism, they turned to explanations depending on the microstructure of substance. Naturally the direct exploration of this microstructure was impossible, though the fascinating discoveries already made with the microscope seemed to promise that it might not always remain so, but its characteristics could be clearly deduced from a suitable body of experiments.

None of the dozen truly great scientists of the seventeenth century was hostile to the mechanical philosophy, which survived as a less controversial substratum to scientific theory in the eighteenth. None wished to picture himself as merely describing the natural world, or as a mathematical drudge and compiler of heaps of experimental data. Despite certain aspects of the Baconian tradition, the age of Newton did not distrust theory, or even likely speculation: having rejected Aristotle's rationalization of the Universe, it was very eager to construct its own, with due attention to the verification of hypotheses by experiment and calculation.

In emphasizing the theoretical trend of the scientific revolution, however, and the fact that the revulsion from scholasticism was not merely characterized by crude empiricism, it must be added that observation and experiment also were distinct and prominent features of the new programme. As such they absorbed a large part of the capacity of many scientists, and yielded much information that was valued for its own sake as much as for its contribution to any new theory. Even Descartes, the most speculative of seventeenth-century natural philosophers, and the one who valued experiments least, performed some and spent much time on dissection. Newton's optical experiments are classical; he made many others in mechanics and chemistry. Even with such a great theorist as Boyle, and more so with other writers, chemistry was as wholly experimental as astronomy was observational. Minor work in varied fields consisted mainly of discovering and recording facts whose relevance to the understanding of the microcosm or of the Universe as a whole was not immediately clear; much that seemed important to contemporaries in pneumatics, hydraulics, mineralogy, metallurgy and meteorology was of this kind. Occasional instances of scientific interest in the applications of such sciences as mechanics to engineering, and astronomy to navigation, have already been mentioned: more consistent was the attention scientists gave to the invention and improvement of instruments of research, which brought them closely in touch with some problems of technological innovation. Astronomers and microscopists necessarily interested themselves in the manufacture and working of glass; in many instruments accuracy depended on the skill with which screws or gear-wheels could be cut by the mechanic; others still required devices for dividing lines or

circles into exact fractional parts; for much apparatus uniform glass
tubes, flat surfaces, heat-resisting vessels, strong solders and so on were
required, such as commerce did not normally supply. The tools of science
increased both in diversity and in perfection during the age of Newton.
They could be made only by the most skilful artisans, whose co-operation with men of science was novel and creative. To this extent scientific
discovery was really conditional upon at least the refinement of
techniques.

These developments promoted, as Boyle pointed out, the growth of
the specialist trade of the scientific-instrument maker, a trade divided into
two chief branches concerned respectively with optical devices and with
those whose construction involved mostly work in brass and copper.
Instrument makers of the latter class, together with the clockmakers
whose art had also become more exacting and elaborate, formed an
important reserve of technical skill. Theirs was an advanced engineering
in miniature. Its products were small-scale, and not made in quantity;
they were designed for the care of the laboratory rather than the rough
handling of the workshop; the lathes and other tools used by these
craftsmen were only suited to serve a luxury trade. Nevertheless, in skill
and precision the engineering progress of the industrial revolution was
partially anticipated. In the early eighteenth century the shop of the
instrument- or clock-maker was probably the best school of practical
mechanics.

Such schools were to bear fruit a generation later. More conspicuous
to contemporaries were the results of the continuing process of craft
evolution. Shipbuilding may be taken as a typical example. There
was a steady secular tendency towards an increase in the size of ships,
so that what had been exceptional in one generation became usual in the
next; the principles of construction of the hull by scarfing and pinning
together large numbers of relatively small timbers were unchanged. Rig
was adapted to give greater handiness and speed, but the marginal interest
of scientists in problems of design seems to have gone unregarded by
practical men, like Sir Anthony Deane, who were their friends. The
drawing of the 'lines' of a new vessel, and the methods of realizing these
lines in the shipyard, followed traditions a couple of centuries old at
least. Even the draught and tonnage of a new vessel were estimated only
with uncertainty from her drawings. Schemes that bear a flavour of
'scientific' inventiveness proved quite unpractical. Just as the ship-
builder tended to perpetuate with little variation save in scale and
possibly sail-plan a design that had proved successful, and that was itself
the product of gradual evolution, so in building-construction experience and style were the dominant considerations. In large buildings the
thickness of pillars, arches and beams was determined by consideration

of the stability or otherwise of existing structures, or by reference to traditional rules which erred generously on the side of caution. Structural analysis and experiments on the strengths of materials were virtually unknown among practising architects, though some progress was made in the mathematical theory of the arch. Even the works of such a mathematically equipped architect as Christopher Wren appear to have no more foundation in exact calculation than a Gothic cathedral.

The same might be written of many other constructive crafts, like those of the millwright, the wainwright and coachmaker, or the iron-founder. The works of skill that most men knew changed little between birth and death: the most obvious exceptions were the products of luxury trades—watches and clocks, firearms, table-services, furniture. When such exceptional trades are examined, however, the changes in craft methods are seen to be slight. The manufacture of porcelain demanded more skill and care than that of earthenware, but it was not essentially different; the craftsman who could make a wheel-lock pistol could as easily make a flint-lock. Differences in elegance of the product are far more obvious than differences in basic technique. Tools were improved and rendered capable of more accurate work, but machine-tools like the clockmakers' for cutting gear-teeth were late in invention and slow to spread. The emphasis still lay more strongly on dexterity in handwork than on the invention of devices more precise than human hands. Attempts, as by some early inventors of textile machinery, to imitate the repetitive motions of the manual worker were cumbersome failures. Strangely enough, it was in the little-understood processes of chemical industries that most progress was made, and that the connection with science is most demonstrable. The English glass industry, for instance, by its adoption of forms of melting-pot and furnace fitted to the use of coal fuel, and by the invention of lead-crystal (c. 1670), developed an industrial unit distinct from that of the continent. Its products were cheaper, though less prized, than the famous Venetian glass. Scientists (Merret, 1662; Kunckel, 1679; d'Holbach, 1752)[1] found much of chemical interest in glass: in the variety of materials from which it could be made, and in their coloration by minerals and metallic salts. Probably this scientific interest added little to the elements of glass-making, but it contributed something to the elegance of the glass-workers' art. A single innovation, like the introduction of the 'salting-out' process in soap-making, could effect a real improvement in yield, and give one region where it was known commercial advantage over others. Thus the invention of the scarlet 'Bow dye' (cochineal applied with a mordant made by dissolving pewter in nitric acid), probably by

[1] The dates refer to successive translations of Neri's *L'Arte Vetraria* (1612), to which Merret and Kunckel added extensive notes.

Cornelius Drebbel[1] about 1620, conferred a temporary precedence on the London dyeing industry. The new scarlet was employed in Holland about 1647, and at the Maison des Gobelins soon after 1660. It was looked upon as one of the outstanding technological discoveries of the century. There were other changes in dyeing techniques, partly brought about by the search for brighter finishes through the use of new mordants, partly by the greater availability of indigo when direct trade with India began, partly by the use of dyestuffs like logwood and brasil obtained from the New World, which combined to make this industry, like glass, of particular interest to chemists.

Not less interest, ascribable in part to the lingering alchemical significance of gold, silver, mercury and antimony, attached to the metallurgical industry. Chemists still pored over the great sixteenth-century treatises on minerals and metals (p. 101). The heavy sections of the industry, concerned with the smelting of copper and iron, were little modified by technical invention, much by increases in the size of furnaces and in the efficiency with which they were operated. The production of these two metals grew steadily, especially for military purposes. Some iron (for cannon, for instance) was cast directly from the smelting-furnace; more was worked by further treatment into wrought iron, from which in turn the steel for implements and weapons was made. The cementation of bars of wrought iron in charcoal was described in detail by Robert Plot, a physician, in 1686; cast steel was first made on a fairly large scale by Huntsman (1740), but it was already known in the seventeenth century. The lesser metals were more affected by innovation. Lead was rolled into thin sheets, with which the bottoms of ships were sheathed. The tin-plate manufacture, long localized on the borders of Bohemia, was established in France and England. The smelting of zinc from lead-silver ores at Goslar, in the Harz mountains, was begun. Bismuth, antimony and arsenic became increasingly important in alloys of tin and copper. In metallurgical knowledge, academic scientists were generally content to learn rather than teach, though some (like Newton) studied the physical properties of alloys, and many related the crystalline structure and other characteristics of metals to the ideas of the mechanical philosophy. Réaumur (1683–1757) was outstanding in the latter group. The title of his great work, the first scientific monograph on the ferrous metals, *L'art de convertir le fer forgé en acier et l'art d'adoucir le fer fondu* (1722) is self-explanatory. In it, while leaving the nature of his fundamental particles obscure, Réaumur 'clearly under-

---

[1] Drebbel (1573–1633) spent much of his life in London. Besides his military inventions (including a submarine), he originated many other 'scientific' devices, such as a thermostatically controlled furnace. Like other similar inventors, he made no contributions to science.

stood that, to explain the properties of matter, it was necessary to have parts with varying geometries and attachments to each other and that different materials could diffuse into each other and aggregate or disperse, depending upon the temperature.'[1] This is a perfect illustration of the application to practical technological problems of abstract scientific theory, which was still rare: and even here, despite the great merits of Réaumur's investigation, its immediate benefits were few. The company formed to exploit his methods failed, and the metal industries developed far more rapidly in England than in France, though with some obligation to Réaumur's work.

An industry which owed much to scientific chemistry, though in techniques rather than theory, was the manufacture of porcelain. The last phase of ceramic art before the eighteenth century had been dominated by tin-glazed earthenware, brilliantly decorated with bright enamel colours (produced by adding metallic oxides to the glaze) in the Italian maiolica industry, or ornamented with cobalt blue on a creamy-white ground in the Delft manufacture, which was imitated in England.[2] The desire to emulate Chinese porcelain, already evident in blue-and-white earthenware, stimulated many experiments on the composition of a whiter, harder, and finer ceramic 'body'. The earliest of these, made in Italy and France by practical potters, led to the successful manufacture of 'soft-paste' porcelain, especially at St Cloud (1693) and Vincennes (1745), the latter being re-established at Sèvres in 1753. Examination of earths and minerals likely to serve in the preparation of porcelain, and of glazes and pigments for its decoration, became a major occupation of French chemists. In 1710 Frederick Böttger, a chemist or rather alchemist kept virtually a prisoner by Augustus II of Saxony, discovered that 'hard-paste' porcelain could be made from a fine white Saxon clay, later known as kaolin. A factory to make it was built at Meissen. The distinction between the soft and hard porcelains was drawn by Réaumur in 1727; he found that the soft-paste made from sand, salts and other minerals was a fusible kind of semi-vitrified glass, while oriental porcelain was infusible. The French chemist P. J. Macquer (1718–84), head of the royal factory at Sèvres, recognizing that the Saxon porcelain was also infusible, instituted a search for a suitable raw material in France. The fabrication of true porcelain, worked out under his direction, was begun at Sèvres in 1766. The experiments of many others in the same direction, among them the German chemist J. H. Pott (1692–1777), commissioned by Frederick the Great to unravel the

---

[1] *Réaumur's Memoirs on Iron and Steel*, trans. A. G. Sisco, introduction and notes by C. S. Smith (Chicago, 1956), xxvii.

[2] The other principal varieties were the common lead-glazed ware, and Germanic lead-glazed stoneware. An important English invention, *c.* 1680, was that of salt-glazing, applied to much industrial pottery.

secrets of Meissen, and the great English potter Josiah Wedgwood (1730–95), whose constant aim was to apply scientific knowledge to the benefit of his manufacture, enhanced the beauty and range of the ceramic industry in Europe.

At this point ceramics enter the industrial revolution. The contrast between the potters' trials resulting in one kind of porcelain, and those of the chemists resulting in another, affords a convenient point of transition. Eighteenth-century chemists had negligible insight into the complex chemical changes associated with the firing of clay, or knowledge of the nature of the materials used in the ceramic industry. What they could offer in the way of science to industry was much humbler: firstly, the ability to classify minerals, and compare the properties of one with another; secondly, a systematic method of making empirical experiments and of learning from their outcome. This was enough to put into the chemists' hands a new process. For its discovery, scientific knowledge was not essential (the Chinese had made it without that) but scientific skill could certainly hasten it, and did. Other discoveries were made in a similar way, more frequently as time passed. A new invention might be partially scientific, the product of fragmentary (perhaps even false) scientific knowledge, and of the application of scientific method. The mechanical aspects of the industrial revolution remained, however, very much at the mercy of purely empirical invention.

# VI. *Biology, Medicine, and Health*

After the growth and transformation of industry, the expansion of population is the most enigmatic factor in eighteenth-century economic history. Attempts to explain it have usually turned upon developments in medicine, but before these can be discussed something must be said of the biological sciences, especially in their relation to medicine. The situation here is not unlike that prevailing in the interaction of the physical sciences and technology. Eighteenth-century medicine was still very largely empirical; its major 'inventions', like those in industry, were made without deep foundation in exact science—inoculation and vaccination, for example. Medical, like industrial, experience suggested problems of general biological importance; and some of the work done in biology was reflected in medicine, as work in the physical sciences was in industry. But the physician, like the manufacturer, was only marginally a scientist, though he received training in science. Most medical problems, like technological ones, were still too complex for scientific analysis and solution.

Interest in living things was split into two largely unrelated activities, natural history and the medical sciences, that is, non-human and human biology. Cross-connections, provided by botanical pharmacology and the fact that many naturalists were physicians by profession (though some of the greatest were not), do not upset this generalization. Moreover, until about the mid-eighteenth century, natural history was dominated by botanists, and even in the second half of that century the outstanding naturalist, Carl Linnaeus (1707–78), was primarily a botanist. From the late sixteenth century to the time of Linnaeus botanists were chiefly preoccupied with taxonomy: after the microscope became scientifically effective (c. 1660) a few naturalists, like Nehemiah Grew (1641–1712), studied plant histology, but the average botanist regarded description and classification of species as his object. Thus, despite much accomplishment within this limited range, botany could have little importance for the wider affairs of men. There were specialized discoveries, like that of sexual reproduction in plants, of great scientific importance but even these did little to enlarge the horizons of thought, and nothing to facilitate the efforts of the practical pioneers in agriculture. A potentiality of wider significance came with the challenge to traditional ideas on the fixity of species presented by such naturalists as Charles Bonnet (1720–93), the Comte de Buffon (1707–88) and Erasmus Darwin (1731–1802), but the history of biological evolution belongs rather to the nineteenth than the preceding century.

Some new trends appear in zoology, which was very largely the province of physicians. Animal dissection was an ancient aid to the study of human anatomy: the second half of the seventeenth century saw much good work in comparative anatomy, as well as improvement in zoological taxonomy, largely due to John Ray (1627–1705). Even more exciting were the wonders of microscopy. It was now possible to anatomize the 'parts' of insects and to trace their life-histories. A further world of totally unsuspected living things was disclosed, the 'eels' in vinegar, animalculae in rainwater, spermatozoa. This, like the cellular structure of organic matter and the corpuscles seen in blood and milk, was ocular evidence of the minute fabric of things, which science had formerly imagined, but with unaided senses could not detect. Some new ideas were immediately formulated—the most notable theoretical result of microscopy being the dispute between the animalculists (who regarded the spermatozoon as an immature foetus) and the ovists (who, following de Graaf's reputed discovery of the mammalian egg, took that for the embryonic form), which was only resolved in the early nineteenth century.[1] This question of the mechanism of reproduction held as much human interest as any in biology; before it was settled much information had been collected about the strange habits of microscopic

[1] The true mammalian ovum was first observed by von Baer in 1827.

creatures: an outstanding monograph was that of Trembley on the hydra (1744), which was experimental as well as descriptive. The microscope proved to be the decisive tool of biological science, radically changing its development, but the optical defects of the instrument, together with the lack of chemical means of investigation to supplement its use, obstructed studies of minute structures and their physiological functions.

For these reasons, the maturing of knowledge about the functioning of the organs common to human and animal species could occur but slowly, and it was here that ancient concepts and terminology ('humours', 'spirits', 'coction' and so forth) lingered longest. The different branches of medical science (anatomy, physiology, pharmacology, pathology) were almost exclusively pursued by physicians, who kept practical requirements constantly in mind, though chemists also contributed many new ideas. Of these branches, anatomy was the best founded; for most of the period this meant describing the arrangement of bones, muscles and organs with their blood-supply and nervous connections, but towards the end of the eighteenth century it was possible superficially to describe the differing structures of muscle, liver, heart, brain and so on. Yet even at that date 'physiology' was still largely a matter of gross description: it was possible to give only a very crude and uncertain account of what the stomach does in digestion, or the kidneys in excretion. Perhaps the best of it was that men were less ashamed to confess their ignorance than to invent imaginary explanations. Modern physiology is commonly said to begin with Harvey's discovery of the circulation of the blood, published in 1628—a majestic discovery indeed, but one that long remained without parallel or consequence. For physiological theory Harvey's most valuable legacy was his scientific method and his manner of reasoning, which were extended by his successors. His was one of the major influences in diverting medical science from fancies to facts.

If physiologists were to derive explanations less incomprehensible than those already prevailing, how were they to proceed? The seventeenth and eighteenth centuries favoured two allied approaches, the mechanical and the chemical, and in so doing opened up at least the possibility for a coherent science. The mechanical approach had the authority of Harvey (who had proved that the blood-supply of the body was a simple matter of hydraulics), of Descartes (who believed that animals were organic machines), and of the mechanical philosophy. It was possible, for instance, to describe the mechanism by which certain muscles effect the motion of the lungs, and to show that the purpose of breathing was to bring air into contact with the blood. Stephen Hales (1679–1761) made careful and important studies of the pressure of the blood in animals, and of the cognate motion of the sap in plants, using hydrostatic apparatus. He also discovered that large volumes of 'fixed air' could be generated from organic materials—a fact more immediately suggestive to chemists, than to physiologists. More complex versions of mechanical physiology were adopted by Albrecht von Haller (1708–77), for whom the central action of the body was a kind of filtering, by which the appropriate nutritive particles were either added to or subtracted from the blood-stream where necessary, and harmful particles similarly removed from it. However much the body might be affected by the 'passions of the mind' (whose seat in the body was an insoluble problem) the body itself was a highly involved mechanico-chemical system, the parts of which could carry out only the functions for which they were designed. The maxillary and sebaceous glands might be deranged by disease, but nothing could make them secrete bile instead of saliva and sweat, any more than the hands of a clock could sound the chimes.

The chemical approach was likewise based on analogy. Certain results follow from putting reagents together *in vitro*; similar results must ensue in similar circumstances in the body. Thus, acids are powerful solvents; the gastric juices are strongly acid; therefore food must be dissolved in the stomach by the familiar chemical action of acids. This was a promising path but it was blocked by the deficiency of chemical knowledge which, for instance, rendered attempts to analyse the various chemical compositions of bone, muscle and fat, or even of plant materials, productive of very crude statements. The laboratory analogy could also be very misleading. Chemical experience showed that reactions proceeded differently, or did not occur at all, according to the degree of heat applied; this induced the mistaken notion that the varying temperatures of different parts of the body had decisive effects on the processes taking place there. The best results were gained in the study of respiration. Harvey had left the function of the circulating blood a mystery. Richard Lower, in 1669, pointed out the difference between venous and arterial blood—the former could be made in all respects like the latter by shaking in air. Since air was equally essential to life and combustion, as experiments in the air-pump proved, it seemed plausible to suppose that something in the air was imparted to the blood by respiration, and carried round the blood in the arteries. Typically, this ingredient was thought to be a class of particle contained in the atmosphere which also acted on the 'sulphureous' particles of combustible bodies to produce fire. These interesting conjectures, however, were not confirmed by precise interlocking experiments, nor were they approved by all eighteenth century physiologists: the chemistry of respiration needed the elucidation of Lavoisier's oxygen theory of combustion.

The impulse to construct physiology on mechanical (or physical) and chemical principles was undoubtedly a sound one. It was a laudable endeavour to explain highly complex phenomena from knowledge of simpler ones—the true procedure of science. Unfortunately too little was known of the apparently analogous simpler phenomena. The direction of existing chemical techniques to physiological research was like trying to operate on the eye with an axe. The physiologist who attempted to use all such ideas that came to hand also suffered under the disadvantage that the mechanical and chemical levels of explanation were not strictly compatible—he might find it useful to think of blood as a complex of dissimilar particles, each serving a specific physiological purpose, but then at the chemical level this explanation proved deficient, when he had to trace the origin of these particles in the digestive process. For, despite Boyle, the useful statements of chemistry were not couched in particulate terms. And, finally, pathology applied a destructive test to mechanistic physiology. If the processes of the body were purely mechanical or chemical, what was the cause of their disorder, manifest in disease? The physician's problem is the sick, not the healthy body, and in the tradition of medicine continued through the eighteenth century everyone was sick unless he took physic. The body did not seem to be a machine that worked perfectly; under the conditions of normal life it broke down continually, 'degenerated', and so required regular adjustment and repair. Hence the physiologist was forced to compromise:

The blood of the renal artery . . . being brought by the serpentine arteries of the kidneys, deposits into the rectilineal tubes of the papillae a great portion of its water, and the oil incorporated with it, and the salts, and any thin fluid it may contain. But the small diameter of each uriniferous duct at its origin, and its firm resistance, seem to exclude the gross oil, and the chyle, and the coaguluble lymph. Hence the increased celerity of the blood so easily forces the red globules through these tubes, and, by morbid relaxation, they transmit the true fat and the chyle, and the salts of the meat and drink. But when the strength of the kidneys is restored by astringent medicines, the urine returns to its natural state.[1]

Thus Haller expresses the explanation of a defect in the filtering action of the kidneys, and of the counter effect of suitable remedies. But he is forced to invoke a vague 'morbid relaxation' as the root cause of the disorder. It was very difficult to handle pathological conditions mechanistically, for though the concept of infection of the healthy organism by 'ferments' or other agencies was discussed in the eighteenth century, it was usual to attribute disease to disturbances of the normal functions which could not be accounted for either mechanically or chemically.

[1] Albrecht von Haller, *First Lines of Physiology* (Troy, 1803), 383.

In practice, a 'scientific' physiology at this stage was of little help to the medical man, who wanted first to be able to identify a diseased condition, and then to know the remedy for it. Progress in these respects depended, as in the past, on clinical experience. The scientific approach is evident in the writings of such clinicians as Thomas Sydenham (1624–89), but it was hampered by the inevitability that the physician's attitude to his art should be predominantly empirical.

Probably the primary need in medicine is for the accurate description of diseases, so that they can be recognized by the physician. There was notable work of this kind in the second half of the seventeenth century— among conditions carefully studied, some of them for the first time, were skin diseases (Roilau, 1648; Willis, 1670), rickets (Glisson, 1650), apoplexy (Wepfer, 1658), diabetes (Willis, 1670), gout (Sydenham, 1683), and tuberculosis (Morton, 1689). Sydenham's books were particularly instructive in this respect: he was a great teacher, as well as a great physician. Medical training was improved at the schools of Leyden and (later) Edinburgh, and by the excellent works of some of their professors, of whom Herman Boerhaave (1668–1738) justifiably enjoyed the highest reputation. The same period was marked by a wiser use of chemical remedies, and of exotic drugs like cinchona (quinine)—the first specific of modern medicine. But the progress of an art which had no theory ('All that has been written', declared Sydenham, 'has been hypothesis'), or even a solid body of fact on which to base a theory, was bound to be slow; and what was gradually gained was even more gradually diffused for the benefit of the population at large. Not the physician, but the local wise woman, delivered, physicked and laid out the peasant masses of Europe.

Two causes of death indeed diminished during the eighteenth century. There were no widespread epidemics of plague, such as had occurred frequently in the first half of the seventeenth. Plague was rare in the British Isles after 1666, and unknown after 1679. The plagues at Marseille (1720) and Messina (1743) were begun by infection brought from surviving centres in the Near East, and were limited in extent. No other outbreak spread beyond the fringes of Austria. Smallpox, whose ravages had grown steadily more violent during the last century or so, was at last subjected to control, first by inoculation (1717) and later by vaccination (1798). In neither case can much credit be assigned to medical science. Probably the quarantining, favoured by medical opinion, of vessels and goods coming from suspect areas was effective in preventing the spread of plague into western Europe after it had ceased to be endemic there (though Britain had no quarantine laws before 1720): the disappearance of endemic plague seems to have been mainly due to the superior vigour of the brown rat. Inoculation was an empirical procedure long familiar in Turkey, introduced into Europe by Lady Mary Wortley Montagu. Vaccination was another empirical prophylactic of country-people in several parts of Europe, made medically respectable by Edward Jenner (1749–1823). The relatively rapid acceptance of vaccination speaks for the willingness of the medical profession to exploit sound empirical observation, rather than for its ability to discover remedies through the study of disease.

Other factors commonly alleged to have contributed to the improvement of health in the eighteenth century are hygienic rather than medical. In essentially social reform of this kind a leading role was played by laymen some of whom, like John Howard, found it necessary to criticise the sloth of the profession. New hospitals (including isolation hospitals) were founded; attempts were made to increase the cleanliness and conscientiousness of old ones, and to make the state of the prisons less dreadful. Towards the end of the century urban sanitation was improved by paving streets, supplying piped water, and sewerage. Benevolent societies provided better medical aid for the poor. The draining of marshlands reduced the ubiquitous malaria. Only in England, however, had there been measurable progress in all these respects before 1800.

Unfortunately there is also much to be said on the other side. Inoculation, for instance, gave a reasonable chance of security to the patient at the expense of his friends: it was fairly thought that it *increased* total mortality 'inoculation destroying more than it saved, by spreading [smallpox] to places which would otherwise have escaped'. Hence it was forbidden in Paris in 1763.[1] In any case, the number inoculated was always small. Vaccination was long restricted by popular prejudice. Hospitals remained dirty, unventilated, the dead and the living sometimes sharing a bed. Few could be entered without charge. Yet it was only for the destitute that admission to hospital was a real act of charity— even the humblest dwelling was likely to be a healthier place. Sepsis and fever are notoriously easily spread in lying-in hospitals. The streets of towns were still filthy and noisome; piped water spread disease far, if the source became tainted; the 'hygienic' water-closet was a potent means of infection of subsoil and river water, drunk untreated. Cities claimed more people, and shortened their lives.[2] At the end of the period, living conditions in the new factory towns were becoming especially bad. In spite of all that was done, the horrors remained for mid-nineteenth-century reformers to describe, such that one can scarcely imagine the

---

[1] Quoted by K. H. Connell, *The Population of Ireland, 1750–1845* (Oxford, 1950), 214.

[2] Even in Sweden, the net reproduction rate per thousand of the *small* towns was zero, that of Stockholm was —6·6, and that of the countryside +7·3, in 1802 —15. Towns, it was said, were like a pestilence.

pre-industrial state to have been worse. Even if it had been, the result of a larger fraction of the whole population becoming urban would inevitably have been to increase the death-rate.

To recognize the sad impotence of medicine in the eighteenth century—which was no greater than it had been in preceding ages—quaintly expressed in the gibe against the respectable English physician John Coakley Lettsom:

> When any sick to me apply,
> I physics, bleeds, and sweats 'em:
> If, after that, they choose to die,
> Why, verily, I Lettsom;

is not to deny that medicine made some contribution to increasing longevity. But it was still (as always) very much safer not to contract a disease, than to hope for its cure, and the best medicine was the body's own resistance to infection.

The hypothesis that medical progress had a great effect in reducing the death-rate was invented by demographers who sought to explain the rise of population in Britain in the eighteenth century, which they attributed to a decrease in mortality (among infants especially), the live birth-rate remaining constant. Having decided upon this explanation, they then looked into the history of medicine for evidence to support it, though historians of medicine have justifiably been more cautious in their assessment of the same evidence. From medical considerations alone no one would have predicated such a prodigious increase in population as occurred in England and Ireland, especially after about 1780, in a period of distress and war, nor would such a prediction be supported by contemporary testimony.

The events in Ireland have been carefully studied, and furnish a conclusive test of the value of this medical hypothesis.[1] Ireland lay out of the main stream of endeavour in science and medicine, and its population of peasants lacked urban amenities; nevertheless this increased from some 2¼ million at the end of the seventeenth century to about 4 million in 1780 and 8,175,000 in 1841. If medicine had any connection with this increase it would be expected that in the towns the death-rate would be lowest and the birth-rate highest—since the peasant was worse off medically than the townsman. In fact the reverse was the case: the peasant produced more children and had a longer life. And in Ireland it is untrue that the birth-rate remained constant: it increased. More children were born, because the Irish were marrying earlier, and at this time children were not regarded as burdens upon their parents.

[1] Connell, op. cit.

As Arthur Young said, the peasants 'found their happiness and ease generally relative to the number of their children, and nothing considered such a great misfortune as having none'.[1] It might be anticipated that the Malthusian restraint on the growth of population would apply, as indeed it did with catastrophic force in the 1840's and later; that it did not before the population had multiplied several times over was due to the availability of a new source of food, the potato. A heavy consumption of potatoes, with a fair amount of milk, which constituted the normal diet of the peasant, was ample for health. The mother was in good physical condition for bearing and rearing children, and there was nourishment for an expanding family because potatoes required less land than an equivalent quantity of corn, and could be grown on otherwise unproductive soil. Ireland's case was also stated by Malthus: when the food supply potentially increases, the population will tend to enlarge to eat it.

More recently, this explanation of population growth as a response to economic opportunity has been applied to England also, *mutatis mutandis*.[2] It can hardly be believed that English cities were less baleful than Irish, and there is good reason to suppose the statistical argument false that has insisted on the constancy of the birth-rate. Generally, a high net reproduction rate seems to be associated with multiplicity of births, rather than fewness of deaths.[3] The favourable economic situation that encouraged early marriage, and hence a high birth-rate, was more complex in England than in Ireland: beginning with the good harvests and cheap food of the period 1730–55, it involved the employment provided by industrialization, the ability of improved agriculture to supply a growing demand for foodstuffs, the decline of guild and similar restrictions on the earning capacity of the young, and the system of parish relief. Economic growth furnished economic opportunity: it is certain that if children could not have been employed in the new factories, however dreadful the circumstances, they could not have survived at all. Thus the economic historian endorses the equation set out by Adam Smith—'the reward of labour must necessarily encourage in such a manner the marriage and multiplication of labourers, as may enable them to supply that continually increasing demand by a continually increasing population'[4]—which the history of medicine has no reason to dispute. For if medicine had kept more people alive, it could not have fed and employed them—as happened in both England and Ireland.

There can be little doubt but that over the whole of Europe the

[1] Quoted by Connell, *op. cit.*, p. 15.
[2] H. J. Habakkuk, 'English Population in the Eighteenth Century', *Economic History Review*, 2nd ser. VI (1953), 117–33.
[3] *Ibid.*, 123.
[4] *Ibid.*, 118.

population was capable of expansion, as soon as resources allowed. Growth was effectively limited by hunger, not disease. In Sweden, writes Professor Heckscher, 'food-supply was the deciding factor in influencing the rate of mortality, counting far more than medical causes.' This is evident, for example, from the correlation between deaths from contagious diseases and the yield of the harvests. He believes that conditions were substantially the same elsewhere in Europe: in fact they were probably more extreme than in Sweden, with both birth- and death-rates higher.[1] It is significant that in the nineteenth century those countries in which economic expansion was most rapid were also those in which population increased fastest. Modern experience has been that where mortality falls owing to medical intervention, without an accompanying diminution in the birth-rate, the expanded population presses heavily on its resources and the standard of living falls, for the effect of medicine is to reduce the threshhold at which the Malthusian check operates. That this did not happen in the eighteenth century, that the standard of living remained constant or even rose, suggests that economic conditions were not so much the factors limiting numbers, as factors permitting numbers to increase.

Since there can be little doubt of the enhancement of the English farmer's ability to produce foodstuffs during this period (perhaps more markedly than that of farmers in other countries, though elsewhere the trend was similar), it is reasonable to inquire whether agricultural development owed anything to science. There is little evidence for an affirmative argument. The Royal Society did something to stimulate an intelligent interest among the gentry, though it received few replies to its lists of queries on farming practice and failed in its propaganda on behalf of the potato and cider-apple. Nearly a century later the prizes offered by the Society of Arts promoted local growing of such crops as lucerne, and new designs for agricultural implements, but the total results of its efforts do not seem to have been great. Apart from changes in land-distribution and the reclamation of waste-lands (probably the greatest factors in increasing total yield), the main impulse to agricultural reform in England, as elsewhere, seems to have come from the desire to emulate the complex rotations of Flemish husbandry, which avoided the loss of crop in fallow years and enabled larger numbers of cattle to be kept. It is certain at least that whatever the reasons for growing turnips, artificial grasses, legumes and so on as field crops, their function in an agricultural cycle could not yet be understood. It was argued by some that different crops took different forms of nourishment from the soil, but this was no more than an empirical observation. Chemical analysis

[1] E. F. Heckscher, 'Swedish Population Trends before the Industrial Revolution', *Economic History Review*, 2nd ser., II (1950), 266–77.

was still too crude to separate out the ingredients of vegetable matter and could do little more than indicate its composition of water, 'oil', 'salts', and a little 'earth'. The beneficial action of marl, dung, lime and other fertilizers on different kinds of soil defied explanation. The idea of plant nutrition most discussed by farmers in the eighteenth century was that of Jethro Tull (1674–1741) who asserted that fine particles of the soil entered directly into the structure of the plant. If the soil were divided finely enough by implements, no manuring was necessary. This is an example of a simple 'mechanical' theory denying attempts at chemical types of explanation. It has justly been emphasized that Tull's 'new husbandry' was rather founded on dogma than on any scientifically demonstrable theory—for the scientific knowledge of the time favoured a chemical approach to the problem; yet science was inadequate to expose Tull's fallacy. The work of such pioneers in plant physiology as Nehemiah Grew (1641–1712) and Stephen Hales (1679–1761) was important, but it provided no answers to the questions which the practical, experimental farmer was apt to ask. The first observations on the carbon-oxygen cycle in plant life were described by Joseph Priestley in 1774; understanding of the nitrogen cycle awaited the nineteenth century. Until the role of atmospheric gases in the formation of plant tissue was understood, scientists were simply groping in the dark and left the progressive farmer with no guide save empiricism.

# VII. *Science and Technology in the Industrial Revolution*

Not every manufacture that changed its character in the eighteenth century was modified by important technological changes. Logically there is a valid distinction between changes in economic structure and organization on the one hand and modifications of processes on the other, though historically the latter tended to accelerate the former. An industry like brewing was an example of economic change occurring without accompanying technological stimulus: the pattern of events was similar to that associated with the major manufactures but the methods by which beer was brewed altered only in scale. The steam-pump was a new device in the brewery, but one introduced only *after* brewing had become industrialized. Perhaps even more striking is the sudden value attached to inland water-transport, and the resulting canal-mania especially notable in England. The necessary engineering techniques had been perfectly applied in the Languedoc Canal of Louis XIV's reign, and nothing but lack of economic incentive had delayed their use everywhere. Conversely, it seems that the absence of technological drive caused certain manufactures, like that of nails or boots and shoes, to stay close to the domestic level. When machinery to supplant handwork appeared in the later nineteenth century, factory organization followed swiftly. At that stage, however, the inventors of such new machines had the intention to make factory production possible, whereas the earliest inventors of the industrial revolution had not foreseen the factory as a consequence of their efforts.

Reviewing the whole of industrial activity in the early eighteenth century, the problems to be solved by technological invention fall into three classes: those in which the object was to perform by mechanical linkages operations normally effected by the hands of an artisan; those concerned with the use of power; and those related to metallurgical and chemical processes. The first class is typified by Kay's flying-shuttle; the second by Watt's improved steam-engine, and the third by the manufacture of synthetic soda. By 1700 the situation in each class was acute, if a long history of unsuccessful attempts in each is a measure of the realization of the need for technological progress and of the desire to bring it about. Every major success of the industrial revolution was foreshadowed by a series of earlier failures; and it is natural to suppose that success was due to an intensification of the need for invention, prompting greater persistence in the search and greater willingness to risk capital in it. To this must be added the fact that a gradual, general progress in technology permitted spectacular advances to be made at particular points in turn: the relation of the superiority of Watt's engine to the development of hollow-boring techniques is a well-known example. And in the third class of invention something was owing to the gradual progress of science.

Inventions of mechanisms of the first class are the most difficult to discuss, because a logical pattern is indiscernible; yet such invention was a most conspicuous feature of the industrial revolution in the textile industries. So much seems to depend upon the experience and resourcefulness of the individual inventor that consideration of the steps leading to his achievement is rather a biographical than a general technological problem. Thus it happened in time that different men devised very dissimilar mechanisms working to the same end—such as making a yarn for weaving—one of which might be used here, another there, with little to choose between them. In some cases experience might decide that yarn for the warp was best produced by one machine, that for the weft by another, even though the work done by both machines was essentially identical. One can point to features common to all machine-building, and therefore to the success of invention, such as the greater availability of iron and steel, the higher skill of the mechanic, and the improved tools at his disposal. Many things were possible with iron gears that were impossible with loose-fitting wooden cogs. If it is reasonable to suppose that the textile machinery of 1800 could not have been built successfully at a much earlier date, it is less easy to account for the appearance of the ideas appropriate to its design at the moment when it could be built. Certainly attempts at mechanical invention were more frequent, and probably mechanical knowledge was more widespread, than formerly. The simple elements that, compounded together, form a machine (gears, ratchets, springs, cams, eccentrics, cranks, rollers, detents, guides and so on), in their different guises and uses, were more familiar than they had been a couple of centuries before. Sometimes, as with the use of pairs of drafting-rollers in the spinning-machines of Lewis Paul (1738) and Richard Arkwright (1769), an important mechanism may be traced back to its antecedents, in this case the use of heavy steel rollers to draw out and reduce strips of metal. How, on the other hand, can one account for the invention of the punched-card system of 'instructing' a machine (Bouchon, 1725)? This appears to be a totally novel conception. Few of the new machines embodied any single feature of such ingenuity as Paul's or Bouchon's; the originality of most lay in their re-combination of familiar devices and some (such as gig-mills) were extremely simple. Many industrial operations, like crushing, mixing and stirring, or stamping were easy to mechanize once the incentive existed and the scale of production justified the expense of a machine, which might be no more complex than the ancient corn- and fulling-mills.

At least one can say that the debt of Arkwright, Hargreaves, Crompton, Vaucanson, Jacquard and the like to science is immeasurably small. The science of mechanics had by this time little to do with machine-design. Popular lecturers demonstrated the screw, pulleys, inclined plane and so forth, but all these devices were too well known to practical mechanics—from experience, if not theory—to require further publicity. Roemer's premature study of the optimum shape for gear-teeth, in the previous century, had been without influence or succession. Again, seventeenth-century scientists had given much attention to both thermal expansion and time-keeping; but it was left to such clock-makers as Harrison, George Graham and Pierre Leroy to correct the effect of temperature-changes on a pendulum or balance spring. With the exception of John Smeaton (1724–92) none of the inventors of new productive machines had affiliations with organized science.

In the remaining classes of invention the situation was otherwise. The improvement of prime-movers was mainly the work of men sensitive to the ambitions and methods of science, and far more sophisticated in their attitude than the purely mechanical inventors. For hydraulic engineering the scientific writings of B. F. de Belidor (1693–

1761), Leonhard Euler (1707–83) and others were by no means irrelevant, and some of their results were absorbed in practice. John Robison (1739–1805), in fairly non-technical articles, could show from theory that it was a waste of money to install large pipes for a water-supply system, if the flow was obstructed by small control-valves; and that, with a given supply of water, it was preferable to design a water-wheel to turn slowly rather than fast.[1] Yet he was well aware of the general deficiency of theory, especially as it had penetrated among engineers, who were usually taught only to understand the operation of a machine in static conditions:

But when the equilibrium is destroyed by the superiority of one of the forces, the machine must move; and the only interesting question is, *what will be the motion?* Till this is answered with some precision, we have learned nothing of any importance. Few engineers are able to answer this question even in the simplest cases; and they cannot, from any confident science, say what will be the performance of an untried machine.

The two most notable engineers of the new technology, Smeaton and James Watt (1736–1819), were both trained as scientific-instrument makers; both were Fellows of the Royal Society, Smeaton receiving the Copley Medal for his *Experimental Enquiry into the Natural Power of Wind and Water to turn Mills*[2] and Watt being known for his chemical interests; both talked freely with their scientific friends. Smeaton and Watt were as near to being scientific engineers as eighteenth-century conditions allowed, but as was the case with the industrial chemists, it was the method of science that was useful to them, rather than any of its particular insights. Their investigations of actual engines brought them close to such concepts of nineteenth century thermodynamics as *work* and *energy*, though the science of their own day provided an inadequate theoretical structure. In fact the formulation of the scientific theory whose lack caused Smeaton and Watt to stumble in the dark sprang, during the first half of the next century, from the attack with great rigour on the very problems with which they had been concerned as practical engineers. These concerned the efficiency of prime-movers. A water-wheel has a given fall and volume of water available: a steam-engine burns so many pounds of coal in a day: the question was to find out how to measure the performance of different engines, and ascertain the best possible design. Smeaton constructed model water-wheels of different types and in his experiments measured power-output by finding the

[1] Robison wrote on engineering for the third edition of the *Encyclopedia Britannica* (1788–97); the articles were reprinted in his (posthumous) *System of Mechanical Philosophy* (Edinburgh, 1822), cf. II, 574, 601–12, 708.

[2] *Philosophical Transactions*, 1759.

distance through which a weight was raised in one minute. As a result he was able to lay down some useful principles of design. The common reckoning of the 'duty' of a steam-engine was the number of million foot-pounds of water raised for each bushel (84 lb.) of coal burnt, but Watt returned to Smeaton's definition of power, taking 33,000 foot-pounds as the 'horse power'. Somewhat obscurely behind their experiments and discussions seems to lie the ideal of the perfect engine which would convert all the energy of fuel or falling water into mechanical energy, and to which existing engines only approximated; but the expression of such notions in precise language followed much later.

At least their investigations taught them that a large fraction of the power that was potentially available for pumping water or driving machines was wasted, partly through the inevitable friction and inertia of the parts, still more through bad design, and most conspicuously in the steam-engine. Smeaton's improved Newcomen engines were about twice as efficient as the early type. Watt, by his introduction of the separate condenser and his application of steam-pressure above the piston, further raised efficiency three to five times; his method of obtaining rotary motion from a steam-engine vastly extended its usefulness. Newcomen had invented a pump, Watt a source of power for factories and transport.

It has often been supposed that Watt's inventions—themselves far more vital to the second stage of the industrial revolution than to the first—owed much to the work on heat of the Scottish chemist Joseph Black (1728–99).[1] Watt himself, in 1814, while paying graceful tribute to Black's superior insight into the science of heat, denied this suggestion.[2] Although he admitted that he derived the concept of latent heat from Black, he claimed that he had already discovered this property in steam empirically, that all other facts needed to account for the weakness of the Newcomen engine were available previously, and that though Black's theory explained all these facts, the explanation was not at all material to his own improvements of the engine. 'These improvements proceeded upon the old-established fact, that steam was condensed by the contact of cold bodies, and the later known one, that water boiled in vacuo at heats below 100°, and consequently that a vacuum could not be obtained unless the cylinder and its contents were cooled every stroke to below that heat.'[3] This is a fascinating instance of

---

[1] This was Robison's opinion, to which Black himself had lent support.

[2] Watt to David Brewster, May 1814, printed in Robison, *op. cit.*, II, iii–x. Watt wrote, 'I never did, nor *could*, consider my improvements as originating in those communications [from Black].' However, he did acknowledge that he learnt much of scientific reasoning and experiment from Black, and the two men carried out a joint investigation of the latent heat of steam.

[3] *Ibid.*, viii.

parallelism in science and engineering, one that brought Black to a major discovery in physics, Watt to the effective invention of the modern steam-engine. Watt clearly indicates how he needed empirical facts, in order to draw useful consequences from them; Black, having devised a theory accounting for the facts, had no concern with useful consequences. There could hardly be a neater instance of the difference between science and technology. Watt's assertion of his entire independence of Black in his major invention is totally credible, and it shows how much more important for technology empiricism still was, than scientific theories from which no specific deductions of utility had been drawn. After Watt's time the divergence between science and craft continued. The engineering development of the steam-engine was continued by practical mechanics like Arthur Woolf (1776–1837) and Richard Trevithick (1771–1833) while study of the theory of heat-engines evolved (in France, chiefly) in the hands of mathematicians. A long time passed before thermodynamics acquired any useful significance.

It was the last branch of science to spring from such empirical roots. In the chemical manufactures the reverse, more modern relationship is at last fairly apparent, first, as might be expected, in the simpler processes. Until about the mid-eighteenth century the preparation and use of chemicals were primitive, although the list of industries in which chemical processes figured is impressive. Besides textile-finishing—bleaching and dyeing—it includes tanning and paper-making, certain metal-trades, and the manufacture of soap, glass, gunpowder, sugar, paints and varnishes, glues, ink and the like. Most of the materials required were either organic, obtained from organic sources, or prepared by simple heat-treatments. Organic 'chemicals' were urine, sour milk, water in which bran had fermented, blood, soot, horn and bone, oak-bark and galls, animals' dung, vinegar, and tartar scraped from old wine-casks. In all these the active reagents were mingled with a mass of putrescent substance. Soda and potash were obtained from plant-ashes, saltpetre from the floors of stables and pigeon-houses. The valuable mordant alum was prepared from the mineral by an ancient process of repeated roasting; other important articles of commerce like sulphur, salt, the vitriols, charcoal, lime and chalk were either won directly from natural deposits or prepared by fire. Acids—of which the sulphuric was by far the most important—were made by essentially pharmaceutical methods. These, with alum and saltpetre, were the only tolerably pure chemicals of commerce.

Progress in chemical technology during the later eighteenth century involved improved methods, larger scale of operation, and the substitution of relatively pure factitious substances for messy organic materials.

The price of acids was much reduced by the production of sulphuric acid from burning sulphur, first in large glass vessels and later in lead-lined chambers (Roebuck, 1746). Gunpowder was rendered stronger by carbonizing wood in iron retorts. In such instances as these the product was unchanged; more elaborate technological modifications were the use of sulphuric acid and bleaching-powder in place of sour milk and other acidulous liquors, and of soda manufactured from salt in place of vegetable alkalis. Organic sources of supply were costly and ineffective. Bleaching with the aid of sour milk and exposure to sunlight occupied many months and large areas of ground; in northern climes it was limited to the summer months. Plant-ashes contained only a low percentage of alkali, and (until the short-lived kelp industry grew up in Scotland) both England and France relied heavily on imports from Spain. Hence there was a strong incentive to the discovery of new materials and methods. The bleaching action of chlorine[1] was discovered by the French chemist C. L. Berthollet (1748–1822) in 1785; at this time, when the chemistry of gases was in its infancy, the discovery was of little practical use. Attempts to make a liquid chlorine bleach failed in France. In 1789, however, Charles Tennant (1769–1838) successfully prepared one by absorbing chlorine in lime, and later made a dry chloride of lime bleach in large quantities at a Glasgow factory. The enormously increased product of the looms could hardly have been handled by the bleachers but for this discovery. Artificial soda has a longer history, and the problems of its manufacture were harder to solve. Chemists had long studied the nature of alkalis; Joseph Black's investigation (1756) was outstanding in the immediate past. Black later joined with Watt and the Birmingham industrialist John Roebuck (1718–94), who was already making suphuric acid, in attempts to synthesize soda. Several patents for effecting this synthesis from common salt were taken out in Britain after 1770: the problem was to convert sodium sulphate (Glauber's salt) into sodium carbonate (soda), for the derivation of the former from the chloride (salt) was well known.[2] Similar researches were pursued in France, and several processes worked out after 1777; synthetic soda was marketed as a by-product, however, for the natural material was still the cheaper. None of these processes involved anything very new, until in 1789 Nicholas Leblanc (1742–1806) discovered that which formed the basis of the heavy chemical industry throughout the nineteenth century.[3] Leblanc, it has been pointed out, could only have discovered his process by empirical experiment, for it was unpredictable by the chemistry of his time; nevertheless, his experiments could only

[1] First described by the Swedish chemist C. W. Scheele (1742–86) in 1774.
[2] All the patentees were hampered by the heavy duties on salt.
[3] The sulphate is heated with limestone and coke.

have been pursued by a man of scientific skill. Leblanc's own factory failed, and the success of his process was confirmed only after his death; meanwhile in England soda manufacture (which in turn owed something to the French chemists) began on the Tyne about 1796, and soon spread to other places. Thus the synthetic material had been on the market for many years before the Leblanc process was extensively worked in Britain, after the removal of the salt tax in 1823.

There are many other examples of experiment in chemical industry. The ceramics manufacture has already been mentioned; Wedgwood, who was its greatest industrialist, was also constantly active in the investigation of new methods and materials, in which he was assisted by his scientific friends, notably Priestley. Distillation of tar from coal was initiated by Lord Dundonald (1749–1831) in 1781;[1] the same process yielded coal-gas, used as an illuminant by 1805; phosphorus matches were introduced; rags for paper were bleached chemically, so that coloured as well as white rag could be used; and the dyeing of textiles received the constant attention of chemists who, though they could not solve the mystery of the processes, added to their number with such pigments as Prussian Blue.

Many of the greatest chemical philosophers, like Priestley and Black, acted as advisers to their manufacturing friends, testing the products from new processes, suggesting new reactions, even computing costs; for some, like Macquer (Director of the Sèvres Porcelain Works, and Inspector of the Dyeing Industries of France) and Berthollet (Macquer's successor in the latter post) government service provided a livelihood. Others, like Scheele and Baumé, were apothecaries;[2] others again like Bergman (who initiated the Swedish 'soda-water' industry), Baumé (the first manufacturer of sal-ammoniac in France, and otherwise engaged in productive enterprises), Chaptal (who set up works making acids, alum, white-lead and so on), and Guyton de Morveau (an adventurer into the synthetic-soda business) entered into chemical industry on their own account. The greatest of all the eighteenth-century chemists, Antoine Lavoisier (1743–94), was never far detached from practical questions though these had nothing to do with his major researches; he examined the purity of water-supplies, was concerned with agrarian reform, was director of the government's Régie des Poudres, and was constantly consulted on all chemical matters of interest to the state. Hence it is not surprising that in this respect the relations of science and technology were especially close. It must be remembered,

[1] He also made varnishes and sal-ammoniac from the tar-liquor. Dundonald was the most active chemical entrepreneur of the age, prominent in the synthetic soda business, but it does not seem that his efforts met with financial success.

[2] In this period ambitious pharmacists like Baumé turned to the manufacture of chemicals, generally those of medicinal use.

however, that in all these instances it was the quality of the man that counted. A scientist could be of great value as an industrial consultant or as an entrepreneur, when science in the abstract meant little. This was particularly true of chemistry; a good chemist could see his way through a problem, with the aid of experiments, that he could not solve from his knowledge or by reference to the best books on the subject.

In chemical industry it was almost inevitable that those who attempted new processes should either themselves be notable chemical experimenters, or at least have had some training in chemistry. Hence the interchange between academic and manufacturing chemists was natural enough. Nor does the employment of scientists by governments require much explanation where, as in France, there were state-controlled industries, or where special skills (mainly in mathematics) were required for such purposes as hydrography, survey, and the training of military and naval officers. Such posts hardly required research ability, but they provided an opportunity for its exercise. Eighteenth-century governments were awake to the occasional usefulness of the national scientific academies, and to the prestige attaching to support for such major scientific programmes as were arranged to observe the transits of Venus in 1761 and 1769. The most striking display of governmental recruitment of scientific support occurred in France during the Revolutionary war, when so many celebrated French scientists were called upon to reconstruct the explosives industry, and to advise on other warlike matters. The Académie des Sciences was re-formed, and the École Polytechnique was founded to provide an adequate number of engineers who were drafted into the military service. It was far more difficult for science to impinge upon private industry. Universities offered some teaching in physics, chemistry and mathematics: but as the subjects were taught—or more often in practice neglected—they did little to prepare the student for an industrial career. Nor did the structure of industry afford a niche to the scientist, unless he founded a new firm of his own. In the various European countries societies for the encouragement of agriculture, and prizes offered for the solution of technological problems, gave him only a meagre opportunity to apply his knowledge usefully. Communication at the personal level between science and manufacture effected more than formal institutions. It is significant that in Britain, where such communication played an important part, the most famous meeting-ground of the two was a private club, the Lunar Society of Birmingham composed of Wedgwood, Boulton, Watt, Samuel Galton (manufacturer and scientific dilettante), Erasmus Darwin, James Keir (chemist), Priestley (the only distinguished scientist in the group, and not an original member), William Withering (botanist) and a few more. Yet this club subsisted mainly on the individual relationships of its members, who appear to have attempted no corporate function. Thus even the Lunar Society can scarcely be qualified as a 'technological research organization', precisely because any information that passed between its members passed privately, as it would if no club had existed. Nothing like organized technological research seems to have existed in the eighteenth century, except perhaps in such state manufactures as Sèvres. This was a world of small-scale private enterprise, and even of deliberate concealment of the truth, in science and technology as in commerce. Discoveries were disseminated slowly; new processes were tested behind locked doors, and if they spread abroad for the general benefit of an industry, it was despite, not because of, the efforts of the first inventor. Men like Wedgwood, Boulton and Watt might pride themselves on the use they made of science, yet they were as jealous of their secrets as their least enlightened rivals. In such an atmosphere co-operation was out of the question, and however much the usefulness of science to industry might be proclaimed in the abstract, any particular benefit of that kind was to be kept as quiet as possible.

With the industrial revolution the trinity of scientist, technologist and entrepreneur becomes even harder to interpret than formerly. For at this time the function of each was becoming acutely necessary to the progress of manufactures, yet no one was dominant. Science had at last something to offer—even though it is important, still, to place method and experience over theoretical insight. Technological skill was required to make a new invention or process workable on the industrial scale, whatever its source. Business enterprise was required in the raising of capital, the choice of a factory, and the exploitation of the market.[1] Sometimes, as with Boulton and Watt, the experimental and craft genius of one man was aptly allied with the commercial acumen of another; sometimes, as with Leblanc and the Duc d'Orléans, a scientific inventor depended on the more old-fashioned pattern of patronage; rather rarely a scientist like Chaptal plunged direct into industry; but perhaps the most usual event was for a scientifically-minded entre-preneur like Wedgwood, Roebuck or Dundonald to try to solve his technological problems as best he might, with such advice as he could get, and work up his own 'pilot-plant'. Not infrequently experimental development lived parasitically on some older enterprise until in time, if successful, it swallowed its host. Setting aside the familiar names of the inventors of textile machinery, the proportion of those contributing to the transformation of manufactures who associated themselves, more or less, with contemporary science is certainly impressive. Such men

[1] My former colleague, Mr Neil McKendrick, has discovered the extent to which the success of even such an advanced technologist as Wedgwood could really arise from his even greater capabilities as a salesman.

commonly regarded themselves as introducing the spirit of science into industry, and as applying its discoveries. Thus, before the industrial revolution was well under way the champions of its cause were calling attention to the wonders that science had already wrought, and that more applied science would work in the future.

No doubt such proclamations sprang from confused thinking. Science and technology have very often been mingled by careless or optimistic writers, and the paternity of science in an invention has often been illegitimate. After a century and a half the history of the industrial revolution seems rather to reveal the frailty of science's claim to change the world, than its strength of which contemporaries boasted—though they were indeed better off, in their turn, than their ancestors. Compared with what is now seen to be involved in the full scientific analysis of a lump of cast iron, or the strains in a ship's hull, or even a simple chemical reaction, how shallow was all that could then be said on such topics! There has been a vast change of perspective, produced by the development of science itself. To contemporaries, it was the grand novelty of subjecting technological problems to rational and systematic enquiry that was significant; the modern historian is inclined to ascribe success less to the scant and lame results of such enquiries, than to persistence in a long, costly grind of converting them into economic methods of manufacture. Even so, it is often easy to take the shadow for the substance, the language of science for the reality. The logic of science has no place for 'accidental', unpredictable discoveries (though these have often occurred in practice), yet the most 'scientific' inventions of the industrial revolution possessed this fortuitous character—they were made, but they could not be understood. Problems, whether those of the engineer or those of the industrial chemist, had to be solved on their merits, not by knowledge of the bits of scientific theory that would yield the answer to them. The usefulness of science lay in its empirical, not in its theoretical character—hence chemistry was of greater value than mechanics. The method of experimental inquiry, even with the sketchiest basis of general ideas, was as likely to hit upon the solution of a manufacturing problem, as to make a scientific discovery. Empiricism, experience, intuition—all that enables a man to answer a question without knowing quite how he did it—constitute the philosophically least reputable aspect of science, but it was at the same time its socially most useful one. Empiricism, not theoretical comprehension, was the attribute of science most firmly established in the minds of the founders of the industrial revolution, and most highly valued by them.

# CHAPTER III

# Transport and Trade Routes

## I. *The Mediterranean Trades*

The Mediterranean at the beginning of the sixteenth century was still very much a world of its own. It was still a large world, not yet dwarfed by comparison with the world of great oceans beyond Suez and Gibraltar. A ship—an ordinary merchant ship, with reasonable weather —took up to two months to make the passage, say, from Cartagena or Alicante to Alexandria; perhaps two or three weeks from Messina to Tripoli of Barbary; ten or twelve days from Leghorn to Tunis. There was plenty of space, plenty of elbow room; and the area as a whole was almost self-supporting. The sixty million or so people who inhabited the countries bordering the inland sea produced between them most of the food, many of the raw materials and almost all the manufactured goods which they consumed. They built their own ships and carried their own trade. The richest, liveliest and most varied economic activity of the region was concentrated in the relatively small area of northern Italy comprising Milan, Florence, Genoa, Venice, and their smaller neighbours and satellites. Florence and Milan were primarily manufacturing centres—Florence had little success in developing its own trading fleet, and Milan never possessed one—but Venice and Genoa, both great industrial centres, were also major naval powers and bases of great merchant fleets. Outside Italy, Ragusa specialized in very large ships for carrying bulky goods, grain, salt and wool. France, growing in unity and prosperity, attracted an increasing volume of Mediterranean traffic into the Rhône Valley by way of Marseilles, with its busy fleet of light lateen-rigged craft. The Adriatic, the Tyrrhenian Sea and the Gulf of Lyons were major arteries of international trade. The shipping of these coasts carried a great part of the internal trade of the Mediterranean region. The harbours were centres from which the rest of Europe drew —by sea, river, or mountain passes—its supply of Mediterranean products, and of still more valuable luxuries from the East.

The Mediterranean countries for the most part were not by nature lands of plenty. Light rainfall, light soils denuded by generations of peasants and their goats, gave light and variable yields. Every city sought to draw as much food as possible from its own immediate neighbourhood.

The local imperialism of many cities, their constant concern to extend their jurisdiction, arose largely from their urgent desire to control neighbouring supplies of food. The transport of bulky food-stuffs by waggon or pack-animal, however, was slow and costly, and the radius within which grain could be carted economically to a central market was very small.[1] Local sources of supply were rarely adequate, therefore, even in good years, and were obviously unreliable in a region of frequent and unpredictable local drought. Most of the larger cities, even in normal times, imported part of their requirements by sea and river over considerable distances, and in times of local failure were often obliged to increase their imports heavily and at short notice. Accordingly, there existed in the Mediterranean a specialized, complicated, necessarily flexible sea-borne trade in grain, concerned with shifting an overall annual surplus of, perhaps, some 50,000 modern tons from places of relative abundance to places of scarcity, whether permanent or temporary. The ships—Venetian, Genoese, Ragusan—were large, were designed to carry grain, and usually carried nothing else. Wheat, barley and millets were the grains most commonly carried and used for bread and biscuit. Rye and oats were comparatively rare in the Mediterranean until the arrival of northern traders in the late sixteenth century.

The most regular importers of sea-borne grain were the cities of the western and central Mediterranean. In the East, it is true, Constantinople —an immense city by European standards—was a great maw engulfing all the grain that came its way; but Constantinople could, and did, monopolize the exports of the fertile regions on the shore of the Black Sea. Only in years of harvest failure was the Ottoman government obliged to draw heavily upon Mediterranean sources for the victualling of its capital. Cairo, the other urban colossus, was even better placed. The Nile valley could always feed Cairo and Alexandria, with plenty to spare. Similarly the thriving commercial cities of Syria had supplies of grain at their very doors. In the West, more populous and less productive, the situation was more difficult, though there again some cities were more fortunate than others. Milan drew from its rich surrounding country, and could even send grain by pack train up into the Grisons. Marseilles could draw upon Provence and the Rhône valley—sources which had supplied by sea the armies of Charles VIII and Louis XII in Italy. Significantly, as Marseilles grew in size and wealth in the sixteenth century, less and less grain coming down the Rhône was available for the Mediterranean pool. Florence, Genoa, Venice, Ragusa, Naples, the cities of the east coast of Spain—these last mostly set in country

---

[1] F. Braudel, *La Méditerranée et le Monde Méditerranéen a l'époque de Philippe II* (Paris, 1949), 347. For Florence the extreme limit was about twelve miles. See G. Parenti, *Prime ricerche nella rivoluzione dei prezzi in Firenze* (1939), 82.

producing wine, or oil, or wool—all were importers of grain by sea, usually in ships belonging to local owners or owned or chartered by the city governments.

In all, or nearly all, of these cities, the assurance of a steady supply was the first preoccupation of government, and became the responsibility of a permanent government organization for purchase and storage. All practised, on occasion, a species of cereal piracy, sending out their armed galleys in times of shortage to intercept grain ships and bring them into their own harbours. The knights of Malta, in particular, shamelessly victualled their island fortress in this way, cruising in the Sicilian channel or the Straits of Otranto for grain ships bound for Venice or for Spain. Such prizes were paid for, but at the captors' prices.

The principal western sources of exportable grain were Apulia and Sicily, both controlled politically by the rulers of Spain. Apulia was part of the kingdom of Naples and much of its grain went to supply the city of Naples. Had it been possible economically to carry grain across the peninsula by land (as the Spanish government suggested in the 1560's) Naples might have monopolized this source of supply; but costs were prohibitive. Apulian grain went by sea, and Naples had to compete with interloping buyers from Venice and Ragusa. Sicily, however, was the chief granary of the western Mediterranean, exporting amounts which varied greatly from year to year, but which averaged, between 1532 and 1578, about 10,000 tons,[1] mostly to Spain and to Spain's ally Genoa, but also in varying quantities to all the hungry cities of Mediterranean Europe and North Africa. The grain was grown mostly on the south side of the island, and was shipped from a limited number of officially licensed wharves (*caricatori*) coastwise to Messina. Messina was a specialized grain port, exporting the product of Sicily, and also transshipping grains brought from the East. The commercial houses in the export trade, however—Genoese and Florentines mostly—had their head offices at Palermo, where lived many of the larger landowners, and the officials who, on behalf of the viceregal government, issued the precious *tratas* or licences to export grain. These permits were not given freely. The fee charged for an export permit ranged from a quarter to a half of the cost of the grain itself, increasing according to the prevailing price. To the cost of the grain and of the permit had to be added the cost of transport, and if the price of the grain in Sicily were 10 Spanish *reales* the *fanega*—a normal price in mid century—the export licence would

---

[1] 120,000 *salme*. The best year of this period was 1532, about 260,000 *salme*, the worst 1557, about 20,000. L. Bianchini, *Storia Economica-Sociale di Sicilia* (Naples, 1841), I 240. The equivalence of 12 *salme* of grain to 1 modern ton weight is, of course, very approximate. It depended on the kind of grain.

cost 5 *reales*, transport from supplier to dock-side 3 *reales*, freight from port of departure to a Spanish port 3½ *reales*, insurance at 9 per cent a little less than 1 *real*; price delivered at Alicante 22½ *reales*.[1] Yet even at these heavy charges, the issue or refusal of a permit could be made a means of favour or political pressure; so constant was the demand for grain and so great the opportunity of profit.

The western Mediterranean was rarely self-sufficient in grain, even with Sicily as its granary, and the importing cities also had constant recourse to the cheap and plentiful grain of the Levant. Venice, in close trading connection with the Turk, particularly relied on eastern grain. Its colonies—Corfu, and some of the towns of Crete—got supplies from Patmos and neighbouring islands in the Aegean, and sometimes re-exported part of their purchases. The Republic itself regularly imported grain from Egypt. Alexandria, Volo, Salonika, Valona, Prevesa, all exported grain to the West. Naturally such open commerce needed the permission of the Turkish government, and naturally applications for permission to buy grain were often refused, either for economic reasons, because Constantinople was short, or for political reasons, or from sheer caprice; but besides the authorized exports, there was at all times a flourishing illicit trade carried in the fast, light *caramusalis* of the Greek islands. Without this trade, Venice would have fared badly. The Turco-Venetian War of 1570–3 caused a major crisis in Venetian food supply; the Republic was driven to apply to Spain—of all places—for grain, and to seize, reckless of consequences, the grain ships bound from Apulia to Naples.

Even in peace, however, the grain trade was full of surprises and anomalies, arising from local crop failures or unexpected bumper harvests. Spain in the sixteenth century was normally an importer; but in 1555 Andalusian wheat was sent to Rome, in 1564 to Genoa. In 1587 Sardinia, unexpectedly in surplus, released a large consignment to Genoa. Even Algiers and Oran occasionally produced a surplus for export.

In the second half of the sixteenth century the grain situation in the western Mediterranean, always precarious, grew steadily worse. Famines became not only more frequent—they had always been frequent—but more severe. Naples suffered six major famines between 1560 and 1600—in 1560, 1565, 1570, 1584, 1585, and 1591. Most serious of all, exports from Sicily began to fail. In 1575–7 a famine occurred there —three bad harvests in succession—and corn had to be brought from Apulia to Messina at famine prices; in 1591 came a still worse famine. From 1592 Sicily ceased almost entirely to export grain and became an importer. A general increase in population, especially the urban population, seems to have been the chief cause of this worsening shortage. Of a

---

[1] Cf. Braudel, *La Méditerranée et le Monde Méditerranéen*, 451.

decline in productivity there is no certain evidence, though decline due to cumulative over-grazing and erosion seems likely. The massive scale of Turco-Spanish hostilities in the 1570's, and the association of Venice with Spain, also dislocated the normal trade in grain and at the same time increased the demand for victualling navies, armies and garrisons. Even when hostilities ceased, the Turkish Government was both unwilling and unable to resume export to the West. Population was increasing in the countries of the Levant also. Famine threatened Constantinople in 1589, in 1597, and again in 1600. The whole Mediterranean area, in varying degrees, was affected; and this growing hunger was among the potent factors in the invasion of the Mediterranean by the shipping of northern Europe, for the Dutch and English vessels, which brought much-needed grain, stayed to share in still more rewarding trades.

Though by far the most essential, grain was by no means the only bulky article of daily use to be carried by sea in the Mediterranean. Salt, and food preserved in salt, were both considerable articles of trade. Mediterranean peoples, it is true, have never been great meat eaters, and the salted-fish and meat trades in the Mediterranean never assumed the immense volume and importance which Sombart rightly attributed to them in northern waters.[1] Salt or dried fish, nevertheless, was an essential article of food. Tunny was the most important local fish; Sicilian waters (in particular the Straits of Messina) and the coastal waters of Provence the richest sources. Mediterranean supplies of salt fish, however, never fully met the demand, and the cities of Italy and Spain also imported fish caught and salted in Atlantic waters. Throughout the century the Portuguese brought the tunny from their own home waters and cod from the Newfoundland Banks; and from about 1585 barrelled herring from the North Sea began to come in great quantities in Dutch ships; yet another example of commercial invasion from the North.

The Mediterranean climate and the relative absence of tide encouraged the manufacture of salt by the cheapest and easiest means, the evaporation of sea water, wherever the coast was suitable. As with grain, a long-haul trade existed to supplement inadequate local supplies. The Venetians were the principal carriers of salt; Istria and Sicily (Trapani) the chief exporting sources, except in the years when Venice controlled the salt pans of Cyprus.

The other chief articles of food which went by sea in quantity were oil, wine and cheese. Cheese travelled by complex, criss-crossing routes, in many different varieties—from Auvergne, from Parma, from Milan, and above all from Sardinia, whence whole shiploads were carried to

[1] W. Sombart, *Der Moderne Kapitalismus*, I, 315.

France, Italy and Spain. Southern Italy and southern Spain were the
principal sources of oil; both, but especially Italy, exported it in exchange
for grain, even as far as to Egypt. The long-haul Mediterranean trade
declined in the course of the sixteenth century, partly because of the
diversion of Andalusian oil to the Indies, where it fetched very high
prices; but throughout the century large quantities of oil, and of soap
made from oil, were shipped regularly from Bari up the Adriatic to
Venice and Ragusa. The Mediterranean wine trade—since viticulture
was spread throughout the region—could not compare with the great
fleets which left the Gironde and the Guadalquivir for Atlantic destinations; but Naples supplied, by sea, the needs of Rome and of cities further
north. Neapolitan wines were for daily use. More highly prized, as
expensive luxuries, were the sweet, heavy wines of Cyprus and of Crete
—home of the famous Malvoisie grape—which were sold in small
quantities, at high prices, all over the Mediterranean from Constantinople to Genoa, and beyond Gibraltar to England. With these
rarer wines went a trade in Greek dried grapes—raisins and 'currants'—
by the same routes, in Venetian and Genoese ships. Sugar, even in the
Mediterranean, was still a luxury in the sixteenth century. In the eastern
Mediterranean, Crete and Cyprus were the chief sources of supply;
in the west, south-eastern Spain, where sugar was shipped from Malaga,
Alicante and Cartagena to Genoa and Leghorn, and Sicily, which with
Crete and Cyprus supplied most of the needs of Venice.

A busy and—by the standards of the time—densely populated urban
concentration, such as that of northern Italy, had to import not only
food but many of the raw materials of industry, in particular of
textile manufacture. The Italian cloth industry no longer depended
heavily upon English wool, which, indeed, was no longer available in
sufficient quantity. Most of its wool came from Spain, and at the
Spanish wool fairs the Italian buyers had to compete with buyers from
another great industrial area, the Spanish Netherlands. In the middle
years of the sixteenth century a little over half of Spanish wool exports
were shipped to Flanders, through Bilbao and other Atlantic ports.[1]
Towards the end of the century more wool went to Flanders and less to
Italy, and in the seventeenth century Flanders took nearly the whole of
an export which had probably also diminished in total amount. Florence
and Milan had then to get their wool where they could, from North
Africa, the Balkans and the Levant, all sources of second-quality wool;
and their cloth production declined both in quality and quantity.
Throughout the sixteenth century, however, nearly half of the Spanish
export of fine wool was still being shipped through Malaga, Alicante,
Cartagena, more rarely Valencia and Barcelona, to Genoa, Leghorn and

---

[1] Cf. Carande, *Carlos V y sus banqueros* (Madrid, 1943), 64.

Venice. The big ships of Ragusa, as well as those of Venice and Genoa, were prominent in this trade.

The north Italian silk weavers were more fortunate than the cloth manufacturers in their supplies of raw material, and maintained their position well into the seventeenth century. Many countries in the Mediterranean area produced raw silk, and, as with grain and wool, part of the supply of the West was drawn from the East. The chief centre of distribution in the western Mediterranean was Messina, where raw silk was offered for sale from places as far apart as Valencia and Tripoli of Syria. Naples, which manufactured silk, was also a distribution centre for the surplus of raw silk from Calabria. From Messina and Naples the bales were shipped to north Italy in Genoese or Tuscan ships.

Mediterranean Europe used prodigious quantities of leather for a great variety of purposes: saddlery, harness, protective clothing, shoes and boots, gloves, furniture, covers of books, and so forth. As with wool, silk and grain, the trade in leather cut across the division between Christendom and Islam. North Italy was the principal importing area; North Africa, possessing fewer people but greater flocks and herds, the chief source. Hides went by the ship-load from Algiers, Sallee, Goletta, to Messina, Ancona, Ragusa, Venice, and many other Christian ports. Central Spain, a largely pastoral country, naturally produced hundreds of thousands of hides annually; but many Spanish cities were centres of leather manufacture, producing not only articles for local use but also a variety of specialized fine wares, suitable for export, particularly *guadameciles*, the elaborate gilded hangings widely used in the sixteenth century as wall coverings. Saragossa, Toledo, Granada, were all famous for their *guadameciles*, which were exported through Malaga and Barcelona all over the Mediterranean, as well as to northern Europe. Spain, therefore, was an importer of hides and an exporter of leather goods. In the second half of the sixteenth century the western Mediterranean as a whole ceased to be self-sufficient in hides, and imports reached Italy and Spain in large, ever-increasing, quantities from sources as far part as Poland, Russia and—most important of all—the New World; yet another example of the increasing dependence of the Mediterranean upon the Atlantic for its most essential needs.

Compared with the volume and urgency of the trade in animal and vegetable products, the mineral trades in the sixteenth-century Mediterranean were relatively small, but of growing importance. Among the most important was that in alum, a cleansing agent indispensable in the cloth industry, which at the beginning of the century came mostly from Asia Minor in Genoese shipping. Early in the sixteenth century, however, extensive deposits were developed at Tolfa, near Civitavecchia—whence alum could be shipped coastwise to Leghorn and Genoa—and in eastern Spain. The alum trade between East and West declined in consequence. In the second half of the century a lively export trade developed from Italy to England and the Low Countries, initially in Genoese ships, but later tending to fall more and more into the hands of Dutch and English.

In most other mineral products the stream of trade set throughout the sixteenth century from west to east. Coral, prized almost as a precious stone in some parts of the East, was the object of a lucrative trade, virtually a monopoly of Genoa. Natural coral was brought in by Genoese fishermen, and worked at Genoa into ornaments which found a sale in Egypt and passed thence to the countries from which spices continually came in the reverse direction. The trade in non-precious metals also set in the same direction, towards the east. Iron deposits, it is true, were so widespread that most Mediterranean centres of iron manufacture could use ore found near their own doors; but copper, tin and lead were always valuable objects of long-haul trade. Demand for all three increased throughout the Mediterranean largely as a result of increasing use of artillery; and for the first two, additionally, because of the replacement of old-fashioned, iron-bound, moulded iron gun-barrels by cast pieces of bronze. The copper came largely from south Germany overland, and was exported to the eastern Mediterranean in Venetian ships. England was—as it had been for centuries—the chief source of lead and tin, brought into the Mediterranean throughout most of the sixteenth century by Venetians and Genoese, but also increasingly, towards the end, by Dutch and English ships.

The manufactures of the cities of northern Italy, southern France and eastern Spain found widespread markets; in particular, the fine, light woollens of Florence were sold throughout the Mediterranean and reached the interior of Asia through the bazaars of Aleppo. Milan remained throughout the sixteenth century the principal Mediterranean centre of the manufacture of arms and armour. Venice, in its own ships, and Lyons by the way of Marseilles, poured into Mediterranean circulation a steady stream of books, and Genoa provided the Mediterranean world with paper. From Venice, too, came a steady flow of glassware of all sorts, not only fine table glass, looking-glasses and the like, but also such workaday articles as sand-glasses, which were the only way of marking the passage of time on board ship. All the ocean-going shipping in the western world used—and constantly needed to replace—these fragile Venetian glasses. Pottery was less of an Italian monopoly; the blue wares of Talavera de la Reina, the white and yellow faïence of Triana, near Seville, were sold in England, in the Indies, and in the ports of North Africa; but the majolicas of Ferrara and Savona also were in sufficient demand to justify the cost of long-haul transport. It is true that these towns, especially the four great capitals of northern Italy, no longer enjoyed the easy mastery, the firm predominance, of a hundred years before. Throughout the century the weavers of Florence, Venice and Milan had to compete with cheap fustians from south Germany; the armourers and gunsmiths of Milan, faced with competition from south German towns, tended more and more to specialize in parade armour and tournament weapons, in the making of which they were unrivalled, but for which there could be no very wide market. Nevertheless, even when their industrial predominance was challenged, the northern Italians long retained their commercial dominance. South German manufactures—fire-arms, for instance—might compete with Italian; but they travelled south over the Brenner, and reached the Levant in Venetian ships; for in carrying manufactured goods, land transport, though more expensive than sea or river, was still cheap enough and efficient enough to tie south Germany to the Mediterranean.

The Mediterranean was the scene of a rich and varied commercial activity throughout the sixteenth century. But the richest trade of all, and the most sought after, was in commodities originating outside the Mediterranean: in spices, particularly in pepper. Except for 'Malaguette', the coarse false pepper of West Africa, the spices of European commerce all came from the East. Throughout the later Middle Ages a long chain of commercial exchanges had connected the spice growers of India, Ceylon, and Indonesia with the merchant senators of Venice. At its eastern end the trade was handled by Chinese, whose junks collected the nutmeg and cloves of the East Indies and carried them to the great Malayan port of Malacca. From Malacca across the Bay of Bengal to India the trade was in the hands of Muslim merchants, whether Indian, Malay or Arab. In India, the far-eastern cargoes, together with the cinnamon of Ceylon and the pepper of India itself, were sold in the spice ports of the Malabar coast—Cochin, Calicut, Cananore, Goa—and further north in the ports of Gujerat, particularly Diu. The trade of these ports with the rest of the Indian Ocean littoral was mostly in the hands of the Arabs; from Malabar their teak-built ocean-going *baghlas* cleared with their precious cargoes for the harbours of Persia, Arabia, and East Africa, maintaining sailings whose regularity derived from the regular alternation of north-east and south-west monsoons. At the end of the fifteenth century, there were two alternative routes from the Indian Ocean to the Mediterranean, and two ports of transhipment: Hormuz and Aden. From Aden, the way up the Red Sea, that heated funnel of reef-bound water, was slow and hazardous, and the big *baghlas* rarely ventured beyond the Bab-el-Mandeb. Red Sea trade was carried in a great number of small coasting vessels, *zaruqs*, *sambuqs*, and many other

lateen types, plying from one small port to another, up to Suez, the Red
Sea harbour for Cairo and the Nile Valley. In the Persian Gulf, the large
doubled-ended *boums*, still characteristic of the region, carried eastern
and East African goods from Hormuz up to the Shatt-al-Arab, whence
caravans conveyed the spice shipments overland, either through Asia
Minor to Constantinople, or through Mesopotamia by way of Baghdad
to Aleppo, the great spice bazaar of Syria. At Alexandria, Mediterranean harbour for Cairo, or Tripoli, the outlet for Aleppo, Venetian ships
loaded for Venice; and from Venice the spices were distributed, by river
or pack train, to north Italy, across the Alpine passes to south Germany
(which in this respect, as in many others, formed part of the hinterland
of Venice), by sea to Marseilles and up the Rhône to central France, by
sea to Barcelona, Alicante, Malaga, through the Straits to England, the
Low Countries and the North. With spices travelled other eastern
products which commanded high prices in Europe and went there by
the same routes: Chinese and Persian silks, greatly superior to Italian
or French; Indian cotton cloth; rhubarb, grown in China and much
prized as a medicine; and precious stones—emeralds from India, rubies
from Burma, sapphires from Ceylon. These were the 'rich trades'
which aroused the envy of all Europe and made Venice one of the great
sea-ports of the world.

At the beginning of the sixteenth century, the Mediterranean spice
trade passed through a severe crisis, in consequence of the opening of a
direct Portuguese trade with India by way of the Cape of Good Hope.
The Portuguese quickly replaced the Venetians as the chief purveyors of
spices to the countries of the Atlantic seaboard. Portuguese cargoes
reached Antwerp in 1501 and Antwerp became the chief distribution
centre for north-western Europe. In 1504 the first Portuguese shipments
reached England. Western Germany and western France soon turned to
Antwerp for their supplies. Spain—curiously—took longer to change
its commercial habits, but by the 1520's the pepper offered for sale at
Medina del Campo fair was mostly Portuguese, brought from India. The
Portuguese even invaded the Mediterranean spice trade for a time. The
Genoese began early in the century to buy pepper from them. Even the
Venetians were obliged, in 1515, to buy spices in Lisbon in order to
fulfil the orders of their own regular customers. The trouble, from the
Venetian point of view, was not that the Portuguese competed by selling
spices cheaper; it was that the Portuguese, by violence and threats of
more violence, by seizing ships and bombarding harbours on the Malabar
coast, by establishing themselves at Goa, Hormuz, Socotra and Malacca,
and endeavouring to suppress all ocean trade in spices but their own, had
succeeded temporarily in interrupting the regular Arab sailings which
supplied the ports of the Persian Gulf and the Red Sea. In the first few

years of the sixteenth century very few spice shipments reached the Levantine markets, where the Venetians normally obtained their supplies.

The Portuguese monopoly, however, proved short-lived. Formidable though they were at sea, the Portuguese could not hope, with a few warships operating from widely scattered bases, to suppress permanently a whole flourishing commerce which supplied Egypt and the Turkish empire as well as European customers. They failed to capture Aden, one of the key points of the trade. Their short-lived base at Socotra was not adequate for an effective blockade of the Red Sea. They could not make full use of their footing at Hormuz, because they needed Persian support against the Turk, and so were obliged to allow the passage of cargoes up the Persian Gulf. In both places they tended to become collectors of tolls, encumbering Arab trade rather than preventing it. The Indian Ocean spice trade—or the greater part of it—soon re-entered its old channels; with it revived the Mediterranean trade in Venetian ships. In straight competition over price and quality, the advantages were by no means all on the side of the Portuguese oceanic trade. The costs and risks of the Cape route were great, and tended to increase; and the Portuguese had no goods to offer which could make a profitable outward freight. They bought spices with bullion, and the proceeds of the home-ward passage had to cover the costs of the outward passage also. The Arab merchants, on the other hand, carried goods which found a ready sale in India: horses from Mesopotamia, copper from Arabia and the Mediterranean, arms, light woollens, coral ornaments. The Venetians, forming the last link in a well-established, regular chain of inter-mediaries, had similar advantages. They had goods to sell in the bazaars of Cairo and Aleppo; and had the advantages of experience and good-will in a complex but highly profitable commerce. There was little, if any, difference between the price of pepper brought from the Levant and pepper carried by the Cape route, once it had reached the western Mediterranean. There may have been a difference in quality. Arabs and Venetians were probably more discriminating buyers than the Portu-guese. It was widely believed, moreover, that spices tended to spoil and to lose their aroma on the long sea voyage. This, no doubt, was a story put about by the Venetians, but it probably had some foundation in fact, since the Portuguese cargoes were carried in bags, in leaky ships, through latitudes where the weather could be violent. Soaking in sea water is bad for any cargo.

Political events, in addition, took a turn which favoured the Red Sea route, and enabled the Venetians to recover at least their Mediter-ranean and South German monopoly. The second quarter of the sixteenth century was remarkable for a rapid advance of Muslim power, and of Turkish power within Islam, on all fronts. In 1526, at Panipat, Babur laid the foundations of Mughal power in India. A Turkish fleet achieved what the Portuguese had failed to achieve, the capture of Aden, so making the Red Sea a Turkish Strait; for Egypt had already been over-run in 1517. In 1538 and again in 1546 the Portuguese were heavily attacked in their fortress at Diu. Their own trade continued, but diminished; Arab trade went unhindered, and the Levantine harbours flourished. Immense quantities of pepper entered the Mediterranean between 1550 and 1570; some 1500 to 2000 tons a year by the Red Sea route alone, according to some estimates.[1] Well-informed contemporaries were in no doubt that the volume of trade was as great as it had ever been, and at least as great as that which the Portuguese carried round the Cape. During the Turco-Portuguese war of 1560–3, Turkish galleys intercepted Portuguese spice ships in the Indian Ocean, and diverted them to the Red Sea. Off Hormuz, it is true, Portuguese arms were more successful, and the Persian Gulf trade suffered considerably from Portuguese depredations while the war lasted. The Venetians, however, had always the advantage of a choice between two rival sources of supply. If Aleppo failed, then Cairo could supply them, and vice versa. The Portuguese had reason for anxiety over their vulnerable ocean trade. In the negotiations for peace with the Turk, in 1563, they even sought—unsuccessfully—an agreement whereby they should themselves ship spices from India to the Red Sea; so permanent, so surely profitable did the Levantine trade routes seem.

About 1570 the tide of events again turned in favour of the Portuguese and the Cape route. In 1568 a widespread Arab rising against Ottoman domination interrupted trade in the Red Sea. This revolt was not suppressed until 1573; and meanwhile Venice became involved, with Spain, in the war of 1570–3 against the Turks in the Mediterranean. The old political and naval rivalry between Genoa and Venice was submerged in the greater rivalry between two giants, the Turkish Empire in the eastern Mediterranean and the Spanish in the western. This combination of circumstances caused a sharp decline in Levantine trade. In 1577 the Venetians were again reduced to buying pepper in Lisbon, and in order to do so lifted the import duty which they had levied since 1519 on spices coming from the West.

Business in the Levant grew worse in the early 1580's, probably as a result of intermittent hostilities between Turkey and Persia. The time was propitious for the curious offer which Philip II, newly possessed of Portugal, made to the Venetian Senate in 1585: the offer to sell the greater part of the annual Portuguese imports of pepper to the Venetians, at a relatively low price, together with a promise of naval escorts for the

[1] Braudel, *La Méditerranée et le Monde Méditerranéen*, 429.

Venetian ships visiting Lisbon, and a share of the Sicilian grain trade. If accepted, the contract would have bound Venice securely to the policy of Spain: would have ensured the distribution of Portuguese spices through Europe by internal routes, safer and surer than an Atlantic increasingly infested by Dutch and English privateers and pirates; and would have dealt a mortal blow to the Levantine trade. The offer must have tempted the Venetians, in view of the scarcity and high price of spices in the Levant at the time; but it was refused, and events proved the wisdom of the refusal. Levantine trade revived. One part of it, indeed, greatly increased: the trade in Persian silks through Aleppo and Alexandretta (which in 1593 replaced Tripoli as the Venetian depôt in Syria). The 1590's were a period of almost unbroken peace in the Indian Ocean, and brisk trade in the Levant; while in the Atlantic, Portuguese shipping suffered from repeated blockades, and constant attacks by corsairs operating off the Azores and Cape Verde Islands.

The Mediterranean spice trade, then, continued to flourish throughout the sixteenth century. The Venetians, far from being put out of busines by the Portuguese discovery of the ocean route, competed successfully with the Portuguese as purveyors of spices to a great part of Europe; and continued to get their spices mostly by the old routes. It was not the Portuguese, but the Dutch, and to a lesser degree the English, who destroyed the pre-eminence of Venice in this trade.

## II. *The North European Trades*

The pattern of trade in northern Europe at the beginning of the sixteenth century differed most obviously from the corresponding pattern in the Mediterranean, in that there were no 'rich trades' except, perhaps, the trade in Baltic furs, then the livery of dignity and wealth. A trickle of spices and other eastern products passed from the shores of the Caspian by slow rivers to the great fairs at Novgorod, whence they were carried down the Baltic in Hanseatic ships; but most luxury articles were brought to northern Europe from the Mediterranean in Mediterranean shipping, or overland, or else, increasingly, from the East by way of Lisbon and Antwerp. Northern trades handled chiefly bulky commodities for daily use. This fact in itself tended to confine long-haul trade to water routes; and northern Europe was in any event deficient, by Mediterranean standards, in facilities for overland transport. Its legacy of Roman road-building was poorer, its rainfall higher, its lands wetter and more densely forested, so that wheeled traffic, and even pack-traffic, was useless for much of the year in many places. In shipping, northern Europe was much better equipped; but the northern shipping industry

—again by Mediterranean standards—was still relatively primitive, lacking in methods for the easy mobilization of capital and the rapid transmission of market intelligence. Ships were still relatively unspecialized, even as between freighting and fishing, or between peaceful avocations and fighting.

Against these obvious contrasts must be set obvious analogies. Like the Mediterranean, northern Europe possessed a thriving and well-developed industrial area—chiefly cloth-working—in the southern Netherlands, which imported most of its raw material and much of its food, and exported a good part of its finished products. Like the Mediterranean also, northern Europe included areas which produced a reliable surplus of exportable food and raw materials. In this respect, indeed, the north was potentially very well placed; its climate and its great areas of fertile soil—much of it yet untilled—would in time produce vastly more than the overworked, eroded lands of the Mediterranean basin, and its fisheries were the richest in the world. Finally, in two respects the potential 'transport assets' of northern Europe were superior to those of the Mediterranean: in quantity of easily available timber, and in navigable rivers. In the course of the sixteenth and seventeenth centuries, opportunities for commercial profit, abundant resources, and growing maritime skill, were to combine in a technical revolution which made northern Europe the principal centre of the world's trade.

Northern Europe in the early sixteenth century had no Venice, no Genoa, but it included two distinct areas—or rather groups of port towns—whose merchants specialized in seaborne trade. These were the towns of the North German Hanse, and the ports of the Netherlands. At the end of the fifteenth century the merchant fleets of these two areas were approximately equal in carrying capacity.[1] In the fourteenth century and throughout most of the fifteenth, Hanseatic traders had predominated in the trade of the North Sea, Scandinavia and Iceland, and had been to the Baltic what the Venetians and Genoese were to the Mediterranean. The challenge of Dutch competition, however, was delivered in the Baltic a full century before it was felt in the Mediterranean. Changes in trade routes and trade relations in the later Middle Ages had tended to favour the Dutch at German expense. The sea route into the Baltic through the Sound, first pioneered by the Dutch, had come to be preferred to the old overland route from Hamburg to Lübeck; and Lübeck, the old headquarters of Hanseatic strength and policy, had suffered in trade and importance. Bruges, the principal foreign centre of Hanseatic trade and influence, had declined, chiefly

[1] W. Vogel, 'Zur Grosse der Europäischen Handelsflotten im 15, 16 und 17 Jahrhundert', *Forschungen und Versuche zur Geschichte des Mittelalters und der Neuzeit* (Jena, 1915), 277 ff.

because of the silting of its harbour, and Antwerp, where the Hansards had no particular privileges, had become the chief commercial port of northern Europe. Antwerp enjoyed astonishing prosperity throughout most of the sixteenth century; but it was not a major shipbuilding centre, and eventually war and dependence on foreign shipping proved its undoing. The 'Spanish fury' of 1576 damaged Antwerp severely. Parma's siege and capture of the city in 1585 resulted in the removal or bankruptcy of many business houses and the exile—mostly to Amsterdam—of thousands of Protestant artisans. Dutch traders deserted the port, and Parma's attempts to revive its trade by means of Hanseatic shipping were defeated by the Dutch blockade of the Scheldt. The Dutch kept up this blockade, unofficially but effectively, throughout the Twelve Years Truce and the succeeding war, and eventually secured a clause in the Treaty of Münster closing the Scheldt to commerce. Throughout the seventeenth century the wharves of Antwerp were used only by inland shipping and by a few Dutch grain ships. The sea-borne trade which Antwerp had handled moved to Amsterdam. The Hansards, down to the end of the sixteenth century, were still a force to be reckoned with; they were still active in English and Iberian trade; but they were fighting a losing battle against Dutch aggressiveness, which combined flexibility, cheap freight rates and commercial enterprise, with increasing naval force. When the Thirty Years War paralysed the economic life of Germany, the Dutch were left as virtual monopolists of northern international trade.

The fields of Hanseatic–Dutch competition were the trades in bulky foodstuffs, particularly grain, salt and salt fish; in woollen cloth; in furs, iron, and timber. In northern Europe, as in the Mediterranean, there was both a permanent and regular trade, and a casual and variable trade, in grain. England, normally more or less self-supporting in grain but liable to occasional wet summers which could ruin much of the harvest, might import grain one year and export it the next; or might import into one part of the country and export from another simultaneously. The rapid expansion of London in the late sixteenth and early seventeenth centuries necessitated the import of corn, mostly from the Baltic, first in Hanseatic and later in Dutch ships; but after about 1660, foreign imports almost ceased and London was able to rely upon an expanding domestic supply. As for the outports, they only imported corn from abroad in times of great scarcity. England, then, was only a casual importer, and towards the end of our period ceased to be an importer at all. France, likewise, exported in good years and imported only in very bad ones. The regular importers included Spain and Portugal, which imported grain from both France and the Baltic and relied heavily on German and Dutch shipping to carry it, even during the war with the United

Provinces. The seizures of Dutch shipping in Iberian ports in 1595 and 1598 each involved between 400 and 500 ships. At the other extreme, in the far north of Europe, Norway, barren and forested, was a good customer for Baltic grain. Bergen was a harbour of some importance, to which Hanseatic ships plied regularly, importing grain and exporting 'stockfish' and forest products. The biggest importers of grain, however, were in the industrialized areas of the Netherlands; these densely populated areas required imported grain for their own support, and also for a large and growing brewing industry which exported beer to England and Scandinavia. Some of the wheat and barley supply of the southern and central Netherlands came from northern France by way of the Somme or the Scheldt. More wheat and, more important for the mass of the population, great quantities of rye, came by sea from Poland and east Germany, from the wide plains on the south shore of the Baltic. The grain was sent by boat and barge down the big slow-flowing rivers of the region to the ports which stood at their mouths; most particularly, down the Vistula to Danzig. For the merchants of Danzig and the other eastern Hanse ports, faced with the problem of exporting bulky commodities—grain and timber—in large quantity, the assistance of Dutch shipping was a positive advantage. Naturally it was extremely unwelcome to the Wendish towns; this was one of the questions upon which Hanseatic unity split, since Lübeck and its neighbours could never secure the co-operation of Danzig in attempts to exclude the Dutch from the Baltic.

The successive increases in the rate of the Sound Tolls and the increasing aggressiveness of the Danish government in collecting them, never offset the lower cost of the all-sea route. The overall number of vessels passing the Sound in the sixteenth century is astonishing. It increased from an annual average of about 1,300 at the beginning of the century to one of over 5,000 at the end.[1] Admittedly one ship might make several passages, in and out, in the course of a year. Admittedly, also, most of the ships were small. Tonnages were roughly classified, not precisely recorded; but some ships were certainly under 60 tons; the great majority were registered as between 60 and 200, a very few as over 200. In the seventeenth century the number of ships dropped to an annual average of about 3,000 at mid-century, but the ships were larger. The number of vessels registered as over 200 tons exceeded that of smaller craft for the first time in 1620. This sudden increase was more apparent than real, being due largely to the introduction in 1618 of stricter methods of assessment; but strictness in itself encouraged the use of larger ships. Tonnage classification ceased in 1645; but of a gradual increase in the

[1] Nina Ellinger Bang, *Tabeller over skibsfart og varetransport gennen oresund 1497–1660* (Copenhagen, 1930), I.

size of ships there is no doubt, and by any reckoning the weight and bulk of cargo shifted throughout the two centuries was formidable and constantly growing. The first years of the Sound Toll Register, in the 1490's, show Dutch ships already a majority of the vessels passing the Sound. The proportion increased steadily in the sixteenth century. Throughout the seventeenth century Amsterdam was the principal grain market for the whole of Europe. When, in turn, the Dutch came to be challenged by other competitors—the English—using the same route, they were ready with political and diplomatic weapons of defence: the Redemption Treaties with Denmark for farming the Sound Tolls. In 1670, before their shipping was heavily affected by war, the Dutch had about 735 ships regularly engaged in the Baltic and North Sea trades (excluding the fisheries and small coastal craft), of an average tonnage of about 280; a total of roughly 207,000 tons. This was between one-third and one-half of the total Dutch merchant fleet,[1] and more than twice the capacity of the total English merchant fleet at the same date. Dutch predominance in the Baltic grain trade was not effectively challenged until the eighteenth century.

The Baltic at the beginning of the sixteenth century was the chief northern source of another vital article of food in northern Europe: salt fish, especially salt herring. The principal fisheries were those of Skania, the southern tip of Sweden, and off the island of Rügen. The fishing itself was an offshore operation in the hands of local fishermen, and the salting and packing were done on the beach. The salt chiefly used in the Baltic fishery was either mineral salt from Lüneburg, shipped down river and supplied by way of Hamburg or Lübeck, or sea-salt from the Biscay coast of France. Hanseatic shipping brought not only salt, but provisions for the fisheries and casks for barrelling the catch; and Hanseatic merchants distributed the final product throughout northern Europe and down the Atlantic coasts of France, Spain and Portugal. The disposal of herrings thus involved long voyages and the use of big sea-going ships, and was a very important part of Hanseatic trade.

In the course of the sixteenth century Dutch fishermen developed new fishing grounds and new methods of fishing; the Baltic fishery, and with it the Hanseatic share of the fish trade, declined both relatively and absolutely. The decline was gradual; as late as 1537 Skania produced 50,000 *last* of barrelled herring; but 1537 was a good year, and already by that time the rival grounds of the Dogger Bank and elsewhere in the North Sea and off the Scottish coasts were being regularly fished, and the Dutch were competing strongly as purveyors of fish to the whole of Europe. Unlike the Hansards, the Dutchmen not only fished and packed,

[1] 568,000 tons or 284,000 *last*. according to Vogel, *op. cit.*, 319.

but also peddled the catch. In order to exploit fishing grounds far from shore, they developed a class of sturdy, highly specialized but cheaply-constructed drifters known generally as busses (*buizen*), which were large enough to allow fish to be gutted, salted, and barrelled on board. A buss could bring ashore forty or fifty *last* of fish each voyage; each buss in a good year would make three voyages between mid-June and December, the duration of the legal 'open season'; and the number of busses engaged in the business was generally estimated at about 1,000 at the height of the trade's prosperity.

One of the secrets of the Dutch maritime success was their willingness to build ships cheaply and drive them to death; and about the middle of the sixteenth century they began to develop a system for carrying fish to market, which enabled the busses to remain at sea continuously throughout the season, instead of returning to port when their holds were full. Fast ships known as *ventjagers* (sale-hunters) put out from the home ports to meet the returning busses, to take their catch on board, and to carry it into harbour, leaving the busses to fish. *Ventjagers* were mentioned in legislation as early as 1556; though at that time they were not venturing much beyond the mouths of the rivers. A law of 1604, however, describes the fully-developed practice of sale-hunting on the fishing ground, by fast ships designed to carry the first herring of the year to market in the shortest possible time. The first of the catch always fetched a high price; on the day when the first *ventjagers* arrived at Rotterdam or Vlaardingen the Dutch—usually no great horsemen—used every means of speed in a race to sell the first barrels of 'new herring' in the Hague and Amsterdam. Dealers kept light carts and fast horses for this purpose—a matter of honour as much as of profit. The distribution of salted herring to the rest of Europe was one of the principal foundations of Dutch maritime ascendency throughout the seventeenth century. Constant complaints were made to government in England against the Dutch, who sold in British ports the fish which they had taken in British waters; but the repeated plans put forward for ousting, or at least imitating, them, came to little, because the English could never in our period compete with the Dutch in the construction of economical vessels for the trade.

The North Sea herring fishery—the 'Grand Fishery'—was not the only Dutch fishery, though it was the most important. In the North Sea, herring busses line-fished for cod out of the herring season; and smaller keel-less vessels, such as the Scheeveningen 'pinks' and well-boats, fitted with wells for keeping fish alive on board, combined the Dogger Bank cod fishing with the 'trade of the fresh' in the Netherland ports. The Iceland cod fishery required larger ships, and could not be combined with herring fishing, because the seasons were the same.

Iceland cod was not sold fresh, but was salted, or dried ashore, and found its markets chiefly in Spain and the Spanish Netherlands. Both herring and cod trades suffered—since the ships had to pass through the Channel to reach their best markets—from the attentions of the Dunkirkers, who were to the fishery what the dogfish is to the herring. The busses went armed, and from 1589 onwards usually got heavy convoy. Despite depredations and the expenses of convoy, the trade increased steadily until the middle of the seventeenth century; but the wars with England and France after 1652 damaged the trade severely. From that date alternate convoy and prohibition summarize the history of the Dutch fisheries. English warships and French privateers caused a gradual decline in the north European dried fish trade, and southern Europe came to rely more and more upon supplies from further afield, from New England and from Newfoundland.

A third branch of the Dutch fisheries which created a big export trade was the Spitzbergen whale fishery. The *Traankokery* at Smeerenburg Bay was started about 1612, and the Dutch Arctic Company chartered two years later. For about twenty years the fishery flourished greatly, and the fleets of whalers anchored in the Bay attracted still further fleets, carrying provisions to the flensing stations ashore and taking train-oil back. A ship could make two trips between Smeerenburg and Amsterdam in the season with 1,000 quarters of train-oil each trip. By 1641, however, over-fishing made the Smeerenburg station unprofitable, and the company was wound up. The English and French wars, the pressing of trained men and the commandeering of ships, depleted the Dutch whaling fleets. Many Dutch shipowners, to avoid commandeering, sold their ships to the English; and whaling moved out from the coastal waters of northern Europe to follow the unpredictable movements of whales in the open Atlantic and the loose pack-ice of the Arctic.

By far the most important manufactured commodity in the trade of northern Europe in the early sixteenth century was woollen cloth. Cloth of one sort or another was made in many places, but the chief areas of manufacture were in north Italy, northern France, Flanders, Brabant, Holland and eastern England. Of these areas, Flanders was by far the most important. Other manufacturing areas prospered in so far as their products were complementary to those of Flanders, and could be marketed there; indeed, the clothing areas together formed a more or less continuous region held together—despite constant internal friction—by geography, by economic interdependence, and by easy and cheap transport by sea and river.

The port of Antwerp, the centre of the Flemish cloth industry, throughout the first three-quarters of the sixteenth century was also the centre of the international textile trade, and in consequence the commercial and financial capital of the greater part of northern Europe. London, economically a satellite of Antwerp, climbed to prosperity along with Antwerp; and the same was true of many of the Hanse towns, especially those of the western group.

The wool which was woven upon the looms of Flanders came partly from the Low Countries themselves, but chiefly from Spain and from England. England was the principal source of high-quality wool in northern Europe, enjoying so high a reputation that Italian merchants, in the early sixteenth century, bought considerable quantities of wool in London and shipped it to Italy by the way of the Rhine. Foreign buyers of wool, however, whether Italians or Flemings, were discouraged by discriminatory export duties from buying in England. As far as possible, the export trade was retained in English hands. The continental market, the Staple, was at Calais so long as that town remained an English possession. Flemish dealers bought their wool at Calais and took it to Antwerp in their own ships. After the loss of Calais in 1558 the Staple was removed to Middleburg, and then to Bruges, where it remained until the early seventeenth century. In 1617 the export of wool from England was finally prohibited and the foreign Staple abolished. By that time the harbour of Antwerp had become a ruined backwater; the English industry was absorbing all the native wool production and itself importing wool from Spain. Throughout the sixteenth century, however, and especially throughout the period of Antwerp's ascendancy, England continued to export, as it had done for centuries before, large quantities of wool produced in excess of home manufacturing requirements.

The organization of the wool trade and the transport of raw wool across the North Sea was a relatively simple affair. The cloth trade was more complex. Different manufacturing centres produced different types and qualities of cloth, and often exchanged their products. Both cloth and wool were readily portable; they could be made up in bundles and bales of convenient sizes and carried to and from local centres by pack animal at reasonable cost. It was, indeed, this portability which made possible the development of the domestic system by which much of the cloth of western Europe was produced. Within Flanders and Brabant, cloth and the raw materials for making it could be moved readily about a net-work of inland waterways, natural and artificial. From Antwerp, cloth went out in all directions, by sea to England, Iceland, Scandinavia and the Baltic, in exchange for grain, fish, timber and raw wool; by sea also to Spain and Portugal. It went by inland waterways, of which the Rhine was the most important, to central and southern Germany. The Rhine carried great fleets of horse-drawn barges which took Dutch fish and Flemish cloth as far as Frankfurt-am-Main, and returned with linen 'fustians' from central and southern Germany, with Rhine wine, steel, hardware and weapons, and spices and silk from Mediterranean and eastern sources. The barges were of considerable size, with permanent living quarters on board. Many of the bargees were Dutchmen: and for carriage by sea also, especially towards the northern parts of Europe and into the Baltic, the export of cloth from Antwerp depended heavily and increasingly on Dutch shipping. Towards the end of the sixteenth century, with the devastation of Flanders and the decline of Antwerp, with the development of Leyden and Amsterdam as textile manufacturing centres of importance in their own right, Dutch control of the carrying trade in cloth naturally increased still further.

The Low Countries, however, were not the only large-scale exporters of cloth in sixteenth-century northern Europe. England had exported cloth for centuries, and during the sixteenth century English exports— though with heavy fluctuations—more than doubled. They went in two principal directions: to Antwerp: and to northern Germany, Scandinavia and the Baltic. The purchases made in London by Italian, Ragusan and French merchants were a relatively minor matter. The very large exports, chiefly of undyed and unfinished cloth, which English industry supplied for Flemish finishers, were handled chiefly by English exporters, who had long been organized in a corporate body, the Merchant Adventurers, for the protection of their particular monopoly. The headquarters of this regulated company was at Antwerp, where the Adventurers were an influential and respected body. On the other hand, the heavy, hard-wearing woollen fabrics which went from England to the north were exported almost entirely, in the first half of the sixteenth century, by the merchants of the German Hanse, who in return for their carrying services enjoyed exceptional privileges in London—a highly favourable position in the matter of export duties and the virtual extra-territoriality of their Steelyard. The Germans had long used their maritime strength to impede English penetration of the Baltic. In the early sixteenth century they began, in addition, to compete with English merchants in the Flanders trade; for the centripetal tendency which had drawn the Londoners towards Antwerp was felt by the Hanse merchants also. English economic nationalism, accordingly, made more acute by the depression of the early fifties, demanded and obtained first the reduction, eventually the abolition of Hanseatic privileges in London. Meanwhile, however, worsening relations between Spain and England interrupted the Flanders trade. Antwerp was closed to English goods in the early sixties and again in the early seventies; and the

disasters which befell the city thereafter prevented a full resumption of
the trade. The Merchant Adventurers were driven to seek 'staples'
elsewhere, in one or other of the Hanse towns—an attempt which
naturally exposed them to retaliation against their London policy—or
in the United Netherlands, or both. After many changes, and as a result of
intricate negotiations, the Adventurers in 1611 fixed their German headquarters at Hamburg, which proved a good market for the recently
developed production of high-quality finished cloth. There they remained until the nineteenth century. The willingness of the Hamburg
authorities to welcome them was symptomatic of the decline of the
Hanse both in unity and in commercial aggressiveness. The English
Adventurers, however, could not do without their Netherlands market
for unfinished cloth, whatever exactions the Dutch might impose upon
them. They never returned to the Spanish Netherlands, but their
Staple moved between Middleburg, Rotterdam, Delft and Dordrecht
and was permanently fixed at Dordrecht in 1655. By that time their
privileges were being challenged more and more openly by English
interlopers as well as foreigners, who shipped English cloth to Amsterdam for warehousing and re-export in Dutch ships.

The decline of the Hanse and the revocation of German privileges in
London encouraged English Baltic merchants to seek privileges in their
turn. The Eastland Company was incorporated in 1579 to export dyed
and dressed cloth to countries beyond the Sound and to import linen,
flax, grain and naval stores into England. Its foreign staple was first at
Elbing, later at Danzig. Its membership overlapped with that of the
Merchant Adventurers, but its volume of trade was smaller than theirs,
and very much smaller than the Dutch business in the same area. Even
more than that of the Adventurers, its story through the first three-
quarters of the seventeenth century was of a losing battle against Dutch
competition. Throughout the century its members carried much of
their business in ships bought or chartered from the Dutch. The result of
all these changes and developments was that in the seventeenth century
the cloth export of the Low Countries was carried almost entirely by
Dutchmen, whether by sea or by inland waterway. That of England,
which formerly had been largely in the hands of Germans, was now
shared between Englishmen and Dutchmen, the Dutch, without benefit
of monopolies or chartered companies, securing the larger share. In
1601, of a total of 714 ships entering the port of London, 207 were
English, 40 were German, 360 were Dutch.[1] Admittedly most of the
Dutch vessels were small and engaged only in North Sea trade; but they
were large enough to carry English cloth to Holland and to Germany,

[1] L. R. Miller, 'New evidence on the shipping and imports of London, 1601–1602',
*Quarterly Journal of Economics*, 41, p. 740.

and many went further. In 1620 the Dutch were reported to be operating 200 ships between English ports and the countries beyond the Sound.[1] They seized the opportunity of the English Civil War to develop still further their own woollen industry and to extend their trade in German and Baltic markets. Sir Josiah Child declared in 1688 that English trade to the Baltic was no more than one-tenth of the Dutch.[2] Dutch shipping carried throughout northern Europe the greater part not only of cloth exports, but nearly all the manufactured products and raw materials of industry: the pottery of the Low Countries, German weapons and hardware, Swedish iron and copper, Russian and Polish flax and hemp, Baltic timber, pitch and potash.

Coal was to some extent an exception. It was mined in various places in the north of France and the southern Netherlands, but the main exporting area was the Tyne coalfield, and English colliers carried not only the coastal trade between Tyne and Thames, but also much of the export trade to the Low Countries. Coal in the first half of the seventeenth century was still chiefly a domestic fuel. It became an important industrial raw material in the second half, and the great increase in its use and transport was a potent factor in the rapid growth of English merchant shipping at that time.

In general, however, in the carriage of bulky and varied cargoes the Dutch were unrivalled. They served England, France, Germany and Scandinavia alike. The English Acts of Trade and the French tariffs of 1664 and 1667 were equally ineffective in capturing European trade from the Dutch. The purpose of the Navigation Act was defeated by licensed exemptions; by the clauses in the Treaty of Breda which included the whole of the Rhine in the hinterland of Holland; and by the inadequacy of English shipping, despite numerous captures and purchases from the Dutch. The French, in the Treaty of Nymwegen, were obliged to grant substantial tariff rebates to the Dutch. At the end of the seventeenth century the whole carrying trade between France and northern Europe, and most of the corresponding English trade, was still in Dutch hands. It was not until the eighteenth century that English shippers—by then largely freed from the restrictions of regulated companies and established as exporters of fully finished cloth of all types and qualities to many parts of the world—seriously challenged the Dutch lead in the trade of northern Europe.

The history of transport is necessarily closely connected with the history of the timber trade. Timber was, until the middle of the nineteenth century, the principal raw material in the construction of the means of transport. It is one of the most difficult commodities to carry

[1] *State Papers, Domestic, 1619–23*, 157, 211.
[2] *A New Discourse of Trade*. (4th Edn.), 113.

economically, because of its bulk and its rigidity. Nevertheless, in the sixteenth century, and even more in the seventeenth, timber proved more mobile than skill and capital; those European countries whose people devoted themselves most thoroughly to a carrying trade, lacked timber and had to import it. The Dutch never had any supply of natural timber worth mentioning. The natural supplies of northern Spain and of England, excellent in quality, but depleted both by ship-building and by iron smelting, began to run short by the middle of the sixteenth century. France, naturally better supplied, felt the effects of shortage in the seventeenth century. For all, but especially for the Dutch, an un-interrupted supply was essential for the maintenance of maritime strength, and control of the timber trade was a major preoccupation.

Three areas in northern Europe produced large quantities of export-able timber. All three possessed forests which had been exploited and roughly conserved for centuries. Western Germany produced oak of fair quality, floated by way of the Elbe to Hamburg and by the Weser to Bremen. Much timber, including Swiss masts, also came down the Rhine. Norway was an important source of pine and fir, chiefly for masts. The chief source of shipbuilding timber, both fir and oak, how-ever, was the forested land on the south shore of the Baltic.

The advantage common to all these areas was not the mere existence of good timber, but its accessibility. In the international timber trade, the cost of timber on the stump was a small matter—usually about 5 per cent of the delivered price. Transport costs were the determining factor. Timber could be moved economically only if the greater part of its journey was by water. Twenty miles was usually considered the maxi-mum economical haul by land, in the most favourable conditions. Accessible timber, therefore, was that which grew within twenty miles of the sea or of a fair-sized river. The Baltic forests were particularly well placed in this respect, with many navigable rivers, and well equipped harbours at their mouths. The Vistula and the Dwina were the major timber rivers, Danzig and Riga the principal ports. The hard winter climate made it possible for winter-felled logs to be dragged or sledged by ox-teams across frozen snow to the river banks. Delivery on timber contracts was often made subject to suitable winter weather, for logs could not be moved in the miry conditions of mild winter or sudden thaw. Floating logs down-river to the sea was a simpler, though slow process. On the smaller streams the logs were rolled in singly. In Norway they usually made the whole trip down the swift-flowing torrents in this way: but on the Baltic rivers and on the Rhine they were collected at the main confluences and made up into rafts. These rafts, often formed of a thousand logs or more, carried the families of the lumber-men with their huts, cattle, poultry and waggons. They drifted downstream for weeks and months, steered by great sweeps over the stern and often accelerated by oars or sails.

On reaching the sea, the rafts were broken up. The crews returned home, on foot or in the waggons they had brought. The logs were floated into 'mast ponds' formed by booms in the river, sorted and 'bracked' or marked according to size and quality. The best fir sticks were exported with the bark on for use as masts. Other timber might be sawn at the port of shipment, and shipped as 'plank' or 'deals'; or else shipped in baulks, merely trimmed so as to take up less room in the hold. The term 'wainscot' applied to oak referred originally to the form in which logs were shipped from Danzig and Riga, and with two sides of the log hewn flat. The Dutch usually shipped timber for their own use in this form, and cut it up in the sawmills of Zaandam and other ports; but timber for England was usually sawn at the Baltic ports, whose windmills performed this operation more cheaply than it could be done in England.

As merchant ships went in the seventeenth century, timber carriers tended to be fairly large. Their size was limited chiefly by the sand-bars which obstructed many of the Baltic harbours. From 200 to 400 tons, by seventeenth-century reckoning, was the usual size. Timber was reckoned in 'loads' of fifty cubic feet. A load corresponded roughly to a ton of shipping, assuming a judiciously mixed cargo of oak and lighter, bulkier fir, so that most ships carried from 200 to 400 loads. The construction of a single 'great ship'—a ship of the line—required, in the later seventeenth century, at least 1,000 loads, not counting masts and spars. In view of the immense increase of naval armaments in the seventeenth century, of the increase also in merchant shipping (using admittedly timber of smaller scantling, but in great quantity) and of the continuing demand for timber for building ashore, these figures give some idea of the scale of the north European carrying trade in timber in the seventeenth century, and the large number of ships needed to carry it. In the late seventeenth century about 250 timber ships sailed annually from Riga, and twice that number from Danzig. Occasional crises produced sudden and urgent demands; the Fire of London, for example, was a Godsend to the Norwegians.

The timber trade was singularly wasteful of shipping. Timber could be shipped safely by sea only in the summer, partly because a cargo large enough to be profitable had to be carried above as well as between decks, so increasing top-hamper; partly because some forms of timber—baulks and masts—so stiffened a ship as to make her extremely dangerous in a head sea. There was a strong temptation to employ old and worn-out ships in the trade, which in turn tended to raise insurance rates. A difficulty of a more purely economic kind was that of securing freights into the Baltic. A well-assorted cargo of manufactures and 'colonial goods'—tobacco, sugar and the like—would purchase sixty or seventy cargoes of ordinary timber at Danzig. Most timber ships had to enter the Baltic in ballast. It is not surprising that transport costs, with the associated duties and insurance charges, accounted for at least two-thirds of the price of imported timber at its final destination. The methods of transport moreover affected the quality and durability of the timber. After lying in water for months, timber was loaded in summer into the hot holds of ships, where it steamed for weeks; for the voyage from Danzig to Zaandam or London took at least a month, and much longer in wartime, when ships had to wait for convoy. Such conditions bred fungus, particularly the dreaded 'dry rot'. This was the basis—the only real basis—for the loud English prejudice against foreign timber, and the preference for properly seasoned native oak, when that much-advertised commodity could be had. Ships built of imported timber usually had a short life—twenty years at most; and so the avid demand for timber was maintained.

Like the grain trade, the trade in Baltic timber was carried partly in Dutch, partly in Hanseatic ships in the sixteenth century, and almost entirely in Dutch ships in the seventeenth. The English Eastland Company's share in the trade was a relatively minor one. The same general distribution of trade held for sources of supply outside the Baltic. Norway ceased to be a Hanseatic preserve as early as 1550. Norway had, for the English shippers, the advantage of being only a short distance away; say a week from Bergen to Hull. Even so, the Dutch by 1600 were handling most of the Norwegian timber exports, and in 1670 they had some 40,000 tons of shipping in the Norway trade. The Chancellor expedition to the White Sea in 1553–6 opened for the English a new supply of masts from the hinterland of Archangel: but the supply was neglected, because transport costs were thought to be too high, until the Dutch began to exploit it about 1610. American supplies were never a serious consideration in the seventeenth century, because of transport costs. The Baltic remained throughout the century the chief source of timber, Danzig the chief timber port; though Danzig throughout the century sent out two cargoes of grain to every one of timber, unlike Riga, which had only timber to offer.

The trades of Hansards, Dutchmen and Englishmen from the Baltic to the North Sea had one important feature in common. All traders depended on the good-will of the power which guarded the Sound—Denmark throughout most of the seventeenth century, but Sweden towards the end. The passage of the Sound was especially important for the timber trade, since timber was a vital munition of war, and was too bulky for overland carriage *via* Lübeck. No traders succeeded in regularly avoiding the payment of Sound Tolls (though the Dutch farmed them, for their own shipping, for part of the century). Baltic timber was too indispensable. Hence the constant concern of both English and Dutch with the stubborn wars and tangled diplomacy of the 'Northern Crowns'. The one advantage which the English held in competition with the Dutch was that they tended, throughout most of the century, to back the eventual winner—Sweden—while the Dutch relied on good relations with Denmark, the eventual loser; but that advantage did not become apparent until the end of the century. Throughout the incessant wars of the seventeenth century, the timber fleets of the principal naval powers needed—and got—heavy naval convoy, and the passage of the Sound was repeatedly demanded by the minatory despatch of battle fleets. Both England and Holland risked present fleets to ensure the supplies needed to build future fleets. Eventually—but not till the eighteenth century—England secured by competition in armaments a commercial predominance which it had formerly failed to achieve in competition over transport costs.

## III. *The Trades of the Atlantic Coasts*

The importance of the two inland seas, the Mediterranean and the Baltic, with their characteristic and indispensable trades, suggests a picture of sixteenth-century sea-borne commerce polarized between these two extremes. Such a picture would be misleading. The trade of sixteenth-century Europe cannot be divided neatly between north and south. The long stretch of Atlantic coastline from Seville to Rotterdam with its many coastal and riverine harbours, carried a port-to-port trade at least equal in variety and volume to either the northern or the Mediterranean sectors. The nautical tradition and capacity of the Iberian peninsula should not be underrated. In the second half of the sixteenth century the Spaniards were the second ship-owning nation of Europe; the combined merchant fleet of Spain and Portugal was at least equal to that of the Netherlands, and much larger than that of England or France or Germany. The Iberian fleet was divided, it is true, between the Mediterranean and the Atlantic; but in the sixteenth century the Spanish-directed shipping of Cataluña was in decline. Philip II's government tried unsuccessfully to revive it in 1562-3, by transferring shipwrights from Bilbao. Bilbao was by far the most important Spanish harbour, with a volume of shipping considerably exceeding that of Seville, despite the trade of the Indies, and far exceeding that of Barcelona, Alicante or Malaga.[1] In the sixteenth century it was a great ship-building centre,

[1] A. P. Usher, 'Spanish ships and shipping in the sixteenth and seventeenth centuries', *Facts and factors in economic history* (Cambridge, Mass., 1932), 212.

whose mountainous hinterland produced oak of excellent quality and a considerable—though never quite adequate—supply of pine masts and pitch. Many ships used in the Indies trade were built in the Biscayan ports, including most of the largest, which were beyond the capacity of Andalusian shipyards. Unfortunately for the shipping industry, however, the lack of navigable rivers made much useful timber inaccessible; and since the area also produced iron, the smelting industry competed with shipbuilding for the available wood. It was the depletion of forests, as much as conservatism in design and growing shoddiness in construction, which caused the decay of the Biscay shipyards in the seventeenth century. Mast timber ran out before oak, and was already being imported in large quantities from the Baltic in Dutch, Flemish and Hanseatic ships in the last quarter of the sixteenth century; but the massive oak logs needed for keels and stem and stern posts also became increasingly hard to find and costly to transport. Sailcloth and cordage were always imported; the Biscayans never developed their own industry, but got their sailcloth from France or Portugal, their hemp cordage from Italy or from the Baltic by way of the Netherlands.

The shipping of Bilbao, and of Biscay generally, like that of the Netherlands, lived not by 'rich' trades, but by a bulk traffic in ordinary commodities. The chief export was wool, the high-quality wool of the uplands of northern Castile, especially the provinces of Segovia and Soria. The ancient city of Burgos was the chief collecting centre for this highly-priced product, and significantly one of the few towns in Castile to possess a Guild Merchant. From Burgos the bags of wool were carried by pack-train to Bilbao, where they were shipped either in Biscayan or Flemish ships. Most of the wool went, naturally, to the Spanish Netherlands, but a large quantity also went to Hamburg, some to northern France and some—in the seventeenth century an increasing amount—to England. When, as a result of political conditions in the late sixteenth century, trade with the Netherlands declined, the losses were largely offset by a steady increase in the trade with England and with Brittany. To the same destinations Bilbao exported high-quality iron, though in relatively small quantities, and considerable quantities of cheap and not very good wine. Apart from naval stores, its principal imports were Flemish and English cloth.

The other Spanish port prominent in Atlantic trade was Seville. Seville —later supplanted by Cadiz—was famous chiefly as the terminus of the official Indies trade, and the source, for the rest of Europe, of New-World foodstuffs, dyestuffs and drugs—sugar, cacao, cochineal, indigo, logwood, tobacco, and quinine. Andalusia, like Biscay, had extensive forests, and ships were built on the banks of the Guadalquivir and the Rio Tinto. The ships were not as numerous, or as good, as those of Biscay, but the area had a fishing and seafaring tradition, and Seville had long been a major port, with close trade connections in England and the Low Countries. Large quantities of West of England cloth were shipped from Bristol to Seville; and the whole of Andalusia was a good market for the chief exportable commodity of northern Europe—fish, whether salted herring from the North Sea or dried or salted cod from Iceland and the Banks. In the seventeenth century, Seville also imported a large quantity and variety of French manufactured goods, for re-export to the Indies by the monopolists of the *Consulado*. Apart from American products, Seville exported raw Andalusian wool—a coarse and cheap variety—and several other raw materials of the clothing industry: Castile soap, olive oil, and *barilla*—an alkali used in soap making, derived from the ashes of salt-wort scrub. It supplied northern Europe also with much of its winter fruit—oranges, raisins, figs and almonds especially, which had formerly been articles of rare luxury but which in the sixteenth century were becoming fairly general and the objects of a substantial trade.

The most famous native export of southern Spain, however, was wine. Wine was a bulky, heavy and valuable commodity, and one very difficult to transport satisfactorily by land. The only feasible method was to carry it in skins—the normal method in countries which, like Spain, have few navigable rivers. Jolting in malodorous goatskins on the backs of mules was not only expensive; it also spoiled the wine. Wine in cask, on the other hand, though almost immovable by land, was relatively easy and convenient to carry by water; a wine-laden ship needed no other ballast; and wine improves in cask. Hence the double importance of the wine rivers of Europe—Rhine and Rhône, Garonne and Guadalquivir. The markets opened by the Garonne and Guadalquivir and their tributaries, however, were limited in extent. Much of the wine of Gascony and Andalusia found its best customers not at home, but in countries closely linked by sea. England and the Low Countries, but England especially, were the most dependable European markets, since they produced no wine themselves but had acquired, by close political connection with countries that did, a firm taste for it.

By the sixteenth century the ancient trade in claret from Bordeaux had lost, for political reasons, the easy primacy it had enjoyed in the later Middle Ages, and was tending to decline; though Bordeaux at the beginning of the century was still supply three-quarters of the English consumption of wine, and claret remained an important item in English trade until William III taxed it out of the market. Bordeaux had little shipping of its own, and its wine was usually carried in English, Flemish or Dutch ships, or else exported by Breton carriers to northern France. The relative decline of the northern trade from Bordeaux was the gain of

Seville and Cadiz; for English taste for the potent wines of south-western
Spain and of the Canary Islands grew steadily throughout the sixteenth
century and has persisted ever since. The trade, cloth one way and sack
the other, was the making of sixteenth-century Bristol. Antwerp too,
took large quantities of sack in the sixteenth century, carried in Spanish
or Flemish ships. The Dutch, though they would carry any wine for
freight, imported for their own use mostly Rhine wines by river
shipping: and when, in the course of the Thirty Years War, the Rhenish
vineyards suffered widespread damage, the Dutch turned not to sack but
to locally brewed beer.

The sweet-wine trade was of much smaller bulk than that in clarets
and sacks, though sweet wines fetched high prices in northern Europe.
They came, in the sixteenth century, mostly from Mediterranean
sources, and were shipped in jars, not casks, from islands long stripped of
their timber. After the capture of Crete by the Turks in the seventeenth
century, however, the supply of Malmsey was cut off. The Malvoisie
grape, from which it was made, had already become naturalized in
Madeira, but the excellences of Madeira wine were not fully appreciated
in northern Europe until the early eighteenth century; nor did Genoese
attempts, in the sixteenth and seventeenth centuries, to sell sweet Italian
wines in England and the Low Countries, meet with much success,
because these wines would not keep on the long voyages. The answer to
the English demand for sweet wine, in the later seventeenth century, was
the growth of a trade in port, carried from Oporto to London, a three-
or four-week run, in English or Dutch ships.

The third great staple of Atlantic coast trade was the salt used in the
meat-preserving and fish-curing industries of northern Europe. There
were many European sources of salt: the mineral salt of Lüneburg, which
largely supplied the Skania fishery; 'moor-salt' made from the ashes of
darinck, the salt-impregnated turf of the Dutch estuarine shores; the sea-
salt obtained by evaporation at many places between the mouths of the
Loire and the Gironde, but chiefly at Brouage and Bourgneuf Bay; the
similar sea-salt of southern Portugal, especially that made at Setúbal.
The Dutch, those ingenious specialists in bulky freights, were the masters
of the international salt trade as well as the principal users of salt. In the
early sixteenth century the imperial regulations governing the Grand
Fishery had insisted on the use of moor-salt, but as the supply of darinck
became exhausted the herring curers were obliged to import sea-salt,
which was coarser and dirtier than moor-salt, and had to be refined,
before use in fish curing, by solution and evaporation by boiling. After
the middle of the century they were commanded to use only Spanish or
Portuguese salt, and Setúbal became a principal source of supply. The
revolt of the Netherlands, the union of the Spanish and Portuguese

Crowns in 1580, and the embargoes on Dutch shipping at Lisbon and Setúbal in 1585, 1595 and 1598, caused interruptions and difficulties in the trade. The Dutch could get salt from Bourgneuf Bay, but not enough. They needed salt in such large quantities, and had made themselves so indispensable as carriers, that they continued to trade with Lisbon, with Setúbal, and with Spanish ports also, almost throughout the war, by more or less transparent subterfuges. The Spanish connived at it, because of their dependance on Dutch shipping for imports of grain and timber. Even in the embargo years, when exasperation and shortage of shipping drove the Spanish government to seize enemy vessels in Spanish harbours, most of the Dutchmen managed to bribe themselves and their ships out. The conditions of the trade became so uncertain, however, and the cost of Spanish connivance so high, that in the last decade of the sixteenth century and the first decade of the seventeenth it became worth while to exploit salt pans much further afield, in the Cape Verde Islands and eventually in the West Indies. In this way the Dutch, like the Spaniards and Portuguese before them, graduated from the Atlantic coast to a trans-Atlantic trade.

Throughout most of the sixteenth century north Italy and Flanders were the two chief areas of industrial and commercial activity in Europe, and contact between them was essential to the prosperity of both. The Italian maritime cities imported eastern goods by sea from the Levant, and exported them, along with goods of their own making, to Flanders for distribution throughout northern Europe. Besides money, they received in return manufactured goods from Flanders and Germany, raw materials from England, Scandinavia and the Baltic. This varied and vital traffic went both by land and by sea. The land routes, of which there were several, depended on the conjunction of rivers and mountain passes. The string of prosperous small towns on and near the upper Adige—Verona, Trento, Bolzano, Merano—owed much of their prosperity to the traffic going from Venice over the Brenner to the manufacturing and commercial centres of South Germany—Augsburg, Nürnberg and others. These German cities were in turn linked by way of Ulm and Stüttgart, or Würzburg and Frankfurt, to the great north-western artery, the Rhine. What the Brenner was for Venice, the Saint Gotthard was for Genoa and Milan, a highway, passable at least for mules, to the Swiss heart of Europe and thence—though not by very easy ways—to the upper Rhine.

For all except very bulky goods, these overland routes had many advantages. They were safer than the sea route, especially from the 1530's, when the rulers of the north African towns were steadily increasing their maritime strength and waging increasingly aggressive war against Christian commerce. The Strait of Gibraltar, in the middle of the sixteenth century, was a very dangerous stretch of water. It is true that in Germany the toll exactions of riparian landowners approximated to piracy at times; but on the other hand, developments in land transport were increasing its efficiency, so that traffic was not confined to rivers. In Germany there was a steady development throughout the century in the number and efficiency of carts and waggons. In the Mediterranean countries the sixteenth century was the heyday of the mule, that humble but indomitable beast of burden which, commercially speaking, was conquering the New World for Spain. Its value was curiously little appreciated in Europe. Spanish writers in Charles V's day joined in a chorus of complaint against the increase of mule breeding in Spain and Italy, which, they said, diminished the stock of saddle-horses fit for war. Nevertheless the mule throve, and played a part in reducing the costs of transport; and in many parts of the Mediterranean world there is evidence of an increasing preference for land over sea transport in the second half of the sixteenth century.

The flourishing trans-Alpine trade between north Italy and southern Germany did not long survive the sixteenth century. It was cut off, or at least seriously diminished, by unforeseen and uncontrollable physical changes. The later Middle Age was a period of increasing climatic severity, which reached a peak in northern Europe and the Alps at the end of the sixteenth century and in the first half of the seventeenth. At that time, villages which had been in existence for hundreds of years were overwhelmed by rapidly advancing glaciers—glaciers which until then had been so small and so far up among the peaks that no-one had ever thought that they might become a menace. High mountain passes, which had been used from time immemorial as summer trade routes, became blocked by ice. South German trade with the Mediterranean, and through the Mediterranean with the outside world, was increasingly forced in the opposite direction, down the Rhine to the Netherlands and the Atlantic. Trade by land between Italy and the Netherlands almost ceased.

There remained the sea route. Sea-borne trade between Mediterranean and northern Atlantic at the beginning of the sixteenth century had been carried almost exclusively in Venetian and Genoese ships. This Italian predominance was maintained during the first half of the century, but with increasing difficulty, because of the depletion of timber supplies and the consequent rise in the cost of shipbuilding and repair. Venice had formerly relied entirely on its own hinterland for timber; on Istria for oak, on the Rhaetian and Carnic Alps for fir masts and larch beams. A fair supply of mast timber was obtained from the Upper Adige until well into the sixteenth century, but the depletion of oak forests gave cause for concern before the end of the fifteenth century. In 1520 the arsenal obtained extensive powers to reserve oak timber for naval use. It used these powers to protect large tracts of forest not only from charcoal-burners and goats, but also from commercial ship-builders. Private shipyards were obliged to import oak from places outside Venetian control, from the Dalmatian coast and the eastern slopes of the Appenines; but these areas lacked navigable rivers for the transport of logs, and the available supply was limited. Shortage of timber became general throughout the western Mediterranean in the second half of the sixteenth century.

Venetian ship-building was retarded not only by shortage of material, but also by a conservatism in construction and design hard to explain in a people of such pronounced commercial acumen. The Venetians employed galleys in the Flanders trade down to the 1530's. Galleys were valued in the Mediterranean because of their speed and independence of wind. In the Atlantic, they could be used only in the summer; and they were necessarily uneconomical. They stowed little cargo. Oarsmen, slave or free, were hard to find and expensive to feed. Eventually, even oars became almost unobtainable in Venice, because the arsenal reserved for its own use the beech wood from which they were made. In 1532 the Flanders galleys discontinued their sailings. The Italian ships left in the trade were mostly large carracks. Venetian shipyards had long specialized in building the largest class of merchant ships. Their answer to the timber shortage was to build fewer ships of small and medium size, but to continue the old practice of laying down four or five very big ones each year.[1] More of these monsters were being built at Venice in the middle years of the sixteenth century than ever before, many of them over 600 tons and some over 1,000—much larger than most ships built for the Atlantic trades. They were solid, well fastened, old-fashioned in lines and rig, costly to build and to operate. In the second half of the century they competed less and less successfully with cheaper northern vessels of more moderate size; by the end of the century commercial shipyards had almost ceased to build them. In the seventeenth century, only the naval arsenal still upheld the ship-building tradition of Venice. Venetian merchants were compelled to buy ships from northern Europe, from Spain, and from the Aegean islands, to keep their trade afloat.

The invasion of the Mediterranean by Atlantic shipping was the work of the English, the French, the Hansards, and inevitably—but somewhat belatedly—the Dutch. The English, already long active in trade to Seville, were the first to push beyond the Straits and to establish, about 1511, regular trading relations; a handful of ships out of Bristol and Southampton, sailing to Leghorn, to Sicily, Crete and Cyprus, eventually

[1] F. C. Lane, *Venetian ships and ship-builders of the Renaissance* (Baltimore, 1934), 106 ff.

pushing as far as Beyrout and Tripoli of Syria, bringing woollen cloth—'kerseys'—and tin, much in demand for the gun-founding industry; buying silk, pepper, sweet wine and fruit, oil and carpets. They were too few to compete seriously with the Venetians, and often entrusted freights to Venetian ships. Their visits ceased abruptly in the early 1550's, for reasons which can only be guessed, since other shipping, Italian, French and Flemish, continued to ply through the Straits. Possibly Turkish aggressions had something to do with it; more probably the reasons were specifically English. The early 1550's in England were a period of commercial crisis and contraction of credit: a period also when attention was being diverted, by the enterprise of Richard Chancellor, to the north-eastern search for 'Cathay', which led to the opening of a trade to Archangel. The English returned to the Mediterranean about 1573; by 1578 they were in negotiation with the Turk; and in 1581 the Levant Company received its charter and began to drive a profitable trade in the Levant in competition with Venice. It was a small beginning. The English reputation for piracy at the end of the sixteenth century shows them to be still preying on the fringe of a great trade, rather than making it their own. The first real conquest of Mediterranean trade by an Atlantic power was made not by the English, despite their early start, but by the Dutch.

The English had entered the Mediterranean to sell cloth and tin. The Dutch first came in force to sell fish and grain. Their trade with Lisbon and Seville, though inconvenienced by war, had never entirely ceased. In these southern harbours they could not fail to learn of the growing shortage of grain throughout the western Mediterranean, and particularly the famine resulting from the series of bad harvests in Italy from 1586 to 1590. They were not, indeed, alone in rushing to Italy to sell grain at famine prices; their old competitors, the Hansards, were also early in the field. The German merchants had grain to sell, from the Baltic. They had also the political advantages of neutrality in the war, and the active favour of the Spanish government, who were anxious to exclude the Dutch. In 1590 the Grand Duke of Tuscany, unable to fulfil his grain *tratas* from Sicilian sources, had sought supplies from Danzig, Lübeck, Holland, France and England, in that order. The Hansards, moreover, had an urgent reason for looking to Spain and Italy for markets, for Dutch competition was pressing them hard in the north, and in 1579 they had lost their privileges in England. They hastened to Italy, armed with Spanish safe-conducts. In 1593, of a total of 219 ships arriving at Leghorn, seventy-three brought grain from sources outside the Mediterranean. Of these, thirty-four belonged to various Hanseatic towns, twelve were Dutch, seven English, four Flemish, two Norwegian, one from Riga; thirteen remain unidentified. It is significant, however, that of the seventy-three, only twenty-nine actually loaded at Hanseatic ports, chiefly Hamburg and Danzig.[1] The seven English ships all loaded at English ports, and the Riga ship at Riga. Of the rest, all the Dutch, all the Flemings, both the Norwegians, five of the Germans and five of the 'doubtfuls' loaded at Amsterdam; a further indication of the importance of that city as the centre of the international grain trade. All these voyages were made in the first five months of the year, and the passage time from Amsterdam varied from five to twelve weeks; indication, also, of emancipation from the old fear of winter voyages.

Hanseatic competition in Mediterranean trade was short-lived. By the Anglo-Spanish treaty of 1604 and the Dutch-Spanish truce of 1609, the Germans lost their advantage as neutrals. Having no important manufacturing centres in their immediate hinterland, they had less to offer to Mediterranean purchasers than the Dutch. In technical matters of ship design and commercial organization they were falling behind the Dutch; and in the second quarter of the seventeenth century Germany was ravaged by a war of unparalleled destructiveness. For all these reasons, in the early seventeenth century, trade between the Mediterranean and northern Europe was left chiefly in Dutch, French and English hands, the Dutch here as everywhere carrying the larger share. Having broken into the grain trade, the Dutch stayed to seize a great part of the 'rich' trades also, accompanying their commerce by acts of violence as efficient as they were ruthless. They demonstrated that ships built for Mediterranean conditions could no longer compete, even in the Mediterranean, with Atlantic shipping of better design and far cheaper construction. They had reached Syria by 1597; in 1598 they had been granted by Henry IV the right to trade under the French flag to Turkish ports. Their trade was fully legitimized in 1612, when they secured their own capitulations with the Turk.

The expansion of Dutch trade in the Mediterranean coincided with an even more spectacular irruption into the Indian Ocean. Houtman sailed in 1595 and the East India Company was incorporated in 1602. In the next twenty or thirty years the Dutch gained control of the principal spice-growing islands of Indonesia and diverted the greater part of the spice trade to the Cape route. The result was a division of eastern trade into two sections. Dutch and English traders went to the Far East for spices, calicoes and muslins. They went to the Levant to buy silks, sweet wines, currants and carpets. Both trades were profitable; in England in the early seventeenth century the Levant Company's trade was thought by many to be more advantageous than that of the (English) East India Company, because Turkey was a market for cloth, tin and weapons, whereas far eastern goods had to be paid for in cash. The Venetians, on the

[1] See tables in Braudel, *La Méditerranée et le Monde Méditerranéen*, 499.

other hand, found their supplies of far eastern goods, through Aleppo, cut off or greatly increased in price; and their trade in near eastern products faced with fierce and increasing competition. Venetian shipping long continued to carry a considerable volume of trade between the Adriatic, the Aegean and the Levant; but the accumulated wealth, and ultimately the naval strength, of Venice was sapped by the long wars with Spain and Turkey, and its trading position was greatly weakened by the loss of Crete to the Turks in 1669. Gradually, almost imperceptibly, the Adriatic became a somnolent backwater.

The ports of the Tyrrhenian Sea profited by the change in the direction of trade and the influx of northern shipping. The number of ships entering Leghorn, in particular, grew astonishingly in the early seventeenth century.[1] Genoa despite its relative decline in shipbuilding and ship-owning, retained its importance as a harbour and business centre, with a prosperous and industrious hinterland. There was a steady growth in coast-wise trade with southern French ports, largely in ships owned and built at Marseilles. Marseilles flourished increasingly as a small-craft harbour—Colbert made it, indeed, a subject of reproach—especially after 1681, when the Languedoc canal was opened to traffic. This canal, the most ambitious of the many inland waterways undertaken in the seventeenth century, provided the French with a route of their own between the Atlantic and the Mediterranean, but a route passable only by comparatively small ships.

The sea-going ships which entered the Mediterranean through the Straits in the seventeenth century, though smaller than the big Italian merchantmen, were large by northern standards. Vogel[2] estimated that in 1670 the Dutch were employing about 200 ships in the trade, the average size being about 180 *last* or 360 tons. The reason for this high tonnage figure was the need for defence. Piracy and frequent war made the Mediterranean a dangerous sea for unarmed merchantmen, and the goods carried were valuable enough, in proportion to their bulk, to pay for crews large enough to defend them. The Dutch, who specialized in unarmed, light, but capacious merchantmen, had to renounce some of the excellences and economies used in the northern area of trade. The English, who habitually built ships more heavily timbered and more extravagant in man-power, competed much more successfully in the Mediterranean than in the Baltic. Their Mediterranean trade in the seventeenth century was much smaller than that of the Dutch, but it increased steadily, especially at the end of the century, and was in-

---

[1] F. Braudel and R. Romano, *Navires et merchandises à l'entrée du port de Livourne, 1547–1611* (Paris, 1951).

[2] 'Zur Grosse der Europäischen Handelsflotten in 15, 16 and 17 Jahrhundert', *Forschungen und Versuche zur Geschichte des Mittelalters und der Neuzeit*, 319.

creasingly supported by naval force, by treaties with the Barbary rulers and later by the establishment of bases. It was this combination which eventually, in the eighteenth century, produced that unlikely paradox, an English Mediterranean.

# IV. *The Ocean Trades*

The establishment of regular trade by sea between Europe and the rest of the inhabited world was, in the main, a sixteenth-century achievement. Before the last years of the fifteenth century the only habitual users of trans-Oceanic routes had been fishing-fleets operating in Icelandic waters, and a few traders between Spain and Portugal and their respective Atlantic island possessions. By the end of the sixteenth century, oceanic voyages, if not commonplace—for they were always hazardous—were frequent. European merchant ships were carrying goods regularly across the Atlantic and the Indian Ocean, even in small quantities across the Pacific; and many of the distant harbours to which they plied were under European control.

The two main oceanic trades, from Lisbon to India and from Seville to the West Indies, had much in common. Both were governed as to course and sailing dates by characteristic and fairly predictable wind systems. Both were monopolies in law—one public, the other private, neither complete in practice. Both monopolies became, in the seventeenth century, the objects of repeated and largely successful attack by other maritime people who were able to develop greater naval strength, more flexible trading methods, and cheaper and more efficient means of transport.

The Portuguese secured fortified bases and a place in eastern commerce in the first two decades of the sixteenth century by the use of naval force; and naval power, particularly the superiority of European shipborne artillery, enabled them to protect their trade against the attacks of oriental competitors. Goa, their Asian capital, was a naval base of considerable strength. It is an exaggeration, however, to speak of Portuguese 'domination' of eastern trade routes. They dominated the sea route from Europe to India, because for a hundred years they had no competitors; but in Asian waters they soon accepted the position of one among many groups of traders. They preyed on Muslim shipping in time of war, and from their strategic bases at Hormuz and Malacca they levied duties on it in time of peace; but Arab dhows, as we have seen, continued to cross the Indian Ocean, Chinese and Malay shipping to ply in the China and Java Seas. Portuguese merchants sometimes shipped goods in Chinese junks, and vice versa. The commercial successes of the Portuguese were due not so much to naval strength—formidable though their ships were by eastern standards—as to the great diversity and geographical range of their activities. From the point of view of the 'grocer king', the Portuguese organization in the East had but one main function: the regular shipment to Lisbon of oriental spices, chiefly pepper, but also cinnamon from Ceylon, nutmeg from Celebes, camphor from Borneo and—most valuable of all—cloves from the Moluccas and the Banda Islands. To pay for these cargoes, however, a whole network of ancillary trades had to be developed, since Portugal had little of its own to offer, and little trading capital.

The basis of this local commerce was the export trade in cotton textiles from the ports of Gujerat and Coromandel. These textiles found a ready sale in Indonesia, where they were exchanged for spices, and in East Africa where they were bartered for gold and ivory. The populations of all these regions provided as profitable a market for Indian piece-goods in those days as they did for the products of the looms of Manchester and Osaka in more modern times. Equally profitable to the Portuguese was the acute demand in Japan for Chinese manufactured goods. Direct commerce between the two empires had been permanently forbidden by the Ming Emperor about 1480, because of the depredations of Japanese *Wako* pirates along the China coast. Smuggling no doubt went on; but in official trade the Portuguese, as intermediaries, held an important advantage. Although the annual Macao carracks had a shorter history than their more famous contemporaries, the Manila galleons—sixty years as against two hundred—they were no less profitable. Many of them were built in India of Malabar teak. They must have been efficiently run, for in sixty years there is only one record of ship-wreck, and that in a typhoon. Sailing from Goa by way of Malacca, they carried assorted European goods to the Portuguese settlement at Macao, where they loaded silk goods, raw silk, and porcelain purchased in Canton. These were sold in Nagasaki, the returns being made, as a rule, in silver bullion. Since the value of silver was higher in China than in Japan, a further profit could be made by exchanging silver for gold on return to Macao. The practice of sending one very large ship to Japan each year was abandoned in 1618, because of the danger of Dutch attack, but larger numbers of smaller and faster ships continued in the trade down to 1639. Silks were carried also from Macao to Macassar— a source of spices—and to Manila, where they were sold for Mexican silver. There were many other local trades: the sandalwood trade, for instance, between the China coast and the Lesser Sunda Islands; the slave trade, whether in African negroes or in Chinese and Japanese *muitsai*; the import to India of horses from Mesopotamia and copper rom Arabia; the export from India to China and Japan of hawks, pea-cocks, and even an occasional caged tiger. The Portuguese were the first world-wide traders. For over 200 years Portuguese was the *lingua franca* of Asiatic maritime trade. Pidgin English was derived from Pidgin Portuguese.

The 'country trade' was far more extensive and probably far more profitable than the trade of the royal fleets which it helped to finance. Ironically these fleets, connecting Goa with Lisbon, formed the weakest link in the chain of empire. Their weaknesses—so pitifully revealed in that chronicle of disaster, the *História trágico-marítima*—can be grouped under three heads: the inherent difficulties of the route; the defects of the ships; and the weakness of the system of manning and command.

The Portuguese pioneers, lacking detailed geographical knowledge, had established their chief oriental base on the first coast they came to, the Malabar Coast of India, which notoriously is deficient in sheltered habours. Most of their other bases were on the ancient routes of Arab trade, on the north shores of the Indian Ocean. Their successors rarely entered the southern hemisphere, except to round the Cape or to visit Timor or the Moluccas. In sailing to the China Sea and the Spice Islands they followed the northern route long used by Malay shipping, through the sheltered waters of the Malacca Strait. Goa was both the economic and administrative centre of their organization, and the terminus of the fleets. As at all the Malabar ports, the sailing traffic of Goa was governed by the alternation of south-west and north-east monsoons. For three months every winter ships could not, without difficulty, approach Goa harbour, and for three months every summer they could not leave it. Malacca and Hormuz, the most important subsidiary bases, were cut off from Goa for long periods every year; the seasons during which spices could be brought to Goa for trans-shipment were restricted; and the sailing dates of the royal Indies fleets were fixed within narrow limits. They left Lisbon in March for an estimated arrival at Goa in September; they sailed from Goa in January or February for the direct run to the Cape, or in December for the longer but safer passage through the Mozambique channel, in order to reach Lisbon in August or September. Failure to sail on time meant delays of many months, and might mean disaster on the way. The route had its dangers at all times: frequent heavy weather off the Cape, and corsairs off St Helena, the Cape Verde Islands and the Azores, especially after the union with Spain, when Portuguese shipping became fair game for Spain's enemies. Victualling stations—Brazil, Luanda, Mozambique outward bound, St Helena or Luanda or the Azores homeward—were many weeks apart, so that the dangers of scurvy and typhoid were added to the perils of the sea and the violence of the enemy.

The fleets which made these hazardous passages were small, rarely more than five or six sail, sometimes only one or two; but the ships which composed them were very large. The *Madre de Deos*, taken by Burroughs in 1592, was rated by Hakluyt at 1,600 tons, and she was by no means the only colossus in the trade. They were carracks of Mediterranean type, built for maximum cargo capacity rather than for fighting or sea-keeping qualities. Portuguese shipyards, in Portugal and in India, could and did build reliable intermediate types, which were used in other trades, and were recommended for the Indies by a succession of experienced commanders, notably João Pereira Corte-Real; but the carracks remained in use, and between 1550 and 1650 their size steadily increased. A small fleet of very large ships was cheaper to build than the equivalent tonnage in smaller ships—a major consideration in Portugal, where timber was scarce and construction costs high. In theory, also, such a fleet was more economical to man and operate, on a regular fixed run with predictable cargoes. In practice, the *naós da Carreira da India* grew too large for safety, without any corresponding improvement in construction or design.

Safety was sacrificed to commercial profit in other ways. The anxiety of officials and merchants to get the fleets away on time with a maximum cargo led to scamped maintenance work and careless, hasty stowage. Worn-out ships were sent back to sea, and ships were habitually overloaded, partly because of the practice of granting permission for private ventures to officers and men, instead of paying wages. This, of course, was not confined to Portuguese ships. The Dutch and the English worked their ships to death, and overloaded them, for the same reasons. In the *Carreira da India*, however, ships were more readily sent to sea in an unsafe condition, because of lack of professional knowledge in those responsible for major decisions. The Portuguese never, in the sixteenth and seventeenth centuries, adapted their medieval social structure to the needs of sea-going command. Portuguese navigators and sailing-masters were among the best in the world—so shrewd a judge as Sir Richard Hawkins had only admiration for them;[1] but they were usually men of humble origin, and in the ships of the royal India fleets they served under noblemen whose training was military rather than nautical. Many captains and admirals acquired considerable experience of sea-going command, but they were not professional sailors. Almost every account in the *História trágico-marítima* reveals divided counsels among the officers, lack of professional *esprit-de-corps* in the ships' companies, and serious lack of discipline at moments of crisis.

The incidence of shipwreck rose steadily with the increase in the size of the ships. The incidence of capture rose more erratically, depending

[1] Richard Hawkins, *Observations*, ed. J. A. Williamson (London, 1933), 57–8.

on political circumstances. The heaviest losses, from all causes combined, occurred in the four years 1620–3, when of thirty-four ships sailing from Lisbon or Goa, eight were wrecked, two captured, and nine forced to return to harbour. Exact overall figures are unobtainable; but between 1550 and 1650 the total number of losses was not less than 100 and may have exceeded 125. Very approximately, the proportion of sailings which ended in disaster was one in eight during the first half of the sixteenth century, one in five between 1550 and 1650.[1] The most careful observers of the trade in the late sixteenth century, the Portuguese chronicler Couto and the Dutch interloper Linschoten, agree in pointing out the implications of these mounting losses.

The Portuguese, as might be expected, had difficulty in manning their Indies fleets, and took seamen where they could get them— Lascars, Scandinavians, Englishmen, Dutchmen. The Dutch were well informed on Portuguese shipping routes in the East, therefore, not only as distributors of spices and providers of shipbuilding capital in Europe, not only through writings such as Linschotens' *Itinerario*, but also through the personal experience of sailors. The groups of Dutch adventurers who began voyages to the East on their own account in 1595, and who in 1602 coalesced in the Dutch East India Company, made a deliberate and radical departure from Portuguese practice by leaving India on their flank and establishing direct contact with the Indonesian sources of spices. It was a fixed principle of Dutch commercial policy to go behind the middleman where possible; and prudence initially suggested that fleets whose purpose was declared to be peaceful trade should keep well clear of Goa and Malacca. The Dutch, therefore, from an early date used the alternative entrance to the Java Sea, through the Sunda Strait, which lies south of the monsoon latitudes and in the belt of the south-east trade winds, and is difficult of access for a sailing ship approaching from the west or north-west but readily accessible at all times of year to ships coming from the south. In sailing from the Cape to the Sunda Strait they soon discovered the cardinal principle of navigation in the southern Indian Ocean—that of 'running the easting down' before westerly gales in the thirties and forties of south latitude, before shaping north to catch the trade wind for Java or India; a principle which held until the last days of sail. Such a course had its dangers. It demanded seaworthy ships; and in a time when chronometers were unknown and longitude was computed by dead-reckoning and guess-work, a ship might drive too far east. The west coast of Australia, though in lesser degree, became in time a graveyard for Dutch Indiamen, as the shore of Natal was for the Portuguese.

[1] See H. Quirino da Fonseca, *Os Portugueses no mar* (Lisbon, 1926), 724–32, and M. de Faria e Sousa, *Asia portuguesa* (Oporto, 1945), III, 525–60.

The southerly course also posed trading problems. Ships sailing directly from the Cape to the East Indies, unsupported by a network of local trade, unless they were to export large quantities of bullion, must offer goods of European origin acceptable in the Indonesian market. The Dutch, with industrial towns at their back-door in Europe, solved this problem by carrying cargoes of German manufactures—helmets, armour, fire-arms, linen, velvet, glass, and a range of ingenious toys compendiously called *norembergerie*.

In the five years 1598–1602 fifty-one ships left the Netherlands for the East. With the exception of one fleet of nine sail (which attempted the western route by way of Magellan's Strait, and by a series of misfortunes became an almost total loss) all these expeditions were successful as navigational experiments, and most were moderately profitable —one very profitable—as trading ventures. The fleet commanded by Jacob van Neck in 1598–9 reached the Moluccas, loaded spices, and returned to its home port in fourteen months—a remarkable turnround. The United Company, in the first four years of its existence, sent out some fifty ships, all armed for fighting, and although several were destroyed or severely damaged by enemy action, only two were lost in other ways. Like the Portuguese, the Dutch grew more careless as time went on; but the ships which they employed were better suited to their tasks, and more efficiently and economically operated, than Portuguese carracks. The Dutch extended to the East the policy of operating large numbers of medium-sized ships, which had served them well in Europe. As the seventeenth century progressed, the Dutch built bigger Indiamen, but the increase in size was kept well within the bounds of operating efficiency. In 1670, according to Vogel,[1] about a hundred ships were regularly employed between the Netherlands and the East Indies, mostly of about 600 tons—much the largest class of merchant ships in Dutch possession, but still smaller than the sluggish Leviathans of the *Carreira da India* fifty years earlier.

From its foundation the Dutch Company possessed greater resources in money and ships than were commanded by the Portuguese Crown or the English Company; and in 1619 that far-sighted seaman, Jan Pieterszoon Coen, established at Batavia a fortified base to windward of Goa and Malacca, which gave the Dutch fleets a permanent strategic initiative. He and his successors used their advantage deliberately to eliminate buyers' competition and to establish as nearly as possible a monopoly. They sought first to capture the 'country trade' from the Portuguese by means of the forcible seizure of their factories, and to stop, by blockade or capture, the long-haul trade between Portugal and India; then, to exclude other traders, European or Asian,

[1] *Op cit.*, p. 319.

from the most remunerative trades of the archipelago; and finally to reduce to vassalage the petty rulers of the chief spice-producing areas, in order to control production and prices in the Dutch interest. What the Dutch left, the English snapped up. Of the chief Portuguese fortresses, Hormuz was taken by Shah Abbas, with the help of an English fleet, in 1623. The trade which it controlled was already drying up, and the place soon became a mere village. Malacca, after many attacks and counter-attacks and eleven years of blockade, was taken by the Dutch in 1641, and similarly left to decay. The trade which it had handled went to Batavia. The Portuguese ports in Ceylon and South India were taken, to be used as ports of call by the Dutch. Goa was never captured, but a Dutch fleet blockaded it for eight successive winters from 1637 to 1645, the monsoon maintaining a natural blockade in summer. The export trade of Goa was largely diverted to other ports under Dutch and English control, and never recovered. The chief native centres of Indonesian trade, Atjeh, Macassar, and others, suffered a like fate, their rulers undertaking after defeat to restrict their seafaring subjects to trade in rice and similar necessities, except with the Company's permission. English traders, the strongest European competitors, were driven from most of their stations in the Archipelago in the 1620's; and most of the chief spice-producing islands—Amboyna, Ternate, the Banda Islands—were brought under direct Dutch control, either by outright conquest or by foreclosure on trading debts.

In speaking of the Dutch, as of the Portuguese, too much should not be made of the word 'monopoly'. The Dutch East India Company, by controlling the producing areas, established a virtual monopoly of the trade to Europe in spices, and later in coffee, which it introduced from Arabia into Java at the end of the century. Conversely, it monopolized the sale of European goods in Indonesia. This long-haul trade, however, was only part of its activities. Elsewhere in the Indian Ocean and throughout the East it traded in competition with Chinese, Malays, Arabs—all skilled traders by sea—and with other Europeans. Even in the Java Sea a large volume of native shipping persisted, tolerated, indeed encouraged, by the Dutch so long as it respected the Company's monopoly of certain commodities. Elsewhere Dutch business acumen and shipping efficiency were widely, though by no means universally, successful against trade rivals. Dutch traders supplemented Portuguese and Arabs in southern Persia, supplying cloth and firearms, diverting considerable quantities of silk and carpets to Batavia for trans-shipment to Europe. By their control of harbours in Ceylon, they got the greater part of the foreign trade of the Kandy Kingdom into their hands. They took over the Portuguese trade to Formosa, and handled the small amount of trade permitted, after 1639, to Europeans in Japan. On the other hand, they made little headway on the China coast. The Portuguese at Macao continued to trade with India, with Europe and with Manila, but the Chinese authorities would allow no other Europeans in the Canton River. In India the Dutch shared the field not only with the remnants of Portuguese trade at Goa, but with the English and later the French. The Dutch exported piece goods from Pulicat and other places on the Coromandel coast to Indonesia, but never came near to a monopoly of export.

The true heir of the Portuguese in India was the English East India Company. The English discovered, as the Portuguese had done in China, that their best defence against Dutch competition was the protection of a powerful prince. They obtained trading privileges at Surat by making themselves navally useful to the Mughal emperor. In 1643, by agreement with the king of Golconda, they secured and fortified their first territorial possession, Madras. Bombay came with Catherine of Braganza's dowry, and Calcutta was founded on the mud of the Ganges delta in 1690. From these ports the Company shipped cottons, muslins, indigo, and saltpetre to England, paying for them—since in the seventeenth century it had very little 'country trade'—chiefly in cash. Towards the end of the century the Company began tentatively to reach out towards China. At first it made its purchases of tea from Chinese merchants at Bantam or the Malay ports. Its first cargo to be shipped directly from China was loaded at Amoy in 1689; but many years were to elapse before the English Company could succeed where the Dutch had failed, and finance a China trade by exports from India.

With these qualifications, the naval aggressiveness and commercial enterprise of the Dutch in the early seventeenth century worked a major revolution in the trade system of the Indian Ocean and its adjacent waters. A great volume of trade deserted the northern half of the ocean for the southern. The Red Sea and the Persian Gulf became commercial backwaters. Their ports, and those of East Africa, cut off from the valuable products of the Far East, subsisted largely on a local trade in slaves and dates. Their decline was accelerated by the depredations of the sultan of Muscat, who after the eviction of the Portuguese from Hormuz and Muscat itself, had become the principal naval power on that coast. The only harbour immune from his rapacity was the Dutch trading post at Bandar Abbas. Similarly, the Malacca Strait lost much of its former importance and for a time was almost deserted by European shipping. Trade between south-east Asia and Europe went from Batavia to the Cape, south of the Equator all the way. In 1652 the Dutch colony at the Cape was established for the convenience of this trade. Even trade with India followed, as far as possible, a southerly route. By mid-century, Indian Ocean trade had become fixed in routes it was to follow for more than two hundred years. The square sail had triumphed over the lateen, the trade wind over the monsoon.

The transatlantic trade between Spain and Spanish America in the sixteenth century employed far more shipping and moved far more goods than the trade from Portugal to India—paradoxically, since the one served the needs of, at most, a few hundred thousand Spanish settlers, *mestizos* and Hispanicized Indians, while the other connected western Europe directly with the great populations of the East. But precisely because it was a colonial society, Spanish America, much more than the highly developed societies of the East, was the economic complement of Europe. The settlers imported from Spain the goods they needed to maintain their Spanish mode of life in an American environment. They developed, to pay for these imports, a ranching, planting and mining economy, producing goods for sale in Europe. For their plantations they required slaves, and so created a market for a whole new trade with West Africa. Finally, in the middle of the century they stumbled upon the richest silver mines in the world, which enabled them to pay for still more imports, and which nourished trade with the East by supplying the specie needed for the purchase of eastern products.

The trade to Spanish America was in law a close monopoly, confined —with certain limited exceptions—to the port of Seville, and participation in it was restricted to the merchants of that city, organized from 1543 in their *consulado* or merchant guild. The early voyages to the Indies had started from Andalusian ports, and Andalusian capital was early attracted to the trade. Seville, the chief city of Andalusia, was the most highly developed port of Castille; was, indeed, the only major harbour in Castillian territory. Seville had already a flourishing trade with the Canary Islands, of which the Indies trade seemed a natural extension. By taking his final departure from the Canaries, the transatlantic navigator could not only top up his fuel and water at a point well to the west of Spain; he could make his passage in the north-east trade belt, which gave him his best chance of a favourable wind. This important, if inadvertent, discovery had been one of Columbus' main achievements on his first voyage. Seville, moreover, was the most convenient port of shipment for the goods which new-world settlers most needed. The American trade in the first half of the sixteenth century was principally a bulky trade in articles of daily use, in tools and pottery, above all in foodstuffs, the wine, oil and wheat-flour which European taste in America continued to demand. These were mostly the local produce of Andalusia. Most of the ships, too, were local vessels of the caravel type used for coasting voyages, and were astonishingly small, rarely more than 200 tons, usually much less. A royal order of 1522 fixed the minimum for the Indies run at 80 tons. Ships of this size, however, in the right latitude and at the right season, could and can make the crossing with perfect safety, and in the early days, when a ship in the West Indies might have to go 'tramping' to a number of small settlements, small size was an advantage. The Seville monopoly at that time was no hardship. Other Spanish ports showed no particular desire to participate. By mid-century, the monopoly was firmly established and changing circumstances failed to break it.

The great silver discoveries of the 1540's produced a revolutionary change in the transatlantic trade. The European population of the Indies mounted rapidly, and its purchasing power increased more rapidly still. The demand for Andalusian wine and oil persisted, but outward cargoes included a larger and larger proportion of more valuable manufactured goods—clothing, weapons, household utensils, glass, paper, books—which were not products of Andalusia, nor even necessarily of Spain. Return cargoes, in addition to hides and sugar, included large and increasing quantities of silver bullion, and also sundry luxury goods of American origin such as cochineal and tobacco, the use of which was spreading in Spain. The average annual tonnage sailing from Seville increased from less than 10,000 tons in the 1540's to over 20,000 in the 1580's, representing perhaps one-tenth of the total shipping capacity of Spain. The peak year was 1608, with 45,000 tons; but this was exceptional. The number of ships clearing from Seville varied greatly from year to year, but the annual average, decade by decade, remained fairly steady, about 60 or 65, from 1550 to 1610. The size of the ships in the trade, however, increased steadily, dictated by the needs of self-defence as well as by the interest of exporting merchants. The Spaniards never went to such extremes as the Portuguese in this respect, because the Seville river was a geographical as well as a legal bottle-neck, and the bar at San Lúcar imposed limits on the draught of ships entering. Various legislative attempts were made to keep tonnages down, partly for that reason. The maximum tonnage permitted was never officially higher than 550. The minimum lawful tonnage, though it also went up by stages, was not raised to 200 until 1609. The average tonnage of ships actually sailing to the Indies was about 240 in the 1550's, about 265 in the 1580's, about 400 at the turn of the century.[1] Many small ships remained in the trade, including ships from the Canaries, which were allowed to sail to the Indies, and which carried much of the less lucrative trade in agricultural products to the smaller settlements. On the other hand, the fleets in the late sixteenth century included an in-

---

[1] Usher, 'Spanish ships and shipping in the sixteenth and seventeenth centuries', *Facts and factors in Economic History*, 206–9. H. and P. Chaunu, *Séville at l'Atlantique*, Paris, 1655–6, I, 146, VI, tables 13 and 149. See note on ships' tonnage, below, p. 218.

creasing number of ships of over 600 tons, and in the seventeenth century vessels of over 1,000 tons occasionally crossed the Atlantic.

The construction of marine monsters was not in the Atlantic tradition. The shipwrights of the Atlantic ports of Spain, like those of Portugal, were especially skilled in the design of light caravels—the only true Iberian type of sea-going vessel. Faced with a demand for very large ships, they turned to Mediterranean models. Neither the commercial *naos* nor the fighting *galeones* of the Indies fleets, wherever built—in Andalusia, in Biscay, or in the Indies themselves—showed much advance in lines or in economy of handling upon the corresponding types evolved, say, by the Bressan family in Venice in the first half of the sixteenth century. Adequate for fair-weather sailing in the Mediterranean, these large, unhandy, overloaded ships were dangerous in the Atlantic, especially in the open harbours which the Indies fleets had to use. Among the most serious disasters were those of 1563—seven ships driven ashore at Nombre de Dios, fifteen wrecked in Cadiz harbour, five lost in the Gulf of Campeche; 1587—six ships grounded and broken up on the bar at San Lúcar; 1590—fifteen ships driven ashore by a 'norther' in Vera Cruz harbour; 1591—sixteen ships wrecked at Terceira; 1601—fourteen at Vera Cruz, again by a 'norther'; 1614—seven wrecked on Cape Catoche. The frequency of groundings in familiar harbours provides a significant comment on the handling qualities of the ships. Not all these lost ships were large, it is true, nor were all Spanish; for ship-owners in the Indies trade often employed foreign-built ships, Flemish, Dutch or Portuguese, when they could get round the law. Nevertheless, the evidence is overwhelming that in Spanish, as in Portuguese shipbuilding, size outran design.

Increase in the size of merchant ships was not an adequate answer to piracy and privateering when the attackers carried artillery. Convoys were first organized during the war with France which broke out in 1542. From the 1560's most shipping for the Indies sailed in convoy. A fleet for New Spain was supposed to leave San Lúcar every May, and usually entered Caribbean waters by the Mona Passage. Once inside the Caribbean, ships for Honduras and the Greater Antilles parted company; the main body passed south of Hispaniola and Cuba, through the Yucatán channel, across the Gulf to Vera Cruz. The Isthmus fleet left San Lúcar in August, and set a slightly more southerly course, passing through the Windward Islands. Some ships put into small ports on the Main, but the main body anchored off Nombre de Dios (later Puerto Bello) where it unloaded goods for Peru and loaded silver. It then retired to the fortified and sheltered harbour of Cartagena. Both fleets normally wintered in the Indies. The Isthmus fleet began its return voyage in January, steering north-west—usually a comfortable reach with the wind on the starboard beam—until it could round Cape San Antonio and put into Havana. Meanwhile the Mexico *flota* in February made its tedious three- or four-week beat against the trade wind from Vera Cruz, for a *rendez-vous* at Havana in March. Havana guarded the only convenient exit from the Gulf of Mexico for sailing ships. The fleets refitted and victualled there, and endeavoured to sail in company for Spain in the early summer in order to get clear of tropical waters before the hurricane season. Delays and failures to make *rendez-vous*, however, were frequent. The fleets beat out through the Florida channel—a tedious and dangerous stretch—and then stood to the north until they could pick up a westerly wind for the transatlantic crossing.

Each convoy was escorted by armed galleons, from two to eight in number according to the international situation and the shipping available. These warships also carried trade goods, often on the private account of the captains-general and their staffs; on one occasion a flagship was reported to be so heavily loaded that her lower gun-ports were under water. On the whole, however, the convoy system served its purpose. Reasonably regular sailings were maintained for a century and a half, during which Spain was frequently at war with powerful maritime states. Stragglers from the convoys were often captured, but only three times during that period were whole fleets intercepted and defeated, once by the English and twice by the Dutch. The main objection to the system was its expense. The cost of the escorts was met by a heavy additional duty on the goods carried. The unavoidable delays of convoy made the economical use of shipping impossible. The predatory activities of naval officers and fiscal functionaries intensified what a recent French writer aptly calls a 'psychosis of fraud', and added still further to the costs. High transport costs, restrictive regulations, chronic shortage of shipping, and the general failure of Spanish industry to expand in the later sixteenth century, together made it impossible to meet, from Spanish sources, the mounting demand for goods in Spanish America.

The trade of Portuguese America suffered less from over-regulation. In the first half of the sixteenth century the small settlements on the Brazilian coast had served merely for watering the India fleets and for victualling slavers with cassava bread; and later, a trade conducted through many small ports, scattered along 2,000 miles of coast, defied regulation. Sugar, in keen demand in Europe, was the object of this trade. In the late sixteenth century and the first half of the seventeenth, Brazil supplied most of the sugar consumed in Europe, and imported considerable quantities of manufactured goods, not only for the use of the 50,000 or so Portuguese planters and settlers, but also for illicit re-export to Spanish America. Goods were shipped from the southern ports of Brazil up the Río de la Plata, and carried by mules across the uplands of

Tucumán to Potosí and even to Cuzco and Lima, where, not having paid Spanish customs or convoy duty, they competed with lawful imports *via* the Isthmus. These goods consisted chiefly of cloth and hardware which—since Portugal had little industry—came originally from northern Europe; and slaves.

The slave trade formed a commercial link between the Spanish and Portuguese empires long before the union of the Crowns. The Portuguese were the only Europeans in the sixteenth century who possessed barracoons in West Africa and maintained regular contacts with the slave-dealing rulers. Portuguese slavers not only supplied the Brazilian plantations; they were also, unofficially before 1580 and openly thereafter, purveyors of slaves to the sugar planters of the Spanish Caribbean, to the mines of New Spain, and by way of Buenos Aires, to the mines of Potosí. Since slavers, with their perishable cargoes, could not be expected to wait for convoys, they were licensed to sail directly from Lisbon to Spanish America; and many of them went a step further, and sailed directly, unlicensed, from Guinea. The temptation to evade duties by smuggling other, denser goods was obvious. Hence the strict regulations stating the number of slaves to be carried: approximately one slave per ton of shipping. The figure was not a maximum imposed for reasons of health or humanity, but a minimum, to ensure that the ships were filled with slaves and carried nothing else. None of the regulations or *asientos* made by the Spanish Crown, however, succeeded either in checking smuggling or—because of the shortage of shipping—in ensuring an adequate supply of slaves. The opportunity was seized by foreign traders, already active in lawful trade to Madeira and the Canaries. The English were the first to extend their Atlantic voyages to the Guinea coast, trading for slaves, whom they smuggled, along with cloth and other manufactures, into the Caribbean settlements in return for sugar, hides and silver. Planters welcomed the trade, and local officials connived at it. The four voyages of Sir John Hawkins in the 1560's were only the earliest and most notorious of many.

The Dutch intrusion into American trade began later than the English, but was on a much larger scale. Dutch traders began to appear off Brazil, trading cloth for sugar, about 1587, and their share in the trade increased steadily. They began to visit the harbours of the Greater Antilles about 1595. In 1608 their hide trade from Cuba and Hispaniola was said to employ twenty 200-ton ships. The first Dutch slaver recorded in the West Indies appeared off Trinidad in 1606. The commodity which first attracted Dutch shipping in force to the Caribbean, however, was salt. From about 1598 Dutch salt traders, unable to secure this vital preservative in Portugal, began to exploit the immense deposits round the lagoon at Araya, near Cumaná in Venezuela. An astonishingly large volume of shipping quickly concentrated on that desolate place, despite losses inflicted from time to time by Spanish warships. According to the Spanish governor, from 1600 to 1606 his province was visited every year by about 120 foreign ships, most of which were Dutch salt carriers of an average capacity of some 300 tons.[1] This was a total annual tonnage comparable with that of the combined official fleets from Seville to Mexico and Puerto Bello. Besides the salt ships, some general traders, Dutch and a few English, came to Cumaná bringing cloth and hardware, taking Venezuelan tobacco and Margarita pearls. Many of these vessels carried letters of marque, and were prepared, when they could, to take goods by force if the owners refused to trade. The salt belonged to nobody and was never paid for; though transatlantic transport for so bulky a commodity must have been extremely costly. In 1609, with the Truce, the old Setúbal trade was resumed and the special reason for the Araya voyages disappeared. Dutch smugglers and traders continued to operate in Brazil and in the Caribbean, however, and when hostilities were resumed, the States General prepared to back their trade in American waters, as in the Indian Ocean, with powerful naval armaments.

The Dutch West India Company was chartered in 1621. For the next twenty-seven years it pursued a course of plunder and conquest, as well as competitive trade. As a result, the official shipping between Seville and the Indies shrank by 1640 to less than 10,000 tons annually, and continued to shrink throughout the rest of the century. With more efficient shipping, Dutch traders stepped in as carriers for Spain and Portugal in the New World, as they already were in the Old, and Amsterdam became a market for logwood, cochineal and cacao, for Peruvian silver and Brazilian gold, as it was for eastern silk and pepper. As a base for the greater convenience of their trade with the Spanish Main, the Dutch in 1634 seized the island of Curaçao, which also possessed valuable salt pans. They conquered, at least temporarily, a long stretch of the northeast coast of Brazil, from which they exported sugar and braziletto, and to which they imported slaves from factories in West Africa, seized from the Portuguese.

The victories of the Dutch in the Caribbean had far-reaching indirect results. They provided a naval screen, behind which other northern Europeans, English, French and Scots, built up new colonies of settlement in a long string down the Atlantic coast from Newfoundland to Barbados. These new colonies called new trades into being, by importing manufactures and producing exportable staples. The Dutch themselves settled New Amsterdam, which became the centre of a lucrative trade

---

[1] E. Sluiter, 'Dutch-Spanish rivalry in the Caribbean area, 1594–1609', *Hispanic American Historical Review*, vol. 28 (1948), 179.

in beaver fur. The furs were brought in canoes from the Lakes region down the Hudson by Iroquois middle-men, and were shipped to Europe, chiefly for use in the hat industry. New Amsterdam also developed a flourishing entrepôt trade between the other North American colonies and the Caribbean. Other important sources of furs were the French settlements on the St Lawrence and, towards the end of the century, the English trading posts established by the Hudson's Bay Company on the southern shores of Hudson's Bay. Further south, Virginia in the 1620's became the principal English source of tobacco. The English and French settlements in the Lesser Antilles also tried tobacco, but without much success. About the middle of the century, however, they began to produce sugar for export. Dutch traders, knowing that every successful new settlement meant a new demand for shipping, first introduced cane from Brazil and instructed the planters in its cultivation and use. They supplied the rollers, coppers and other equipment needed for manufacture, on credit against the future crop; and a little later they supplied slaves from West Africa for the field operations. Within a few decades the island settlements had changed from struggling communities of small farmers to groups of prosperous planters employing slave labour and exporting sugar. The colonies of Surinam, Essequibo and Demarara, which the Dutch retained after their expulsion from Brazil, were developed in much the same way. The New England colonies, devoted mainly to small-scale mixed farming, had no staple product for export to Europe. Their timber cost too much to transport, their fish could not compete with the Dutch catch (though some New England fish went to Portugal and Madeira in return for wine). As the sugar colonies grew in wealth, however, the New Englanders learned to pay for their imports of European manufactures by trading in their own small ships to the West Indies, selling grain, beef, horses, barrel staves and salt fish, returning with rum or molasses from which rum could be made, and sugar, much of which was re-exported to Europe. The Dutch island of St Eustatius became a useful entrepôt in this trade.

In the steady expansion of transatlantic and inter-American trade, the Dutch were at first the principal carriers. Their predominance, however, was not unchallenged. The Portuguese, in a remarkable burst of naval and commercial vigour, succeeded in recovering not only their Brazilian territory, but a great part of its trade, together with the indispensable slaving stations in Angola; an ample compensation for their losses in the East. From 1663, English shippers also re-asserted themselves in the slave trade. It is true that the Royal African Company was constantly in financial difficulties; but these were due less to Dutch competition than to the fact that the Company was undercut in its own markets by English interlopers and cheated, as all the great monopolists were, by its own agents. Slavers required large crews, so that in the slave trade the Dutch genius for economy in manning was a less important advantage than in many other trades. The total volume of English merchant shipping increased enormously between 1660 and 1730, in contrast with periods of relative stagnation between and after. Rough estimates are: 90,000 tons in 1663, 178,000 in 1688, 261,222 in 1701.[1] This rapid increase was partly achieved by the purchase of foreign ships; in the 1680's between a quarter and a third of the English merchant marine was admitted to be Dutch built.[2] A good part of the increase, nevertheless, was of English construction. The increase was heavily concentrated in the coasting trade and in the trade to the American colonies. Between 1660 and 1690 the English succeeded very largely in monopolizing the trade to their own colonies, with some ships left over for smuggling to Spanish America.

The Acts of Trade were considerably more effective in America than in Europe. Some of the clauses of the Navigation Acts were even welcomed by powerful interests in the colonies, because of the protection which they gave to colonial shipping and ship-building. Naval force was freely used to seize Dutch ships in colonial harbours; and a series of calculated aggressions favoured the purpose of the Acts. The capture of Jamaica provided the English with a convenient base, from which they could compete with the Dutch in smuggling trade with Spanish America. Conversely, the annexation of New Amsterdam in 1664 robbed the Dutch of a base for illicit trade. By the Treaty of Breda in 1667 the Dutch accepted the English seizure of Cape Coast Castle and abandoned their claim, long violently upheld, of a monopoly of trade on the Slave Coast.

In 1690, of a total of about 178,000 tons of English merchant shipping, about 28,000 tons were employed in the American trades;[3] rather less than one-sixth. The Dutch employed a much smaller proportion of their merchant fleet in these trades: according to Vogel[4] about 40,000 tons out of a total of 568,000 or rather more than one-fourteenth. The English ships, including colonial-built sloops, were more numerous than the Dutch, but most of them were much smaller. Their average capacity was only some 120 tons, as against a Dutch average of 250 to 400;

[1] A. P. Usher, 'The growth of English shipping 1572–1922', *Quarterly Journal of Economics*, XLII (1927–8), 467.

[2] V. Barbour, 'Dutch and English merchant shipping in the seventeenth century', *Economic History Review*, II (1930), 2.

[3] Usher, *op. cit.*, p. 467. G. L. Beer, *The Old Colonial System* (New York, 1912), Pt. I, vol. I, 43.

[4] 'Zur Grosse der Europäischen Handelsflotten in 15, 16 and 17 Jahrhundert', *Forschungen und Versuche zur Geschichte des Mittelalters und der Neuzeit*, 319.

but this difference was tending to disappear, as a result both of English purchase of Dutch vessels, and of English improvement in the construction of moderately large merchantmen. The whole trade of the Americas, however, was expanding so rapidly at the end of the seventeenth century that a considerable increase in English and French shipping was possible without any corresponding decrease in Dutch. The absolute superiority of the Dutch, though less in this trade than in most branches of seaborne commerce, nevertheless lasted into the eighteenth century.

For all regular commercial purposes the Pacific was inaccessible to Atlantic shipping throughout the sixteenth and seventeenth centuries. The passage of Magellan's Strait was prohibitively slow and dangerous; the doubling of Cape Horn, in the teeth of the prevailing westerly gales, normally impossible for ships not fitted with fore-and-aft sails. The discoverers of Peru had coasted south from Panama, and trade followed the same route. Goods from Europe were unloaded from the galleons at Nombre de Dios or Puerto Bello, and sold to Peruvian merchants. They were lightered up the Chagres to its headwaters, and thence packed by mule-train to Panama; loaded into ships built and owned on the Pacific coast; landed at Callao and other Peruvian and Chilean harbours; and then, if they were destined for inland towns such as Cuzco or Potosí, packed again over high and difficult mountain passes. There was, as we have seen, another route, via Buenos Aires, up the Río de la Plata into the heart of South America, and by mule train across Tucumán to Potosí. This back-door trade involved fewer trans-shipments and, being illicit, paid no duties; but it never became the main channel of supply, for good reasons. Official prohibition of the Río de la Plata trade was a minor reason; more important was the poverty of the immediate hinterland of Buenos Aires; most important of all, the difference in distance. In those days of small ships and slow passages, sheer distance mattered much more, portages and trans-shipments mattered much less, than they do to-day, in all except very bulky trades. The trade in oriental goods via Cairo or Aleppo survived by a hundred years or more the opening of the all-sea route to India. Similarly, trade via Panama, manufactured goods one way, silver the other, held its own against the competition of the peruleiros; and those shrewd interlopers, the Dutch, found it worth while to smuggle goods in at Puerto Bello.

Another reason for the survival of the Isthmus trade was that it could draw upon the services of shipping engaged in coasting trade between the two viceroyalties. Both Mexico and Peru produced silver; it was their chief value in Spanish estimation. But Peru produced much more silver than Mexico, and in the sixteenth century produced little else, other than its bare subsistence needs. Civil wars, Indian revolts, and the difficulties of the terrain combined to prevent the interpenetration of Indian and European ways and the acquisition of European crafts by Indian artisans. The *conquistadores* in Peru remained a small Spanish community with a good deal of specie at their disposal and an avid desire for consumers' goods. In Mexico, on the other hand, Spanish and Indian communities quickly began to mingle and to fuse. Mexico was industrious and productive, and was short of specie, because of the efficiency of *quinto* collection and the large private remittances made to Spain. From the 1530's it became profitable to import goods of Spanish origin from Mexico to Peru, to supplement the costly trickle of supplies across the Isthmus. With these trans-shipments went a much larger volume of Mexican products; mules, sugar, preserved fruit; European-type wares made in New Spain by Spanish or Indian craftsmen; and an interesting assortment of Indian wares—polished obsidian mirrors, lacquered gourds, feather-work tapestry, and the like. The return cargoes were almost entirely silver, except for a period in the 1560's and 1570's when large shipments of mercury from the Huancavelica mine were sent to Mexico. The ships in the trade, or at least their hulls, were built at Huatulco and other small ports on the Pacific coast of Nicaragua, a region which produced not only timber but *pita* and *cabuya* fibre from which rope and even sails could be made. Discarded sails and rigging from the *flotas*, and all necessary iron fittings, were also imported from Vera Cruz. In the second half of the sixteenth century a ship-building industry also developed at Guayaquil. Some of the ships were as large as 200 or 250 tons, and as many as a dozen might make the Mexico–Peru voyage in a year.[1] Though built in Central America, most of the ships were owned in Peru, whence came the capital to build them. From Callao they were sent tramping to Panama when the galleons were at Puerto Bello, at other times to Mexico, or anywhere that a profitable cargo could be had.

The greatest profits of the coasters, however, were in connection with the trans-Pacific trade. The 1564 expedition to the Philippines was planned at a time when the Portuguese spice trade was in great difficulties, and when a new route to the Far East offered even more attractions than usual. The project of opening a spice trade by way of the Philippines and Mexico was quickly dropped in face of the immediate and jealous reaction of the Portuguese in the East, but Legazpi himself suggested the alternative of a trade in silk, which could be bought readily from Chinese junks which frequented the islands. Over the next thirty years the jealousy of the Portuguese changed to a willing naval and com-

---

[1] W. W. Borah, *Early Colonial trade and navigation between Mexico and Peru (Ibero Americana* no 38) (Berkeley, 1954), 67, 116 ff.

mercial co-operation. The Spanish settlement at Manila became a principal market for the merchants of Macao, who, in defiance of prohibitions, sold Canton silk for American silver, and soon controlled a large part of the business of the Philippines. When, in the seventeenth century, the Portuguese lost their access to Japan, and when the Dutch closed the Malacca Strait against them, the Manila trade helped to save Macao from commercial extinction.

The trans-Pacific trade established direct contact between a society in which silver bullion was in high demand, and one in which it was plentiful and cheap. The Spaniards were able, therefore, to buy silk in Manila at prices which justified an appallingly long and hazardous voyage between two very hot and unhealthy places. Acapulco, the Mexican terminus, was the best harbour on the Pacific coast; but like Vera Cruz and Puerto Bello, it was only occupied when the galleons were in; for the rest of the year its population moved to higher and healthier ground. From Acapulco to Manila was a trade-wind run of some eight or ten weeks. As in the Atlantic, the return passage was the dangerous one. After leaving Manila the ships spent some two months struggling north-eastward, in a region of normally light and variable winds but subject to frequent typhoons. This was the worst region of shipwreck. In the thirties or forties of north latitude, the latitudes of Japan, a westerly wind could usually be found which would take the ships to the coast of California and thence south-east to Acapulco. The whole return voyage took from four to seven months, and on the longer passages hunger, thirst and scurvy could reduce a ship to a floating cemetery. The ships used in the trade were mostly built in the Philippines, of local teak, by European designers and eastern craftsmen. They had the reputation of being the strongest and most durable ships in the world. Their size was limited by legislation in 1593 to 300 tons, and their number to two sailing in any one year, in a characteristic attempt to keep the export of bullion within bounds. The number was, in fact rarely exceeded, and often not attained; but the ships were often much larger than 300 tons. Their size was governed by the requirements of the trade at the time of building.

The best years of the trade were the last decades of the sixteenth century and the first decades of the seventeenth. During these years a considerable part of the silk landed at Acapulco was packed across Mexico and re-exported from Vera Cruz to Spain; so insistent was the European demand for silk, and so inadequate the supply from all sources. Still larger quantities were trans-shipped from Acapulco to Peru, since the Pacific wind system prevented direct passage from the Philippines to Peru. In the peak year, 1597, the amount of bullion sent from Acapulco to Manila—most of which came from Peru—reached the enormous total of 12,000,000 *pesos*; a figure approaching the total value of the official transatlantic trade.[1] This was very exceptional, however. In the last decade of the sixteenth century the annual export of bullion was usually between 3,000,000 and 5,000,000 *pesos*, of which perhaps two-thirds came from Peru. Trade soon declined from these high levels. Silk brought to Europe by so long and complex a route could not compete indefinitely with the increasing quantity, both Persian and Chinese, imported into Europe by the Dutch. After 1640 shipments of silk from Mexico to Spain ceased altogether. As for the trade to Peru, it had always been disliked in official circles in Spain, because it diverted Peruvian silver to New Spain and thence into the specie-hungry Orient, and because it flooded Peru with Chinese goods and spoiled the market for textiles from Spain. From 1631 trade between the viceroyalties was prohibited in an attempt to isolate Mexico, to control the leak of silver, and to reserve at least the Peruvian market for Spaniards. No doubt smuggling went on; but trade *via* the Isthmus remained the principal channel of Peruvian imports. The silver production of Peru declined sharply in the middle decades of the seventeenth century, and this alone might well have reduced the purchase of silk. The trans-Pacific trade shrank to the volume which Mexico alone could absorb.

The Manila galleons continued their hazardous but always profitable sailings to the end of the eighteenth century. The Spaniards in the Philippines, relying entirely for their contact with Spain on this tenuous line of communication, held out against all enemies, European or Asian, throughout the seventeenth century. Manila remained all this time the meeting ground, halfway round the world, of the heirs of Columbus and Vasco da Gama; a triumph of maritime communication in defiance of probability.

# V. *The Means of Transport*

Throughout the sixteenth and seventeenth centuries the total volume of European shipping steadily increased. The rate of increase was slow in countries bordering the two inland seas—Mediterranean shipping may not have increased at all—much faster on the Atlantic coasts, fastest of all, especially in the seventeenth century, in countries bordering the North Sea, particularly the United Netherlands. The volume of Dutch shipping increased nearly ten-fold in 200 years. In 1670 the volume of Dutch-owned shipping—some 568,000 tons—considerably exceeded that of Spanish, Portuguese, French, English, Scottish and German combined; and the preponderance of Dutch-built shipping was even

[1] Borah, *op. cit.*, p. 123. C. H. Haring, *Trade and navigation between Spain and the Indies* (Cambridge, Mass., 1918), 169.

greater. It is true that at that date the remarkable late seventeenth-century increase in English shipping was already under way; but even at the end of the century the volume of English-owned shipping was still only one-third to one-half that of Dutch-owned, and probably more than a quarter of English-owned ships were Dutch-built.

Many circumstances contributed to this extraordinary predominance, but two characteristics of Dutch ships call for particular comment here: cheap construction and specialized design. All contemporary observers remarked on the skill of Dutch shipwrights, their economy in the use of materials, their willingness, for example, to use fir instead of the more expensive oak, whenever the less durable material would serve. Equally important was the use of labour-saving devices in the shipyards: winches, cranes for handling heavy spars, wind-driven saw-mills, and so on. These economies were among the advantages of large-scale standardized production. To them were added the advantages of large-scale purchasing materials, and cheap transport of these materials in Dutch ships. The cost of construction in Dutch shipyards was commonly reckoned to be 40 or 50 per cent lower than in English in the middle years of the seventeenth century.[1]

Dutch ships were not only cheaper, but also, for their particular purposes, better. Throughout the later sixteenth century and the whole of the seventeenth the Dutch were the leaders of Europe in the design of merchant ships. The story was one of steady development rather than of revolutionary inventions. No revolution occurred in the rig of ships, comparable with the marriage of square and lateen sails in the fifteenth century which had produced the Iberian square-rigged caravel. Highly inventive in the rig of small craft, the Dutch were relatively conservative in rigging ocean-going ships. The three-masted ship, square rigged on fore and main with lateen mizzen, was more or less standard throughout the period; the bonaventure mizzen was quite extinct by 1640, and two-masted ships were rare, at least in northern Europe. For most merchant ships a simple five- or six-sail plan sufficed. Striking topmasts, with fids and caps, began to appear in Dutch ships about 1570; but many merchant ships throughout the period had no fore-topsail. Jibs and stay-sails—great labour savers, conferring some measure of mobility in contrary winds—did not begin to oust the old and clumsy spritsail until the very end of the seventeenth century.

The most striking innovations in our period were in hull design. Dutch shipwrights addressed themselves systematically to the problem of increasing the carrying capacity of the ship, reducing her operating costs—which meant principally her crew—in relation to her dimensions,

[1] Barbour, 'Dutch and English merchant shipping in the seventeenth century', *Economic History Review*, II (1930), 249.

without undue loss of sailing qualities. They developed vessels with much greater length but less depth, in proportion to their beam, than was usual in other countries; with a very full section and almost flat bottom; with a high proportion of keel length to length overall—that is, with much reduced overhang fore and aft; with bluff bows and a full round tuck to the stern instead of the massive transom usual elsewhere. Such were the *fluyts* which began to appear in the last decades of the sixteenth century, which were launched in great numbers when the Twelve Years Truce gave some respite from attacks of the Dunkirkers, and which throughout most of the seventeenth century dominated the trade of northern Europe. They had a length from four to six times their beam.[1] To minimize longitudinal weakness, their superstructures fore and aft were reduced to the barest necessities of cabin accommodation. *Fluyts* were, indeed, little more than floating holds. Their masts were stepped well apart to allow room for a capacious main hatch. Their rigging was simple, working through winches or tackles as far as possible in order to save labour. Most important of all, for keeping down crew and operating costs, they carried few or no guns. With ships of this type, the Dutch were able, in peace time, to offer freight rates 30 to 50 per cent lower than their English competitors. There is no evidence that wages were lower than in English ships (though interest and insurance rates usually were). The difference was chiefly due to cheaper and more economical ships, to shrewd business sense, to experience and care in handling, stowage and delivery of cargoes.

The *fluyt* represented a major advance in the design of merchant shipping. It is true that it was not widely imitated outside the Netherlands, because English, French, Scandinavian, even Spanish traders found it cheaper and more satisfactory to buy Dutch-built *fluyts*, either from Dutch owners or from the Dunkirk prize market, than to commission imitations from their own shipyards. Nevertheless the success of the type and the great economies which it represented necessarily influenced ideas on merchant-ship design all over Europe. The general proportions of the *fluyt* became the standard for cargo carriers down to the introduction of iron hulls. It revealed the advantages, in most trades, of the medium-sized merchant ship between, say, 200 and 500 tons over both the flimsy caravels and the ponderous carracks of southern Europe. Warships grew steadily in size and power; but the very large merchant ship fell rapidly from favour. From the middle of the seventeenth century to the middle of the nineteenth a wooden merchant ship of over 700 tons was something of a rarity.

---

[1] B. Hagedorn, *Die Entwicklung der wichtigsten Schiffstypen bis ins 19 Jahrhundert* (Berlin, 1914), 102 ff. For comparisons see tables in Usher, 'The Growth of English Shipping 1572–1922', *Quarterly Journal of Economics*, XLII (1927–8), 467.

The introduction of the *fluyt* marked the first clear distinction between the functions of the warship and those of the merchant packet. This specialization of function could not, it is true, be carried through in all trades. In the dangerous conditions of Mediterranean trade, for example, the *fluyt* was as out of place as a Thames barge, and there, as in the Indian Ocean, the Dutch used somewhat larger heavily-timbered armed ships, resembling small men-of-war, which contemporaries often called *pinasse*, pinnaces—somewhat misleadingly, as these stout vessels had nothing in common with the little *pataches* of Spain and Portugal.[1] The Dutch *pinnass* had, relatively, a deeper draught than a *fluyt*, but much the same proportion of beam to length. As we have seen, it was in the more dangerous but more profitable long-haul trades that rivals such as the English, using similar ships, offered the most serious competition. The English, far more conservative than the Dutch, maintained their liking for armed merchantmen much longer; but in the second half of the seventeenth century the armed merchantman, at least in northern Europe and the Atlantic, was becoming an economic anachronism. The Dutch perceived the distinction clearly and accepted it boldly, with its corollary, the provision of convoy in time of war.

Specialization went much further than the mere distinction between freighting and fighting. The *fluyt* was never a fixed type; its proportions varied according to the trade in which it was to be employed. The *noortsvaerder* in the Bergen timber trade could stand two or three more feet of draught than the *oostvaerder* which had to cross the bars of the Baltic rivers to load grain. Timber-carrying called for special modifications. Long spars in the early seventeenth century were loaded into the hold through the rudder-port; but later in the century it became the custom, for the sake of water-tightness, to carry the head of the rudder well up into the counter, so that the tiller was entirely inside the ship. The rudder-port then became small and vertical instead of wide and horizontal, and special loading-ports had to be cut in the sterns of timber-carriers. Whalers also needed special adaptations, particularly the bracing of their stumpy masts to bear the heavy tackles by which carcasses were handled. In the sugar trade ships required a high deck-head allowing room for a double tier of hogsheads, or alternatively for temporary additional decks for carrying slaves. All these specialized types, however, had in common simplicity, buoyancy and avoidance of waste space; the characteristics to which their commercial success was largely due.

In navigation, as in ship design, the sixteenth and seventeenth centuries were a period of steady development rather than of revolutionary innovation. The essential instrument, the compass, was improved early in the sixteenth century by being slung in gimbals; and knowledge

[1] Hagedorn, *op. cit.*, 115.

of magnetic variation was steadily enlarged by sixteenth-century explorers. In the sixteenth century, also, a method was devised of measuring speed—formerly a matter of experience or guesswork—by means of chip-log, knotted line and sand-glass, thus greatly improving the accuracy of dead-reckoning. A ship's position at sea was determined by a combination of dead-reckoning and observed latitude. The basic methods of calculating latitude, from Pole-Star altitude, or from solar altitude using declination tables, had both been worked out in the fifteenth century and continued in use unchanged, except that in the sixteenth century improved instruments were devised for measuring altitudes: the cross-staff, and for solar observations its refinement the back-staff. The tremendous advances in knowledge of mathematics and astronomy in the later seventeenth century affected practical navigation very slowly, and methods of finding a true observed position, including longitude, had to await the introduction of the chronometer and the sextant in the eighteenth century. On the other hand, the construction of mariners' charts advanced steadily throughout our period. In the second half of the sixteenth century the old type of portolan coasting chart began to be replaced, for purposes of ocean navigation, by projected charts, suitable for plotting dead-reckoning and observed positions, and showing parallels and meridians as straight lines. Mercator published his planisphere, embodying the first maps on 'Mercator's projection', in 1568. The projection was much improved for working purposes by Edward Wright in 1590, and was in fairly general use among up-to-date navigators by about 1630. Just as Lisbon in the sixteenth century had replaced Venice, so in the seventeenth century Amsterdam replaced Lisbon as the principal centre for publication of charts, atlases and navigation manuals. The average seventeenth-century skipper, however, was no book-navigator. Generally speaking, the steady improvement in the safety of navigation and the confidence of navigators owed more to widening experience and personal knowledge of the seas than to scientific innovation.

No sharp distinction divided salt-water sailing from inland navigation. Many passages, especially in the coasting trades, included both, and even ocean-going ships, especially in Holland, finished their voyages gliding between fields of growing crops by river or canal. Mention has already been made of the immense importance of river navigation. In Holland, a land built up through the centuries by piles and polders, dikes and dams, artificial waterways were of at least equal importance. To a lesser extent the same was true of Flanders and some parts of north Italy. The lock—the key to successful canal construction—was known in these areas before the end of the fifteenth century. Elsewhere, navigable canals were rare, except for a few open cuts, such as the Foss Dyke in England, which had remained more or less usable since Roman times. In the seventeenth century, however, a veritable mania for canal-digging developed in western Europe, particularly in France. The Canal de Briare, connecting the Loire at Briare with the Loing at Montargis, was begun by Sully in 1605 and completed in 1640—not indeed, by the state, but by a company to whom it had been granted. The canal from St Omer to Calais was constructed by Colbert's order as part of his scheme of internal reconstruction. The still more famous Languedoc Canal has already been mentioned. This great work was a pioneer undertaking in large-scale canal construction in western Europe. It has 119 locks in 148 miles, rises to above 620 feet above sea level, and is 6½ feet deep. In the seventeenth century, however, it proved difficult to maintain. Its navigation was always confined to relatively small vessels and was often obstructed altogether by silting. In Prussia, the Frederick William Canal, named after the Great Elector, was opened in 1669. In England, the draining of the East Anglian fens required a system of cuts which could be used by barges and which enabled the port of King's Lynn to draw wool and wheat from eight counties.

Inland waterways were used by a bewildering variety of local craft. Witsen[1] lists for Holland alone thirty-nine types of river and canal boats. It was in devising craft which could manoeuvre in narrow channels, yet face the pounding of coastal seas, that Dutch shipwrights acquired the experience which they applied so successfully to deep-water ships. The round tuck and the flat bottom of the *fluyt* betrayed its barge ancestry. Nowhere did the Dutch display greater versatility and originality than in the rig of their barges and other small craft. The sprit-mainsail, used in river barges to this day; the balance-lug, admirable for drifters and fishing boats generally; the jib and the gaff-mainsail, both introduced into sea-going ships with great effect in the eighteenth century—these were all sixteenth- or seventeenth-century Dutch inventions, first employed in inland and coastal craft. All tended to the same ends—manoeuvrability in confined channels, better performance on a wind, economy of crew.

Skill in designing small craft was not, indeed, confined to the Dutch. Long after Mediterranean trade had been captured by Atlantic shipping, many Mediterranean ports retained their characteristic and often very efficient local types. Such were the *tartanes* of Marseilles—an elegant compromise between lateen tradition and fore-and-aft innovation—and the *navicelli*, the beautiful fine-lined river boats of the Arno, the use of which Dummer advocated for English rivers.[2] The English had their

[1] N. Witsen, *Aeloude en Hedendaegsche Scheeps-Bouw en Bestier* (Amsterdam, 1671), 165, 169–71.
[2] 'Dummer's voyage into Mediterranean Seas', 1685. *King's MSS.* 40, 142–3 ff.

own types also. The Thames barge was an imitation from the Dutch; but the Severn trow was, and is, 'mere English'. All over Europe such stout, serviceable, highly individual local craft distributed bulky goods and supplemented the work of larger sea-going and coasting ships.

Inland waterways had one serious disadvantage: the ease with which riparian land-owners could obstruct traffic, whether by fish-weirs and other physical obstacles, or by the exaction of tolls. The attempts of seventeenth-century governments to remove or reduce these hindrances to trade, particularly weirs, had little lasting success. A particular water route might be made so expensive that traffic—except for very heavy or bulky goods which could be moved economically only by water— would take to a parallel land route as a cheaper alternative. Land transport was more flexible. Except in towns, and on a few trunk routes which had been maintained in more or less serviceable condition since Roman times, a road was not so much a prepared and engineered way, as a right of passage from place to place. If road traffic found itself obstructed by bad going or unduly heavy tolls, it would find a way round the obstacle, as river or canal traffic obviously could not do. Land and water transport, therefore, competed in many parts of Europe throughout our period, and both expanded steadily. Traffic shifted from one to the other, as variations in time of year, weather conditions and toll exactions, affected the costs.

Harness changed little in our period. The three most essential devices of heavy horse traction—nailed shoes, rigid shoulder collars, and a method of harnessing beasts to a waggon in file—all date from the tenth or eleventh centuries and were in general use throughout western Europe well before the sixteenth. On the other hand, in the design of carts and waggons, as in that of boats and barges, sixteenth- and seventeenth-century Europe displayed great inventiveness. Three important improvements first made their appearance in Germany at the end of the sixteenth century: the 'fifth wheel' or turning-front carriage; the suspension of the body by leather straps, a rudimentary form of springing; and the protection of the wheels by means of iron tyres contracted on to the rims. These devices first appeared in passenger carriages, which were beginning to be built and used by great men in the late sixteenth century. The carriage in which Henry IV was assassinated had none of them; Louis XIV's state coach had all three improvements. A great increase took place, in the first half of the seventeenth century, in the number of passenger vehicles, both private carriages—whose use both Louis XIII and Louis XIV tried unsuccessfully to discourage—and public coaches. Dechuyes[1] gives for 1647 a list of forty-three towns

[1] *La guide de Paris, contenant le nom et l'addresse de toutes les rues de ladite ville et faubourgs avec leurs tenans et aboutissans etc. etc.* par le sieur Dechuyes, Lionnais, Paris, 1647.

throughout France, for which coaches left Paris at regular intervals varying from every day to once a week. Stage waggons had had an earlier beginning. The number of waggons in use increased steadily throughout our period, and in the late seventeenth century their efficiency increased also, as iron tyres and the 'fifth wheel' spread from carriages to carts.

The cutting and pounding action of this growing weight of iron-bound wheels caused a serious deterioration of existing roads, such as they were, and called the attention of governments to the necessity of creating an organization to build and maintain roads, instead of leaving traffic either to beat its own paths or to use the ruined and broken remnants of the Roman roads. These roads, in any case, were uncovered and usable only in Italy and in a few places in southern France and Spain. In northern Europe most of them had long been broken up by frost, overgrown, or buried. The Roman road along the left bank of the Rhine, for example, lies under more than ten feet of riverine mud at Mainz. Medieval road builders had never followed the Roman method of laying down thick, solid cemented causeways of stone, designed for the use of marching men rather than of heavy waggons. Roman roads were wasteful of material and labour, and peculiarly vulnerable to frost. The late mediaeval road was more plastic and more suitable for wheeled traffic. It consisted either of paving blocks set in a bed of sand, or cobbles rammed into sand or loam. Both these types of road, though cheaper than the Roman types, were still expensive to build and maintain, and few roads were so paved, outside the towns. The first serious attempt in Europe to establish a state organization for the maintenance of roads was made by Sully as Grand Voyeur de France. The office was suppressed in 1626, having achieved little; but the matter was taken up energetically by Colbert, who by exacting *corvée* labour succeeded in surfacing most of the main roads of France with broken stones—a remarkable achievement, but a short-lived one, because most of the roads had no proper foundation and no weather-resisting surface. After Colbert's dismissal his roads were neglected and the stones were in time pushed into the mud by the weight of the traffic. It was not until the late eighteenth century that the virtues of a relatively thin but elastic road surface, formed of graded broken stone, and sealed by sand watered into the crevices, were discovered by English (or rather Scots) engineers; and that heavy rollers enabled road builders to achieve the necessary degree of compaction. Throughout the sixteenth and seventeenth centuries, just as constantly improving types of boats and barges had to ply on neglected, weir-obstructed, toll-impeded waterways, so constantly improving types of beasts and vehicles were held back by unimproved tracks, or at best neglected and often unsuitably constructed roads. The badness of roads and the obstruction of waterways throughout most of Europe reflected the weakness of governments in the mercantilist age. They were among the chief reasons why the development of inland transport, throughout this period, lagged behind the remarkable growth of transport by sea.

## NOTE ON SHIPS' TONNAGE

In the sixteenth century in most European countries the unit used for the computation of freight charges and port dues was presumed to represent the dead-weight capacity of the vessel, if loaded with some standard commodity regularly carried in the area. The commodities most commonly taken as standards were wine, oil, grain, or salt. A ship carrying general merchandise or dry goods would not be loaded to her dead-weight capacity, even if her hold were full; conversely, a cargo of iron might load a ship to her full dead-weight capacity but leave her hold half-empty. Such freight was normally charged in terms of arbitrarily determined units of weight or volume, presumed to represent the space which would be occupied by the standard unit of cargo in grain, wine, oil, or salt. At some ports—at Seville for instance—the authorities kept lists of equivalents for the classes of goods most commonly shipped. Goods were reckoned by bales, by cubic content or by weight, as might seem most convenient. The standard commodity at Seville was wine, and the standard unit the *tonelada* of two pipes. Two pipes held from 35 to 40 cubic feet of liquid; they occupied an average space in hold—allowing for the bilges of the casks and waste space at the ends of the ship—of about 60 cubic feet; and they weighed, with the casks, about 2,300 pounds. In the Bordeaux wine trade the *tonneau* was the weight (or the volume in hold) of four Bordeaux *barriques*, a little less than two Spanish pipes. The Bay salt trade had a unit of its own, the *brouage*, about one-sixth of a ton. In the Baltic grain trade the unit of weight used was the *last*, theoretically the maximum load of a large four-wheeled waggon; it varied from port to port, but was usually between 4,000 and 4,500 pounds. The specific gravity of different types of grain varies considerably, and the presumed volume equivalent in a ship's hold also varied, according to the type of grain locally regarded as standard, from about 120 to nearly 200 cubic feet. Rye was the grain most widely regarded as standard, not only because it was the commonest grain in northern Europe, but also because its specific gravity was such that a ship's dead-weight capacity in rye was usually found to occupy the whole cubic capacity of the hold. The various grain-*lasts* must not be confused with the Dutch herring-*last*, which also varied from port to port, but was most commonly 12 or 14 barrels, amounting to about five-sixths of the average rye-*last*.

The ratings of vessels were usually determined empirically, sometimes by direct experience in loading with particular types of cargo, sometimes by crude calculations from the main dimensions. The need of a rating not dependent upon the sworn statement of the owner led, in the late sixteenth and

early seventeenth centuries, to attempts to formulate general rules for computing the cubic content of the hold. A unit that was originally conceived of as
a direct statement of dead-weight capacity thus became a unit of volume that
was only roughly equivalent. An early example of such a rule was that
issued in England in 1628, to the effect that the King's ships and ships hired by
him should be measured by taking the length of the keel, leaving out the false
post, the greatest breadth within the plank, the depth from that breadth to
the upper edge of the keel, multiplying together and dividing by 100.[1] Other
more elaborate and more accurate rules were suggested in the course of the
seventeenth century, and attempts were made to devise methods of computing the tonnage of loaded ships, whose depth could not be ascertained. The
divisor used was sometimes 100, sometimes 94 or 98; and fierce controversies raged over the question of the most accurate divisor. The general
effect of the adoption of computation rules was to reduce the apparent tonnage
of ships—as governments, the chief charterers, naturally intended—and, in the
case of British ships at least, to bring the capacity ton nearer to the 100 cubic
feet which is now its internationally accepted value. Analogous changes
occurred in the computation of the Spanish *tonelada* and the Dutch *last*.

Among so many different units computed in so many different ways,
precise equivalents are clearly impossible. A number of attempts have been
made to establish rough bases of comparison. Chaunu (*Séville et l'Atlantique*,
I, 125–46), demonstrates the steep increase in the value of the Spanish *tonelada*
in the late sixteenth and early seventeenth centuries, and suggests corrections
for converting the ratings of ships in the Indies trade into terms of modern
capacity tons. Van Driel (*Tonnage Measurement*), described the complexities
of the northern European measures. A more recent general discussion is in Lane,
*Tonnages, medieval and modern*. In the foregoing chapter, tonnages are expressed
as far as possible in capacity tons of 100 cubic feet. The figures are necessarily
only approximate. Much of the story remains obscure. All statements about
the relative capacities of ships of different countries and different periods
must be accepted with caution, unless actual dimensions are known.

[1] S. P. Dom. xxxii, 119–121.

# CHAPTER IV

# European Economic Institutions and the New World; the Chartered Companies

Up to the end of the Middle Ages the world was divided into a number of almost self-contained regions which only made contact through strictly limited channels of trade. It is indeed possible to maintain, as Fritz Rörig has done in a brilliant article, that the medieval world already enjoyed a world-economy, for the spice trade and the silk trade, the voyages of the Norsemen and the explorations of the Arabs, even the wanderings of occasional travellers and missionaries, gave external contacts of varying importance. Nevertheless western Europe, the Near East, India and Indonesia, the Far East, to mention only the great and obvious divisions, each followed its own particular way of life.

Then, from the end of the fifteenth century onwards, contacts were increased and became more and more active, slowly helping to produce a single market for the whole world. Faced with new tasks, the European peoples who bordered on the Atlantic developed and applied new economic techniques. They changed the framework of their economic organization, created new methods of co-operative action and new state departments and above all new merchant companies. They improved their techniques and their methods of using capital, changing their methods by a new organization of property and by a re-introduction of slavery. The states intervened more directly in economic affairs and slowly created modern colonies; their methods, in general terms, became accepted as *Mercantilism* and eventually developed into modern capitalism.

The beginnings of colonization are clearly marked by the dates of the Discoveries. But history knows no absolute innovations, and the activities which carried western European enterprise overseas were inspired by the methods and habits of earlier periods. Even if they did not follow those techniques closely, no clear chronological division separates the new methods from the old. Medieval Italian colonization in the East—the overseas world of those days—and experiments by the English and French in the fourteenth and fifteenth centuries, and by the Portuguese in the fifteenth, set the example for the founders of the new settlements in America and in Asia.

Italian colonies were to be found all along the coast of the eastern Mediterranean. The Genoese had their own privileged quarter in Antioch from the time of the First Crusade, from 1098, even before the capture of Jerusalem. Thereafter the merchants of the various towns formed companies to administer and develop their colonies. In the fourteenth century the Genoese formed a joint-stock company, whose shares soon had their regular price, for the administration and trade of the isle of Chios; another was then formed for Cyprus, and both were still in existence when the great Portuguese colonial movement began. The Italian city-states had transplanted feudal customs for the settlement of their distant territories, where the colonies spread outwards from cities—seigneuries, fiefs, vassalage, and a whole organization based on privileges, both collective and individual. From the sixteenth century onwards the colonial possessions of the many different countries were often based on these same principles.

Agricultural development was guaranteed thanks to slavery, which had always persisted on a domestic basis round the shores of the Mediterranean and which had spread in the Latin kingdoms of the Middle East; and the sugar industry, which was for long years to be the mainstay of several of the new lands, was developed in those overseas territories on the same lines as in the Levant. Sea-borne communication between the home-lands and the colonies, especially the Spanish *flotta*, the treasure-fleet, was organized after the model of the convoys of galleys which Venice had developed since the thirteenth century. Often the overseas possessions of the Italian city-republics were more or less directly ruled by the metropolis; Genoa, for example, had set up an Officium Gazarie and an Officium Romanie (an Officium Corsice too), of which the former administered her colonies on the Black Sea and the second her colonies situated in the Byzantine Empire. Such institutions and habits were taken into the countries which engaged in colonization, directly and by the Italians themselves.

For the Italians played an active part in the process of colonial expansion. Scattered throughout all the countries of western Europe, they stimulated interchanges both of ideas and of goods. In the fifteenth century they took an active part in the voyages of exploration down the coast of Africa, and after the great discoveries were over their role remained of the greatest importance in the Iberian countries, while John Cabot in England and Verrezano in France, with many of their compatriots, suggested to rulers the idea of voyages which proved decisive and of which the Italians undertook command. Later, in 1555, Sebastian Cabot was one of the chief instigators of the English voyages to Muscovy. In these ways Italian schemes were everywhere put before the rulers, the fortune-seekers, and the adventurers of the western world.

All the same, the Italians took only a secondary part in the great movement which was to change the face of the world and to alter the rôle of Europe in that world. Despite constant threats, Venice managed to keep her possessions in the eastern Mediterranean; but until the seventeenth century she remained their prisoner. Genoa had already lost hers before the period of the great discoveries, and her citizens took a notable part in the voyages to the New World. Certainly the Italians remained economically the most powerful group of merchants, and the most widely scattered too, during the fifteenth and sixteenth centuries. But apart from the fact that the Italian ports were to prove badly sited in relation to the new routes, their city-states, strengthened but yet riven by their various traditions, were not large enough to undertake the effort which was necessary to set up durable institutions overseas. The incompetence of the Italians in the movement of European expansion, coming after their activity in the Middle Ages, is one of the features which most clearly marks the break in the steady process of evolution caused by the great discoveries and their consequences. The supersession of Italy, coming at the moment when she ceased to rank as a major market and became the battle-ground of Europe, was a factor which was destined to confirm the shift in the economic balance of Europe.

The nations which now began new careers approached them with unequal chances. The Portuguese already had behind them three-quarters of a century of miscellaneous trading voyages down the African coast. The Spanish monarchy imitated the Portuguese, but also developed its own new institutions. Both these countries, and all other states seeking extra territory overseas, had recourse alike to methods which had not been tried, and to a variety of experiences acquired in the course of long experiments.

The English had a custom of forming privileged groups, the prototypes of the future companies. The Merchants of the Staple had bound in a common discipline all who used the national mart established by their king on the continent—normally at Calais from 1359 until 1558. The Merchant Adventurers had formed a corporation since the middle of the fifteenth century; their headquarters was established in the Low Countries—at Antwerp, with numerous exceptions. They were not to receive their charter until 1564, when they had passed their zenith, but they lasted until the nineteenth century. Numerous other companies were created during the course of the sixteenth century. With some modifications, the English companies for colonization and trade took shape according to patterns which were already in existence.

Yet it was France which, a little before the great discoveries, developed the model which most nearly anticipated the great companies for overseas trade. It was Louis XI, a king who made many innovations, and who was always seeking economy as none of his predecessors had done, who supplied the initiative. Throughout his reign he tried to set up a national company for trade to the Mediterranean, which was the normal region for long-distance trade in his time. He would have given such a company a monopoly of that trade by a charter. After starting a Franco-Genoese company he then set up two such companies, both purely French. He himself supplied them with ships and with capital, and secured for them a footing in the ports of the Mediterranean. But the merchants of France set themselves against the establishment of a monopoly, and brought about the failure of these efforts. From this time onwards French efforts were clearly marked by state intervention and by the grant of a monopoly by the state (and also by the opposition of interested parties).

From all these activities nothing emerged which was precisely appropriate to the needs of the New World. But early experience had foreshadowed the methods which the great enterprise of the merchants and the colonizers of western Europe was to use and to develop.

# I. *The Background for Expansion*

The white races have expanded overseas for about five centuries, but this movement should be divided into two portions. The dividing line corresponds with the Industrial Revolution at the end of the eighteenth century and the beginning of the nineteenth. That revolution was itself closely bound up with the great movement for colonization; it was at least in part set going by the produce from overseas territories and by the markets which they offered. On the other hand, the coincidence of the Industrial Revolution with the intellectual movements of Europe, with political unrest and with its spread in the colonies (especially in America), prepared the way for a breakdown of the status of Europeans in the countries which they had subordinated. The political situation was changed in the colonies at the same time as new methods of production were adopted, based on the nature of modern capitalism. Everywhere colonies became more simply the outposts of their metropolis, and political considerations controlled economic developments more directly.

Here we are concerned with the first period of this expansion when, from the end of the fifteenth century to the end of the eighteenth, five states embarked on major colonial careers—Portugal and Spain, followed by England, Holland and France.[1] The first two employed methods and constitutions which differed from those of the other three. The most typical, and indeed the essential, factors in the colonization of the second group were the chartered companies. Their organization was a necessary link in the chain of institutions which in turn gave birth to modern capitalism and to its network of international relationships; and by their monopolies they prepared the way for the states to take over the colonies and to merge them into empires.

Of the three centuries which composed the first period, the sixteenth century has its own individual characteristics. General European expansion overseas was still extremely slow, partly because an increase in Mediterranean trade and in trade to the Baltic and to Muscovy all helped to slow down the overseas movement. A number of other factors tempered the spirit of enterprise which might have led merchants and adventurers in the direction of the New World; the legal pretensions of some states, derived from their achievements in the first period of the Discoveries; the risks attendant on voyages to 'the Indies', which made them attractive only to the most adventurous or to the most enterprising capitalists.

The very magnitude of the Discoveries upset the first discoverers, the Iberian states. They were not equipped for so immense a task. The initiative for their overseas voyages came largely from their governments; and the governments quickly ensured that they would get most of the profits. In Portugal the development of state-intervention was marked by a whole system of measures which were already customary in that country—by the organization of shipping into convoys, the system of granting away domains and jurisdictions, and then by the Casa das Indias; in Spain the Casa da Contratación marked the same development.

Other countries could only make their first tentative efforts in the sixteenth century. From England Henry VII sent John Cabot to America as early as 1496, a sign of the speed with which Christopher Columbus's voyage had attracted attention. Then for three-quarters of a century no other officially-sponsored expedition left England for America or for Asia. From France, after a subsidy for a voyage by Verrezano in 1524, the first voyage to receive royal support was that of Jacques Cartier to Canada in 1535. A progressive change in government policy, more purposeful from this time forward, doubtless reflected a change in public opinion. If Jacques Cartier and those who surrounded him were already planning the establishment of permanent settlements overseas, François

---

[1] Denmark, Sweden, Kurland, Brandenburg and the Hanseatic towns, even the Emperor, fascinated by the prospects, started movements which were sometimes interesting, but which produced no significant results.

I, jealous of the treasure which made a grandiose policy possible for Spain and Portugal, was already concentrating his thoughts on spices and precious metals. This was to be a matter of prime policy with Henry IV also; but Henry II and then Catherine de Medici dreamed, with Coligny, of the peopling of overseas settlements. The motive forces behind French efforts were a mixture of political and economic factors.

In England the great maritime enterprises were taken up again under Elizabeth. They were bound up with the urge to win wealth by piracy, which had by then become habitual, and with the pressing need for exploration, which was at that time both more natural and more essential than we would normally think. But if the English government was already making plans for the establishment of true colonies overseas, the initiative for the voyages had almost always to come from private citizens and from merchants.

In England, as in France and indeed in all the maritime countries, maritime and overseas activity was associated with plundering the Spanish galleons. This took place with or without the pretext of warfare or of political strife, and it was the origin of many voyages and the object of many merchant companies.

When the great discoveries had been made, all the states which were in the process of formulating their administrations and centralizing their authority hoped to profit from the wealth promised by the New World and to secure thereby some of the riches which had become more than ever necessary for them to fulfil their enlarged civil and military tasks. The overseas expansion of Europe ran on parallel lines to the development of national states; but this development of national states was accompanied by the survival of many old institutions, which often played their part alongside institutions which were created overseas.

Local and municipal authority necessarily declined before the growing authority of the states; but the states were at various stages of development, and faced with a great variety of tasks. Portugal, for example, enjoyed a common system of law from the thirteenth century onwards, and a common system of taxation from the fourteenth. Her economic administration was already advanced and varied; but Spain completed her unification by the capture of Granada only in the very year of Columbus's first voyage, and never developed popular institutions. England and France were more advanced constitutionally than other countries. When the United Provinces, a century behind the other states, joined the colonizing powers (and immediately took the lead over them) they had only just established themselves as an independent state, and organized authority still remained in the hands of the towns and provinces while the Estates General were only an assembly of delegates who could decide nothing without the authority of those whom they represented. The career of the United Provinces as a colonial power was settled by an agreement of Oldenbarneveldt, as Pensionary of Holland, with the Estates General. They produced the constitution of the United East India Company (Vereenigde Oost Indie Compagnie, or V.O.I.C.) which was a fusion of the several companies (the Compagniën van Verre) which had preceded it. When the Scandinavian and Baltic states were dragged into colonial rivalries by their European ambitions they set about strengthening the machinery and the institutions of their governments. In fact, for all the countries of Europe, overseas expansion accompanied a movement for strengthening and reorganizing their internal administration and government.

Yet the old municipal economies exercised a declining influence for many years, as witness the protests of the ports of Spain against the privileges which the king granted to Seville. The habitual opposition to London of the English 'outports' (that is, York, Hull, Newcastle, Exeter, Southampton and Bristol), the peculiarly London stamp which the East India Company bore for many years, the foundation of the rival Plymouth Company and of the Newfoundland Company—these things show how long local forces continued to matter in England. So, in France, did the frequent and sometimes successful protests of the ports of the Channel coast and of the Atlantic seaboard against the privileges which the king granted away; above all against the great privilege that the cities of the interior, such as Lyons, should have their independent chambers within the companies. In direct succession to such municipal influences, the independent Chambers within the Dutch East India Company carried on their local tradition.

Despite the growth in the power of the monarchies and of central governments, feudalism still dominated men's minds and their habits, and the normal relationship between lord and vassal was envisaged by all countries, from the time when Henry VII of England granted a charter to John Cabot up to the time when Louis XIV granted charters to the several companies founded during his reign. In the sixteenth century, from 1533 onwards, the king of Portugal granted hereditary captaincies in Brazil—as he had done even before the great discoveries were made, in Madeira and in the Azores. Two of them prospered, at Pernambuco and at São Vicente.

The chartered companies accepted the feudal suzerainty of their governments; they fulfilled their obligations as vassals, and even in the eighteenth century they themselves granted away fiefs according to the traditional forms. The French occupation of Canada was largely organized according to a seigneurial régime which had scarcely been brought up-to-date at all. Even in the eighteenth century the Compagnie de la

Louisiane can be seen organizing duchies, marquisates, counties and baronies, subject to the king's confirmation. The English did the same in several of their American colonies; Walter Raleigh created fiefs in Virginia, and the two Carolinas were both feudal states. But the Dutch companies furnish the most typical examples of this tendency. The Protestant burgesses, having revolted against the Spanish kings, in the seventeenth century then set up a feudal régime in their American possessions. The *patroons* established by the companies were forced to do homage but were allowed to dispense justice. The English and the Dutch sometimes added to this feudalism a collegiate organization and municipal institutions which themselves had their own firmly established traditions.

The determination of the states to secure profit from the wealth of the New World can be seen everywhere at the time when the princes still effectively represented their states. Manoel, and then Jean III, of Portugal only needed to develop and enlarge the practices of the fifteenth century; Jean III himself announced that he was 'the true spice-merchant of the Indies'. Isabella of Castile put up seven-eighths of the money for the first two voyages of Columbus and reserved the revenues for herself in the same proportion. The two dynasties were to keep a tight hand on the economic development of the whole of their colonial empire. As early as 1496 Henry VII of England had favoured the expedition of John Cabot, and Elizabeth contributed from her private purse not only to Drake's piratical expeditions but also to the formation of the Africa Company (in 1588), from which she was to get a third of the profits. James I, in 1624, and Charles I, in 1628, tried in vain to grasp a share in the profits of the East India Company, and the rival company set up by the second of these princes was expected to pay him for his support. In France, François I promised himself considerable profit in spices or in precious metals from the voyages to America which he encouraged, but Coligny and Catherine de Medici, under Henry II, probably counted mostly on the acquisition of new territory. Henry IV himself arranged with certain Dutchmen for the formation of an East India Company, and granted a royal charter to companies for mining, while of Richelieu it could be written that he was the only French politician of the *ancien régime* who seemed to have grasped the importance of colonies. He formed or encouraged companies whose appearance was certainly important and perhaps decisive—the Compagnie du Morbihan and then that of the Cent Associés, designed for Canada, the Compagnie des Îles d'Amerique for the Antilles, and the Compagnie d'Orient. After Richelieu, Colbert was the real creator of about ten chartered companies which Louis XIV supported, in many cases, with his authority. In particular, Colbert founded the two Compagnies, des Indes Orientales and des Indes Occidentales, both in 1664, and then the Compagnies du Sénégal, de l'Acadie, du Guinée, du Cap Vert, and de la Chine, many of which underwent major changes either during his ministry or at some later date.

But no-one in any of the three great colonizing states, or in any of the states which were to follow their example during the eighteenth century, dreamed of creating a colonial empire. The prime urge among all the protagonists of expansion, whether they were governments or private persons, was essentially to acquire riches from precious metals and from trade. The Dutch, the last to join the great states and the colonizing powers, were the first to imitate the Iberian monarchies. By indirect means, using conventions and alliances with native princes, they gained their positions; they only began to assert a title to territories after 1610, in the time of Jan Pieterszoon Coen, their second governor-general. The French, after making several false starts in the sixteenth century in Canada, in Brazil, in Florida and in Guiana, only began to make permanent settlements again after 1610; in Canada and in Guiana, then after 1630 in the Antilles, then at Madagascar and, at last, in India. The English, after profitless experiments in North America at the end of the sixteenth century, only got a firm hold there at the start of the seventeenth century, and only got a footing in India after 1640.

At the end of the sixteenth century, therefore, the Portuguese and the Spaniards were still the only nations to occupy important overseas territories. The Portuguese were penetrating further and further in central Africa, and into Brazil, where a viceroy had been set up at Bahia; they had scattered their posts along the seashores of the whole world, from Morocco to Macao, and were especially to be found in India and Indonesia. Their possessions in the Indian Ocean were all under the authority of a distant viceroy, whose seat was at Goa. The Spaniards ruled over almost the whole of South America except Brazil, the vast domain of the Portuguese, and had set up two viceroys, at Mexico and at Lima; they were also masters of the Philippines. The English and the French had barely tried to set up any colonial establishments; from the beginning of the sixteenth century onwards a few English had occupied some places on the mainland in Virginia, and Elizabeth had granted a charter in 1597. The French, after several fruitless attempts, had failed to maintain their posts in Brazil, on the north coast of South America, and in Florida; but they were persisting in their efforts in Canada.

The Portuguese and the Spaniards were, moreover, alone in that they had created institutions to regulate the relations between the metropolis and the overseas territories. The contemporary background of their efforts, the political histories of the different states and the parallel development of economic organizations, all explain the different methods which the chief colonizing powers employed. The Iberian powers created institutions of a public character, directly subordinate to the state; the other countries used companies which, in their semi-public organizations, left more of the initiative to private citizens.

## II. *The State Institutions*

From the middle of the fifteenth century onwards the Portuguese monarchy had granted away the monopoly of the trade of the African coast, for certain areas and in certain commodities, to private persons under a variety of titles. Then, first a Casa de Ceuta, then a Casa da Guinea, and then a Casa da Mina was created at Lisbon under the authority of the Vedores da Fazenda, who were the officials who regulated the whole economic life of Portugal as well as the general national life. The last two *casas* were soon united in a single institution which controlled the whole trade of the African coast. When contracts with the Indies were established the king created a Casa das Indias, or da India, while in India a Treasury was established in 1517, to be speedily followed by a complete state system, administering the factories and official warehouses.

For several years after the Discoveries any merchant might freely send his merchandise to the Indies or bring trade from the Indies so long as he paid the customs dues on their return, but from 1450 onwards the rules for currency were modified. In 1506 the state reserved for itself the monopoly of precious metals and spices, especially pepper, cloves, mace and civet. Shipment had to be protected by fleets organized either from royal ships or those of merchants who had accepted the régime which the state imposed, and all expeditions were controlled by the *casa* both on their departure and on their return. Imports were subjected to customs dues according to a varying scale; but the *quinto*, a due of 20 per cent imposed in the early days by Henry the Navigator, became the common scale. This due later became normal in all countries.

Soon a single administrator, the *feitor*, controlled two distinct *casas* within the single establishment, the one the Casa das Indias, the other da Mina and da Guinea; and he had under him three treasurers, of whom one was responsible for the control of spices, a second for the goods bought from the sale of spices, and the third for the Casa da Mina and da Guinea. There were five secretaries—*escrivães*—three for the first and two for the second of the two *casas*.

The *casa* itself was set up near the royal palace, with the result that the kings and governments of Portugal could always see the caravels which supplied their revenue and could easily know their size. Besides the *casa* were set up the naval dockyards where hundreds of workmen carried out their tasks and where the *provedor* had to organize the equipment of the fleets which the *casa* sent out, examine the pilots, the under-pilots, the ships' masters and mates and members of the crews whom he put forward at the nomination of his administrators, and where he had to provide the pilots with the charts which were essential for them to be able to navigate.

The numbers and the subdivisions of this personnel were soon modified. A *provendor* was put over the *feitor*; the treasurers were reduced to two and the secretaries became six, who, with an assessor of weights and a keeper of the books, controlled a small department of about sixty employees, including a chaplain. In fact, the *casa* became more and more an organization for controlling trade with all the Portuguese possessions. But the official rules always allowed the ships' officers and crew, and officers and administrators of the colonies, to ship on their private account, aboard the royal vessels, as much merchandise as sometimes equalled the regular cargoes in value.

During the Spanish occupation of Portugal, in 1591, Philip II set up a Conselho da Fazenda, whose powers were extended to cover the whole economy of the Portuguese kingdom and of its possessions overseas; in 1604 a special organization, the Conselho da India, was set up to deal with the colonies. This split into two sections, of which one dealt with Brazil and Africa, the other with the Indian Ocean. The Conselho da India shared the revenues of the whole Atlantic territories and control of colonial trade with the Conselho da Fazenda, an arrangement which led to many disputes and to many abuses. But the thing which most seriously interfered with government control over relations with over-seas territories was the constant, and always tardy, intervention of the Consejo do Portugal, which sat at Madrid.

After the restoration of its independence in 1640, the genuinely Portuguese institutions remained largely unchanged. The Conselho da India became the Conselho do Impero and administered the whole of the overseas possessions (except for the posts in Morocco, Madeira and the Azores). But the organization of fleets and the enjoyment of royal monopolies for the Indies were granted to the Council of Finances, and for Brazil they were granted to juntas specially created, or to privileged companies. Yet these institutions normally lacked authority, and in the colonies the governors and the local officers controlled the trade and the economy almost at their will. In addition, the Portuguese state seemed to grow more and more incapable of maintaining its monopoly. After 1640 the Portuguese crown was tempted by the success of the Dutch East India Company, at that time firing mens' imaginations, and it created companies which were subordinate to the *casas* in the seventeenth and eighteenth centuries. They achieved but indifferent success, and at the end of the eighteenth century trade between Portugal and her colonies was almost free.

Spain, unable to profit from the experiences of Portugal in the fifteenth century, followed the same methods as her neighbour. The Discoveries carried her headlong into new tasks, with new rights and new responsibilities. The needs of the Spanish state were to dominate her conduct more and more as she became involved in international diplomacy and won for herself preponderance in Europe. The Spanish government hesitated to take control over trade. Aliens were always forbidden to trade in Spain and were only allowed to engage in trade through the medium of Spanish natives. For a certain period the Castilians emigrated freely to America, but already the government reserved to itself one-tenth of the tonnage of the ships of private traders and it set up a Casa de Aduana 'in the Indies'; and from 1501 onwards the Spanish government began to regulate trade. It reserved to itself one-fifth of the precious metals which might be found in the Indies and it granted the monopoly of trade to Seville, the greatest city of Castile and situated pretty well in the centre.

To organize trade, the Spanish government created the Real Audiencia y Casa de Contratación, under a treasurer, a controller and secretary, and a 'factor' whose special duty was to control the shipments of merchandise (the first to hold the office was a Genoese, who had drawn up the blue-print for the *casa*). The institution was intended to be at the same time a court of justice, a trade administration and, a necessary element at that time, an academy of hydrography. The Casa de Contratación kept record of the merchandise exported, the merchandise brought from the colonies and the many and varied details which affected trade with Spain's overseas territories. It soon began to organize convoys, which were made compulsory from 1526 onwards, it chose the captain and the clerk of each ship, arranged the composition of the fleets, and regulated their time of sailing and their route. An identical institution was set up in Hispaniola; a small caucus of royal factors, who were to gain complete power over all trade and who, to maintain a regular correspondence with Seville, was to take under its control all the Spanish possessions and was to get for itself the monopoly of trade, which was in the king's gift; in fact, the offices of these factors were nothing more than customs offices. In 1510 a complicated ordinance about the inspection of the offices, about the registration of merchandise and about the organization and conduct of business, fixed the character of the *casa* for the next two centuries. In 1524 the creation of a Council completed this organization by giving it an appelate jurisdiction.

The royal monopoly was made more flexible in 1512, but it was still maintained and its regulations were revised in 1534, in 1536, and again in 1543. Later, one of the most important tasks of the *casa* became that of organizing the fleets (the *flotas*) and, more and more, that of organizing their defence against pirates and enemies. Seville soon found its monopoly challenged by Cadiz, which was better placed for trade but more exposed to maritime attack. Seville was forced to share her commercial control, but the organization set up at Cadiz always remained subordinate to the *casa* at Seville. The monopoly of the Castilian port was also challenged by other ports which by tradition had their own 'admiralties' and the power to regulate the trade of their merchants; but they were never able to get more than a minor share in trade to the colonies.

The *casa* made great efforts to unite all the overseas territories in a single organization for the purposes of finance and for the securing of precious metals, as well as for defence and the organization of convoys. From 1542 onwards the *casa* was directly subordinated to the Consejo Real y Supremo de las Indias, which had been set up in 1542 and was a committee for legislation, administration and justice, and which really carried on the government of the overseas possessions. The Consejo de las Indias became a complete ministry in itself; it came to occupy an important place in the machinery of Spanish government as an essential element in the Spanish economy.

The importance of its role necessitated a change in the functions and the character of the *casa*. From the second half of the seventeenth century onwards it became a complex bureaucracy whose offices began to be filled by grand personages who were themselves unacquainted with economic affairs. In the first half of the seventeenth century under the government of Olivares the aristocratic character of the *casa* became more marked. Already its administration was failing; its personnel, its state-controlled and oligarchic tendencies, developed within it that passivity and sterility which were to be the signs of the decline of the Spanish empire.

From the end of the thirteenth century several Spanish ports, and some inland towns such as Burgos, had a *consulado* (a Consulatus maris or Consolat do mar, to distinguish it from municipal administration) which served both as a judicial tribunal and as a merchant corporation. From 1525 onwards the merchants of Seville, who traded to the Indies, asked that such a *consulado* should be created for them. They secured in 1543 the creation of the Universidad de los Cargadores a las Indias (distinct from the Universidad de Marcantes in which the shippers of the town were organized). The tribunal of this Universidad de los Cargadores a las Indias, the *consulado*, gave its name to the whole institution. Similar *consulados*, and often similar *universidades*, were established in Mexico at the end of the sixteenth century, at Lima at the beginning of the seventeenth, and in five or six major ports (even at Buenos Aires) in the eighteenth century. The role of these *consulados* was sometimes considerable, especially in Mexico. The *consulado* of Seville, in the meantime, assisted the *casa* in the administration of justice. It was composed of a prior and two consuls chosen by their predecessors, of a judge of the *contratación*, and of thirty merchants chosen by lot. Its role was formally set out in 1556. The *consulado*, as intermediary between the merchants and the administration, was a permanent help to the *casa* in sorting out the details of all the practical affairs under the direction of one of the *casa's* officials. It was housed alongside the *casa*.

From a strictly economic point of view the *consulado* belonged to the ranks of regulated companies; invested with some public duties, it had something in common with the chartered companies. But its completely subordinate character gave it a unique position among the political and economic organizations of the *ancien régime*. Its singularity emphasized a factor which was common in the institutions of the Iberian lands for dealing with their colonies.

The Portuguese and Spanish regimes were the first to be established, the only ones organized during the whole of the sixteenth century, and they always retained characteristics which distinguished them from the institutions which came to be set up by the other states. The *casas* were state departments and were parts of the administrations, which throughout knit them together in organizations which were increasingly coordinated; and they had direct control over trade from their countries to the colonies, they did not delegate any part of their authority. Further, the states reserved to themselves a share of the trade; in both lands the state carefully reserved the trade in precious metals to itself, and in Portugal it reserved normal commercial monopolies. The strict subordination of trade matters to the states gave to these regimes a strongly mercantilist character. But the participation of the *casas* in trading activities indicated neither vigorous evolution nor even progress. Both *casas*, to the extent that they provided capital for overseas development, simply used resources which the state had procured by taxes or by contributions which were scarcely ever voluntary; but they did not use capital which had been permanently invested and which necessitated a return on the capital. So the *casas* had little influence on the formation of colonies or on the formation of groups of producers. On the other hand, their remarkable feat of organization, imperfect though it may have been, made possible the first efforts at expansion on a global scale.

In so far as general development is concerned, the action of the *casas* presents some contradictory features. They put the benefits of overseas production directly at the disposal of their states. But their excessive rules and controls, which were powerless to prevent the many abuses, retarded development both in the parent states and even more so in the colonies. Their almost inevitable incompetence when faced with their vast tasks put a serious check on their usefulness. The piracy of the sixteenth century led naturally to a widespread contraband trade which helped to undermine the desired regularity of trade, and more or less openly acknowledged evasions created large gaps in the closed trade systems which the governments tried to enforce between the mother-countries and their colonies.

The start of the seventeenth century marked a decisive change in European expansion. The French were then still at the stage of sending out exploring expeditions and of military occupation, occasionally making attempts at settlement and colonization, while the English, who had set up several companies with trading privileges, had not yet enlarged them for the needs of the New World. But in a few years new institutions were set up alongside the state-mechanisms of Spain and Portugal. Chartered companies, normally private in origin but occasion-ally state-inspired, set going projects for trade and for colonization which derived directly from the earlier companies for trade but which were to develop into new forms.

England established the first of them in 1600; the East India Company, which had been created by merchants who asked for a royal guarantee of their monopoly of trade. The Vereenigde Oost Indie Compagnie (the V.O.I.C.), founded in Holland in 1602, was the result of the fusion of about ten Pre-Compagnies. It owed its origin entirely to merchant enterprise, but its field of action lay at the heart of the Hispano-Portu-guese empire, and the United Provinces were at war with Philip II. So, for reasons which were as much political as economic, the authorities pressed for a firm constitution for the Dutch Compagnie and then in turn granted it. The Dutch East India Company was reinforced in 1621 by a Dutch West India Company, which played an important part in waging warfare in Brazil and which was even more closely tied to government. Almost from the start, the Dutch East India Company aroused envy and admiration; its prosperity, and the power which it soon won, gave it an unrivalled prestige throughout the seventeenth century.

The examples of the Dutch and of the English re-awoke French ambi-tions, which private initiative had sustained with many scattered ventures for the last three-quarters of a century. Nevertheless, in France the urge to form great companies was markedly governmental. Henry IV was personally responsible for the formation of an East India Company, and he took a part in setting up several other companies, while at the same time he granted out privileges for the colonization of Canada. He achieved no general success, and perhaps Henry IV was still concentrating on the search for spices and for precious metals; perhaps, following the English and the Dutch example, he was seeking general commercial benefits; he certainly was moved as much by political as by economic motives. Later on, Richelieu and Colbert were to incorporate their colonial ventures into a political plan which went much further than a mere conquest of territory.

In all these countries a similar movement was steadily changing the character of their overseas settlements. Economic motives had been always of the greatest importance in starting movements for colonies, and from the economic point of view colonial products were required, more and more explicitly to fit in as complementary to the output of the metropolis, while the states ran their monopolies together into national systems of exclusive trade (*l'exclusif*). From the political point of view, the vicissitudes through which the European states were passing had their repercussions in their overseas possessions, which were reduced to the role of national colonies. But this process, again, followed a very uncertain course. The wars of the reign of Louis XIV, for example, spread out to the colonies, but even during the War of the Spanish Succession the three rival East India companies managed to maintain a kind of neutrality among themselves.

At the end of the seventeenth century the expansion of European countries into other continents was beginning to produce more important and more coherent units. If Portugal had seen her possessions in Asia diminish a little, as by the loss of Ormuz and Malacca, she had extended her occupation of Brazil on the American continent; and in Africa she had confirmed and enlarged her grip on Angola and Mozambique. In the Antilles Spain had only kept possession of a few great islands, but she had vindicated her claim to immense possessions on the American continent and in the Philippines. England had expanded her colonies along the Atlantic coast of North America, had got a footing in Hudson Bay, and had occupied several of the Antilles islands. At the end of the seventeenth century, at a time when both speculative thought and capitalistic enterprise were intensely active, England's colonies were already considered as 'a main branch of England's wealth'. The Dutch, established at the Cape, had secured a series of protectorates which ran from the Persian Gulf to Singapore, and they dominated, more or less directly, the greater part of Indonesia. The French, firmly established in Canada, were thrusting down the Mississippi even as far as Louisiana, and they also had taken possession of some of the Antilles. In Africa they had extended their authority to Senegal and the surrounding country, and in Asia they had already begun to try out a policy of intervention and alliances with Indian princes and had made the beginnings

of an empire which was destined soon to be interrupted. Several
other North European states had embarked on haphazard attempts at
colonization in Africa, in America and in Asia.[1]

Neither the methods of administration nor of economic development
had been changed in the Spanish and Portuguese possessions. They were
essentially practical and empirical, especially where the Portuguese were
concerned. They reacted against systematization and varied from one
colony to another, from one regime and one governor to another.
But from the beginning of the seventeenth century the 'terrae ultra
marinas' were reckoned at Lisbon as 'members of the same kingdom as
Algarve and of the same status as the provinces of Alentejo and Antre
Douro and Minho'. But in the colonies of almost all other European
countries both political organization, in so far as it existed, and above all
economic development were in the hands of the chartered companies,
although the companies' organization was still in the experimental stage.
After the Revolution of 1688, as company development flourished in all
manner of economic activities, England saw a great growth in the number of companies for trade and colonization; they increased in numbers
right up to the time of the South Sea Bubble, in 1719–20. A similar
movement, though less violent, developed in France, connected with
Law and his 'System', from 1717 to 1720. European national wars
spread more actively to the colonies, although neither in their beginnings
nor their endings did they coincide between Europe and the other
continents. In this period England greatly extended her dominions in
America and in Asia, while France lost Canada and India, and in general
terms the metropolitan countries bound their colonies ever closer in a
stricter policy of 'l'exclusif'. Already, in 1719, an English author could
write, 'I take this kingdom and all its plantations to be one great body.'
Colonies were becoming empires, whose subordination, pushed too far,
was to be attacked from the middle of the century onwards. The
companies, overwhelmed by tasks which were too vast and too important, themselves passed more and more into dependance on their states.

But, from the strictly economic point of view, the growth of trade
increased the interchange of hitherto unknown foodstuffs, raw materials,
and manufactures between the different areas of the world and helped
development towards the economic unity of the world. This development was controlled by general circumstances which must be summarized
briefly.

The demographic structure of the countries of Europe was quite
different from that of the nineteenth century. In Portugal the small
number of the inhabitants (1,400,000 in 1527) was an unpromising background for the gigantic tasks which faced her. In Spain, the considerable

[1] Cf. p. 6, n. 1.

emigrations of the middle of the sixteenth century noticeably lessened that country's productive capacity. The Dutch, few in numbers, did nothing which might encourage emigration. In France, emigration took place mostly from Normandy, Brittany, Poitou and Saintonge; even the efforts of Colbert to achieve settlement produced little result. The English, who emigrated in the greatest numbers proportionately to their population, went to North America. Nowhere was emigration dictated, as a necessity, by excess population. Everywhere, even in lands which were almost void of people, the extent of European settlement was very moderate.

So emigration, motivated by forces which had very little power behind them, played only a relatively small part in the general developments of the time. Europe remained essentially an agricultural area, and the vast effort of those who opened up the new sea-routes was, from some points of view, a marginal activity, not a central element in the European economy. The number of those who, in all the different countries, took any active interest in colonial economics, was small, except perhaps in Portugal; and colonial production was regarded as subordinate to that of the metropolis. The interest of the whole of western Europe had been stimulated by the search for precious metals, and it had been kept going by exotic products such as sugar and cotton. The economic development of the New World speeded the formation of our industrial civilization, accelerated the change in our economy, helped its development from a primary to a secondary stage; but until the end of the eighteenth century this movement remained very slow.

This slowness was due in large part to the means of communication. Navigation was still a most difficult art; in 1660-62, and again between 1698 and 1702, two trading voyages from France to China each took almost two years. Similarly, at the beginning of the eighteenth century, it took five week to get from Lisbon to Loanda, five weeks from Loanda to Bahia; and the same missionary took 80 days to get from Bahia to Lisbon in 1708 and 138 days in 1721. Even as late as 1756, the voyage from Portsmouth to Charleston alone took seven weeks. Dangers of all kinds, including piracy (which was common everywhere), ignorance of the routes, the delays and the evasions which were possible, all explain the secrecy in which the voyages were surrounded. Such secrecy was jealously kept, above all in the sixteenth century and even into the seventeenth, and helped to limit knowledge of trade and development, and so to limit their exploitation.

Of equal importance was the vast size of the territories to which most of the chartered companies were committed; for years they could do no more than make tentative experiments in such territories. The various East India companies, in their different countries, were all given a monopoly of trade from the Cape of Good Hope to the Straits of Magellan; the West India companies got monopolies in the lands which bordered on the Atlantic Ocean and even on the east coast of the whole American continent. A Compagnie d'Orient, founded in France in 1642, tried to develop the possibilities of Madagascar for more than twenty years and then gave up, defeated; the great Compagnie des Indes, created by Colbert in 1664, was founded in order to develop the same island and only turned from Madagascar to set itself up on the Indian mainland in 1669–71. Five or six years later, as the outcome of all its efforts, the Compagnie had achieved no more than the establishment of seven or eight posts, scattered from Surat to Chandernagore; but it nursed ambitions to set itself up at Ceylon, at Sumatra, Java and Bangkok.

Examining these doubtful ventures closely, one can better understand how, after the project of du Noyer had failed despite encouragement from the highest authorities in France from 1613 to 1633, and then the officially-sponsored Compagnie du Morbihan and the Compagnie de la Nacelle de Saint-Pierre-fleurdelysée had foundered, plans for colonial companies might easily involve programmes for developing the whole French economy, ranging from the sewers of Paris to the canalization of the Seine and the forests and quarries of the Pyrenees. This sort of thing can be seen at various periods in French history—first at the start of Richelieu's ministry and then, much later, under the influence of Law, when a single colonization-company was designed to control the whole of France's trade with non-European lands. Again, in Sweden at the beginning of the seventeenth century, the company which Usselincx then suggested would have extended its powers to the uttermost parts of the world. It was only in the second half of the seventeenth century that it was possible to see the state, in France and in England, announcing from time to time that the territories which had been ascribed to the companies in Asia, in Africa or in America, were too vast, and setting up commercial organizations which were better adapted to more limited tasks. The immense territories in which the companies were called upon to perform their tasks explain the absolute need which they felt for the guarantees which they demanded of their governments.

The constant efforts of the states to unify themselves on a national basis had a variety of effects also on one of the essential elements in colonial expansion. While some states deliberately favoured emigration for religious reasons, others provoked it by persecution. The idea of spreading the Gospel had its place in the motives which animated Columbus and the early discoverers; in France, missionaries were often associated with the foundation of companies, and the monarchy often laid tasks of a missionary nature on the companies. Though Protestants were generally excluded from the French colonies there were many

Frenchmen who would have liked to create in the colonies religious asylums for the Huguenots. Large numbers of nonconformists emigrated from England to America for conscience' sake, and they took into the New World (often in organized communities) a spirit which still inspires the institutions and the society of the United States of America. The Council of Amsterdam officially took some account of the religious affairs of the Dutch overseas territories, but the Dutch companies took no serious interest in such matters.

The part which the nation-states took in promoting overseas expansion set the pattern for their efforts, in modern times, to maintain control over all aspects of their national lives. Mercantilism was the economic expression of this desire and was everywhere to be found dominant. The ruling economic thesis from the fifteenth to the eighteenth century, mercantilism was a mixture of beliefs, theories, and practices aimed at increasing the wealth of nations. This was to be achieved by the action of states and for their profit, at first by the accumulation of precious metals and later (at the beginning of the eighteenth century) by accumulation of all monetary instruments; and mercantilism played its part directly in the organization of the relations between the parent states and their dependencies, in particular for the production and the circulation of the precious metals, the importation of primary commodities and the export of manufactured goods, and the part to be played by industry in the new lands.

These characteristics were common to the European states, but they were to be seen in efforts which were directed to widely different countries. Africa and America, generally speaking, were practically empty of inhabitants, but the former remained closed to white settlement while the second, until it secured its emancipation, and itself took the lead, became an annexe to Europe. Asia, on the other hand, was occupied by relatively dense populations which had their own traditions, and organizations which were stable enough to maintain their own character and to remain, in a passive sort of way, resistant to European penetration.

The Europeans worked out their tasks of development and innovation within the framework of these different conditions. They did not deliberately distinguish between their political and their economic tasks. Where they moved into empty continents they were able to exercise their political roles alongside their economic roles, and they did so for a long time without rousing any serious opposition. But the economic functions, which were quite essential at the beginnings of expansion, were the only roles which they assumed in Asia for a considerable time, and it was only in the eighteenth century, when expansion gave place to conquest, that the old chartered companies gave way to the empires of the future. The two tendencies, political and economic, were represented by the two unequal forces which worked together for the development of the new lands. Merchants and speculators were there, anxious for immediate profits; so were states, eager to secure more power.

## III. *Membership and Finances of the Companies*

Membership of the companies and organizations which developed the New World may be divided into two categories. The active members were, naturally, merchants; but capitalists with a wide variety of interests, nobles with a great variety of privileges, officers, and city-dwellers joined with the merchants in widely different arrangements.

Normally it was the merchants who agitated for the formation of the companies. London merchants prepared the way for the formation of the East India Company during the period from 1579 to 1600; the founders of the Dutch company had already embarked on a number of Voor-Compagniën in the period from 1594 to 1602. Even in France it was the merchants, above all the merchants from the sea-ports, who demanded the formation of a great company for colonization in 1663. Everywhere merchants provided the bulk of the capital for overseas voyages, and it was they who carried the companies into the new lands.

The merchants who stayed in their metropolis and directed trading operations from there had seldom any experience of administering on a large scale and had to patch together their enterprises from many different expedients. Those who went overseas in the sixteenth and seventeenth centuries were really moved by a desire for adventure, and the great majority of them were still, in fact, almost nomads. Up to the eighteenth century it was the common custom in all lands that young merchants should serve their apprenticeship under a qualified merchant, normally in a foreign land. In the middle of the sixteenth century the great merchants of Paris had proclaimed that the feat of merchandise consisted 'en travail de corps et d'esprit, et au danger et péril continuel de naufrages, détroussements et autres cas fortuits'. The English 'mere merchants' and the French 'bons marchands', both anxious to distinguish themselves from the artisans and the retail merchants, only qualified for their title by the same distinction of a period of residence overseas. Even in the seventeenth century, import trade with foreign lands normally entailed considerable absence from home, and the founders of overseas posts hardly needed to introduce any novelties when they crossed the oceans in search of trade. They were already accustomed to travel under arms; to risk attacks from pirates, to defend themselves, and to wage war in the factories which they now built in distant lands was not much of a change. Nor was there any novelty when they commanded the ships which were carrying their merchandise and, as happened in France under Richelieu and Colbert, challenged the authority aboard of naval captains; nor was it a novelty when the merchants claimed the administration of a colony, at all levels of rank, as they did in Saint Domingue in 1713; or claimed command of troops, as they did more or less everywhere in the eighteenth century. The titles borne by officials in overseas settlements emphasized the importance of the merchants and underlined the nature of authority and competence there. These titles were common to all the colonizing countries—upper merchants, merchants, partners, assistants. For the rest, if some merchants did indeed begin to specialize in their trades, the majority continued to buy and to sell all sorts of commodities, and they hardly changed their practice when they undertook their risky voyages in search of the wide variety of colonial produce.

Perhaps from necessity, perhaps from simple self-interest, perhaps because the authority which gave them their charters suggested or required it, the merchants took an interest in scientific discovery in addition to their basic mercantile problems. In the same way as Fernão Gomez had secured the farm of the trade of Guinea on condition of exploring a hundred leagues of the coast in each year, in 1550 Fernão de Loronha got a trade permit for Brazil on condition that within three years he should explore 300 leagues of the coast, and at Amsterdam at the end of the sixteenth century the merchants of the future East India Company were in constant contact with the geographer Plancius. Barentz, Lemaire, Hudson worked for merchant companies; even in the eighteenth century, Captain Cook was as much moved by commercial plans as by the search for purely scientific discoveries.

Such common features resulted in tendencies which were similar but not identical, according to the country concerned. The practices of the fifteenth century had accustomed the Portuguese to official controls, to royal monopolies and to a system of farming out the trade, sometimes on a regional basis, sometimes on a basis of commodities. The Spaniards, faced with a new task, were immediately moulded by the institution of the Casa de Contratación. The English, driven to take to the sea in pursuit of trade, had formed local guilds for hundreds of years and had traditionally carried on their life behind the shelter of charters and collective privileges. Bacon declared that 'trading in companies is most agreeable to the English nature'.[1] Their group-organization was strengthened in most cases by something of a religious tie; the heads of the factories of the East India Company were ordered to bring together their 'family' —the men under their command—for morning and evening prayers,

[1] Cf. E. Lipson, *Economic History of England*, II, 193 and n. 6.

and this spirit (which ultimately produced some purely religious settlements, such as those of the Pilgrim Fathers) gave English enterprises for many years something of the character of a 'mixture of piety and of profit'. In Holland, with the habits of local autonomy and of civic freedom which had been asserted in the struggle for independence, the merchants were allowed to organize themselves as they wished, virtually free from state control although they represented the state in external affairs. The Dutch colonial companies provoked the remark, in France in 1663, that 'What must be appreciated is that everything is arranged and carried out by means of the merchants alone'. While in England and in Holland the part played by merchants was overwhelming in the formation of the companies, the French were divided between their maritime interests and their territorial ambitions. In 1664 it was expected that three quarters of the members needed to set up the Compagnie des Indes Orientales would have to be merchants. Among those who took part in overseas enterprises there was always an active element which consisted of representatives of the interior of the kingdom; Paris, Lyons and other towns normally took their part. Throughout, the national spirit of individualism resisted the dominance of the French state, but in the end movements begun by the state were on balance more important than those begun by merchants. In states in which colonization was only of secondary importance the role of the merchants was always subordinate to that of the public authorities.

There was also always a certain number of purely private ventures, evading the restrictions of the chartered companies and of state regulation, sometimes legal, sometimes illegal, varying in number from period to period, and occupying a half-way position in the matter of grants from public authorities to individuals. The interrupted story of the early discoverers of the sixteenth century was taken up again by the Dutch Voor-Compagniën, and many merchants continued to run independent expeditions, either as individuals or joined together in private partnerships. Sometimes they even managed to prevent the foundation of great national companies. These parallel activities of the merchants could not be suppressed, and they gave evidence of the enduring importance of merchant participation in expansion.

The part played by merchants was reinforced by the action of other kinds of collaborators, direct or indirect, who supported the companies. The proportion of merchants which was anticipated in France in 1664 was characteristic; of the members of the Compagnie des Indes Orientales about a quarter might be non-merchants.

Princes of the blood-royal took an interest in expansion for a variety of reasons. Here we can only point to the profits which the Spanish and Portuguese monarchies drew from the organization of their respective *casas*. The kings of England hoped to draw profits in their private capacities from the revenues of the great companies, and we have seen how James I and Charles I tried to secure some of the profits of the East India Company. After the Restoration, as early as 1660, Charles II managed to set up a rival company for the East India trade without meeting any opposition. Sometimes, it is true, the states took a contrary attitude; in 1621 the Estates General of the United Provinces underwrote half of its capital for the Dutch West India Company, and Louis XIV provided most of the capital necessary for many of the enterprises which he created.

Like the princes, and often following where the princes had led, nobles and grandees of various ranks took their share in the foundation of great companies for overseas developments. Apart from the *hidalgos* who secured fruitful sinecures in the *casas*, both in England and in France a number of members of princely families and of courtiers took up membership of the companies. Further, nobles of the highest rank often took the lead in the companies. In France, for example, during the minority of Louis XIII the dukes of Damville and of Montmorency, and during the minority of Louis XIV the maréchal de la Meilleraye, lieutenant-general of Brittany, directed large and ambitious companies in person and lent them the support of their names. In England Prince Rupert was governor of the Hudson's Bay Company in the second half of the seventeenth century. Lower down the aristocratic scale, a great number of full-blooded nobles were shareholders of the companies which were formed in England and in France. The English Royal African Company contained a great number of aristocrats at the start of the seventeenth century; out of thirty-eight members only five were genuine merchants, and special conditions were drawn up to allow the children of shareholders to become members. The Dutch bourgeoisie which ruled the two great Indian companies of that nation did not, it is true, consitute a genuine nobility; but it established a narrow oligarchy. And behind these noble groups must be ranged the members of Parliament, the numerous members of the courts attached to the legal profession, whom the governments invited (more or less ordered, in France) to take their shares in the great merchant companies.

Others also took their parts in the companies, men more directly concerned with the business of finance and production. In seventeenth and eighteenth-century France the great financial potentates who acted as Fermiers-généraux of the kingdom were often put under contribution by ministers who wished to found companies. In France, and in other countries also, it is possible to distinguish a group of men to whom, from the time of the reign of Henry IV, the modern term 'colonizers' may be applied. Gathered round Henry IV, round Richelieu, round Colbert and continuing into the eighteenth century, they were equally involved in Africa, in America, or in the Indies. Examples, taken at random from many such, are high officials or officers on the border-line between politics and administration such as Bellinzani and Berryer, merchants from Paris like Poquelin, merchants from the great sea-ports such as Fermanel of Rouen, bankers like Formont, or industrialists like Cadeau. It is difficult to distinguish them from the other capitalists of their time, and the intermingling of their activities with the general movements of their periods is characteristic both of the lack of specialization in most economic activities and of the vagueness which characterized colonial projects.

Over and above these economic and social groups, on the margins of the movement, an interest in trade and in colonial affairs spread to a fairly considerable element in the general public, once the practice of buying and selling shares on the exchanges had been established. During the seventeenth century dealings in the shares of the two India companies were among the chief business of the Bourse at Amsterdam; in France and in England, significantly at about the same time, the South Sea Bubble and the System of Law stirred all classes of society—they were feverish movements with no important financial future, but they were not without results in preparing public opinion to take an interest in colonial matters.

There is one class of supporters of the companies which must be considered under a different heading; apart from England and (for different reasons) Spain and Portugal, aliens were an important element in most countries. It is not necessary to emphasize the example of Magellan in Spanish service or the part (already mentioned) which Italians played in all the overseas expeditions at the start of European expansion. The Dutch spread everywhere in the seventeenth century; they were to be found in France under Henry IV and then under Richelieu, actively pushing for the formation of companies, and they were likewise to be found in Denmark, in Sweden and in some of the Hanseatic towns. The Dutch supplied ships' captains and, when it was not forbidden officially by their government, some of the ships; at times they even supplied some of the higher administrators in other countries' colonies. The Protestant Caron, a native of Brussels, and François Martin, a Parisian, who had begun their careers in the service of the Dutch East India Company, transferred later to its French rival. Capitalists invested their money in all countries; in France under Richelieu some companies got financial help even from England, and under Colbert they got help from Germany. Despite an official ban on the practice in the Dutch East India Company's statutes, aliens were admitted as servants. These changes of service, from one company to another in an alien country, show that purely national incentives were far less compulsive than they are nowadays; tolerance made possible the freedom of movement which had continued from the Middle Ages and slowed down the economic tendency to canalize men's efforts within national limitations, as organized by the growing power of the national states.

By comparison with the *casas* of the Iberian countries, the chartered companies maintained a real autonomy of their own. The states, while developing their own powers, had long since granted away part of their authority to the companies to whom they gave commercial privileges, and therewith they often granted away part of their sovereignty. In countries which so far had no overseas possessions, state and individuals joined together in the eighteenth century, in more or less strict partnership, under the guarantee of charters granted by the governments. Such partnerships of states and individuals for many years heavily accentuated their economic aims.

A deeply-rooted tradition assigns to England priority in using this method, which had been known there since the Middle Ages. During the sixteenth century chartered companies had been set up in England; for the Eastland trade (the Baltic, in 1408 and in 1579), for the Muscovy trade (1555–66), for the Levant (1581), and for Africa (1588 and again in 1618). Merchants had taken the initiative; and they were London merchants, as we have seen, who founded the first of the great colonial companies, the East India Company, to which Elizabeth granted a charter in 1600. Other companies were promoted by men who mixed in politics, such as Walter Raleigh, or by aristocrats, especially where the object was to create colonies in North America, at the beginning of the seventeenth century; of later creations the most important were the Hudson's Bay Company (1670) and the South Sea Company (1710) whose territories stretched from Malacca to the Straits of Magellan, and therefore included the whole of Indonesia.

In Holland, since the start of the War of Independence, the Dutch and Zealand merchants had planned to reach the Far East, either by a north-west passage or by a north-east passage. When eventually they made their way round the Cape, from 1594 onwards, several companies 'for distant voyages' (Compagniën van Verre) sprang up. Their voyages entailed serious dangers—for example in 1598 only fourteen ships got back to Europe out of twenty-two, belonging to five companies, which had set out for the Indies—and they created a harmful trade-rivalry among themselves in the Indies, and again when they had returned to Europe. The United East India Company (Vereenigde Oost Indie Compagnie) in which they were joined received its charter from the States General in 1602, granting the monopoly of trade between the Cape of Good Hope and the Straits of Magellan. Some twenty years later, in 1621, thanks to the energy of William Usselincx, a West India Company was created, and to it was granted all trade of the Atlantic seaboard, of the American continent and of the two Americas, north and south, from the Tropic of Cancer to the Cape of Good Hope.

These were the two greatest chartered companies in Holland; but other companies, clearly of lesser importance, existed alongside them. Small and great alike existed only by authority of the state, which always maintained the principle of its sovereignty, even under traditional feudal forms. But, from the very nature of their structure, and from the way in which their officials were indistinguishable from public officers, the two great companies, especially the East India Company, for many years were veritable states within the state and were for all practical purposes independent both in Europe and in the Indies. This was particularly true of the first, the East India Company.

In France, the chartered companies normally bore a deeper and clearer imprint of the state than they did in Holland or in England. Under Henry IV, under Louis XIII and Richelieu and under Louis XIV and Colbert, it was customary for the government not only to take its part in the foundation of companies, even to take the initiative, but for government to recruit members, to name directors, to amass the capital needed, or at least to procure a large proportion of it; it was habitual for the French government to provide shipping and, as happened almost everywhere, to help by exemption from customs and by other privileges. The incorporation of the French companies in a governmental organization during the seventeenth century underlined this special feature while at the same time it gave them considerable diversity; while the colonies which were directly under the Crown were under control of the admiralty, those which were under chartered companies were controlled by the treasury.

Similar arrangements could, nevertheless, be found, and were characteristic, in the northern countries, where the companies were only set up as a result of state action—as for example, the Danish East India Company of 1612, 1634, 1686 and 1728, the Danish West India Company at the end of the seventeenth century, the Swedish South Sea Company of 1611, the Swedish Africa Company of 1630, the Swedish East India Company of 1626 and 1731, and the Swedish West India Company of William Usselincx and then Louis de Geer. There was also a Prussian Africa Company at the end of the eighteenth century, and a Courland Company. Despite their artificial origin some of these companies managed quite well, some in India, some in Africa, especially on the Guinea coast; but their careers were brief.

Their charters ensured that these various companies should remain autonomous through a period of about two centuries. Derived from medieval practices, they remained characteristic of the legal system of the *ancien régime*. They were guarantees of liberty and they cast their cloak round the innovations which were preparing the way for the economy of our days; in particular they sheltered all kinds of partnerships, which for centuries had been suspect of producing monopolies and cornering the markets. Their charters had for many years been the means of assuring the solidarity and discipline of trading companies; for companies who voyaged afar, the charter was a gauge of security against hostilities from enemies and against competition from rivals.

Sometimes supplemented by an edict, sometimes by letters patent or by a solemn declaration, the charters gave to the companies a clear legal position, the position of a semi-public body invested with special powers by the public authority but within which the individual members worked for their own profit, perhaps under common rules, perhaps working for a joint profit. This kind of institution, which can still be found working in Anglo-Saxon countries, had its existence interrupted in the countries which were deeply affected by the French Revolution, but it has now come back into active life almost everywhere. Their legal title enshrined the companies' personality and made them a 'body politic'. Nevertheless, in 1724 an English court of justice can be found disputing the right of the Dutch West India Company to plead at law, although it was then a century old, because its name had not been expressly written into its foundation charter—an abuse which underlines the importance of formalities, and the bitterness of trade rivalry.

The charters defined the territory within which the grantees were to act. This was a geographical area in the case of all the great companies; for others it might be the exploitation of a particular object or trade—furs, fishing, tobacco, slaves etc. The vast size of the areas assigned to the great companies is evidence of the commercial ideas which dominated men's minds up to the start of the eighteenth century. We have already seen what boundless lands were granted to the various East India companies. The Dutch partitioned the whole world between their two great companies. It is true that the geographical knowledge of the founders of the companies and of colonies was very limited; merchants and capitalists were indeed to establish themselves, but first they had to make the discoveries. Law's Compagnie d'Occident, whose object was at that time to control French expansion into all parts of the world, was the last company to put forward claims which clearly exceeded the capacity of a company, even of a semi-public company, of those days.

The privileges which the charters secured may be divided into two classes; those of a purely economic nature and those of a political nature, which often entailed a delegation of sovereignty.

The state always granted a trade monopoly—as in Portugal in the fifteenth century—for a fixed period. This was always at least a dozen years, and in France it was forty and fifty years respectively for the West and the East India companies. Renewing the monopolies gave an opportunity for the state to make profits and to re-affirm its authority. In England monopolies had been granted as early as the later years of the fifteenth century in the letters patent which were granted to John Cabot. Less obviously than the restrictions imposed by the Spaniards and the Portuguese, such monopolies paved the way for the restrictions of the '*pacte colonial*'. They always aroused protests from those who were excluded, and the breaches caused by the contraband trade of interlopers were largely responsible for the movement of public opinion which led to modifications, and ultimately to the abolition, of the monopolies in the second half of the eighteenth century. Most charters also gave pecuniary advantages, especially exemption from customs dues, or at least reductions in the rates. In certain countries—in France as a matter of course—the companies received subsidies, sometimes directly, sometimes in proportion to the growth of their trade. Occasionally the state gave them support in kind, in particular the use of ships for carrying their trade. Often the state granted to the companies ownership of the lands which they were to develop, and this was a right which bore upon the question of the sovereign powers which the state itself intended to exercise in the distant lands.

In fact, the state habitually delegated to the companies a part, large or small, of its sovereign power. Its authority in infidel lands arose in the first place from occupation, the natives being considered as having no rights. For this Christian princes could vouch numerous precedents; the Portuguese could claim by a papal bull of 1455, and the Spaniards by the arbitration of Alexander VI, at the request of both kings, between them and their Portuguese neighbours, later sanctioned by the Treaty of Tordesillas, signed in 1494. Other princes could claim to have the same rights as those who had thus guaranteed their positions. The rest was a matter of the strength available.

The conditions under which the states entrusted some of the attributes of sovereignty to semi-public companies were determined by a variety of circumstances and by immediate necessities. For the Dutch the first vital necessity was to secure a foothold in the midst of the possessions, actual or claimed, of the Portuguese and the Spaniards. Henry VII had instructed Cabot to set up his banners and insignia in all the lands and places of which he might take possession, with full seigneury and jurisdiction. To establish themselves and to order their trade, the companies were instructed to make treaties with the established rulers (those holding '*dominium, titulum et jurisdictionem*'). They had to be able to defend themselves against their European enemies, against foes roused by their intrusion into economies which were already established; they had to guard their posts with fortifications and to be ready to defend them, and they armed themselves, signed conventions, raised soldiers, furnished warships, contracted alliances and became involved in all the complexities of inter-state diplomacy. For the administration of the territories given to them they had to exercise a jurisdiction which was at first confined to their own nationals, but which spread slowly to include the natives as well. The heads of their posts, whose main task was economic, developed into governors with wide powers but still remained the appointees of the companies, as did the military officers, even when they were officially invested with their offices by their governments.

The charters gave the companies a very real autonomy. From this point of view the most characteristic were the Dutch companies. While the West India Company, founded in 1621, was the more closely dependent on the States General, the older company, that of the East Indies, no longer required the agreement of the Estates General to the nomination of its Governor-General in Asia from the middle of the sixteenth century onwards. It could, at this period, write to the Estates of Holland that 'The colonies of the East Indies are not acquisitions made by the state, but by private traders who may sell them if they wish, even to the king of Spain or to any other enemy of the United Provinces.'

Normally, in exchange for their privileges, the companies were only bound to pay the same customs and taxes as other members of their states but, often enough, they were bound to make some feudal acknowledgement of suzerainty and sovereignty when they renewed their charters. In return for the particular advantages which they enjoyed and which placed them in their peculiar and privileged position they were expected to increase the national wealth.

It was by no means exceptional either in France or in England, for different reasons, that a charter should be compromised by the issue of a second charter to a rival company. Under Henry IV, under Louis XIV, under Charles I and under William III, this phenomenon can be seen in the companies for trade to the East Indies; and from a legal and technical point of view the great English East Indies Company of the eighteenth century was the successor of a rival company, founded in 1698 and merged with the first company in 1708, rather than of the original seventeenth-century company.

The continuous development of the state in all countries during the *ancien régime* led it to intervene directly in the operations of the companies, even when they had their charters. In England, from the early years of the seventeenth century onwards, the principle of delegating state rights ('ordering of State affairs') to commercial companies was subject to challenge, and there were some who asserted at that early date that the creation of colonies was an affair for the Crown. This sort of feeling was allied to the movement in thought which was to find expression with Locke, and in the insistence on constitutionalism which was a permanent feature of the seventeenth century. The Crown, it is true, ran into trouble when James I and Charles I made claims which were thought derogatory to the East India Company, but in 1660 Charles II got part of their profits with very little trouble. The growing preponderance of London helped to unify commercial action and to emphasize the national character of English expansion in distant territories: the 'Governor and merchants of London trading into East India' became 'the English Company trading into' East India in 1698. And Parliament took increasing control over colonial affairs; in the first half of the eighteenth century the English Company was more and more absorbed in the machinery of government.

In France, royal authority, remote under Henry IV, came into direct control under Richelieu and under Colbert, who were the effective founders of most of the companies of their period. Louis XIV secured the election of Colbert as one of the directors of the Compagnie des Indes Orientales (and that company was offered an office within the château of Versailles), dissolved companies, himself named the members of the Compagnie de Guinée, and in 1684 ordered several companies to pay out dividends so as to enhance their credit. The minister certainly intended to establish direct administration, installed it in Canada and in the Antilles, and recommended the application of the forms which were in use in France, especially for legislation and the administration of justice. In the eighteenth century, following the example of the Compagnie d'Occident of 1717, nomination of the directors in the successive constitutions of the Compagnie des Indes came more and more under political control. In 1723 the Compagnie was directly governed by the Conseil des Indes, a Council composed of twenty members named by the king and ten elected by the shareholders, a Council whose president was the chief minister Dubois and whose leader was the contrôleur-général Dodun, while the Council was itself one of the 'Conseils Supérieurs' of the government. A little later 'rien ne se décidait au Conseil des Directeurs qui n'eût son écho au Conseil des Ministres', and during the Seven Years War the administration of the Compagnie became the 'bureau de la guerre au département de l'Inde'. Little by little the governors and the military chiefs, nominally appointed by the companies, were in fact appointed by the ministers. The organization both of trade and of production became an affair of state.

In Holland, where state-action was least effective, the Dutch East India Company surrendered a thirty-third of its revenues to the stadthouder William III, and in 1747, yielding to a campaign against its abuses, it granted a post as Director-General to the young stadthouder William IV. His death in 1751 prevented him from using this office for the good of the general public.

Everywhere in the first half of the eighteenth century the '*pacte colonial*' was being tightened. The rivalries of the different countries for the use and the mobilization of capital, for the choice of members of the companies, for officers even of the highest rank, had not yet taken on the bitterness which they were to have in the next century, but the tendency to give a narrowly national character to enterprises, in Europe and overseas, was marked and increasing.

Some of the chartered companies became the most important commercial organizations of the *ancien régime*. Their prosperity made the three East India companies, Dutch, British and French, into political powers, and their vicissitudes played a great part in the history of the world. Their brilliant histories give them a notable place in the evolution of groups which were to foreshadow the formation of limited companies, those essential ingredients in modern capitalism.

When European expansion began, joint operations by merchants were organized according to two formulae; private partnerships, traditional since the Middle Ages throughout the whole of western Europe (and still under suspicion in Germany at the start of the sixteenth century, even when organized on a strict family basis, because of their monopolistic tendencies); and privileged organizations, the direct ancestors of the chartered companies, and particularly active in England. Monopolies and other privileges, political in their origins, bridged the gap between the two categories in many subtle ways. The distinctions which anticipate modern types of organization first appeared, as the companies evolved, in England. But even in that country these forms only emerged slowly; a wide variety of arrangements was tried out with an empiricism which resulted in considerable confusion. Among the partnerships which had received privileges, some had got them simply as reward for carrying out economic tasks; others enjoyed rights which nowadays belong to sovereignty, rights of jurisdiction, of diplomacy and military power, with a great variation in their degree of autonomy. On the borders of these organizations, semi-public or private, the Portuguese *casas* and their Spanish counterparts were organizations for regulation and administration which had political origins. The Portuguese *casas*, moreover, took a considerable part in trade; but in both kingdoms they left to individuals the peculiarly economic tasks of land-development. Still, as we have seen, the Universidad de los cargadores a las Indias at Seville must be accepted as very similar to the semi-public companies, especially to the regulated companies.

But other aspects of their juridical and financial positions make it possible for us to divide the chartered companies into two classes. It is traditional to divide them into two—regulated and joint stock companies—and in fact this division marks real differences. The regulated companies were essentially groups of persons, while in joint stock companies a permanent capital ultimately became the unifying basis for corporate action. Regulated companies derived from a traditional form, collective in character but at the same time not unlike a modern cartel in some respects; they set out the common conditions for trade, but not for a common trade. Joint-stock companies began the movement which was to lead to our limited companies; the three great East India companies belonged to this group. Only 'mere merchants', 'good merchants', were admitted to the regulated companies, sometimes at the end of their apprenticeship, sometimes by right of heritage, by payment of a '*hance*' or at least of a caution-money payment made by an existing member of the company. All members were subjected to moral discipline and all had to accept identical practices for their trade; for example the 'stint' fixed the quantity of merchandise which the members might buy or sell. But, subject to such limitations, each member retained his initiative and ran the risks of his own trade. While the regulated company normally admitted only qualified 'mere merchants', the companies which were based on a common capital welcomed those who had invested their money; and capitalists of all classes, bourgeois or aristocratic, could take a part in their trade, or at least could share in any profits.

To our eyes, these contrasts mark a clear distinction between different kinds of companies; but it was a characteristic feature of the *ancien régime* that men did not make such clear distinctions and that the structure of the companies for trade and for colonization, moreover, did not seem novel among the general mass of economic organizations of that period. For about two centuries, from the middle of the sixteenth century to the end of the eighteenth, all companies were constantly experimenting to try to find an appropriate form of organization; groups of men might act together, for the purchase and the sale of merchandise, for setting up a factory or for the occupation of a colonial post, without overmuch care to define in legal terms the manner of their corporate action. It is only by degrees that distinctions arise and that companies of traditional form disappear before their successors, who laid the foundations of colonies, ready for them to become the empires of the nineteenth century.

This evolution can best be seen, and the salient points picked out, in England. But it is important to remember that only the salient points emerge, after tentative experiments which are not always followed up. Their empiricism allowed English merchants, more than those of any other country, to attach little value to statutory and governmental formulae. Even as late as about 1640 the East India Company members were expressly asked, on many occasions, what form they wished their company to take. Should it be a regulated company, a company with a separate joint-stock for each voyage, a company for general voyages which entailed a continuous joint-stock, or should it be a limited company similar to our modern companies? Less obviously perhaps, certain characteristic traits show that Holland, France, and the other countries of northern Europe developed in the same direction, with the same lack of definition of economic forms.

This development seems to us all the more complicated because the major distinctions of our days fit badly into the realities of former times. The root principles of the companies had no common base in any economic plan, and in the long run the methods of grouping men into regulated or joint-stock companies derived from different ages. The regulated companies, heirs of customs and traditions which had come from the middle ages, derived their character basically from their statutes; the joint stock companies, looking to the future, took their character from the formation and method of using their capital. Chartered companies belonged with regulated companies, for the simple reason that they had statutes which gave them existence; but one and all they either started out with a permanent capital or were forced to acquire one. So the two types of companies were able to live side by side until the eventual triumph of capitalism;[1] further, the same company might pass from one type to the other—as, indeed, the companies which had preceeded the great colonizing movement had done. The Levant Company, founded in 1581 as a joint-stock company, became a regulated company in 1605; we have seen the indecision among the members of the English East India Company as to which form of organization their company should take; the Guinea Company, a joint-stock company set up in 1618, suffered a series of changes before, at the late date of 1750, its successor the Royal African Company became a regulated company with an explicit veto on trading for the common concern.

More remarkable still is the fact that the companies habitually confused their characteristics.

In all cases where they were set up by official ordinance their composition varied but little. There was nothing remarkable in the fact that a

[1] As late as 1733 the merchants of London, Bristol and Liverpool demanded the abolition of the East India Company and its replacement by a regulated company in which each merchant could trade with his own private capital. Although they took no part in the work of colonization, it is interesting to note that regulated companies lasted into the first quarter of the nineteenth century; the Company of Merchant Adventurers, which dated back at least to the fifteenth century, lasted till 1806 and the African Company lasted till 1825.

regulated company, half-way between a corporation and a cartel, should be open to all who wished to join it; it was enough to pay the entrance fees and, as often as not, to be proposed by a relative[1]. Even in the joint-stock companies the same situation was to be seen for many years; they had no fixed number of members. The English East India Company had 218 members enrolled on its books; in Holland all who were members of the Voor-Compagniën could become members of the Dutch East India Company, and from the start it was accepted that all citizens of the United Provinces could become members; in France the companies which were set up under Henry IV and later under Colbert were normally open to all who were willing to subscribe capital for a year, eighteen months or even three years after the return of the first ships sent to America or Asia. In 1664, before the Compagnie des Indes Orientales was set up, more than 300 people were present at a preliminary meeting, and a 'great number' of them subscribed to the company's capital. In addition, fees for admission to the English companies were insisted on in the seventeenth century as though they were corporations, and this applied to the joint-stock companies as well as to the others; the members were called 'brethren' and their wives were 'sisters'; they bore the title of 'free men of the company' or simply 'freemen'; sons of members paid smaller entry-fees than other candidates; in the great East India Company the young employees were called apprentices, and, as we have seen, the personnel of a factory constituted the 'family' of the chief.

Yet within the companies there was no equality between the members. Paradoxically, it was in the companies with a permanent joint capital that the differences in the status of members were most formally set out. Doubtless in England and later in France the rights of the members of the companies were often proportionate to their financial contributions; but in England and in Holland (and according to a custom which was already widespread, in Germany also) the members of a single company can be divided into two types. Some of the members were fully enfranchised and their names alone figured on the registers of the companies; others, who paid their shares of the capital through an intermediary, only appeared as members under the intermediary's name and could not exercise any personal control.

Even the unity of the companies was less clearly secured than we are led to believe. Members sometimes grouped themselves in such a way as to create and give power to almost autonomous organizations within the companies. In fact, not only was there seldom any limit to the numbers of members but the members saw no reason to limit their activity to one company. A considerable number of the merchants who formed the

---

[1] The Company of Merchant Adventurers had 7,200 members in the middle of the seventeenth century.

English East India Company were already members of the Levant Company, and continued to be members; some of the East India Company's members were Merchant Adventurers about the year 1640, although the Merchant Adventurers did not normally trade outside Europe. In Holland, the Dutch West India Company welcomed members of the older company, that of the East Indies. In France, especially under Colbert, all who wished could become members of both the Compagnie des Indes Orientales and of the Indes Occidentales; the members of the Compagnie des Indes Orientales set up other companies, such as the Compagnie de la Chine of the period from 1660 to 1698, and several others for the Africa trade. This, as we shall see, was a common practice in all colonizing countries.

Even within the companies groups (more or less homogeneous) enjoyed a form of autonomy, sometimes simply as a matter of fact, sometimes as a matter of formal and statutory arrangement. In England, where opposition between the merchants from the various ports was traditional, the Londoners persistently claimed a privileged position as against the outports. This can be seen even within the East India Company. But local divisions were most pointedly maintained in Holland, within the Dutch East India Company, which in its time was the most modern company and which for many years was the most envied and most frequently imitated. That company was, in fact, composed of six chambers, one for Amsterdam, one each for Middelburg, Rotterdam, Delft, Hoorn and Enkhuizen, deriving from the Voor-Compagniën. The powers and capacity of these chambers were not equal; Amsterdam was responsible for half the debentures of the company, Middelburg was responsible for a quarter, and the other four chambers between them were responsible, in varying proportions, for the other quarter. Each chamber enjoyed real autonomy; it fitted out its own ships, chose the men both for the ships and for the Indies, and gave them their instructions separately; it selected the merchandise which it sent to the Indies and it sold the returns on its separate account, setting on one side certain commodities which were only to be traded by agents of the company acting for the company as a whole. Each chamber could raise loans on its separate account and it was even possible for the financial situation of one chamber to be quite different from that of others. The chambers only made liaisons among themselves very slowly, and the unity and survival of the company were normally assured by intervention from the most active chamber, that of Amsterdam, which presided for six years out of eight.

The uncertainties and delays caused by such a loose organization did not prevent the Swedish East India Company, when it was set up in 1626, from following the Dutch example and setting up chambers in the principal ports of that country. And, after almost two thirds of a century, the prestige of the Dutch company produced another imitation in France; when the Compagnie des Indes Orientales was established by Colbert, in addition to its main Paris office, it was expected to consist of chambers for Lyons, Rouen, Le Havre, Nantes and Bordeaux, based on the subscriptions of members from those towns. In fact these chambers were never created; the organization of the Compagnie was unified, but the Dutch model had almost been followed. The members of a great company might therefore figure in many clearly different capacities. Nevertheless, from its earliest days the Dutch East India Company had run on a permanent capital, it had been founded in a land where the state was newly created and where there was no tradition of regulated companies to hinder possible innovations.

It is not surprising that the character of the companies remained unsettled for so long a time. Their corporate status was by no means clear. The same men might be active members of more than one company; the English East India Company and the Levant Company had for many years the same President, and a common register or agenda served for them both. In France the common name under which they were described had no precise definition; under Henry IV companies for trade and for colonization were sometimes called companies, sometimes societies, but Jacques Savary, the collaborator of Colbert and author of the treatise *Le Parfait Négociant*, kept the name of company for the greatest ones.

This hesitant development of the companies derives very largely, if somewhat confusedly, from the part which capital played in their activities. Not only the ways in which capital was used, but the very concept of capital caused many uncertainties.

The name joint-stock company described a new form of partnership. The meaning of the term has developed as the function of the money placed at their disposal has changed, and it has finally come to describe something quite different from its meaning when it first became a term in common usage. Groups which were genuinely autonomous, or subgroups formed within companies with a corporate character, had for long worked with financial resources which had been jointly subscribed by their separate members. Groups based on a common capital, however, increased their scope at the start of the modern period, acquiring charters and securing powers of the utmost importance; their novelty, at that time, did not consist in their working with a common capital, but in the permanence of that capital. The words joint-stock therefore express, even in English, a dual nature. All the more, when we nowadays translate the term into French as *compagnie par actions*, as we normally do, we commit an anachronism; our *compagnies par actions* are the latest developments from the joint-stock companies formed in the sixteenth and eighteenth centuries. The formation of capital, and above all the employment of capital, was directed according to peculiar methods at that time.

The capital of the great companies was amassed under a variety of conditions and according to a variety of principles. The English East India Company had £30,000 sterling in 1600; the Dutch company had 6,459,588 florins in 1602; in 1604 the minimum individual subscription for the proposed French company was 3,000 livres, but the total seems never to have had any limit. A series of increases brought the total for the company founded by Colbert in 1664 up from six to fifteen million livres. Clearly the purposes to which these sums were to be put varied considerably.

In fact, the concept of capital, and above all the notions of the ways in which it should be employed in a collective enterprise, were still uncertain; the utility of a sum of money placed for a long term at the disposal of a company was not exactly appreciated. It was traditional that each separate operation of buying and selling, and still more, each distant voyage, should be considered as a separate account. The members of a company who took part in such a transaction used their funds as a common stock; at the return of the expedition the merchandise brought back would be sold, the profits divided, and each participant regained his money and his freedom. This method of operation was long used by members of chartered companies. The English East India Company worked in exactly this way from 1600 to 1612. For each of its voyages it got together the necessary capital, and a separate ordinance wound up each operation. Sometimes a series of voyages might lead to competition between them, but such competition was controlled (not always completely) by the fact that the participants were very often the same merchants. For half a century the company varied between treating each voyage as a separate concern and carrying forward the balances to finance later voyages. Thus the same company used both temporary and permanent capital.

In Holland a formal regulation, Article 9 of the statutes of the Dutch East India Company, authorized the members to withdraw their capital at will, together with their proportion of the profits for the period during which their capital had been at the disposal of the company. In such cases the Company's registers noted the end of the 'action' together with the name of the person who had acquired the right. But at the same time, in 1612, both the English and the Dutch companies refused to make such repayments since the capital was invested in buildings, ships and land, and could not be realized. From that time the Dutch company made it possible for the owners to sell their shares

freely, especially on the Bourse. In 1621 the statutes for the new Dutch
West India Company, and in 1623 the statutes of their East India Company
(then renewed) forbade actual withdrawals of capital though the
shares might be sold. It was not until 1658 that the English East India
Company's capital was declared to be fixed, and then it was only a
declaration of principle since the members, with some delay, could still
withdraw at least a part of their investment.

At that time in France, where the examples of England and Holland
were under constant scrutiny, the same ideas about the nature of a great
company were accepted in circles interested in matters of trade and
colonization. In 1660, the Compagnie de la Chine was set up with the
modest capital of 220,000 livres, obviously contemplating only a single
voyage; this was a company with both commercial and religious objects,
whose chief advocate was an ennobled merchant of Rouen, one Fermanel,
and it only sent out a single ship. The company foresaw in its statutes
that, when this first ship came home, the question would be on what
terms a second voyage should be financed.

In all countries, the facts dictated something of a common practice in
this matter of the permanence of the companies' capital. But, at this
time, the chief problem of the directors of the companies was to secure
running cash. It is possible to maintain, in fact, that the most imposing
of the great colonizing companies, the Dutch East India Company, did
not vary the sum of its capital from 1602 to 1788. When current cash
was needed, it habitually issued short-term loans; this was a procedure
which was most used after 1676 and was one which the separate chambers
of the Dutch company had used from 1638 onwards. Moreover although
the Dutch company drew up an annual general statement of its goods
and possessions in the Netherlands, at least from 1638 onwards, yet partly
because of the difficulties in its communications, it never produced a
comprehensive balance-sheet. Its statements never amounted to a
complete picture of its position throughout the world.

The shares of the capital among members were only subjected piecemeal to exact rules. To begin with, the capital of a company was made
up of a more or less strictly defined number of *shares* whose value varied;
the number of members accepted by their colleagues was fixed. Later,
these shares were split into *fractional* shares of fixed value, which became
known as *stocks* (or *actions*). The unequal contributions of the members
of the English East India Company were at first divided into £50 shares,
and this was raised in 1676 to £100. At first no share-value was set out
for the subscriptions to the Dutch company. In France, in 1604, the
minimum share for the projected Compagnie des Indes Orientales was
to be 3,000 livres; in 1664 the capital of that company was divided into
shares of 1,000 livres and half-shares of 500 livres.

The rights of the shareholders also were only fixed as time went on. We have already seen that, especially in England and in Holland, a section of members of the companies only took part through the covert intervention of fully official members. In the English East India Company each member's voting right was in proportion to his investment. From 1623 onwards in the Dutch East India Company the big investors got a dominant position by statute; the small stock-holders were deprived of all effective power. Such a distinction tended to show up more or less explicitly everywhere. All the same, in England it was ordered that a £300 share in the Hudson's Bay Company should carry a vote. In France, after Law, the capital of the Compagnie des Indes, 112,000,000 livres, was split into 48,000 shares of 2,000 livres each and 80,000 tenths of a share at two hundred livres.

From the moment that the capital began to be split into shares it became easy to deal in them. In the seventeenth century, as we have seen, the business of the Bourse at Amsterdam consisted largely in dealings in the shares of the two Dutch Indies companies.

The voyages undertaken by the colonizing companies brought very different rates of profit. The English East India Company carried the profits from its first voyage to the second venture, and the profits on the second voyage amounted to 195 per cent; profits from the third voyage, which were considerable, were carried to the fifth voyage; the fourth voyage resulted in a loss as a result of the wreck of two ships. Eight other voyages, from 1609 to 1613, gave respectively 334, $221\frac{2}{3}$, 318, 311, 260, 248, 320, $233\frac{11}{12}$ per cent. Between 1651 and 1690 the dividends varied between $12\frac{1}{2}$ and 60 per cent, and the most brilliant period was from 1687 to 1736.

Dividing the profits, which over a period were rich in most companies, remained an uncertain business. The same rule, admittedly a vague one, was applied in England and in Holland; dividends must be paid whenever a certain percentage of the sales from the 'returns' had been paid into the coffers. Law made an innovation when he proposed to pay a steady interest of $7\frac{1}{2}$ per cent plus a variable dividend; in general terms the division of the profits depended on the discretion of the directors of the companies.

Putting the capital to work therefore takes the form of a series of hesitant experiments in all countries during the whole course of the *ancien régime*. Even the eighteenth century did not as yet reveal any standard methods of using capital.

The development of administrative machinery within these companies was equally slow and experimental, even in the greater companies whose importance compelled them to make innovations. For the principles on which their forerunners had worked were of no value as models; the general body of the Merchant Adventurers, despite the preponderance of the Londoners, was split between the Londoners and their colleagues from the outports, and their official establishment was not even in England but in some port on the continent.

The English East India Company, the first among companies chartered for overseas trade, was from the start organized in a modern form. A 'court of Proprietors' was the supreme authority in the company, and a 'court' of twenty-four 'assistants' named by the 'court of Proprietors' directed the affairs of the company under the authority of a governor and a deputy governor. The members were split into several committees, each charged with special duties.

The Dutch company was organized in a much more empirical manner. The seventy-two directors of the Voor-Compagniën were kept on at the head of the united company. Later reduced to sixty, these *bewind-hebbers* were allotted according to the capital brought in by the different chambers: twenty for Amsterdam, twelve for Middelburg, fourteen respectively for Delft and Rotterdam together and for Hoorn and Enkhuizen together. They nominated a 'college' of seventeen members, de Heeren XVII (Zeventien), which ruled the company. The shareholders, divided into two categories from the start, and clearly so from 1623 onwards, were formally so divided in 1647; only the greatest investors enjoyed any real power. Control of the various chambers became, in fact, a function of the urban and provincial authorities.

We have already seen how far the autonomy of the chambers extended. Their interchanges were always slow and difficult among themselves, and their relations with the XVII had no common form. The XVII met whenever they thought it necessary, rarely more often than three times a year. Nevertheless from about 1640 onwards a bond grew up between these apparently irreconcilable institutions. The company had its own solicitor; from 1652 to 1706 this was Pieter van Dam, whose *Beschrijving*, written from 1693 to 1701, constitutes one of the principal sources of the company's history. Around him, at the Hague, a sort of secretariat, soon known as 'de Haagsche Besogne', concentrated the correspondence, especially that with the colonies, took charge of the payment of dividends and of other matters of common interest, especially of the accounts and of reports which had to be made to the XVII. In addition, the presidency which the Chamber of Amsterdam exercised for six years out of every eight, and its habitual intervention in any business which bore upon the general welfare of the company, had a permanent influence on the company's progress and gave it continuity.

In fact, the XVII and the class of wealthy bourgeois, from whom the *bewindhebbers* were recruited, governed the company according to their own good pleasure for two centuries, and the administration was at the same time regular and almost secret.

The Dutch West India Company, founded in 1621, had a similar organization, but with the difference that its directors were XIX, and that an official representative of the Estates General figured among them.

The French companies founded by Colbert took the great Dutch company as their model; coming later, they were able to make use of slightly better-organized arrangements. We know what the organization of the French Compagnie des Indes Orientales was supposed to be under Colbert, and what it actually was; the five local chambers which were supposed to be erected in the provinces would have sent a report of their activities to the Chambre de la Direction générale every six months. A general meeting of the shareholders was supposed to be held every year; to have a vote in the Compagnie it was necessary to hold six shares and to be eligible for election to a chamber it was necessary to hold twenty shares in Paris or ten in the provinces. The shareholders named the twelve Parisian directors, who were to be assisted by nine directors from the provinces; and the directors were elected for seven years and retired from office in rotation. Each chamber was to have a cashier, a secretary, a book-keeper, elected by the shareholders, and each year a general statement of accounts was to be submitted to the directors and to be made available to all subscribers. Three departments or colleges, administered by the directors, undertook the administration of day-to-day business. Nine separate books were specified for the accounts. In 1668-9, Colbert carried his care for orderliness so far as to lay down the tasks of each director and to specify that they must devote themselves to work for the company on four days of each week from four to seven o'clock in the afternoons.

In the eighteenth-century companies the staffs were normally over-numerous and their duties were even more narrowly specified. The Compagnie d'Occident only had six directors, named by the king, but the Compagnie des Indes in 1719 had thirty, reduced in 1724 to twenty-four, all nominated by the king.

These directors had under their command specialized departments, and they were controlled by commissioners from the Conseil Royal. In 1723 as we have seen, when it had been reorganized after Law's System, the company was directly governed by the Conseil des Indes. Through all the re-shufflings, the directors became, more and more, either simple officials or representatives of the shareholders, nominated more or less directly by the king. In the northern countries of Europe, where the companies were directly set up by the governments, their administration was indistinguishable from public organizations.

The metropolitan administrators extended their authority into the overseas possessions by means of arrangements which were pre-eminently empirical and extremely diverse.

It is obvious that those who were responsible for organization and action in the Portuguese and Spanish possessions must be considered separately; they directly represented the state. The strictly economic tasks, distinguished only vaguely from the functions of government, as everywhere, were (in fact, if not always legally) directly regulated by administrations controlled from above by viceroys and, under the orders of the viceroys, by hierarchies of officials and functionaries. In France, it was not until the reign of Louis XIV that cadres of functionaries, viceroys, governors or lieutenant-governors and intendants, were substituted for the personnel who had been appointed by the companies. This was particularly the case in Canada and the Antilles, but it happened at first in an intermittent manner.

The great companies, in general, themselves organized their own services. The first company to bring its departments into a single organization was the Dutch East India Company—and even that company showed considerable divergencies for many years. In its early days it had only isolated posts in the Indian Ocean. In 1609, by agreement with the Estates General, the company created a governor-general and very soon it habitually nominated him on its own sole initiative. The organization of the Dutch West India Company in America showed considerable variations.

In France the important companies imitated the Dutch East India Company; in fact, they also nominated their own governors-general, but they required the assent of the king. Among companies in general, the dispersal of territories and of posts led them to set up local governors, more or less effectively under the control of governors-general. Many of these leaders were assisted by councils or colleges, some 'sovereign', some with only local and restricted authority. All members of such superior cadres were invested with the powers which their charters had conceded to their companies.

Under these chiefs and organizations, in most companies, the 'upper merchants', 'merchants' and 'junior merchants', exercised authority in all spheres, even in military and judicial matters (and the judicial was normally subordinate to the military). Their names, eminently appropriate to their tasks, were astonishingly similar from one country to another. They were assisted by a complement of subordinates with a variety of titles—book-keepers, commissioners, assistants and so forth. Seldom or never did the companies set up a rigorous hierarchy; from one district to another employees boasted a great variety of titles, not all of them always to be found at any one post. For the most part the bonds between these agents and their companies were exceedingly tenuous; distances were often immense, and everywhere the companies' representatives of all ranks were empowered to carry on trade for their private accounts and were often, in effect, the most dangerous rivals of their own companies.

It was not only their internal organization which was uncertain in the chartered companies. Their general characteristics also were not capable of precise definition. Between the state-organizations and the great enterprises endowed with a privileged charter on the one hand, and private associations which ran the risks of distant voyages on their private account on the other, there was a range of commercial organizations with a wide variety of rights, and reaching widely different statures. Some of these, also, were chartered companies of only secondary importance, sometimes even directly subordinate to the great companies, sometimes limited to a narrow regional activity, perhaps to trade or production of specified commodities. Others secured licences, or limited permits, either from the state or from the companies themselves. They might nevertheless possess considerable powers and a reasonably efficient organization; from 1595 onwards a private company of merchants of Rouen and Dieppe, created for trade to Guinea, Angola and Brazil, managed to carry on warfare with the Portuguese along the Brazilian coast.

Even the organizations set up by the state in Portugal and Spain made use of the process of granting out charters, and set up companies under their authority. In 1623, inspired by the new but already brilliantly successful Dutch East India Company, and using the same name, the Spanish minister Olivares set up a company for trade with the Portuguese Indies. This company was to work under the control of the Casa da India of Lisbon, and it was still in existence in 1633. After the restoration of Portuguese independence, a certain P. Vieyra, one of the chief councillors of the king, worked out a plan to create two companies, one for the Indies and one for Brazil, but he was only able to get one company formed, and that (the Compania Gĕral do Comércio do Brasil) took charge of the monopoly of shipping between the metropolis and Brazil from 1649 to 1720. Other companies were created in Portugal under Pedro II (1667–83) to handle trade with Africa, and others followed at later dates with a wide variety of forms and purposes. Pombal, minister from 1750 to 1777, was to create new companies for trade to Para and Maranhão (1755), then for trade to Pernambuco and Parahiba (1759). In Spain the government granted many monopolies both to companies and to private persons, aliens as well as nationals, especially for the supply of negroes to the American colonies.

While even in the two Iberian kingdoms, private enterprise found methods of operating in companies, this was the common procedure in all other lands. In France several Compagnies de la Chine were splintered off from the bigger East India companies; the first, of 1660, lapsed like its parent company; the second, of 1698, was created by royal decree expressly limiting the rights of the existing company. Successive Compagnies du Sénégal, and South Sea Companies, derived from each other or else were, like the Asiento Company for the slave trade, closely allied among themselves. And it often happened, for a variety of reasons, that charters encroached on concessions which had already been granted.

At least from the start of the seventeenth century, in all countries private citizens might get authorizations from the chartered companies to practise certain branches of trade. In France, in 1682, the Compagnie des Indes Orientales granted to a 'société' the right to trade in its own ships on payment of 10 per cent of the value of the goods transported; in 1701, provided the money was forthcoming, the king established a group of financiers within the Guinea Company, which was to permit participation in the slave trade to any merchants who wished. And the companies of all countries adopted a similar system of concessions.

From such diversities it is obvious, once more, that trading organizations were experimental; obvious too that methods which seem to have been regulated by precise rules, such as charters and the rights conferred by them, left room for a great deal of uncertainty.

This general uncertainty explains the precariousness and the great number of the chartered companies, the variations in their powers and in their activities. For France alone a list of seventy-five known companies between 1600 and 1789 is certainly incomplete; there were seven for the East Indies, three for China, six for Canada and Acadia. Some companies had limited objects and limited means, or were strictly subordinated to public authorities, and this applied particularly to the Iberian countries; some became a 'state within the state'. Diverse but fundamentally identical, they were the first means to hand for the white expansion of the seventeenth and eighteenth centuries. They showed the same contrasts of diversity and identity in their methods of developing the wealth of the New World.

# IV. *The Economic Development of the New World*

In overseas territories methods of economic development varied according as the land was directly taken in hand by the state or was granted out by the state to companies. They varied also according to whether the land was adequately populated or not, and according to whether the products were complementary to those of the metropolitan country or not.

For a considerable period one guiding principle governed all overseas enterprises. They aimed in the first place at gaining wealth; the companies sought this aim by trading. Even in the eighteenth century the difficulties which Clive and Dupleix encountered from their respective companies arose from their failure to accept this basic notion of their directors and shareholders; in the middle of this century a governor of the English East India Company wrote to the court of directors that he had placed his merchandise to advantage, and La Bourdonnais called Dupleix 'this merchant'. The controller-general Silhouette declared in London that 'It is not proper for the Company to make itself into a military power in India and it ought to limit itself to commercial objectives'; and in 1756 the government at Versailles declared that 'The Antilles are in the last resort nothing more than trading establishments'.

It is true that America, from the Discoveries onwards, opened up large territories to the Spaniards and the Portuguese and then, in the sixteenth century, placed before other colonizing powers temptations and (in the seventeenth century) opportunities to make vast settlements. But it is equally true that no company, and no country after the Iberians, tried to seize territory in Asia or to set up an empire in Asia and its dependencies. In 1617 the instructions which the Dutch East India Company sent to its agents clearly ordered them to cultivate the friendship of the native princes so as to get from them facilities for trade; in the seventeenth century 'the Dutch avoided all continental establishments with the greatest care' and for over 150 years this great company only possessed isolated posts. Even when it was at the height of its power it only exercised direct administration in and around Batavia, in Ceylon, in a small number of posts and at the Cape. The Dutch Company was typical; it was only at the end of the seventeenth century and during the eighteenth that the Dutch, English and French empires began to take shape, under the cover of a variety of conventions and alliances. Alongside these empires there came to be ranged the possessions of other European powers, some extended, some not, some lasting, some short-lived. It is only at this period that one can distinguish two types of company, the company for pure trade and the company for colonization.

The peoples of Europe set up their colonies across the seas in a wide variety of conditions. The Spaniards emigrated to America in considerable numbers. The French, who had wanted to set up populous settlements in their possessions under Francis I and Henry II, followed this policy systematically under Colbert. The English had made a start with Raleigh and they continued to set up homogeneous communities, especially in America. The Dutch set their faces against any substantial emigration to the Indies.

Relations with the natives were equally diverse. The Spaniards intermarried vigorously with the peoples whom they ruled while the French tried the policy which we nowadays should call 'assimilation'; the English and the Dutch held themselves apart from the native populations. In some countries such relations were affected by the religious outlook.

As far as the settling of a population in the new territories was concerned a novelty which followed after the Discoveries was the transplantation to America of African negroes. The institution of slavery had never entirely disappeared from the Mediterranean. For the vast territories of America slavery provided numerous labour-gangs, as it had done in ancient times. Most of the companies who traded across the Atlantic were obliged to supply this kind of labour-force, and charters were granted expressly for this purpose in many countries from the end of the seventeenth century onwards.

Occupation of the soil was undertaken according to generally-accepted principles. First occupation of vacant lands gave a strong claim, for non-Christians were held to have no rights in the soil. States expressly gave to the beneficiaries named in their charters a propriety in the soil; thus, in England, Henry VII made such a grant to John Cabot in 1496 and James I in 1606 granted to the members of the Virginia Company the full ownership of such lands as they might discover. In France, in 1628, Louis XIII granted Canada to the Cent Associés 'en tout propriété', and in 1633 he gave divers lands in America to the company of William of Caen, likewise 'en tout propriété'. Louis XIV gave Madagascar to the Compagnie des Indes Orientales in 1664 on the same terms. The companies certainly considered themselves as owners of their lands; about 1651 the French Compagnie des Îles d'Amérique sold piecemeal the Antilles islands which had been granted to it in 1635, and in 1670 the Dutch West India Company sold the island of Surinam to the city of Amsterdam.

This custom of granting away soil, in itself, derived from traditional usages. The first explorers, some of whom arrived with a clientèle of followers, were anxious to set themselves up as seigneurs within a feudal framework established by the state. The Portuguese Fazendeiros and the Spanish Haciendados were masters both of their lands and of their servants, and medieval methods of working the land were perpetuated in the way in which land was divided up into *encomiendos* and in the forced labour of the *repartimientos* which was exacted from the Indians. In Canada, individual holdings of land were allotted out according to the seigneurial system, whose character was being constantly changed. In the London Virginia Company the shareholders, who were mostly great lords, had a right to allocations of land in proportion to their investment. Sometimes companies reserved to themselves the ownership of lands of which they had granted away parts. Thus the Plymouth Virginia Company was a rival to the London Company for its territory. At the end of the seventeenth century the custom gradually spread that the lots of land given to new settlers should be determined according to a uniform system.

Settlers were normally recruited by the companies in a methodical manner and many of the companies, especially in France, were bound by their charters to bring out a specified number of colonists to their lands. To this practice may be traced the system of 'indentured labourers' who were obliged to remain in the service of the colonizing company which brought them out from the mother-country for a specified time— usually from a year and a half to three years.

The chartered companies, like the institutions set up by the states, organized the output of their territories within the general framework of mercantilism and adjusted their practices to its overriding rules. One and all, they had been set up in hopes of a mythical Eldorado. This myth dominated men's imaginations, but the actual wealth revealed in the new lands transformed the vision into a very different reality.

The activity which followed the first discoveries was primarily directed to the search for spices and for precious metals. In the scale of values, pepper was soon surpassed by cinammon, then by cloves; then spices slowly lost their comparative importance though they remained vital for the Dutch East India Company which continued to be the chief distributor of them. Gold and silver dropped to the second rank in the seventeenth century, but the rush to Minas Geraes gave new life to the movement for their production; at the start of the eighteenth century the French Compagnie de la Louisiane, though under the control of that skilled financier Crozat, still claimed to exploit mines and minerals. This was an attractive feature in company prospectuses, and the popular pictures of Law's time, which were at the same time a stimulus and a reflection of opinion, emphasize the hopes which were always roused by precious metals.

It is necessary to emphasize another source of riches which was often sought by the great companies. Piracy is more reprehensible in our eyes than it was in theirs, and raiding the Spanish galleons was a branch of piracy often combined, more or less openly, with normal trade. The buccaneers in the Antilles, in the first two-thirds of the seventeenth century, continued this kind of operation, which had already spread along the coasts of Europe.

Search for, and development of, mineral wealth slowly gave place to wider and more methodical development of the resources of the colonies. First came the exploitation of particularly valuable commodities. The Dutch East India Company, using native authorities as its intermediary, organized the production of spices in a most methodical way, involving a great number of regulations; it often ordered the destruction of crops which exceeded the needs of the market, even when it had ordered them to be grown. The French companies in the Antilles, like their foreign rivals, greatly extended the growth of sugar-cane; in 1698 the settlers were ordered to abandon sugar for the growth of tobacco, cacao, indigo. In many cases the companies, like their governments, dedicated large regions to a single crop in their own interest, and the state of the European markets did not always provide a satisfactory outlet. Transplantation from one continent to another spread the areas of production for plants and commodities which had hitherto been confined to more or less isolated zones. Even fishing, as on the North American coast, and fur-hunting in Canada, became increasingly normal complements to European export trades, and the mercantilists tried with great trouble to work out a balance for such trades.

Industrial activity also upset the traditional order of production and brought with it a testing-time for ideas, which were changing too. In general terms, the vast and varied changes which resulted from the influx of precious metals had less influence on the chartered companies than on the Spanish and Portuguese *casas* which it stimulated into activity.

But manufacturing industries posed multiple problems. In general the companies, closely allied with the economic circles of the home countries, took but little trouble over planting old industries in the colonies; the Dutch deliberately abstained from doing so, and English statutes tried to prevent industrial growth. But French charters of the seventeenth century, especially those for Canada, set out to organize emigration of artisans and promised a master's privileges to emigrants, with the right to set themselves up in France as 'maîtres de chef-d'oeuvre' after a stay of a certain number of years in the colony—six years was the specified time in 1628, ten years in 1642. So, in many lands, strife soon arose between the colonies and the metropolis. When Canada tried to subsist on her own under the Intendant Talon, during Colbert's ministry, the metropolitan authorities did not oppose it; when individual colonists, under the régime of the chartered companies, tried to develop the sugar and rum industries, the home manufacturers stirred up the French authorities and, in 1684, secured a ban on refineries in the Antilles. The prohibition of cottons, then of china and porcelain, of curios and furniture from the Far East, all of which were important articles of trade for the Compagnie des Indes Orientales, stirred up quarrels and controversies which lasted for more than half a century and which spread to several European countries. In England, an act of 1733 forbade importation of hats made in the American colonies and limited to two the number of apprentices which American hatters might take. When the struggle between England and her colonies was already imminent and the colonies were determined, and for the most part proud of their chartered rights, Lord Chatham cried out 'If America decided to make a horse-shoe or a nail I would bring against her the whole power of England'.

Attempts to co-ordinate such unequal and scattered economies were pushed on with the utmost rigour and determination in all matters of trade. As the states took these problems in hand they impinged on the activities of the chartered companies, which were constantly confused with those of the states themselves and of private individuals. The companies had been set up primarily to conduct trade, and the English governor who had 'placed his goods to advantage' was typical. But their autonomy, which was fundamentally economic, was bound to give way before the authority of the state, which tended to resume the rights which it had delegated to the companies and to place their operations under the same laws as applied to all other subjects.

The king of Portugal had been the first to subject trade to strict regulations when he imposed the monopoly of the royal fleet on all shipments between the mother-country and the colonies; after 1640 a chartered company was to supplement this official service. Spain always forbade access to her colonial ports to all foreign ships, subject (as in all such cases) to the exceptions, permits and licences, of which the *asientos* were the most continuous and profitable examples. The method of using convoys, which were controlled and protected, was in the logic of the times; wars and piracy dictated the policy to Spain from 1526 onwards, and shipments were forced to be made only in common voyages; two squadrons, plus a third squadron of galleons, set out each year. Chartered companies also always sent several protective ships on most of their distant voyages.

Such a discipline was all the more easy to enforce because the ships remained for a long time the property of their captains, who were naturally anxious to ensure a safe voyage for them. From the middle of the seventeenth century the French companies were constantly trying to get their ships made in Holland or to buy Dutch ships, but this was because of the better workmanship of the shipyards of that country. Like the great majority of merchants, the companies did not always own their ships. Even the English East India Company did not bother to acquire ships until the second half of the seventeenth century.

But all the companies exerted themselves to maintain the monopolies in trade which their charters promised to them in their territories. Of all the problems in the history of colonial problems in the *ancien régime* the most hackneyed is that of the companies' monopolies and of the national monopolies. These were as much political as economic in character, and dependent on the system which was then called '*l'exclusif*' and which has often in later times been called the '*pacte colonial*'. For Colbert it was an important element in his policy of seizing the trade of the Antilles from Dutch hands. Monopolies, as we have seen, could be most unequal in their scope; for some they were of world-scope, for others regional, and they indicated the varied power of the companies.

From the end of the seventeenth century onwards the position of the companies became more complicated. In France the '*pacte colonial*' was more strictly enforced after the ordinances of 1698 and of 1727. In England and in Holland the companies perhaps were more willing to grant licences or concessions to individuals or to private companies, but the policy of those states was not therefore any more liberal as far as foreigners were concerned.

The way in which the judicial and economic conditions under which the chartered companies worked was tied up with the mercantilist system. This made it seem reasonable that various trade zones should be allocated and that the companies should have their separate régimes. Trade between Europe and the Canaries on the one hand and Madeira on the other always enjoyed something of a special status; the slave trade gave rise to a complicated criss-cross of companies and of state-regulations; relations between the Antilles and the American continent were subjected to a variety of different regulations. Voyages between America and the Far East were always subject to particularly close regulation. In southern Asia the Europeans had come upon a system of trade-relationships which was more or less organized; Arabs, Indians (the Parsees) and Chinese met each other in the ports of Indonesia and of southern India; they went their rounds and the trade 'of India to India' was a fruitful branch of their activity for all the companies.

The many-sided activities of the companies constantly intersected with the diplomacy and the legislation of the states; and, from the middle of the seventeenth century, despite the predominance of mercantilism, the two did not always harmonize. In addition, the results achieved by the companies and by the states were always being spoiled by the contraband trade of interlopers (often organized by alien rivals and often maintained by their governments) and all alike without exception were given trouble by the permits which the companies granted to their agents, allowing them to trade on their own account.

There was, moreover, one problem which posed a question affecting the whole economy, and all companies: the problem of payments in bullion, allied to the greater problem of the Balance of Trade. Bullionism, everywhere accepted, forbade the export of gold and silver. In all countries colonial trade called forth lively criticism, all the stronger in that the critics could cry out against the carrying away of gold and silver from the mother-country. Charles V had already reproached the Portuguese for taking the treasures of Christianity to pagan lands. Throughout the seventeenth century controversy on this point was fierce throughout western Europe; on many occasions the House of Commons upbraided the companies for exporting gold and silver, and in the eighteenth century Defoe and Voltaire both brought the same arguments to bear on this problem. Supporters of the companies retorted in vain that in the long run their trade produced a nett gain for their countries, and the dispute was still not played out in the second half of the eighteenth century.

## V. *The End of the Companies*

The eighteenth century steadily undermined the organizations which controlled the relations of European countries with the colonies, while the economic situation of the colonies itself underwent changes. The destruction of the earlier system was started by the liberal movement and, in continental countries, was completed by the French Revolution and its successor-movements.

Monopolies granted to the companies had always roused lively opposition. In England the various ports had traditionally been jealous of each other, and from 1604 the House of Commons protested against the monopoly of the East India Company centred in London. In France the États-Généraux protested against all proposals for trade monopolies; provincial merchants embarked on expeditions to all the continents of the world at their own risks and perils and persistently protested, one after the other, against the creation of companies. In Holland the situation was different: the Dutch East India Company was the outcome of a compromise between groups who had been in strong rivalry, and its directors had a very positive sense of their common interests; they belonged to a homogeneous class which gave unity to the political direction and the economic activity of their land—but which soon fell into the faults of oligarchy.

The end of the seventeenth and beginning of the eighteenth century saw protests arising everywhere. In 1688 in England a company which had already been established with a capital of £100,000 was unable to procure a charter because a private company offered to carry on trade with North America. Soon the development of the overseas possessions of European countries challenged the habitual ways of proceeding, and checked the tightening of rules. The colonies claimed some liberty of trade, they created their own industries. The movement of ideas, with the physiocrats and Gournay in France and Adam Smith in England, tended irresistibly towards freedom.

European institutions, including chartered companies as organs of state policy, were outmoded by changes in the economy itself, both in the overseas establishments and in the mother-countries. The companies were no longer capable of adapting themselves to the situation, still less of controlling it. One and all, they were lost in the complexities of their own bureaucracies, and favouritism multiplied abuses at all levels. The inadequacy of their equipment and of their administration, as against the vast tasks with which they were confronted, condemned them to disperse their strength and rendered them ineffective: more and more, despite the distribution of dividends, sometimes generous but usually irregular, their existence became precarious. Their essentially mercantile purpose was too confined to allow them to bring the colonies effectively into production. The states were finally destined to take in hand the colonies' political organization, and private citizens, under orders from the states, were to exploit their resources.

Conflict between the states and the groups endowed with rights and privileges developed slowly and first came to a head in the English colonies. From 1619, 1625 and 1633, the Virginia Company had placed restraints on the royal governor; in 1629 that company, still retaining its rights, transferred its direction to North America and, instead of being a commercial company, became in effect an independent provincial government. Moreover, political power became more and more important; Parliament constantly busied itself with colonial matters. In the middle of the eighteenth century Parliament conducted enquiries into abuses committed in India, and in 1773 passed the Regulating Act, in 1784 the India Act, reorganizing the East India Company and making it subordinate to the Crown.

In France it is possible that about 1670–2 Colbert was moving in the direction of a system of general control in imitation of Spain, or at least of supervision by the state of colonial movements which had hitherto been relatively independent. If on the one hand he maintained the Compagnie des Indes Orientales, on the other hand he favoured the dissolution of the Compagnie des Indes Occidentales and the partition of its lands by bringing Canada under the Crown and splitting the rest among smaller companies. At the same time as he set up the Compagnie de Saint-Domingue he appointed a Conseil Supérieur for Martinique, and elsewhere in the Antilles the company's servants were taken into direct government service. In the eighteenth century the Compagnie des Indes, as reconstituted by Law, became, after many vicissitudes, virtually a government institution. Its misfortunes during the wars, and its ill-fated rivalry with the English company, along with the attacks of the supporters of freedom in trade, caused its suppression in 1769. A new company was set up in 1785, with the same name and under direct control from the government; it was suppressed in October 1793.

In Holland the Dutch company, while recognizing the supremacy of the state from time to time, had managed to retain a great measure of autonomy. But from 1726 onwards it made steady losses in trade and grew ever weaker; at the end of the War of American Independence the company no longer owned a single ship, and in 1784 it yielded to its English rival the right to trade in its territories and bit by bit abandoned its lands and its rights. A new company, formed in 1790, met with no success, and in 1796 the Dutch East India Company only retained Java and Ternate in its possession. Then in 1798 the Batavian Republic suppressed the company and annexed to itself the minute remnants of the glorious company which had been founded in 1602.

Of the great companies the English East India Company lasted till 1858, when it was abolished after the Indian Mutiny; the Staple Company of England and the Merchant Venturers of Bristol and of York still survive in some sort; and the Hudson's Bay Company still conducts an active trade.

The state-institutions of Spain and Portugal disappeared when those two countries were occupied by Napoleon's armies.

# VI. *Conclusion*

The expansion of the white races has changed the world and has made a significant contribution to the world's economic processes. Disparity of methods, and even the set-backs in achievement during the period, are witness to the divisions and the inequality of the various parts of Europe under the *ancien régime*. Defects in the administration of even the most active enterprises, the chartered companies, are signs of the archaic empiricism of the methods adopted until modern times, and of the slow developments which changed them.

If it is true that, in the two countries which saw the start of the great discoveries, the state had taken in hand both the political organization and the economic development of the new world, it is equally true that in the countries which became the chief powers in international politics the state fell back on close association with private persons by granting out charters. But the later development of these states led them to resume everywhere the powers which they had delegated and to unify methods of working with the new lands in the modern colonial system.

On parallel lines, economic development slowly led to more rational organization of the contacts between Europe and the overseas territories while at the same time the internal structure of all the great companies was re-organized. Domination of European interests was more and more stressed, and relations between the European countries and their colonies became more and more closely regulated. But economies which were for many years in a subordinate position nevertheless took on a character of their own; their needs and their demands alike could not be over-looked.

The contrasts became less important. Increasing ease of communications played a decisive part in the growth of economic and intellectual bonds. Populations of white emigrants were the first to claim their freedom, first on an economic basis, then in politics. Multilateral trade brought into contact economies which had formerly been isolated and, very slowly, tended to build up a world-economy—still at this day very imperfect! Methods of organization conformed more and more to a pattern; the companies of former days, with all their inequalities, slowly gave place to organizations which everywhere had relatively similar machinery, until the time came when there was little to distinguish one industrial or commercial organization, slowly built up since the start of the Industrial Revolution, from its rivals.

# CHAPTER V

# Crops and Livestock

It must not be thought that European agriculture, before the great voyages of discovery, was stagnant as regards the introduction of new crops. The conquests of Alexander, the Arab invasions, the Crusades, had in turn familiarized Europeans with many exotic products. Since the beginning of the Christian era, introductions to Europe had included rice, sorghum, sugar-cane, cotton and several citrus fruits; amongst animals, the water buffalo and the silkworm had found an economic niche in southern Europe. Some of these introductions were still quite recent. Rice and cotton only reached Italy from Spain in the fifteenth century, and buckwheat was still spreading in France at the same time; hops, spreading slowly through northern Europe, were not planted in England till the early sixteenth century, when Englishmen first supplemented 'ale' with 'beer'.

The Europeans of the fifteenth century were therefore well aware of the potential value of crop introductions. The group of crops in which their own agriculture was most deficient was the spices, which were in especially heavy demand in northern Europe where dried and salted foods perforce constituted so much of the diet in the winter months. To meet this demand, spices from Asia were imported overland at enormous expense. The conjunction of gold and spices in the quest of the early explorers is more understandable when we find Garcia da Orta recording in 1563 that 100 lb. of Ceylon cinnamon was worth 10 lb. of gold. Vegetable drugs were a subsidiary object of their quest; a medicine so much in esteem as rhubarb, for example, had to be imported from Asia and was quoted in France in 1542 as being ten times the price of cinnamon. Peres, the first Portuguese ambassador selected to go to China, where he arrived in 1517, was an apothecary who seems to have been expected to bring back useful plants.

In the event, few important plant introductions were made from Asia or Africa to Europe. It was the unforeseen discovery of America which changed the agricultural map of the world. As Columbus and his successors became familiar with the agriculture of America, they found that the only crops common to both the Old and New Worlds were cotton, coconuts and some gourds. The crops hitherto unknown outside America included maize, cassava, potatoes, sweet potatoes (which may or may not have reached some of the Pacific islands by this date), groundnuts, French beans, tobacco, cocoa, pineapples and tomatoes. The dog was the only domestic animal common to both hemispheres;

otherwise the Americans had only partially domesticated the llama, the guinea-pig, and the turkey.

Thus at one stroke the potential vegetable resources of the known world had been doubled. The dispersal of crops and livestock which followed was the most important in human history, and perhaps had the most far-reaching effects of any result of the Discoveries. Without the American crops, Europe might not have been able to carry such heavy populations as she later did, and the Old World tropics would not have been so quickly developed. Without the European livestock, and especially horses and mules for transport and cultivation, the American continent could not have been developed at the rate it has been. But these processes were not sudden, and not all of them took place in the period of history we are now considering. Some of the most important introductions, such as rubber and cinchona to Asia and cocoa to West Africa, did not take place till the nineteenth century, and others have continued to the present day.

# I. *Introductions into European Agriculture*

It is logical to start with the new introductions into European agriculture, whose effects would be most immediately apparent to the Europeans of the time.

The early explorations of the Portuguese along the West African coast yielded only one plant product of immediate interest, grains of paradise (*Amomum melegueta*). These were already in use in Europe as a pepper substitute and for making the spiced wine known as hippocras. They could now be obtained more cheaply than by the overland trans-Saharan route, and the trade gave its name to the 'Grain Coast'; but the plants could not be acclimatized in Europe. The further explorations of the Portuguese in the East likewise brought to light plant products in abundance, but did not result in any important introductions of living material.

Very different was the case with the American crops; but even these only came in slowly. Some crops which were widespread, like maize and cassava, were seen by Columbus on his first voyage to the islands; others, such as cocoa, were not discovered until Central America had been broached; still others, native to the interior of South America like potatoes and tomatoes, had to await the conquest of Peru.

Maize was brought home by Columbus from his first American voyage, and described in a pamphlet published in Italy in 1494; but the first widely-read description would be that by Peter Martyr in 1511. At first regarded in Europe as a garden curiosity, it was soon accorded the status of a crop, and spread quite rapidly; a locally-grown specimen was placed in an Italian herbarium in 1532. The rapid spread of this and other American crops to North Africa and the Turkish Empire would have been facilitated by the numbers of Moorish refugees who at this period were leaving Spain for Muslim lands; another herbarium specimen of maize was collected on the Euphrates in 1574. In Spain itself, maize was first grown in the Guadalquivir valley; but its economic importance in the south of Spain and of Portugal was limited by the fact that, having to be grown in the summer, it demanded irrigation water which could often be more profitably applied to other crops. During the seventeenth century however it spread to the wetter mountain regions of north-west Spain and northern Portugal, revolutionizing agriculture and diets as it replaced rye and millet (*Panicum miliaceum*). In Italy too it was soon recognized to out-yield local grains, and had become a staple crop by the first part of the eighteenth century. The same century saw it an established crop in the Morea. In the territories now comprising Rumania, a country which later became Europe's leading maize producer, no effective introduction was made until about 1700. Since maize was then reported as being introduced by Italian and Turkish traders, it would appear that the crop reached this region from the East and the West simultaneously. Once introduced, its adoption as the main article of the peasant diet was very rapid. But in Yugoslavia, another country which now has an important maize production, its promotion from garden plant to field crop did not take place before the nineteenth century. Over-reliance on maize in the diet was tragically accompanied by pellagra, a disease due to a vitamin deficiency which was first described from Asturias in Spain about 1730, and shortly afterwards from northern Italy.

Columbus introduced the sweet potato (*Ipomoea batatas*) into Spain at the same time as maize. Helped perhaps by its reputation as an aphrodisiac, it soon became popular as a garden vegetable and minor crop. It could not be grown much further north, but small quantities were imported at a luxury price into England from Spain in the sixteenth and seventeenth centuries.

The tobacco plant was also first introduced to Europe through Spain and Portugal. In 1561 Jean Nicot, the French ambassador at Lisbon, took to France tobacco seed imported from Florida. In Paris the use of the leaf was popularized as a panacea for many diseases; it was taken as snuff, or in syrups and other decoctions. The habit of smoking was first introduced by the English. The bringing of tobacco leaf into England, by at least 1587, has been variously credited to Hawkins, Drake and Lane. But it was Sir Walter Raleigh who made smoking fashionable by his own example. The habit spread so fast that Paul Hentzner, visiting

England in 1598, wrote that 'the English are constantly smoking tobacco'. From England the Dutch and Germans soon copied the habit of smoking through a pipe. The Spaniards, on the other hand, adopted the use of cigars direct from the Indies. Not till about 1796 did a fashion for cigar-smoking in Hamburg lead to the establishment of cigar factories in northern Europe. It thus came about that the 'Havana' type of wrapper leaf produced in Cuba was a valuable article of commerce long before a demand for cigar leaf in Holland induced a similar type of production in Sumatra.

The French were also responsible for certain introductions to Europe. Cartier in 1535 found beans (*Phaseolus vulgaris*) growing in Canada and probably brought home seed; the English, at any rate, first obtained them from the French and have ever since called them 'French beans'. The Jerusalem artichoke was brought from Canada by Champlain and Lescarbot early in the seventeenth century, and for a time attained in France a vogue which is explicable only by the paucity of palatable root crops at that time in Europe. During the eighteenth century, these artichokes were probably more widely grown in France than were potatoes.

The potato itself (*Solanum tuberosum*) was being cultivated in Spain by 1573, when it figures in the accounts for provisions bought by the Hospital de la Sangre at Seville. In 1588 it was described as an established garden vegetable in Italy. But cultivation in northern Europe soon overtook that in the south. The botanist Clusius received in 1588 tubers from potatoes brought into Belgium by the suite of a Papal Legate. An independent introduction of potatoes from America to the British isles does not seem to be in doubt; but the tradition that Raleigh brought them to Ireland cannot now be verified historically. Gerarde in 1596 was certainly growing potatoes in his London garden. The new crop, however, spread much faster in Ireland than in England; within fifty years of its introduction it was the staple article of food of most of the people of Ireland—the most rapid acceptance in Europe of any of the American crops. The somewhat slow adoption of the potato elsewhere can be partly explained by the fact that the varieties of the period had knobbly tubers with deeply sunken eyes, much more laborious to peel than the smoothly-rounded tubers of the modern improved varieties.

Of the American fruits, pineapples were exhibited in Europe in the sixteenth and seventeenth centuries, but were not grown to fruiting until nearly the end of the latter. During the eighteenth century the fruit became an exceedingly fashionable one for rich men to grown in their hot-houses in France, England and Holland. Tomatoes were introduced in the sixteenth century and their cultivation became established in southern Europe. In the northern countries they aroused surprisingly little interest, and were still very rarely grown in England at the end of the eighteenth century. The only spice plants which proved amenable to cultivation in Europe were the American capsicums (red peppers or chillies). These were described by Fuchs from specimens grown in Germany in 1542, were common in Spain in the second half of the sixteenth century, and were grown by Gerarde in England before 1597. They constituted a useful addition to the dietary of southern Europe.

Certain American trees were successfully grown in England at quite an early date: *Thuya occidentalis* in the sixteenth century, and the swamp cypress and pencil cedar in the seventeenth. But introductions to Europe of trees which are now important in commercial forestry were mostly postponed until the nineteenth century.

The turkey was the only American livestock which found an economic place in Europe. Its English name, like that of the guinea-pig, shows how vague were the ideas of our ancestors as to the source from which they got their introductions. First brought to Europe by the Spaniards, turkeys spread so fast that they reached England by the 1530's and Tusser mentions them as already a popular Christmas dish in 1573.

Some livestock importations of significance also took place from the Old World. The foundations of the English thoroughbred horse were laid by the importation of the 'Byerley Turk' in 1689, the 'Darley Arabian' in 1702 and the 'Godolphin Barb' about 1784. When Europeans reached China they found that, in that region where pigs had first been domesticated, some useful breeds had been evolved. With the English interest in livestock improvement in the eighteenth century, Chinese pigs were imported from about 1770, and in 1800 were described as 'very common in England'. They have left their mark on certain of the modern English breeds, particularly the Middle White and Berkshire, which have again been transported to other parts of the world.

## II. *Introductions of European Crops and Livestock Overseas*

The first transferences of European crops and livestock overseas were to the Atlantic islands. During the fifteenth century, the Spaniards probably took sugar-cane from their own country to the Canaries, and the Portuguese fetched it from Sicily to plant in Madeira. In both places flourishing sugar industries soon developed. It was from the Canaries that Columbus took sugar cane setts to Hispaniola in 1493. It is now uncertain whether these plants survived, but further consignments were sent and the first sugar was made in Hispaniola in 1506.

The Portuguese meanwhile had colonized Sao Thomé in the Gulf of Guinea, where by 1522 there were sixty sugar mills; with the Madeiran production, this is claimed to have made Portugal the leading sugar producer of the time. In 1526 Brazilian sugar was paying customs duty at Lisbon, though an introduction of cane from Madeira to Brazil is recorded as late as 1532.

It was unfortunate that all the introductions to America were of the thin type of cane then grown in Europe, which has been identified with the Indian variety 'Puri' and the 'Algarobena' of modern Spain. The introducers were aware of the need for the best stocks, for Columbus wrote in 1494 to his sovereigns 'May it please your Highnesses to instruct Don Juan de Fonseca that he send here only the best sugar-canes'; but there was not much choice open to them. It was not till the eighteenth century that this 'Creole' cane, as it came to be called, was superseded by the far higher-yielding thick or 'noble' canes. The low yields of sugar per acre obtainable from the thin cane necessitated the use of much ground and were one cause of the avidity with which the European nations scrambled for suitable land.

Columbus, at the same time as sugar cane, took with him seeds of the commoner Spanish crops, but these did not for the moment become important. The repeated introduction of the vine, with the object of wine-making in America, by this and other expeditions, is a reminder that the introducers had their disappointments as well as their successes. The establishment of the temperate cereal crops in North America is no part of the present story, for they did not enter into trade outside the Americas or affect the European economy during the centuries now under discussion.

The introduction of European livestock into America is of more significance, since in this branch of agriculture the continent was almost totally deficient, and a more immediate trade developed as a result. The Portuguese and Spanish had already had experience in introducing European livestock to Madeira, the Canaries and the Azores, though this had taught one sharp ecological lesson. Rabbits introduced to the island of Porto Santo in the Madeira group had become so destructive of vegetation that by about 1420 it was complained that farming there was impossible.

The Portuguese were also particularly active in landing breeding stocks of pigs and goats to run wild on uninhabited islands where they might be useful for provisioning ships and for shipwrecked sailors. Thus to take the single example of St Helena, Cavendish visiting the island in 1588 reported thousands of goats and 'great store of swine' and also turkeys which had been introduced from America. In other cases the introductions were not deliberate but resulted from animals escaping from wrecked ships. Such is the presumed origin (and the wrecks were there in both cases as evidence) of the pigs of Bermuda upon which the shipwrecked May in 1591 and Gates in 1609 subsisted, and of the wild cattle and sheep of Sable Island off Nova Scotia which are recorded from 1598 onwards.

Columbus on his second voyage to America took with him cattle, sheep, goats, pigs and fowls, which he loaded at Gomera in the Canaries. Cattle were multiplied rapidly in Hispaniola, their number in 1520 being estimated at 4,000. An export trade to Spain in hides and tallow developed at an early date from Hispaniola, Porto Rico and Cuba, and was important in providing a steady income for the colonists while they were building up their settlements as a springboard for further conquests. In 1587 Santo Domingo (Hispaniola) exported 35,444 hides and Mexico 64,350. The cattle population of South and Central America remained almost exclusively of Spanish and Portuguese origin until the nineteenth century. The introductions were largely of black Andalusian cattle and other long-horned Spanish types, which are of remotely African origin. This origin may partly account for the relative success in the tropics of these cattle, which gave rise in America to some later well-known types such as the Franqueiro breed of Brazil and the Texas longhorns. The foundations of the Argentine cattle industry were laid when Aguirre brought cattle into that country in 1543 from Chile and Peru. In the West Indies there were later introductions of English, French and Dutch cattle which contributed to the amalgam eventually known as 'creole' cattle, more or less acclimatized but not very productive.

In the North American settlements, cattle brought in by the Dutch to New Amsterdam and by the Swedes to their short-lived colony on the Delaware achieved a high reputation and were sought after by neighbouring English settlers; though it was noticed that the harsh rigours of the frontier settlements were better tolerated by the then less-improved English cattle. All these introductions were made before the great era of cattle improvement began in the eighteenth century. There was not time for the development of stable breeds in North America before the types of stock there were outclassed by the new European breeds which, though later introductions, have largely superseded them.

Pigs naturally multiplied more rapidly than cattle in the New World, and droves of these animals and of sheep on the hoof were an important element in provisioning the expeditions of the Conquistadores. It is nevertheless surprising that Gonzalo Pizarro, on an eastward expedition from Peru in 1541, was able to take with him four to five thousand pigs, only eleven years after the country had been entered by the Spaniards. In a similar way Coronado, on a northward expedition from Mexico, drove with him 5,000 sheep in 1540.

Horses were another very important introduction, in the first place as instruments of conquest in Mexico and Peru by terrorizing the Indians who had never before seen such animals. At a later date the tables were turned to some extent when this resulted in the horsing of the Indians. Many Spanish horses ran wild and bred freely on the American ranges, and there were Indian tribes who became expert horsemen before they had seen a white man. Apart from the uses of horses and mules for transport and cultivation, horses were indispensable to the gaucho and the cowboy for the herding of cattle on fenceless ranches.

In Africa and the East there was not the same need for the introduction of crops and livestock from Europe, since the same types were usually already present wherever they would thrive. Nor did Europeans settle as agriculturists until the Dutch did so in South Africa in 1652. These latter indeed took their European cereals with them; but for cattle, they made the Hottentot animals serve their needs. From these they selectively bred the Afrikander type, which so competently fulfilled their purposes for trek and for beef.

Only in a few islands were livestock found to be lacking. The most important of these was Mauritius, where cattle introduced by the French settlers originated the present 'creole' breed which has performed better than many such types in the tropics.

# III. *Inter-Tropical Movements of Crops and Livestock*

As they explored the tropics, the European colonizing nations naturally became anxious to extend the cultivation of export crops to new and favourable areas. Inter-continental introductions were made easier by the fact that the Portuguese had possessions in South America, Africa and Asia; while the Spanish, besides their American colonies, had an Asiatic foothold in the Philippines. For over two centuries the annual round-voyage of a Spanish government vessel between Acapulco on the Mexican Pacific coast and Manila would have made plant introductions easy.

As this transference proceeded, it led in due course to the foundation of botanic gardens to facilitate the introduction and multiplication of plants. The first of these was founded by the Dutch at Capetown in 1694, as a staging-post for plants from the East on the long voyage to Europe. The French established a botanic garden at Pamplemousses in Mauritius in 1735; the British at St Vincent in the West Indies in 1764,

Jamaica in 1774, Calcutta in 1786 and Penang about 1796. The first botanic garden in North America was founded by Bartram near Philadelphia in 1730; in 1781 Charles III of Spain sent a scientific expedition to Mexico, one of whose objects was to establish a garden. Botanic gardens in Europe also played a notable part as clearing-houses for tropical crops: Amsterdam and Paris as early as 1706-23 in the case of coffee, and Kew from the date of its foundation in 1760.

One crop, tobacco, proved so instantaneously popular on the introduction of smoking into the Old World that it spread with little encouragement, sometimes actually against the wishes of governments. Moslems quickly introduced it from Europe into Turkey and Persia, where by 1622 the Persians had already invented the art of smoking through water. The crop is recorded in India in 1609, in Java in 1601, and the Chinese soon obtained it from the Portuguese. In Africa, tobacco is reported as being commonly grown and used in Sierra Leone in 1607. The Europeans, who seem often to have been singularly blind to the importance of varietal differences in their crop introductions, soon recognized differences of quality in tobacco. The local sorts first grown by the English settlers in Virginia were not good, and were soon replaced by the 'Orinoco' and 'Trinidad' varieties. It is quite likely that these latter had been obtained by Raleigh on his South American expedition of 1594-5, and had passed through intermediate generations in England or Ireland, where the crop was then being cultivated.

The case of spices is rather different. Exploration of the American tropics showed that they only yielded three spice plants: capsicums, vanilla and pimento. As these were unfamiliar to Europeans, they did not spread until a taste for them had been established. This happened first, as already recorded, with the capsicums. Pimento was not imported into Europe until about 1601; vanilla was not grown in Asia until the nineteenth century. The Asiatic spices were more highly prized by Europeans because they were already familiar. But exploration revealed that, with the exception of ginger which was widely dispersed in Asia, each spice was only indigenous to a rather limited region. Ginger was therefore early taken to America; but with the other spices, the Portuguese and later the Dutch conceived it to be in their interests to continue to limit cultivation to the areas where they had a near-monopoly of the trade. These botanical monopolies were not broken until the French traveller Le Poivre succeeded in establishing pepper and cinnamon at the Pamplemousses botanic garden in Mauritius in 1767. Later expeditions, sent out by him as Intendant of Mauritius in 1770 and 1772, landed on unfrequented coasts of the Moluccas and brought back enough plants and seeds of cloves and nutmegs to distribute from Mauritius to Réunion, the Seychelles, and the French colony of Cayenne in South America.

The clove industry of Mauritius remained important until it was superseded by that of Zanzibar in the nineteenth century. In 1796 the British East India Company obtained nutmeg and clove plants from the Moluccas for Penang, which became another centre of their cultivation.

In the sugar industry, the introduction of the thick high-yielding 'noble' canes to the American tropics was an event of the first importance. It was not until European navigators began to frequent the Pacific islands in the eighteenth century that they were struck by the value of these local canes. Bougainville on his voyage round the world in 1766–8 is believed to have brought the Tahiti cane to Mauritius. Passing thence to Réunion (Bourbon), the cane was brought to Martinique in the French West Indies in 1792. Almost simultaneously, in 1793 Captain Bligh brought four varieties of cane direct from Tahiti to Jamaica. Under the name of Bourbon or Otaheite (Tahiti), these canes rapidly displaced the existing Creole variety and raised sugar yields to a level hitherto impossible.

The dispersal of the great tropical beverage crops—coffee, cocoa and tea—was a slow process because it was a long time before a mass demand for them arose in Europe. Coffee (of the type first used in the trade) is native to Ethiopia, but had been put into cultivation in Arabia before the era of European exploration. From here it was introduced to India at a date unknown, and by the Dutch to Ceylon in 1658 and Java in 1696. In 1706 one coffee plant from Java reached the Amsterdam botanic garden, and from its progeny the whole vast coffee populations of America, the greatest coffee-growing continent, were until recently descended. This came about partly through a direct introduction from Amsterdam to Surinam in 1714, and partly via the Jardin Royal (later Jardin des Plantes) in Paris to Martinique in 1716 and 1723. The result was a botanically uniform population with little variability to give scope for improvement. Cocoa is recorded to have been introduced to Celebes in 1560, but effective cultivation remained limited to its native continent of America until well into the nineteenth century. Tea too remained an export product only of China to the end of the eighteenth century. A similar limitation applied to quinine, a product derived from the bark of the Cinchona tree. The drug was popularized as a febrifuge for Europeans by the cure of the Countess Chinchon, vicereine of Peru (after whom the plant is named) in 1639. But for another 200 years the wild trees of the South American forests were able to supply all the demand that arose.

The distribution of native food crops did not interest Europeans nearly so much as that of the export crops. A great deal of the dispersal that occurred seems to have come about more or less accidentally, and probably through the voyages of slave ships between Africa and

America. It is understandable that the provisions taken aboard such ships would include maize, sweet potatoes, groundnuts and French beans on the American side, and sorghum, yams and cowpeas on the African. On arrival, the holds of the ships would be cleared and provisions which would not keep for another voyage would be sold or thrown away; some might well be tried by local people for planting. At any rate, it is certain that each of the crops named soon made its appearance on the other side of the Atlantic. Yams were a particularly popular food crop of the negro slaves in America, many of whom came from the eastern part of the Guinea coast where these are a staple food. It is less easy to account for the introduction into Africa of cassava, a crop which is planted from stem cuttings and not from roots, and which was in any case often loaded as flour. This introduction is presumed to have been made from Brazil, because the Portuguese in the sixteenth century were in constant touch with the kingdom of the Congo. Portuguese residents may perhaps have introduced it for their own use, since Merolla describing a visit to Congo in 1682 says it is 'more used by the Portuguese than blacks'. Crop introductions also took place direct to the east coast of Africa through the Portuguese settlements; it is recorded in 1634, for example, that maize was being grown in Zanzibar by Portuguese planters.

The effect of the introduction of these new food crops and tobacco into Africa was far-reaching. Tropical Africa had hitherto had the poorest selection of indigenous food crops of any cultivated region of the world. Cereals were limited to sorghum, several small-grained millets, and the indigenous 'red' rice (*Oryza glaberrima*) in parts of West Africa. Root crops included only yams and the low-yielding 'kaffir potato' (*Coleus*). Cowpeas, and in West Africa the Bambarra groundnut, were the only significant legumes. Of the new introductions, maize was, in the high rainfall areas, a better yielder than the indigenous cereals. The two new root crops, cassava and sweet potatoes, must have been particularly welcome because they increased the small number of available crops which escaped locust damage; while cassava, which keeps for long periods in the ground, is the best famine reserve crop for the wet tropics. These new crops must in the course of time have prevented thousands of deaths from famine. They spread through the continent at a rate which there were no historians present to record.[1] By the nineteenth century, when Europeans first penetrated the interior of Africa, they found the new crops already completely integrated into African farming. This revolutionizing of African diets is in retrospect one of the more striking results of the economic expansion of Europe.

[1] Some of the presumed early records of maize in Africa are erroneous, due to the use of the Portuguese word *milho* at that time to denote not only maize but also other cereals.

For crop transferences between Asia and Africa and America, the Portuguese are again presumed to have been largely responsible. To them, for want of other evidence, are attributed the introduction of coconuts and Asiatic rice to West Africa, of eddoes (*Colocasia*) to America, and the fact that in India such American plants are recorded as pineapples in 1583, papaya in 1600 and sweet potatoes in 1616. But Asia, with a much wider range of indigenous foodstuffs than Africa, was slower to adopt the American crops and has still not done so in the same measure. Thus cassava (here known as tapioca) was only introduced to Pamplemousses in Mauritius in 1736, whence it came to Ceylon in 1786 and to the Calcutta botanic garden in 1794. Potatoes (*Solanum tuberosum*), perhaps introduced from England, seem to have been first grown in India during the governor-generalship of Warren Hastings (1772–85).

There is only one transference of a food crop during this period where we have a clear record that it was done as an act of government policy. The scientists accompanying Captain Cook's expedition to Tahiti in 1769 were apparently so struck by the virtues of the breadfruit tree that they thought it would be a useful food plant for the slaves in the West Indies. Accordingly in 1787 Captain Bligh, who had served with Cook, was sent in the *Bounty* to collect plants from Tahiti. The voyage ended in mutiny and disaster; but Bligh, after narrowly escaping with his life, was sent again to Tahiti. Thence in 1793 he successfully brought breadfruit plants to the botanic garden at St Vincent, introducing the Tahiti sugar cane to Jamaica at the same time. Unfortunately the breadfruit failed to live up to expectations and did not become a popular food in the West Indies.

Transference of livestock between the tropical continents seems hardly to have occurred during this period. Some animal geneticists have surmised a West African origin for the Mocha breed of cattle in Brazil, and for the sheep and goats of the Bahamas; but if such movements occurred they must have been rare.

In summary it may be said that the vast post-Columbian dispersal of crops, which came so intimately to affect the daily lives and economic occupation of people in all the tropical continents, was not carried out by the inhabitants of those continents but was almost entirely the work of Europeans going about their own economic business.

## IV. *The Economic Effects of Crop Dispersal*

The first Europeans to take a close interest in the new plants were the surgeons and apothecaries, seeking to discover what 'virtue' each might have for medicinal use. The sweet potato, they decided, was an aphrodisiac; pineapples stimulated the appetite; kidney beans must be good for strengthening the kidneys. Potatoes were long distrusted because of their relationship to the poisonous deadly nightshade. Garcia da Orta's *Colloquios dos Simples e Drogas da India* was the first European book to be printed in the East, at Goa in 1563. The arrival of so many exotic plants in Europe shortly preceded, and perhaps partly inspired, the golden age of the great herbalists. During the sixteenth century the German Fuchs, the Frenchman Clusius and the Englishman Gerarde all gave us some of the first descriptions and drawings of American plants. In the following century more scientific work was carried on in the tropics themselves. Hernandez, in his *Rerum medicarum Novae Hispanae Thesaurus* of 1651, gives the first description of vanilla. Sir Hans Sloane, later secretary and president of the Royal Society, collected plants in Jamaica in 1687–8 and published a Latin catalogue of them in 1696. Rumphius (1626–93) in the service of the Dutch East India Company produced in his *Herbarium Amboinense* the first sound work on Asiatic botany.

But scientific interest in exotic crops was soon overtaken by economic. A number of false starts were made before the great staple trades settled into their strides. Some of the early European traders to the eastern Guinea coast in the sixteenth century loaded cargoes of cotton cloth and palm oil. But it was soon found that cotton goods could be had in better quantity and quality elsewhere; and the oil trade lapsed until, with the industrial revolution, small regular shipments to Liverpool began again in 1772. Barbados started its colonial career as an exporter of tobacco, cotton, indigo, ginger and fustic wood; but with the beginning of sugar manufacture in 1642, all these were soon superseded.

Almost as soon as any massive trade developed in a particular commodity, tropical agriculture found itself faced with a problem that remained characteristic, over-production for the market. This was largely due to the fact that the majority of tropical products, then as now, were articles of luxury consumption with a limited demand. Already in 1496 the additional production of cane sugar from Madeira and the Canaries led to a fall in price, and in 1498 King Manoel of Portugal limited Madeira to an export quota. Tobacco production at an early stage ran into the same trouble. In 1639 a slump in price induced the English and French settlers who shared St Kitts to agree to a year's holiday from tobacco planting. In the same year, the Virginia planters agreed with their Governor to limit production for that year to 1,500,000 lb. of tobacco and for each of the next two years to 1,200,000 lb. In the spice trade, due to over-production, an immense quantity of nutmegs and mace was burned at Amsterdam in 1760 to maintain prices; cinnamon stocks were also burned in Holland at periods of low prices. Over-production could however be equally frustrating when it consisted in produce of the temperate zone, which was then in adequate supply in Europe and which no colonial power particularly wished to encourage overseas. In Connecticut in 1644 over-production of wheat led to a fall in price to 2s. a bushel. The remedy adopted was to appoint two monopolistic buyers who were to pay 4s. a bushel and export the wheat overseas. That they were not successful in finding a market is suggested by the lawsuits brought against them for recovery of debts.

The further economic developments arising from the new trades in agricultural products are best followed by considering each trade separately in more detail.

## V. *The Spice Trade*

In order to understand the historical development of the spice trade, it is necessary to define the areas in which each of these spices was produced. Pepper was indigenous to southern India but had been introduced to the Malaysian region before the advent of Europeans on the scene. It was in bulk the most important item in the spice trade, and was the staple of early European trade with India. A corner in pepper by the Dutch in 1599, raising the London price from 3 to 6 or 8 shillings a pound, was a proximate cause of the founding of the English East India Company in 1600. Cinnamon and cardamoms were both native to southern India and Ceylon; but Ceylon cinnamon bark was much more highly valued than the Indian article, and made Ceylon a tempting prize first for the Portuguese and then for the Dutch. The nutmeg tree (which also produces the spice mace) was limited in distribution to the Moluccas, while cloves were still more restricted in distribution to a few small islands of that group. Thus the Moluccas became the richest bone of contention between the European powers. This was also the point where European penetration of the globe from the west and the east respectively met and clashed. The Portuguese, arriving from the west, acquired their first base in the Malaysian region by the seizure of Malacca in 1511, and soon pushed on to trade in the Moluccas. Here in 1521 the survivors of Magellan's Spanish expedition, circumnavigating the world from the east, encountered them. In 1526 and 1528 more Spaniards arrived from the east, fighting a desultory war in the Moluccas against the Portuguese until the Treaty of Saragossa in 1529 finally ceded the islands to the latter. The Dutch, consolidating their conquest of the Moluccas from the Portuguese in 1609, were no more willing to tolerate interlopers. In 1623 they perpetrated on English traders in the islands the 'massacre of Amboyna' which for so long embittered relations between the two nations.

Each of these powers, controlling in turn the source of the most lucrative trade in spices, took care to make the trade a monopoly within its own nation. In Portugal the whole spice trade became, almost from the start of the eastern voyages, a royal monopoly. In Spain, during the brief period when she grasped at the conquest of the Moluccas, a Spice Board was set up in 1524 to handle the commerce, with a depot at Corunna which was calculated to supply the profitable markets of Flanders, Germany and England. The Dutch, uniting their eastern trading interests in 1602 into the Vereenigde Oost-Indische Compagnie, declared a government monopoly of spices and delegated it to this company, which became practically a department of state.

During the period of Dutch rule in Indonesia, control of the production of spices was carried much further by local measures. The Company decided to limit the production of nutmegs to the small Banda Islands and that of cloves to Amboyna. Annual expeditions were sent out by the local administration to destroy these trees in the other islands of the Moluccas, and though these never succeeded in entirely fulfilling their task, they did not finally cease until 1824. The first result of these operations was that the production of the two spices is said to have declined to a quarter of its former volume. When at a later date the demand for spices in Europe increased, it was impossible to restore the production by voluntary means. In 1656 the people of Amboyna were made to plant 120,000 more clove trees, and 60,000 in 1658; but in 1667 further planting was forbidden, and in 1692 and 1697 trees were cut down. A further regulation from about 1720 compelled the cultivators of Amboyna each to maintain 125 trees.

For spices other than cloves and nutmegs, it was not possible to attempt to adjust production so closely to the market because their growth was not limited to a single territory. Pepper in the eighteenth century in those parts of Java under the closest Dutch control came within the system of forced deliveries from particular areas, which were bought by the ruling company at a price fixed by itself. From 1763 in Bantam overseers were sent round to see that the required plantings were made. A similar system was applied to cinnamon in Ceylon under Dutch rule. The British, from their occupation of Ceylon in 1796, continued the government monopoly of cinnamon until 1832. That the system did maintain world prices at an artificially high level was shown in this case by the increase in exports of cinnamon and the fall in price which followed the removal of the monopoly.

# VI. *The Sugar Trade*

The first result of the extension of sugar cane production to Madeira and the Canaries in the fifteenth century was severe competition with the existing European producers. This was accentuated as the American colonies came into production. By 1580, in spite of some fiscal help, the industry in Sicily was moribund. Attempts were later made to revive it by increases in protective duties in 1684 and 1732, which did make the island for a time self-supporting in sugar, but by the end of the eighteenth century production had ceased. In Spain the industry had been a Moorish one, and languished after the conquest of Granada, receiving a further setback from the expulsion of the Moriscos in 1609. Though production never entirely ceased, it was reduced by 1800 to 1,225 acres of cane served by four mills. The small medieval sugar industries of southern Italy, Malta, the Morea, Rhodes, Crete and Cyprus all underwent a similar decline and eventually disappeared.

In both Madeira and the Canaries sugar production involved the use of African slave labour, to which both Spaniards and Portuguese were already accustomed on a small scale in their homelands. In 1552 there were 2,700 slaves in Madeira. This use of slaves may have helped the islanders to undersell other European sugar producers; but Madeira and the Canaries in their turn succumbed respectively to Brazilian and West Indian competition. During the second half of the sixteenth century sugar production in both island groups passed its peak, and was gradually succeeded by the planting of vines and the establishment of wine exports. These islands and the Azores had nevertheless played their part, in this as in other spheres, in providing Europeans with an apprenticeship to the development of wider lands beyond.

In the American tropics the history of sugar and slavery is even more intimately linked. Of all the tropical export crops of this period, sugar cane demanded the most manual labour, especially for harvesting. The necessity for a mill in close proximity to the fields, to which the transport of cane must be organized within a few hours of cutting, required for the first time the establishment of the plantation system. For such regular work the native Indians were neither numerous enough nor suited by temperament; and the Spanish system of the *encomienda*, a grant of the land with its inhabitants' labour, proved inadequate. Without doubt sugar cane was primarily responsible for agricultural slavery in the tropics. In 1518 the first *asiento* or licence was granted to Lorens de Gominot to import 4,000 African slaves into the Spanish colonies between that year and 1526. This was sublet to Portuguese merchants. The Spaniards, being debarred from Africa by the Treaty of Tordesillas (1494), could not conduct their own slaving expeditions and consequently had to entrust the importations to foreign nationals. From 1552 onwards the contracts were given to Portuguese, with the Dutch taking a share in the seventeenth century. From 1701 to 1713 the French held the coveted monopoly, which passed at the Treaty of Utrecht to the British. On their behalf it was exercised by the Royal African Company, who already had a monopoly of supplying slaves to the British West Indies. The last *asiento* was held from 1786 to 1789 by the firm of Baker & Dawson, British merchants in Havana, for the import of slaves to Cuba. From 1789 the slave-trade into Cuba was unrestricted; but in 1778 Spain had acquired from the Portuguese, with Fernando Po, the island of Annobon in African waters as a slaving depot of her own. These developments in the slave trade in turn reacted upon sugar, for it was due to them that Cuba first became a major producer, with a resultant collapse in sugar prices in 1801.

The close link between sugar and slavery is even more clearly demonstrated in the history of the English colony of Barbados. From the settlement in 1627 until 1639 the main crop was tobacco, grown on small holdings with indentured white labour. The great tobacco slump of 1639, to which reference has already been made as it affected other colonies, induced a number of planters to turn over to sugar. So successful did this prove to be that it revolutionized the island's economy. Estates increased in size, and land values rose prodigiously. The white population fell greatly by emigration to other colonies; but whereas in 1640 there had been only a few hundred slaves in the island, by 1651 there were 20,000.

The see-saw fortunes of the sugar industry in the seventeenth and eighteenth centuries are largely bound up with the exhaustion of the original fertility of the West Indian soils and the extension of the crop to new lands. In Barbados it was complained in 1714 that the soil now needed manuring every year to produce a cane crop, and at about the same date that the slave labour required was four times greater than in the French islands where soils were less exhausted. In 1667–70 the price of raw sugar fell by nearly half when the French islands of Martinique and Guadeloupe first came into serious production. Again during the period 1713–33 markets for British sugar were greatly narrowed by the increasing sugar production of St Domingue (now Haiti, the western half of the island previously known as Hispaniola) which the French had acquired from Spain in 1697. This directly led to the passing by the British Parliament, under the influence of the powerful West Indian lobby, of the Molasses Act of 1733 which imposed heavy duties on foreign sugar imported into any British territory. By the time of the French Revolution St Domingue was exporting more sugar than all the British colonies together. But a converse process was now to work. The rebellion which took place in St Domingue in 1791, and the cutting off of the other French islands from Europe during the ensuing wars, caused a rise in sugar prices, which nearly tripled between 1793 and 1798.

The smaller British West Indian islands were the first countries in the world to carry agricultural specialization so far that they devoted most of their land to the export crop and found it more profitable to import food than to grow it. Thus in the late seventeenth and in the eighteenth century the West Indies imported quantities of foodstuffs from the British Isles. These came largely from Ireland, which contributed beef and pork, herrings, butter and potatoes. Potatoes were also exported to Jamaica from Lancashire. In such trade of course Scotland had no part before the Union with England in 1707. The Navigation Acts confined trade with the English colonies to English ships and English ports; and it was not till long after the Union that Glasgow became an important port for colonial produce and a centre for sugar refining and tobacco manufacture. The West Indian colonies did however also import large supplies of the foodstuffs of the temperate zone from the British North American colonies, a trade convenient to both sides. From this source came supplies of beef and pork, flour, bread, and smaller quantities of rice, maize and salt fish among other articles.

Meanwhile an entirely different system of sugar production was being developed under Dutch rule in the East Indies. Sugar growing and milling was here in the hands of Chinese immigrants and could not be regulated in the same way as the production of crops by the native peasants. Manipulation of the supply was mainly by altering the prices at which the Chinese were compelled to deliver their sugar to the Company. Shipments to Europe began in 1622. During the seventeenth and eighteenth centuries they never attained a very large volume; Holland's imports of sugar from all her possessions in 1770 were only 12,500 tons. But there were alternative markets in Asia, including a steady trade in low-grade sugar to Japan.

The sugar industry was associated with the first exports of specialized agricultural machinery to the tropics. In the 1650's iron-cased rollers first replaced wooden ones in the vertical three-roller mill of the time, and the earliest of these were made in England by George Sitwell at his foundry near Derby. In time they were superseded by horizontal rollers, of which the first of modern type was made by Collinge of London in 1794. A mechanical device to direct the cane to its second rolling was patented by Fleming in England in 1773, and a similar machine, made by Varettes Frères, was in use in St Domingue in the eighteenth century. The same century saw the first application of steam engines to sugar milling in 1768 in Jamaica and in 1797 in Cuba, but their use did not become effective till the nineteenth century.

A more important item in Europe's economy was the sugar refining industry; though the individual units or 'boiling-houses' were usually very small. Sugar refining had been carried out in the fifteenth century in Venice and Bologna, with imports of raw sugar coming from as far afield as Cyprus. As Venice declined, Antwerp became the chief centre of the industry. The Antwerp merchants also had a stake in sugar production, individuals among them owning in the 1560's plantations in the Canaries and Brazil. In 1556 Antwerp had nineteen refineries; but the Spanish sack of the city in 1576 put an end to the industry. Its next centre was Amsterdam, where there were sixty refineries in 1661. Holland refined most of the sugar from the English and French colonies until the Navigation Act of 1660 in England and a similar restriction by Colbert in France stopped this trade. The next centre to rise into importance was Hamburg. Here 8,000 men were employed in sugar refining in 1690, and in 1750 there were 350 refineries. France had twenty-nine refineries in 1683, Rouen being the busiest centre; Colbert himself was a partner in one of the Rouen refineries, perhaps by way of encouraging the industry. In 1700 sugar was quoted as the most important export of France. In 1788 imports of raw sugar to France were 81,000 tons, which compares with 103,800 tons to Britain in 1785. Denmark established refineries in the late seventeenth century to deal with sugar from her West Indian colonies. In England, refining only became important after 1660. In 1753 there were eighty refineries in London, twenty in Bristol, and a smaller number elsewhere. In Scotland, Glasgow could boast two refineries before the union with England; but at Greenock, the later centre of the industry, a refinery was not built till 1765.

## VII. *The Tobacco Trade*

Tobacco was at first welcomed in Europe as a valuable drug. But as the habit of smoking spread, it began to attract condemnation as a pernicious and dissolute practice. In England, James I himself wrote a 'Counterblaste to Tobacco' in 1603. A short-lived French law of 1635 prohibited the purchase of tobacco except from an apothecary's shop on a doctor's prescription. At various dates in the seventeenth century smoking was made a punishable offence in Switzerland, Turkey, Persia and Russia. In the latter country the prohibition lasted until the end of the century, and the penalties included amputation of the nose.

Nevertheless the demand for tobacco grew so strongly that the crop formed the basis for the original settlement of certain European colonies, such as Virginia, Maryland and the French West Indies. Since it could be grown both in Europe and overseas, the history of its cultivation and importation for each of the European countries is somewhat chequered. Each country naturally wished to be supplied either from its own cultivation or from its colonies. Sir Edwin Sandys complained in the English Parliament in 1620 that it was unnecessary for the nation to be spending £120,000 a year on tobacco imported from Spain.

This was also the year in which James I, in consideration of the Virginia Company agreeing to higher import duties and the consignment of the whole tobacco crop to English ports, prohibited the growing of the crop in England. The prohibition was later extended to Ireland, and was re-enacted by Parliament in 1660. It was nevertheless not at first strictly enforced, and there were said at one time to have been 6,000 growers in the western counties of England. In the 1660's, when enforcement was undertaken, the military had to be used in several places to support the destruction of the crop, and in 1666 there were riots in Winchcomb and Cheltenham. Not until about 1690 was the cultivation extinguished for the time being. This was not, however, the end of the matter. The Act of 1660 did not apply in Scotland, where during the American War of Independence a shortage of tobacco caused its cultivation to be taken up until stopped by an Act of George III. At the same period an illegal cultivation of tobacco sprang up in the vale of York, which was put an end to when the growers were fined a total of £30,000 and the tobacco publicly burned.

Tobacco production in the British colonies suffered from the same periodic over-production and fluctuations of price as did sugar. The Virginians at times had to adopt restriction of acreage or to destroy the lower grades of leaf. Virginia reached its highest eighteenth-century production in 1758 with an export of 70,000,000 lb. The Maryland leaf was of somewhat different quality and found its chief market in the Low Countries. The trade at home was strictly controlled. James I made it a royal monopoly and tobacco dealers had to obtain his letters patent, from which he derived a considerable revenue. As time went on and the demand for tobacco in Europe increased, re-exports from Britain became more important. In 1770 it was said that tobacco imports into the kingdom were evenly divided between England and Scotland, but that four-fifths of the latter's share was re-exported. The high duties on tobacco throughout this period, with the rebate on re-exports, tended to systematic fiscal frauds which grew into a major abuse. Walpole's attempt to introduce a reformed system in his Excise Bill of 1733 aroused the opposition of vested interests, shook the government, and had to be abandoned.

In France very similar problems presented themselves to the government as tobacco cultivation began to be taken up. In 1674 the cultivation and sale of tobacco were made a state monopoly, which like others was farmed out. In 1719 however a new policy was adopted in the interests of the tobacco industry which it was hoped to develop on a large scale in Louisiana. All cultivation of the crop in France was prohibited, save in Franche-Comté, Flanders and Alsace, to which this law did not apply. The prohibition was enforced on pain of fines, the galleys, and even death. This lasted until 1791, when the revolutionary Assembly freed the cultivation and manufacture of tobacco, subject to a simple excise on the product.

Portugal and Spain, with their immense tropical possessions, did not during any part of this period find it expedient to encourage tobacco production at home. In Portugal the cultivation of the crop was prohibited in the eighteenth century. In Spain, local production was not developed until after the loss of her American possessions. Tobacco for local consumption was being grown in parts of the Turkish dominions in Europe, such as the plains of Thessaly, during the eighteenth century. But it was not until later that the development of a western taste for 'Turkish' tobacco caused the growth of an export trade.

# VIII. *The Beverage Trades*

The first non-alcoholic beverage with which Europeans came into contact was cocoa, which Cortez found in use among the peoples of Mexico. As prepared by the Aztecs, it was a bitter porridge. It was some time before the Spaniards learned to make it more palatable with sugar and milk. In the early seventeenth century chocolate became an appreciated drink among them, first in America and then in Spain. The early chocolate factories were all in Spain, and the Spaniards long sought not only to monopolize the trade but to keep the method of manufacture secret. From Spain, the practice of drinking chocolate first spread to Italy. In 1640, the substance figures in a German apothecary's price-list. A chocolate house was advertised in Bishopsgate Street, London, in 1657; and chocolate was being drunk in Amsterdam in 1660. In France, it was made fashionable by Louis XIV's Spanish bride, Maria Theresa, of whom it was said that 'Le roi et le chocolat furent les deux seules passions de Marie Thérèse'. A monopoly for the preparation of chocolate was granted to Chaillon David in 1659 and transferred to one Damame in 1692. But at this time chocolate was too dear to be more than a luxury for the aristocracy, though chocolate houses were numerous in London in 1700. Not till the middle of the eighteenth century, when the price fell considerably, did it become a more common drink.

At first solely an export of Mexico, cultivation was next taken up in Venezuela; here, as in other American countries, introductions of seed were made although wild trees were also present, and it is not always clear from which the plants were derived. Venezuelan exports of cocoa began in 1634, and although the trade was legally limited to Spain, a large share was soon obtained by the Dutch who were then the ubiquitous carriers of the Caribbean and took this 'Caracas' cocoa straight to Amsterdam. Plantations were developed during the seventeenth century in Trinidad, where the first introduction had actually been made in 1525; in Martinique, where cocoa was introduced by the Jew Benjamin da Costa from Venezuela in 1664, and the first exports were sent to France in 1679; in Hispaniola; and in Jamaica, where the English found an established production when they captured the island in 1655. But in 1727 the cocoa plantations of all the West Indian islands were devastated, apparently by a hurricane. Cultivation took many years to become re-established, and in Jamaica this was not done till the nineteenth century. Cocoa exports from Surinam commenced in 1725. By contrast, in Brazil only small plantings were made in the eighteenth century.

The drinking chocolate of this period was different from the modern 'cocoa', from which excess fat has been removed. The defatting process was clearly described in France in 1763, but did not come into common use till the following century. The grinding of cocoa beans was at first done manually. This was superseded by the use of water-power in the factory of Fry & Sons, founded by Dr Joseph Fry of Bristol in 1728. The same firm applied the first steam engine to cocoa manufacture in 1795. By 1800 there were said to be chocolate factories in all the principal cities of Germany. But the trade was still on a small scale. Imports of cocoa to Great Britain in the closing years of the eighteenth century did not exceed 100 tons per annum. There was as yet little incentive to extend the cultivation of the crop from America to other continents.

Coffee was not an ancient drink like cocoa. Its use as a beverage, first invented by the Arabs, only spread through the countries of the Middle East during the early sixteenth century. In the following century the practice was introduced into various European countries by travellers using the beans of Mocha. The establishment of some of the earliest coffee houses of Europe can be dated at 1650 at Oxford, 1652 at London, 1671 at Marseilles, 1684 at Leipzig. Thenceforward the trade grew rapidly. But the sources of supply were very different from those of today, when the greatest bulk comes from South America. All the trees were of the 'arabica' species, 'robusta' not being planted until the twentieth century. The Yemen coffee, exported from the port of Mocha, reached Europe through the markets of Alexandria and Smyrna. In France, the importation was limited to Marseilles, and in 1723 a monopoly of coffee sales was granted to the Compagnie des Indes. The early Dutch introductions into Ceylon and Java have already been mentioned. The first export of one ton was made from Java in 1713.

Frantic efforts during the succeeding decades to adjust supply to demand resulted in compulsory orders for the Javanese peasants at one time to plant coffee trees, at another to uproot them and substitute pepper. Dutch 'coffee-sergeants' went round to enforce these regulations. In Ceylon, coffee failed in the lowlands and its production was left to the kingdom of Kandy in the interior, though the export was a monopoly of the Dutch Company.

In 1718 the French introduced coffee from Mocha to the island of Bourbon (Réunion), whence was named the 'Bourbon' variety which was later so widely spread around the world. In America, the coffee first established in Surinam supplied plantings in northern Brazil in about 1726. The first estate in the neighbourhood of Rio de Janeiro was established in 1774; but Brazil did not become a substantial producer in the eighteenth century. Costa Rica did not receive plants till 1779, nor Colombia till about 1784. In Jamaica, however, coffee was introduced from Martinique about 1730, and her Blue Mountain coffee became the chief source of supply for the British market.

In 1750 the total import of coffee into Europe was estimated at 66 million pounds. By 1789 the French colonies alone were supplying more than this, principally from St Domingue. Jamaica exported 2 million pounds in 1784, but by the end of the century its production was rising steeply. This was partly due to Pitt's reduction of the United Kingdom import duty from 1s. 6d. to 6½d. per lb. in 1783, and partly to the destruction of the St Domingue plantations by revolution. In the later part of the century, North America as well as Europe was providing a substantial market. Imports of coffee into the United States during the years 1793 to 1799 fluctuated between 30 and 61 million pounds annually; in the latter years six times as much coffee as tea was imported.

The tea trade differs from those in coffee and cocoa in that consumption became so much greater in one European country, Great Britain, than in any other. Tea was first imported into Europe by the Dutch in 1610. This consignment was from Japan; but as the trade developed, supplies came almost entirely from China. The trade remained for some time a Dutch monopoly, tea being re-exported to France from about 1635, England about 1645, and Germany and Scandinavia about 1650. Meanwhile the Russians received their first tea by the overland route from China in 1618. Regular supplies by this route did not begin until after the Treaty of Nerchinsk in 1689; the journey to Moscow took about eighteen months, which was actually longer than the sea voyage to western Europe. The English East India Company, having obtained footholds in Canton and Amoy, sent their first tea to England in 1669. Tea went through the usual stages of being first sold by the ounce from apothecaries' shops and alternately blessed as a remedy for illness and reviled as a dissipation. The price of tea in England in 1650 was from £6 to £10 per pound, according to quality. By 1703 the average price had dropped to 16s. In the closing years of the seventeenth century the average import into England was about 20,000 lb. a year; in 1703 it reached 100,000 lb. In spite of Wesley preaching vehemently against its use as late as 1748, by the end of the century consumption had reached the formidable figure of 2 lb. per annum per head of the population.

Throughout this century the legitimate tea trade remained a monopoly of the East India Company, shipping almost entirely from Canton. The high rate of duty imposed, and the strong demand, made tea a particularly profitable commodity for smugglers; and it is estimated that half of all the tea consumed in eighteenth century England was smuggled. Smuggling of tea into the North American colonies was also on a large scale.

Tea was at first drunk in the coffee houses, enjoying a common price with coffee of 2d. a dish. These places were male preserves; but in 1717 Thomas Twining opened the first tea-shop in Devereux Court, London, to which great ladies flocked. A further development was 'tea gardens', Vauxhall being first developed in this respect in 1732. Ranelagh, founded in 1742, became equally famous. Some of these gardens combined tea-drinking with spectacles and sports; Marylebone offered carnivals and fireworks, Bermondsey exhibitions of paintings, Cuper's Gardens concerts, and the White Conduit House cricket. At the eighteenth century peak, there were over thirty tea gardens in London. The craze also spread to the colonies. New York had its tea gardens, of which the most famous was the Tea Water Pump Garden, whose natural spring water was said to be particularly suited for making tea, and was sold as 'tea water' all over the city. Thus with tea as with the other new beverages, one of its most important effects was to soften the manners of elegant society and, as it became cheaper, to provide an alternative to gin-swilling for the masses.

The involvement of tea in the politics of the American Revolution was to some extent due to misunderstanding. The East India Company had hitherto landed all its tea in England, where British duty was paid on that proportion which was eventually marketed in America through English and American merchants; the numerous smugglers were a third party to the situation. The Tea Act of 1773 had various purposes, one of which was to help the Company to dispose of an unsold surplus of some 17 million pounds of tea. The method was by giving the Company the right to import tea directly into America in its own ships and to sell there through its own agents. By thus eliminating the British duty, the cost of tea to the American consumer would have been halved. But the Act aroused the resentment of shippers, American importing agents, and the smugglers. More political capital was made out of it than it was worth; but the economic effects of the 'Boston tea party' were far-reaching in permanently making the American nation drinkers of coffee rather than of tea.

# IX. *The Potato in Europe*

The double introduction of the potato to Europe, through Spain and through the British Isles, has already been recorded. The first country in which the crop assumed importance was Ireland. That island was in the seventeenth century tormented by rebellion and its suppression, while many of the Irish peasantry were reduced by the system of the English landlords to living off tiny plots of land. In these circumstances the particular merits of the potato were pre-eminent. The crop gave a much higher food yield per acre than was obtainable at that time from cereals; and its great fungus enemy, the 'late blight' disease, was unknown anywhere in Europe before 1842. Potatoes in the field were furthermore much less easily destroyed by the soldiery than were corn crops. The first certain mention of potato-growing in Ireland is in County Down in 1606, but its spread thereafter was rapid. By the end of the seventeenth century potatoes were the chief article in the diet of all the poorer classes in Ireland. It was from Ireland that the potato, although a native of the American continent, was first introduced to the North American colonies. Its cultivation seems to have been begun by Irish emigrants to New England in 1718. Ireland also provided an introduction of potatoes in 1728 into St Helena, where they became a most important product, especially for victualling ships.

The adoption of potatoes in England and Scotland was much slower. In the seventeenth century they were still in most areas only an unimportant garden vegetable. In Scotland in the eighteenth century they assumed the same role as in Ireland, of a preserver of life to the miserable and impoverished crofters of the Highlands and islands. The introduction of the potato also led to an increase in the raising of pigs; while, replacing grain in human diets, it made more barley available for sale to the distillers. In England, field cultivation first developed in Lancashire, perhaps because of its intimate contacts with Ireland or because of the presence of Irish immigrants who demanded potatoes. Field cultivation here began before 1700, posing a problem for the Church authorities who were anxious to claim tithe on the new crop. By 1750 there was a considerable export trade from Liverpool to Ireland. Potatoes in England in the eighteenth century were in competition with the turnip, another root crop which was newly introduced to field cultivation in the early part of the century. In some ways this helped the spread of the potato, as it familiarized farmers with the field husbandry of root crops and made them aware of their cleaning value in the rotation. But turnips also competed against the potato by providing an alternative cheap food for the very poor. In eastern and southern England the spread of the crop was slow, and it was not till the nineteenth century that really extensive acreages of potatoes were grown. In Jersey, potatoes became a field crop about 1780, replacing parsnips which had hitherto been the chief root crop for feeding both people and pigs. A small export trade in early potatoes to London was already established by the first decade of the nineteenth century.

On the continent, Germany was the first country to become, as she has since remained, a great producer of potatoes. Frederick William I of Prussia (1713–40) and his son Frederick the Great both applied compulsion to the cultivation of potatoes. But it was the famines caused by the Seven Years War that first really established potato cultivation. Again in 1770, famine conditions following a series of bad corn harvests caused a further extension of the crop. In 1778–9 was fought the so-called 'Potato War' (*Kartoffelkrieg*) between Prussia and Austria. This took its name from the fact that the armies manoeuvred to secure food supplies for themselves and deny them to the enemy, and only desisted from hostilities when they had eaten all the potatoes available in Bohemia. In 1853 the town of Offenburg in Baden erected a statue of Sir Francis Drake, whom they erroneously regarded as the introducer of the potato to Europe, on which were carved the words: 'The precious gift of God allays bitter want as the help of the poor against need'.

The potato was much slower in achieving popularity in France, and was of slight importance until late in the eighteenth century. In 1772 A. A. Parmentier, who had been a prisoner of war in Prussia, won a prize offered by the Academy of Besançon for a new famine-relieving food with a treatise on potato culture. Louis XVI gave him 50 morgen of land on which to plant the crop; and the resultant propaganda, with the king wearing potato flowers in his button-hole and Marie Antoinette in her hair, did something to further the cultivation. The Revolutionary War period extended the crop much more widely.

In Hungary the crop was introduced about 1654 by students returning from Germany. But some outlying parts of Europe were late in receiving it. In Sweden the introduction was made about 1725; in Norway the first record of cultivation is from 1758. Russia and Poland probably first obtained the plant from Germany in the latter part of the eighteenth century.

The great economic contribution of the potato was to make Europe able to feed her growing population from internal sources for longer than would otherwise have been possible, and to provide a cheap food from small acreage for the urban masses, thereby helping to lay the foundations of the industrial revolution.

The long story of crop and livestock dispersal was rounded off, before the eighteenth century closed, by one more significant episode. In 1788 the first European settlement was made in Australia, the last of the habitable continents and one where the natives cultivated no crops at all. Seeds of cereal crops were carried by the original expedition from England and the Cape of Good Hope, but it is noteworthy that in 1793 the acreage of maize planted was five times that of wheat. However the wheat harvest of 1796 produced 40,000 bushels, a twelve months' supply for the colony and enough to make it self-supporting. Complacency was nevertheless reduced when in 1799 the colonists experienced their first crop failure due to an Australian drought.

The art of colonization had by this time progressed somewhat beyond the amateur stage, at least among far-sighted men. Such a one was Captain John Macarthur of the New South Wales Corps, who in 1792 was prescient enough to write: 'A petty population, established at so vast a distance from other civilized parts of the globe, could have no prospects of ultimately succeeding unless by raising as an export some raw material which would be produced with little labour, be in considerable demand, and be capable of bearing the expense of a long sea voyage.' The product which would best fit the circumstances, he decided, was fine wool.

Sheep had been brought to Australia from the Cape by the first expedition, but they were types with fleeces of hair rather than wool. In 1797 however an importation of Merino sheep was made from the Cape, and of these Macarthur was able to obtain two rams and four ewes. With the progeny of these animals he was to establish Australia's wool export.

While these events were not of immediate economic importance, they were highly significant as pointers to the future. The European exploration of the world had originally been largely motivated by the quest for spices. But in the long run it was not the luxury products of tropical agriculture which were to be the most significant importations for Europe. They were to be overtaken in volume and importance by a flood of the staple products of temperate agriculture—wheat, wool, meat and dairy produce—derived from the new lands which had been opened up by European enterprise.

# CHAPTER VI

# Colonial Settlement and Its Labour Problems

Amid the many motives which led Europeans to take part in the overseas movements of the fifteenth and sixteenth centuries, the need to provide some overspill for redundant population was negligible. Men wished, perhaps, to strike the infidel a blow, to strengthen their native state, to ascertain the shape and the nature of the earth, to gain great wealth or to escape from a humdrum existence—or perhaps a mixture of these things. Seldom was the hope of access to the trade goods, the spices and the silks and cotton of the sophisticated East far from their minds. But they neither wished to settle overseas themselves to earn their livings in alien lands nor to provide opportunity for their compatriots to do so. They were not colonizers, but, usually, traders or would-be traders. The desire to colonize, to settle or even to organize production, came late, and was accepted reluctantly.

Any estimate of the population of Europe as it came into the modern age, still more of the different states of Europe which were becoming increasingly the effective units, must be largely a matter of guesswork in which such data as the number of hearths, of communicants, of ship-owners, of serviceable military men or even of corpses, are subjected to multipliers and distributors. Figures got by such processes can be closely related to contemporary estimates, but they remain slightly conjectural, and they are largely irrelevant from the point of view of overseas expansion. The general picture, however, has begun to emerge with reasonable clarity and to gain in significance. It is a picture which starts with a widespread and catastrophic decline in population in the fourteenth century and in which any sustained recovery was delayed by endemic plagues and constant warfare until the last quarter of the fifteenth century. Then 'after 1500 evidence of sustained demographic growth becomes overwhelming in all countries'.[1] The period of increasing numbers was marked by genuine and widespread concern for the unemployed poor—a concern which may well prove to have left a greater mark on historical writing than it did on contemporary society, for it brought fine writing from such diverse and able men as Vives, Von Hutten, Robert Gray and Walter Raleigh, and a host of others. But unemployment was a product of many factors besides an absolute increase in population: of wars, technical improvements, religious and sociological changes in outlook and habits, and of increased urbanization. Certainly population was more mobile than was formerly imagined,

[1] Cf above, p. 20.

and the wandering vagrant was the chief source of uneasiness for the statesman giving thought to the problem. But, although there is clear evidence that rural population moved quite freely, there is very little evidence of what might be called rural colonization; that is to say, invasion of the marginal and waste lands of western Europe, a remedy which was always to hand and which both in logic and in fact (by the precedents of the later Middle Ages) was the obvious remedy for agricultural over-population.

If anything the agricultural evidence points to a decline in rural population at the turn of the fifteenth and sixteenth centuries, with a marked tendency to labour-saving methods and with emphasis on agricultural bye-employments to supplement standards of living, rather than on invasion of the rural wastes as a long-term remedy for serious rural over-population.

The probability (for it cannot be more) is that the increasing population went to the wars or to the cities. Its wanderings, its needs and its capacity for crime, harassed and embarrassed statesmen. But it is clear that by the Period of Discoveries western Europe had not reached anything like saturation point in its population, either by modern standards or by the standards of that age. The troubles were sociological and economic rather than demographic; they derived from changes in methods and customs in production and in consumption rather than from any absolute surplus of people, when town and country are taken together. So far were the governments of the period from feeling any serious need to provide a vent for excess population that the current doctrines tended in the opposite direction, with emphasis on conserving man-power as a matter of military necessity in the constant wars of the period. The nation-state was working out its *credo*, more swiftly in the realms of dynasticism, of law, liturgy and defence than in the realm of economics; but in defence and in economics alike it knew the basic value of a healthy and numerous population, and when the Discoveries revealed the possibilities of deriving wealth and of achieving economic power from overseas, the object of statesmen was to secure these benefits without weakening the man-power available in the home country.

From the start the tone was set by the Portuguese. The discrepancy between the small size and meagre population of Portugal and its magnificent achievements is one of the most marked and interesting features of the period. Portugal's ambitions have been summarized as a desire to replace Venice in the Eastern Trade; this overlooks the many religious and personal factors which drove the royal house of Braganza to foster and to organize the explorers, and it overlooks the sheer urge for discovery. But yet, as the shape and the potential value of the eastern

Discoveries came to be realized, the object of Portuguese colonization was not the possession of the Indies themselves, but of the trade of the Indies. Their approach was based on a concept of a *mare clausum*, secured to them under papal authority, which should save them from the inroads of other Christian states, and on a system of forts and garrisons which should save them from native opposition. Numbers of men, even for defence, could not be provided. The forts were strategically sited, and sea-power soon came to be accepted as the link which gave coherence and strength to outposts which without it would be weak, dispersed and vulnerable.

The result was that the Portuguese posts were hardly colonies at all. They controlled strategic points on the trade-routes to the east. But even the garrisons were in great part locally recruited. There was little machinery of government, few possibilities of the growth of a society, and Portuguese power seldom extended a day's march from their ships. Portugal lacked the people for any significant migration, and the circumstances of her eastern expansion fitted her lack of capacity with a strange appropriateness. For on the mainland of India the Muslim powers were distracted by wars and the Portuguese never came into hostile contact with any of the great fighting races of the sub-continent; protection in India itself therefore demanded no great man-power, and further east and in the islands sea-power counted for much. For trade, too, the Portuguese found large numbers of men unnecessary. They came to a sophisticated economy which for centuries had been able to provide luxuries for the European market, and they had no desire to engage in the businesses of production or of manufacture, merely to divert to their own sea-routes a trade which was based on a competent native economy. Their purpose was to make the king of Portugal the only merchant trading between India and Europe; but not to impinge on the domestic background of that trade. There to their hand on the Indian mainland stood a Muslim trading system, ranging through the necessary forms of capitalism to culminate in the great export merchants who could provide cargoes for the Portuguese ships. For trade, and for the protection of that trade, therefore, Portugal seemed able to manage with no great emigration.

But the very success of their system made changes inevitable, and brought a peculiarly Portuguese contribution to the conjunction of the Old World and the New. As European rivals with equal maritime power challenged the Portuguese claims, the defence of the vast trade which had been won demanded close organization, and the garrison posts needed troops who would stand up to European attacks and who could hold on when naval support was lacking. The Portuguese answer was worked out in thesis form by their Governor, Affonso Albuquerque, who developed a plan for a series of independent forts and for channelling trade through the entrepôt of Goa on the Malabar coast and to Europe through the sole port of Lisbon, who concentrated his defensive system on the vulnerable area of the Persian Gulf and the Gulf of Aden, and who advocated a solution to the man-power question by the evolution of a half-breed population.

The Portuguese, lacking emigrants, showed a strange mixture of tolerance and of religious intransigence in their relations with the native peoples with whom they came in contact. Where the natives remained obstinately heathen they were often treated with cruelty and treachery. But this was not a racial discrimination, and they knew no such thing as a colour-bar. From their earliest contacts they brought natives back to Portugal, treated them as equals, and often entered into marriages with them. There is record of a negro bishop, from the Congo, in the early sixteenth century, and though missionary activity was particularly strong in the Congo this is but one sign of the way in which the Portuguese were prepared to overlook differences in race and in cultural standards. Along with the concubinage which was almost inevitable when men of active blood were stationed for long periods away from their own women and in close contact with scantily dressed natives, used to domestic slavery and polygamy and for whom fornication as such was not a particularly sinful activity, there went a great deal of mixed marriage within the church; and Albuquerque evolved a theory of the Portuguese empire on the basis of a society of mixed blood, unconcerned whether the native element were Arab, Negro, Hindu or Indonesian. This was something more than a concession to the weaknesses of the flesh; this was a clear and coherent theory of empire, and the basis of it was that Portugal could not of herself produce the men, still less the women, to people an empire.

Even so, Albuquerque's theory was designed for an empire of trade in the East Indies, and perhaps in Africa en route to the Indies; for a trade system in which the cargoes were brought by native traders to the shore, ready for sale and shipment. Where these conditions did not apply, any such system would be impossible, for the Europeans would have to organize the supplies of goods, and perhaps would even have to engage in the techniques of production. These were the conditions which the Portuguese met in the Atlantic islands, the Azores, Madeira, Cape Verde and São Thomé, and which they also met on the American mainland, in Brazil. There agricultural settlement was a necessary preliminary to maintaining any sort of establishment, and any produce for export or for consumption would have to be the result of European effort. The need for emigrants was much more severe than in the east, and the sort of mixed society which might there have provided garrisons and administrators would be inadequate for the heavy work of production.

For this the Portuguese had three remedies—a legal system which enabled grants of land to be given on condition that the land was brought under cultivation (the *Donatarios* system); a criminal law which enabled them to banish their *degredados* to their colonies; and an acceptance of the institution of slavery. Of the three institutions, that of banishment had the least effect, for although the quality of Portuguese emigrants was later held by Protestant nations to be one of the reasons for the decline of their empire, the defects were rather defects in the maintenance of the social and moral conventions of European society than defects which were due to definite criminal tendencies. In any case, the *degredados* were comparatively few in numbers, and they mostly went to the East Indies to garrison and to serve, not to the colonies of settlement to work and to produce. The semi-feudal grants of land, combined with acceptance of slavery, did however enable productive European-owned and European-managed estates to be developed both in the Atlantic islands and in Brazil.

Although many different definitions of colonization may apply to different phases of the movement, the one definition which almost universally applies is a definition in terms of land and labour. Relative plenty or scarcity of capital, and managerial capacity, cannot be left out of the account; but in-so-far as land and labour are the basic elements of any system of production, a colonizing movement is a movement from an area in which land is scarce and labour is plentiful (even to the point of redundancy) into an area in which land is plentiful (even to the point of having no value) and labour is scarce. Emigration occurs naturally when labour seeks a better market; and as soon as colonization ceases to be such a spontaneous movement to a better labour-market and becomes a matter of state or of capital development, then the government which desires colonies has the task of organizing the necessary labour-supply. In the so-called 'colonies of exploitation' the minimum number of European administrators and traders have 'colonized' by adapting native population to the needs and customs of a European trade. At the other extreme, in 'colonies of settlement' European immigrants have themselves supplied the necessary labour. Between the two extremes the immigrants have not been numerous enough to perform the whole work of production, nor have the native inhabitants been capable or willing to perform these tasks. The immigrants, as settlers rather than administrators, have there been faced with the choice either of turning native peoples into their labour force, or of introducing to the colony their own alien labour force.

The methods adopted in this quandary have varied with the backgrounds and institutions of the various colonizing powers. But to the extent that colonies have been based upon the desire to profit from the productive capacity of overseas territories (and this is to an over-whelming and not necessarily reprehensible extent) the problem has been the same and the answers have not differed in fundamentals. Portugal had to face this problem as a pioneer, without precedents to follow; and her answer was first to try to organize the native peoples into an adequate labour force and then, as a second resource, to import supplementary labour. For this she used negro slaves. This was, in fact, the pattern of modern colonization until the nineteenth century brought a revulsion from the institution of slavery at the same time as liberal doctrines and the steady accumulation of colonial experience brought both the desire for and the possibility of colonial indepen-dence.

On the basis of the large estates which the Portuguese legal system made possible, São Thomé was producing sugar for export by 1522, Madeira was selling sugar and wine, and the Azores were exporting cheeses in considerable numbers and were capable of acting as a provision depot for the Portuguese fleets. Angola and Brazil were the two main areas on which the Portuguese system rested, and of the two Brazil was the more important as supplying the resources without which Angola would have been insignificant. In Brazil the Portuguese found both earth and man in a crude state; so far were the Indians from producing the fine manufactures and the spices of the Far East that they had no domestic animal tamed for service and their agriculture at best was no more than the casual growth of small quantities of peanuts. The Portuguese who came there were for the most part not agriculturists, for the Portuguese nation had become commercialized as the trade of the East flooded into Lisbon and the early emigrants were fortune-seekers, not farmers. But in Brazil they had perforce to turn to agriculture; and they had to organize the agriculture for themselves. Attracted by the great rivers of the country, and helped in their agriculture by the smaller and gentler streams, they had easy opportunities to establish under their legal system a widespread plantation economy. Of this, one marked feature was dispersion, a lack of density and depth of settlement, a tendency towards so-called 'self-colonization' (a feature not unlike what has come to be called 'the frontier' in American history), and dependence on forced labour for the necessary toil. Land was danger-ously plentiful, labour almost non-existent.

The dispersive mobility of the Portuguese was offset by their political maturity and coherence, by the lack of division between church and state, and by the unifying influence of the Jesuits and the educational missions which they sponsored in Brazil. The result was that dispersion as a geographical feature was not accompanied by disunion or even serious divergency as political or economic features. These were peculiar virtues in the Portuguese, and they were common to their settlements in the East as well as in the West; equally peculiar and important was the fact that they 'went forward without the colonizers being concerned with racial unity or racial purity'.[1] In Brazil, as in the East, the only barrier was that of religious orthodoxy; alien blood and diseased blood were alike free to enter, but unity of religion and of law were insisted on from the start and were maintained throughout.

Settlement, and the beginnings of serious agriculture in Brazil, date from the foundation of the colonization of São Vicente, near the present port of Santos, in 1532. By that time their experience in the East had left the Portuguese confirmed in their characteristics as a nation of merchants rather than farmers, and their approach to the possibilities of agricultural development in Brazil was not that of farmers, who delight in a fertile soil and in bringing it to production, but that of merchants who aim to get the maximum reward by organizing the labour of others, and selling their products. Even those who had behind them a training in agriculture in Portugal or in the Atlantic islands had been conditioned in a system in which the heavy work was often performed by servile labour.

# I. *Slaves from West Africa*

Portugal was, in fact, a slave-owning country before she became a colonial power. At the time when the settlement of Brazil was just beginning, the humanist Clenardus wrote of her that 'All services are performed by Negro or Moorish captives. Portugal is being overrun with this race of people. One could almost believe that in Lisbon there are more slaves, male and female, than there are Portuguese of free condition'.[2] The spread of Mahommedan power had revealed the resources of Africa as a supplier of negro slaves, and from about the year 1000 a steady supply of slaves was annually being secured by Mahommedan raids and wars, to give soldiers, labourers, and domestic servants to European masters. The Crusaders, and their successors the Christian merchants in the Levant and African trades, took to the slave trade with as little compunction as the Mahommedans, though they normally secured the slaves by trade rather than by capture.

In slavery, as in the spice and luxury trades, the aim and the achievement of the period of the Discoveries was to divert to a western and Christian route a business which already flourished in Mahommedan

---

[1] Gilberto Freyre, *The Masters and the Slaves* (New York, 1946), 40.
[2] Quoted Freyre, *op. cit.*, p. 245.

hands. The trade itself was regarded as necessary and acceptable—so much so that it was reckoned that there were about 3,000 negro slaves in Venice alone about the year 1500—and from the earliest contacts with the west coast of Africa the Portuguese habitually brought back some seven or eight hundred slaves a year, to work the estates which had been taken from the Moors or for which domestic labour was inadequate.

No question of conscience was involved in the traffic, or in the subsequent working of slavery, for all the inhabitants of north-west Africa were assumed to be Moors, against whom Christians had the duty of waging war, and whom it was legitimate to reduce to slavery after capture. As it became clear that the explorers had brought the Portuguese into contact with peoples who were not involved in the struggle between Christianity and Mahommedanism the problem of conscience was solved by the Papal Bull of 1454, in which Nicholas V encouraged the Portuguese to press on against the Moors (who were not finally expelled from Europe until 1492) with a permit to 'attack, subject and reduce to perpetual slavery the Saracens, Pagans, and other enemies of Christ southward from Capes Bojador and Non, including all the coast of Guinea'. The slaves must indeed be converted to Christianity, and this approach, coupled with the lack of colour prejudice which was a marked feature in the Portuguese, resulted in some strange anomalies. Slaves were baptized *en masse* as they were shipped aboard; but they remained slaves. In contrast stood the native sovereigns of the Congo, who accepted a nominal Christianity which did not prevent them from keeping their wives or from serving their fetishes, but which entitled them to be accepted as legitimate monarchs with whom the Portuguese could (and did) make treaties which laid down the necessary conditions on which trade posts could be maintained and on which the slave trade could be based.

The discovery of the Gold Coast would seem to have brought the Portuguese, in the last quarter of the fifteenth century, within reach of one of their major objectives in opening up the coast of Africa. But the attainment of gold (reaching something like a tenth of the world's annual supply of new gold in the early years of the sixteenth century) led to a renewed interest in discovery and so, ultimately, to Portuguese voyages round the Cape and their penetration into the rich trade of the eastern seas, so that knowledge of the Gold Coast diverted attention from Africa rather than increasing it. Yet as the Portuguese had come past the Senegal River and Cape Verde in 1446, a few negroes had been taken back to Europe, at first as catechumens. They attracted merchants to the African trade, for negro slavery was already known and accepted in Portugal. Regular cargoes of slaves soon followed, and a steady trade was established by the death of Henry the Navigator in 1460.

Such slaves soon proved to be a commodity which helped the Portuguese in their trade with the Gold Coast, for although they built the stone fort of Elmina (São Jorge da Mina) there, and lesser forts at Axim and Shama, they did not dominate life on the Gold Coast but traded there on conditions set by the native peoples. The Portuguese were accepted on sufferance, the ground occupied by their posts was leased to them by agreement, they had little or no influence over the tribal life of the peoples among whom they settled even when their trade had brought considerable native settlement into the coastal areas near the posts. Above all, they were not allowed to trade direct with the inland territories which were the original sources of the gold and the gold-dust. The pattern was to become a familiar one, repeated throughout the world as non-European peoples quickly brought a lively sense of economic strategy, and a wakening appreciation of value in trade as against value in use, to their contacts with Europeans. The coastal Africans, as later the Iroquois of North America or the Hong merchants in China, claimed and vindicated a right to be sole intermediaries between European traders and the producers of the hinterland. The Portuguese were therefore forced to bring commodities which the coastal Africans desired; and slaves were one of the things which the peoples of the Gold Coast were ready to take in trade.

A steady trickle of slaves was procured from Upper Guinea south of the River Senegal, but this went for the most part to the Cape Verde islands, which lay just off this coast and whose settlers dominated the trade on the coast between Sierra Leone and the Senegal. This was almost a self-contained trade, while the great source of slaves for the Portuguese, apart from those destined for the Cape Verde islands, was the Slave Coast, the area later called the Oil Rivers, between the Volta and the Niger Delta. Here, when the Portuguese first reached Benin about 1483, the kings of Benin were engaged in a series of local wars in which they consolidated their authority over the tribes of the Niger Delta; and from such wars they derived a supply of slaves which the Portuguese gladly traded from them and which they later traded to the peoples of the Gold Coast. They brought them also to Europe, to their plantations in the Atlantic islands, and later to Brazil.

The Portuguese took to their overseas possessions the habits and attitudes derived from their European economy, an economy in which the pre-existing familiarity with slavery had been strengthened by their early experience in trade on the African coast. The Gold Coast, the Ivory Coast, the Grain Coast (which really produced 'grains of paradise' or malagueta pepper) each in turn offered great attractions to the Europeans; but it was the Slave Coast which became essential in their spread to America and the West Indies. With growing dependence on slave labour in Portugal—dependence both on Moorish craftsmen and on negro labourers—went ostentation in public life combined with apathy and idleness, and a great deal of penury, in domestic life; and a marked lack of economic activity. These attitudes, together with their acceptance of negro slavery, the Portuguese took with them where they settled, and it is difficult to exaggerate the importance of the fact that they opened up the coast of Africa and its supplies of slaves as they explored their way towards the wealth of the tropical and sub-tropical lands which they sought, and which they at last discovered and developed.

The climate of the Niger Delta proved too unhealthy for the Portuguese to establish permanent posts there, and their post at Gwato was withdrawn early in the sixteenth century. But this did not mean that the slave trade was abandoned, for the islands of São Thomé and Fernando Po had been settled by the Portuguese, and on these islands ideal conditions for development of sugar plantations had been found. From these islands a constant trade to the mainland persisted. Largely conducted through the agency of Africans and half-castes, to whom the climate was less lethal than to Europeans, the trade provided the island planters with slaves for their sugar growth and the merchants with slaves for Portugal herself and for her new territories. The islands, São Thomé in particular, remained as bases from which slaves could be got even after the sugar plantations there had lost their attractions, when towards the end of the sixteenth century several of the planters had begun to follow those from Madeira across the Atlantic to Brazil.

## II. *Slavery and Sugar*

Portuguese settlement in Brazil tended to be restricted to the coastlands because access to the interior was difficult. The great rivers are not axes for advance into the depths of the land; nor was there any reason why the Portuguese should turn their backs on the coast and boldly turn away from the sea and the support of their ships. In the coastal strip there was land to spare.

The first step towards colonization was taken with the creation of ten captaincies, each extending for about fifty leagues along the coast. But of the ten only three proved successful—that of Pernambuco in the north, that of Bahia, and that of São Vicente with the city of São Paulo in the south. Both Pernambuco and Bahia found it necessary to fight the Indians for possession of their lands, and although São Vicente came to terms with the neighbouring Indians by reason that a Portuguese sailor had married the daughter of their chief, the Paulistas (from São Paulo) were led in their search for slaves into expeditions which took them up into the Matto Grosso. On the whole, the Indian was required in the coastal districts to clear the ground, to defend the great house, and to engage in the domestic work of the house. His own way of life was largely naturalistic; he was robust and healthy, and delighted in felling trees and carrying them to the ships, but he did not till the earth, save perhaps for a few peanuts or a little manioc grown by the women, nor did he breed cattle. To be of value to the settler he had to pass in one stride from a nomadic to a sedentary way of life. He had to accustom himself to continuous activity and to a changed diet, and he had at the same time to survive the new diseases which the settlers brought with them—catarrh, smallpox, syphilis, dysentery—and still to maintain his vitality. It was asking too much, especially if it had all to be accomplished at the first contact, as the country was brought into production. The Indian lost his vitality; he withdrew himself, 'became enveloped in the sadness of the introvert', and the settlers quickly looked for a more satisfactory and industrious source of the labour which they needed if the potential wealth of their land was to be developed, and if Brazil was to retain its attractions as a home for emigrants.

The negro, already well known as a part of the social and economic system in Portugal and in the Atlantic islands, was the obvious answer; indeed some of the Portuguese settlers who came to Brazil from the islands seem to have brought their slaves with them. They certainly brought the culture of sugar, and negro slavery seemed the almost inevitable counterpart of sugar cultivation. Much of the soil of Brazil was peculiarly suited to sugar cultivation, especially in the three great captaincies which survived the initial difficulties of settlement, in the neighbourhood of Pernambuco, the Reconcavo area near Bahia, and the São Vicente captaincy where the first sugar canes were planted and the first cattle bred from imported stock. Sugar prices in Europe were high. There was an almost insatiable demand to be met, and the thin Creole canes on which the first colonial period's sugar industry was based spread outwards from the Middle East to the Iberian peninsula and thence to the Atlantic islands and to Brazil.

Sugar in Brazil was a thing of which all settlers dreamed, once the 'first improbable hopes of rich mines' had been exhausted and plans for substantial trade in luxury goods had failed. Sugar would be a cash-crop for which a ready market was waiting. For the Crown and its officers early emphasis in Brazil lay, as elsewhere, on hopes of wealth to be got from minerals and spices; but as it came to be accepted that agriculture would have to be the source of wealth, the official object was for the Crown 'to populate the wilds of America without burden to itself, to clear the land of jungle, to defend it against corsairs and the savage, and to transform it into a productive region, all at the expense of those persons who were daring enough to deflower so rude a portion of the earth'.[1] The legal system worked towards large grants of land, suitable for plantations; and the Crown in some sort undertook the duty of fostering sugar-cultivation in that feudal lords to whom grants of land were made were urged to undertake agricultural work. They were given the exclusive possession of sugar-mills and of water-wheels to drive them; and this, together with the natural advantages of the soil, and the fact that sugar was their most probable source of wealth and comfort, was enough to turn their interest in agriculture into devotion to sugar. Before the end of the first century of settlement it was accepted that 'it is the judgment of God that, as the result of the money gained in Brazil, through sugar and cotton, woods and parrots, Your Majesty's treasury should be enriched with much fine gold'.[2]

The number of plantations devoted to sugar rose from thirty in 1576 to seventy-six in 1584 and to 180 at the end of the first quarter of the seventeenth century. The amount of sugar produced was more than the mills could deal with; it was estimated that there was enough cane on hand to keep the mills solidly at work for three or four years if agrarian production should cease completely, and Portuguese shipping, though it amounted to thirty or forty vessels a year, was unable to carry away all the sugar from Pernambuco. These might have been features of a glutted market, but the price of sugar remained high throughout the period, and the accumulation of stocks was rather the outcome of incompetence in processing and in marketing than of any over-supply of the commodity.

Cultivation of food-stuffs was to some extent sacrificed to sugar. But the lack of balance which the sugar-trade revealed was the result of ineptitude rather than of any inherent weakness in the trade, for the Portuguese were remarkable, and remarkably fortunate, in that they had to hand not only previous experience in this trade and knowledge of the machinery and of the techniques needed, but a source of the labour which was required.

The first shipment of negroes was made in 1525, and although this was some years later than shipments to Spanish colonies it was at an early and formative period in the settlement of Brazil. The trade began slowly, for the negro was a capital investment for the settler and not all settlers could afford such investment, especially in the early period when emigration was apt to be undertaken only by social and economic failures. In the south the *Paulistas* continued to hope for Indian slaves, and to penetrate into the interior in search of them, until a royal decree in 1570 declared all Indians free save such as should be taken in war by command of the king or governor, or such as were aggressive cannibals.

---

[1] Freyre, *op. cit.*, p. 252.
[2] Freyre, *op. cit.*, p. 252, quoting João Lúcio de Azevedo, *Épocas de Portugal Ecônomico*.

At Pernambuco and at Bahia the negro dropped more easily and early into a predominant role. By 1585, when Brazilian society and the Brazilian economy had developed the patterns which they were to maintain through the seventeenth century, it was estimated that the colony contained about 57,000 inhabitants, of whom about 25,000 were whites, 18,500 were 'civilized' Indians, and 14,000 were African slaves. Within the total figures there were considerable local variations. Pernambuco was reckoned to have about 10,000 negroes and Bahia about 3,000; it was estimated at about this time that Olinda, the capital of Pernambuco, had 700 inhabitants and had round it fifty sugar works, each with twenty to thirty residents, and employing altogether over 4,000 negroes. Elsewhere, where sugar was not so much grown and the negro slave not an investment, they were not so numerous.

The Atlantic islands were reduced to a secondary role in the sixteenth century, as Brazil became the great colony of settlement for the Portuguese. There he engaged in the work of primary agricultural production; and there, as formerly in the Atlantic islands, he found the negro slave ready to hand, able, vigorous, and often used to an agricultural life, to perform the heavy work in the fields.

Yet, strangely, the trade in negro slaves had become an important source of profit to the Portuguese even before the negro became so great an element in the Portuguese colonies themselves. While it was the middle of the sixteenth century before agricultural development in Brazil began to open up a constant and prosperous traffic, to supply negroes to the settlers there for the purposes of the sugar plantations, already from the first decade of that century Portuguese merchants were engaged in shipping slaves to the Spanish possessions in the New World. For a great contrast lay between Spain and Portugal. While it meant a great deal that Portugal should be able to provide the slaves which she needed for overseas development from areas which were under her control, it meant as much that Spain was always forced to go outside her own empire to get the slaves which she needed. Spain had no possessions on the African coast.

## III. *Indian and Negro in the Spanish Empire*

The Portuguese moved into their new possessions under a strong monarchical leadership but with few articulated notions of the way in which they should modify their institutions in the face of new needs. Spain, in contrast, had throughout a marked and legalistic theory of empire. This entailed regular, and at times successful, inquiries into administration, and it embodied a clearly defined policy of care for the native peoples. The theory of a deliberate imperialism with a duty of political, religious, and economic tutelage had, however, to be applied by the actual persons who were prepared to emigrate; and their interests were primarily to make the new territories profitable. Despite monarchical authority, the tight control of all contacts with the New World by the Casa da Contratación and the close screening of emigrants, many undisguised fortune-seekers soon found their way to the Spanish colonies, and they were early reported to be full of 'broken or desperate men'. By no means all were criminals; but even the Conquistador, with his *hidalgo* background and with that fine and determined purpose of expansion which carried the Spaniards from Nova Scotia to Cape Horn, from Oregon to the Straits of Magellan, by 1550, was more of an individualist, more purposeful and less humane, than would have been required for the Spanish crown's policy to be realized.

In settlement as in discovery, Columbus was the great innovator. Realizing early that the lands which he had discovered would require settlement to bring them into production (that he had not come to the fully developed economy of the Far East) he proposed that the settlement of Hispaniola should be undertaken on the basis of a common farm, with restraints on gold-seekers, with some three or four towns endowed with municipal rights, with control of all trade to Europe via Cadiz, and with a limit (he suggested 2,000) on the numbers of immigrants. Emphasis was upon agriculture and the development of a firmly-based society. Yet if production had to be organized and trade with an already existing system could not be got, the bases of the new system would have to be paid for. Columbus proposed that the cattle and other stock should be paid for by the sale of slaves. The proposal not only casts a significant light on labour conditions in Spain, where the slave was as well known as he was in Portugal; it also reveals Columbus's own views of the Caribbean Indians at his first approach. Under the Capitulation of 1492 he had been made hereditary viceroy, governor, captain-general and admiral of the Spanish colonies, but his proposals ran counter to the set policy of Spain and to the will of his royal mistress. While a panel of jurists declared in 1494 that the Indians were free although they were not fit to govern themselves, Isabella sent back to the islands a cargo of Caribbean slaves which Columbus had sent home. Columbus's settlers, such as they were, were revealing that work for a common farm was unacceptable, and his difficulties came to a head with a revolt of the Indians in 1498. This provided the solution, at least for the time being, for the legists had produced the theory of the 'Just War', by which Indians who rejected the rule offered to them forfeited their natural rights and could legitimately be made slaves. The remedy came towards the end of Columbus's career, when he was removed from office and brought home in manacles in 1500. Hispaniola had lapsed into licence in his last years, as the possibility of Indian slavery was accepted and as the third outward voyage, of 1498, brought new immigrants, many of them criminals, attracted by offers of a year's free supplies.

Columbus as governor had sought remedies for his troubles by abandoning all pretence of a common farm and by setting up the immigrants in *repartimientos*, allotments of land, or of labour, or of both; normally a semi-feudal grant of land with the labour on it on a para-military basis, a *peonia* of 100 acres, more or less, being the portion for an infantry soldier, a *caballeria* of about 500 that of a knight. The innovation led to a great outcry, and Columbus was abused (as so many colonial governors have been since his time) alike by the settlers whom he tried to curb and by the humanitarians who took up the case for the Caribs. The Church was loud in its protests, and from Ovando and from Las Casas comes much of the information which has seemed to make of the Spanish régime a selfish exploitation of land and labour for the short-sighted benefit of the immigrants. Ovando, however, when he arrived in 1502 on a special mission with full power over all officials and with the task of rectifying abuses and vindicating justice, found only 300 settlers in Hispaniola. They had assumed considerable estates on which to live, and in order to bring their estates to production they had secured heavy drafts on labour, so that villages and native society were breaking up and even the stability of Spanish rule seemed under threat. Ovando was ordered to put the Caribs back in their villages once more, to ascribe reserves of land to them, and to give them protectors and build them schools.

Yet the Caribs had to be used as a labour force if any production was to be achieved, for the settlers themselves were too few in numbers, and too apathetic towards manual labour, to perform the heavy work of agriculture themselves. Something of the quandary was conveyed in the royal order that although the Indians might be compelled to work on buildings, in mines and in agriculture, yet they were to work for wages, and as free men. The solution, full of controversy, was found when Ovando began the system of requiring the Carib chiefs to supply quotas of labour and of giving out this labour to the settlers in *encomiendas*. There was in the *encomienda* system some undoubted element of 'trust', and the Spanish *encomiendero* was given the custody of the Indians ascribed to him. Implicit in the institution was the conviction that in-corporation as a labourer into a white and Christian community was in itself an educational process by which habits of industry and a Christian sense of values would replace their heathen counterparts. There was also the fact that the system seemed the most likely means of supplying the labour force which the settlers required, and without which they could with difficulty survive. The settlers, being nearer at hand than the Spanish government or even, at times, than the missionary priests, turned the system to their purposes.

The *encomienda* system was destined to play its part on the mainland as the great mineral wealth of the Spanish colonies resulted in a steady demand for labour in the mines. There the system, modified and developed and known as the *mita* system, came to involve almost permanent exile from their villages for those Indians who were nominated for the task, with longer journeys to distant mines, lengthier absences and a resultant breakdown of family life. In its way it was not ungenerous, for the Indian servant could secure a new master, could buy his freedom, and could live with his wife and family. But it was shiftless, and it amounted to virtual slavery. In view of the type of men involved it was, moreover, almost inevitably subject to constant abuse; and it received the equally constant care of the Church and of the Crown and its servants. With all its abuses, the *mita* system lasted in Central America until well into the eighteenth century, and it left the Indian there as an important and vigorous element in economic life, mingling his culture with that of the Spaniard to produce the precious metals on which the economy rested and to evolve a fine series of cities and of educational establishments, and a tolerant 'colour-blind' Latin-American society.

The virtues of the Spanish approach lay partly in personal indifference and tolerance, partly in governmental principle. With strong, if spasmodic, urging from the Church, the Spanish Crown stepped in with a notable series of enactments (not all fulfilled to the letter) to prevent abuses of the *encomiendas* and the *mitas* and to try to create a society in which the Indians should have their proper place, their rights as owners of much of the soil, and their duties as the source of labour. The Laws of Burgos, in 1512, reformed many abuses and, in particular, ordered that no women or children should be forced to perform the heavy work of the fields. These laws were followed within a couple of years by a commission under Cardinal Ximenes to enquire into abuses, by a re-distribution of the *encomiendas*, and by a change to grants for the term of two lives (since a tenure for a single life led the holder to get the most he could from his privilege and to exploit his Indians unmercifully). Reserves for the Indians were also set up by Ximenes, and the period clearly revealed the clash of interests between Church and government on the one hand, and settlers on the other. The differences came to a head again as the mines of Central America began to attract more attention, towards the middle of the century. In 1538 a Papal bull forbade the (formal) enslavement of Indians, and in 1542 the Recopilación of the Laws revised the whole system.

The Recopilación, largely under the influence of the Dominican Las Casas, the 'Apostle of the Indians', denounced the idea of Indian slavery and built upon the experiment which the monk had achieved when he had secured that no Indian in the province of Guatemala should be 'commended' and had secured the submission of the Indians there, as freemen, by missionary effort. So convinced was the Spanish Crown that the Indians would see their proper interest in submission to, and co-operation with, the Spaniards that the Recopilación ordered that no further *encomiendas* should be granted and that all which existed should end on the death of their present holder. Nor was any Indian to be held as a slave, even when taken in a 'Just War'. In the meantime, as the *encomiendas* died out, none was to be held by any government or ecclesiastical official, and the Indians were to be drafted back to live in their villages under their native *caciques*. Compensation for the ending of *encomiendas* was to be paid, especially to the widows and children of the holders, from the revenues of the Crown; but the settlers knew well that without labour their lands were worth nothing, and they would have conquered in vain. Some officials refused to promulgate the new laws, armed rebellion broke out in Peru, revolt threatened in Mexico, clergy and officials were alike defied, and there was every prospect that a general rebellion would set up independent states in the New World and would deprive Spain of that flow of wealth which was just beginning to assume international importance. Charles V, beset with manifold troubles in Europe, withdrew the new laws in 1545, and henceforth the Spanish Crown accepted the *encomienda* as a necessary institution and devoted its efforts to mitigating its defects.

The *encomienda* system was spread to the Philippines when they were conquered by Spain in 1565, but the combination of the accepted need to perpetuate the system, or something like it, with the need to control it in the interests of the Indians, led to development towards a system of segregation, in which Indian agents were attached to each colonial government to protect the interests of the Indians, and the Indians were segregated from contacts with Europeans except their official instructors and guardians. They were to live in groups in their own villages and their *encomiendero* was forbidden to reside there with them, as was his fore-man or overseer; when they were wanted for labour they emerged, otherwise they were to live their own lives behind (protective) barriers. They were not to be household servants, were not to be supplied with spirits, and the master was responsible for seeing that they had their Christian priest. No single *encomienda* was to exceed 300 souls. Such amendments of the system carried it down to the end of the seventeenth century and into the eighteenth. They were not always observed to the letter, but though they admitted of abuses which entailed a serious decline in population, they secured the survival of the Spanish-American Indian on the mainland and they gave to the Spanish settler adequate labour for the mines and for the more normal business of agriculture and development. The system left large Indian groups on their own lands, to become free villages; and it left numbers of 'commended' Indians who, when the *encomiendas* came to their ends as the grants expired, were nevertheless tied economically and socially to the estates on which they had grown up and who, though legally free citizens, emerged as the Spanish-American peons.

The *encomienda* went forward with the frontier of Spanish conquest on the mainland, and in effect it was the *encomienda* which enabled the *conquistador* to bring into production the territory which he won. In the meantime, in the islands, the *encomienda* had played itself out almost before the march into the continent had begun. The reason for the contrast in experience lies partly in simple chronology, partly in social institutions. For the islands saw the first untrammelled experiments in using the Indians as a labour force under this system; and they also saw the impact of the Spanish demand for labour on a primitive and unco-ordinated society, whereas in Central America the Spaniards met strong and competent tribes and kingdoms, fully integrated and based on economies in which the heavy work of agriculture and of building and mining were accepted aspects of life. The Central American peoples did not revolt from the very thought of constant labour in the same surroundings. But the less developed Caribs, with their 'natural economy' based on fishing and hunting, found the sort of labour which the Spaniards required intolerable, as had the Indians of Brazil when faced with the Portuguese demands. The Caribbean Indian 'withdrew' from the white man and his demands. Not only did he provide unsatisfactory service; he died, with such aversion from life that within a generation sheer lack of numbers made him quite inadequate for the settlers' needs. Figures for such a movement are impossible to establish with accuracy; but the outcome was clear, and estimated figures give a pointer to the process. It has been reckoned that at the approach of the Spaniards, in 1492, total Carib population in Hispaniola was about 300,000. By 1508 it was reduced to about 60,000. A great decline had brought it to about 14,000 by 1514, as serious settlement began; and by 1548 it had reached a figure which indicated virtual extermination, about 500.[1]

European diseases had played their parts in this decimation of the Carib population, but the main cause was without doubt a passive revulsion from the changes which white occupation brought. The Carib, long accustomed to the effortless life which natural conditions in the West Indies make possible, had not the resilience needed either to

[1] E. G. Bourne, *Spain in America*, 1450–1580 (New York, 1904), 211–14.

repel or to co-operate with the European settlers. As family life and social stability were undermined by the demands of the *encomiendas*, the Carib withdrew and died. His place was taken by the negro slave, robust, capable of heavy labour in tropical conditions, and magnificently resilient in his response to adversity.

The first known shipment of negro slaves to the Spanish islands was made in 1505. But before that date, indeed from the very start of Spanish settlement, there is every likelihood that negroes had been taken out, for they were well known and accepted in Spain and the instructions to Ovando in 1501 had emphasized that, although Jewish or Moorish slaves would be barred from the colonies, he was to encourage the importation of negroes. Moreover he complained as early as 1503 that refugee negroes spread bad habits among the Indians. Queen Isabella seems to have been quite genuinely concerned over the problem, even to the extent of ordering that none but white slaves should be brought into the islands! This, however, was in the last year of her reign, when licences to import negroes can clearly be traced, and on her death Ferdinand made no bones about encouraging and developing the trade. In 1505 came the definite shipment of seventeen negroes, together with a cargo of equipment for opening up mines, and the change coincided with a plea from Ovando that more negroes should be sent.

The development came in part from an early interest in mining on Hispaniola, for Isabella had bequeathed to Ferdinand half of the royal dues from the Indies. But Hispaniola was not the only territory concerned. That island was, however, the normal entrepôt through which shipping to Spain went in the early days, and from there slaves were taken to other islands as Spanish settlement spread. Thus, Puerto Rico was settled in 1509, and slaves were soon taken there; Jamaica was settled also in 1509, and slaves were certainly there in 1517, and probably some years earlier; and Cuba was similarly settled in 1511. On the mainland Darien was the first settlement, in 1511, and negro slaves can be seen there as early as 1513.

This was an unorganized introduction of the negro slave to the Spanish possessions. But it demonstrated the value of the work which the negro could perform, and the way in which he could supply the defects of the Carib Indian. In 1510 the Casa da Contratación was ordered to organize a supply of negro labour, and the officials were ordered to send them to work in the mines, since the Indians were inadequate for this work. Here, with orders that cargoes of 100 negroes, and then of 200, should be shipped out by the Treasury, to be sold on arrival to the settlers, was the beginning of a new feature, the development of a speculative trade in slaves, quite different from the haphazard shipments of the few negroes who had hitherto been taken out on the personal account of their known masters. The negro slave thereby became an article of commerce, and the essential feature of the slave trade was thereby established; it was an organized *trade*.

As yet the negro slave for the Spanish possessions was acquired in the Iberian peninsula. A further development came when the transport route ran direct from the African coast to the Caribbean. But most noteworthy was the fact that Spain, in contrast with Portugal, had to look outside her own possessions for this essential supply. Revenue licences or *asientos* were required for the importation of this 'merchandise'. Herein lie the origins of the *asiento* system; and the Portuguese, with their experience and with their possessions on the African coast, inevitably became the principal source of supply and inevitably became involved in a smuggled trade to evade the dues. A licence to ship negroes had a considerable value both because it gave access to an active market and because it gave a remission of dues; and from the beginning of the reign of Charles V, in 1516, such licences were freely given by the young monarch as signs of personal favour. They went, for the most part, to his Flemish favourites, and they roused the opposition of the Spanish courtiers, and particularly of the regent, Cardinal Ximenes. But whether Ximenes was more concerned over the dissipation of a possible source of revenue or over the humanitarian problem, over the preferment of Flemings or over the dangers of a servile revolt if too many slaves should be brought into a sparsely-peopled settlement, remain open questions. Certainly the numbers of slaves had become considerable, and certainly the trade had assumed an importance in which revenue and national interests were concerned.

Fears of a servile revolt were in part allayed by looking to the example of the Portuguese settlements, where it was alleged that even defenceless widows were able to live at peace surrounded by as many as 800 negroes; with firm handling there was no danger, said the interested parties. Policy was also influenced by the religious orders and their care for the Indians. The Dominicans of Hispaniola declared that negroes were essential to relieve the demands on the Indians if the latter were to be kept in *repartimientos*, and to replace them if they were to be freed. The idea of using the negro to lighten the lot of the Indian was later put with force and effect by Las Casas; it was not a peculiar or an original idea but was the commonplace of most functionaries and the demand of most settlers. From the settlements on the mainland, as on the islands, came reiterated demands for the licensed importation of negroes. Partly because the Indian was inadequate for the purpose, partly because the Indian appealed to a sense of law and justice, the negro slave was defended as the only means of protecting the Indian. That the negro did not so appeal to a sense of justice is one of the inexplicable anomalies which marked three centuries or more of world history and which shaped the mould in which the pattern of European expansion overseas was created.

For Las Casas the basic need was for a satisfying influx of white settlers. But when Ximenes had died and the friar took his pleading straight to the throne his idea was that each new settler must be allowed to bring with him a dozen negroes so that he might not need the work of Indians. The principle once conceded that the negro might be enslaved so that the Indian might be spared, it became a question how many negroes would be needed to stabilize the settlements, and the Casa da Contratación produced the figure of 4,000 for the Antilles. In 1520 much the same process was followed for the mainland; an initial arrangement for three slaves per settler (later to be raised to seven) and then a bulk demand for five or six hundred. In the early years the proposal, and the practice, was for Spanish merchants to take goods from Seville to the Guinea coast, trade there for slaves, and under the terms of their licences ship them to the Spanish settlements. This, however, required the permission of the Portuguese monarch, and it meant that some Spanish merchants engaged in the trade without such Portuguese licences and in despite of Portuguese authority. It was possible, and profitable, to engage on this basis for limited cargoes. But a major commitment, such as the great licence which was granted for 4,000 slaves to the governor of Bresa in 1518, required different treatment. It was not possible to combine a privileged monopoly-grant from the Spanish authorities with a smuggled trade in defiance of the Portuguese authorities.

The licence to the governor of Bresa took the form of an order from the king to the Casa da Contratación to allow the 4,000 slaves to be taken without interference to the Spanish Indies, and the beneficiary was also empowered to go and seek his slaves on the African coast and to take them direct to the Indies without touching back at Seville. This last was an exceptional privilege, not accorded in other lesser licences which were issued at about this time and whose beneficiaries were required to get their slaves from Spain. But such minor licences were of little importance compared with that to the governor of Bresa, who was clearly intended to have a monopoly of the trade, and who was allowed to sub-contract his licence. The monopoly was the more significant and the more dangerous both because it carried no terminal date and because it placed the supply of a labour-force, which had been shown to be essential to the Spanish planters, in the hands of a courtier-concessionaire. There was nothing to prevent the monopolist from sub-contracting this essential supply-service to non-nationals or even to enemies of Spain; and this was a weakness which was to mark the entire period of Spanish imperial power.

## IV. *The Slave Trade and National Rivalries*

The whole problem of labour was but one aspect of the economic approach of Europe to the New World; and that general economic approach was worked out in the context of the assertive nationalism of the fifteenth and sixteenth centuries. The emergent nation-states of that period took much of their character from their monarchies, and in large part the economic approach to the New World was conditioned by the strength and the weakness of the monarchy. Thus the voyage of Columbus was financed (as is well known) by the sale of Queen Isabella's jewels, and the overseas possessions of Spain became part of the appanage of the Crown of Castile; the Portuguese explorations were the personal ventures of the House of Aviz and the commerce of the Indies was the property of that house; and Queen Elizabeth took shares in the voyages which set out from England in her reign, and hoped (in vain) for a share in the profits. In the new appraisal of the European diplomatic situation the House of Habsburg stood as the central support of the old régime; the emergent nation-states were necessarily to some extent committed to a defiance of Habsburg claims or ambitions. It was not a new thing that economic factors should be taken into account as the diplomatic and military balances were weighed, for that had been the common practice in the later Middle Ages. But the extra importance which attached to national wealth during the Period of the Discoveries was unprecedented. Increased dependence upon the mercenary soldier, increased dependence of the monarchies upon cash revenues (with consequent weakness if that revenue were not available), increased tension and intolerance between the states as religion and national self-consciousness added to the dynastic quarrels of the previous period; these things go far to explain the new emphasis. But no explanation can be satisfactory which leaves out of account the fact that in the fifteenth and sixteenth centuries statesmen, secular and ecclesiastical, thought more of economic factors than they had previously done; and though this may seem to be an attempt to explain the problem merely by stating it, yet the change in attitude was supremely significant. The result was that the Discoveries were brought into the diplomatic balance in a new way, best epitomized when Hakluyt exhorted his fellow-opponents of the Habsburg power to 'Strike him in the Indies, you strike him in the apple of his eye'.

In such a context the Spanish lack of labour was something to be exploited by opponents and to be guarded against by the Spanish government. The Habsburg monarchy and its advisers could no more be expected to regulate the affairs of the overseas dependencies of Spain without regard to the accepted and current maxims of political economics than they could be expected to plan their European diplomacy without regard to the current maxims of military strategy. It is indeed true that as the wealth of the American mines began to pour into Spain that country was not in the same quandary to preserve precious metals, as the sinews of war, as were the other countries of Europe. Consequently care for a Balance of Trade, and for preventing an outward flow of bullion, was not a marked or consistent feature of Spanish policy. But this was merely one card in the game, which it was not necessary for Spain to play. She fully realized the extent to which diplomatic and military affairs could be influenced by economic factors, and in trying to arrange her economic life so as to produce diplomatic and military results she was as 'mercantilist' (if that is the correct term to apply to this inter-action of economics and statecraft) as the rest of sixteenth-century Europe. Spain hoped, for example, to use an embargo on the import of English goods into the Netherlands in such a way as to provoke riots and rebellion in England, and so to overthrow Elizabeth's government, or at least to compel it to restore the Roman Catholic religion in England.

The *asiento* trade in slaves fell neatly into this picture, all the more neatly because at the heart of it lay a grant of a monopoly subject to certain conditions; and such grants and privileges, with their abuses, came to be the distinguishing features of the later 'mercantilist' system. But it was a highly disputable way of managing one of the requisites for survival in the New World, and a constant cause of grave uneasiness to the Spanish authorities. For favouritism and incompetence in the granting of licences, and ignorance of 'the trade' and sub-contracting in the exploitation of the licences, led to many abuses, to inadequate supplies and high prices, to connivance, smuggling and corruption. The first great grant, of 1518, was due to expire in 1527, and although in practice many shipments were made after that date under this licence, the period of true *asientos*—licences (mostly to non-Spaniards) in return for payment—begins in 1528 with the licence to two German merchants for 4,000 slaves to be imported within four years in return for payment of 20,000 ducats into the royal Treasury. This was a monopoly, and it placed the settlers at the mercy of the monopolists, whose alien interests were to recover their contribution to the Treasury, and as much more as could be got, from their grant within a limited time. Hispaniola was quite the best-supplied market, but even there (where a fresh gold-mine had just been opened in 1531) slaves were so scarce, dear and ill-conditioned, that outcries were endless, from Church and state alike. This despite the fact that the Germans had sub-contracted their *asiento* to Portuguese merchants who had developed it into a means of setting up a direct trade between Lisbon and the Spanish possessions, or between the islands and the Portuguese posts in West Africa.

The defects of the *asiento* system were so glaring that, apart from the left-over repercussions of former grants, the system was abandoned from 1532, when the grant to the Germans expired, until 1580 when Spain took control of Portugal and of the Portuguese possessions overseas. The intervening years saw an increase, rather than a decrease, in the demands for slaves, and the demand was met by the expedient of issuing a series of licences of brief duration and for a limited number of slaves—usually about 300. Clearly distinct from a great and monopolist *asiento*, these licences brought a certain amount of revenue to the Crown, and they brought a supply of slaves to the settlers. But they did nothing ever to remove the great weakness of the Spanish imperial economy; they did not provide a steady and controlled supply of the necessary labour-force. The number of negroes, and their preponderance over white settlers, did indeed increase over the period, and the reason why a lasting and satisfactory *asientist* arrangement could not be made to satisfy Spanish needs was because no Spaniard could undertake it though the Spanish authorities would, it appears, gladly have attempted a long-term *asiento* if there had been a promising bidder. In addition, the needs of the Crown were such that there could be no certainty that a grant which had been paid for would be respected over the years, and so the utmost which the Crown could sell was a short-term licence, usually to an active merchant rather than to a courtier.

It was almost an inevitable feature of dependence on slave-labour that the demand should never be fully and cheaply met, for the labour-force is the most easily expended factor in a slave-owning system; and by the end of the reign of Charles V official correspondence between Spain and her colonies contained many complaints of the shortage of negroes, and of their necessity for the colonial economies. But restrictions, in theory or in practice, did nothing to put this vital trade into the hands of native Spaniards. It is indeed true that a number of Spanish merchants took out quite considerable licences, but they were outnumbered by aliens, and there is reason for thinking that many of them were no more than intermediaries for aliens, who thereby circumvented the law that all trade with Spanish colonies must be conducted only by Spanish citizens. The rule was, however, maintained in that it ensured that the colonists themselves should not engage in the trade, going to Lisbon or to Africa to fetch the slaves which they needed.

In such circumstances it is not surprising that smuggled and connived shipments should be numerous and attractive, nor that such shipments should have been undertaken with something of a moral assurance that the shippers were doing no wrong and were, indeed, supplying the settlers with the essential labour of which the government ordinances deprived them. In general it was assumed that such shipments would seriously invade a real property of Portugal when they went to the African coast to get slaves, but that in taking them to sell in the Spanish possessions they would be merely evading a formal veto; Portugal was the serious bar to a free trade rather than Spain. So far did this approach to the slave trade carry sixteenth century merchants that a powerful group of English merchants saw the possibility of setting up an Anglo-Spanish partnership for the trade in such terms as would satisfy the settlers' demands for slaves, the Spanish government's desire for economic strength and control, and the English merchants' desire for the profits entailed. This would seem to cut right across the dominant politico-military alliances of the period, but it must be remembered that in the early years of Elizabeth's reign England and Spain were not yet arrayed in clear hostility, and indeed that such hostility arose largely from the depredations of English corsairs on Spanish shipping in the Narrow Seas, a series of depredations which stemmed to a large extent from incidents of the slave trade. Something of the old alliance with Burgundy still sweetened relations between England and Spain, France was still the prime enemy of both countries, and in the Treaty of Cateau Cambrésis Philip (who thought a marriage between himself and Elizabeth neither impossible nor unattractive) insisted, as against the claims of the French-sponsored Mary Queen of Scots, that Elizabeth was the rightful queen of England.

Yet it requires an effort to realize that John Hawkins began to trade in slaves to the West Indies in the hope that he might establish a regular commercial co-operation between England and Spain. There were already strong trading connections, and there was a strong colony of English merchants resident in Spanish ports, and trading from those bases. Hawkins, and his father William, had already traded and had made good fortunes and attained considerable stature, on these traditional lines; and it was on voyages to the Canaries and to Madeira that they had begun to appreciate the mercantile opportunity which the Spanish lack of slaves offered. The bullion trade of the Guinea coast seemed at times equally attractive; but Portuguese ships were on guard there and even with something of royal support the English merchants failed to break in. In 1562 John Hawkins and his associates, after the failure of such an attempt to break into the bullion trade from Guinea, set out to stake a claim in the slave trade. Taking on board a Spanish pilot at Teneriffe, Hawkins secured some 300 slaves at Sierra Leone in defiance of Portuguese opposition and then made his way to Hispaniola. His concept was that, as far as Spain was concerned, he was justified in trading his slaves to the labour-hungry settlers, justified by 'the freedom of the high seas and the reciprocal rights of trade enjoyed by Spaniards and Englishmen in each other's ports, in virtue of the old commercial treaties between England and the House of Burgundy'.[1] So confident was Hawkins that his actions, however debatable as far as Portugal was concerned, were acceptable in Spain that, having made a most excellent trade, he sent two ships loaded with the produce to Spain for disposal. The Spanish authorities, however, could not see the episode in the same light as Hawkins, and his ships sent to Spain and some slaves which he had left to pay any Spanish dues were all impounded. When, disgruntled but convinced of the great opportunity for mutual profit, he embarked on his second voyage in 1566, Hawkins found that he had to face both opposition from the Portuguese on the Guinea coast and a direct embargo on the Spanish Main (for this time he went to the mainland rather than to the islands).

Much though his slaves were desired, Hawkins on this occasion could get no custom until, protesting that all he wanted was honest trade, he had landed a hundred men at Borburata (Burborough Water); and again he had to make a show of force to get payment for his bills at the Treasury of the Indies at Rio de la Hacha. The settlers' misgivings silenced by Hawkins' show of force, he made a good trade, managed about 60 per cent profit on his venture, and drew off with certificates of his good behaviour both from the governor of Borburata and from the treasurer of the Indies.

By honest trade, smuggling with connivance, or downright armed intrusion into Spain's dominions, Hawkins had shown that he, and others like him, could easily defy Spain's economic and military control of her overseas territories. In so doing he deprived himself of any special consideration as an Englishman, not hostile to Spain. For the Spaniards felt that, given the opportunity, he and his like would inevitably turn to attack the treasure fleets which annually brought across the Atlantic the bullion from the mines of the New World. The danger brought the Spanish ambassador in London into the field, and the official power of Spain behind him; and Hawkins' famous third voyage, to San Juan d'Ulloa, brought down on him official Spanish reprisals and so started an irremediable rancour between Drake (who was aboard) and the English sea-dogs and the Spaniards. This in turn went far to make inevitable the struggle which led to the Spanish Armada, and the changes in the balance and the purposes of European diplomatic and military power of which the Armada was at once a cause and a feature. The slave trade had played its part in bringing Spanish and English into endless hostility, and in provoking the English to accept a policy in which they challenged the Spanish pretensions to exclusive possession of the New World. As yet, by the end of the sixteenth century, English statesmen and merchants alike were pre-occupied with the possibilities of actual plantation in

[1] J. S. Corbett, *Drake and the Tudor Navy*, 1 (London, 1917), 81.

northern Ireland, with their age-old trade-contacts with modern Europe and with the Levant, and with the transition from fishing to plantations which Newfoundland and parts of the coast of North America offered. Only Raleigh and a very few like-minded speculators had begun to conceive of English possessions on the American mainland or in the islands; but their adventures were ill-fated, and their careers were marked by the opposition of Stuart statesmen who hoped still to revive the Anglo-Habsburg alliance to which John Hawkins and his successors had dealt such an unforgettable and unforgivable blow.

Certainly one thing which emerged clearly from the Hawkins episode and its aftermath was that the English, as a people, could not hope to step in and fill the gap in the Spanish imperial economy by managing the slave-trade, in despite of Portugal and in alliance with Spain. Indeed, before the climax had been reached in the Armada year, the Spaniards had sought their remedy in the conquest of Portugal. This, with efficient exploitation and with the goodwill of his new subjects, should have given into Philip's hands all the labour which his realms required. Joint sovereignty did not, however, bring unity to the two realms, certainly not a unified economic policy, any more than it brought the Netherlands and Spain into an economic unity. By royal decree the Portuguese were explicitly denied the privileges of Spanish nationality, especially the privileges of trading to the Spanish possessions, and since they owned the whole coast-line from which slaves might be derived and were themselves actively engaged in the traffic to supply their own settlers in Brazil, this drove them to connivance and defiance in order to perpetuate their interests; interests which had become so organized over the years as to bring a steady revenue to the Crown from licences and customs. They had also built up an important body of concessionaires and of merchants whose wealth and consequence made them politically significant.

The influence of this class of Portuguese merchants was great on the west coast of Africa also. There, interest was in trade rather than in settlement, and normally settlement did not extend beyond small posts on the coast or (for better defence) on islands adjacent to the coast. In Upper Guinea, north of the Senegal, the Portuguese met opposition from Muslim merchants, and their only permanent settlement, at Arguin, soon fell into decline as trade shifted to the easier area of southern Upper Guinea, from the Senegal River to Sierra Leone. Here they came up against no great Muslim influence, and here the Cape Verde islands, with their settlements and their increasingly prosperous sugar plantations, provided a background from which trade on the coast spread inland up the Gambia and the Senegal rivers. This was a prosperous trade, in which gold-dust, pepper and gum arabic, supplemented the traffic in slaves; but it fell into the hands of a rather disreputable half-caste society, with no particular virtues and with no particular national characteristics. From Sierra Leone to the Gold Coast the lack of good natural harbours was a deterrent to trade, but from the Gold Coast there was a flourishing trade to Portugal in gold-dust, and the Portuguese posts at Elmina, Axim and Shama, were well-built and defensible. Even here, however, direct Portuguese influence on native affairs was limited to a narrow area near the posts, and the coastal peoples effectively resisted Portuguese attempts to make direct contact with the peoples of the interior. They also resented the claim that trade with Europeans was, or should be, a monopoly of the Portuguese, and given the opportunity they were always ready to trade with ships of other nations. Yet Portuguese influence was so strong, and the attractions of trade were so great, that the Portuguese posts caused considerable migration among the negroes and the development of migrant and de-tribalized communities, dependent on the European posts.

Serious as was Portuguese influence on native society on the Gold Coast, it was much more serious in the Bight of Benin, for there they made contact with the rising power of the king of Benin, and from the wars waged by that monarch in asserting his power over his neighbours came ample supplies of slaves for the Atlantic islands and for the New World. Though the Bights of Benin and Biafra were so unhealthy that from about 1520 onwards no attempt at permanent stations in the Niger Delta was made, yet the trade continued, for it proved easy to manage from the islands of São Thomé and Fernando Po, and there also extensive sugar plantations were developed, to flourish until the latter half of the sixteenth century, when the dangers of servile revolts and exhaustion due to monoculture drove many of the planters across the Atlantic to Brazil and left the islands to act as depôts for the collection of slaves for the Atlantic trade.

The result was that, although their claim to exclude all other Europeans was not accepted on the coast, and although determined rivals such as Hawkins could always take away slaves to the Americas, in effect the Portuguese dominated the slave trade throughout the sixteenth century and supplied both their own settlements and those of Spain with the labour required. The supply was never enough to quiet the complaints of the settlers, and probably was always genuinely inadequate. In fact the numbers seem to have averaged about 13,000 a year. The demographic significance of this number cannot be ascertained in the absence of any accurate estimate of the numbers of the social units from which the slaves were drawn—tribes reaching far into the heart of Africa—but it was certainly adequate to enable Spanish and Portuguese settlements in the New World to take a shape dependent on slavery, and therefore entailing a continuous and urgent quest for slave labour through the ensuing centuries.

Yet the weakness of the Spanish economy remained, for the trade was predominantly in the hands of Portuguese merchants, with their control of the African coast, and the differentiation between the Portuguese and the Spanish subjects of Philip perpetuated the weakness of the régime. Attempts to organize the traffic in such a way as to bring it under the control of either the Spanish régime of the Casa da Contratación or of the Portuguese régime of the Consulado alike failed. There was in effect a struggle between the interests of Seville and of Lisbon, which epitomized the different interests of the two nations, and the Portuguese and their sub-agents had a practical grip on the trade which made them the only reliable purveyors on whom the settlers could depend.

This Portuguese predominance through the period of licences was emphasized even more when, in 1595, the system of a general *asiento*, comprehensive and monopolist, was revived in the grant to Pedro Gomez Reynel, a Castilian who carried off the contract in opposition to Antonio Nunez Caldera, *fermier* of the trade of Cape Verde and of Angola, an experienced and reliable merchant. The object of the revived *asiento* was to utilize the facilities of the Portuguese possessions without allowing the Portuguese to share in the wealth of the Spanish Indies. It was, however, clear (as it had been with the projects to bring the trade under the control of the Consulado) that the Castilian would have to rely upon the services of merchants actively engaged in the trade, and that his chief function would be to farm the system of licences; yet he was permitted to engage in the trade himself, and the trade to Buenos Aires was reserved to him. From the Spanish point of view there was such a need to keep the flow of slaves constant, and to direct the ships to certain areas, that although merchants were free of the more vexatious restrictions which compelled them to use only certain ports in Europe, they were nevertheless severely hampered in their trade and there was much scope left for a contraband and fugitive trade. In particular, the *asientists* were in general forbidden to ship slaves to the mainland, they were forbidden to employ agents of alien nationality, and they were only allowed to bring home the produce of the colonies, excluding precious metals, in exchange for their slaves. Such rules could easily be evaded, and it was particularly difficult to enforce them when the *asientist* employed a colonist, already engaged in trade on his own account, as an agent. The rules nevertheless give a clear insight into the way in which Spain approached this vital trade, even after the conquest of Portugal, and tried to regulate it in such a way as to contribute to national economic strength and independence. Desire for national strength, and for revenue, together with the fact that the actual trade to Africa was separately licensed out and that the *asiento* only gave access to the Indies and America, so undermined the value of the privilege that this great *asiento* was surrendered voluntarily in 1601, when it should have run till 1604.

Failure and difficulties notwithstanding, some such system seemed so necessary and so attractive that there was little delay or difficulty in negotiating a new *asiento*, though the advantages of placing it in the hands of Portuguese nationals, who in any case had control of the first stage in the trade, led to a grant to the Portuguese Governor of Angola and farmer-general of the dues of Africa, Juan Coutino. Here was a triumph for reality, acceptance of the simple fact that Spaniards did not command access to the Slave Coast. Acceptance of that fact, and of the corollary that the Portuguese would not easily tolerate alien intervention in the trade of their territories, led to the conclusion that a gap in the policy of exclusivism must be accepted. But the gap was accepted with bad grace, as a defect, and the *asientist* was forbidden to grant out his licences to aliens; only Portuguese and Castilians were to be allowed to take part in the trade. By the death of Coutino in 1603 the *asiento* was in such a complicated and difficult predicament that it was abolished *in toto* and a new contract created, to run for the remainder of the prescribed period, till 1609. This, and succeeding contracts, left so many loop-holes for a contraband trade (not only in slaves) and left the settlers so short of labour and the colonies so troubled by aliens, that the disadvantages were universally recognized, and the Portuguese were at one time in danger of being forced to bring their slaves to Seville, which would act as the entrepôt through which all shipments to the Indies must pass.

More important than the ineffective efforts of the Spanish authorities to find a remedy within the system of *asientos* was the way in which the system invited merchants of other nationalities to do as Hawkins had done and to defy the system with the connivance of the Spanish settlers and the Spanish colonial administrators, both of whom depended on a more generous and regular supply of slaves than the *asientos* produced. Here there were three major contestants, the French, the English and the Dutch, and of them all the Dutch were by far the most effective and dangerous. The commercial importance of Antwerp, and then of Amsterdam, had been largely based on Dutch control of trade to the Baltic and the Rhineland, and on Dutch ability to supply to northern Europe the spices and luxuries of the eastern trade which the Portuguese brought to Iberian ports. With the Spaniards they drove less trade than did the English, but for the Portuguese they supplied the outlet to the markets of Europe.

First, for the Portingall, we know, that like a good simple man, he sayled everie yeare full hungerly (God wot) about 3 parts of the earth almost for spices, & when he had brought them home, the great rich purses of the Antwerpians, subjects of the King of Spaine, ingrossed them all into their own hands, yea oftentimes gave money for them before hand, making thereof a plaine Monopoly.[1]

So wrote the Secretary of the English Merchant Adventurers, with an intimate personal knowledge of the Dutch success. But until the early years of the seventeenth century the Dutch were prevented by their own separatist organization, and by their normal trading access to the Spanish possessions, from taking a very active part in breaching the exclusiveness of the Iberian powers. Until then the main protagonists against the Habsburgs were the French.

French corsairs had preyed upon Spanish shipping in the New World before Hawkins roused fears that the English were only awaiting an opportunity to do the like, and the first threat to Spanish possession of the mainland came from the French. Their colony at Florida, established by Ribault, was early destroyed even though Hawkins had succoured it on his second voyage. It was weak and ill-supplied in itself, and it was suspiciously well-sited for preying on the Spanish treasure-fleets as they made their way out from the Caribbean to Europe by way of the Florida Channel. French trade, under duress, with Spanish settlers took much the same form as had the voyages of Hawkins, and the French captains turned naturally and easily to buccaneering and piracy. But no French colony was set up in the Caribbean until 1625 (the same year as the first English colony there) and such national efforts as France made went into settlement near the mouth of the St Lawrence.

For this the reason was in part a natural reluctance to add an overseas dispute with Spain to the exacting demands of the Wars of Religion; in part it was the simple lack of a powerful and purposeful government in France. But when France emerged from her civil wars with a unified policy under Henry IV, and with a coherent economic policy prescribed by Sully, that policy gave but little place to overseas possessions. It was indeed a policy imbued with notions of national economic self-sufficiency, but the great extent, diversity and wealth of 'la belle pays de France' dominated French thought. Expounded by Sully, Razilly, Barthélemy de Laffemas and Montchrétien in turn, the major theme did not greatly vary. 'Ce grand royaume, composé de pays differens de solage et de ciel, mais tous bien correspondans entre eux-mesmes, est non seulement fourni de tout ce quil faut pour l'estre, mais encore pour

---

[1] John Wheeler, *A Treatise of Commerce*, ed. G. B. Hotchkiss. Facsimile Text Society (New York, 1931), 36.

le bien estre.' 'Ce royaume est si fleurissant, si abondant en tout ce que l'on peut désirer, qu'il n'a que faire d'emprunter rien de ses voisins.'[1] Such phrases could be many times repeated, with minor variations; they swelled to a chorus of belief that for France foreign trade, unless carefully controlled, was always a means of drawing away her own produce, and colonies were unnecessary and potentially dangerous for France. Such commodities as she could not supply, like lead, could easily be got by a well-ordered trade, and there was no necessity to indulge in colonial ventures in order to obtain them. The major theme was emphasized by Sully's thesis that little profit could be got from colonial lands lying to the north of 40° (and any lands south of that latitude would entail rivalry with Spain) and it says much for the enterprise of individual Frenchmen that the Canada and Newfoundland ventures received any support at all. The 'insupportable dominance of Spain' played its part, together with the desire for adventure and for easy plunder, in stimulating individual Frenchmen, and it was from individualist efforts (sometimes under licence from the Crown) that the French made their approach. Jacques Cartier had indeed been sent on his voyage of 1534 to discover 'certain isles and country where it is said one may find a quantity of gold' *au nom du Roi*, but he had been financed by private supporters despite the royal interest, and so had his successors.

For the English also it must be accepted that not until the Stuart period did any serious national efforts at colonial expansion take place. Ulster and Newfoundland between them took up such energy as the Elizabethans had to spare from defence and from piracy, and the ill-fated attempts to settle in Virginia and in Guiana speak all too clearly of a lack of national support, or even of co-ordinated private support, for such ventures. 'Pride in the spectacular achievements of the Elizabethan adventurers (and the hot air generated nowadays about the New Elizabethan Age) should not blind us to the fact that it was the Dutch and not the English who broke the back of Iberian sea power during the first half of the seventeenth century'.[2] Already entrenched in the trade to Portugal, the Dutch moved to dominance in the all-important trade in slaves in three stages; first, trade to Brazil; second, trade to Guinea; and third, trade to the Spanish possessions. The order was not so much chronological as logical, for the three phases overlapped in point of time.

Although the first Dutch impact came by way of trade, both to the Iberian ports and to the New World, a fresh point was reached when, at the end of the sixteenth century, they began to think in terms of setting up their own agricultural colonies in the New World as counterparts to

[1] A. de Montchrétien, *Traicté de l'oeconomie politique*, ed. Th. Funck-Brentano (Paris, *n.d.*), 131, 240.
[2] C. R. Boxer, *The Dutch in Brazil* (Oxford, 1957), 1.

their European economy. Here the theorist was Willem Usselincx, the example was Brazil with its supplies of sugar, cotton, and dye-woods to Portugal; and the outcome was the establishment of the Dutch West India Company in 1621. This came after considerable delays, during which the truce of 1609 between Spain and the Dutch gave them much more free access to the trade of Brazil and a marked preponderance in the trade to the Guinea coast (for gold and ivory rather than for slaves) despite the Portuguese and their fortified posts. The West India Company as chartered in 1621 was, moreover, marked in its origins by clear hostility to Spain; it aimed not merely at peaceful colonization but at war and conquest, and it was largely inspired by the 1617 voyage of Lemaire into the Pacific and by the idea of uniting the East and West India trades in a joint attack on the Habsburgs. Yet the West India Company made a slow start, and although by 1623 it had fifteen ships at sea these were all bound on trading voyages and the directors (the Heeren XIX) were still at that date slowly making up their minds to an attack on Brazil.

The great Portuguese colony was by this time populated by about 60,000 to 70,000 settlers of European or mixed blood, of whom the majority were in the captaincy of Pernambuco, where sugar predominated. The planters needed about 8,000 slaves to be brought into the country in each year, and the slave trade was almost entirely in the hands of Portuguese contractors and Jewish merchants, working under *asientos* or licences to bring the slaves from the Portuguese possessions in Angola; they also controlled the bulk of the equally lucrative trade in sugar. Many of the Portuguese merchants were, however, merely cover-names for enterprising Dutchmen, who had by this means evaded Spanish embargoes and had so improved their position during the Eleven Years Truce (from 1609 to 1621) that at the end of that period they carried between a half and a third of all the trade between Brazil and Europe. By 1622 there were twenty-five sugar refineries in Amsterdam alone. There was strong feeling in favour of leaving such an important trade intact, but the urge to strike a blow at Spain was too powerful. At the end of 1623 a strong Dutch expedition set sail for Bahia and easily took the city in the following May. This was an important strategic move, and if Bahia had been held the rest of Brazil would surely have fallen. But while the Dutch garrison of the key city fell into evil ways under poor leaders their naval strength was dissipated by an expedition to Angola in 1623, an expedition to Luanda (under Piet Heyn) in 1624, and a disastrous attempt to capture the Portuguese fort at Elmina on the Gold Coast in 1625.

The result was that a combined Spanish and Portuguese fleet of over fifty ships had little difficulty in recapturing Bahia at the end of April

1625. Successful commerce-raiding, with Piet Heyn to lead and encourage the Dutch, kept the West India Company solvent and purposeful, and despite their failures to capture the Portuguese posts their trade in gold and ivory from the Guinea coast continued active and prosperous. The company had for the moment failed in its major purpose of capturing a colony and the slave trade which went with it. But in 1628 Piet Heyn crowned his career when he captured the Spanish treasure fleet with eight million guilders' worth of silver aboard and much besides, gold, pearls and silks—the only time in the long history of the Spanish colonies that this was accomplished. Other booty also flowed into the company's coffers; on booty it throve, and on booty it financed a renewed effort to capture a colony and its trade, complete.

This time the Dutch turned against the northern, sugar-producing, captaincy of Pernambuco. But although they captured the two major cities of Olinda and Recife they were then hemmed in by guerilla bands, and in 1631 they were forced to abandon Olinda and to concentrate on Recife. With the great advantage of ability to move their troops from place to place by sea, while the Portuguese had to march inland, and with the power in their hands to devastate the plantations, the Dutch seemed to hold the whip-hand by 1637. But resistance was not over; the shoulder of Brazil was indeed called New Netherland, but it could not be claimed that a colony had been established. The war had cost the company even more than it had won in booty, and it was heavily in debt. The appointment of the efficient and enlightened Count of Nassau-Siegen, Johan Maurits, as governor brought unity and efficiency, and something of the sense of purpose which had ensured such outstanding success for the Dutch East India Company. Early military success was followed by enlightened administration, but as trade recovered and it was made possible for individuals to breach the monopoly of the West India Company (except for the trade in slaves, dye-woods and munitions) attention was concentrated on the fact that Brazil needed a constant supply of slaves if her natural resources were to be developed. The original idea held by Usselincx, that the Dutch tropical colony which he desired should be peopled and worked by north Europeans, held few attractions, and the actual situation in northern Brazil, as the Dutch had got it, was quite inextricably tied in with the slave trade.

Though in the first period of activity of the Dutch West India Company the Guinea coast had been the object of three important but useless expeditions, it was the trade in gold and ivory rather than in slaves which had attracted the Dutch there. The Calvinist conscience was uneasy over slavery, there was a precedent in which a cargo of slaves brought to Middleburg in 1596 had been freed on arrival, and it was not until the success of Johan Maurits in getting possession of Pernambuco faced them with the immediate problem that the Dutch entered at all largely on the slave trade. Then, with cover from Calvinist divines who argued that the trade was justifiable as long as the slaves were instructed in Protestant doctrines and were not sold to Spaniards or Portuguese who would make them into Papists, the directors began to attempt large and regular shipments from Africa, and in 1637 the great Portuguese fort at Elmina was captured in order to give to the Dutch control of the supply-point on the Gold Coast. But slaves from the Gold Coast were less prized than those from the Congo and Angola, and those from Luanda were the chief source of labour for the Spanish mines in Mexico and Peru. Even the accession of John IV at the end of 1640, and the break-up of the Spanish-Portuguese combined monarchy, did not prevent the Dutch from regarding the Portuguese as still their enemies, nor the Portuguese from continuing their persistent efforts to recover their lost lands. As a truce between the States-General and Portugal was in process of negotiation (it had been concluded in Europe but was not yet effective overseas) Johan Maurits despatched an expedition which gave to the Dutch possession of Luanda, Benguela, São Thomé, Annobon, and even Axim, the last Portuguese fort on the Guinea coast, in 1641–2. The new acquisitions, however, were not placed under the Brazilian administration, to which they were economic adjuncts and which had effected their conquest, but were given a separate Governor, directly under the Company in Europe.

Despite its great successes, and the developments which Johan Maurits secured in peaceful development when the work of conquest was over, the West India Company had by no means ended Portuguese resistance in Brazil. Seven of the fourteen captaincies still held out, including Bahia and Rio de Janeiro; and war to complete the conquest steadily cost more than the profits which the company got from its possessions in Guiana, Curaçao, Aruba, West Africa and at the mouth of the Hudson River in North America. Even the profits from the slave trade were ultimately swallowed in the costs of warfare; and these were very considerable. Although there were complaints that the company kept the number of slaves imported under control in order to maintain high prices, it has been estimated that during the period 1636–45 over 23,000 slaves were shipped into Recife; but the planters had little cash in hand to pay for their purchase, and when it was ordered that slaves must only be sold for cash the chief result was to put their distribution into the hands of Jewish speculators, with a resultant rise in price for the planters and drop in profits for the West Indian Company.

In the actual production of sugar in Brazil the Dutch took little part, either in growing or in processing it. They were above all merchants and factors, and the Portuguese retained control of production, remaining

as technicians and managers even when the Dutch owned the plantations
or mills, as many of them did in the optimistic period which followed the
appointment of Johan Maurits. The result was that the countryside
remained predominantly Portuguese—a tendency greatly helped because
guerilla resistance to Dutch rule was never entirely overcome—whereas
the Dutch congregated in the towns; and though efforts were made to
encourage immigration of Dutch and German agriculturists, little could
be achieved in this direction and the main basis of the Brazilian economy
remained the Portuguese planters with their negro slaves. Efforts were
made to raid Spanish possessions in Chile and at Buenos Aires, but sugar-
exports from Brazil remained the main source of income for the West
India Company, and emphasis on this single crop perpetuated the unbalance of the Brazilian economy, with its need to import grains, meat,
flour and wine as well as slaves. In all, the result was to produce a disastrously high cost of living, to lead the West India Company to expedients of economy, and to undermine whatever chance of founding a
lasting colony in Brazil the Dutch might ever have had. With the recall
of Johan Maurits in 1644, and the refusal of the Estates General to
restore conquered territories, the way was open for a strenuous and
organized revolt against Dutch rule. Though retaining their predominance at sea, the Dutch were thrown on the defensive on land; but the
garrison at Recife managed to hold out until a relief fleet, tardily
organized, raised the siege in the summer months of 1646. Eventually
King John IV of Portugal reached a decision to intervene directly in the
rebellion against the Dutch, in part because Dutch ships were raiding
the Portuguese sugar-caravels and without the sugar-revenues from
Brazil Portugal could not pay for the defence of her frontier with Spain.
'The loss of Brazil would involve the disappearance of Portugal as an
independent nation'.[1]

So, while the Dutch delayed in uncertainty due largely to their
internal dissensions and to jealousy of the West India Company, the
main Portuguese fleet was sent out to the relief of Bahia. This did little
to alter the balance of force in Brazil; but it tied down the available
Dutch ships off the Brazilian coast while the Portuguese were able to
send a fleet of fifteen sail to recapture Luanda. But this exploit did no
more than save the Portuguese from completely losing their hold on
Angola, for they had suffered heavy reverses there, and privateers from
Zealand wrought havoc on Brazilian trade while on land the Dutch
forces remained strong and effective enough to ravage the sugar plantations of the wealthy Reconcavo area at the end of 1648 and early in 1649.
Faced by the maritime predominance of the Dutch, and the need to
supply Brazil with trade and shipping if the colony was to be saved, the

[1] Boxer, *The Dutch in Brazil*, 186.

Portuguese in 1649 founded their own Brazil Company, to which aliens and heretics were permitted to subscribe although the merchant community of Lisbon was given special status and Lisbon was originally named as the only European port to which the convoys, whose supply and organization was the chief public duty of the Brazil Company, were to sail. Much of the shipping used by the Company was hired from the English (anxious to deal a blow at the Dutch); alien merchants in Portugal were worked upon to subscribe to the Company. Much of its capital was Jewish, and it received a monopoly of supplying Brazil with its food imports, but not the slaves, and the right to levy an impost on the exports of sugar, cotton, tobacco and other produce. Such privileges did not make the Brazil Company a profitable concern. But in Brazil Dutch power sank lower and lower as disputes between the provinces prevented their West India Company from following a clear and forceful policy and as poverty led it to starve and neglect its soldiers and sailors and to concede freedom of trade to outsiders—even freedom to trade slaves in 1648. The situation nevertheless did not change decisively in favour of the Portuguese, for the strong convoys organized by the Brazil Company failed to reduce the Dutch garrison at Recife; and as the Cromwellian fleet under Blake gained command of the seas it blockaded the Tagus, took out the English ships from the Brazilian convoys, raided the sugar fleets and inflicted heavy losses on the Portuguese. On the other hand, the English fleet was at grips with the Dutch from 1652 onwards, when the Dutch War broke out, and when the Brazil Company sent out an armada of seventy-seven sail at the end of 1653 the Dutch garrison at Recife was at last subdued and all Dutch possessions in Brazil were surrendered.

## V. *West Indian Sugar and Slavery*

The end of the costly Brazilian venture, which had seemed so likely to succeed under Johan Maurits, marked the failure of Dutch efforts to establish a colony on the mainland of South America. But it marked the start of a new phase in the history of colonization as it was affected by the problem of labour supply. The first half of the seventeenth century had not only seen the Dutch defying the power of Spain and setting up their East and their West India companies in a Protestant counterpart to the division of the New World by the Roman Catholic Treaty of Tordesillas; it had also seen them establishing colonies of settlement at Manhattan, Orange, and New Amsterdam in North America; and it had seen the first great emigration from Europe, to the Puritan New England colonies.

The New England colonies had a driving force of their own, but they were established within the framework of royal charters and grants, and chartered companies; and the same machinery saw also the beginnings of English settlement in the Caribbean. Something of a start was made in Barbados in 1620, and the Bahamas saw occasional mariners and buccaneers spending their winters on the islands; but the first serious attempt at English settlement in the Caribbean was when Warner took possession of St Christopher's in 1624. The general interest of the non-Iberian states in the West Indies may be judged by the fact that in the same year as Warner, a one-time English buccaneer, made his stop on St Christopher's the island was also settled by Esquemeling, a one-time French buccaneer. For both French and English the basis of settlement in the West Indies was the tobacco-crop. This proved within the competence of the small family farmer, and tobacco led to a remarkable period of settlement, lasting perhaps for a quarter of a century and producing in the islands a rapid influx of small-holders, in marked contrast to the slave-owning plantation system of the Spanish and Portuguese colonies.

Tobacco, introduced into Virginia in 1612, had already proved the salvation of that colony and, together with the abandonment of the early system of common farming on behalf of the community and of the company, had effectively galvanized the economic life of that apparently moribund colony. In the British and French West Indies tobacco had much the same effect. In the seventeenth century, as in the twentieth, the 'West Indies' was merely a common phrase of European terminology to cover a wide diversity of economies separated by thousands of miles of sea. But the isles had the common feature that they were first settled by small proprietors who depended on tobacco farming for their cash crop. For the rest, the settlers lived and held their lands within the framework of the proprietary patents of the period, and the grantee-proprietors were as much concerned as were the farmers with the problem of organizing a supply of labour. For this the machinery was two-fold—a system of land-grants on condition that a quota of labour was taken out by the grantee (a system which was to be worked out to something of a logical, but ineffective, conclusion in the British colony of Carolina and in French Canada); and a system of assisted emigration by indentures. The essence of the indenture was that the labourer was given his passage by his future employer in return for an indenture to serve him, on stated conditions and for agreed pay, for a period of years. Often a man who had accepted a grant of land in return for taking out a certain number of labourers got his men on the indenture system, and the two elements intertwined in this way. Through them wove the criminal law, and the ability of a felon, or of a political prisoner, to secure his freedom on condition he went as an indentured man to the colonies.

Between them, these methods of recruitment, and of defraying the costs of emigration, played their parts in providing the European labour which made the English, French and Dutch colonies in North America into colonies of settlement in the fullest sense of the word. That was a result which was partly attributable to climate, partly to religious intolerance, and which took till the middle of the eighteenth century to reach fulfilment. More remarkable, especially in the middle years of the seventeenth century, was the way in which tobacco, the small-holder and the indentured labourer, built up a white labouring population in the sub-tropical West Indian islands.

Emigration was not confined to the West Indies. By 1640 the population of New England had risen to over 40,000 while Virginia numbered some 7,500. The reasons for emigration from England vary, from the economic consequences of the Thirty Years War, with their overthrow of the European market for English woollens, through the rise of the Dutch to their new economic predominance, the ecclesiastical policy of Laud and the Arminians, to simple vagrancy and a plentiful supply of cheap shipping. At base was the fact that life in Stuart England was uncertain, limited by privileges and an outmoded social and constitutional system, and that the New World offered prospects of better fare and freer status. So motivated, the movement overseas was largely spontaneous, and was marked by clear social and religious characteristics. But religious dissidents were in a minority among the emigrants (even on the *Mayflower* itself), and social and economic dislocation which made available a plentiful supply of indentured labourers was of paramount importance.

The resultant division between colonies dependent on slave labour, and colonies following a subsistence agriculture on a family basis, is one which has to this day diversified the society of North America. In the West Indies the division is no less important because it is a chronological division instead of a latitudinal one. The small-holding society gave way before the advent of the slave; tobacco and coffee gave way before sugar. The turning point came in the middle of the seventeenth century. The significant act was the withdrawal of the Dutch West India Company from its pre-occupation with founding its own tropical colony in Brazil, and its turning to the economic development of the West Indian colonies of other western European nations, on the basis of the shipping, trading, slave-supplying and sugar-growing techniques which it brought from Brazil.

The result was two-fold; a rise in the trade and the prosperity of the West Indies, and a great development in the importance (largely strategic) attached to those islands. The seventeenth century saw ventures, such as Lord Rich's Providence Company and the endless efforts to develop the stronghold of Tortuga, which had little incentive save to secure strategic bases. But the new and important feature, round which the concepts of imperialism were built for a century and a half—until the fall of the so-called 'Old Colonial System'—was the volume and the value of the trade which could be got from the West Indies. They became 'the hub of the British Empire, of immense importance to the grandeur and prosperity of England'.[1] By the end of the seventeenth century they supplied more of England's total imports than all the mainland colonies (9 per cent as against 8 per cent), and they also took more of our exports. It was reckoned that this country derived a higher proportion of its income from the West Indies than from its trade with the whole rest of the world, and even Adam Smith, decrying the 'Old Colonial System', admitted the splendid profitability of the plantation system which lay at the back of it all. While Arthur Young calculated that one Englishman employed in the West Indies was worth eighteen times as much to the English economy as one employed in the 'Bread colonies' to the north, Adam Smith allowed in more general terms that 'the profits of a sugar plantation in any of our West Indian colonies are generally much greater than those of any other cultivation that is known either in Europe or America'.

Much of this emphasis on the West Indies is, of course, the verdict of later generations on the fulfilled system. But contemporaries were equally emphatic. Jamaica, for instance, placed in the forefront of his policy by Cromwell, was praised as the key of the Indies, 'lying in the very Belly of all Commerce', and in 1625 and again in 1637 Coke drew up a memorandum advocating the formation of an English West India Company in emulation of the Dutch, with whom, should the problem prove too serious for the English company, he proposed to amalgamate, to borrow Dutch skill, experience and capital, to help in an attack on Spain.

Dutch methods and organization had been closely investigated, and the English politicians had before them detailed analyses of their rivals. With sixteen slave posts under its control, the Dutch company paid so much attention to this aspect of its trade that the Guinea trade was kept as a separate capital project and the various local chambers of the company were ascribed different areas in the African possessions. One of the most significant points in the English favour was that when in 1654 they made their peace with the Portuguese they secured free access to Portugal's overseas possessions.

As yet, however, the Dutch rode high. While we kept the elements of our West Indian policy separate, the Dutch gained by combining them. We allocated the settlement of Bermuda to the Bermuda Company and gave patents for St Christopher's in 1623, for Barbados in 1624,

---

[1] E. Williams, *Capitalism and Slavery* (Chapel Hill, N.C., 1944), 52.

Santa Cruz in 1625, Nevis in 1628, Providence in 1629, Montserrat and
Antigua in 1632. But we set up a separate Guinea Company in 1618 and,
when the first had failed, another such in 1631. The difference from
Dutch practice was justifiable on the ground that these settlements were
indeed not designed to be worked on negro slave labour but on the basis
of English indentured servants. Available figures for the shipments of
indentured servants come for the most part from the last quarter of the
seventeenth century and the subsequent period, and it is clear that after
about 1689 (despite the considerable numbers of political prisoners from
the western counties who were indentured after the failure of Mon-
mouth's rebellion and the Bloody Assize) there was a considerable
falling off in emigration. Yet, apart from the puritan migration to the
New England colonies, something between a half and two-thirds of all
white emigrants to the colonies were convicts, indentured servants, or
redemptioners—a redemptioner being a comparatively free servant who
contracted with a ship's captain to enter into indentures on arrival in the
colony for such a period as would enable the plantation-owner to pay
the shipper for the passage, whereas an indentured servant had already
entered into a contract for service before he shipped aboard, and his
master was financially responsible throughout. The system had produced an estimated 1,078 servants out of a total population of 12,000 in
Maryland by 1660, and during the years from 1633 to 1680 it has been
reckoned that over 21,000 servants were imported into that colony. In
the Virginia census of 1624–5 the total population was only 1,227, and
of these 487 were servants and only 23 were negroes. It was estimated that
in this colony the number of servants had built up to 10,000 by 1665,
that the total population had built up to about 40,000 by 1671, and that of
these 2,000 were black slaves while about 1,500 servants were brought in
each year. From Carolina no satisfactory figures are available, but it is
clear that in the mainland colonies of the south the white labourer was
more numerous and more important than the negro in the middle years
of the seventeenth century.

In the islands the change came even sooner. As 'swarms of English
and French colonists poured like flies upon the rotting carcase of Spain's
empire in the Caribbean', figures for white population surged forward,
to reach a high point, which has never since been passed, by the middle of
the century.[1] Generalization for the islands is, as always, difficult but the
significant trend seems strongly enough indicated by outstanding
examples. Barbados, for example, emerged from a tangle of proprietary
grants in which it had been tied in with St Christopher's in an English
grant to Warner and in a French grant to d'Esnambuc in 1625 and then

---

[1] Cf. H. I. Priestley, *France Overseas through the old Régime* (New York, 1939), Ch. VII.
Sir A. Pym, *Colonial Agricultural Production* (Oxford, 1946), 87–9.

in an English grant (along with Trinidad and Tobago) to Courteen in 1628, to be taken up by James Hay, Earl of Carlisle, and a London syndicate in 1630. Despite these difficulties, by 1631 some 3,000 to 4,000 English settlers had been shipped out to the island by the efforts of the proprietors; by 1636 it boasted over 6,000 English settlers; and by 1642 had risen to over 37,000. This meant a density of 224 whites per square mile. Then decline began, the whites dropping to 23,000 by 1655. St Christopher's and Nevis by this time had a white population of between 20,000 and 30,000, with no negroes. But although white population had reached this peak with such speed the islands were not prosperous. The type of settlement has indeed stimulated a rousing thesis that the history of the islands during this period shows that there is no physical reason why white men should not undertake the heavy work of agriculture in the tropics, for the changes came not with the debilitation of the white population but with the failure of their economy.[1] The small planters with their white servants cultivated plots of from five to thirty acres, and maintained something of a standard of life until, in 1639, the tobacco market broke. The islands' tobacco was accepted as inferior to that of Virginia, and what with fever and scurvy, royal grants and tobacco taxes, and the hostility of the monarchy in England, not even the veto on the tobacco growths of Gloucestershire and the other English counties could rescue the industry. The glut of 1639 produced complete stagnation and then a change in the agricultural system and of all that went with it.

Even during the tobacco period our West India islands had been closely tied to the Dutch Company. The large number of small ships under the Dutch flag, which cleared up Spanish booty and trade in the wake of the great and organized fleets, showed the Dutch ability to supply goods (and slaves if required) and to freight back to Europe the export staples upon which the islands depended. Thus, to take an extreme example, our exiguous little settlement at Providence Island sold the year's crops *en bloc* to the Dutch company in 1632, in 1638 the Providence Company sought and obtained permission to trade with the Dutch despite embargoes, and in 1639 the Dutch offered to buy the island outright. Providence Island was something of a special case in which booty from the Spaniards predominated in the economy, few white servants were shipped out, and the settlers grew such crops as they could with the labour of slaves bought from the Dutch. Elsewhere the connection was less emphatic. But both the French and the English settlements on St Christopher's were set on their feet by the Dutch after a Spanish raid in 1629. They were then started off on a system in which

[1] Cf. A. Grenfell Price, *White Settlers in the Tropics* (American Geographical Society, 1939).

slave labour played an important part, and they struggled along largely because they were able to sell their tobacco to the Dutch. So dependent were they that in 1659 the English sent in a petition that the trade of the island had been completely engrossed by the Dutch, to the discouragement of the English. Barbados, despite its increase in population, was so unprosperous in the tobacco régime that the proprietors demanded nothing from the settlers, and it was not until 1640 that things changed. Then, under the governorship of Captain Philip Bell, 'a very honest man with a plentiful fortune', good laws were made and also 'the Dutch came and taught the art of making sugar, and having free trade and plentiful supplies' brought the island to rapid prosperity. By 1643 there were over 6,000 negro slaves on the island and the value of land was rising rapidly. By 1660 the negro population had risen to 50,000 and the value of land had risen to seven times its price in 1640. Instead of the meagre homesteads of the tobacco-farmers of a generation previously, the island was marked for its well-built houses, full of rich plate and household goods, there were usually sixty to seventy ships there awaiting cargo, and altogether the trade to Barbados occupied about 400 ships and 10,000 seamen, took out a yearly supply of about 10,000 tons of European goods and took home the produce in sugar, cotton, indigo and tobacco. Sugar predominated, and of a customs revenue of £12,930 from this island in 1654–65 brown sugar produced over £10,000 and white sugar £1,400.

In the vital change at Barbados it is easy to distinguish the formative part played by the Dutch, for they 'came and taught the art' of sugar-growing, and then supplied the necessary slaves. When the Cromwellian forces captured the island they found sixteen Dutch ships in harbour there, in 1651; and the Governor reported that trade was mostly carried on with the Dutch. They stimulated, financed and supplied, the change to sugar and a plantation system—a change for which disease, and the poverty of small-holders who could neither afford soil conservation nor experiments with alternative crops, had prepared the way. They supplied the machinery and the slave labour, and were reported to have taken planters to Brazil to show them the correct methods of cultivation.[1]

Jamaica showed the same features, if with important differences. After its capture from the Spaniards the Commonwealth government tried to settle the island with disbanded troops, giving them small holdings (inappropriate for sugar). Attempts to settle with indentured labourers, in the circumstances of the Civil War, merely filled the island with rogues and vagabonds, and society was dangerously unstable because of the scarcity of women. This resulted in an interesting Chancery case in which an enterprising Welshman, Owen Evans, was

[1] *Calendar State Papers, Colonial*, 1661–68, 541.

charged with riding round the West Country with pretended authority to seize upon girls who might make wives for the settlers. The scandal came to light when the church wardens complained that girls would not come to church for fear of being taken up by Evans, and it then proved that his authority was based on forgeries. But the market was there, and was a sign of the unbalance of colonial society. There were over 7,000 men 'in the hills' in Jamaica by 1655, and there was no stability until Governor Modyford (who acted on occasions as the agent of the Dutch Company) introduced the culture of sugar in 1664. White population then settled at a level of about 7,500 while negro numbers soared from 9,500 in 1673 to 74,000 in 1728, and Jamaica entered on a period of prosperity which was, however, marked by a growing disproportion of blacks and whites, by 'deficiency laws' which compelled a proportion of white servants to be kept by the planters, and by a dependence on militia and troops dictated by fears of a servile revolt.

## VI. *English and French Slave Trades*

If, as contemporary evidence shows, it was the Dutch who taught the English and French planters in the West Indies to grow sugar, and who then traded the sugar from them until discriminatory laws were passed (and sometimes after that date), it was the English who took up the slave trade which was thereby stimulated. Despite Hawkins and his voyages, and the chartering of a Company of Senegal Adventurers in 1588, English trade to the African coast had been obscure and unimportant until a Company of Adventurers trading to Guinea and Benin emerged in 1618 with a monopoly of the trade. But this company, although it established the first English post on the African coast, at Kormantin, and saw the beginnings of regular English participation in the slave trade, was not a serious rival to the Dutch. English factors undoubtedly maintained themselves on the Gold Coast, set up some kind of building at Cape Coast Castle, and kept the company going (with a reconstruction in 1631 and a renewal of its monopoly in 1651) until the Restoration. But it appears that as the West Indian demand for slave labour rose during the middle years of the seventeenth century the trade driven by the English Guinea Company was never a dominant, seldom a significant, element. Interlopers, and private merchants under licence from the company, kept interest alive and avarice on the boil. But steady and organized supplies were in other hands, and the English company seems to have been concerned with the search for gold rather than with a regular slave trade.

When the Royal Adventurers into Africa were chartered in 1660, the pre-occupation with gold persisted and the slave-trade was not taken into account as a prime objective until the re-organization of the company, with a new charter, in 1663. Then the slave-trade, and the new pattern of labour-demands in the West Indies, were taken seriously into account. In 1663 over 3,000 negroes were delivered in Barbados, and the English company undertook to supply 3,500 to the *asientist* for the Spanish colonies. This was a contract which could not be fulfilled, for the company was in difficulties over selling its slaves (cash being short in the West Indies), it was severely criticized by English rivals, and it was actively opposed by the Dutch. Ostensibly peace reigned between the two Protestant powers; but in 1661 Robert Holmes had taken a strong naval expedition to the Gold Coast and had taken over a small Courlander post in the mouth of the Gambia and had confirmed the company's posts on the Gold Coast and near Sierra Leone. Then the Dutch captured six English ships, Holmes took the Dutch post at Cape Verde, their castle at Cape Coast and their other posts on the Gold Coast, and in 1665 de Ruyter turned the English out from all their posts on the Gold Coast except Cape Coast Castle. This remained in the English company's hands as open war with the Dutch began in 1665— very largely a war for the lands and the trade of the overseas world. But the English company was already too entangled to be able to fulfil the needs of the trade for which it claimed a monopoly. Licences to private traders were freely granted for trade to Cape Coast while the subsidiary company of the Gambia Adventurers was set up to run the trade to Gambia and Sierra Leone, with a lease of the trade of north-west Africa. The Gambia Company's area produced chiefly goods for export to England, and though some slaves were got from the Gold Coast the English, like the Portuguese or the Dutch, found that the Bight of Benin produced the best, and the most, slaves.

The Company of Royal Adventurers was reduced by its difficulties to the position of a *concessionaire*, holding a chartered privilege but farming it out, by a system of licences, to merchants engaged in the actual trade. As a profit-making concern it had completely failed in 1670. But it had seen the beginning of serious English rivalry to the Dutch in the slave-trade and the impetus, with government desire to put the trade on a reliable and organized footing, was strong enough to carry it through into the formation of a new, and stronger, company, the Royal African Company, in 1671–2. Negroes were accepted as the chief objective of the new company, and there was about its formation an element of purposeful imperial planning and of rivalry with the Dutch, with the knitting together of possessions in Africa and in the West Indies as counterparts to the supply-system of the metropolis—something of Shaftesbury's notion of binding the component parts into such an empire of trade that 'they may be most serviceable one unto another, and as the whole unto these our kingdomes, so these our kingdomes unto them'.

The Royal African Company, chartered in 1672, had therefore a definite role to perform in a British imperial economy. It had also hopes, derived from the Royal Adventurers, of sharing in the still-unsatisfied slave-market of the Spanish colonies. It was to meet a serious need, and it was founded in a fortunate hour. For whereas the second Dutch War had arisen largely from conflicts in colonial trade and had played a great part in bringing down the Company of Royal Adventurers, the Third Dutch War (beginning in 1672) was largely a result of European dynastic intrigues, the French were deeply committed, and the Royal African Company was able to embark on its business while the Dutch were preoccupied elsewhere. Numbers of slaves fluctuated considerably from year to year, and the causes of the fluctuations were rather African than European in origin. The existence of a steady demand from the planters did not always suffice to make the ships' captains go on to their secondary sources of supply for slaves; and difficult conditions on the Gold Coast, caused by local wars, by European opposition or by unimportant personal troubles, often meant that the captains did not proceed on to the Bight of Benin but took inadequate cargoes to America and the West Indies.

Even so, it has been reckoned that between the years 1672 and 1711 the company sold some 90,000 slaves in the West Indies by auction—nearly a half at Barbados and over a third at Jamaica. Making allowances for those sold direct to planters, in addition to the auctions, and for those who died on the voyage, the company during these years must have delivered in the islands about 100,000 slaves, and must have shipped out from Africa about 120,000–125,000.

During this period by far the heaviest trade was during the years 1674 to 1689, during which nearly two-thirds of the grand total was shipped. Barbados is something of a special case in this, for there the decisive step of the change to a slave-owning plantation economy dependent on sugar had been taken under Dutch auspices before the advent of the Royal African Company. In Barbados, therefore, in the period of Dutch rivalry the Royal African Company successfully and purposefully undertook the business of keeping the numbers of the slave population up to the demands of the planters (and in excess of the numbers demanded by the 'deficiency laws' with their insistence on a proportion between blacks and whites). But in the other islands, especially in Jamaica, economic development had not gone so far as in Barbados; and under the company's auspices the slave population of Jamaica rose fourfold, to 40,000 by 1700, doubled to 80,000 by 1722, and stood at 130,000 by 1754. Of the smaller islands Nevis resembled Barbados in being near to maturity by the time the company began to exercise its monopoly, while St Christopher's, Antigua, and Montserrat required slaves for expansion and change rather than for maintenance of their economies. Making allowances for interruptions in the trade, it seems that the Royal African Company met the reasonable needs of the islands, justified its monopoly, and played its part in developing and maintaining the sugar economies until its affairs were thrown into confusion by the outbreak of war in 1689—this time war in alliance with the Dutch and with the French as enemies. Scarcity and high prices then drew a series of complaints from the islands, especially from Barbados, although the company probably served that island better than any of the others.

In the peculiar conditions of the sugar islands the results of the monopoly-control of essential labour by the Royal African Company were that slaves were probably cheaper than they would have been under a system of free trade, since the company bought at controlled prices on the African coast. But distribution of the slaves was diverted to the easy and clamorous market of Barbados while Jamaica and the smaller islands were undoubtedly short of labour and their social and economic stability was to that extent undermined. Part of the trouble was that slaves were, so to speak, capital expenditure which was needed to bring the islands into fruitful cultivation, and so the trouble of the British islands during these years was not so much a lack of labour as a lack of capital with which to purchase that peculiar kind of labour, of which one of the most important features, especially in the field of colonial development, is that it requires a heavy initial outlay of capital whereas more normal labour demands very little initial outlay but considerable running costs. Jamaica, a late acquisition, suffered heavily from this, and many were the petitions that the company should be forced to supply slaves on credit. Nevertheless it is evident that Jamaica suffered from the preferential treatment which the company accorded to Barbados, and that lack of slaves held back the development of the island. Nevis, in broad terms, reflected the position of Barbados, while the other islands were in the same situation as Jamaica.

The British Parliament was therefore bombarded with petitions against the Royal African Company—for even Barbados and Nevis were far from satisfied—and the company itself was in too precarious a position to organize an effective defence of its privileges. Yet some controlling organization, and some form of protection on the African coast, was essential if the trade was to continue, or if the British colonies were not to fall into dependence on aliens for this vital trade. So when in 1698 Parliament at last took the company in hand, the basis from which the Act started was that the forts and castles in Africa were necessary and that all who shared in the trade must contribute to their maintenance.

This was to be achieved by the company levying a duty of 10 per cent on all exports to Africa and on all exports from the northern parts of West Africa. Apart from this, the trade to Africa was free and was open to all subjects of the Crown. The Act left the company open to competition from private traders who had previously maintained their trade despite the company's charter, and this called for more determined trade methods, with the result that the colonies were vastly better supplied with labour during the years following the Act than they had previously been. Within a few years its efforts had exhausted the company, while the private traders prospered and even shipped out to Africa the goods with which the company's factors bought their slaves there. By 1705 the company was taking its case to Parliament and was seeking modification of the 1698 Act, for the independent traders were carrying the greater proportion of the trade; they delivered about five times as many slaves as the company to Jamaica during the years 1698 to 1708, and far outpaced the company.

Much as they had harmed the monopolistic company, the private traders had left much to be desired in the colonies. Slaves were still inadequate in numbers during the period of private trade, and prices were higher since slaves were dearer to buy, in competitive conditions, in Africa. Yet for the planters the independent traders at least brought slaves in greater numbers, and the increase in cost was a less serious defect than had been the inadequate supplies which the monopolist régime had entailed. The company had played its part in the transformation of the economies of the islands; but the particular manner in which it had played that part had made a slave-owning, sugar-growing, economy less profitable and stable than it otherwise might have been. Wars, conditions in the native states of West Africa, and the chances of English political life, all played some part in producing these results. The company alone was not responsible. But the undoubted difficulties in which the company worked would have had less effect in the British West Indies if the company had devoted all its efforts to those islands. This it did not do—in part because there seemed good chances of profitable trade elsewhere; in part because it was a genuinely national policy to usurp the Dutch and Portuguese business of supplying slave-labour to the Spanish colonies.

After the successful revolt of Portugal the lack of direct access to West Africa revealed once more the basic weakness of the Spanish imperial system. In the absence of Spanish supplies, the government made no formal arrangement for slave-trading to its settlements until 1662. The intervening years were a period in which the Spanish settlers freely traded with Dutch smugglers, for since the trade went to the most efficient merchants and this was the period of undoubted Dutch primacy

there could be but one result. The first consequence of the veto on
Portuguese shipments was a lack of labour so noticeable that mines and
farms alike went out of production. Dutch manoeuvres to gain the
*asiento* were turned down, even when masquerading under Italian
colours, and so were the offers of English merchants and even of the
English ambassador at Madrid who, seizing the opportunity of the
restoration of Charles II to the throne, sought to get the contract for two
ships a year for an English company. So strong was the exclusivist element in Spanish policy that *all* offers to supply slaves were declined.
Failing a Spanish source of supply, the colonists would have to go without. But after their first outburst the Spanish colonists were singularly
complaisant; for once the impossibility of negotiating an open trade had
been accepted, the smuggled trade soon supplied all their needs—so
much so that it has been reckoned that they were able to buy more
negroes, at lower prices, than at any time hitherto. The urgent needs of
the colonists were satisfied; but not in such a way as to implement the
doctrines of empire, for neither revenue nor shipping power, nor a
self-controlled source of labour, was produced.

It was the prospect of getting shipping for the Atlantic, rather than the
need to supply labour, which led to the revival of the *asiento* system in
1662, with the Genoese merchants Grillo and Lomelin as the *asientists*.
Both the Dutch West India Company and the English Company of
Royal Adventurers set out to secure a sub-contract from the *asientists*
(who had full permission to act in this way), and the English company
undertook a contract to supply 3,500 slaves a year. This was more than
they could fulfil, and their failure merely underlined Dutch supremacy
in the trade. The supply of slaves to the Spaniards, both during the lifetime of the Grillo and Lomelin *asiento* (to 1671) and later, was utterly
dependent on Dutch merchants. But the English Royal African Company, from 1672 onwards, had inherited ambitions to share in the
Spanish trade, and negotiations were constantly in hand for this purpose
although the company would not commit itself to supplying any substantial number of slaves regularly to the Spaniards. Yet the Spaniards
seem to have traded for slaves, first at Barbados and then at Jamaica, in
considerable numbers. The Spaniards, or their agents, were ready to pay
higher prices than the English planters; and, although the Spanish trade
was sporadic and fell off after 1685–6, it gave fair profits to the company
and it roused criticism since it was alleged that the company starved the
English colonists in order to make profits out of the Spaniards, who were
even favoured to some extent by the British government since their
trade was on a cash basis and brought much-sought bullion to the
English balance.

English and Spanish governments alike were, therefore, willing to twist the essential supply of labour so as to conform to their trade theories; and behind the backs of both governments the needs of the planters, their ability to pay in cash or in kind, and the merchants' ability to provide ships and to supply cargo, really set the pattern of the trade. The pattern was such that the English company felt constant temptation to make an arrangement which would give it an edge over the independent traders, and at last in 1689 it reached an agreement to supply 2,000 negroes to Spanish agents in Jamaica. This would have been in contravention of the Navigation Acts, but the British government overlooked that. No government help, however, could make it possible for the company to fulfil the contract in times of war, and the company did not, in fact, play any important part under this arrangement in the supply of slaves to the Spanish settlers, although there is no doubt that individual English merchants played their part in that trade.

The English company nevertheless nurtured and perpetuated ambitions to share in the Spanish trade, and when the chances of the Spanish Succession placed the *asiento* in French hands the ambitions of the company became a matter of national rivalry. For France had stepped into this trade after much the same sort of apprenticeship as the English had served, with early semi-piratical voyages followed by settlement in the West Indies, and with the culture of sugar largely undertaken under Dutch auspices. The profits of the trade, and the need to integrate it into something of a national and imperial economic policy, ensured that the highly individualistic voyages of the 'armateurs' of the Atlantic seaboard were followed by organization of the trade into companies, and the French slave trade was allotted out in succession to the Senegal Company in 1673, the Guinea Company in 1685, and the Asiento Company in 1703. The same sort of complaints were constantly uttered against the French companies as the English companies had evoked—high prices, lack of slaves, and lack of dividends; complaints from planters, from private traders, and from share-owners. The companies, although they dominated the scene in succession, were in reality continuations and expansions one of the other, and it was the Guinea Company which secured the grant of the *asiento* from the Spanish government in 1702, an *asiento* which was to last for ten or twelve years and which tied the Asiento Company (as successor to the Guinea Company) to ship out 38,000 slaves during that time if the War of the Spanish Succession persisted, or 48,000 if peace should be achieved.

But peace brought the end of the Asiento Company's monopoly, for the negotiators at Utrecht took the *asiento* from it and handed to the British (and so to the South Sea Company) the right to supply the Spaniards. This was matter of high diplomacy rather than of practical merchandising, for the Asiento Company had devolved its rights upon individual French merchants (largely from the port of Nantes), and there was little change in the actual trade when the privileges of the Guinea Company were withdrawn in 1716. The trade to French possessions continued, tied to the ports of la Rochelle, Bordeaux, Nantes and St Malo, and though the monopoly was again granted to the Compagnie des Indes in 1721 that company used its position only as a means of securing revenue from the merchants who conducted the trade. So through the eighteenth century a flourishing French slave trade, based upon Nantes and upon the French possessions on the Guinea coast, supplied the French colonies with the labour which they required and played its part in bringing the French West India islands to the peak of prosperity which they enjoyed at the outbreak of the revolutionary wars—a peak at which Guadeloupe was reckoned as equal to Canada in importance and St Domingue was recognized as 'the pearl of the Antilles'.

But though the achievement was striking and attractive, there were many unsatisfactory elements in the situation. The trade was based on no common feeling between the participants. For the merchants payment in cash rather than in kind, controlled supplies, and the exclusion of alien competitors, were the essential features; and they were always ready to challenge for a position in the *asiento* trade to the Spanish colonies, if necessary at the cost of proper supplies for the French planters. For the planters a regular and generous supply of slaves at cheap rates, payable either in produce or at long terms, was a necessary feature of their agricultural economy; and if they could get better terms or better slaves from interloping aliens they were always eager to do so. The eighteenth century moreover was a period of endemic colonial warfare, and both the slave trade as an ocean-borne commerce, and the West Indian islands as prosperous outposts, were constantly vulnerable, and constantly raided.

Within the French islands, as within the British, the state of development regulated the demand for slaves. By the end of the War of the Spanish Succession and the beginnings of the organization of the French slave trade under the banner of the Compagnie des Indes, Guadeloupe had already almost reached saturation point whereas St Domingue was as yet hardly in production and was constantly bringing fresh land under cultivation. The principal markets for the French merchants' slaves were therefore St Domingue and Martinique, with the latter steadily absorbing the greater numbers. In metropolitan France the bulk of the trade fell to the merchants of Nantes, and was subject to endless minor fluctuations due to personal or shipping conditions. Yet through the eighteenth century there appear to have been three major recessions in the French trade, overriding the minor year-to-year fluctuations—the period from 1725 to 1726 during which direct exploitation of its privileges by the

Compagnie des Indes and its subsidiaries reached its lowest level; the period from 1747 to 1748 during which the War of the Austrian Succession completely upset the trade; and the period from 1758 to 1763 when the colonial war with England was drawing to its climax in the Treaty of Paris. The peak period lay between the years 1750 and 1755, when the yearly average from Nantes was something over 9,000 slaves a year bought in Africa.

Within the general picture the variations are of considerable interest. From 1715 to 1728 the Nantes merchants averaged only about 2,570 slaves a year (35,968 slaves bought, 6,497 casualties on the voyage, 633 stolen and 28,856 sold in the islands over the period); but these figures are from the official returns of the ships' captains and are of no absolute validity. The trade was an expanding one during this period, the individual shippers were challenging the monopoly of the Compagnie des Indes and expanding into fresh territories, and the profits to be got drew ever more and more shippers into the trade. When the Congress of Soissons and the Treaty of Seville gave French merchants freer access to Spanish markets (always reserving the *asiento* itself to the English) their trade-figures rose but slowly, and it was not until about 1733 that expansion began; indeed the years from 1729 saw a decline. Expansion levelled off during the years 1734–7, but the period from 1738 to 1745 was one of great growth, the yearly average shipment rising to about 7,000 and the high figure of over 9,000 being reached in 1743. This was a period in which the trade to St Domingue quite outpaced that to the other French islands; the luck of immunity from the hurricanes which devastated the other islands was part of the cause, but continuous prosperity and the possibility of opening up new estates, if only labour were available, were the more weighty explanations.

So flourishing a trade could not escape from the conflict between France and England; it was a temptation to privateers, was urged in both countries by powerful interests, and was in both countries rightly regarded as the very basis of the colonial system which they practised. From 1737 onwards the French ships found themselves opposed and interrupted on the African coast. The formal hostility of the War of the Austrian Succession was but the open continuation of a hostility which had long been manifest; but open war allowed the full naval power of Britain to be deployed against the vulnerable and vital French trade, and privateers and commerce-raiders blockaded French ports, lay off the African posts, and cruised at will in the Caribbean with Jamaica as their base and with the blockade of St Domingue as their object. Strategically the French trade, with its three focal points, was easy to molest, and by 1748 it was at a complete standstill. This was due to British naval superiority only, for the economic situation remained unchanged, the

French merchants well knew the profits to be got, and the colonists offered an eager and constant market. Petitions for the re-establishment of the trade were already being organized as the delegates met for the Peace of Aix-la-Chapelle, and as soon as peace was secured French ships swarmed into the trade once more, to bring it to its highest peak in the years between 1749 and 1756, when trade ran at an annual average from Nantes of over 8,000 slaves bought on the coast, and almost 7,000 sold in the islands, for the six years from 1749 to 1755.

The stringencies of the war years, and the almost inevitable trends of a flourishing commerce, led during this period to a drop in the number of merchant houses engaged in it and to amalgamations between them, to the use of a smaller number of larger ships, to exclusive concentration on the two great markets of Martinique and St Domingue, and to the spread of the trade from the Gold Coast to the kingdom of Angola. Here the formation of the French Company of Angola marked both the trends of the trade as it revived from the war years and a new attempt at capital organization to deal with the trade. The Company of Angola was a well-supported joint-stock venture, projected by experienced merchants; but the quality of the negroes from Angola was poor and the machinations of the leading traders cast suspicion on the stability of the company, so that it made only one successful voyage. The distinguishing feature of the French trade remained the individual 'armateur' rather than a joint-stock company although the Compagnie des Indes kept its privileged position, from which it derived the right to issue licences to the shippers.

Though the Company of Angola failed, the French trade as a whole prospered, and it was an essential part of the well-being of the whole French empire. It was as much involved as India or Canada, or the West Indies themselves, in the warfare for imperial predominance waged between France and England, and it was as much affected as those areas in the struggle for position which the inter-war years witnessed. Parallel with the building of forts on the Canadian-American border and with the struggle of Dupleix and Clive in India, the slave-traders had to run the gauntlet; but the trade prospered, and so did the French islands, whose sugar returns rose steadily until the Seven Years War broke out, and which reached a peak of prosperity that the British islands could not emulate. This was, however, a prosperity which depended on a slave-trade which needed either peace or sea-power, and when the uneasy peace gave way to open war the French trade ceased almost overnight. The Seven Years War witnessed a seven years' interruption of commercial intercourse between metropolitan France and her West Indian possessions. But the inter-relation of the slave-trade with the wealth to be derived from the colonies may be judged from the fact that, with all her command of the seas, and with all her victories in the Caribbean (at the capture of Guadeloupe in 1759 and of Martinique, Granada, St Lucia and St Vincent in 1762) England never tried to capture St Domingue, which was unquestionably the wealthiest of the French islands. The first task of the British forces in the West Indies was not the capture of French territory but the interruption of French trade and the protection of British trade; and it was because it released so much French power from the Mediterranean to prey on trade in the Caribbean that the loss of Minorca was regarded (probably with justice) as such a disaster. Yet by the end of the war, especially after the declaration of war with Spain, the British triumph in the Caribbean was complete.

Nevertheless, when terms of peace came to be discussed, not only was Guadeloupe returned to France (and Canada retained by Britain), but the argument brought out some home truths about the sugar-and-slave economy of the islands. The dependence of the islands, and of the southern plantation colonies of the mainland, on slave labour and on constant reinforcement of the slave bands by importation, had left the planters dependent on capitalists and ship-owners in Europe, and had left this vital supply under the control of the metropolitan government. The slave-owning economy was in the fullest sense a dependent economy, and the way in which the islands were held in high esteem was but a sign that such a dependence could be mutual. The slave trade nevertheless left the planters economically dependent on the merchants in a way which was quite apart from political and military dependence on their mother country; for the merchants who brought slaves also took away, often in payment at fixed rates, the sugars, cottons, coffees and dyewoods which the system produced. If a dependent empire was what statesmen had in mind, then the sugar islands, with their constant demands for slaves, filled the role to perfection. But, in the debate as to whether Guadeloupe should be returned to France or not, Shelburne (from whom Pitt claimed that he had learned much) voiced the opinion that although the sugar islands weakened and depopulated the mother country yet 'wherever sugar grows population decreases'. There developed a strong argument, with a rising humanitarian and anti-slavery accompaniment, that the dependent sugar-islands were a constant responsibility, for they never would maintain a white population adequate for their defence and administration. The benefits of empire without the cares of government could best be got from the sort of settler-colony, based on individual subsistence-farming, which had arisen to the north. That the whole argument of empire was not dictated simply by the type of labour on which the colonies were based may, however, be judged from the fact that it was the southern, slave-owning, colonies of the mainland who were most eager in their search for new lands and who led the drive by the Mississippi valley to the new lands of the west, and that they did so in evasion of British laws, and in due course took an active and formative part in phrasing and in leading the opposition to British rule.

The defects of the British traders had played a full part in creating the antipathy from which the sugar islands suffered as the imperial systems of the world came to their hour of trial in the last quarter of the eighteenth century. Having won the privilege of the *asiento* from Spain at the Treaty of Utrecht, together with the right to send one ship a year to the Spanish colonies, the British government granted away both privileges to the South Sea Company. The annual ship was guaranteed to be the only exception which the Spanish government would make to its rule excluding all aliens from trade with its possessions, and the perpetuation of this exclusiveness was insisted on in the Treaty—as a discrimination against France. There was no period set to this British invasion of Spanish imperial trade, but the *asiento* was to run for thirty years.

The *asiento* in English hands marked a clash of interests between planters and merchants, and something of that subordination of the economic interests of the colonies to those of British merchants which led to the Old Colonial System being decried as Mercantilism. The supply of slaves to the Spanish possessions could indeed be defended as a means of bringing Spanish bullion into the English Balance of Trade; but the slave trade to the Spaniards, and still more that to captured French islands, could only bring profits to the merchants at the cost of competition to English planters—competition both for shipments of slaves and for sales of sugars and colonial wares. So to Malachi Postlethwayte, and to many more, the *asiento* clauses of the Treaty of Utrecht were iniquitous; 'a treaty could scarce have been contrived of so little benefit to the nation'. While the South Sea Company so exploited its right to send the annual ship to the Spanish possessions as to provoke endless complaints, and ultimately to lead to the War of Jenkins' Ear, British planters complained that it merely raised the price of slaves sold in the islands, and illicit traders both complained of the monopoly and defied it to an extent which evoked strong national opposition. The South Sea Company was a creation of the moment, the epitome of England's desire for an ordered imperial trade, conducted within the framework of a chartered and exclusive corporation. In itself it had no experience of the slave trade and, with the Royal African Company still in existence, the South Sea Company contracted with the Royal African Company to supply slaves, deliverable when and where the *asientists* should direct.

The Royal African Company, however, had but barely survived. The Ten Per Cent rule of 1698, which provided that individual traders must pay dues to the company as their contribution to the cost of maintaining the forts on which all depended, expired in 1712. It had led to a flourishing trade in private hands, and when it ceased it left the company to carry the cost of the forts as an overhead charge which did not fall on the private traders. On this basis the Royal African Company could not compete, and although a government subsidy for the forts was voted in 1730, even that help did not enable the company to run a profitable trade. The private traders had too much start, and by 1730 were too numerous and well-established, for the company to have any prospect of winning from them the bulk of the trade. In fact, the South Sea Company itself had taken to contracting out its *asiento* to the private traders, and almost from the start of that company's enjoyment of its privileges a new régime had started in the trade, a régime in which the great slave-trade ports of Bristol and Liverpool (with Lancaster also doing a flourishing, if unexpected, volume of trade) predominated.

As the outports, and the independent traders, rose to dominance in the trade, regulations and the preservation of alleged national interests (other than the Balance of Trade) fell into the background and the conflict of interests between trader and planter became more undisguised. This should not be taken as any indication that the planter had right on his side; but he was without doubt in a vulnerable position, liable to exploitation at both ends of the trade—and while the traders on the whole made fortunes and died prosperous, the planters spent what they got and died either in debt or in an ostentatious affluence which was but one step removed from ruin. The planter, moreover, could on occasions indulge ordinary human feelings towards his slaves whereas to the trader they could be nothing but 'pieces' of merchandise. The planter is, on the whole, the less unattractive figure; the trader was responsible for the horrors of the 'Middle Passage', which were the commonplace of the anti-slavery orators (who did not lack for eloquence) at the end of the eighteenth and the first part of nineteenth century. But the planter himself was wide open to criticism both for his normal way of life, for his neglect of opportunity and maintenance of privilege, and for his treatment of the slaves upon whom he depended for the unenterprising agriculture which he practised. Yet if a national economy had any meaning (and without it there was no logical defence of the sugar colonies or of the slave trade) the planters had a legitimate complaint against the way in which the traders supplied alien and rival planters with the slaves whom they would eagerly have bought themselves.

The defect in the system from the British planters' point of view was perhaps excusable, but more common and more serious, when the chances of war placed rival territories under British control. Thus, during the Seven Years War we held Cuba for about nine months; during that brief period, it has been reckoned, over 10,000 slaves were shipped in, more than a sixth of the total for the previous 250 years, since Spanish settlement had begun. Similarly, in their three years' occupation of Guadeloupe the British shipped in 40,000 negroes. As the Old Colonial System came to its climacteric in the last quarter of the century, two-thirds of the slaves carried by British merchants were disposed of to foreigners, the merchants of Liverpool managed almost a half of the slave trade of all the European powers, and during the century British traders had provided the sugar planters of France and Spain with half a million negroes.

The climax of the system was essentially the product of individual enterprise, not of a regimented trade. In its way the 'Old Colonial System' had cast away its form as a necessary step towards achieving its object. The colonies were indeed dependent on Europe, utterly dependent for supplies of slaves who were essential to their way of life. But it was English and French merchants who supplied the New World, regardless of nationality; and within the national frameworks of those two countries it was the individual merchants who carried on the trade, not the great chartered companies erected to maintain national objectives. Yet national regulations were not altogether valueless. When, for example, the *asiento* was surrendered back to Spain in 1750, the Spanish government agreed to pay the considerable sum of £100,000 sterling in compensation to the company; and the sugar islands and the southern colony of Florida were essential parts of the national rivalry which came to its head in the Seven Years War.

# VII. *The North American Colonies*

In the meantime, while the slave trade had been knit into the southern colonial economies, with all its consequences in monoculture and in dependence, and in the inter-relation of European trade to Africa with expansion in the west, two other major areas of overseas trade and settlement demanded attention. To the north, Canada was still, in effect, confined to the mouth of the St Lawrence. Explorers, fur-traders and missionaries, had indeed penetrated to the foot of the Rockies before the French régime ended, and so had Englishmen starting from Hudson's Bay. But apart from the French settlements on the lower river there was no industry, no agriculture, and no problem of labour. The fur trade, in French or English hands, dominated the vast expanse of the Northwest, and in the fur trade the Indian played his part but could not in any sense be called the worker for the white man. Behind the shipments of furs to Europe lay a whole series of trading contacts, and the Europeans slowly realized that the furs were brought in to trade, not by the actual hunters who had made the catch, but by intervening tribes of traders, who might contribute something of their own to the returns but whose main function (of which they were increasingly jealous) was to take European goods inland and to bring furs down to the trade-posts, whether those posts were within reach of the sea or whether they were sited inland, up the rivers and even (by the end of the period) on the prairies. The Indian, however, increasingly dependent though he undoubtedly was on constant importations from Europe, only allowed this dependence to affect his way of life in its non-essentials. He remained a wanderer, a hunter, and—at the cost of great precariousness—independent. Essential though he was to the fur traders, he was not at their disposal, and even the individuals who took paid employment with traders did so only for short periods and in such form as left them independent. For the fur trade there was no *maine d'oeuvre* in the ordinary sense of the word.

Nor did the settled parts of Canada boast of any recognizable labour-force. In its early days French settlement on the lower St Lawrence had been predominantly masculine and military, these being the inevitable results of attempts to implement a system of indentured settlement in return for the grants of land and of privileges with which the various Companies of Canada were endowed. Shipments of orphans and of 'honest girls', often under the tutelage of religious orders, balanced and stabilized society. But there was in the French theory something of the idea of forming a mixed society with native blood in it, and of creating vast numbers of new subjects of France by inter-marriage; and the French approach was such that constant social and economic contact with Indians, whether by trade, by missionary endeavour, or by exploring achievement, was a normal feature of life in Canada. So mixed marriages and a recognizable half-breed element (the *métis canadien*) became a factor in Canadian society and in the French-Canadian economy. With fishing, and with voyages into the forests in pursuit of Indians with furs (not often in order to trap furs themselves) as constant and attractive adjuncts to the heavy work of agriculture, and with agricultural work almost impossible for long periods of the year, the French-Canadian economy was in constant danger of over-extension. While industry remained small and local, designed merely to satisfy the minimum demands of the agricultural and fur-trading population, the farms which were set out along the river-front were in constant danger of neglect as the men went off to sea or to the woods. But the balance was not rectified by drafting into Canada such numbers of subservient labourers as would enable the owners of the land to develop agriculture on some other basis than their own care and labour. Seigneuries and estates were created, laws were passed against trading in the woods, or even against long absences; but the picture remained one in which the land-owner could at best produce the basic necessities for subsistence—perhaps for some sales, from time to time, on the local market—and in which the labour of himself and of his family and of the comparatively few household servants of European extraction was the mainstay of exiguous agricultural development.

Between the semi-arctic conditions of Canada and the sub-tropical development of the southern colonies and the Caribbean lay those areas which had most appealed to the theorists of colonization in the sixteenth century, the temperate parts of North America from which the statesmen hoped to produce all the commodities which a European economy could require to supplement its own resources. Equally attractive to the free settler as to the statesman, the English and Dutch colonies of North America alike provided early evidence that when a colony is able to stand on its own feet economically (especially in the vital matter of labour) it is necessary to give it the most courteous political attention.

The Dutch West India Company had taken out its first ship-load of settlers to Manhattan in 1623. The West India Company had taken over from the New Netherland Company its meagre fortifications at Nassau and its treaty with the Five Nations of the Iroquois confederacy (by which the Dutch agreed to supply fire-arms in return for furs) and the Dutch maintained a small garrison on Manhattan Island despite the protests of their neighbours from the English colony in Virginia. Dutch settlers took possession of Long Island, of the site of the modern city of Hartford on Connecticut River, and of the site of modern Philadelphia—in effect they founded the extensive colony of New Netherland—and cattle and sheep followed in the next year. But although the Indians of Manhattan Island sold their land to the Dutch, neither they nor any of the neighbouring tribes succumbed to the lure of settled employment and became labourers on the farms or *bouweries* which sprang up on the island and on the mainland. Considered merely as an alternative agricultural country, New Netherland had few advantages over the Netherlands if the farmer had to do the heavy work himself, and settlement was correspondingly slow.

Remedy by granting the title of *patroon*, with a suitable landed estate, to any who brought out fifty emigrants, promised to bring forth something between the Portuguese *Donatarios* system, the Spanish *encomienda*, and the English and French indentured labourer. But even the charter of 'Privileges and Exemptions' which made these offers to would-be *patroons* in 1629 envisaged a period in which the Dutch colony would only be able to survive if, at any rate for an interim period, the settlers were liberally supplied with slave labour; and the prospect of becoming tenant to a *patroon* in fact offered little inducement to Dutch agriculturists to emigrate. So although a few flourishing estates were founded under the charter, many of the *patroons* who came out soon turned to the fur trade rather than to agriculture. Yet a few flourishing estates were established, and in particular the cultivation of tobacco (a crop with slight demands for regular labour) took a hold at Manhattan. A colony in the full sense of the word was not, however, grafted on to the traders and shippers who lived in New Amsterdam and the surrounding district, and the *patroons* were refused their request that convicts and paupers should be shipped out on an indentured system. Instead, in 1638, the West India Company ordained that the fur trade and the right to hold land should be thrown open to all settlers, inducements in grants of land and provision of stock were promised to immigrants, and the colony took a great stride forward. Englishmen from England, and some also from the English colonies, came in alongside Germans and Huguenots, Piedmontese, Waldensians, Scots, Anabaptists and Jews. The experiment was marred by a disastrous Indian war, but by 1653 New Netherland had a polyglot population of about 2,000 souls, and by 1664 the total was up to almost 10,000, of whom the great majority were farmers who had gone to settle on the land.

Neither the religious toleration nor the rising demands for municipal self-government which went with this policy were easily acceptable to the Dutch West India Company or to the Estates General. But New Netherland was sufficiently Dutch-nationalist to suppress the rival Swedish colony in Delaware River and to get involved in the wars between England and Holland which marked the Commonwealth and Restoration period. The outcome was the capture of the Dutch settlements and their absorption by their English neighbours, the actual title to the land being granted to James, duke of York. But although there was sufficient affinity for the colony to be involved in the disputes of the mother-country, and Governor de Stuyvesant would have resisted if he could, New Netherland had but 10,000 population and the burghers were not sufficiently Dutch in feeling to hold out against the numbers which were brought against them, and against the feeling that they were neglected by the West India Company and the Estates General.

The rule of Holland in America came to an end with the inhabitants ranged against the governor and insisting on surrender. This in itself was perhaps not surprising, for resistance would have been foredoomed to failure. But the attitude which led to this lack of action deserves comment. New Netherland was in any case a polyglot community as a result of the policy of toleration. For the same reason its local nationalism was stronger than its European loyalties; and since the policy of recruitment which had dictated this complexion had been adopted in order to induce a population of working agriculturists, it was this basic economic approach which dictated the pattern of settlement, and the political indifference of the colony.

The English, on their approach to New Amsterdam, had made an offer that the colony should be open to future settlers from the Netherlands, that present settlers might freely depart, and that Dutch ships should have free access to the colony. Such an offer of trade-freedom went far to reconcile the settlers to surrender, and when the surrender had been completed the Dutch were even allowed to infringe the Navigation Acts in order to carry their trade (especially goods designed for the fur trade) to the colony. They were, in fact, an economic entity, self-supporting except for the European goods which they needed for the fur trade. To them the Netherlands was not essential either as a purveyor of slave labour or as a market for export staples which plantation agriculture might produce—and as for the fur trade, that could proceed just as easily under English rule. So New Amsterdam became New York with no great difficulty.

The English expedition to capture the Dutch colony had to some extent concealed its objective since it was also designed to reduce to order the New England colonies. Boston was the ostensible destination of the little fleet of four ships which left England in 1664, and part of the purpose of the expedition and of the four commissioners who sailed with it was to impose royal authority and Anglican episcopacy upon Massachusetts and the confederate states. There also the economic background had been such as to make mixed subsistence farming, and the local manufacture of domestic necessities, both possible and desirable. The economic autonomy of the New England colonies was, of course, powerfully fomented by the social and religious independence of the English colonists. At this stage it would be impossible to unravel the contributions of the economic and the religious elements in creating the independent spirit of the New England settlers. To seventeenth-century minds it was not an entirely attractive independence, for it was both obtuse and intolerant; but it was deeply interwoven in the pattern of colonial life, and one of its strongest threads was the fact that European labourers were the basis of society and of the exploitation of the lands which were being brought into use. Here was no dependence upon imported slave labour, nor upon an indigenous labour force; climate, soil, and social pattern alike fostered mixed subsistence farming, and although tobacco diversified the economy, and large and wealthy estates were not unusual, with some dependence upon indentured labour, the social pattern was dictated by the economic foundations of New England society; and, as with the Dutch, these foundations were those of a

European community dependent on white family—or hired—labour to develop wheat and cattle lands in a temperate northern climate. This, as much as the pressure of religious opinion, explains why the whole history of the New England colonies is a history of rebellion or near-rebellion against the economic and constitutional tutelage of the mother-country. Massachusetts sustained a bitter quarrel with Charles II throughout the whole of his reign, and he ended by confiscating the charter of that colony.

In the meantime, while the New England colonies were strongly marked by dependence on their own servants and by independence in outlook, the colonies which developed to the south showed clearly different characteristics. The 'trade' in indentured servants continued and developed through the seventeenth century. 'The Puritan communities, scanty in their agriculture, chary of favors, hostile to new-comers as they were, received few. Farther south, on the contrary, they were hailed with delight by planters and farmers who wanted cheap labor, by speculators who needed more settlers to validate their grants of land, by colonial proprietors who wished to build up the population'.[1] More than half of all those who came to the southern colonies at this time were servants; the State Papers of the period are full of the theme that labour is the prime necessity to bring the colonies into the imperial economy as productive areas, and not until the eighteenth century was white indentured labour superseded by negro slaves in the southern mainland colonies. As late as 1755 the Governor of Maryland could write that 'The Planters Fortunes here consist in the number of their Servants (who are purchased at high Rates) much as the Estates of an English Farmer do in the Multitude of Cattle'; and this was but the reiteration of the Virginia dictum of a century and a half previously, that 'our principal wealth consisteth in servants'.

By 1755 only in South Carolina did the number of negro slaves exceed the number of whites. In Maryland there were at that time 107,000 whites as against 42,000 blacks; in Virginia 173,000 whites as against 120,000 blacks, and in North Carolina 50,000 whites as against 30,000 blacks. In South Carolina some 50,000 negroes preponderated over 25,000 whites, and in Georgia also the white servant was of far less importance than the slave.

Tobacco as a crop, military defence as a pre-occupation, and the social disturbances and economic dislocation of eighteenth-century England, go far to explain the importance of the white indentured labourer. But the southern colonies were above all plantation colonies, producing tropical or sub-tropical staples for export on a system in which the large estate (often the plantation) was the norm. Servile or semi-servile labour

[1] A. E. Smith, *op. cit.*, p. 4; cf. also pp. 27, 332.

was a necessity; the slave-trade became all important when the South Sea and Royal African Companies, and the merchants of Liverpool, London, Bristol and Lancaster, made that trade more easy and practicable for English planters as the eighteenth century wore on. But these developments did not vitally affect the nature of the southern economy or its close dependence on the metropolis. Although before the eighteenth century had run its course it was the expansive and improvident agriculture of the southern colonies which began to drive the American frontier of settlement up the Mississippi and the Ohio, inland from the seaboard, yet the southern economy was tied to the metropolis both in its need for a market outlet and in its need for shipping and supplies, especially in its need for supplies of labour, whether that labour was black or white.

# VIII. *Labour and Rule in the Spice Islands*

Across the Atlantic the European settlers had, in their different ways, firmly and forcefully developed a social and economic structure in which they undertook the organization of production. Their efforts were variegated according as they tried to organize the indigenous peoples, their own household servants and families, indentured white servants or negro slaves, as the basic labour for primary production, whether from the mines or from the fields. In the East the situation had from the start been radically different, for in the East the Europeans had always met with economic and social systems which were sufficiently advanced and integrated to organize for themselves the production and the marketing of the goods which the Europeans sought. Portuguese, Spanish, English, French and Dutch, therefore came as merchants, not as primary producers reduced, in the end, to supply their own labour force. There were, of course, many local exceptions to this general contrast between East and West; and there was one major example in which European influence penetrated backwards from the traffic in surplus products of a native economy into the organization of labour to supply those products.

The Dutch brought to their East India trade the knowledge and the realism which had already made them masters of the distribution of East India products in Europe. They brought, too, a knowledge of the profits which could be got from efficient operation of the shipping routes and of the trade-contacts in the East, for between 1595 and 1601 some fifteen Dutch expeditions had defied the Portuguese ban and had traded direct with the East, and there were four Dutch companies in existence for that trade. The organization of the composite Dutch East

India Company in 1602 gave extra financial stability, firmer direction, and monopoly control. It gave, too, ability to make peace or war, to acquire lands and build fortifications, and a markedly national approach.

At the heart of the matter lay the necessity to defend the Dutch trade and possessions against the Portuguese; and the Dutch proved far more valiant in action, and far more shrewd in their naval strategy, than their rivals. The Portuguese were driven from Johore and Amboyna in 1605, and the Portuguese position was completely undermined except at the port of Macao, the one place through which Europeans were allowed to have access to China. There the Portuguese were secure in the friendship of the Chinese authorities, and a Dutch attack in 1623 was beaten off.

Already, before the advent of the Dutch in strength, the Portuguese were in grave difficulty. They had found that the great entrepôt for the spice trade was at Malacca, and that behind Malacca lay a network of merchants and traders who enhanced the prices at each stage as they brought the spices to Malacca. In 1511 the Portuguese took possession of Malacca and set up their form of plural government there, with separate administrations for Hindus, Moors and Javanese; but they also resolved to go behind the market at Malacca and to make direct contact with the spice-growing areas. So they moved out from Malacca to the Moluccas (or Spice Islands) and in 1522 built a fort at Ternate by alliance with the prince of that island, and thereby acquired the monopoly of the trade in cloves, which at that time grew only in Ternate, Tidore, Amboyna and a few small islands. The move, however, brought the Portuguese into conflict with Tidore, with the Javanese traders who had hitherto profited by taking the cloves to Malacca, and with the neighbouring islands to which the cult of the clove spread as the possibilities of the European market began to be appreciated. Moreover, the Portuguese never managed to achieve predominance in the democratic Banda islands, where the trade in nutmeg was concentrated. For nutmeg they had to depend on the Javanese traders who brought the spice to market, and upon their position in Amboyna, where they had been established since 1511. That island had the great advantage that it grew both cloves and nutmeg, and that its rulers did not resent the missionary efforts with which the Portuguese constantly complicated their relations with the native peoples.

The complication of religion was more important when, as so often happened, earlier Buddhist and Brahminist beliefs had been replaced by Islam. The earlier culture had been the result of commercial colonization by Hindus from India and had been challenged when, from the ninth century onwards, Muslim penetration brought eastern trade into the orbit of the great changes in world economy of which Muslim expansion was the most notable feature. The Muslims were established in North Sumatra by about 1250, and from there they extended southwards; they reached Ternate in 1440, and by 1450 they were masters of Malacca. In Java, however, the native Majapahit dynasty, basing its power on the social hierarchy of the Brahminist beliefs, was at this very time at the height of its powers, in control of the plains on the north coast of that island from which rice was got, and manipulating a widespread and complex system of trade in spices and minerals and manufactured goods to which islands as far apart as Timor and Palembang contributed their products.

The capture of Malacca by the Portuguese had therefore been a shrewd blow against Muslim influence. But at Ternate Muslim influence was dominant, and Portuguese efforts to establish in that island a base from which they could go behind the entrepôt at Malacca were constantly harried by religious, as well as personal, rivalries. Muslim hostility also closed to the Portuguese the pepper trade of Bantam and denied them access to the Shivaitic kings of the interior of Java. The Portuguese position was precarious at the end of the first quarter of the sixteenth century. Malacca, indeed, they held. But to the south the Sultan had set himself up in implacable hostility at Johore, on Sumatra the Muslim dynasty of Atjeh defied the Portuguese and denied the pepper trade to them, and the port of Brunei in Borneo was a flourishing Muslim rival to the trade of Malacca. Even at Ternate their position was undermined by the religious dispute, and hostility from the Javanese Muslims made passage of the Straits of Malacca dangerous. Little effort was, in any case, made to control or use strategic sea-routes, and when the Portuguese fort on Ternate at last fell in 1574, after a five-years' siege, no help had been sent in all that time from Malacca or from Goa.

Portuguese power and trade in the East Indies therefore seemed on the decline before any serious challenge came from Europe. Muslim rivalry at Johore, Brunei, Sumatra and Ternate, was made the more threatening when the inland states of Java also adopted Islamic beliefs and the powerful kingdom of Mataram, though split by constant dynastic wars, spread its authority over the east and centre of the island. The scene was ripe for European intervention, and there were feuds and rivalries enough to promise strong local support to any European challenger of the Portuguese position. Outstanding was the rivalry between the predominantly agricultural state of Mataram on Java and the commercial power of Sumatra. While its rich soil gave to Mataram the power to supply rice to the islands, it also looked north to Sunda Strait, dividing it from Sumatra and offering a route between east and west which was little inferior to the way by the Straits of Malacca—and Malacca was under Portuguese control. Sumatra, less wealthy in agriculture, had the great advantage that she controlled the Sunda Strait from her southern coast and the Strait of Malacca from her northern shore. So situated, she inevitably depended for her wealth and power on the commercial opportunities which her position gave her, and equally inevitably came into constant strife with Mataram as each state tried to control the Sunda Strait by occupying the opposite shore. But Mataram had not won control of the whole of Java. Many of the Hindus who had rejected Islam had migrated to the neighbouring island of Bali, but the virtual predominance of Islam did not bring unity to Java. The split ran along the lines of a division between commercial and agricultural interests, and while Mataram in the interior represented the agricultural predominance of the rice-growing areas, Bantam, on the Sunda Straits, represented and led the commercial interests.

It was this rivalry between the agricultural and the commercial elements of Java which gave to Dutch interlopers their chance to overthrow the Portuguese power and to take its place. From the first the Dutch profited from the warlike situation which they found, and from the attitudes of the native states; for whereas the ruler of Mataram welcomed them because he relied upon agriculture and had no fear for them as rivals in trade, the people of Bantam also were friendly, because they hoped to profit by their trade. On their first voyage to the East Indies, under Cornelis de Houtman in 1596, the Dutch made a treaty of alliance with the sultan of Bantam, and although their general behaviour was so overbearing that the Portuguese felt they need fear little from such rivals, they were bound to be involved in the hostilities between the Dutch and Spain, and they found it necessary to prepare not only for commercial rivalry but also for armed attacks on their posts. Yet Portuguese attempts to intimidate the sultan of Bantam into rejecting all similar European rivals were largely responsible, in their failure, for a marked decline in Portuguese dignity and stature. Triumphant over the Portuguese fleet, Bantam hoped that later Dutch voyagers would assist in the expulsion of the common enemy. But although Dutch enterprise and enthusiasm brought many ships to the islands during the years following de Houtman's voyage, their aims, at this period of individual enterprise, were predominantly commercial. So they set up trading posts at Ternate and on Amboyna, accepted the friendly trade of the islands, but declined to join the Indonesians in their struggles against the Portuguese.

Dutch supplies, Dutch shipping, and Dutch trading methods were so much in advance of anything the Portuguese could offer that they had a firm hold on the trade by the end of the sixteenth century. They made a formal treaty of alliance with Amboyna in 1600, and from that time onwards they inevitably found themselves involved in the native wars of the islands, and in the common hostility to the Portuguese. The new turn was decisively marked when a small Dutch fleet of only five vessels intervened and drove off a Portuguese fleet of twenty-eight which, in December 1601, came to assert Portuguese control over Bantam. The Dutch were indeed unable to prevent the Portuguese from conquering Amboyna, but the Portuguese failed in a similar attempt at Ternate and they were forestalled and driven off by the Dutch in an attempt at Johore.

The situation was therefore propitious as the separate Dutch interests were united into the single Dutch East India Company in March 1602. But trade was already inextricably bound up with warfare. Further, it had become clear that the spice trade was conditioned by the fact that the Spice Islands wanted very little of the produce of Europe save firearms. Rice was the chief need of the islanders, since the islands were heavily populated and for the most part grew only sago as a food-crop; and cloth from the Coromandel Coast could also find a market, but not cloth from Europe. Here the Dutch came up against the same problem as their fur-traders were to meet in North America. Once their immediate wants were satisfied, the islanders were indifferent to trade. Consequently, enhanced spice-prices cut down returns instead of increasing them, as would have happened in a European economy. Requiring only certain quantities of goods, the islanders lost their incentive when their limited demands had been met, and after a certain point there could be no certainty that trade would be forthcoming, whatever the terms offered. So although their own internal monopoly, coupled with their superiority over the Portuguese and their good relations with the Indonesians, enabled the Dutch to make great profits when their ships escaped wreck and piracy, and even to seize a virtual monopoly of the European pepper market in 1599, they were soon forced to acceptance of the thesis that in the East Indies 'You cannot have trade without war, or war without trade'. This was not only because they had got involved in the wars of the archipelago, and found that the supply of arms was the trade which came nearest to providing an open-ended market, but also because they were not alone in the field as challengers to the claims of Portugal, and of the Spanish monarchy which had successfully occupied the Portuguese throne since 1580. An English East India Company was also in the field from 1600 onwards, stirred in part by the tradition of Drake's passage through the islands and his call at Ternate, in part by the profits gained by Sir James Lancaster and other later adventurers, and in part by the spectacle of Dutch profits and of their pepper control. A French expedition had reached Bantam, too, in 1601, and a French East India Company had been formed in 1604.

But the Dutch Company easily predominated over its rivals, and it took a strong initiative against them. It was from the start 'a great instrument of war and conquest', and the mighty fleets which it sent out—thirty-eight ships in the first three years—were no longer destined primarily for commerce. They were to attack the Portuguese, and they easily drove them from Johore and then from Amboyna. Dutch success was naturally followed up by a treaty with Amboyna, in 1605; but the treaty not only gave a monopoly of trade to the Dutch, it also recognized the suzerainty of the Dutch over the island. A similar acknowledgement would have followed from Johore if the Dutch had managed to oust the Portuguese from their control of Malacca; but there they failed, and at Ternate their posts were overrun by a Spanish expedition from the Philippines. The sultan of Ternate in consequence drew even closer to the Dutch, took them into complete alliance, and promised that when they had together beaten the Spaniards he would recognize the Dutch company as his protector. But before this alliance could bear fruit, and confirm the Dutch position at Ternate as at Amboyna, the war had to be won.

Spanish and Portuguese hostility would clearly not be overcome without carefully-planned operations, and this would necessitate a stronghold from which Dutch control could emanate. So the Dutch company moved from desire for trade, and for locations in which trade could be conducted, to desire for military dominion; in 1609 Governor Pieter Both was ordered to seek out a place convenient for a fortress which could act as a rendezvous for the whole of the Dutch fleets in the Indies. The strategic and commercial importance of Bantam on the Sunda Strait made it an obvious choice; but English and French posts were also sited there, and rival Muslim rulers were trying to embroil one European nation against the others in their search for alliances. The Dutch turned to the adjacent city of Jacatra, but some years passed before they could secure satisfactory terms from the local ruler, and in the meantime the English followed them to Jacatra, as they generally followed the more enterprising Dutch round the islands. When the French also seemed likely to set up their establishment at Jacatra the forceful Dutch governor, Jan Pieterson Coen, began to build his fort despite the fact that he had not yet reached the end of negotiations with the local regent; and when the English also began to build he destroyed them and, although the two countries were at peace in Europe, followed this up by excluding them from Banda, Amboyna and the Moluccas. He beat off a serious English attack on Jacatra in 1618–19 and, since the regent of Java had favoured the English, he imposed Dutch rule throughout Java, with Jacatra as his fortress and the centre of dominion.

Diplomats in Europe agreed a peace between the two Protestant nations as Coen spread his authority and turned the city of Jacatra into the Dutch emporium of Batavia. There also the English joined the Dutch.

But they were unable to maintain force enough to run parallel with their rivals, unable either to prevent or to share in a punitive expedition to the islands of Banda, which Coen 'pacified' in 1621 by massacring all who had sided with the English; and unable to maintain anything of a hold in the islands after their expulsion from Amboyna in 1623. With the French offering little by way of serious competition, the Dutch were masters of the archipelago and in process of changing their mastery into dominion. The Spaniards, it is true, had not withdrawn from the Moluccas until 1663, Malacca was not taken by the Dutch until 1641; and the Dutch found the extension of their power a problem which involved them in constant and dangerous warfare. Piracy followed in the wake of prosperity and of the weakening of native authority which went therewith. But although the Dutch were forced to maintain forts at numerous strategic points, it was only on Java that they made any attempt to extend territorial control outside of their fort or, at most, the town and its immediate precincts. Even on Java they aimed first and foremost at trading privileges and reluctantly, for the purpose of controlling trade, undertook the rule of the ports, then of a narrow strip of coast, and then over the hinterland of the island; this not until the middle of the eighteenth century.

But the way in which they evaded the responsibilities of rule did not imply that the Dutch left the native states in sovereign control—merely that Dutch intervention stopped short at the point at which commercial interests ceased to be involved. For the most part land was left in native possession, but where it seemed opportune the same sort of concept of a 'Just War' and of forfeiture for rebellion came into play as in America. On Banda, for example, after the 'pacification' of 1621, the lands of those who had supported the English were parcelled out in 'parks' among servants of the Dutch Company on condition that they supplied to the company the spices produced. The same sort of arrangement was followed as the centre of Java was brought under authority, the nominees of the company being known as 'regents' and occupying much the position of feudal lords, with rights over people as well as over land. Most of the 'regents' were natives, vassals of the company as they had formerly been of their own princes, and their degree of political subordination ranged from virtual independence, limited by alliance with the company, to complete dominance by the company in the immediate vicinity of Batavia.

For the most part the 'regents' were left alone to rule and administer all save Europeans, with separate systems of law and of land tenure. They could count on the Dutch company to support their quasi-feudal authority, and they were left with very little interference until well into the eighteenth century—except in commercial matters. Here they were under strong control, bound to obey the orders of the representatives of the company, who came to be known as 'residents', and tied to deliveries of specified quantities of named products, including timber, cotton, indigo and coffee. It was a flexible system which evolved, and a strong factor was always the distance from central control at Batavia. In essence it meant that the Dutch company took up the position of overlord to the native princes, supported them in their rule, and controlled the produce of their lands by means of a 'resident', who also exercised authority over the company's servants and over any other Europeans.

As the system had its origin in the need to control production and to monopolize trade, it was natural that the border-line between governmental and trade controls should be fluid, and constantly moving towards further interference in the interests of trade. This indeed happened, although it did not remove from the Dutch régime that dual character which on the one hand left the Indonesian under laws and governors which seemed appropriate to him, and on the other hand gave to the European something of a privileged position in that separate laws, separate law-courts, and ultimately separate educational and social systems, were administered for his exclusive benefit. There is much to be said for and against such a dual society, but whatever merits it may have in allowing constitutional and cultural development on autochthonous lines, in Dutch hands the system did not leave the basic agricultural life of the people to follow its own natural development. Not only were the regents directed and controlled in the amount of produce which they had to supply, their territories were also rigidly controlled in the actual crops grown. So-called 'inspection tours' were organized in which the Dutch monopoly was preserved by the destruction of all produce in excess of the estimated demands of the controlled European market, and resistance to such destruction brought reprisals and, as at Amboyna in 1647, complete absorption and control of its cloves trade. From about 1680 onwards Dutch 'sergeants' in charge of outlying districts were given the duties of supervising the production of crops due to be paid to the company, and a system of overseers or 'coffee-sergeants' developed on this basis. The 'coffee-sergeants' were closely concerned with an important side of the activities of the regents, and developed into subordinate controllers of political and administrative business. But their chief and primary duty was to ensure that the growths required were planned and cared for throughout the agricultural cycle.

With 'inspection tours' and 'coffee-sergeants', and with the overriding advantages of controlled utterance of limited quantities of spices and other produce on the European market, went a steadily increasing regimentation of the native economies. Not only were more 'coffee-sergeants' appointed as the eighteenth century wore on, but the islands were often directed to the production of one commodity only. The growth of cloves, for example, was confined to Amboyna and the Uliasses in 1656, and more and more trees were ordered to be planted until saturation of the market dictated vetoes on further planting, and even destruction of the trees. Similar regimentation was practised for the growth of coffee on Java, and then of pepper; and in all of these crops, as in the generality of the spice trade, a persistent interference with normal economic processes lay behind the ultimate ordering of the growths. The Dutch took crops sometimes direct from the cultivator or from the native regent, who held his lands on condition of paying an annual tribute of spices; where prices were paid they were often the result of forced deliveries in which the price was set over a long period of years and on terms favourable to the Dutch.

In addition to all of this the Dutch exacted compulsory service from the native cultivators. Sometimes this was directly rendered to the company, but more often it was exacted through the agency of the regents. It was in either case but the last and most obvious sign of the way in which the Dutch had contrived to subordinate the native agricultural economy to their purposes. Without themselves engaging to any great extent in the actual business of agriculture, and while leaving the natives in possession of the vast bulk of their lands, they contrived a system in which the labour force of the native-born peasant was harnessed to their purpose. This certainly did not mean that they allowed native society and institutions to develop naturally and spontaneously in their own way. Dutch economic power penetrated through the whole of the life of the peoples of the islands, it resulted in a decline in native trading, in considerable changes in the growths of many of the islands, and it made Indonesian society more authoritative, and Indonesian standards of living more precarious, by support for the regents and by insistence on staple growths. In places, too, as on Banda (where nutmegs were the favoured crop), slave labour was substituted for free peasant agriculture, and a local slave trade grew up in which the neighbouring islands were raided for slaves.

This, however, was exceptional. In general, the distinguishing feature of the Dutch régime in the East Indies was that it was distinct from the subsistence farming of North America with its dependence on white labour, and equally distinct from the plantation farming of the West Indian Islands and of the mainland colonies of the south. The Dutch acquired a labour force by their own methods of using the indigenous peasantry, methods which resulted in a plural society which was as much a distinct result of the overseas expansion of Europe as were the slave-owning societies of America. The great difference lay in the fact that although they were slowly forced to accept more and more responsibility for rule, even when they left the actual exercise of authority to the regents, the Dutch did not form Indonesian colonies in the same sense as even the slave-owning plantations did. They lived as merchants, administrators or soldiers, not themselves engaged in primary production; and although Jan Pieterson Coen had planned that a society of Vryburgers of Dutch extraction should grow up and be the nucleus of an overseas society, the Vryburger never attained any social or economic importance in Indonesia. In Ceylon and at the Cape of Good Hope circumstances were different, but where it proved possible to erect a dualism between Indonesian society and Dutch suzerainty, and to use that system to make native authorities responsible for organizing the necessary labour force, that basic economic condition affected the whole of society.

A dualism of a different sort had arisen in the slave-owning plantation-societies of the West Indies and the American mainland—a dualism based upon the lack of status of the slaves. Midway between the dual societies, with their frank discrimination between masters and labourers, Europeans and 'natives', and the legal and juridical homogeneity achieved in the North American colonies of settlement, stood Latin American colonies. Here the labour force was in part got from the American Indians, in part from imported slaves, within the framework of a social and legal structure marked by a strong missionary influence.

The result was that the need to secure a labour force, while clearly a vital factor common to all European overseas ventures, was a factor which reacted differently according to the European background and motives of the settlers, and according to the habits and numbers of the native peoples. Modified in these ways, the need to secure labour formulated the economic, social, and judicial characters of the European colonies.

# CHAPTER VII

# Prices in Europe from 1450 to 1750[1]

The history of prices in Europe from the mid-fifteenth to the mid-eighteenth century is a very large problem indeed, and not to be undertaken in a single chapter without some trepidation. It is easy enough to outline the framework for such a history, but there is little possibility in the present state of our knowledge of discovering all the facts, or even of interpreting them with confidence. The principal advantage of such an enquiry is to establish once more the validity and basic characteristics of price history.

The first difficulty is that the economy under review is *old*, and now largely superseded, with structures and rhythms very different from those of industrializing Europe in the nineteenth and even more in the twentieth century. A readjustment of basic concepts is thus required on the part of the reader and of the historian of this economy.

Then again, price history has not yet succeeded in acquiring its own tools of analysis. For better or worse, it must rely on those provided by economists and statisticians. This has meant a constant effort to define terms, and in turn as a result, the methodological refinements have imposed uncertainties and repeated changes of view. It is as though each scholar believed in the persuasive value of a single method—his own—which 'in the name of Science' made him free to dispense with, and even reject, the contributions of his predecessors.

These, indeed, are not inevitable difficulties in the history of prices: they are difficulties which the historians have created for themselves. And they are legion. All the great names among the early writers on the subject are silently set aside or passed over with glib and negative criticism: Georg Wiebe, François Simiand, Franciszek Bujak, Lord Beveridge, Wilhelm Abel, Earl J. Hamilton, Ernest Labrousse . . . but for whom, it must be remembered, price history would hardly exist. Since their pioneer work, the subject has made little appreciable progress at the basic level of problems; rather the opposite has been the case. Price historians rest content with verifying this or that point of detail, the general significance of which has already long been established or

---

[1] In this chapter, Frank Spooner undertook the calculations. I have contributed only to setting them in context and to their interpretation; this retains my full responsibility and puts strict limits on whatever merit I may claim. The graphs have been drawn by Jacques Bertin and his colleagues. F. B.

suggested. The subject threatens to degenerate into a sterile exercise in logic.

Without stopping to enumerate the various controversies, we think, for our own part, that these debates have tended to obscure the crux of the problem. Price history is not and cannot be the only explanation of history. It merely attempts, from one standpoint, to simplify the complex realities of human activity in the past. It is a partial assessment of this historical reality, but has the advantage of employing the impersonal and complex evidence of statistics. Historians no doubt find some difficulty in becoming accustomed to this particular language, or in accepting its tools of analysis, however simple. Prudence and caution are therefore appropriate where there are serious differences of opinion. But they have meaning (and price history itself has meaning) only when we transcend such discussions in order to encompass and then explain the full range of history.

That is the precept of Ernest Labrousse's work: it is the recapitulation that matters. A price series certainly has its own reality but is not established *for its own sake*. It has significance only in contributing to knowledge, as a reappraisal of historical realities. As a result, price history must find its place in the context of general history, of which, after all, it is simply an ancillary science.

In this return to 'universal' reality, is there only *one* correct series, only *one* acceptable method? If so, there would be good cause for wonder. The authors of this article each in turn canvassed the opinions of mathematicians interested in economics—in England[1] and in France[2]—in the hope that they would settle the argument about the best method. 'There is no single method' they both quickly answered, in roughly the same terms. Any graph that gives a good or fairly good answer will serve the purpose of analysis. Try them all and see for yourselves! And so we did: encouraged to do so, it is true, by a particular example. One of the authors of this chapter collaborated with Ruggiero Romano and Ugo Tucci[3] on a long series of prices of cereals and wine in Udine. This series lends itself to every kind of calculation, for it provides weekly prices, in the same market, for 212 consecutive years, for a wide range of grainstuffs. Every method was tried, each serving to emphasize some particular aspect of reality.

So, with open minds, we decided to follow procedures best adapted to the task in hand, beginning with the available long series of data, and

[1] C. B. Winsten, Oxford University.

[2] G. Th. Guilbaud, University of Paris.

[3] Ruggiero Romano, Frank Spooner and Ugo Tucci, *Prix et conjoncture à Udine, 1450–1797*, of which one section has been published under the title 'Le finanze di Udine e della Patria del Friuli all'epoca della dominazione Veneziana', *Memorie Storiche Forogiuliese*, XLIV (1960–1).

by their comparison grasping the aggregate reality of price movements in Europe. The attempt was at once complicated by having accepted such a vast field of study; and more so by the presence of not one but several Europes—often very different—existing together at the same time.

Economic historians have long since noted that the European continent was organized by the division of labour; that is to say, much of its activity was designated by the confines of a common life. In 1400 Europe was certainly divided up according to zones, as in a von Thünen model. Nevertheless, before that date, great 'industrial' zones and some general organization of markets can already be observed in the eleventh, twelfth, thirteenth and fourteenth centuries.

Some evidence of this can be seen in the expansion of Venice's official trading network (see Fig. 3, showing the movements of the *galere da mercato*), in the pre-eminence of the industrial and commercial cities of Italy, and finally in the fluctuations experienced in the cloth industries of north-western Europe (the Low Countries, England and northern France). This concentration and industrial specialization, producing under well-established privileges, surely imply that Europe and its labour-force had achieved a large measure of unity. The great problem, as J. A. van Houtte[1] has suggested (though not for the first time) is whether Bruges was or was not an international port in the fifteenth century, as Antwerp certainly was to be in the sixteenth century. In sum, through the centuries, a certain unity had been established in the life of Europe, and was destined to be consolidated still further.

In the initial stages, therefore, it is logical enough to think of prices as though under the control of a conductor of music, who from London to Constantinople, from Moscow to Lisbon compelled them to conform to his directives. But in the course of this study, we shall see that the conductor is not always at his rostrum, that sometimes he shows signs of caprice, and that the musicians themselves are undisciplined: in short, that the music, wherever played, is full of individual initiatives. As in the language of economic theory, it is possible to say that the period from 1450 to 1750 was a régime of imperfect controls.

Beyond the great trade across the Alps in the fifteenth century, Venice exerted her influence over the maritime economies, tense and agile to a greater or lesser degree, which found another focus in Bruges. Here was a brilliant international economy, already showing modern characteristics, but with certain limitations. Not all the seas and not all continental regions were affected by it. So we must be careful not to confine our attention to the advanced sectors concerned with luxury goods—to the cloths of the north, which from the mid-twelfth century

---

[1] J. A. van Houtte, 'Bruges et Anvers, marchés, "nationaux" ou "internationaux" du XIV° au XVI° siècle', *Revue du Nord*, XXXIV (1952).

onwards were exported to the Mediterranean; to the spices which the Venetian galleys brought from so far away to Aigues-Mortes, to England, to Bruges; to the international trade in wheat. For there was another factor, no less impressive even though obscure, constituted by the lags and backwardness of economies, which were closed or still only partially penetrated by a money economy. Yet on occasions that international economy could crush them, when it really burst in (as in the case of Poland, where violent monetary devaluations and inflation accompanied the large-scale exports of grain). Barter (that is, transactions in kind) still prevailed even in the seventeenth century—as in the case of Beauvais, near Paris. There, only the wealthy had gold and silver coin: the 'black' money fell to the lot of the poor, and even they had very little of it. All this creates a picture of countless small local centres of activity, where coins, true in weight and fineness, were rarely seen. But this image was also valid for whole regions of Europe.

For this reason, among others, we have provided ample illustrations in graphs and maps. They serve to emphasize and isolate disparities in price levels which at the same time initiate, hinder, or perhaps further a unified way of life. This was surely maintained—in the very real sense of the word—by such differences of levels: by the low value set in this place or that on human toil? For, the corn exported from Danzig or the Balkans, the silver from the mines of Central Europe and later from the New World, the gold of the alluvial deposits of Brazil (after about 1670–80) were in the final analysis the work of the poorest and most oppressed of men, cheap labour thrown onto the international market.

Not all the difficulties, contradictions and problems, which we must consider, are open to solution. As Ernst Wagemann[1] aptly remarked, prices (one set of data among many others) make a good 'detective'. We will often set it on the trail, but only in detective stories does everything find a perfect solution. In reality, we will try in four separate ways to throw more light on problems all too often obscure:

(a) The first consideration, by way of precaution, must be money—both currencies and precious metals.

(b) The second section is directed to establishing the secular movements. This turns the discussion to the history of 'long duration',[2] which devotes more attention to recurring phenomena than to what is incidental, to structures than to particular fluctuations.

(c) Thirdly, we must concern ourselves with short-term movements, with their demarcations and periodicities, for their varying titles often bring them—wrongly—very close to traditional history.

[1] Ernst Wagemann, *Die Zahl als Detektiv* (Munich, 1952).
[2] Fernand Braudel, 'Histoire et sciences sociales: la longue durée', *Annales: Economies, Sociétés, Civilisations* (1958).

(d) Lastly, we must summarize the possible conclusions: that is, assess the data, problems, theories, graphs, estimates—but with the admonition, under the present circumstances, that the last word still remains to be said.

# I. *Currencies, Precious Metals, and Money Markets*

Prices indeed can be understood only within the monetary systems which serve as framework and means of expression. No currency, no prices! But currency was 'a mystery which few people can understand', as the Sieur de Malestroit wrote as early as 1567.[1] And even today there is little agreement about the importance to attach to arguments based upon monetary considerations.

At the risk of over-simplification, we must recapitulate the much-discussed problem of the moneys of account: it is not that complicated, but it does demand a certain mental effort. Moneys of account (in the sense of being distinct from the currency in everyday circulation) exist today as accounting systems, but in the form of complex, specialist techniques, of which generally only experts are aware (for instance, in the case of the dollars used as the money of account for settlements between Common Market countries). On the other hand, in the period with which we are concerned, 'imaginary' currencies were part of everyday life across the whole of Europe. For those unfamiliar with the subject, it is difficult to understand how necessary such moneys of account were.

All prices, all accounting systems (even the most rudimentary) and all contracts—or at least almost all—were formulated in terms of an accounting unit, that is to say in a money which was 'not necessarily represented by metal currency', but which acted as a measure for the coin in circulation. Each country had its own particular version, with its subdivisions: in France the *livre tournois* was worth 20 *sols* (or *sous*), and each *sol* was worth 12 *deniers;* in England the pound sterling was divided into 20 shillings and the shilling into 12 pence; in Germany the *Mark* (or *Pfund*) was divided into 20 Schillings and the Schilling into 12 Pfennigs .... In this manner, all payments were a conversion into currency from prices formulated in a money of account. Take for example the year 1574: a debt of 65 *livres tournois* (the money of account in France) paid in silver *testons* (which were current coins worth officially 13 *sols tournois* each) would have meant a payment of 100 *testons*.

But why these apparent complications? They existed simply because

[1] Sieur de Malestroit, 'Mémoires sur le faict des Monnoyes proposez et leus par le maistre des comptes de Malestroict au Privé Conseil du Roy tenu à Sainct-Maur-des-Fossez, le 16 jour de May 1567', *Paradoxes inédits*, edited Luigi Einaudi (Turin, 1937).

they proved to be unavoidable, because they rounded off the monetary system and gave it coherence. A metal coin 'of full weight which rings true' represented so many grams of gold and silver: that is, of a commodity—bullion—of which the price varied like that of any other merchandise. Doubtless, governments always endeavoured to have a real money which corresponded to the accounting unit (which, indeed, originally had also been a real coin). But as a result of the fluctuations in the price of precious metals it was necessary to readjust constantly the intrinsic weights of this money, so as to keep the current coins in line with the money of accounts. This adjustment was more or less regular in the case of coins of small denomination (we will return to this) and after a fashion also of the larger coins, by the frequent issue of new currency, lighter than its predecessors, and so on. . . . As a result, the circulation soon consisted of coins which often differed considerably in weight, fineness, stamp, wear and tear, or illegal clipping (which often meant that they had to be weighed). Furthermore, there was everywhere the insidious presence of numerous foreign coins, often debased and extremely diverse. Under such conditions, how was accounting done in everyday transactions?

Take, for example, the ordinance published by the Republic of Venice on 24 September 1551: it lists the foreign gold coins to be current in Venice, and provides a facsimile picture of twenty-one of them for ease of identification, together with their equivalent rates in Venetian *lire*, the money of account. Exchange rates were also fixed, whenever necessary, for the 'effective' coins issued by the Venetian mint—the *Zecca*. Thus everything was organized: if a Venetian had a debt of 100,000 *lire* to pay, he could use any of these coins available, Venetian or otherwise, and could refer to the most recent exchange rate for the exact sum required. In short he had to do just as we ourselves would, if the occasion arose to pay 100,000 French francs in gold coin. We would have to divide the sum by the most recently quoted rate for the gold *napoléon* on the Paris Bourse, and then work out exactly how many coins we would be required to give. Incidentally, in this case our modern banknote would more or less fill the role of the old money of account, though the fact that it is represented by a piece of paper guaranteed by a State bank, which is legal tender and can be hoarded (at a fixed rate), gives it the characteristics of a real currency in all respects.

A money of account is thus a scale, a measure. It makes possible the classification of prices and creates a continuous accounting procedure. It is a unit of measurement for gold coin, silver, *billon* (that is, small change coined from more copper than silver) or copper; it brings them into a valid relationship with one another and itself becomes part of that relationship. Thus in everyday life, *billon* (the 'black money', as it was called) was constantly expressed in terms of money of account and its sub-units. At Milan[1] for example, *terline* were always worth one fortieth, and *sesini* one eightieth, of the *lira imperiale*, the money of account in the city. But all too often they were coined in excessive quantities. They were such small coins, containing little silver, and with each progressive devaluation their intrinsic content and weight deteriorated.

The *lira imperiale* was thus followed by a latent devaluation, simply demonstrated by the debasement in the coins of small denomination. In this devaluation of the *lira*, inevitably by reason of the 'internal exchange', the full-bodied gold and silver coins also continued to increase in face value. The same process went on in Germany, where the Pfennig, a copper coin, was fixed at $\frac{1}{240}$ of the Mark, the money of account. The Turkish *asper*, a small coin almost entirely of copper with hardly any silver, also served as the money of account. Devaluations, more frequent after 1584–6, inevitably involved the circulation and value of the rest of the currency; they affected the stability of the Osmanli power no less than the social peace of Constantinople and the vast Turkish territories, thrown into confusion by progressively destructive inflation.

The same conditions obtained in Muscovy. The rouble, once a real money, had already become little more than a money of account by the fifteenth century, with its sub-divisions of silver kopecks and half-kopecks. From 1656 to 1663 Muscovy went through an inflation of copper: a copper kopeck was substituted for the silver kopeck, and thereby the rouble was quickly devalued. In 1701, Peter the Great had some silver half-roubles coined and then, in 1704, some silver roubles. So the money of account became a reality once more, though not permanently so, for the new money was finally stabilized only in 1762.[2]

What, in fact, were governments trying to achieve as they struggled with these monetary problems? Certainly they wanted to fix the values of all the currency, the small coins as well as the large, and maintain a stable system of accounts which directly concerned their taxes and revenues. Governments thought they succeeded in their manipulations (often devoid of sincerity) or at least they pretended to think so.

To conclude, no better example could be found than the 'classic' ordinance of 1577 in France compelling all the king's subjects to reckon not in *livres tournois* as formerly, but in 'gold *écus*' (*écus d'or en or*), which were *real* coins, known as *écus d'or au soleil*. Each *écu* was henceforth worth 3 *livres tournois*, or—in other terms—60 *sols*.

In theory, this tying of the *livre tournois* to the *écu*, and so to gold, lasted officially until 1602; but, from the time of the League, the balance

---

[1] Carlo Cipolla, *Mouvements monétaires dans l'Etat de Milan* (1580–1700) (Paris, 1952), 15 *et seq.*

[2] W. Lexis, 'Beiträge zur Statistik der Edelmetalle', *Jahrbücher für Nationalökonomie und Statistik* (1879), 368; and information communicated by G. Spassky, Keeper of the Department of Russian coins, Hermitage Museum, Leningrad.

was upset. In the open market, the rate for the *écu* went well above 60 *sols*, and at the same time prices rose at a furious pace. When peace was restored, the new ordinance of 1602 re-established the system of account-ing in *livres tournois*. At the same time the rate for the gold *écu* was raised to 65 *sols*: but naturally it was later to go beyond this level. All the same, one vestige of this experiment remained: namely the practice of reckon-ing foreign exchanges in *écus*, which stayed fixed at 3 *livres* (or 60 *sols*). Here, there is a striking example of a real money, which continued to circulate, becoming a money of account (and thus shows, once more, how all moneys of account originated). Again, the same fate befell the Venetian ducat in the fifteenth century. Fossilized—it may almost be said—in March 1472 at 6 *lire* 4 *soldi*, the ducat became the principal Venetian money of account. The sequin (or *zecchino*) on the other hand, until then its counterpart, continued to be used as a current coin. The fate of the Spanish ducat in the following century, fixed at 375 *maravedis*, was another case in point.

The reader who has followed these explanations without losing the argument will have realized long since that the devaluation of the money of account—or, as it was often put, the 'raising of the face value of real money'—was the crux of every currency and price problem throughout the period covered by this study. Did it cause or was it the result of those violent disturbances which almost always accompanied it?

Figure 4 shows the devaluations year by year of the chief moneys of account between 1440 and 1760, and in effect the progressive and simultaneous reduction of the equivalents of these moneys in grams of silver. We could equally well have expressed this equivalence or 'intrinsic value' in gold or even in copper. We have chosen silver, in the first place because we have better basic data for it; and secondly because silver, more than gold, reveals the larger and more real perspectives of economic activity. Silver is a good indicator in the centuries under review, although the word is regretted as soon as spoken. To tell the truth, there is no single criterion: not the wheat chosen by Jean-Baptiste Say (1818); nor the rye chosen by Johannes Falke (1869); nor the minimum wage chosen by Hermann Grote (1864); nor even, we may add, gold and silver. The greater the number of graphs and indicators, the more solid are the conclusions.

The picture given by this graph (Fig. 4) could hold our attention for a long while if we wanted to follow one by one the transformations of each of these currencies. Clearly, for the time being, we need only concern ourselves with the overall characteristics. What are they? The process of devaluation, already under way before 1440, continued well after 1750 and indeed down to the present day. Every one of the moneys of account deviated from the general trend, but sooner or later was bound to surrender to this basic movement. With few exceptions, the intrinsic value of all currencies declined, sometimes catastrophically, sometimes in a succession of small losses. The *maravedi* was an exception until 1642—at least officially; so from 1601 was the pound sterling, the heaviest and most stable of these currencies, despite some violent upsets, for example in the 1540's; and the Neapolitan *carlino* (if the available information is in fact correct; often it must be accepted with reserve).[1] In the final analysis, not a single currency escaped the general devaluation. In the three centuries covered by this study, the pound sterling lost only 43·42 per cent of its equivalent weight in silver, a remarkable performance; the *livre tournois* 82·68 per cent; the Genoese *lira* 72·98 per cent; the Polish *grosz* 90·10 per cent; the Dutch guilder 68·74 per cent. Over the whole of Europe in 1750, the devaluations appear in retrospect to have been particularly severe in three huge political systems: in Poland, Turkey and France. In France, after the reform of 1726, the *livre tournois* was skilfully stabilized—though at a much lower level— in the immediate sequel to the operations of John Law.

In many ways, it is possible and indeed useful to derive a monetary typology from these graphs. In the graph already mentioned (Fig. 4) it will be noticed that each currency is represented by its real weight in silver, but these weights are extremely varied. Did the different currencies share a common fate, when grouped according to their respective 'weights'; or to be more precise, was there a collective destiny of the heavy currency group (the pound sterling was its only example); of the 'middle weight' group; and lastly of the 'light' currency group?[2]

But in this matter, there are two other questions to be raised: what were the determining factors in these lags, slow declines and catastrophic falls; furthermore, what exactly did they signify in economic activity, and particularly in price movements?

The 'crying-up of money' (that is, raising the face-value of coins in terms of the money of account, which is the counterpart of devaluing the money of account in terms of bullion) attracted currency from abroad. Currency movements were bound to be affected by devaluation of any money of account whether of the *livre tournois* or the mark or some other imaginary unit. The circulation of money was at once speeded up.

In effect these devaluations of the moneys of account inevitably had repercussions on the price level, both in the short and in the long term. We can often see obvious lags in these returns to scale, it is true. If every

---

[1] Giuseppe Coniglio, 'Annona e calmieri a Napoli durante la dominazione spagnuola', *Archivio storico per le provincie napoletane* (1940).

[2] These terms refer to the bullion equivalents of the different units of account and not to the relative stability of the currency systems they represent.

devaluation (as we maintain) was preceded or accompanied by alterations in the foreign exchanges, it is still to be expected that it did not at once produce its full effect on domestic prices. The English crisis—or rather, succession of crises—between 1522–6 and 1555 but notably in the 1540's is discussed in an important article by F. J. Fisher.[1] The violent devaluation of the pound sterling had immediate effects on the Antwerp exchange. English cloths therefore fell in price on this vital market, from which they were redistributed, and an export boom ensued (the record year was in 1553: 133,000 cloths). At home English prices rose, though relatively slowly: they lagged behind the debasement of the currency. Protests against rising prices, and financial difficulties of the governments of Henry VIII and then of Edward VI at seeing the total royal debts contracted abroad inflated by such speculations, finally gave way to measures of currency reform under Elizabeth in 1560.

So tampering with the money of account—its debasement—had an effect on prices, but often imperfectly in the short run. And moreover in different ways according to the metal affected by change in currency rates. In practice, sometimes gold currencies were raised in face value, sometimes silver ones, sometimes both together. The long series of prices available for the market in Udine appears to allow some conclusions on the subject. In the case of a raising of gold currency rates only, it seems that short term cyclical rises tended to be retarded. If Venice (for Udine was a Venetian dependency) raised the price of gold, it meant in effect that the Signoria wanted to attract gold bullion and coin. Naturally in return she was ready to yield some of her silver coin—in a compensatory movement. This deflation of silver, it seems, may have slowed down in the *short term* the rise in nominal prices and gives another illustration of the dynamic role which silver played in economic activity. When silver was plentiful, prices tended to rise; and when it was scarce, they tended to fall. But it is important to note that this was true in the short run only. In the long term movement, each variation in the money of account was reflected in price movements, and moreover lost its separate identity.

The response in price levels to currency changes became more and more precise as time went on. It took a certain volume, a minimum level of circulation,[2] for this interaction between prices and currencies— and inversely between currencies and prices—to be established. And that volume needed to be more than one supposes, for water escapes from the level stretches only when it has previously accumulated there.

[1] F. J. Fisher, 'Commercial Trends and Policies in the Sixteenth Century', *Economic History Review* (1940).

[2] Ruggiero Romano, 'Une économie coloniale: la Chili au XVIIIe siècle', *Annales: Economies, Sociétés, Civilisations* (1960).

Raising the rates of the different currencies was always in short a *demand* for gold and silver. But demand, as we know, is powerless without supply, and supply must respond to and in turn satisfy demand. It seems that up to the beginning of the sixteenth century, the supply in the Western World was relatively inelastic or at least slow to respond.

All this makes a complicated story, difficult to explain, both in itself and in its causation and effects. If we take the period 1450–74 as a base period (= 100) the index numbers of the various national series can be averaged out to give the mean fall in Europe of the intrinsic value of currency in grams of metal. Naturally, to be exact, this ought to have taken certain essential compensating factors into account, assigning weights according to the sizes of the various economies in question. But there can be no question of this in the present state of our knowledge. The resulting graph has only an indicative value, therefore; but even so it is full of interest. The calculations were made both in grams of silver and grams of gold. By taking the reciprocals of these two movements, we obtain an index of the average rise in the nominal price of both silver and gold in Europe.

These two series are remarkable: the prices of the two metals rise at a fairly steady rate over the long term, with level stretches where they slow up from time to time, but except for two instances without any real recession at all (see Fig. 11). This long term progression continued for both gold and silver over the whole period, and seems to be an inseparable part of the monetary system itself. Economists from Cassel to Woytinski, Kitchin, Warren, Pearson, Wilcoxen, Rist and Marjolin have shown a passionate interest in trying to solve this insoluble problem. Demand for gold and silver is uninterrupted. Following up the conclusions from an estimate made for the mid-nineteenth century, could it be that the stock of metal has to be increased regularly for the price level *merely to be maintained*, for which a coefficient of at least 3 per cent per annum during the second half of the nineteenth century was suggested? Otherwise deflation would ensue. So there was a steady demand and consumption of precious metals, even in a period of deflation; and inflation only made this clearer and more emphatic.

We notice, too, as is already well known, that the two metals did not follow the same course. There was a certain interplay between the two metals, more than was generally supposed. In fact, we must always[1] distinguish between the quantities of the two kinds of currency in circulation. Roughly, until about 1550, gold was *relatively* abundant: at mid-century the amount of silver was greatly increased and gold grew comparatively rarer. This gap steadily widened, moreover, as

[1] Frank Spooner, *L'économie mondiale et les frappes monétaires en France, 1493–1680* (Paris, 1956).

silver progressively up to the middle of the seventeenth century was devalued in terms of gold. After that the two metals continued their course along more or less parallel paths.

In addition to the average price of gold and silver we have drawn the graph of the famous bimetallic ratio—or the changes in the value of a gram of gold estimated in terms of grams of silver (see Fig. 5). There was a time when economic theorists wanted to fix it at a 'natural' ratio of one to twelve. The appreciation of gold was evident in the early seventeenth century (which we would willingly call 'the turning-point for gold'): gold then finally exceeded the ratio to silver of one to twelve. At first sight this rise can be explained by the heavy production of American silver, by more modern—almost 'industrial'—methods: whereas gold in this period remained tied to artisan methods of production.

This explanation is valid, by and large. But the velocity of circulation of the two metals must have played a part. Did gold coins circulate more quickly or less quickly than silver ones? Bearing in mind the factor of hoarding, it will be readily appreciated that gold tended to circulate more slowly. This difference in velocity of circulation must have had its effect. In any case, as Frank Spooner has pointed out, after the middle of the century, Europe went over to a system in which gold was relatively less plentiful by comparison with silver, and this trend was to be maintained.

If these general considerations carry weight, the graph which we have drawn, pending something better, may be of some service. Here and there, in the course of their studies, historians have picked out some data on these gold-silver ratios, which show slight but constant variations to the general trend. When we bring these scattered figures together and set them in the context of the *average* movement, they very often take on significance, according to whether they fall above or below the mean. At once light is thrown on the variety of differential movements which constantly animated the monetary circulation of Europe. Thus in 1555 the Spanish 'experts' consulted by Charles V's government pointed out a double movement: Spanish silver persistently left Spain for France, and gold on the other hand just as persistently moved in the reverse direction. And again, as Felipe Ruiz Martin has shown, a vast network existed in the Low Countries for making payments in gold by bills of exchange, notably to the troops in the service of Spain. This leading movement in turn set off others.

In the same way, it is also possible to appreciate the extent to which the statistics collected by Jean Delumeau for Rome[1] in the sixteenth century,

---

[1] Jean Delumeau, *Vie économique et sociale de Rome dans la seconde moitié du XVIe siècle*, 2 vols. (Paris 1957-9) 667-8.

or by Walter Anderssen for Ragusa[1] also in the sixteenth century, in fact concern special cases: Rome was not quite in step with the rest of the West, and Ragusa was constantly caught between, on the one hand, the Western World increasingly affected by abundant supplies of silver, and on the other hand, the Turkish Empire dominated by African gold which came to it by way of Egypt, relayed in the form of gold *sultanins* coined by the Cairo mint.

Up to this point, we have deliberately left aside the fiduciary and fiat moneys: 'paper', as it is imprecisely but conveniently called. This fictive money nevertheless circulated under a thousand forms and gradually invaded the economic life of Europe. It did so furtively in the fifteenth century and cautiously, to a greater degree, in the sixteenth century. By the seventeenth century, its presence was already insistent, as the indispensable concomitant of gold and silver, those two great actors so to speak, prevented from playing their full parts. This was on the eve of triumph in the eighteenth century.

Whatever its nature, paper money was based upon the money of account. The first bank notes merely gave it material form; the backing of bullion acted as collateral and served to bind the whole system to the relative stability of precious metals. Other types of paper emerged, such as government bonds, the Spanish *juros*, the *giuri* or *monti* of the Italian cities, the French *rentes* on the Hôtel de Ville in Paris, the bonds on the town of Antwerp, the English Treasury 'funds', and so on . . . not to mention debtors' promissory notes put into circulation in the form of notes of hand,[2] or private bonds in the everyday sense of the word. These provided ways of doing business which were partly independent of actual coinage but which were by no means exempt from its crises nor, more especially, from the disorders suffered by the money of account.

Consider in this matter, for example, the precautions taken by the middle classes in their contracts;[3] or those which banks offered their depositors, as in the case of the re-established bank of San Giorgio[4] in Genoa, where two *cartularii* were set up: in one the accounts were kept in terms of gold and in the other in terms of silver. From 1625, there was even a third kept in Spanish pieces of eight reals, the *reales de a ocho*, one of the standard European currencies from the sixteenth to the

[1] Walter Anderssen, 'Materialien zum ragusanischen Mass- und Geldwesen', *Vierteljahrschrift für Sozial- und Wirtschaftsgeschichte* (1935).

[2] P. Goubert, *Beauvais et le Beauvaisis de 1600 à 1730: contribution à l'histoire sociale de la France du XVIIe siècle* (Paris, 1960).

[3] Bernard Schnapper, *Les rentes au XVIe siècle* (Paris, 1957).

[4] Fernand Braudel, *La Méditerranée et le monde méditerranéen à l'époque de Philippe II* Paris, 1949), 407.

eighteenth century and indeed a world currency, circulating from America to China.

Were all these papers insidious forms of currency? If confirmation is required, one has only to look at the lucrative transactions, in addition to the *asiento*[1] contracts at the court of Spain (an exceedingly well-documented business), which the Genoese bankers made in the *juros de resguardo*, entrusted to them by the king as 'security' for his loans. They used them, like other *juros*, as a supplementary means of payment. Contemporaries quickly grasped the significance of this ghost money; later, it was even more apparent to the inquisitive Portuguese Isaac de Pinto,[2] when he wrote in 1764 of the increasing loans raised by the European states at war at that time:

> the loans these same powers raise on the strength of their credit are an addition to the currency, which did not exist hitherto: an addition which, created by credit, and by the force of public opinion, acquires a real and an artificial value, both intrinsic and conventional, circulating so long as the credit holds good, and partially fulfilling the same functions as real coin, no matter how elusive and impossible the whole thing may be in reality.

We have little space to study these complicated channels of circulation, nor is it necessary to do so. But one particular example demands our attention: the bills of exchange. They explain many of the important relationships and are of outstanding significance in considering the over-all and integrated history of Europe.

Let it be said, however, that it is not a question of re-examining the mechanics of bills of exchange in detail, nor indeed of pointing out what they concealed: that the profits on arbitrage now and again made it possible to cover up a loan at interest (at that time, as we know, condemned as being immoral). However, taking advantage of circumstances was not the same as creating them. The fundamental character of this activity was the repeated alignment of moneys of account, representing—then as now—the confrontation through foreign exchanges of different economic and monetary conditions.

A single example puts the whole matter in perspective: the Amsterdam money market, between 1609 and 1750. It had two aspects. First, the general relationships of the different foreign exchange rates. The set of maps in Fig. 7 shows selected ten-yearly averages of the exchange rates on Amsterdam for a few important financial markets. The base in 1609 (1619 in the case of Lisbon and Paris) at 100 is conventionally

---

[1] A young Spanish historian, Alvaro Castillo, is working on the papers and has published some of his conclusions in 'Dette flottante et dette consolidée de 1557 à 1600', *Annales: Economies, Sociétés, Civilisations* (1963).

[2] Isaac de Pinto, *Essai sur le luxe* (1764).

the guilder—the money of account of Holland—on which our calculations have been based. The three subsequent maps, for 1640–9, 1700–9, and 1740–9, simply express the relationship between the different foreign currencies and the guilder.[1] It would be surprising if the figure quoted for a particular currency at Amsterdam were not given as a function of its intrinsic worth. As the guilder is fixed at an index base of 100, the exchange rates for these currencies do in fact closely resemble the series for their intrinsic values. A fall in intrinsic value was at once registered on the exchange. It can even be reckoned that whenever some discordance arose between the two series, the exchange rates turned out to be the more dependable, since they followed the market valuations, not those fixed by government. It would thus offer, where necessary, a possible means of checking and correcting the series for currency devaluation.

But a more rigorous demonstration emerges from the second graph in Fig. 8. This deals only with the exchange rate for Danzig quoted on the Amsterdam money market, that is an index of the adjusted value of the Danzig *grosz* in terms of the Dutch guilder. This was the money of account which Danzig shared (up to 1663) with the rest of Poland. On this graph, the guilder serves as the unit of comparison in *three* ways, so that the base line at 100 represents, in effect, a triple line: firstly, the guilder as money of account; secondly, the guilder in terms of silver; thirdly, the guilder in terms of gold. As for the *grosz*, it is also represented by three series which show, in each appropriate case, its value *with reference to the guilder*: (a) as money of account; (b) in silver; and (c) in gold. The result is at once clear. After the violent devaluations of the early 1620's, the same severe collapse was apparent in the exchange value of the *grosz* of Danzig on the Amsterdam Bourse, and normalcy was re-established. This period was marked by a falling, a sagging trend. Also, an important point to notice, the exchange rates kept generally within the limits set by gold and silver values, that is between the gold points and the silver points, but showed a clear tendency to follow the movement of silver.

This particular example could be repeated for other currencies and other exchanges. Keeping within the operations on the Amsterdam money market, it is to be noted that the series for Paris and London give similar results (London showed a preference for gold). In Venice, the movement of the exchange offers an interesting problem: by means of a very high *agio*—about 20 per cent—on converting bank-money (in which all the exchange operations were done in the city) into current money, the Venice market managed to support its currency artificially

---

[1] It should be noted that the *agio* on bank money at Amsterdam has been taken into account.

on the international exchange, at a level higher than the local realities and vicissitudes of the *lira*—in terms of gold and silver—would have allowed.[1]

The exceptional French crisis of the 1590's has already been mentioned. It was a twofold crisis which affected at once both prices and money. As regards prices we have a choice of several graphs which show them spiralling upwards. But what about currencies? It would seem that between the two ordinances of 1577 and 1602, the rate for the *écu*, which was used as money of account at that time in place of the *livre tournois*, was fixed at 60 *sols*. The money of account—whether *écu* or *livre tournois* —in theory kept its intrinsic value. But we have only to look at the 'nominal' movement of price rise from 1587 to be quite sure that this was not in fact the case. As from 1587, the gold *écu*, out of step with the money of account *écu*, was in fact exchanged on the free market at 65 *sols* or more, and at Aix-en-Provence during the League a rate of even 100 *sols* was recorded. But this abnormal tension eased off quickly enough. The *écu* came back to lower levels; but rates of 65 *sols*, 64 *sols* and 63 *sols* were noted by an enquiry before the 1602 ordinance to decide on the extent of the 'devaluation' officially to be made.

But what happened to foreign exchange rates during this period? They were affected by this commercial devaluation, as was only natural. The merchant who accepted a bill of exchange on Lyons made out in *écus* (then the unit of account) and payable in France knew perfectly well that when he was paid in cash the real *écu* would be reckoned to him at the going market rate and not at the official rate. The exchange that he had accepted had to correspond, therefore, with this market level; he had to reckon with the fall of the exchange value of the *écu*. How big was the fall? According to Frank Spooner, from the evidence of the exchanges at the Lyons fairs on Venice, Genoa, Seville and Antwerp, it was in the region of 14 per cent.[2] It was certainly less than the fall of the official rate recorded in Paris during the siege, which may at that time have reached briefly 30 per cent or even 40 per cent. Exchanges record phenomena relative to the activity of the whole economy, and clearly that transcends the events within the walls of a besieged city. But whether 14 per cent or 40 per cent, the rise in the price of bullion affected prices of food: 500 per cent when measured in 'nominal' terms. So if, for the sake of exactitude, we were to adjust the evaluation of prices in grams of silver according to the information provided by the alterations of exchange rates, the violent inflation would have to be reduced also perhaps by even 40 per cent. It would have been severe for the people directly

---

[1] Frank Spooner will follow the implications of these problems in a forthcoming article.

[2] Frank Spooner, *op. cit.* 308.

experiencing it without large cash balances, but in *international* terms it would not have been a much higher inflation than that experienced in several other countries during the same period.

We would end these considerations with renewed praise of the money of account. It was indeed fictitious, but it had a real value, tied to actual, effective gold and silver currency. It was something quite different from a mere 'screen'[1] or an out-of-date, amusing device.[2] Whether it was cause and effect, cause or effect, hardly matters! A study of moneys of account involves not only prices and precious metals, but also the respective levels between the different national or regional economies into which Europe was divided.

To conclude, therefore, was money the dependent or the independent variable? This apparently simple question demands several replies, and they are contradictory on more than one account.... We must remember that everything was inter-dependent: moneys of account, coinage prices, economies, social structures, phases and epochs of history. . . . So it was not just one dominant factor, one single line of study, one self-explanatory operation, but a hundred assessments and many precautions.

For example, devaluation of the money of account is not the simple operation which it might at first sight appear to be. The money of account loses in *intrinsic* value as gold or silver coins gain in face-value, but apparently with different implications.

No doubt every economy—or rather, every political and monetary system—had its own procedure for devaluation, its own usages, weaknesses, and necessities. What do we find in Venice? The value of gold money constantly but slowly rising, and this had the effect of attracting gold. Venice was a factory for making gold coins, for re-minting them as perfect—the *zecchini* or sequins—which were then put back into circulation. These successive revaluations of gold must be studied either as a long-term problem—which we have outlined and to which we shall return—or as a short-term problem.

As for this second point of interest, let us look at the long monthly data for Udine. Let us suppose that they are sensitive (but not over-sensitive) to the masterful pressures from Venice. To raise the price of gold coins, it must be remembered, was to attract gold, but in another sense also to disfavour silver currency. It also meant the devaluation of the money of account in terms of gold. This being so, the series in question do show reactions to a whole mass of pressures. They all point

[1] The term employed by Marc Bloch.

[2] Cf. the definition of Sir James Steuart: Money of account 'performs the same office with regard to the value of things, that degrees, minutes, seconds, etc., do with regard to angles, or as scales do to geographical maps, or to plans of any kind', *The Works*, 6 vols. (London, 1805), II, 271.

in the same general direction: a rise in the value of gold currency always tended to damp down the beginning of a rise in prices, and sometimes cut cyclical rises short in a spectacular fashion. Every lowering of gold values, on the other hand, and in compensation every increase in the price of silver, whether relative or absolute, tended to accelerate the rise in prices. This is a very general rule, more easily verified for other places than for Venice, where manipulations of silver only were relatively rare. A detailed study of this subject would certainly be welcome. Rather than set out to establish the long-term effects of monetary devaluations on price movements—which no longer require demonstration—it should attempt to establish the difference in price-behaviour (in the short term, it must be repeated) according to whether the devaluation affects gold in particular, or silver.

## II. *The Secular Trend*

The term 'secular trend' will be used to denote the longest of the long price movements here under study. It includes all other variations and carries them along just as the tide contains the movements of the waves in its motion—to take the expression, so often quoted, of François Simiand. And just as the tide ebbs and flows, and has periods of slack water, so it is possible to speak of the rise, recession and even pause in the secular trend. To make these things clear, we must turn to the longest time series available.

In Chioggia, for example, a small town where the Adriatic meets the lagoon of Venice, the public account books record, until 1797, the daily quantities and prices of wheat sold in the *Fondaco*—or municipal granary. If we take only one figure a day (either the average or the median), we can eliminate the small variations of that day; if we take only the Saturday quotations, or the average of the six weekdays, the variations within the week are likewise ruled out: and so on for the month, or the year, or group of five, ten, twenty, fifty years. Ten or twenty different and similar procedures allow us, at will, to rule out the brief, the short, the relatively long and the very long movements, leaving only the secular trend outstanding. This is the purpose of quinquennial or decennial averages, of moving averages for longer or shorter operating periods, of the method of least squares, of moving medians. . . . Unless one is content to stretch a piece of cotton across the graph of the data and adjust it *a vista d' occhio* to establish roughly the slope of the possible regression! The result, a mathematician would say with a smile, is not so very different from fitting a regression by least squares, one of the more elegant—mathematically speaking—of the methods for eliminating short-term fluctuations.

Such are the methods used. But what data are to be subjected to them? Either all prices at once, calculating general indices (although it is far from easy to submit all Europe to general indices)? Or separate price series studied in turn, the more important of them closely and individually, the less important by groups? We have chosen the latter procedure, looking first at wheat, on which we have depended heavily, because the data for wheat are by far more abundant than for any other commodity, and because grain represents the basic expenditure of every country of Europe. If we were studying Japan or China we would rely on rice as the principal witness.

The various series of graphs make much use of ten-yearly averages of nominal prices (that is, in terms of the money of account) and of silver prices (that is, nominal prices converted into grams of silver). There are several reasons for this, some good and some less convincing: the pervading unity in a *European* history made it seem advisable, on the one hand, to reduce prices to silver, since it was a means of international payment, and allows broad comparisons between the different economies; and on the other hand, rules out moving averages or medians, which cannot easily be accomplished with the gaps that nearly all the long series contain. Nevertheless we have all along had recourse to series of nominal prices. In the face of any problem it is always preferable, at the outset, to return to the original, unadjusted price series, the least inexact of all.

These decisions are self-explanatory if the basic objectives are kept in mind: (a) to determine with relative precision in the various economies the changing chronology of secular movements revealed in a series of particular instances; (b) to ascertain, beyond the range of particular examples, the full movement of the European economy.

## (I) WHEAT

First then, wheat, the outstanding product of the pre-industrial economies in Europe, and indeed their measure. Even England in the mid-eighteenth century was still predominantly rural. Wheat, grown almost everywhere, recorded almost everywhere, has yielded long series of price data, on which calculations can be based. As a commodity it has undoubted defects. In view of its inelasticity of demand, wheat prices were excessively sensitive to good and bad harvests, and for that reason did not follow directly the general movement of prices. In the long term, the incidence of these short-term fluctuations tended to disappear but the basic difficulties of supply largely remained: in the secular inflations, grain prices as a sector tended to rise more rapidly than any other. Admittedly wheat does not stand alone: other cereals constituted the mass of breadgrains—there were rye, barley, oats, and others. In France,

'les bledz' were frequently mentioned, and in Spain, in the same way,
'los panes'.... In effect, wheat was often mixed with other types of grain,
and the mixtures sold under various names in the different markets. According to the region of Europe, people ate white or not-so-white bread,
and the evidence about the quality of bread consumed in itself reveals
much about a given country. A black bread country was almost certainly
a poor one. In 1579 a fastidious Venetian finding rye bread in an inn in
Galicia—and that not without some difficulty—would hardly have called
it bread. Wheat was exported from Poland via the Vistula, Danzig,
Elbing: but the peasant-producer himself ate rye bread, and in beer, so
to speak, drank his barley. Even noblemen did not always have white
bread on their tables. At Danzig, a wealthy town, four times more rye
than wheat was consumed, according to an eighteenth-century census.
The bakers of Marseilles at about the same time bought for their city
the fine wheat from the plains and hills of Provence, but there in place
of their own wheat the farmers themselves consumed the much inferior
'sea wheat' brought from the Levant or from Barbary to Marseilles by
sailing ships: and this in spite of the cost of freight in both directions.
Even rye was traded from country to country. Along with wheat, the
northern countries exported it in great quantities.

Nevertheless, *wheat*—and what concerns us, the *price* of wheat—was a
superior good in the whole group of cereal prices, which in times of
dearth showed variations in price less marked than the other inferior
cereals. In the case of France, Jean Meuvret wrote recently: 'in the grain
market the dominant factor was wheat', and the data from the *mercuriale*
(or market price-current) in Paris from 1520 to 1698 confirm this. A
portion of the latter data is produced in Fig. 12. In the same context,
Pierre Goubert has been even more categorical: 'Grainstuffs (les bledz),
as the principal food of the people in the seventeenth century, would
suffice, in a statistical study of prices, to give the best and surest idea of the
major economic fluctuations.' Boisguillebert had already said the same
thing in 1695: '...the measure of wheat...sets the price for everything
else.' Were not expenditures on bread in France in the eighteenth century,
as Ernest Labrousse has suggested, equivalent to one half of the total
budget of the poor, and so of the great majority of men?

Wheat was a universal problem, a structure, the central feature of
daily sustenance. As such, it will not come as a surprise that this bulky
commodity, difficult to transport, should nevertheless have travelled
throughout Europe at the beck and call of the prosperous and over-
populated countries of the West or at the order of the quartermasters
of the armies, which always expected to be served with priority. In order
to set this bulky commodity on its journey, towns and governments
often had to take precautions well in advance. They had to appeal to the

great, sometimes international, merchants (as for example to the great international merchants, the Ximenes of Lisbon, at the time of the severe crisis of 1591 in Italy and the Mediterranean) and settlement had to be made in gold and silver. Did not Venice from the thirteenth century onwards pay for her purchases of wheat from Apulia in gold bars? In the sixteenth and seventeenth centuries, the Breton seamen in their small and paltry craft carried wheat from the north as far as Lisbon or Seville. But, with the connivance of the local authorities, they brought back bullion or 'red gold dust from Mina'.

It can be guessed in advance how dramatically these conditions affected the amplitude of fluctuations in the price of wheat: there were often veritable earthquakes, such as are recorded in the long data assembled by Earl J. Hamilton for Spain. We can see our way clearly through the violence of these movements only by smoothing the excesses. They were characteristic of the international wheat market in general, but we cannot take them into account when trying to analyse secular movements.

(a) *Wheat prices*: In view of the nature of the documentary material—often discontinuous—we have followed the example of Georg Wiebe and Wilhelm Abel, and have employed decennial averages. These often made it possible to employ a few existing calculations for which the original data have not been published. They seemed to eliminate the interdecennial variations reasonably satisfactorily, one of the important difficulties in the records. As for the choice of series, clearly we had to give preference to the long ones. There are not so many of them, but they cover the continent of Europe fairly well. We have worked out prices in moneys of account and grams of silver, taking the hectolitre of wheat as the common unit of reference.

Firstly, prices in silver. These have been assembled in Fig. 19. The graphs are for fifty-nine different centres, of which some are given in detail. The lines both intermingle and diverge to a considerable degree. The highest points have been joined up by a continuous line, and similarly the lowest points. These two lines (the *maxima* and the *minima*) form a 'surface', in reference to which the individual graphs each acquire their own particular significance. It is like the channel of a wide river, of which the banks at first are very far apart and then come markedly closer together in the eighteenth century. We can even put part of a graph back into the composite movement: the effect is sometimes to improve the explanation and enhance its value. For example, the extremely useful Venetian price-current for 1575–1609 found by Fernand Braudel finds its place in the upper register of the graph. It is what we might expect in those crisis years, but it is interesting to have it confirmed. The series—open to some criticism—which can be drawn from the data for Orleans assembled years ago by P. Mantellier, also appears there.

This 'test' is particularly valuable for the long and reasonably reliable series given in this graph. The rise and fall of each series differ individually when related to the upper or lower limits, or indeed to the average-line which has been calculated from the total group and drawn between these limits. Here again it should be noted that we set no more value on the average-line than as a guide to help in seeing the picture more easily. But it can be said right away with certainty that the Lwow series constantly follows the lower limit of the whole movement, at least up to the middle of the seventeenth century, and for a long period even remains below the rest of the series for Poland. Exeter, moreover, follows for a long period the average trend of the series in a remarkable way, before it rises towards the upper limit after 1689–90. This has some importance and will not surprise historians familiar with the actual conditions in England on the morrow of the 'glorious' revolution of 1688. As for the Italian and Spanish series, they are much higher than the rest up to the mid-seventeenth century. We shall return to all these matters again shortly, with the help of relevant maps.

Thus we have a tool of analysis which is certainly open to improvement but which, even so, yields a great deal of information. Some of this is unexpected. For example, when the prices of 'American' wheat, in the particular case of Boston, are put on the simplified chart, it is astonishing to find that they were by no means as competitive as is generally assumed, at least until the years immediately following the famine of 1764. Should the conditions in which American wheat reached Europe in the eighteenth century be scrutinized afresh in the light of 'comparative costs' and 'transfer costs', or should the relevant currency and price series be re-examined?

The graphs reveal another problem: the unmistakable closing of the gap between the two lines from the early eighteenth century shows how far prices throughout Europe had begun to converge. If the evidence for wheat has general value, was there not, because of this return to scale, a progressive breakdown in Europe of a certain type of merchant capitalism which could only operate through differences in price levels? These differences arose from differences in economic and social structure and, at the same time, out of historic differences. By over-exploiting these price differentials, merchant capitalism contributed to a process of levelling out, to the creation of a system of channels of communication, and in turn to a diversion of interests looking elsewhere for more favourable conditions. This is forcing the interpretation; but in 1440–9 the gap goes from 6 grams (in Lwow) to 43 grams (in Valencia), whereas in 1750 the figures are 38 and 75 respectively. The change that had taken place is fairly clear.

As a final remark we would add that this balance of prices implies, doubtless, a better circulation of goods and certainly better circulation of coin. Without attributing to the latter what is due to large changes of structure in the eighteenth century, may we not suppose that this contributed, in the special circumstances of Europe, towards putting an end to the terrible, dramatic famines? After 1750, very roughly, only 'suppressed' famines—almost bearable ones—continued to occur.

(b) *An essay in price-maps:* The remarkable tendency of prices to level up concerns only the last phase—and the very last, at that—of the period here under study. It was the fundamental diversity of Europe, its divisions and its disparities, which in contrast assert themselves between the fifteenth and eighteenth centuries.[1] Europe was still far from being that intimate, ardent Europe which we know or think we know on the eve of the French revolution: a Europe in which men travelled easily and frequently or migrated from one country to another. In fact, the important consideration is to map these divisions, these compartments, in so far as wheat prices can show them.

For the sake of clarity in presentation, we have been obliged to reduce and simplify the numbers of cities used for evidence in this sequence of maps. In addition, we have had to make a choice and limit ourselves to a sequence of seven maps at fifty years' intervals (see Fig. 20). A sequence of closer frequency would unfortunately have called for more space than allowed in this chapter. It would also have been too long a diversion from our main subject: the secular movement. But the problem has not been overlooked. The secular movement was in no way uniform and must necessarily take into account the differences in price levels through the economy of Europe.

Like more conventional weather charts, our maps distinguish high and low pressures: that is to say, zones of high and low prices. But whereas cyclones and anticyclones fall on either side of a fixed line, the limit between high and low prices was a moving frontier (for our average price series, after all, follow the general movement). What our maps attempt to show, moreover, through and beyond the decennial samples is the long-term movement. These decennial averages have been converted into grams of silver so as to make possible a range of comparisons between one country and another.

The first map (1440-9), with a narrow base of data, shows marked differences of levels. The ratio of wheat prices between Lwow and Valencia is about 1 to 7. Valencia represents the highest prices; northern and Atlantic Europe represents the zone of medium prices; and eastern Europe (Poland, and also—at its frontier—Austria, with the series of

[1] Its 'non-correlation' as it might be said; see the excellent article of Walter Achilles, 'Getreidepreise und Getreidehandelsbeziehungen europäischer Räume im 16 und 17 Jahrhundert', *Zeitschrift für Agrargeschichte und Agrarsoziologie* (1959).

prices for Vienna) represents the zone of low prices. It should be noted that the prices in Bruges and Utrecht are somewhat inflated. Those of Strasbourg clearly are: in view of the preceding data and the subsequent movements, this figure should apparently be reduced by a third or even a half. But further detailed information on the point is lacking.

For the second map (1490–9), the evidence is more plentiful. It points to a general lowering of prices, although this still leaves the former disparities unchanged. At the highest level, we find the Mediterranean zone (Udine and Naples), which can perhaps be extended northwards as far as Grenoble. These high prices are unknown in Atlantic Europe (except at Utrecht and possibly Bruges), and the difference was about 35 per cent by comparison with the Mediterranean countries. This is more accentuated in the case of England, represented by Exeter; it was still more so in Strasbourg and in Vienna, which represent the lowest points for this second area of Europe. As for eastern Europe, the third area, it remains outstanding for its low prices (5·47 grams at Krakow, 4·77 at Lwow, or $7\frac{1}{2}$ times less than the figure which can be calculated for Barcelona at 35·26 grams). In short, to recapitulate, if an index figure of 100 is assigned to Europe No. 1 (the Mediterranean), then the north and the Atlantic (zone No. 2) stands at 77, and Poland, our reference point for eastern Europe (Europe No. 3), at 16. Naturally, these are rough estimates.

The third map (1540–9), is set in the prelude to the big arrivals of American silver. In the Mediterranean and neighbouring regions we have high prices, as before; to this Old Castile is an exception. But Old Castile, rich in wheat-lands, lies outside the range of the typical Mediterranean countries, where prices show a considerable increase by comparison with the two earlier maps. This wave of high prices covers Italy (Naples, Siena, Florence, Udine), southern—already continental—France, as far as Grenoble. The 'peak' of this anticyclone is in Valencia and New Castile. In fact for these, together with Catalonia, the high prices are overwhelming and almost prevent them from playing an active part in the Mediterranean economy.

Another characteristic zone of moderate prices (leaving aside Utrecht, Bruges and Paris) extends from Vienna and Austria through Germany and France. It ends in England, where the level would be the lowest in this zone (18·17) were there not a lower figure by almost $23\frac{1}{2}$ per cent at Vienna (13·98).

As for the third, continental area of Europe, prices certainly were rising if we accept the figures, often calculated from imperfect data. These prices no doubt rose, as Stanislaw Hoszowski has suggested, in response to increased demand from western countries for cereal products, which resulted in an increase of traffic on the Vistula. The explanation is a likely one. At Warsaw (9·08 grams) the level is low; but at Krakow (18·12) should we not attribute the abnormally high level to local conditions in little Poland, with its relatively heavy population?

The map of the last decade of the sixteenth century, fifty years later, is affected by the biggest diffusion of silver known up to that time. In step with the commercial activity of Seville, the imports of silver fall from 1600 (according to Earl J. Hamilton's data) or from 1610 (in the opinion of Huguette and Pierre Chaunu). But we should also note that this was on the eve of the 'crisis of gold', from which time onwards the whole European monetary system experienced severe trials, with wars, famines, social tensions and economic disorders all becoming more frequent.

The anticyclone of high prices continued to centre over the Mediterranean, that immemorial sea of Europe's wealth but also of Europe's high prices. The peak has moved towards Andalusia, and the reason for this shift is self-evident: Seville has become the centre for dear wheat and dear bread. Still, the price inflation is maintained. It is particularly marked in Italy, in southern France, in the broad meaning of that term, and throughout the entire Spanish peninsula. The process, however, is slightly slowed down in New Castile, and markedly so in Old Castile. But the surge of high prices has overwhelmed the whole of France, despite a few exceptional cases with low levels at Limoges, Poitiers and Buis-les-Baronnies. Dearness has taken hold of the region about Paris, whilst in Paris itself, under siege in 1590–1, the level reaches about 143. But there are other reasons too, already indicated, why that is an unduly high estimate in the cost of living. Thus this Europe of dear bread has changed the picture. Instead of being in comparison to the Atlantic zone of medium prices and the eastern zone of low prices, it contrasted with a single vast area of relatively low prices, which spread out through Krakow (27 grams), Vienna (40), reaching as far as Exeter in England (67). In this zone, the only high levels are at Utrecht and Arnhem, but here too, war has thrown everything into confusion. In a general index, if the South is put at 100, the North would be only about 76 and Poland 25.

The dominating feature at the end of the century is clearly the fact that Polish wheat is now absorbed into the general pool of European prices.[1]

At first sight, this must be attributed to the grain trade on the Vistula and the Baltic. The export of cereals from the port of Danzig increased steadily throughout the sixteenth century and continued to do so in the early part of the seventeenth century. It commandeered more and more Polish produce from the southern regions, and at the same time brought

[1] Or rather, the north of Poland; see Walter Achilles' reservations on this point, *op. cit.*

prices there more closely in line with those of western Europe. Thanks in part to these exports, wheat and other cereals stayed relatively cheap in northern Europe. Nevertheless after 1591 Baltic wheat began to reach the Mediterranean itself, and this trade continued for a long while to come.

The fifth map (1650–9) brings us to the aftermath of the Thirty Years War. At first sight, the evidence seems somewhat confused: on the one hand there is an obvious fall in prices generally, but on the other hand there are wide geographic changes.

In the absence of more adequate and substantial data, some of the conclusions are tentative. Apparently the highest point of the southern zone is in Naples; the lowest in Udine raises some problems, not least by comparison with the rest of Italy.

But it is not in the Mediterranean, where high prices persist, that the decisive changes in Europe are taking place. It is in the north, that former zone of relatively low prices, that a split appears between two vast and different areas. In the first place there is a sort of chain of low prices—relatively low still, of course—between Vienna and Brittany. To the south, this limits a zone of high prices in the Mediterranean, and to the north the high prices recorded from Utrecht to England. The case of the latter is a novel feature. As a result the first quick conclusion from the map is that Europe is divided into two maritime zones of high prices, roughly similar, and between them a central line of low prices, which are largely 'Continental'. In short there has been a marked fall in southern prices, among the *old wealthy centres* of Europe, and a relative rise in grain prices among the *new rich* of the north. Can the explanation be found in the latter, with their henceforth privileged economies? Or can it be attributed to some disturbance of that complex but not inexhaustible organization for producing and distributing cheap wheat, the grain trade in the Baltic?

A German anomaly also stands out. Whilst a line of low prices crosses Central Europe from east to west, it should be noted that in Germany there is a zone of very low prices. This extremely low level for Germany, just emerging from the Thirty Years War, goes far to explain the subsequent rising trend—an abnormality in the context of the falling, or rather static, prices in Europe.

In the sixth map (1690–9) the western Mediterranean has lost its predominant position, if we do not look too closely at the particular case of Genoa. Henceforth France, with Paris leading, is at a higher level. The same conditions obtain in the Low Countries. As for England, after the Revolution of 1688 she has now become the country of dear wheat. Wheat is still cheap in the heart of Europe, and in the east too (Lwow 44·31 grams, Lublin 40·13), despite the inflationary tendencies which showed themselves from the third quarter of the seventeenth century. At Warsaw (though the figure is open to criticism), wheat seems to be selling at 25·24 grams the hectolitre.

The three basic zones in the north, centre, and south are thus still recognizable. The high levels in the south are undermined by depressions which are going to continue (in Siena, New Castile and Udine). 'Continental' prices are maintained from Lwow to Brittany, Germany lagging behind in places and Paris on its own, well in advance. In the north, the *nouveaux riches* of the seventeenth century eat dear bread.

A new equilibrium is established in the last map (1740–9). This map confirms the trends previously established: a main continental axis of relatively lower prices from Vienna to the Baltic and Brittany; one of higher prices in the north; medium prices are maintained in the Mediterranean. But by the mid-century all these differences are becoming less: apparently there was a very strong trend to find a balance. It would be more exact to say, then, that by and large the prices levels in the south, centre, east and west tend more or less to merge into one another and are a little below average, as compared with the slightly above-average prices in the northwest.

(c) *The fluctuations in secular price-movements:* The foregoing explanations have familiarized us with wheat prices and the reasons for their diversity. What of the major problem, the secular movement throughout Europe, and above all, the difficulty of isolating it with any measure of certainty?

The problem is not a simple one. It must always be considered in relation to the diversity of the European economy, which we have already emphasized. The fact is that price historians have tended to study only particular cases. When the assorted fragments of evidence are brought together, it is immediately obvious that it is impossible to extend the varying explanations as general rules for the whole of Europe. It becomes necessary to draw fine distinctions.

We can therefore accept only broadly the chronology of particular price movements recognized by historians. The four long periods are: a fall, or rather stagnation, in the fifteenth century; a rise in the sixteenth continuing into the seventeenth century; then a fall until about 1720–50; finally a renewed inflation in the eighteenth century. But any attempt to date these movements more precisely at once causes some hesitation. In the first place, the dates of the different movements of rise or fall differ in many cases according to whether we take the series of nominal prices (that is, prices expressed in terms of moneys of account) or those of prices expressed in grams of silver. Which of these two sets of evidence is to be preferred? And why the divergencies between them? Any answer can only be approximate and uncertain, especially since the series must in general be accepted with some reserve. Still, it seems useful to raise this complex problem, making use in turn of the data both in nominal prices and those reduced to their equivalents in grams of silver.

(i) *When did the sixteenth century begin?* The first question must be: at what particular moment does the movement begin which has been and still is called the 'Price Revolution' of the sixteenth century? The term is commonly used for the general upward shift in price levels which brought to an end the tense and difficult stagnation of the fifteenth century. The year 1500 was not the decisive year; and if we identify 'price rise' and 'sixteenth century' in a single concept, then there are many dates depending on the locality for the beginning of the century.

To judge by nominal prices, the sixteenth-century Price Revolution apparently was preceded by a Pre-revolution in prices (just as there was a Pre-reformation before the Reformation and a Pre-renaissance before the Renaissance). It was characterized by a slow rise (of about 50 per cent between 1450 and 1500, perhaps 1 per cent per annum), interrupted by sharp cyclical movements which at times imparted a shift of direction: but the upward gradient over the long run can hardly be denied. This Pre-revolution makes itself felt at slightly different times, depending on the place and the economy, and also depending on the incomplete chronological sequence of the data: Paris, 1460 (?); Exeter, 1462; Munich and Augsburg, 1463–4; Utrecht, 1464; *Rome, 1485*; Strasbourg, 1464; Ghent and Bruges, 1464; *France* (according to the data of G. d'Avenel), *1465*; Frankfurt, 1470; Limoges, 1468; *Ragusa, 1482* (?); Lwow (for oats), 1485; Spain (Valencia), about 1500.[1] We have italicized those places and dates which are very approximate; the rest are offered with necessary reserve, since only imperfect data are available as samples for the fifteenth century. Even so in the end we can say that as a factor in the realities of everyday life, this Pre-revolution probably began to extend over all Europe at almost the same date; the exceptions are Spain and probably also Portugal. It is possible to be confident about the Spanish exception but unfortunately there are no reliable data for Portugal.

Despite the cyclical movements to which they are susceptible, nominal prices in Spain—whether in Navarre or in Valencia—have a tendency to stagnate and level out. The rise at Valencia starts only after 1500, and that date will also stand for Seville. Here André Sayous's studies place the beginnings of the sixteenth century Price Revolution about the years 1506–10, though without the evidence of actual data. The Iberian peninsula is thus a zone apart from the European economy, although through the very excellence of Earl J. Hamilton's work we

[1] Earl J. Hamilton, *Money, Prices and Wages in Valencia, Aragon and Navarre, 1351–1500* (Cambridge, Mass., 1936); and *American Treasure and the Price Revolution in Spain, 1501–1650* (Cambridge, Mass., 1934).

have all had a tendency to depict the general European movement in its image.

If we substitute the evidence of prices in silver for this first block of evidence expressed in nominal terms, then at once the Pre-revolution is seen as a movement within certain confined limits. The rise of prices in silver virtually accompanies the rise of nominal prices only for certain German cities: Frankfurt, Würzburg, and Munich. In the case of Lwow the time lag is about ten years; for Exeter and Udine some thirty years; for Bruges and Ghent it may have been as much as thirty-six years. In Spain (Valencia), silver and nominal prices begin to rise together, but not until about 1500.

According to the information so far available, Spain is the chief country standing outside this Pre-revolution in prices. We note, however, that there the money of account suffered little alteration in its equivalent value in silver. In addition, Spain—or rather, the whole Iberian Peninsula—was at that time a centre for redistributing the gold of Africa: that gold was drawn away from it, attracting silver in return through the favourable exchange rate. An earlier graph has shown the disparity in the bimetallic ratios between Spian on the one hand and Germany on the other. Vittorino Magalhães Godinho in his extended work on the turning-point in the structure of the Portuguese empire has set this matter in clear light. In this fifteenth century at the outset of the great discoveries, the Iberian world continued to look to Islam and Africa, towards its gold money, its slaves and its trade, all included in the 'Saharan Mediterranean'. Did not Africa at this time reach as far as the Pyrenees? And once again gold acted to restrain Iberian price movements and the different economic sectors, throwing them out of phase by comparison with the other European economies. All these questions remain without firm answers; but it is possible, however, to explain this Spanish anomaly—the stagnation of its price movements in both nominal terms and silver equivalents up to 1500—only by considering all the relevant factors.

A simultaneous and powerful upswing (both in nominal and metallic terms) was elsewhere the rule whenever the difference between rises in prices and devaluations of the moneys of account was positive: as at Strasbourg, 28 per cent against a weak devaluation of 9 per cent; at Udine 40 per cent against 18 per cent.

These remarks pose another problem: why was devaluation more serious in one place than another? It would be easy enough to say—and the example of Germany bears out the contention—that devaluation was in inverse proportion to the abundance of silver. The rapid spurt in production in the mines of the Tyrol and central Europe, all of them developed early by the Augsburg merchant financiers, would at first sight explain the minor devaluations and at the same time the rise of both series of prices in Germany. Perhaps ten tons a year of bullion may not seem sufficient to have produced this result. Germany presents a further anomaly: the price rise is much more marked there than elsewhere, to such a point that it merges directly into the great sixteenth-century inflation which followed. The word Pre-revolution does not even seem to apply to Germany, but we must also take account of the extent of the German crisis between 1350 and 1450? The *Wüstungen* (deserted villages) were critical there. Germany at that time seems to have suffered more than France or England, even though they were engaged in those long quarrels of the Hundred Years War. Since Germany had fallen much lower her recovery may also perhaps have had a greater potential and so have been accomplished in shifts of greater amplitude. These are only tentative explanations; the hypotheses must be *checked carefully*, and, if need be, rejected.

Another important anomaly remains to be explained, namely the fact that the series of prices for the Low Countries (and indeed for England) are relatively stable when measured in terms of silver: that applies also to Italy, as the modest information for Venice and Udine reveals. Everything taken into consideration, the two most active centres of the European economy—Flanders and Italy—had probably excess demand for silver. Their devaluations (those of Venice, and even more so the repeated devaluations in Flanders) were evidence of this. Silver was in demand and overvalued; and yet it was constantly disappearing to other centres (to Spain, for example, as a letter of 1467 from a Venetian merchant reveals and as is still more explicitly shown in later papers which record big deliveries of Venetian silver exchanged for gold in 1505 at a handsome profit in Spain or in Barbary). In short, the question is whether the devaluations in Flanders and northern Italy are adequate to cancel out the rise in prices when we convert them into terms of silver? In effect, the price rise requires validation from more ample empirical data.

Nevertheless, there can be no doubt that a complex movement—of meagre dimensions, perhaps, but perfectly clear all the same (recorded by the series of nominal prices)—indicates a great wakening of Europe even before the arrival of the first shipments of American treasure. Ingrid Hammarström has shown this to be the case in Sweden, and the knowledge that this was so must cause some reflection.

We are not sufficiently well informed, obviously, for the problems under consideration. There is nothing at all for the whole of Italy (apart from Udine and Chioggia). But Earl J. Hamilton is right in pointing out that at Florence a mass of material is available but not yet put to use. Traditional historians have justifiably concentrated on the Florence of

Lorenzo the Magnificent; but the spotlight which they turn on that privileged city does not illuminate at all the material and economic realities which lay behind its unexampled spectacle. Economic historians know intimately only the sad Florence of the sixteenth century, the Florence of Cosimo. That is to be regretted, for it deprives us of precious evidence in reviewing the whole destiny of Europe.

(ii) *When did the 'long' sixteenth century end?* The end of the sixteenth century is as hard to ascertain as its beginning. The recession set in late, and once again it occurred at different times in different places.

We must again distinguish between the two sets of data—prices in silver and nominal prices. They do not give the same result.

If we consider bullion prices, the 'long' sixteenth century becomes much shorter. The earliest indications of a secular downturn in effect are found in Spain, after the great political changes of the 1580's. The conquest of Portugal (1580) had to be paid for, and then shortly after this came the settlement of the 'bill' for the Invincible Armada (1588). In 1589–92, a short and violent financial crisis can be observed, but it is not easy to interpret.[1] Soon afterwards, the whole of France in its turn seems to waver (Paris, Grenoble, Limoges, Valence, Romans): in reality France somehow had to pay the cost of the League and for the hyperinflation with which it had saddled the whole kingdom. The prospect in Italy also darkened in these last ten years of the sixteenth century, as shown at Siena, Florence or Udine.

It is therefore clear that the highest point of the price series in terms of silver lies successively in Andalusia, at Udine, Siena, Aix, Paris, and Grenoble in 1590–9. The downturn at Genoa appears to be in the decade of the 1620's, but the evidence is doubtful. Thus a concerted and far-reaching movement draws Spain and Italy into an unexpectedly early recession. This long-privileged zone of Europe did not resist the underhand blow of the declining imports of precious metals from America: for the prosperous, almost extravagant style of living called for ever larger shipments from the New World. France also shared in this recession in precious metals, or at least in part. After the short, violent movements of the end of the century, and then sharp declines, there was apparently a slight recovery here and there, which continued during the early years of the seventeenth century, staving off the real collapse. But the clear break at the end of the sixteenth century would seem to have been considerable.

Against this situation, characteristic of the south, must be set the experience of the countries to the north: of Germany, the Low Countries and England. The change for them came several decades later (measured, again, according to silver prices). In Germany, the decisive time seems

---

[1] Pierre Chaunu, *Séville et l'Atlantique (1540–1650)*, VIII, 21, 781.

to be the 1620's and 1630's, after the famous *Kipper- und Wipperzeit*; at Vienna and in Austria generally a similar date seems to be valid; in England and the Low Countries, the downturn is clear by the 1640's. For Poland, and more particularly for Danzig, which remained tied to the monetary manipulations of the kingdom until 1661–3, a clear judgement is not possible: even after the great disturbances of the 1620's, prices reflected inflationary pressures.

The contrast is as sharp as it could possibly be. According to prices in silver, the direction of the secular trend was reversed in the south between 1590 and 1600; in the north, between 1620–30 and perhaps even by 1650. This contrast, according to the distribution of silver, can be explained in part within the framework of the quantitative history of silver bullion, an explanation which will be undertaken when we come to make our final conclusions.

For the moment let us set nominal prices against this first assessment of silver prices. The results are surprising. The reversal of the secular trend apparently takes place on this occasion in three successive movements: towards the 1620's prices in Germany turn down (Leipzig, Würzburg, Munich, Augsburg, 1621; Vienna, 1622; Frankfurt and Strasbourg, apparently in 1636–7 only). The second movement and second series of overall dates are towards the middle of the seventeenth century: Siena in 1649; Exeter in 1647–8; Ragusa in 1648; Naples and Udine in 1649; Aix in 1655; Amsterdam, Arnhem, and Utrecht in 1651–2; Danzig (for rye) perhaps in 1660–4; Beauvais in 1661–2; Paris in 1662. The third and last movement is that of Castile (for nominal prices) in 1678, which is very much out of line, and to which we will return in a moment.

Nominal prices exactly followed silver prices only in the case of England, and very closely in the case of Holland. This coincidence, we should add, is one which expresses a simple arithmetical truth, because of the fixed (or more or less fixed) intrinsic value of the pound sterling in terms of silver. The gap for Germany is wide—one or two decades. In Italy it becomes terribly extended (half a century); in France still more so (but these measures are open to question); and in Castile even more than that—more than three-quarters of a century. Successive inflations therefore are what have kept nominal prices up in these different countries. In Spain they took the familiar form of an inflation by the excessive issue of copper coins. The whole of continental Europe, moreover, or pretty well the whole, had similar monetary disasters. Trading cities, especially in the Mediterranean, tried to get rid of them like the plague. In Castile this copper inflation stopped in 1679 only, with the reform measures taken by Charles II's government. The inflation of nominal prices then collapsed like a pack of cards.

But we need not describe the effects of this picturesque, classic inflation of copper: all contemporary witnesses recorded it, and historians have taken note of it. Our concern does not go beyond taking stock of the reversal in direction of the secular trend. Once more, in the story of the European economies, the rise has not been direct and uninterrupted. The seventeenth century, disturbed by difficulties and misfortunes, is very slow in establishing itself, and the concert of Europe adapts itself by a series of shifts and changes of direction. Ruggiero Romano's claim, that everything was determined by the sharp, particular crisis of 1619-20, is surprising and interesting, but not convincing. Can we believe in sudden, decisive breaks as far-reaching and simple as this?

(iii) *When did the eighteenth century recovery take effect?* A last turning-point: from the stagnation of the seventeenth century to the sudden rise of the eighteenth century. Here again, contrary to what might be expected, the lively eighteenth century was characterized not by a rapid departure, but—rather like the sixteenth century—by many hesitations and doubts.

Silver prices reveal that Europe splits into two groups as the price rise gets under way. The first group, the German countries, set off in the following order: Würzburg and Vienna in the 1650's (at least a first bound forward was apparently made at this time); Frankfurt-on-Main, Leipzig and Berlin in the 1680's. In short, the seventeenth-century depression lasted for just a few decades here, filled only in part with the ravages and sufferings of the Thirty Years War (1618-48).

The second start came later about the years 1720-50—joined by the part of Europe which had maintained itself as best it could whilst the Thirty Years War was going on. In this big group we should note the precocity of Italy (Siena, Naples, Udine in the 1720's), of Castile (in the 1720's), of France (Aix, Grenoble, Strasbourg, Paris, Beauvais, also in the 1720's). In the next decade, Danzig, Arnhem, Amsterdam and Bruges begin in the 1730's; and in the last decade, in the 1730's and 1740's, England (Exeter, Westminster and London).

Nominal prices reveal that there are three movements. German and Austrian prices are first: Frankfurt, Spires and Leipzig (1657); Vienna (1659); Munich, Augsburg, Würzburg (1671); Wels (1672); Weyer (1674); Strasbourg (1655). In the middle of the group is France (in part at any rate): Aix (1673); Grenoble (1689); Buis-les-Baronnies (1690); Milan (1684-8); Amsterdam (1688); Leiden (1690); Udine (1689); Genoa (1690). The last group contains Siena (1721-7), Castile (perhaps in 1721), Danzig (1735-9); England (Exeter, 1731; London, 1734).

In short there is only one anomaly, but it has the greatest importance —Germany. Wilhelm Abel drew attention to this without over-emphasizing it: and it is true that detailed studies are still lacking. Does the Thirty Years War (1618–48) entirely account for this quickening revival? Or do we not find ourselves once more face to face with the recovery of a Germany which had touched bottom in her economic activity? With the apparent depression of her economy, the low level of prices, and the especially significant drop in population, was Germany in a less-encumbered, more favoured position than the others?

The first conclusions must concern only the initial aspects or the framework of the problems, not their solutions. Historians tend to agree, happily enough, about the essential movements of the secular trend. But the exact dates of the turning-points, that is the upswings and the downturns in the secular movement, remain uncertain. In each case—and this has some importance—the reversal, affecting all Europe, has involved significant periods: roughly between 1460 and 1510, between 1590 and 1650, between 1650 and 1750. Europe never turned the corner in just one year, in a single concerted movement; for on each occasion its structures, its basic disparity, its endemic lack of co-ordination intervened.

What is more, these repeated limitations allow the contradictions between estimates in nominal terms and in silver. It cannot be denied that these contradictions are not resolved merely by setting one against the other. In other words, as economists and historians are aware, prices cannot be considered merely in terms of a quantitative or even a qualitative theory of money. Other factors come into play, some of them are almost self-evident.

## (2) PRICES OF COMMODITIES OTHER THAN WHEAT

Wheat, present everywhere, has served as an indicator in the main problems of the secular trend. Now we have to discover in what respects other prices confirm or weaken the first conclusions. Other evidence must be closely scrutinized and where possible related to that of wheat.

Thus working from confirmations and contradictions, we shall draw particular attention to some groups of prices. The greater or smaller range of these, when maintained over a long period, is one of the characteristics or structures of the European economy. It is at the same time, therefore, one of its main explanations. Prices often are most eloquent when contrasted one with another.

(a) *Two important food prices—wine and meat:*

(i) *Wine:* Wine, like wheat, played a very important part. Everything points to an increase in the consumption of wine and spirits between the fifteenth and the eighteenth century.[1] A first increase in the sixteenth

---

[1] It must be remembered that brandy (distilled from wine) and spirits (distilled from grain) in reality first appeared commercially during the sixteenth century.

century involves the towns (those of Spain and Italy at the beginning of the century, of France at the end of it). It is clear that the towns are drinking increased quantities and not paying overmuch attention to the quality of the wine. Then in the eighteenth century a second advance affected this time the countryside. In France in the aftermath of John Law's System, the peasants, who traditionally had lived soberly, making do with 'piquette', turned to drinking more and more wine.

This consumption of alcoholic beverages, from wine to cider, beer and spirituous liquors (brandy, and spirits distilled from grain) increased in the two great phases of economic expansion in the sixteenth and eighteenth centuries. With the increasing number of taverns and other places where drink was sold (their picturesque history is well known) all prices of wine were kept in a state of tension. For this reason we never find them far behind the general fluctuations, rather the contrary.

But if Europe was one so far as wine was concerned, the continent was many in its vineyards. From this point of view there were three Europes at least (Fig. 2).

To the south, Mediterranean Europe had been a land of vineyards for over a thousand years; north of the Mediterranean climate (that is to say, broadly speaking, beyond the northern botanical limit of the olive tree) wine-growing became established under the Roman empire. Little by little, it penetrated deeper into the continent and adapted itself to less favourable climatic conditions. By selection of the types, finally, wines of the highest quality known to Europe were successfully created, in the Bordeaux region, in Burgundy, in Champagne, in Piedmont, and by the banks of the Rhine. This was not achieved, however, without some difficulty, the obstacles being greatest where the vineyards approached very near to the northern limits for cultivating the vine 'commercially', that is, on the slopes of the 'mountain' of Laon or the 'mountain' of Rheims. The grapes ripened badly, as in 1579 at Rheims itself; they were late and a 'keen frost fell on the grape harvest, as a result of which the grapes which were still on the vines were frozen so hard that many harvesters brought in the harvest in sacks'.[1] Why should they have troubled with the customary panniers carried on the back to bring in grapes frozen hard?

The northern limit of the vine may be traced broadly from the mouth of the Loire in France, across the continent to join the Rhine near Mainz, then following the Danube well to the north to reach its most easterly point, the Crimea. Here the Russians established vineyards in the eighteenth century, in regions where the vine had already once flourished in antiquity, despite the terrible, cold winds from the north.

[1] Jean Pussot, *Journalier* (1857), 12.

Beyond this line northwards spread out our third Europe: the Europe without vines. It was not without a lively taste for wine, however, and sometimes as a result of long experience even had a taste for fine wine, as in the Low Countries, England and Germany. Eastwards the taste lost its subtlety. Poland still just passed muster, and here the demand for French wines gave rise to steady price quotations at least from 1700. But at Saint Petersburg in the eighteenth century fraudulent dealings were rife even before the casks and bottles arrived, and even more once they were unloaded.

There were thus three regions. In the Mediterranean the vines were everywhere, all-pervasive; so much so that at Gibraltar in August 1540, for example, the whole town was outside the ramparts during the grape harvest, the citizens sleeping in the vineyards, at the very moment when the Algerian pirates, informed about the habits and customs of the city, were trying to catch them unawares. It is a picture in miniature, but it shows clearly and succinctly the importance of the vine, and gives a glimpse of the choices often imposed on these countries. By and large it is a question of wheat or vines, bread or wine. We see it in the case of the Venetian islands—Corfu, for example—which opted in the fifteenth century for raisins and malmsey. From then on they were often on the verge of famine, waiting anxiously for the food ships to arrive. One of Pierre Vilar's series shows clearly in the case of Catalonia the endless dialogue between wheat prices and wine prices, a dialogue not without bearing on the crops grown. The same conditions prevailed in Provence.

In the second Europe, likewise with vines, the choice lay between the vine and wheat, and also between the vine and industry: Colbert used to say to his agents seeking to foster industrial activities: '. . . between two towns where the locations would be equally suitable for what we want to establish in them, but where the one has vineyards and the other not, you must always choose the one which has no vineyards, for wines are very great hindrances to (industrial) work. . . .'

In northern Europe, devoid of the vine, we have to distinguish further between regions: those on the one hand which were old clients for the wines of the south, and those on the other hand for whom wine was still a luxury, a display of wealth, something relatively new. We have only to think of the Polish nobleman who insisted on drinking wine so as not to be confused with his beer-swilling peasants. It was a luxury, but one which made demands, and—as Werner Sombart would say—one stimulating capitalist expansion: wine fleets were soon bringing barrels northwards from Bordeaux and from the country near La Rochelle: and soon after that they were going to fetch wine from as far off as the Iberian ports, Madeira, the Azores, and the Italian seaports. The history of port, sherry, madeira, malaga and marsala reveals that England was an ever-open market. From the sixteenth century on, white and red 'malmsies' were being exported from Cyprus to England.

A busy fleet of barges was also transporting the wines of Burgundy via the Yonne and the Seine; and the wines of the Paris region were also making the river journey, as far as Rouen and beyond. The roads, too, were called on to help when need be; at the end of each grape-harvest convoys of great German carts, *carretoni* in the Italian documents, crossed the Alps to load up in the south with the new and still 'unsettled' wines of Verona, Brescia and Istria. Venice allowed this part of the production to go off northwards, preferring the warmer wines of the Romagna and Apulia.

No matter where the new wines came from, everywhere in this vine-less Europe they were an occasion for festivity and for excess: perhaps alcoholism was symptomatic of the south and drunkenness of the north? Remember how Montaigne makes fun of Germans draining their glass without pausing for breath. At Krakow the new wines from Moravia or from Hungary arrived every year towards September, and were not allowed to be sold without guarantee of their origin. That is why the consuls ordered branches of greenery to deck the fronts of inns serving Moravian wine, and a shock of straw for those where Hungarian wine was on sale.

We referred above to the diversity of wheat: what, then, of the diversity of wines? There was wine and wine, and normally quality was not forgotten wherever wine was consumed. At Winchester in the fifteenth century there was already a distinction made between first quality chapel wine (for mass) and second quality chapel wine. At Eton at the end of the sixteenth century there was no confusion between sack and claret. At Orleans, in the middle of what was for long an excellent vineyard (it declined in the eighteenth century), there were two qualities of wine from the sixteenth century on, and they differed sufficiently for the better to be priced at twice or even three times the inferior. At Amiens, where there was a big trade, the price-lists between 1565 and 1667 record five to eight kinds of wine. At Amsterdam, we have the price-current of 1669 for eleven kinds of French and Spanish wine.

The price series for Alsace similarly show that buyers distinguished between places of origin. Doubtless it is not always easy for an historian to find his way among the different qualities mentioned in the price lists. At Udine, for example, the *di sopra* wine and the *di sotto* wine always went hand in hand. They undoubtedly corresponded to different parts of the region, the *di sotto* always costing more than the *di sopra*.

At Naples, on the other hand, the discrimination between *Greek* wine and *Latin* wine is clear and the distinction was moreover a very old one. There was a big export of both sorts to Rome. But at Krakow we are again lost in the range of wines offered, and do not find in the series either the Hungarian or the Moravian wines discussed above. In their place, there is malmsey, and the novel liquor distilled from grain, and in addition always present in the series, vinegar, the poor relation of wine, and of beer for there was also malt vinegar. We will limit ourselves to three last examples out of many possibilities in this section on the various wines: first, that of Danzig, which is so revealing that we have reproduced the relevant series (see Figs. 22 and 23); secondly, that of Lwow, where the competition seems to be keen—though not at all clear —between malmsey, unspecified wine and grain liquors; and thirdly the more varied example of Warsaw, where we have Hungarian wine, malmsey, French wine—prices are quoted from 1700 on—grain liquor, and even cinnamon brandy.

But consistent attention to quality seems to have been characteristic of the northern countries, the countries of our third Europe. It was very often the case in the Mediterranean—in Old and New Castile, for example, or at Valencia—that wine was just wine, the *vino de la tierra*, the wine of the locality. A single line is enough to record the price.

Moreover, the countries of northern Europe were distinguished by their high consumption of spirits—brandies, and still more liquors distilled from grain. Europe, which re-discovered or rather generalized the use of the still in the sixteenth century, became a big drinker of spirituous liquors in the seventeenth century. In the eighteenth century, production and consumption both expanded hugely. Could anyone from that time on imagine war and the soldier's or sailor's life without spirits? The north led in this consumption. Amsterdam was the leading capital for liquor, the market both for grain spirits and for brandy (distilled from wine). It was the Dutch who taught Western wine-farmers everywhere the advantages of distilling their wines.

Another characteristic of the countries of the north, and more peculiar to them, was beer. This ancient drink sooner or later came to be made everywhere in the modern way, with the general use of hops. Naturally it would be going too far to suppose that the northern limit of the vine coincided with the southern limit for beer. The fact is that in particular places beer reached far south. Paris had breweries at a very early date and this was not an isolated example.

Obviously there was beer and beer. At Augsburg the price lists distinguished between 'light' and 'brown'; at Vienna, the capital for white wine, there were six different qualities of beer, and their prices sometimes became confused into the bargain. At Warsaw, there were prices of five sorts; at Lwow, two; at Krakow, six. At Munich, a distinction was made between 'March' beer, said to be better and sold at a higher price (though exceptions confirm the rule), and 'winter' beer.

What, then, is important in these data for wine and beer? First, they confirm those broad movements to which wheat first called attention. In particular, the sixteenth century saw an increase in all wine prices, whether the wines were important or not so important, and whether they were produced nearby or far off. They all rose with the price revolution of the sixteenth century, and then were affected by the recession characteristic of the seventeenth century. Beer was equally sensitive to these fluctuations. This is borne out by the selected price series for Alsace, Catalonia and Danzig (Fig. 22), in addition to some data for Winchester, Lwow and Amsterdam Fig. 23.

The first question is: did these prices rise more rapidly or more slowly than wheat prices? The answer is, in general, threefold throughout the three zones of Europe. In order to read more easily the answers given in the graphs, let us imagine that in the selected towns we can compare a hectolitre of wheat with a hectolitre of wine, the prices of both being established in grams of silver.

The first test comes from the series for Spain from Valencia and New Castile (Fig. 23). Both represent the wine-growing Europe, the first zone in our scheme, the Europe with a Mediterranean climate. At the start, wine at Valencia was worth about two-thirds of the price of an equal measure of wheat. So it sets off in second place, follows wheat at roughly the same rate, but does not close the gap. In New Castile wheat at the start was similarly worth more than wine, and its price went up faster than that of wine in the sixteenth century. So there the lead became greater. We cannot continue in this comparison after that date, unfortunately, as the question of a unit of measure for wines poses insoluble problems. Two case-studies do not by themselves, of course, establish a rule. All the same it is probable that these examples give an idea of how prices behaved in countries where vines grew in abundance.

When the experiment is repeated for Grenoble it proves less significant. Grenoble, according to the price lists, drank wine from its local vineyards. Wheat cost more than wine did, but its lead was modest. Moreover wine rose more rapidly than wheat in the last decade of the sixteenth century, and so went into the lead. But presently the price of wheat caught up, only to lose the lead once more. The two series of wheat and wine were more or less at a par, with wheat leading by a small margin.

Further north, the situation was reversed. In England at Winchester College, the price of a hectolitre of 'chapel wine' at the start was six times that of a hectolitre of wheat, and up to the devaluations of the 1540's rose faster. After that, wheat seems to have risen equally quickly. In 1655–9, the wine then called 'chapel wine' (but was it the same as the earlier wine?) was worth ten times a hectolitre of wheat, and continued to rise so steeply that towards 1710, the proportion went to twelve and then in the mid-eighteenth century to twenty times. The same conditions applied more or less to that rich market, Amsterdam. Towards 1630, Bordeaux wine, which was looked on as a luxury wine at Amsterdam, sold at seven times the price of wheat; the proportions went from one to ten during the second half of the seventeenth century and became even more exaggerated during the long war when Holland fought France over the Spanish Succession.

These figures need little comment, although one particular observation must be made: the obvious under-consumption of wine in the northern countries. This luxury item had nothing in common with the jug of wine which any peasant in the south could go and draw from his barrel or any townsman buy from the nearest tavern. To illustrate this difference graphically by means of data (see Fig. 23) we have shown the series for beer in Lwow, the normal drink in the north. The hectolitre of beer was more or less equal in price to the hectolitre of wheat; then this equality was broken in favour of wheat, and afterwards the gap went on getting wider, beer keeping a steady price from the early seventeenth century onwards. In the mid-eighteenth century, it represented barely a quarter of the price of wheat. In the end this meant that in the north as in the south, drink—that is to say the everyday beverage, whether wine or beer—mattered less than food, as is right and proper. The passing example of Beauvais in the seventeenth century more or less confirms this: the town was surrounded by vines at that time, and one price series recorded that wine followed the trend of wheat.

But these are realities which can be observed in the long run. In the short term, the matter was less simple. Prices were subject to random influences and the series became distorted. This is precisely what the Beauvais figures suggest when we look at wheat and wine together. The two products were often contradictory, the one being high when the other was low and vice-versa, as a result of a good wheat harvest together with a bad wine harvest, or the other way about. Their price series agree when both kinds of harvests were bad.

(ii) *Meat prices:* From 1400 to 1750 Europe was a great consumer of bread and more than half vegetarian, before the slow spread and generalization of scientific farming in the nineteenth century. Only this 'backward' diet allowed Europe to carry the burden of a continually increasing population. The population at least doubled, probably even tripled: from about 50 or 60 millions (about 1400) it rose to 140 or 150 millions (about 1750), although it doubtless suffered some setbacks or stagnation between 1650 and 1750.

The consumption of bread put that of meat more and more in the background until the mid-nineteenth century. Then, and only then, was the demand reversed, and meat prices inflated, as a diet of meat gradually became more popular. Europe before 1750 looked to white bread; the Europe of to-day looks to meat. Bread no longer takes a dominant place in our diet, especially as dried pulses, potatoes and the whole range of green vegetables—some entirely new, others improved by selection and wise cultivation—came into wider everyday use during the nineteenth century.

What people are generally less well aware of is that the situation sketched in 1750—large rations of bread and a little meat—which continued by and large for another century until about 1850, was itself the result of a deterioration and does not apply when we go back in time to the Middle Ages. In those days the tables—and not merely the princely tables—were heavily loaded with various meats, the more so as we go further and further back. Wilhelm Abel suggested explicitly in 1937, and his argument on this point confirmed Gustav Schmoller's earlier article published in 1871, that this was a long development from the fifteenth to the eighteenth century. It seems to be irrefutable. In the German towns, according to Abel, the yearly consumption of meat declined from an average of 100 kilograms and more per person (a sort of biological maximum) in the fifteenth century to a consumption of not more than 14 kilograms per person in the nineteenth century. What was true of Germany was sooner or later true of Europe. As a result, the system of limited land-cultivation, with stock-rearing in the great open spaces available, developed into one in which arable farming invaded more and more the pasture land, in its 'obsessive' preoccupation to be able to feed a population which was increasing annually. In the west, regions where stock-raising brought a balance and pleasure to a farmer's hard life became fewer and fewer. As Loisel, a seventeenth century jurist and economist, wrote about the country of Bray: 'it is virtually only those villagers living close to the pastures and commons who tend towards pleasure-seeking and idleness, making do with the food produced by one or two animals.'

Witnesses confirm this decline in stock-raising, which a few more details easily demonstrate: for example, the exceptional demand for leather in the western world, which accounted for so much leather imported from Egypt or from the Balkans, and still more from the New World; or again the recourse to the herds of Hungary, the Balkans and Poland from the fifteenth century, giving rise in these marginal countries of Europe to a real *Viehwirtschaft*, both peasant and seigniorial.

But we must start out from statistical data and prices and see how—the exceptions confirming the rule—they lead back to the big question raised by Gustav Schmoller. In general, meat prices followed the prices of wheat and other cereals, as we see in the series for beef in Andalusia, the no less valuable series for beef in Würzburg and Sand-

wich (Fig. 24), or the unpublished series of the price of sheep in Paris
(based on hospital archives) (Fig. 26). Less in demand than wheat, meat
follows the wheat price movement in the different series, but after a
significant lag. In the group of prices for Paris in the sixteenth century,
the price of sheep thus follows a middle course between all other prices,
between those rising quickly and those rising slowly. Wheat has a higher
rate of inflation than mutton, and the same thing can be demonstrated
from the series for Würzburg and England. If wheat prices and meat
prices are converted into silver equivalents and the comparison made
between them, the results are clear: the dominant position every time is
assumed by agriculture and food cereals.

There are many examples of this. At Strasbourg, the average price of
rye went from 100 in the fifteenth century to 350 in the seventeenth
century, but the price of meat advanced only up to 250 in the same period.
At Duisberg, from 1485–1520 to 1590–1628, rye prices went up by
300 per cent but beef by only 212–42 per cent. In Saxony, the two
percentages are respectively 350 and 250, between the fifteenth century
and the second half of the sixteenth century. There is doubtless no
question here of development in a straight line, without set-backs. The
price of meat at Beauvais in the seventeenth century leads the slight
thirty-year rise ending about 1630. After that it conformed to the average
of wheat fluctuations. In Germany the population declined during the
hard years of the Thirty Years War and opened the way for a temporary
reaction: wheat prices fell behind those of animal products. If for
Würzburg, Augsburg and Munich we compare the period 1619–24
(leaving the untypical year of 1622 out of account) with the quinquennial
period 1669–73 (prices in money of account, 1619–24 = 100), the price
of rye fell to 25 whilst meat prices remained at 85 in Munich and Augsburg, and at 60 in Würzburg. This showed exceptional conditions which
lasted for a long time: it restored the operations of the stockyards and the
cattle fairs. 'The markets are so well stocked now,' reported a Frankfurt
document for 1658, 'that it is possible to choose whatever appeals most
to the appetite. . . .'

It would in fact take many pages to write a history of meat and animal
products throughout a Europe which although remaining immensely
diversified was gradually being forced to follow a common form of
development. This would mean investigating a history of food which
up to now has been composed largely of picturesque details never
seriously classified, measured or compared. The history of food has
hardly begun to rise above the level of anecdotes. What did meals consist
of, what was their calory content, and what was their market cost? Few
of these questions have been considered. In a study in progress, Witold
Kula concludes that the least expensive calories for a Polish peasant in

the eighteenth century were still those he absorbed from the liquor distilled from grain. We may smile at this justification of alcohol, but it is only superficially a joke. The history of prices could doubtless do no more than throw side-lights on this 'realist' history of food, still in its beginnings. But it raises the problems well enough, or rather is the essential point of reference. The other aspects—sociological or biological —of the history of food must always be seen in relation to it. The price of food-stuffs and the range of possible choices are the daily problem *par excellence* that has always beset humanity.

(b) *Prices of commodities other than food:* Coming to non-food prices we have to abandon for various reasons the hope of continuing a coherent enquiry. Firstly, because with few exceptions our data are not very exact. Lime is sold by the cartload. How big a cart? When loads of wood are in question clearly the description can apply to different measures and weights. As for textiles, the confusion defies all explanation. The qualities over the long-run are unlimited; the prices are largely affected by the dye-stuffs and the finishing processes; the rolls have varying dimensions, even for fixed qualities of known cloths (the *kersies* sold in Poland, for example, varied from 32 to 37 ells), and even when it is possible to recognize certain qualities of woollens or silks, precisely designated by trademarks (such as 'one lion', 'two lions' and so on, in the case of the cloths of Leiden) which refer to exact characteristics, they would never be found all over Europe to permit a comparative study. And over the centuries, textile techniques changed and developed under the influence of fashion and public demand.

As for steel, cast iron, iron, copper and other metals, heavy industry was not yet established and our series are all too often inadequate.

In short, we attempt to consider these different sectors only to meet the demands imposed on any chapter on general price history. In each case we will try to give an idea of what the documentation is like, and examine in particular the long series. Whenever possible we will follow the data for a few products, where they are relatively reliable.

(i) *Construction in general:* Housing involves a whole assortment of prices. To build a house, live in it, furnish it, heat and light it—all this implied the use of a variety of materials. Many series have been published for this mass of products but they are usually discontinuous, and rarely cover the whole period dealt with in this study. In many cases—such as laths, shingle-boards, lime, planks, joists—we are left with considerable doubts about the exact nature of weights, sizes, or even the material of which a product was made, and still more about its origin. Are we dealing with goods produced locally, or were they imported, burdened with transport costs? All this gives rise to inexplicable contradictions. In Poland between 1550 and 1750 'rafters' go up tenfold in price at

Warsaw but only five times at Krakow; yet 'laths' behave inversely, going from 1 to 20 at Warsaw and from 1 to 30 at Krakow. We cannot draw firm conclusions, but it is even likely that the words 'laths' and 'rafters' need more exact definition.

(ii) *Bricks:* We can add a few further examples. Bricks are the only product (together with wood for burning) for which we produce graphs —without being sure of their correctness, and without wanting to persuade other people about them. Bricks are products which can be compared from one end of Europe to the other, and they are sold by the thousand or by the hundred. They are more or less widely distributed, though there is also the Europe given to building in stone. Still, bricks do exist almost everywhere, in Siena just as in London, Amsterdam, Danzig, or Paris—in the Place des Vosges, and even more generally in the brick and stone so fashionable in the style of Louis XIII (also common under Henry IV), as also in the Low Countries. Nevertheless an element of disparity can affect this weighty material. Even to-day if you are close to a brickyard you can get cheap bricks. Perhaps this fact is enough in itself to account for some differences in our graph: the most reliable series have been converted here into grams of silver (see Fig. 27).

There are five series in all: for Lwow, Krakow, Würzburg, England and Valencia. We have included in the graph the average price of wheat in grams of silver, as we have already mentioned, only as a point of reference.

Broadly, it will be seen that a hectolitre of wheat, apart from a few exceptions, was worth more than 1,000 bricks: we could support the statement by a mass of references. Again broadly, bricks followed the overall progression of prices, but more slowly than wheat. A period of stagnation was followed by a rise from the mid-sixteenth to the mid-seventeenth century, and again by stagnation.

We could multiply references and comparisons, for each series taking the corresponding local price of wheat, or the general price index when that exists. We will content ourselves with saying that from 1450 to 1750, for example, whilst the general price index in England went from 100 to 600, brick prices advanced up to only 350. The same rate of increase applied also to the Polish series, the two falls in prices corresponding to the devaluation of 1661-3. But only a detailed comparative study between Lwow and Krakow could explain the differences in levels between the two towns.

It should also be noted *en passant* that at the outset Polish prices were by and large at a relatively low level: in 1440-4, 25·7 grams at Lwow; perhaps 77·8 in England; 87·81 at Valencia. The three western series (Valencia, Würzburg, England) remained at a much higher level. It was only in the eighteenth century that the series tended to converge, if we discount the rapid collapse in the series for Krakow. Clearly we must not ask too much of these graphs. Brick prices include a natural, common raw material; they include labour, fuel (generally wood, but also coal in the Low Countries and England), and transport costs. Would the cost of fuel account for the relative fall in brick prices in England as well as in Holland? Or for the use of bricks in paving the streets in these countries?

(iii) *Wood:* Nor must we ask too much of the data for wood, although wood was of immense importance for heating houses, for building, for constructing ships, and not least for charcoal in metallurgy. Wood goes far beyond the sphere of domestic needs and prices, and cannot be restricted to this sector.

It has often been said that up to the eighteenth century, and even to the nineteenth century, there was an age of wood, in which wood was the main source of energy at the disposal of men. Did this source so diminish in England from the sixteenth century that this economy converted first to coal? The conviction of this underlies the famous thesis of John U. Nef on industrialization in Britain.

Wood also signified limits to arable farming: the forests receded before the plough. The struggle of the 'open country' against the forests had gone on for centuries. It still goes on under our own eyes. Such large questions inevitably make for tentative answers.

The graphs (see Fig. 28) for wood for fuel (Lwow, New Castile, Würzburg, Eton) have been established in grams of silver and placed according to their respective levels. We are dealing with 'loads' and 'cartloads' all the time, and this naturally does not allow precise comparisons between them. Würzburg and Lwow offer some similarities, despite the fact that the German series shows early signs of the great price fall in the seventeenth century (by 1620–4, but at Lwow not until the early 1650's). Nevertheless, the Polish prices tended to follow the 'German' pattern. The graph for New Castile, although incomplete, shows a drop characteristic of the falling secular trend in western Europe. Finally, at Eton, there were rising prices after 1600, then a level period from the middle of the seventeenth century. The series for English charcoal (Fig. 29) rises more rapidly than those for wood until the mid-seventeenth century (the reversal of the basic trend was late in England, as we have already discussed). The evidence for Beauvais points to a sharp thirty-year rise (more marked than in the case of wheat) at the beginning of the seventeenth century, then a fall which coincides with the general recession in Europe. But the most interesting fact at Beauvais in the seventeenth century was undoubtedly the movement towards re-afforestation in some regions. The vast study of Michel Devèze on the forests in the Paris basin during the sixteenth century also indicates the settlement of the forests' limits very much as at the present day. Hans Helmut Wächter draws further attention to a turning-point in East Prussia in 1620–5: the grain-growing which had been taking an increasing part in the utilization of the land suffered a setback; marginal land was abandoned, and arable farming gradually confined to the better soils. Wheat-yields at once began to increase and went on increasing, and forest-land was left unmolested. But at any rate in the present state of our knowledge, our price series alone do not permit us to settle the exact limits of this huge problem of the frontiers between arable and forest land.

(iv) *Textiles:* Textiles take us into a vast, complex sector, which is difficult, if not impossible, to prospect. This is a great pity, especially since at that time textiles were the *great* industry, doubtless giving rise to all the 'unbalanced' economic expansion of the period. This undeniably was sooner or later to play an important part in the Industrial Revolution, destined, as it turned out, to exceed by far the conditions in which it originated.

Every region in Europe had textile industries, from before the fifteenth century. According to circumstances, they satisfied mainly either local needs, or an export sector, which sometimes extended to an enormous distance from the centres of production. Some concentrations of the textile industry followed: they can be seen spread over the map of Europe and they continued to increase, from the sixteenth to the eighteenth century. It is true that they sometimes declined, and sometimes there were re-groupings which are not always easy to define. In these centuries, nothing was more fluid than a textile industry, tied as it was to town and country labour even more than to workshops or raw materials. But the great problem of where the centres of the industry were situated and the relative importance of the different zones is not our particular concern. Or rather it would only be our problem if the history of prices could shed new light on it, but for the time being at any rate this is not the case. Our task is to bring a little order to the confusion of evidence by considering three aspects: firstly, raw materials; next, certain finished products which are better known than others; lastly, the outlines of possible distribution, which more detailed enquiry must necessarily improve.

The principal raw materials were wool, cotton, flax, and hemp. Our graph (Fig. 30) giving kilograms of raw material prices in grams of silver, classifies these materials according to their respective prices: at the very top come different types of wool; much lower down come cotton and flax (the latter level with cotton at the end of the seventeenth century); finally, at the bottom of the scale, hemp, together with the particular quality of flax known at Amsterdam as *paternoster* flax. Our graph is further restricted, of course, by the fact that it covers commodities of international trade—excluding silk, however—and takes no account of peasant products for home and local consumption. These latter are more than half-marginal to the money economy, and lie outside the range of our data.

Broadly, the series chosen for study follow the secular trend. The movement of Riga hemp on the Amsterdam market is noteworthy: at first sight it has the shape of series characteristic of continental Europe, apart from the fact that it apparently recovered early, by 1682. Frankfurt flax reflects well the price rise of the sixteenth century. Augsburg flax, curiously enough more expensive, reflects the sixteenth and seventeenth century trend, though after 1750 its movement is, at least apparently, abnormal. As for the eighteenth century price rise which marks the West, Riga hemp and Amsterdam *paternoster* flax and Smyrna cotton and Segovia (a quality wool) all follow the general recovery movement, though this, it is true, begins with a strong advance for Riga hemp.

As regards the relative disparity in prices of these various raw materials, we should note the unquestioned supremacy of Spanish wool. Only the fine wool of Danzig approaches it, and ordinary Danzig wool was at a much lower level. Prices of English wool were at a lower level still, according to the reports of John Houghton, but we should note that these referred to locally produced wools, or more or less local, unhindered by heavy transport costs. For the same reasons, a few prices from Amiens make a rather poor appearance when they are placed on the graph.

The series for finished products (Fig. 31), five in number, which divide into two groups, do not merit too much confidence. Reducing lengths of cloths to metres and the prices to grams of silver allows us to show clearly the difference which existed between the series on the one hand for English cloths which are high quality products, and on the other hand for example fustians—often with a linen warp and a cotton weft, less expensive to produce. English scarlet cloth sold at Frankfurt fell in price in the fifteenth and rose in the sixteenth century (a moderate rise, however, of 55 per cent between 1515–19 and 1600–4); but unfortunately the quotations disappear at the beginning of the eighteenth century. Was the *lunski* cloth—that is, London cloth—sold at Lwow the same as that sold at Frankfurt? We have no idea, but in any case the two series moved in very much the same way. In the seventeenth century they more or less follow the movement of the fine series for *kersies*: this shows a rapid fall from the peak in 1605–9 to the period of stability beginning with the year 1719.

Fustians show an upward trend at Frankfurt after 1519, and then a rapid rise up to the end of the sixteenth century, thereafter continuing at a very slow rate. But can we take the series as correct? For their part, the price of English kersies was stable in the eighteenth century. We have to admit that in bringing these figures together we have not mustered anything very substantial. Can we assume from them that textiles rose in price less rapidly than wheat, but fell as quickly? Even that is a great deal to claim.

This picture lacks a clear demonstration of the price movement of the main textiles, something which would be conclusive. None is available, nor in prospect at the moment. By contrast, we do know that the inter-relationship in the short run between food and textile prices was often contradictory. These contradictions represented crises and distortions. In any case, the short term view, which yields these conclusions, is different. The long term perspective is hidden from us. Moreover, in view of other fluctuations, it is doubtful if there was only *one* pattern of behaviour for textiles. Here again our information does not allow us to reach definite conclusions, but in any case nothing suggests that the behaviour was uniform—rather the contrary. Gunnar Mickwitz long ago drew attention to the double market at Riga in the sixteenth century: a market in high-priced foreign materials on the one hand, and at the same time cheap, local, country cloths. In his recent study, still un-published, Felipe Ruiz Martin rightly emphasizes the difference in the sixteenth century between Segovia, with its high quality cloths intended for export to the New World by way of Seville, and Cuenca, in La Mancha, with its industry destined for the local market. That is not to say that these average or mediocre products did not travel: they sometimes went far, as for example the famous peasant cloths from Aragon, the *cordelates*. But their market was very different from the luxury or semi-luxury cloths, a market with which we are familiar enough. In fact, it is the cheap popular products which are hard to discover, those coarse blue cottons from Aleppo and the surrounding villages which, as a document of 1687 tells us,[1] were imported through the Marseilles trade to be made up into clothing and sold to poor people in the south of France. Should we picture them as being like those blue housewives' aprons now outmoded; or the blue overalls of French workmen today? In the world of these cheaper materials anything made of wool was still a luxury. Did not Shakespeare put into Falstaff's mouth the scorn for men clad in dowlas or buckram? Moheau in the eighteenth century pointed out gladly enough that the wearing of coarse woollen cloth began to spread to the country districts of France: it had been very sparingly used up till then. And the decisive, revolutionary rise of the textile industries in the eighteenth, and still more in the nineteenth

[1] Archives Nationales (Paris), *Affaires Etrangères, Série B. III,* 235.

century, sprang in large measure from the increased mass consumption of their output alongside that of cotton.

The prices of these popular fabrics did not fluctuate in the same way as those of other cloths. At Milan it is possible to establish separate series for high and low grade materials between 1625 and 1660—the latter being fairly stable, the former by contrast falling markedly. In times of difficulty, such as a dearth or commercial crisis, the market demand tended to confine itself to essential purchases, preferably cheap in price. There were shifts along the indifference curves for given incomes. The better cloths had a higher income elasticity. Thus at Milan poor cloths maintained their price, but those of quality tended to fall in price. But again, these are short-term considerations.

Still, this factor tended also to have effects in the long term. Witold Kula is firmly persuaded that this is so, as he has stated in one of his best articles,[1] discussing some of the ideas of Henri Hauser. And it is true that in Poland—and no doubt in other countries as well—such luxury gradually became more accessible, relatively less expensive. What did become dearer, or rather did not become less expensive, were the necessities, the things that were indispensable. This point must be remembered in connexion with eighteenth century Europe, where luxury began to spread and established itself widely among the middle class.

In short, there are few reliable data among the available textile price series, which can throw light on the secular trend. But everywhere there are innumerable piles of documents awaiting study. Perhaps our data could be completed and refined; perhaps in addition to the problem of prices, another could be undertaken, that of the volume of production, about which so little is known. We will come back to this. Finally, it would be worthwhile to follow the prices of a few known articles across Europe, a Europe where the observer must everywhere become conscious of distances and the costs of transport. This would mean more persistent research to consider the flows of trade and identify precisely the various textiles. Then much more could be said towards solving the problem of prices in the most important industrial sector in Europe before 1750.

## (3) EUROPE BEFORE THE RISE OF HEAVY INDUSTRY

If there was unquestionably a textile industry before 1750, it was because there was a vast demand. Clothing was as great a necessity as housing and almost as great as food. Yet between the fifteenth and the eighteenth

[1] Witold Kula, 'Histoire et économie: la longue durée', *Annales: Economies, Sociétés, Civilisations* (1960), 306.

centuries, Europe still could command only limited capacity for heavy industry. It was only to be conceivable much later, after the coming of coal, of coke smelting, and of the use on a vast scale of iron, cast iron and steel: and this itself was hardly possible before the demand was created for steam engines, railway lines, iron and steel steamers, machines and their innumerable tools.

In 1750 that time had not yet come. We must not have too many illusions about mines, forges or foundries. They benefited from some wonderful technical achievements, dating from before Georg Agricola's time (such as the machines for pumping out water from the mine galleries; for hoisting; trip hammers for crushing ore; or machines driven by powerful water-wheels). But wood remained the basic material of these machines, and the transmission of energy was made as often by ropes as by chains: for example, the plaited lime-tree fibres (which resisted the corrosion of salt) in the Wieliczka salt mines near Krakow.

Nevertheless, mines and foundries did lead to heavy inputs of capital, big investments, and concentrations of labour. They were all spectacular achievements for the period, built up under the protection of fiercely defended monopolies, favoured by circumstances and by the state. The vast enterprises and achievements of a Jacob Fugger in the copper mines of the Tyrol and of Hungary are well known; the Copper Company, which Elizabeth created by letters patent in England in 1563, is equally so. Nor need we remind ourselves of the international history of Mansfeld copper, still less recall the success of Swedish copper in the seventeenth century. We should merely be summarizing the classic pages by John U. Nef suggesting the origins of a 'first industrial revolution' in England, the Low Countries, and Sweden: they became privileged countries at an early date.

But these achievements were limited in the context of European economic activity, and some of them—such as the operations in the mines of central Europe—prospered only for a short time. Forges, foundries and mines, apart from exceptional successes, very often remained on a small scale. This was the case with the forges in France from the sixteenth century onwards. Attempts to make a census of them have not yet succeeded. Industry was better served by copper and tin than by iron in its various forms. This was one of the results of the prodigious development of artillery. But in many instances, cannon were produced by methods of craftsmen, like church bells, at least up until the early sixteenth century, when the first cannons were bored out of a whole cylinder from a single bronze casting. In the eighteenth century, further improvements were effected in the techniques of boring.

Our data correspond, more or less, with this rapid outline. They give price differentials over Europe, and the movements in these industrial prices. Particular economic circumstances no doubt govern them, but they are not so apparent as in the case of food prices.

(a) *Iron* (Fig. 6): We have only three series here for iron prices; a fourth—the excellent series for Amiens—is unfortunately short.[1] All these series (with the exception of Lwow) fluctuate widely from the main trend: at Würzburg the highest point is reached in 1613–19, but there is a further recovery in 1680 (an early sign of the subsequent secular trend); Amiens conforms to the general trend in western Europe; at Amsterdam (the series for Swedish iron does not begin until 1609), prices were steady with a marked—though late—upswing after 1750. Lwow shows a very slow rise followed by a short decline and a level stretch to 1661, then finally after 1718 a marked rise which apparently brought its prices closer to the international market level.

(b) *Tin* (Fig. 6): Tin provides a good example. Despite the imperfect data, it is a classic case. Only English tin (mainly from Cornwall and Devon) apparently was on the market up to the end of the seventeenth century. We find it right through Europe and the whole Mediterranean; and the powerful Levant trade spread it still further. After 1695 the Dutch acquired treaty-rights from the king of Siam, which gave them the monopoly of Siamese tin. Tin from Asia, better in quality than English tin, flooded Europe. Its prices were quoted regularly at Amsterdam from 1722. The graphs we have chosen, calculated in grams of silver per quintal, make it possible to rank these prices (see Fig. 6). The price of tin in Danzig was the highest in the early eighteenth century but this was surpassed in the mid-century by the price of Asiatic tin in Amsterdam; English tin was the cheapest on the Amsterdam market. These prices were remarkably grouped together and showed little tendency to wide fluctuations, because of the competition and the restricted markets (which hardly expanded at all until the last years of the seventeenth century). Between 1480 and 1740 prices of English tin only doubled.

We have data on production and production costs for English tin. Though tin prices did not go up quickly on the European market, all the production costs by contrast—iron, ropes, and especially food for employees—rose more readily. Production as a result was impeded. From about 1450, output in England began to climb, to reach a level period about 1520, and then showed a tendency to decline. It advanced again only after 1667, and went on at a lively pace until 1690. After that the expansion was slow. Prices probably doubled, as we have said, from about 1480 to 1740, and production, for its part, went up five times during roughly the same period.

---

[1] P. Goubert, *op. cit.*; we should note the negative correlation *in the short run* between the prices of wheat and iron sold at Amiens. But the farmers were the main clients, chiefly for ploughshares.

(c) *Copper:* Copper, a rival to iron in everyday life, and a third metal for coinage, is of more interest to us. The graph (Fig. 6) treats these series in a special manner. One unit of silver has been compared with its equivalent (i) in gold (this is the bimetallic ratio); and (ii) in copper (from the reciprocal of the premium on silver in terms of copper). In addition, the price of copper in grams of silver is also given. It must be borne in mind that in this, every rise of the price of copper in terms of silver signifies a depreciation of copper. Thus there was a rapid devaluation of this metal in Würzburg after 1460. Was this early inflation peculiar to Germany, or not? Was it connected with the rise in prices in the second half of the fifteenth century? The question remains so far an open one. After this, with the beginning of the sixteenth century, we see a sharp rise in copper prices (we are referring still to the Würzburg data) and after that, if the England and Amsterdam series do not mislead us, there is a trend towards equilibrium and a steady market. Copper was then taking on the role of a monetary metal.

## (4) PRICE-INDEXES AND WAGES

This problem—historically speaking—is better documented than those previously discussed, but infinitely harder to explain. Wages are in reality prices of a very special kind: they recompense a man for his effort, his work, and in general they do so with parsimony. During the period under study, they were relatively inflexible, slow to move either up or down. This can be seen in the differentials between money wages and the cost of living, by converting money wages into real wages, either by using as a deflator the price of a unit of grain (which is the method preferred by Wilhelm Abel, although he is not alone in this), or by applying an index of the cost of living (E. H. Phelps Brown and Sheila Hopkins have calculated a composite unit of consumables).

No one method is perfect; nor when one is added to another do they cancel out each other's faults. A worker in the vineyards of the Paris area in 1510—to take a hypothetical case—earns 10 *livres tournois* for his work on one *arpent* of vineyard (about two and a half acres); but what is the money worth in the progressive price inflation, what could he buy with it? He managed, says Charles Verlinden,[1] facetiously but somewhat hastily; at a pinch, he preferred cheaper products, and in this way faced the rising cost of living. If not, continues our author, the wage-earner would surely have shuffled off this mortal coil. But that is precisely what happened, and with a regularity which cannot be ignored: economic and population crises were never far apart and often 'death settled the

---

[1] C. Verlinden, J. Craeybeckx, E. Scholliers, 'Mouvements des prix et des salaires en Belgique au XVIe siècle', *Annales: Economies, Sociétés, Civilisations* (1955).

score'. Suppose the man did survive, how did he 'manage'? How did he govern his appetite, his purchases, his economies, his extravagances, in such a way that his wages measured up to reality and reflected the true standard of living, sometimes rising, sometimes declining? Even to-day the cost of living is hard to measure; and where contemporaries hesitate, what can a historian do, with all the statistical apparatus on hand, in the face of imperfect information?

The sources for wage movements are not as easy to analyse, nor as helpful as those for prices. The data for wages are not always to be trusted. Even more, it is hard to separate money wages clearly from wages which are more than half lost in a barter economy. Few wages were paid completely in money. There is always the chance of finding only a small number of useful examples under this heading, generally from the building trade. But they were fortunate indeed, these builders and their labourers, if they had work all the year round: there were the long winter months when work was not so plentiful, and the recurrent crises which did not spare the building trade. Much, then, remains in doubt.

It is possible, as in the case of the vast Chioggia inquiry, to investigate the cost of various services, such as the cost of milling a certain quantity of wheat, or of transporting under comparable conditions a given quantity of grain to the municipal granary, the *Fondaco*. But here again it is exceptional to know about such services, and in every case there are attenuating circumstances. The relevance of the information depends, therefore, on the particular region, period, and manner in which the archives have been constituted. Although the wage rate is known, the number of days worked—and so the level of unemployment—is not. The change from the routine of life under the pre-industrial economies to machine-age regularity created difficult problems of adaptation, just because the notion of regular work to the clock was unknown or almost unknown up to that time. As well as lack of work and public holidays, we have to take into account unemployment because of the economic situation or because of the whims of the worker himself; or in more precise terms, the backward bending supply curve of labour. Then again, it is possible that more work was done at a time when real wage rates were falling than when they were rising; and this would imply that the real per capita incomes remained relatively unchanged. In that case, our simplified calculations no longer carry their initial weight. Certain sets of accounts leave much to be desired. Ömer Lutfi Barkan has just directed a careful study of the accounts for the building of the Suleiman mosque at Constantinople. There was an extraordinary movement of workers, of men signing on, leaving and returning to work again. Only a constant supply of new labour made it possible to fill the gaps and attempt to swell the numbers to meet peak demand.

On pay-day, Saturday, after the Friday day of rest, the numbers were at their highest; but from the start of the following new week they fell off and fresh hands had to be hired. Still, returns such as these make it difficult to evaluate the average earnings of labourers. And it is by no means clear how frequent was this intermittent system.

In the present state of our knowledge, moreover, it is not possible to measure a typical budget and average expenditures on housing, clothes and food, at a given moment in the past and in a given country. Obviously no wage-rate can be studied except in relation to the needs it has to satisfy or is supposed to satisfy. E. H. Phelps Brown and Sheila Hopkins settled this difficulty in an arbitrary fashion. They have constructed a model of individual consumption in England during the past seven centuries, with fixed weights (80 per cent for food, $7\frac{1}{2}$ per cent for fuel and light, and $12\frac{1}{2}$ per cent for textiles). This is clearly a simplification, since men's needs, even when reduced to an average, do vary, both in time and place. Simplifications, however, are necessary, and so let us suppose that this composite estimate of consumption patterns is valid, and that it can be divided up into equal daily expenditures (although it is harder to accept this second proposition than the first). When we make these concessions the 'basket of consumables' which they have adopted emerges clearly enough: the consumer fills it every day with his 'farinaceous' products (this includes various grains, bread and pulses), his meat and fish, dairy products and drink, oil for lighting, fuel, cloth, and so on. In reality, this basket, of which the exact contents are given in a footnote,[1] is in effect a way of working out a general index to follow the changes in the cost of living. As a method, it has the advantages and disadvantages of any general index.

And so, in this way, E. H. Phelps Brown and Sheila Hopkins have been able to complete a whole series of operations, establishing series for the

[1] The distribution of household expenditures adopted in the calculation were:

|  | per cent |
|---|---|
| Farinaceous | 20 |
| Meat and fish | 25 |
| Butter and cheese | $12\frac{1}{2}$ |
| Drink (malt, hops, sugar, tea) | $22\frac{1}{2}$ |
| Subtotal (food) | 80 |
| Fuel and light | $7\frac{1}{2}$ |
| Textiles | $12\frac{1}{2}$ |
|  | 100 |

E. H. Phelps Brown and Sheila Hopkins, 'Seven centuries of the prices of consumables, compared with builders' wage-rates', *Economica* (1956).

various items in the 'basket', and in turn by allotting a coefficient to each of the products, to work out a single series for the whole basket. They have then measured wages by reference to this cost-of-living series: thus with the basket at 100 on a basis set in 1451–75, the real wage in England in 1571 is represented by an index number of 63, or almost two-thirds of the original basket. In this way the wage series has been deflated by reference to a fixed unit of consumption. These explanations become much clearer in Fig. 32, which permits the reader to grasp the whole argument.

Using the estimates of E. H. Phelps Brown and Sheila Hopkins, we have before us a number of samples for Valencia, Vienna, Augsburg, Alsace and England. This group, unified in a single method, establishes beyond reasonable doubt the proposition that the real wage-rates of wage-earners deteriorated, when considered in relation to units of consumption. At a time when nominal salaries at least followed the movement of 'industrial' prices, real wages declined by more than 50 per cent, where-ever we take our measurements. With the second half of the seventeenth century began a slow improvement: was it more apparent than real? That is another question.

This collapse in real wage-rates formed the counterpart to the revolutionary rise in prices in the sixteenth century. The operation was fully paid for by the increased toil, hardships, impoverishment, and dejection of the majority. Contemporaries were often aware that the deterioration was taking place. In Normandy, the sieur de Gouberville wrote in his diary in 1560: 'In my father's time there was meat every day, food was plentiful, men drank wine as though it was water. But all that has quite changed to-day: everything is dear . . . the food of the most prosperous peasants is much poorer than the food which servants used to eat.'

But to return to the series offered by Phelps Brown. In England the deterioration went on up to 1610–14, after which, until the mid-eighteenth century, there was a slow, modest, but constant improve-ment. At Vienna, where there was a sudden fall in the second half of the sixteenth century, and then recovery, the decline was broadly the same as in England up to the early seventeenth century. Thereafter ensued a first, very slow, improvement but this hardly continued beyond the 1680's. These years were again followed by a sharp decline and again by recovery.

These statements would seem to call for comment and additional information: the task is too easy for unquestionable result. It is pertinent to point out that these judgments coincide closely with the results established by Wilhelm Abel. They relate to Göttingen, a small centre despite the reputation of its university, reproduce a line which covers four centuries and represent a woodcutter's work in making a bundle or 'Klafter' of firewood. Reducing the cost of this woodcutting to an equivalent quantity of rye cannot be accepted entirely without reservations, but the result nevertheless is practically the same as that of more complex indices. At all events, according to the Göttingen estimates of the woodcutter's labour and the price of rye, real wages fell rapidly between 1475 and 1580–90, then recovered, but rather slowly and erratically.

A final check, excellent despite its limitations in time and space, concerns Beauvais and the neighbouring region in the seventeenth century. Pierre Goubert's recent study[1] deals with a century-long 'phase B' from 1630 to 1730 (to use the expression of François Simiand, familiar at least to French economic historians). This means a century of recession. Prices which were rising in the previous century came to a halt one after another between 1630 and 1637 or at the latest in 1650, the complete fall not being manifest fully until after 1662. The slow, relentless shift of direction is not surprising during this exceptional century of progressively deteriorating prices; and with money wages relatively stable, nothing could prevent the persistent, but very slow rise in real wages. Here was something which *a priori* benefited the mass of wage-earners: in good years, with a drop in prices, the real standard of living tended to rise. But there were the other, critically hard years, the years of very high prices and very high mortality. The result, briefly, was that the short term movement often enough reversed what the long term movement was improving: this is what Pierre Goubert thinks for the region of Beauvais. René Baehrel is less pessimistic about Provence. It is impossible to settle the debate, about which there must be few illusions. From the late fifteenth century until well into the beginning of the eighteenth century, the standard of living in Europe progressively declined. It would be interesting to make a close analysis, where possible, of conditions before this time, in the fourteenth and fifteenth centuries. Broadly speaking, conditions then were better. Did this time constitute a golden age for labour, as so many excellent historians have claimed, before the repeated and violent upsets which we have noted without describing their full extent? If so, then the sixteenth and early seventeenth centuries were indeed a time of impoverishment.

We have now come to the end of this long section on the secular trend. However, we have only just begun to outline its vast movement: only wheat, the essential evidence, and gold and silver for coinage have been examined in detail. This restricts our inquiry and, from the outset, it limits our conclusions to those explanations which have been traditional.

[1] P. Goubert, *op. cit.*

Without thinking, as René Baehrel does, that money in all its forms is merely a cloak thrown over the real movement of the economy, let us agree with him that currency was not everything and that nominal prices alone have the right to be called real prices.

Reducing them to gold and silver alters them or rather makes them conform to a particular type of explanation. All the various sectors we have examined—gold, silver, wheat, wages, all of them to a greater or lesser degree difficult to follow over a long (or a short) period—are only valid when set once more in the context of other prices. They are measured in relation to economic realities: to commodities, and to the constant flow of incomes and expenditures. The revolutionary thesis of René Baehrel on Lower Provence from the sixteenth to the eighteenth century is setting out to establish this. Here, as yet, we cannot judge the validity of its conclusions, but there can be no doubt about the soundness of its objectives.

## III. *Short-term Fluctuations: Cycles and Cyclical Movements*

Along with the secular trend a series of shorter fluctuations is clearly distinguishable. They have their names and descriptions, their own particular identities. The longest, which has a span of about half a century, is called the Kondratieff cycle: and recently Gaston Imbert has devoted a fine book to this subject. Next, in descending order of periodicity, we come to the hypercycle of some twenty years; Ernest Labrousse's *intercycle* of fifteen years; the cycles which often carry the name of Clement Juglar, which vary from ten to eight years, rarely more and sometimes less; then the Kitchin cycle, which would be the shortest of all (about forty months) were it not for the seasonal movement, the smallest unit of the harvest year, which everyone persistently neglects once it has been mentioned.

Because the word *cycle* might be applied to the seasonal movement we should not be misled. The term designates a double movement, a rise and fall, with a peak in between, which in the strictest sense of the term is called a *crisis*; and although the word has a tendency in every language to be used loosely, we shall nevertheless attempt to narrow its application to 'crisis' in the present section. A crisis is a break, a discontinuity, a moment in time.

Clearly, the nomenclature of all these cycles is provisional and gradually will be revised. It is true that each of them has often found favour and disfavour amongst economists and historians. But we would tend to attribute this diversity of opinion not to any spirit of controversy, but to the fundamental diversity of the realities observed. From one economy to another—from the American to the European or from the modern to the pre-industrial and to the time-honoured agricultural economy—could the concept of a cycle appear in the same form? One or other dominates, stands out with greater clarity, according to the period observed; they are often superimposed ... and then we have series of imperfect cycles. Their sequence differs according to whether the secular movement is rising or falling. It also differs according to whether the cycles balance out in the direction of the secular trend or of a long movement of the Kondratieff type. In short, depending on circumstances, this and that cycle may either fade out or become prominent. Economic conditions do not automatically arrange cycles in such a way that two or three Kitchin cycles make a Juglar; two Juglars a hypercycle; and two hypercycles a Kondratieff ... Any such combination appears to lie outside actual experience.

The interplay of cycles amongst themselves and within the secular trend determines a series of actions and reactions, which upset individual movements completely, often changing their duration. In the case of France, the intercycle of Ernest Labrousse from 1778 to 1791, shows how two cycles of varying amplitude could become partly joined, in such a way that half of one was incorporated into the general movement of the other.

But, however irregular they may be, these cycles combine to form a rhythm which is *broadly* periodic or recurrent, as it were the respiration of economic activity. Economists tend to agree on this basic point: whence the increasing attention to mathematical or quasi-mathematical formulations of history, in keeping with economics and economic planning.

In the light of these considerations, a series of tests has been carried out on the monthly grain prices in Udine from 1586 to 1796, as part of the study already mentioned, and in collaboration with the computer centre of the Compagnie des Machines Bull. The calculations by the computers permitted a number of complex operations, in order to isolate the periodicities in serial correlations. The resulting coefficients are given in Fig. 18, together with a minimum of explanation.[1] But the

[1] The statistical significance of the serial correlation of monthly wheat and maize prices at Udine (1586–1797) falls rapidly, but less rapidly in the case of maize (below 0·5 after two years) than of wheat (below 0·5 after one year). The cyclical movement, however, was more clearly marked in the case of the latter. One possible explanation of this is that wheat was a superior good, with a higher income elasticity and a larger outlet in foreign trade. Maize, on the other hand, tended to become increasingly a staple article of food during the period under study. After a relatively stable period (up to a periodicity of 21 years), the coefficients for both series again fall. In this, the approximate coincidence with the hypercycle, or with the long building-cycle must not yet be ruled out of discussion. The

general result is clear: over two centuries there was apparently a succession of cycles and their repetitions. J. Helferich had already suggested this in his pioneer work in 1843.

The rhythms and recurrences at varying intervals interested Lord Beveridge in his early studies on prices. His calculations revealed the reappearance every fifteen years of very curiously similar phenomena. He had a glimpse of the cyclical wave-movement in the more distant past. More recently Pierre Goubert concerned himself with these repetitions, which brought back the good times as well as the bad through history. There was the sombre series, for example, of harvest failures every thirty years at Beauvais—in 1597, 1630, 1661, 1691–3, 1725. . . . 'Does this suggest solar cycles?' he asks, alluding to sunspot theories, favoured a century ago by Stanley Jevons, but until more recently suspect in academic analysis. Why should we not consider the possible influence of solar cycles on agricultural life (more prone, by its nature to

coefficients, nevertheless, are too low to permit exact explanations. The relevant data for wheat and maize at yearly intervals are:

| Time-periods in months | Coefficients of Correlation | | Time periods in months | Coefficients of Correlation | |
|---|---|---|---|---|---|
| | Wheat | Maize | | Wheat | Maize |
| 1 | 0·96 | 0·97 | 361 | 0·12 | 0·20 |
| 13 | 0·53 | 0·70 | 373 | 0·13 | 0·20 |
| 25 | 0·33 | 0·48 | 385 | 0·11 | 0·14 |
| 37 | 0·32 | 0·38 | 397 | 0·17 | 0·10 |
| 49 | 0·33 | 0·35 | 409 | 0·13 | 0·11 |
| 61 | 0·32 | 0·36 | 421 | 0·08 | 0·11 |
| 73 | 0·33 | 0·39 | 433 | 0·06 | 0·07 |
| 85 | 0·36 | 0·40 | 445 | 0·05 | 0·07 |
| 97 | 0·39 | 0·32 | 457 | 0·04 | 0·03 |
| 109 | 0·29 | 0·19 | 469 | −0·01 | −0·03 |
| 121 | 0·30 | 0·18 | 481 | −0·08 | −0·06 |
| 133 | 0·30 | 0·21 | 493 | 0·05 | −0·03 |
| 145 | 0·27 | 0·20 | 505 | 0·13 | −0·01 |
| 157 | 0·24 | 0·21 | 517 | 0·10 | −0·03 |
| 169 | 0·34 | 0·26 | 529 | 0·13 | −0·03 |
| 181 | 0·33 | 0·29 | 541 | 0·12 | −0·05 |
| 193 | 0·28 | 0·27 | 553 | 0·08 | −0·04 |
| 205 | 0·25 | 0·24 | 565 | 0·04 | −0·01 |
| 217 | 0·30 | 0·24 | 577 | 0·01 | 0·05 |
| 229 | 0·34 | 0·29 | 589 | 0·06 | 0·07 |
| 241 | 0·33 | 0·31 | 601 | 0·05 | −0·01 |
| 253 | 0·34 | 0·33 | 613 | −0·05 | −0·06 |
| 265 | 0·29 | 0·31 | 625 | −0·06 | −0·06 |
| 277 | 0·26 | 0·27 | 637 | −0·01 | −0·04 |
| 289 | 0·26 | 0·20 | 649 | 0·02 | −0·04 |
| 301 | 0·24 | 0·15 | 661 | 0·04 | −0·04 |
| 313 | 0·20 | 0·13 | 673 | 0·03 | −0·03 |
| 325 | 0·18 | 0·16 | 685 | −0·03 | −0·03 |
| 337 | 0·12 | 0·17 | 697 | −0·002 | −0·06 |
| 349 | 0·13 | 0·18 | 709 | −0·01 | −0·09 |
| | | | 721 | −0·06 | −0·12 |

such waves than industrial activity), or at least be willing to entertain the idea?

## (1) THE SEASONAL MOVEMENT

Let us begin with the smallest of the cyclical movements. Statisticians, economists and historians are in the habit of eliminating the seasonal movement, since it is predictable. When observations are made, it is a factor more or less taken as given. In 1843, the economist Wilhelm Roscher wrote that 'Cereal prices (whatever the year) are lowest in October, November and December. They gradually rise in spring, reaching their highest point in April, May, June and July.' It was only in the nineteenth century that second harvests were to reach the European market from the Argentine, Chile, and Australia, furnished by the reversed seasons in the southern hemisphere. In this present inquiry which by definition does not go beyond the middle of the eighteenth century, it is possible to discard this monotonous price variation of grain and other agricultural products, and assume that the seasonal movement was always incorporated in the much wider cyclical movements.

For all that, the seasonal movement exists. Every harvest in Udine (from wheat to rye, maize and other cereals, as well as to pulses) meant an abrupt change in prices. And that had an urgency and importance for people whose lives followed the pattern and routine of short intervals of time, whether or not the changes in price were quickly compensated. When there are daily, weekly or monthly quotations, the seasonal movement moreover assumes a character of some importance. An example of this movement can be seen at Udine in the years from 1676 to 1683, when studied with this matter only in mind (see Fig. 13) which shows something of the rhythm frequently encountered. The conse-quences can be imagined for the vast majority of the poor in exceptional times of dearth, when they were obliged to buy from day to day and to bear the full brunt of the fluctuations which made the price of wheat in the mid-seventeenth century change in a matter of months from 14·30 to 32 lire.

The seasonal movement is only completely clearly seen when, as at Chioggia, we can follow the concomitant movement of quantities: those of the wealthy, who kept themselves posted from wintertime onwards about the prospects of the coming harvest, and also those of the government, maintained so as to prevent speculative over-buying and prepare against times of famine.

It will be said, and rightly, that the example chosen is of a particular seasonal movement. There were more moderate periods: everything depends on the basic cycle, which formed its underlying rhythm.

## (2) WERE THERE KITCHIN CYCLES?

The Kitchin cycle is perhaps solely and exclusively a cycle which affects our contemporary economy, and characteristic particularly of the American economy. It appears to have arrived recently from the New World, in this twentieth century, later even than the Colorado beetle. Further, it is sometimes said that this forty-month cycle is a third of the ten-year solar cycle to which some credence is now being given, and that in particular it reflects the movement of commodities.

However, it is possible to reconsider these limitations. In the monthly series at our disposal we have looked to see if a short-term rhythm, of the type of a Kitchin cycle, could be discerned. This would not be the first attempt, however, for Pierre Chaunu has unambiguously stated that he found Kitchin cycles in the series for the transatlantic trade of Seville in the sixteenth century. The Udine series, when studied for serial correlations, shows periodic repetitions; and direct observation of the curve easily allows us to distinguish *during certain periods* successions of short cycles, spread over three or four years.[1] This always seems an accidental, episodic matter, obliterated as soon as the other movements sweep over it. At the very most we would deduce from our observations that the short Kitchin cycle may be found especially in periods of relative calm. As soon as the longer fluctuations become more significant (and they could become extremely violent) the shorter variations disappear almost completely. In the fifteenth century, in the data available for Diksmuide (Dixmude) and possibly also for Chioggia, short term fluctuations reveal themselves clearly enough. The same applied to the series for Udine after 1628, in which a series of small waves can be observed.

Such elusive appearances in the midst of our problematic movements are certainly of economic interest. For the historian the Kitchin cycle is intermittent in its manifestation, less rich in consequences than the long building cycle, or the Juglar cycle, of which the fluctuations have attracted the almost exclusive attention of historians.

## (3) JUGLAR'S CYCLE, LABROUSSE'S INTERCYCLE, BAEHREL'S QUADRUPLE CYCLE, KONDRATIEFF'S CYCLE

The outstanding and 'structural' repetition in the price series—particularly when we have continuous monthly quotations at our disposal (which are not indispensable but highly desirable)—is the incidence of intradecennial cycles. These are equivalent to two or three Kitchin cycles, and all are apparently less than ten years in length.

[1] In the series for Udine, by averaging the intervals, in spite of bad interference, it is possible to deduce a periodicity of slightly less than 39 months.

Pierre Chaunu refers to trade cycles at Seville (1500–1650), Juglar cycles of eleven years, but it should be noted here that it is a question of maritime trade and not of price cycles. An arithmetical average of the duration of these cycles, combining the data of the series for Paris, Beauvais, Lower Provence, Udine and Siena (see the following table) gives a mean figure of about 7½ years.

Table 36. *Arithmetical Average of the Duration of Trade Cycles*

| Place | From | To | No. of periods | Average |
|---|---|---|---|---|
| Aix (R. Baehrel) | 1588 | 1733 | 18 | 8·06 |
| Beauvais (P. Goubert) | 1588–9 | 1727–8 | 20 | 6·95 |
| Paris (H. Hauser and J. Meuvret) | 1588 | 1728 | 17 | 8·24 |
| Siena (G. Parenti) | 1588 | 1727 | 19 | 7·31 |
| Udine (R. Romano, F. C. Spooner, U. Tucci) | 1588 | 1728 | 19 | 7·36 |
| | | | Average: | 7·58 |

This table is given not to fix a scale—for is there one single scale?—but rather to indicate an order of magnitude.

How best can these cycles be measured, what unit should be chosen? The prudent—like Pierre Goubert—stick to the Juglar cycle and to it alone, just once or twice suggesting longer spans, or groups of cycles, which amounts to the same thing. Others have thought that the waves follow on one after another, either the one in conjunction or perhaps the other running in the opposite direction; and that their movement was cumulative. Imagine a faintly marked cycle, though with a long rise and then a short, unstressed fall, followed by a cycle with a long, accentuated rise. It would be tempting to add the whole of our first cycle to the rise of the second as far as the latter's crisis point: the peak of the whole movement.

But a practical example is more demonstrative than a generalization: let us examine the price series for wheat in Paris (see Fig. 12). It shows a classic instance of a Labrousse intercycle. From an index number of 420 (using as base 1610–16 = 100) which is the high point of the cycle, the prices fall to a minimum of 173 in 1593–4. Then let us attach to this the subsequent cycle: this culminates in 1596–7 at a level of about 201, and then finishes in 1601–2 at 79. Thus over eleven years, there is an intercycle marked by a fall in prices, with only a very slight interruption about 1595–7. There is no doubt that these eleven years have a certain unity, from the material point of view. Such a unit or period, like that in the 1778–91 intercycle on which Ernest Labrousse based his classic work, has the advantage of being sensitive to the concordant effects of repetitions. It enlarges the field of cycle analysis and makes it represent relays of either rises or declines. This is not so much a dexterous form of statistical analysis, but rather a way of observing the distortion of the cycle by more powerful and persistent influences.

But clearly it is possible to go beyond this wider approach. In our earlier definition, we could have annexed to the intercycle—the 'Labrousse' cycle of 1590–1602—the upswing of the 1588–93 cycle, and, in this way, combined two cycles: the one soaring (1588–93) and the other almost without impetus (1593–1602) and practically inert. Needless to say, in actual fact it would be a poor combination. The fourteen year long cycle (the double cycle) would not really be a compartment; it would have little interest for an historian in search of a single unit or a single period, as would have been said not long ago. For us there is an operating hypercycle (so called to distinguish the *long cycle* from the Kondratieff cycle) only when two successive cycles are linked without a long break and merge or almost merge into a single movement. At all events, they must be complementary and so replace the rhythm of the normal cycle with one long rhythm. Even so there will be little advantage in grouping successive cycles in pairs. If we compare Gaston Imbert's series for France in the seventeenth century with that of Pierre Goubert for Beauvais, it is apparent that the first with its hypercycles does not offer a chronology which appeals to an historian in search of an explanation.

The same cannot be said, however, of the double hypercycle, or better still the quadruple cycle, of René Baehrel. With the rigorous statistical analysis at his command, René Baehrel has deliberately simplified his problems by setting out from the basis of nominal prices; he has calculated linear regressions representing the long term trend. This method, justifiable in itself, joins several cycles together each time, depending on whether they have a tendency to rise, to stagnate or to fall. At once we are faced with thirty-year phases. These regularly group four ordinary cycles together. We should note carefully that these cycles are logically grouped: for, being all of the same trend, their fluctuations have the tendency to behave alike. They offer us a unit of time, taken in wide slices out of economic activity. Thus for Lower Provence the 1594–1625 phase (a downswing) groups four cycles: 1594–1602; 1602–10; 1610–17; 1617–25. The same applies to the following phases: 1625–55 (an upswing), 1655–89 (a downswing), 1689–1725 (an upswing).

Nor is this regularity the result of some statistical trick, but of simple addition. There are groups of cycles, set in the same direction. That is why René Baehrel's explanation ties in with that of Ernest Labrousse.

To find the historical explanation we must go beyond the cycle. François Simiand had already undertaken this, with his 'A phases' and 'B phases': René Baehrel purposely rediscovered them and also, for good measure, revived the concept of the Kondratieff cycle itself. Thirty years' rise, then thirty years' fall: there can be no mistake about it, it clearly conforms to the pattern of the Kondratieff movement. Kondratieff observed these double movements through the nineteenth century. René Baehrel, setting out from direct observation of the data, found that they existed from the beginning of the sixteenth century, and no doubt they existed earlier than that. Does not an analogous movement from 1339–89 show itself in Gaston Imbert's graphs, or from 1420–70 in France, which he also observed?

### (4) CYCLICAL AND EXTRA-CYCLICAL EXPLANATIONS

And so there are sequences of cycles, so many possible compartments, or frameworks of explanation. But interpreting the movement of the secular trend is already a likely subject for argument. When it comes to short or long cycles, the disputes can be endless, not to mention the insoluble problem of knowing whether the shorter cycles determine the longer, or vice versa. Short or long, the cycles offer the temptation that, all too readily, they can be made to fit the train of 'events': they can insinuate themselves into political, social or economic history, whether as causes or as effects.

No economic study, whether political, social or demographic, should be conceivable without recourse to the movement of prices, with its long and short cycles. But to bring two movements closer together is not necessarily to explain each in turn by means of the other. In any case, any explanation of a cyclical movement by some *local* phenomenon should only be accepted after verification that there is a clear difference between the local movement and the situation in Europe as a whole. To speak of a 'cycle of the League' or a 'cycle of the Fronde', for example, when France is in question, would be to suppose that price fluctuations over the period are to be explained entirely by the political situation in France. Yet during the Fronde, prices went up elsewhere in Europe, and much more sharply in Italy or in Poland than in France.

Does war conveniently provide the eternal 'cause' at work? Gaston Imbert thinks that war is responsible for regular inflations, such as at the time of Agincourt or of Rocroy. Every serious war at once opens the door to reconstruction and to 'building booms'. So it would seem that war leads the way, *bellum omnium pater*, as has often been said. This neglects the possibility that war may as easily be caused by the cycles as the cause of them. Sometimes war may even stand right outside the play of cycles. René Baehrel's detailed study favours this last thesis, in the matter of war and prices in Provence in the seventeenth and eighteenth centuries.

Lastly, if a price cycle is always inadequately accounted for by local factors, it is even less to be explained when isolated in time. It reaches out to the cycle and cycles which went before, and to those which follow.

What is needed is both a comparative cyclical study of the whole of Europe, and then a typology of cycles. Even more desirable is a typology of the sequences or processions of cycles. There is every reason to further the work initiated by Ernest Labrousse or René Baehrel, and for continuing to refer back to the pioneer work of François Simiand.

### (5) THE WHOLE OF EUROPE: IN THE TIME OF THE FRONDE AND OF OLIVER CROMWELL

Europe, so varied in its structures and in the way it has evolved through the ages, has a considerable degree of unity in so far as the international economy is concerned. It appears that we must accept the authoritative, but justifiable views of Ernest Labrousse, Pierre Chaunu and René Baehrel, and talk of *the* economic rhythm (or *Konjunktur* as Ernst Wagemann would say) as against *structures*. Everything was not co-ordinated from one end of Europe to the other by a single command, but rather by each successive impulse in this economic rhythm, heavily dependent as it was at that time on agricultural production. Such impulses quickly reverberated through Europe, although each European movement reacted in a different way with the history and special structure of each region. In consequence, although a rough approximation to the secular trend can be made, the economic activity in Europe requires more exact empirical evidence. It is possible to examine the different problems as Ernest Labrousse has done, by using monthly quotations, and even by preference weekly or daily figures. Progress in scientific knowledge of this type, often if not always, depends on greater precision in the quantities measured. In the case of Europe, cyclical fluctuations are derived from exact measurement.

We can demonstrate this briefly in connection with the cyclical movements which disturb the whole life of Europe towards the middle of the seventeenth century, at the time of the Fronde in France and of Oliver Cromwell in England. No *a priori* reason led us to choose this excellent example: there are others just as revealing. But it has the advantage of lending itself to an exact comparative analysis. Imagine that Europe, with its price differentials, was a sea in motion with waves and under-currents. In the mid-seventeenth century some of these waves and under-currents can be measured exactly, assessing and comparing their relative sizes and strengths. The calendar below shows this in greater detail:

Table 37. *Calendar showing Cyclical Price Movements in Europe*

| Cycle | First Minimum | | | First Maximum | | | Second Minimum | | | Second Maximum | | | Third Minimum | | | Third Maximum | | | Fourth Minimum | | |
|---|---|---|---|---|---|---|---|---|---|---|---|---|---|---|---|---|---|---|---|---|---|
| | Year | Qtr. | Per-centage | Year | Qtr. | Per-centage | Year | Qtr. | Per-centage | Year | Qtr. | Per-centage | Year | Qtr. | Per-centage | Year | Qtr. | Per-centage | Year | Qtr. | Per-centage |
| Beauvais | 1640 | 1 | 100 | 1643 | 2 | 190·13 | 1646 | 2 | 83·20 | 1650 | 1 | 296·80 | 1650 | 4 | 185·87 | 1652 | 2 | 274·13 | 1657 | 1 | 100 |
| Paris | 1639 | 4 | 100 | 1643 | 2 | 298·80 | 1646 | 2 | 88·10 | 1649 | 4 | 285·10 | 1650 | 4 | 191·75 | 1652 | 3 | 305·34 | 1657 | 1 | 107·40 |
| Rozay-en-Brie | 1640 | 1 | 100 | 1643 | 4 | 236·11 | 1646 | 3 | 94·44 | 1649 | 4 | 347·22 | 1650 | 4 | 236·11 | 1651 | 4 | 361·11 | 1657 | 1 | 114·58 |
| Siena | 1640 | 2 | 100 | 1644 | 2 | 207·86 | 1645 | 1 | 181·78 | 1649 | 2 | 436·61 | 1651 | 4 | 183·71 | 1653 | 2 | 331·09 | 1660 | 1 | 118·95 |
| Udine | 1640 | 3 | 100 | 1643 | 3 | 233·77 | 1646 | 3 | 148·77 | 1650 | 2 | 507·50 | 1654 | 3 | 153·82 | 1656 | 4 | 265·37 | 1659 | 3 | 136·51 |
| Lwow (oats) | 1641 | 1 | 100 | 1642 | 3 | 191·67 | 1643 | 1 | 122·22 | 1651 | 3 | 1,051·11 | 1655 | 1 | 333·33 | 1657 | 3 | 916·67 | 1659 | 1 | 263·89 |

The combined map and graph (in Fig. 17) has been designed to emphasize the sequence of three cycles between 1640 and 1660 throughout Europe as a *whole*, and that, in reality, these phenomena transcend local explanations. We may add that the chronological differences between the various minima and maxima of these fluctuations are relatively slight. It would be extremely interesting to measure these differences exactly—sometimes lagging behind the times, at other times ahead of the average. The direction of these cyclical movements, if such exists, is a question that can be established only when more progress has been made in our understanding of these rhythms, which were so important to both the material and the non-material lives of men. In any case, it is clear that the existence of an overall economic rhythm can be substantiated from a broad conspectus of history. It was certainly European, and perhaps even encompassed the world.

### (6) CYCLES IN SEQUENCE BUT DIFFERENT ONE FROM ANOTHER

The rigorous linear movements of René Baehrel have already pointed to a possible solution: cycles are grouped in the general trend. Some rise in the same direction: these can be grouped by an ascending line. Others are receding, so these should be joined by a single descending line. We have said already how these periods conform to the analysis by Kondratieff of the more recent past. This is something more than a single estimate, or a flight of the imagination. In reality, the Kondratieff cycle is the linkage between the rhythm of the economy and the secular trend, between economic activities and economic structures. René Baehrel attempted to demonstrate a cumulative movement built from local movements; and he was drawn inevitably into using this long measure of general economic activity.

But this is not the only chronological approach to recurrent cyclical movements. The pioneer studies by Jenny Griziotti-Kretschmann and Marie Kerhuel, both published in 1935, and the schematic study by Edward R. Dewey and Edwin Dakin are works by economists which unfortunately historians have largely neglected. According to these authors there are different types of cycles, depending on rising or falling periods in the secular trends: some moderate, others violent. Thus the trend of price-rise in Spain which lasted the whole of the sixteenth century, was accompanied by relatively calm cycles; but the fall in prices in the seventeenth century, by contrast, inaugurated a series of violent cycles. To give some idea of the violence possible in the intra-decennial cycles let us remember that at Udine in the seventeenth century we can point to a 500 per cent rise within some critical movements, accompanied by dearth. The short term rise in prices at this time was comparable with that in the trend *during almost the whole of the sixteenth century.*

Pierre Goubert in turn noted these alternating periods of calm and violent cycles. He gives no explanation of them, and under the circumstances a firm solution is not to be expected. Many more studies of long series with preferably monthly, or at least quarterly data, such as those for Udine or for Beauvais would have to be made, and various intercomparisons offered. As can be seen from the graph of cycles between 1640 and 1660 (see Fig. 17), cyclical movements vary in amplitude according to place and period. However, short of firm explanations, we may risk some provisional conclusions. Thus, wide cyclical fluctuations are not mere extrapolations of the secular inflation or recession. For example, at Beauvais, the phases of calm and violent cycles are far from being arranged according to the movement of the trend. Nor does there seem to be any clearer connection with thirty-year phases. Nor, even does Marie Kerhuel's suggestion that cyclical movements are the natural accompaniment of return periods in the trend—what we would call 'hinge' periods—seem any more evident, although this explanation does frequently correspond with observable phenomena. Is there still another hypothesis to be put forward, one that takes account of the known facts and of possible advances in research? It is that perhaps the stocks of bullion and currency in circulation in certain places and at certain times were inadequate. Where gold and silver coins were sound and of true weight, and there was no shortage of 'black' money, prices generally were higher; but—other things being equal, of course—the cyclical reactions were less likely to be unrestrained. It was the relative scarcity of precious metals that would seem to have made fluctuations more dramatic.

But the correctness or falseness of this statement awaits the decision of further study. In such controversies, no single declaration is ever final. But two remarks follow from what we have tried to put forward: (1) the importance of widening the whole scope of inquiry into economic rhythms and fluctuations in order to evaluate the structures; and (2) the need for new, precise and wide-ranging computations.

An example of this can be found in England which has excellent series of prices and where admirable work has been done in this field. But the materials and interpretations are either old, or not yet completely published. So far as possible everything must be done again, or completed by working down to time units smaller than the annual data, to have a firm grasp of the general economic situation and of all that was dependent, permanent or semi-permanent in the English past. The outline of English economic development given by our graphs is in fact only approximate. This is one more reason for paying tribute to Lord

Beveridge, who until the last strove to complete his work long since begun.

# IV. *Conclusions and a Summary of Explanations*

The moment has come for conclusions. But the debate must remain largely open. The possible theories and explanations arising out of the history of prices have merely attempted to grasp a reality which is intractable. It is not so much a question of presenting a new theory, as of summing up what has been said and indicating what requires further investigation.

## (1) THE QUANTITY THEORY OF MONEY

The explanations lead us directly to the quantity theory of money. This theory, clearly expressed in the Irving Fisher equation of exchange, maintains that, in conditions of equilibrium, changes in prices are a function of changes in the supply of money. It may also be said that Earl J. Hamilton, in his first articles on prices in Andalusia, can justly claim to have put the correctness of the definition to the test.

Accepting for the moment the quantity theory of money as an operating definition, how far does it go to meet the case? At the outset, the basic essentials are (1) a general movement of prices in western Europe—and to simplify the argument we can restrict this to the secular trend in the sixteenth century—roughly from the close of the fifteenth century to the early seventeenth century; and (2) an influx of precious metals measured either according to the series collated by Earl J. Hamilton, or by the trade statistics of Huguette and Pierre Chaunu, or again by the output of silver from the mines of Potosi in Peru. The last soared after the application of the amalgamation process (a Schumpeterian 'innovation'), as has been shown by the data published by Moreira Paz y Soldan. Broadly the grouped movements in (1) and (2) follow each other when compared graphically (see Figs. 33 and 34).

But the correlation is not necessarily convincing. Luigi Einaudi,[1]

[1] In giving judgement on the Malestroit-Bodin controversy in France, President Luigi Einaudi favoured neither side. Using the data published by Earl J. Hamilton and Paul Raveau for the period 1471–2 to 1590–8, he came to the following conclusion: the price index during this period (estimated in money of account) rose from 100 to 627·5. In this inflation, 35·47% could be attributed to the devaluation of the *livre tournois* (that is 222·6% of the price rise); and 64·53% of the inflation (or 404·9% of the price rise) to other causes, including the effects of precious metals from America. Of course, there is no need to suppose that Einaudi's calculations are exactly correct. But the method is prudent (for, he says, 'let us suppose that only the devaluation of the livre tournois was effective, then that only the mass of bullion from America was effective . . .'). Each factor in turn has been tested for its effect.

Carlo Cipolla and François Simiand have denied that the correlation was positive and approached unity. Other factors have their influence: for example, the depreciation of the moneys of account, which was effective during the whole period under consideration; the investments required for the reconstruction of Italy after the long wars finally ended by the peace of Cateau Cambrésis (1–3 April 1559); and the important demographic factors.

Then again it must be shown whether or not the various devaluations and the pervasive demographic upswings were as much the result of price inflation as the cause of them, and whether the increases in the output of bullion were not an outcome—as indeed we are prepared to believe—of the expansion in the level of economic activity, of a quickening in its tempo, beginning before the sixteenth century. In this composition of general conclusions, there must be inevitably two aspects to every explanation, cause becoming effect, and effect cause.

After the brief but indecisive intervention of Carlo Cipolla and the data assembled by Luigi Einaudi, it is now pertinent to reverse the process of investigation. In other words, let us suppose that the sudden increase of precious metals was the only factor in the rise in prices, even though in reality this was not necessarily the case. It is then possible to carry out two operations: (1) let us examine the series of the average price of wheat in Europe, calculated first in grams of gold and then in grams of silver, again assuming for the moment that these calculations and graphs (see Fig. 11) *keep within the bounds of prudence* and record faithfully the general movement of prices. Let us also assume within the framework of this 'model' that the equivalent of the increase in the stock of gold is added to the increase in the stock of silver (that is, that the increase in the stock of precious metals is calculated in terms of silver). And finally let us note that the inflation of prices in terms of bullion stopped about 1600 in the case of gold and about 1640 in the case of silver. These 'turning-points' for gold and silver are naturally open to reservations and discussions, but they do point to a fundamental alteration about which there can be little doubt. (2) Without wishing to bring into discussion the vast explanation of Gustav Cassel or his followers, it is possible to examine—within the framework of the inflation of the sixteenth century—both the additions to the stocks of precious metals by the imports from America, and the stocks already existing before 1500. In theory at least, disregarding for the moment the questions of changes in the level of unemployment, it is probable that the price level would remain stable only if there were a steady increase in the supply of money. This varies, of course, according to the level of economic activity (3 per cent was assumed to be an acceptable coefficient for the European economy about the middle of the nineteenth century).

But there is little to assure us that this theory is applicable to the conditions of the sixteenth century. If it does, we should still need to know the rate of interest, the size of the monetary stocks at the outset, and the average velocity of circulation by which its effective volume was increased.

Let us accept the fact that an order of magnitude always offers a useful point of reference, and that an argument based on statistical data is a way of reasoning which, even when the figures remain open to question, is an attractive procedure. Two or three ways of calculating the aggregate money supply are open to us.

(a) *First method:* An old study by W. Jacob, *An Historical Inquiry into the Production and Consumption of Precious Metals* (1830), rightly discredited among statisticians, suggests a method which has some excellent features. The stock of gold and silver in circulation in Europe in 1809 was estimated in terms of silver to be 47,426 tons. If we deduct from this total the amounts produced in the preceding years we will arrive at the earlier stock by extrapolation into the past: on condition, as Jacob reminds us, that we take into account the drain of precious metals from Europe, as well as the consumption for industrial uses, and a certain amount lost through wear: certainly all this could not be more reasonable. But in order to have an impeccable series of calculations the base figure at the start must have been exactly measured. There is no evidence that it was so, rather the opposite. At the end of his calculations W. Jacob arrived at a stock (all converted into silver) of only 4,230 tons at about 1500. What is more, the production figures used for the successive subtractions are much below Soetbeer's estimates (1895); and they are greatly inferior to those of W. Lexis (1897). And these latter in turn are less than the estimates of Clarence Haring (1915) and more particularly of Earl J. Hamilton (1928–34). If we accept the base figure of 1809 as reliable, and ourselves make the necessary subtractions on the base of the evidence now available, we arrive at less than zero for the beginning of the sixteenth century: and the difference is even greater if the yearly exports, and non-monetary uses are taken into account.

(b) *Second method:* Is there any foundation for believing, as W. Lexis does for his calculations of the money supply in Russia in the eighteenth century, that the volume in circulation can be estimated roughly as the total coinage for the preceding thirty years from the date in question? The total money coined in France during the great recoinages between 1631 and 1660 amounts to 267,734,871 *livres tournois*, or at a round figure of 2,259 tons of *silver* (including the equivalent of the gold coinage in silver). As France had about sixteen million inhabitants at that time that would be equal to a *per capita* supply of money of 16·73 *livres tournois*, or if preferred 141·22 grams of silver. Supposing that Europe had ten times the population of France and that France represented the average, then the stock of metal in 1660 would be 22,590 tons of bullion. This is a high estimate. Yet, if we deduct from that total the known or approximate output of precious metals (at least 181 tons of gold and 16,886 tons of silver reached Seville between 1500 and 1650) we arrive once more at a very low level for 1500, especially when—in accordance with the method of W. Jacob—we take into account the exports, wear and non-monetary uses of precious metals. So, once again, our investigation reaches an unsatisfactory conclusion.

(c) *Third method:* This may improve on the foregoing, or at least prove more successful: we have the two masses of precious metals in Europe, one gold and the other silver. Between them is a price relationship, the familiar bimetallic ratio by which the effective values of the two masses *balance each other*. Now, we know that this ratio changed: in 1500 the average in Europe was about 10·5 to 1; and in 1660 about 14·5 to 1. Without taking into account either European production or the contributions from Asia and Africa, the exports, or the exports through the Baltic and the Levant, or again the losses through wear and hoarding, let us assume that the two masses increased only by what flowed in from America. This was certainly the predominant portion (roughly 181 tons of gold and 16,000 tons of silver between 1500 and 1650, according to the data of Earl J. Hamilton). Suppose, further, that we represent the stock of gold in 1500 (in tons) by $x$ and that of silver by $y$, then we arrive at the two following equations:

$$\text{in 1500} \quad 10\cdot5\,x = y$$
$$\text{in 1660} \quad 14\cdot5\,(x + 181\cdot3) = y + 16,886\cdot8$$

When solved, these two simple equations give a value for $x$ of 3,564·5 tons and for $y$ of 37,427·3 tons.

Clearly the premises on which the computation is made are open to question. And considerable question at that! After all, the equation presupposes a basic equality between the effective stocks of gold and silver, at the same time rejecting a third element, that of the different labour requirements to produce each metal. Moreover, it implies that the factors of supply and demand were direct functions of the aggregate stocks of gold and silver. In any case we are so accustomed to thinking of the inflow of gold and silver from America as having submerged Europe that at first sight we are disconcerted by these abnormally high figures. But it is to be remembered that on the one hand the production of about a century and a half is involved and on the other hand a stock accumulated over some twenty centuries, from before the early beginnings of the monetary systems. Heinrich Quiring's book, *Die Geschichte des Goldes*, is not always correct and tends, in fact, to be descriptive rather than quantitative, but all the same we may note that he credits the Roman Empire with a total production in gold of 1,700 tons, and the Middle Ages with a mass of 500 tons. Are these two figures to be added together? They would begin to approach the 3,000 tons of gold which our estimate attributed to Europe in 1500. This is a mere approximation, not a confirmation. But, however imperfect our estimate may be, it conforms to the reckonings of historians: and they tend to overestimate metallic stocks compared with their predecessors. This seems to be justifiable enough, but under the circumstances, what becomes of the quantity theory of money?

Or, more simply, have all these investigations been a waste of time? It is possible, but we plead indulgence. One conclusion emerges from these attempts: namely that, up to 1930 and even later, our predecessors have tended greatly to under-estimate the initial quantities of precious metals produced, and the stocks which existed before the arrivals from America. They assumed that the American mines poured their precious metals into a deprived Europe, and so precipitated an immense and sudden change. But it would seem, on the contrary, that the accumulated stocks in the Old World since early times represented a considerable monetary mass. But the monetary losses were also of no mean size, and these estimates in no way detract from the exceptional character of the new American production, but tend to give a different perspective of the relationship of the two masses of metal involved—the old and the new.

In short, if the inflow of precious metals from the New World did not even reach one half—on the most optimistic hypothesis—of the old stock of European money, then the quantity theory of money and Irving Fisher's equation of exchange must lose some of the force of argument and can be a valid explanation of the sixteenth century price upheaval only on condition that the velocity of circulation at the same time greatly increased.

But then, precisely, everything appears to indicate that this was the case, and indeed requires that it should have been so. If in France the *per capita* money supply about 1660 was *roughly* from 16 to 17 *livres tournois*, the gross revenue *per capita* was at least 100 *livres*. For the gap to be filled coins would have to circulate—or 'cascade' as the Portuguese Pinto said—in order to fulfil their multiple role. During the period under study, this process certainly gained momentum, in France as elsewhere, mainly in the eighteenth century, but also from the sixteenth century.

The question remains whether this coefficient of the velocity of circulation increased sufficiently for Irving Fisher's equation still to be valid as a general explanation of the price-revolution in the sixteenth century. We say *sufficiently*, for few will doubt that the velocity of circulation did increase: but in what proportion? The rapid movement which swept Europe along must certainly have involved a whole range of capital, possessions and reserves, almost without exception. There were certainly 'catchments'—as the geographers would say—of dormant stocks of money, and indeed concentrations of reserves of capital. For example, a hundred years later one would certainly not encounter the spectacle which excited the wonder of the historian Rudolf Sohm, the spectacle of incomes divided between the 7,000 inhabitants of the city of Basle at the beginning of the fifteenth century so equitably that, even though wealth existed, poverty was almost unknown there. A cleavage was set up and the gap widened during the sixteenth century: the rich tended to grow richer and the poor poorer. It is even possible, at least in part, to attribute this to the sudden 'cascade' and diffusion of coin. It would still be necessary to analyse and explain this diffusion. We would have to inquire if the rise in velocity varied between the different regions of Europe as it did between the various sections of the population. It would make a fine subject for a prototype quantitative study, were the necessary data and series available.

In effect, depending on locality, there were scores of different velocities of circulation, and a thousand factors of retardation. In any case, at Seville, the vital redistribution centre, the imports of American gold and silver were the property of the great international merchants and of His Catholic Majesty, the King of Spain. These 'treasures' as a result were either poured into large-scale international trade (which gathered momentum, and thereby pumped the bullion at a rapid rate of circulation through Europe); or else used to pay the costs of Spanish diplomatic ventures (first implemented on a large scale by Charles V in 1552 during the pathetic siege of Metz—as Richard Ehrenberg pointed out long ago). Then, Philip II adopted the same procedure again in the years 1580–90, as Felipe Ruiz Martin has shown. This time Spain opened all the floodgates, and organized silver circulation on a vast scale. Normally, she restrained such circulation as much as possible, in order to avoid the drain of bullion from her territory. But on this occasion the flow of silver was as rapid as it was voluminous and from then on Spanish silver had direct repercussions through all the monetary stocks of Europe.

From that moment, and more than at any previous time, every arrival of bullion from the New World had a powerful effect on the financial and commercial life of all Europe. José Gentil da Silva has published maps to illustrate these rhythms. The moment a silver fleet arrived from America, one money market after another in Europe experienced successively 'largesses' or easy money conditions: that is to say, abundance of coin, of 'ready' cash and bills of exchange, the one usually accompanying the other. Thus the money from Seville circulated from one money market to another, in settlement of commercial and financial transactions often to a value of ten or a hundred times its own value, and then passed on to the next money market for a fresh period of cash advances and trading settlements. Whether as coin or as bills of exchange, money cascaded from person to person and from money market to money market. Sixteenth-century Rome every year handled as much coin as Seville itself did. Between 1575 and 1602 Venice coined 62 metric tons of gold sequins, which was more than the 52 tons of American bullion received at Seville during the same years. Between 1493 and 1660, French coinage rose to 4,133 metric tons of silver (converting both silver and gold issues into their silver equivalents), that is to say more than a fifth and less than a quarter of the 'American treasure' which reached Spain during the same period. We should not be too greatly surprised by these striking figures. In Europe at that time, gold and silver coins were like Offenbach's musketeers on the stage, or like planets in an orrery. Very often they were the same, issued in different guise.

However, symmetry and regularity were lacking in these movements: the circle did not always complete itself. Bullion was constantly drained off by way of the Baltic, the Levant and the Cape of Good Hope to the Near and Far East. Moreover, Spanish silver, for political and commercial reasons, had preferred circuits. They greatly benefited northern Europe, as one of our maps shows (Fig. 10). They also benefited Italy—more so than this map demonstrates—for silver flowed by way of Genoa, Florence and Venice, in compensation for the stream of bills of exchange and gold payments which thereafter went to the Low Countries. At Antwerp, that financial city corrupted by war (like Saigon a short while ago in the trade in piastres during the war in Indo-China), an enormous mass of money collected and thence spread to the countries of the north, first of all to the insurgent Netherlands. These political circuits supplemented those concerned with international trade. The north was one of the directions taken, for Spain depended on the north for wheat, copper, tin, wood, planks, beams, hemp and linen cloth, and for high quality textiles. Every year, almost secretly, from one to two million crowns' worth of merchandise passed from the north to Seville. An unfavourable balance in this sector emptied Spain and Portugal of part of their silver and gold. The same conditions prevailed in favour of Italy, but Italy in her turn exported huge sums to the Levant. Thus in 1595—an exceptional year—Venice alone sent 551,677 ducats or 14,700 kilograms of silver to Syria.[1]

The northern countries for their part had only to account for small losses of silver to the Baltic. So then if the reversal of the secular trend at

---

[1] Museo Correr, Donà dalle Rose, 42, f°. 23 verso, for the years 1593, 1594, 1595, and 1596: 1,045,447 ducats in all, or an annual average of 261,361¾ ducats.

the end of the sixteenth century had its origin in Seville, as everything appears to indicate, it developed in the following way. The northern countries emerged from the war with Spain in 1604 (the Anglo-Spanish peace) and in 1609 (the Twelve Years Truce between Spain and the United Provinces) and so had at their disposal an accumulated mass of money partly because of the persistently favourable balance in ordinary commercial exchanges, and partly as a result of the war. These reserves of the north, put out to profit, functioned until about the middle of the seventeenth century. Moreover, the north was to supplant the Mediterranean countries as exporters of bullion to India and China.

This explanation of the disparity in the secular trend may very well not be the only one possible. Certain regions—such as, traditionally, the Mediterranean—were kept better supplied than others with precious metals, thanks to their inheritance of ancient structures, and above all to their advanced economies more penetrated by monetary conventions than others. Thus Provence studied by René Baehrel was better supplied with currency in the seventeenth century than the Beauvais of Pierre Goubert. Frank Spooner has outlined these monetary disparities in sixteenth century France. Can we assume that for a long time the economies of the north, the exceptions confirming the rule—were in large measure less committed to the monetary network than those of the south? Less silver and less gold would indicate more primitive economies and relatively more barter. The northern urban economies, more subject to vertical integration, lived off a backward or semi-developed countryside. Under these conditions, the north was inevitably a more modest consumer of currency and precious metals—*lato sensu*—than the south. More simply and more solidly constituted, the north was less prodigal with precious metals than the south, at least at the beginning of the seventeenth century and before the full expansion of the eighteenth century when the flow of economic development turned to benefit those who once had been poor and now were the new rich.

Thus, the quantity theory of money has meaning when taken with the velocity of circulation and in the context of the disparities of the European economy. Moreover, according to Werner Sombart and the Brazilian historians, there were five or six hundred million piastres thrown onto the European market by the gold production of Minas Gerais, of the Matto Grosso and the 'Sertão' of Bahia between 1680 and 1720–30. Did the gold thrown into Europe, into the international economy, go directly into circulation? Or did the growing relative abundance of the yellow metal once more stimulate the mining of silver in line with the conclusions of Frank Spooner for the preceding epoch? Thus, the silver from the mines of New Spain enjoyed a second period of splendour, far superior to the first. The sad thing is that these quantitative problems have not yet found their Earl J. Hamilton. Meanwhile, we can be sure of two things: monetary stocks in Europe increased considerably in the eighteenth century, and the velocity of circulation of money in Europe further increased. In France, where our estimate for 1660 pointed to the figure of 267 million *livres tournois* for the stock of money, the classical economists estimated the total circulation in 1789 at 2,000 million *livres*. Even allowing for the depreciation of the money of account and the unreliability of these aggregate figures, it was a considerable advance.

## (2) PRICES, WAGES, AND CAPITALISM

There is a second issue which must be raised: can the history of prices enlighten us about the genesis in Europe of the first experience of capitalism? In effect, capitalism can be seen as a *structure*, at once social and economic, a phenomenon of long-term significance. This being so, the danger lies in explaining it at all costs in terms of short or relatively short duration. These, of course, certainly influence the expansion or deterioration of structures, but to explain the whole perspective of capitalism by these rapid, endogenous factors would not always seem to be justified or sufficient in itself.

In one of his early articles, Earl J. Hamilton rightly emphasized the importance, for the growth of capitalism, of the discovery of America and, even more, of the establishment of a direct trade route by sea between Europe, the Indies and the Far East, from the time of Vasco da Gama's voyage (1497–9). He was also right in pointing out the extent to which a lag between wages and prices during inflation created a bigger margin of profit for entrepreneurs and hence for the concentration of capital. In short, we shall not easily discard the theories of Earl J. Hamilton. But what matters is to pursue them. Every economic fluctuation, even when decisive, or violent, or creative, still remains an accident in a long term, 'structural' history—the development of capitalism— which by its nature transcends accidents. It transcends both those accidents which Earl Hamilton has emphasized, and those we have referred to in the closing of the differentials of wheat prices in Europe in the eighteenth century. In other words the play of capitalism is multiple, both in the short and the long term.

One example will suffice to show the multiple character of capital in the short run. The scene is Venice, at the end of the sixteenth century. Venetian financiers and merchants were less and less willing to accept the increasing risks of maritime ventures. The high seas at the end of the sixteenth century and in the beginning of the seventeenth century were beset by pirates. The fifteenth century had been practically free of piracy: in its place the sixteenth century had substituted wars of religion (Islam against Christendom, Protestants against Catholics), and in the seventeenth century piracies were common practice. What, then, were the sources of profit for Venetian investments at this time? Florentine merchants dominated the city, as a document of the Cinque Savii alla Mercanzia of 1606 tells us: and for a particular Florentine living in Venice, there was speculation in the purchase and letting out of houses to maintain wealth. However, a Genoese merchant, likewise established in the city, gambled on importing bars of silver and speculated on the foreign exchanges. A Venetian of patrician stock, of worthy nobility, not degraded by misfortunes of economic activity into the class of impoverished gentlemen (they were called the *Barnaboti*, inhabitants of the Santa Barnaba quarter of Venice), kept his money safe by gambling on the Besançon market (lending money at interest, even at low rates), as is revealed in the notarial acts. Above all, he also bought and improved land: the enormous increase in wheat production in the Venetian Republic was the work of these men; and it also assured them of profit, for agriculture, we must remember, was the biggest industry in Europe. These Venetians also invested money in the cloth trade, though to a lesser extent. Here the wage demands of the *Arti* at the beginning of the seventeenth century no doubt set limits to entrepreneurial profits, and drove investment away from a sector already subject to competition from the weavers of northern Europe. In short, how is it possible to apply a single rule to this spectrum of investment opportunities? We have not even begun to indicate the infinite variety of possibilities.

Whatever definition we give to capitalism, it was a phenomenon of slow germination. The classic account of it by Earl J. Hamilton and Lord Keynes seized on one particular aspect of its movement, one situation: the change in relative levels of prices and costs. The change may well have worked in favour of profit inflation, but it cannot in itself alone have played the determining role, as Earl Hamilton was the first to recognize. But at this point we have merely reached the threshold of further studies. Price history can open one but not every door.

## (3) PRICE HISTORY AND 'SERIAL' HISTORY

The history of prices is only a chapter—though certainly among the first to be undertaken—in the creation of a 'serial' history[1] (that is, the quantification of historical movements by the comparative study of long series of empirical data). But until the latter has more ample scope or more refined methods, aims and results, price history will constitute only a small sector.

[1] The term is Pierre Chaunu's, see 'Dynamique conjoncturelle et histoire sérielle', *Industrie* (6 June 1960).

For the present, what series—already available, about to appear, or even possible—can widen the base of our conclusions?

(a) *Identical series and related series:* Clearly the initial tasks are to complete and add to the price series; to survey some of those vast regions such as the Balkans or Muscovy, which are still poorly provided with statistics; to take further samples and analyse the non-European countries in whose midst Europe developed; then to complete, where possible, the available series which are deficient—such as the textile sector, for which the meagre data now deprive us of the only important *industrial* check at our disposal; and lastly, to collate the market prices of real estate and land. On this last point, Wilhelm Abel has tried to ascertain the long term changes; H. J. Habakkuk has systematically advanced his promising researches; Aldo de Maddalena recently has devoted an important article to the subject.

The 'related' series are meant to imply those concerned with the borrowing of money, the interest rate. In this sphere, Earl J. Hamilton has projected a vast inquiry—whether it will be realized or not—for the whole of Europe from the fifteenth to the eighteenth century. The term also implies the commercial profit rate. No systematic inquiry has been made on this point; but there is the possibility of finding a good indication of a progress of a capitalism vastly stimulated at the beginning of the sixteenth century, for example, if some idea could be had of the astonishing dividends on Lisbon's trade with Asia. The fortune amassed by the German merchant Lucas Rem revealed this with crystal clarity. A fertile subject for study, if feasible, would be the profits of the Genoese merchant financiers: in the sixteenth century in nearly every trading centre they were accused of profiteering at will by speculating in foreign exchanges and in commodity markets. But will we ever have their papers and account books at our disposal?

Other possible sources for 'serial' studies include inevitably state budgets and data on the general standard of living. The latter objective was entertained by H. Grote when not too long ago he looked for the 'lowest wage' as a basic measure: that is the minimum wage of to-day. It is only of relative utility as a point of reference to know that Pierre Goubert reports the annual standard of living in the region of Beauvais to have been about five hectolitres of wheat for a family of six people, since for his part René Baehrel finds more than twice this figure applied to Provence during the same period. More samples are required. Despite the smiles of the pundits, we ought to be able to reckon in daily requirements of calories, even if the estimates give rise—provisionally or definitively—to procedures as approximate as those which we have used above to review the quantitative theory of money.

(b) *Independent or parallel series:* The group of population series falls naturally under this heading. Good use has been made of such data in Pierre Goubert's book already frequently cited in conjunction with the series concerning economic fluctuations. Population and subsistence crises coincide; periods of dearness and high mortality tended to go together: we knew it already but the demonstration has further clarified the issues. In these accounts of life and death in the past, it has not been shown that long movements and, beyond them, early secular trends existed, but the hypothesis must henceforth be entertained.

However, it is a far cry from this to explaining everything about price movements in terms of population. First of all, the changes—either increases or decreases—in the numbers of active workers must be separated carefully from the aggregate shifts in population. In Provence, for example, the numbers of workers employed increased between 1600 and 1690. Next, we must clarify our notions, within the context of a demanding price theory, about an *optimum* population. Prices are always in relationship both to the volume of money and volume of production. If other factors remain unchanged and the money supply does not increase, population ought logically to bring about a fall in prices. Earl J. Hamilton has given the historical verification for the nineteenth century: then the population rose more rapidly than ever before, and during the greater part of the century except in wartime, prices were falling. They rose after the discovery of gold in California and Australia, fell after 1873 and did not rise again until the end of the century, after the discoveries of gold in South Africa and Alaska. This raises once more the vital question of the quantity of money in circulation. All of which is subject to proof.

In contrast, what is to be said about the social factors? These are sufficiently vague to escape precise measurement, or rather are ill-adapted to this treatment. The great inquiry into social structures proposed at the Rome Congress in 1955 under the direction of Ernest Labrousse, similar to the great inquiry into price movements presided over by Lord Beveridge in 1933, was particularly concerned with the eighteenth and nineteenth centuries. But on what pattern, on what 'model' can social quantification be based, and what coefficients can be isolated to give a true image, scientifically speaking, of a social order or hierarchy? The undertaking is possible. Each secular recession tends to immobilize and stratify a society, to inhibit internal mobility. But further advances along this road will be possible only when a theoretical and applied sociology has been assimilated by historical studies and made an integral part—with the customary prudence and perspicacity—of our own particular field of study. That point has not yet been reached.

(c) *Commerce and production*: Price series are more naturally collated with the series of data for commerce and production. Here, also, many considerations are involved but a discussion is possible only when long series of records are available. There are the pioneer works of Nina Bang and Knud Korst on the customs of the Sound from 1497 to 1783. Other studies have checked the data and clarified their significance. More recently others have interested themselves in this gigantic task. No less gigantic, and still more important from the historical point of view, is the work of Huguette and Pierre Chaunu. They have already documented Seville's trade with Europe and America (1502–1650) and are studying that of Cadiz up to 1784. With these two monumental works they will have measured one of the major maritime trades of the world from its inauguration until almost modern times.

How do prices and trade fluctuate? Happily the answer is simple, whether we look to the Sound or examine the transatlantic trade of the Iberian countries. Trade and prices move in broad unison, without noticeable gaps. Price inflation accompanied—it would be too much to say 'made'—the growth of trade. Prices and trade were synchronized. This widens the scope of the normal discussion on prices.

However, can changes in the volume of shipping tonnage, as shown in port movements, be considered a satisfactory indicator of changes in the level of total output? Pierre Chaunu maintains that indirectly they were: and it is probable *a priori* that one was a function of the other, and vice versa. But we know only very little about production. Thus for the sixteenth century, we have only three main series available, and even these are not sufficient for our liking: there is the output of *sayettes* at Hondschoote from 1378 to 1676; the series for the production of high quality cloths at Venice during two centuries; and the cloth production of Leiden. If need be, the output of silver in the Potosi mines and the production of tin in Cornwall and Devon can be cited. But Potosi already means going beyond Europe, and entering that vast European effort in colonization, which was also part of the framework or matrix of the first international economy.

Under these circumstances, the graphs are eloquent. By comparison with the movements of prices (again those of wheat) these three series, in the form of parabolas, rise and fall steeply (see Fig. 33). For a moment we find ourselves in the classic case of dialectical economics: on the one hand, the irreversible movement of prices, and on the other hand the reversible movement of quantities. If the crux of the problem were contained in one simple system, the conclusion would be relatively easy: the movement of prices provoked, with a time lag, the movement of quantities, and set it in motion. But conversely the slowing-down of prices allowed the rise in textiles or mining to fall back again at a greater speed than the fall in prices. Still, this has not been demonstrated, and a few more new series are required, to see if, in the shifts—first rising, then falling—there was a similar rise and fall which varied in the secular price trend according to the various regions of Europe. What exactly went on in Leiden, for example? The answer on this point is not always clear.

In the same way, we can ask ourselves whether the variations in acreage under wheat in East Prussia, and the increase in land-reclamation in the Netherlands, which are both indicators of agricultural production, vary or not with the secular price movements (see Figs. 15 and 16). The problem can be stated without being completely solved.

It will be clear where these concluding pages are leading. It seems to us that price history has shortcomings not only in the inadequacy but also in the utilization of its sources. It is lacking in having never really been assimilated into the great debate on economic growth (the real merit of René Baehrel's book is that it tackled the study of prices in Provence from this point of view), nor into the fundamental debate on social development. These are two problems which are customarily mingled together, as though economic growth always implied social progress, and vice versa. 'All economic expansion,' M. Marjolin has written about the Europe of the Common Market, 'is beneficial to man in the long run, but the result may be achieved only in the very long run. In the meantime, the accelerated movement threatens to break the traditional structures, modifying the geographical and professional divisions of labour, and displacing the *foci* of activity to the benefit of some and to the disadvantage of others.' Expansion, he more or less goes on to say, can imply social crises, and grave social crises at that.

These reflections on our present predicament apply also to the whole history of Europe since the Middle Ages. We would be very willing to say that economic growth should be studied from a long-term point of view, and for this the price series of the secular trend have rightly been considered as giving unimpeachable evidence. But prices are not just economic evidence. They constitute a factor which sets a positive or negative sign to the wages which remunerate a man for his work. What meaning can a price series have when prices are considered as a measure not of expansion but of a standard of living? They are questions which we could not settle, even with the best sources and the most reliable price series. The problem must be restated. Nothing sets the problem so well as a comparison of René Baehrel's study of Provence and Pierre Goubert's on the region of Beauvais for the same period—the long seventeenth century. Each author divides up these 120 years into four phases, which virtually coincide so far as dates are concerned: but only their dates. For when a period of prosperity reigned at Beauvais, Provence was having a depression. And when Provence once again began to expand, Beauvais was plunged in catastrophe. In effect, René Baehrel considered the problem in the light of economic growth, and isolated 'A phases' and 'B phases', in the line of thought of François Simiand. Pierre Goubert finds periods of prosperity and depression, according to the violence of the cyclical upswings in the context of social crises. The reader needs a certain time to grasp this transposition. In both cases, let us add, the point of departure is in price movements, which develop generally in the same way, but with differences which are to be explained by the different preoccupations of these two authors. The cyclical crises are more attenuated in Provence and growth phases are less sharp at Beauvais. The two authors do not ask the same questions of their series, and as a result the series offer different interpretations.

We will conclude that price history as it has been studied so far gives no satisfactory answer to the basic questions. In its own way, it does provide evidence about pre-industrial Europe, which this volume of the *Cambridge Economic History* sets out to review. It reveals, and indeed could reveal even more emphatically, the extreme diversification of a world split into many units; but it also reveals the ties which grouped some units together; and further, as time passed, it reveals the tendency of Europe to fuse together in a common economic destiny. Lastly, it suggests countless questions and subjects for investigation. Is not the true purpose of research to open up new perspectives? History is never written once and for all.

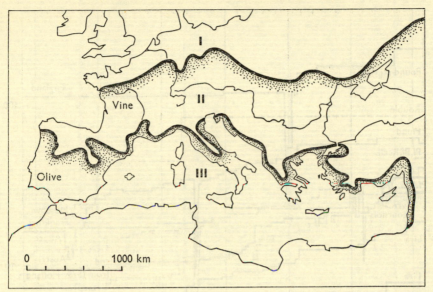

Fig. 2. Three zones of Europe, defined by the present-day limits of the vine and the olive-tree.

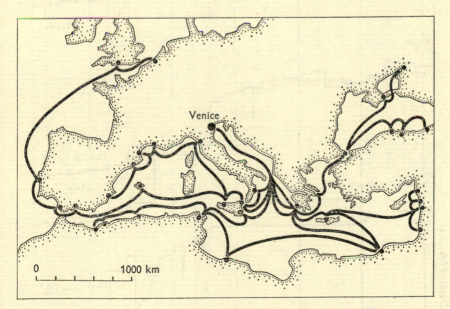

Fig. 3. Venetian navigation in 1442: routes of the *galere da mercato*. (After C. Vivanti and A. Tenenti.)

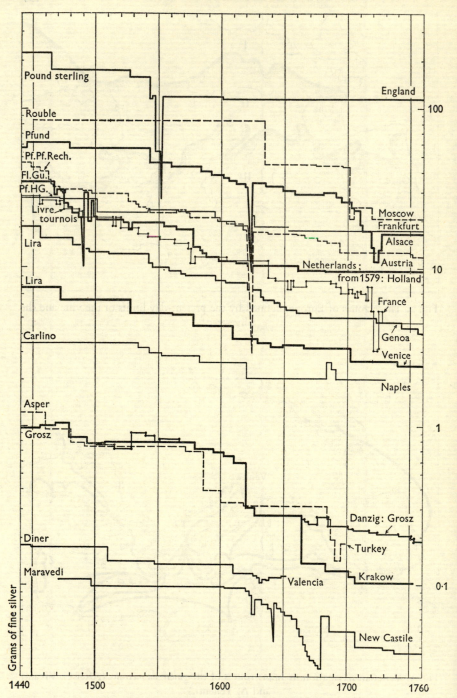

Fig. 4. Moneys of account in Europe, classified by their weights in grams of fine silver. (Pf. Pf. Rech.: *Pfund Pfennig Rechengulden*. Fl. Gu.: florin; from 1579, guilder. Pf. H. G.: *Pfund Heller Gulden*. Approximate values are given for the rouble and the *asper*.)

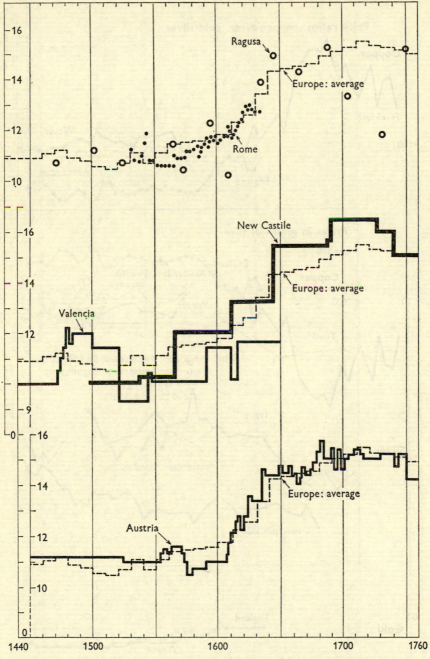

Fig. 5. Bimetallic ratios in Europe (arithmetic scale). A unit in gold = 1.

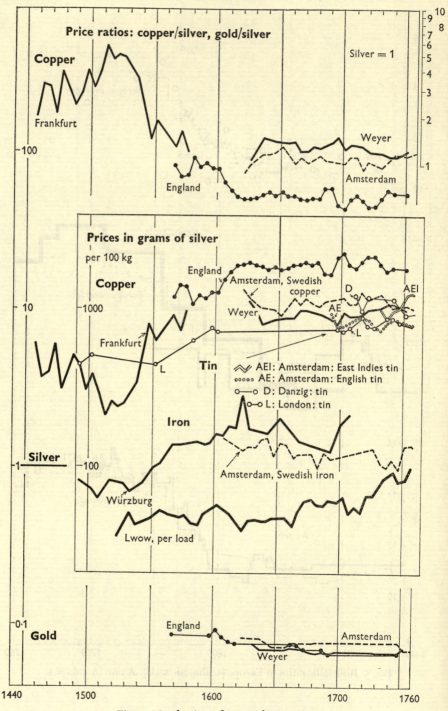

Fig. 6. Metal prices: five-yearly averages.

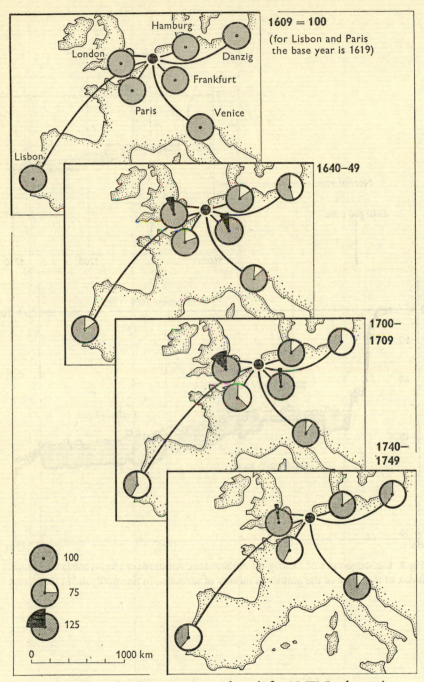

1609 = 100
(for Lisbon and Paris
the base year is 1619)

1640–49

1700–
1709

1740–
1749

Hamburg

London

Danzig

Frankfurt

Paris

Venice

Lisbon

100

75

125

0                    1000 km

Fig. 7. Rates of exchange on Amsterdam. (After N. W. Posthumus.)

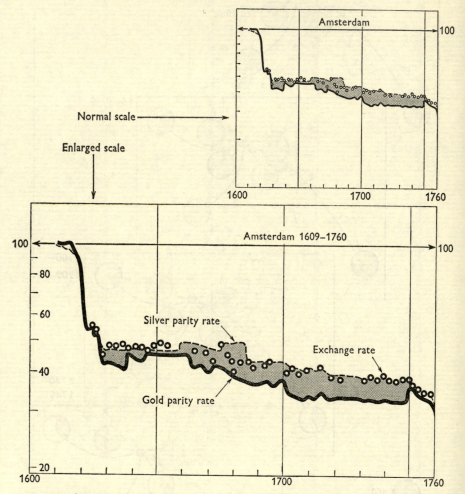

Fig.8. Exchange-rates of Danzig on Amsterdam. Amsterdam 1609–1760 (a composite index of the value of the guilder in money of accounts, in fine gold, and in fine silver) = 100.

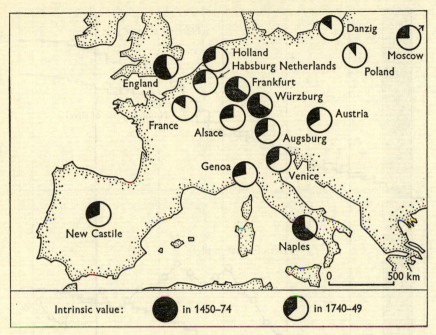

Fig. 9. Index of devaluation of moneys of account in terms of silver, 1450–1750.

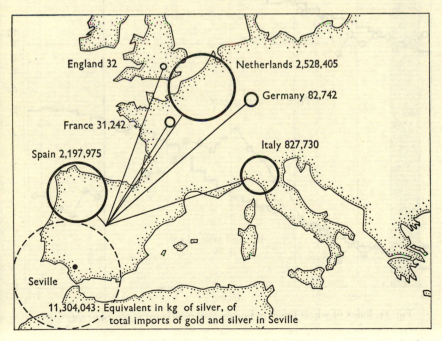

Fig. 10. Payments of Spanish asientos in terms of kg of silver, 1580–1626. (After A. Castillo.)

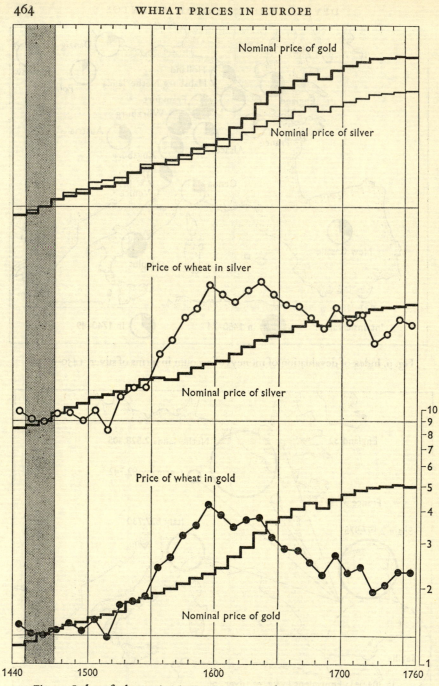

Nominal price of gold

Nominal price of silver

Price of wheat in silver

Nominal price of silver

Price of wheat in gold

Nominal price of gold

Fig. 11. Index of wheat prices in Europe: ten-yearly averages. 1450–74 = 100.

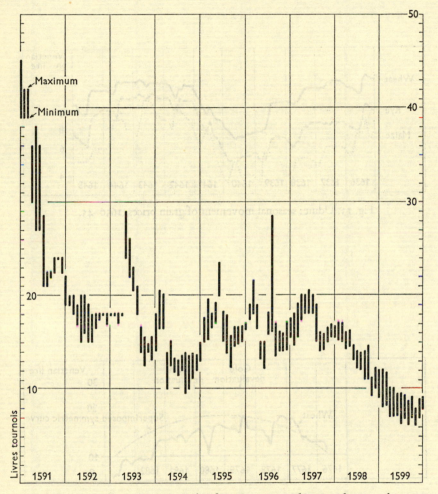

Fig. 12. A section from the *Mercuriale* of Paris, 1591–9, showing the range between maximum and minimum prices of wheat in *livres tournois* at the beginning of each month, in the Halles of Paris. (After M. Baulant and J. Meuvret.)

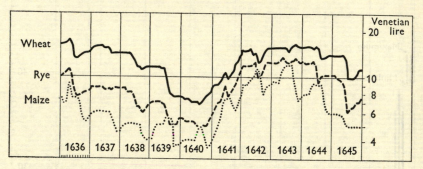

Fig. 13. Udine: seasonal movement of grain prices, 1636–45.

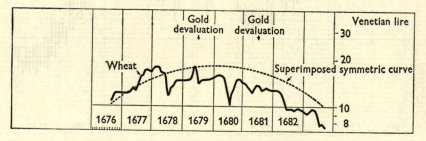

Fig. 14. Udine: a cycle of wheat prices, 1676–83.

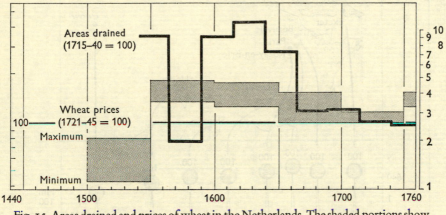

Fig. 15. Areas drained and prices of wheat in the Netherlands. The shaded portions show the range of wheat prices. (After B. H. Slicher van Bath.)

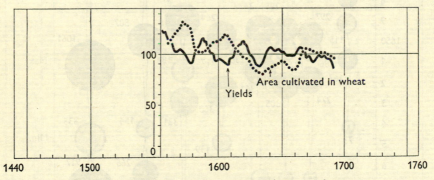

Fig. 16. Trends of grain production in East Prussia: eleven-yearly moving averages. 1550–1696 = 100. (After H. H. Wächter.)

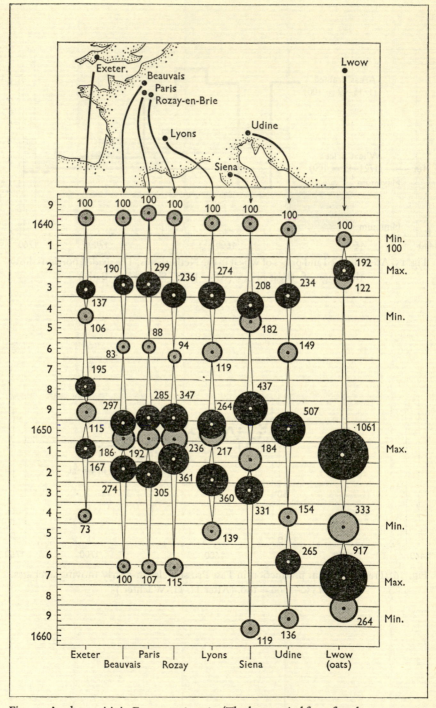

Fig. 17. A wheat crisis in Europe: 1639–60. (The base period from fourth quarter 1639 to first quarter 1641 = 100.)

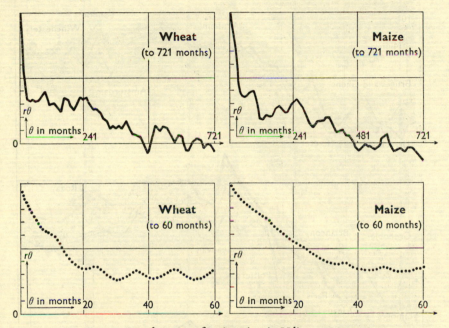

Fig. 18. Correlograms of grain prices in Udine, 1586–1796.

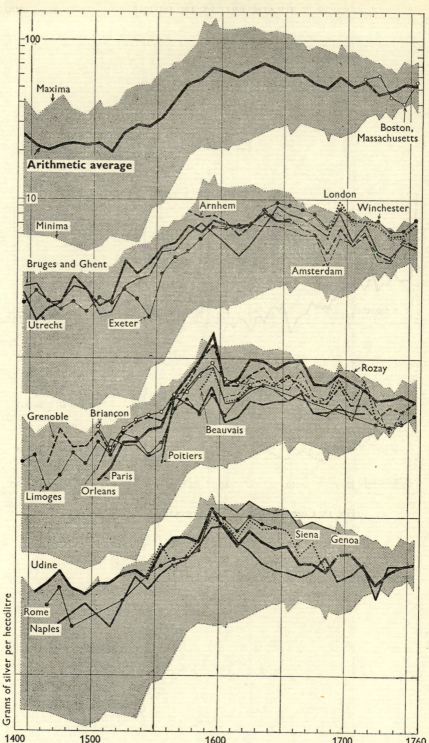

Fig. 19. Wheat prices in grams of silver per hectolitre: ten-yearly averages. The shaded portion shows the range between the maximum and minimum prices.

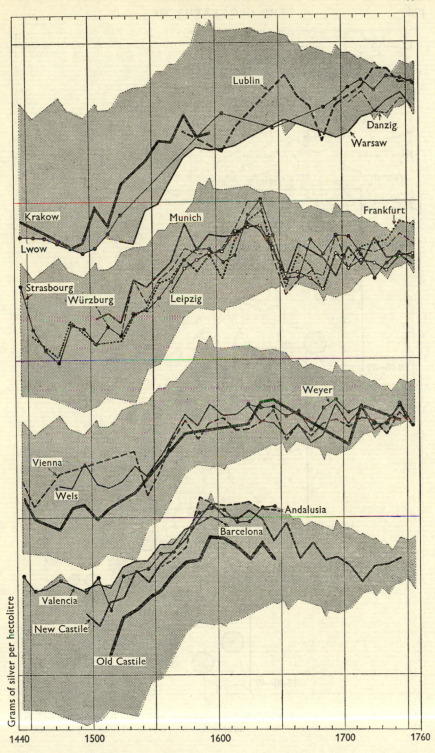

Lublin

Danzig

Warsaw

Krakow

Lwow

Munich

Frankfurt

Strasbourg

Würzburg

Leipzig

Weyer

Vienna

Wels

Andalusia

Barcelona

Valencia

New Castile

Old Castile

Grams of silver per hectolitre

1440    1500    1600    1700    1760

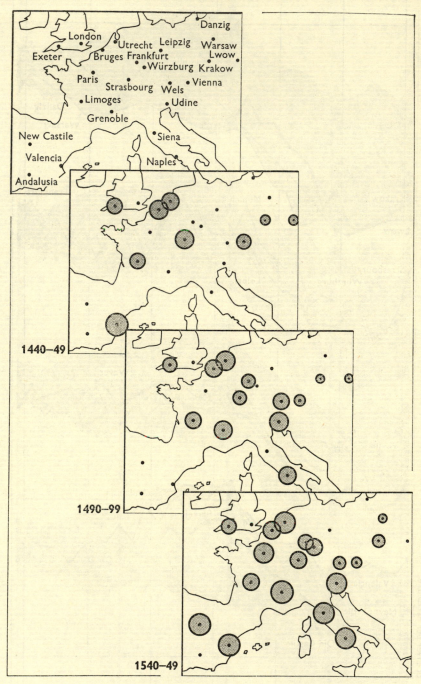

Fig. 20. The geography of wheat prices in grams of silver per hectolitre: ten-yearly averages.

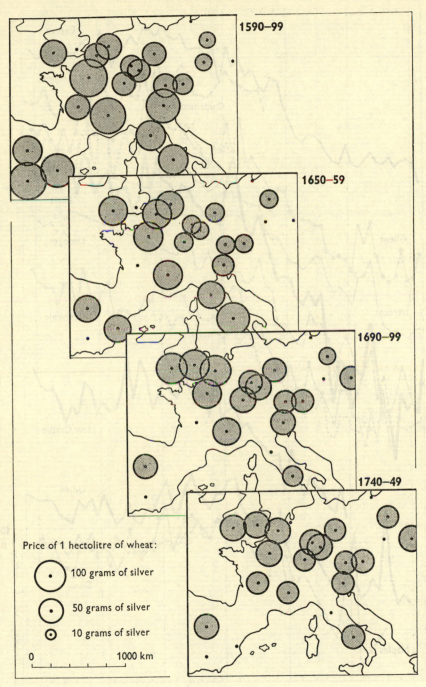

1590–99

1650–59

1690–99

1740–49

Price of 1 hectolitre of wheat:

100 grams of silver

50 grams of silver

10 grams of silver

0                    1000 km

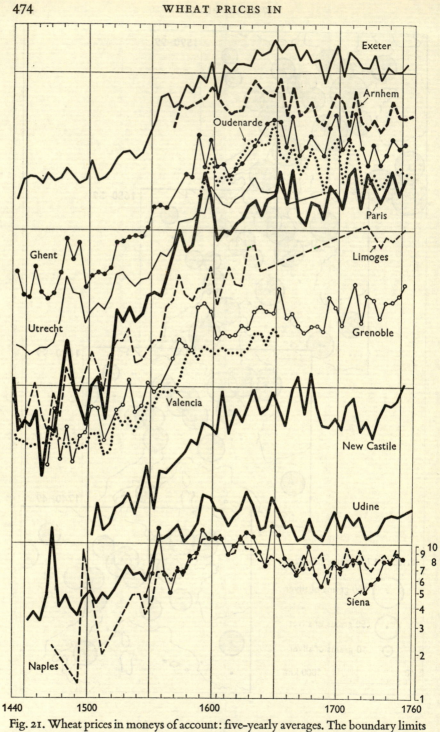

Fig. 21. Wheat prices in moneys of account: five-yearly averages. The boundary limits of the shaded area have been obtained by fitting graphically 59 series of wheat prices in Europe, of which 20 are given separately above.

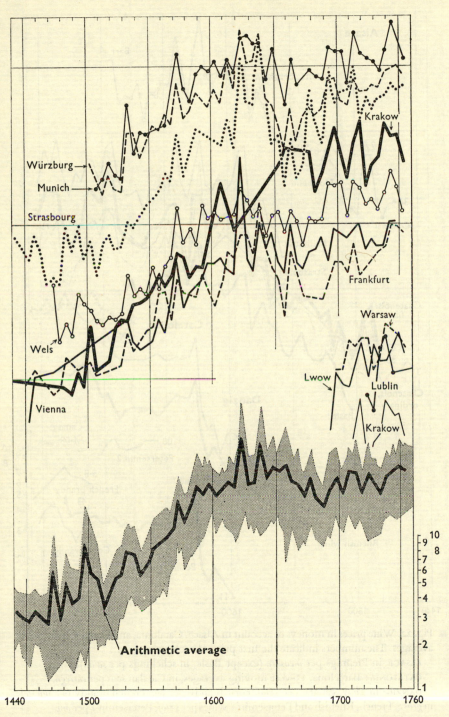

Würzburg
Munich
Strasbourg
Wels
Vienna
Krakow
Frankfurt
Warsaw
Lwow
Lublin
Krakow
Arithmetic average

1440    1500    1600    1700    1760

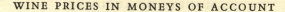

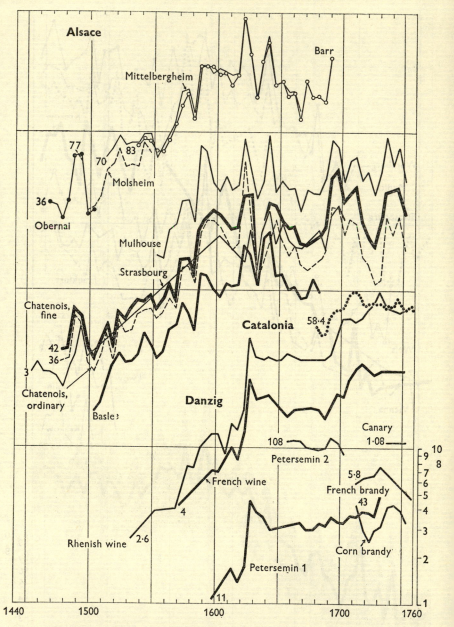

Fig. 22. Wine prices in moneys of account in Alsace, Catalonia, and Danzig: five-yearly averages. The numbers indicate the first price of each series.

ALSACE: in Pfennigs per *measure* (except Basle, in schellings per *saum*).

CATALONIA: Barcelona, 13-year moving averages, in Catalan *sous* per *carrega*.

DANZIG: in *zloty*, canary per *sztof*, corn brandy per *om*, French brandy per *wiertel*; in *grosz*, French, Rhenish and Petersemin 1 wines per *sztof*, Petersemin 2 per *om*.

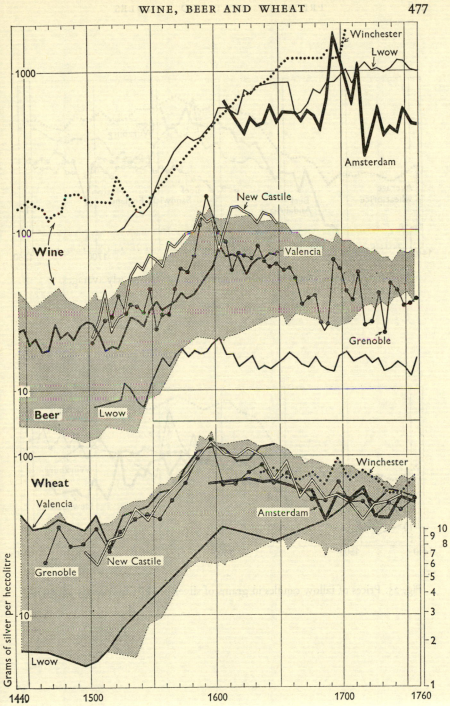

Fig. 23. Wine, beer and wheat prices in grams of silver per hectolitre: five-yearly averages. The shaded areas show the range of wheat prices.

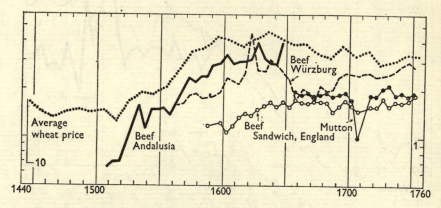

Fig. 24. Meat prices in grams of silver per kg: five-yearly averages.

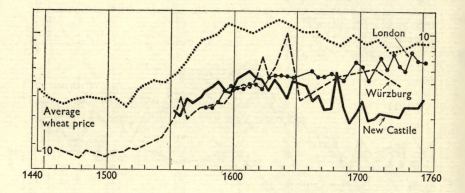

Fig. 25. Prices of tallow candles in grams of silver per kg: five-yearly averages.

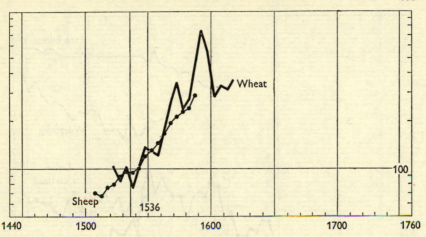

Fig. 26. Sheep and wheat: index of nominal prices in Paris (five-yearly averages). 1536 = 100. (After M. Baulant.)

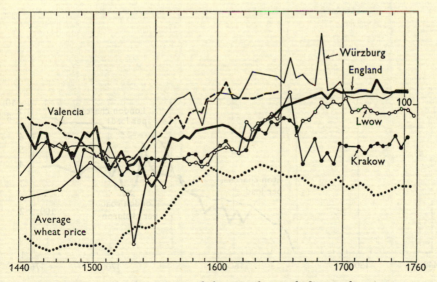

Fig. 27. Prices of bricks in grams of silver per thousand: five-yearly averages.

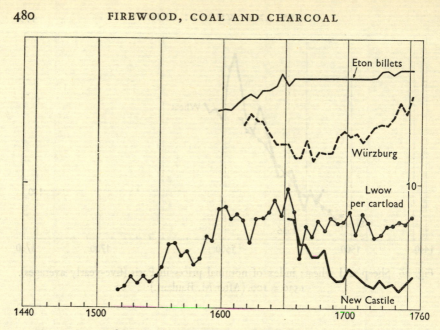

Fig. 28. Prices of firewood in grams of silver per load: five-yearly averages.

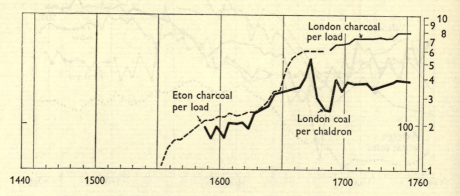

Fig. 29. Prices of coal and charcoal in England, in grams of silver: five-yearly averages.

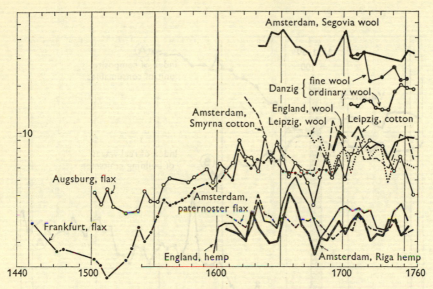

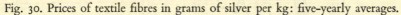

Fig. 30. Prices of textile fibres in grams of silver per kg: five-yearly averages.

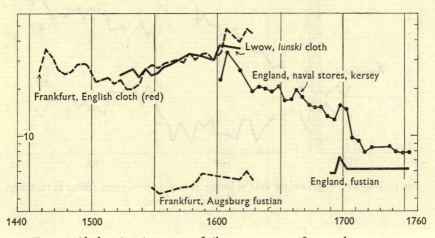

Fig. 31. Cloth prices in grams of silver per metre: five-yearly averages.

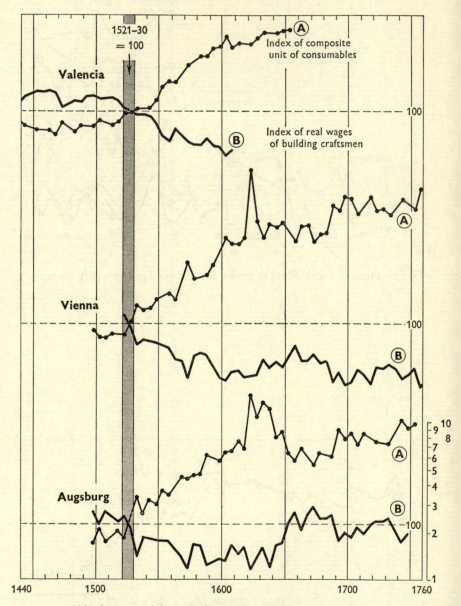

Fig. 32. Builders' wages and the cost of living: five-yearly averages. (After E. H. Phelps Brown and Sheila Hopkins.)

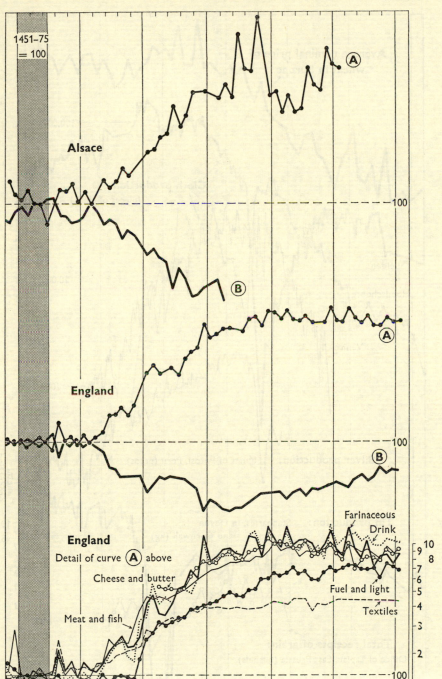

1451–75
= 100

Alsace

A

B

100

England

A

B

100

England
Detail of curve A above

Cheese and butter

Meat and fish

Farinaceous
Drink

Fuel and light

Textiles

10
9
8
7
6
5

4

3

2

100
1

1440          1500          1600          1700     1760

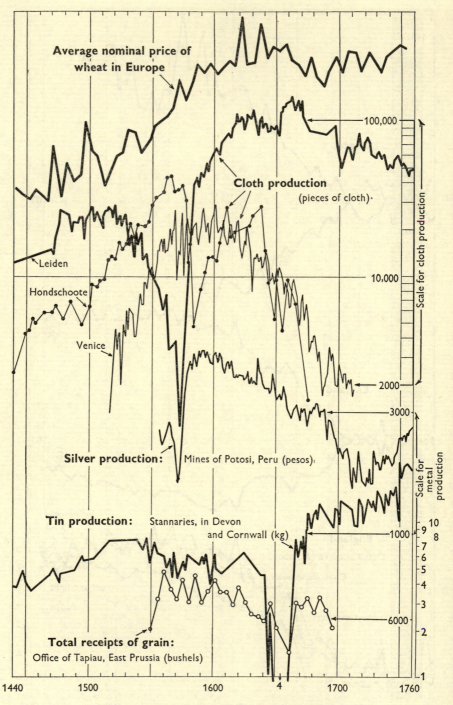

Fig. 33. Trends in prices and industrial output.

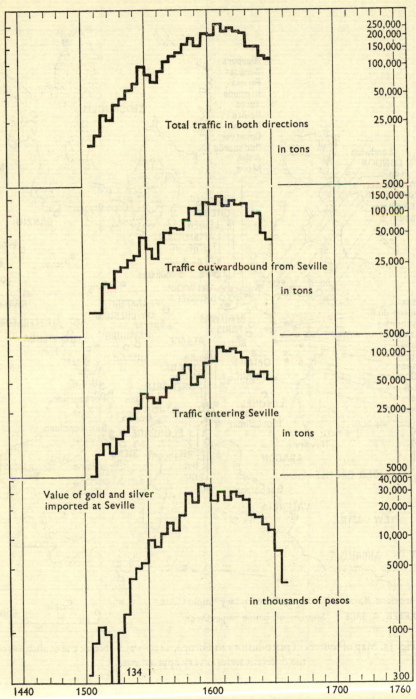

Fig. 34. The port movement of Seville: trade with America (after H. and P. Chaunu);
gold and silver imports (after E. J. Hamilton).

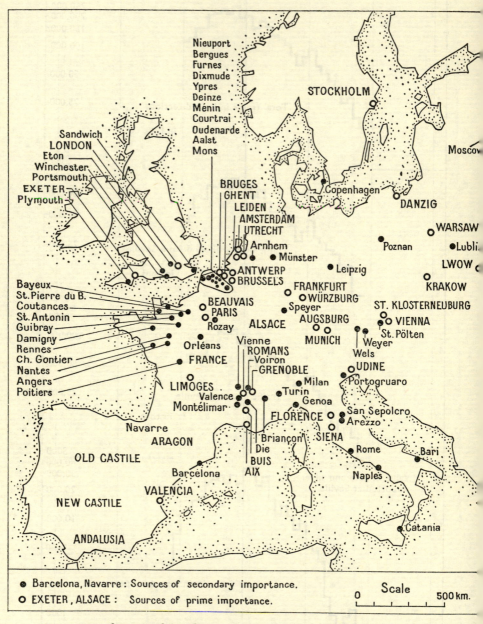

Fig. 35. Map of sources of price-history in Europe, 1450–1750. (Note: the evaluation of the different series is very approximate.)

# CHAPTER VIII

# Trade, Society and the State

The 'mercantilist' age was not idly so christened. Everywhere along the western seaboard of Europe and along the coastline of the Mediterranean from Malaga to Venice, in the centuries that stretched from the Renascence to the Enlightenment the merchants were the dynamic element in society. As the volume of trade grew, as the fleet of international shipping expanded, linking places and trades hitherto isolated, the operations of merchants and manufacturers slowly helped to change the face of western European society partly through the goods and manufactures they made available, partly through the social changes they wrought by introducing new or extending existing methods of manufacture, and partly through the influence they exercised directly or indirectly on the policies of Government. On any statistical basis, most men everywhere were still connected with the land in one way or another: but everywhere in the later Middle Ages and early modern age trade and tradesmen were undermining the crumbling walls of custom that surrounded the economic community of the Middle Ages.

It used to be possible for historians to delineate the major features of this emergent economy under the name of capitalism and it became fashionable to bracket capitalism and the Reformation together with the overt proposal that the latter explained, at all events in part, the former. It was assumed that the sixteenth century saw the birth, specifically in northern Europe, of a novel type of economic society based on energies and ambitions which were themselves old as man but were now in some way released for good or ill on society at large: and that Protestantism—and in particular the teaching of Calvin—was a prime mover in the process. This teaching, it was suggested, made its greatest appeal to, perhaps was even directly and deliberately aimed at, the rising bourgeois class, conferring on their inherent acquisitive spirit the gloss and glamour of a 'calling'. What had been formerly of dubious social respectability now became, in Protestant society, a vocation of which a man could be proud. For the first time, it was suggested, it became possible to talk of economic virtue.

The validity of this suggested link between Calvinism and 'capitalism', however defined, in the sixteenth and seventeenth centuries has more recently been exposed to increasing doubts. And for these doubts there are two main reasons. First, the attitude of Calvin and his followers to such matters as the taking of interest and the nature of usury has been shown to have been exaggerated. In Calvin's own writings the attention given to these matters is reluctant and infinitesimal. While it is true that he replaced theological casuistry by simple moral rule as the basis of economic conduct, there is no warrant for assuming that his rules made capitalist practices any easier, much less that he intended to make them easier. Public policy in Protestant countries continued in traditional fashion to be guided by the idea that there was a fair price for all things; maximum rates of interest were fixed, prices—especially of food—were controlled, middlemen were frowned on, and pawnshops made a public responsibility. The social conservatism of Calvinism can hardly be illustrated better than by the long controversy over the usury problem that went on in Holland, the most advanced of contemporary economies, between Voetius, the *doyen* of the Calvinist divines, a Puritan rigid, austere and uncompromising, and Salmasius. Its origin was this: that Voetius had excommunicated from his congregation a God-fearing woman because her husband was a pawnbroker. She, in turn, was therefore tainted with usury. The more closely the social situation in the so-called 'Calvinist' countries is examined—whether in the Dutch Republic, the Puritan areas of East Anglia, London and the Midlands in England, Scotland, the Huguenot areas of France east of Bordeaux and north of Marseilles, and later in New England—the more dubious becomes the proposition that there was an overt relationship between Calvinism and the rise of the merchant class. It is possible, on the contrary, in each of these areas to discern stresses and strains between merchant community and Puritan authority that arose directly from the conservatism and austerity of Calvinist logic and social outlook. In the Dutch Republic the social tension became a conditioning factor in the alignment of political parties. The merchant class, the regents, the patriciate, liberal and tolerant in outlook, were condemned as 'libertines' by an opposition composed of supporters of the House of Orange and their devoted followers—the Calvinist clergy and congregations in which there was a large element of the lower social orders. Here the dislike of Calvinist for 'Capitalist' was translated directly into a political clash. The same was true in New England where the Puritan gentlemen who founded Massachusetts and Connecticut on the traditional bases of security and status came into conflict with the immigrant city merchants full of cockney ingenuity. 'To be both a pious Puritan and a successful merchant meant to live under what would seem to have been insupportable pressures.'[1]

If the followers of Calvin are to be identified by class or occupation, two groups have better claims to consideration than the merchants, at any rate in the early phases: they are the gentry and the artisanate. In

[1] B. Bailyn, *The New England Merchants in the 17th Century* (Cambridge, Mass., 1955), 44.

France and the Netherlands, as in England and New England later, the Calvinist leadership was recruited from among that class of socially influential but penurious and often disgruntled minor gentry—'landed gentlemen' (as G. M. Trevelyan wrote) of the type of Cromwell, who were not, like the Cavaliers, deeply attached to the soil, who regarded their estates merely as assets in the money market, who had here no rest for the spirit or home for the heart, who so long as they were sojourners upon earth, lived 'in Mesheck, which they say signifies Prolonging; in Kedar which signifieth Blackness'.[1] Such as these formed the *élite*, but they were not numerous enough to form the rank and file of the army of Calvinist faithful. These were recruited in the towns of western Europe from amongst the growing band of artisans. The southern Netherlands, where the ancient cloth towns like Ghent and Ypres were in decline, contained an unstable and inflammable urban population which suffered all the misfortunes of widely fluctuating employment and prices. When persecution drove many thousands from their homes they fled northwards to the ports and industrial areas of the northern Netherlands, France and England. The growth of the population of cities like Leiden, Haarlem and Amsterdam can be traced in detail from the 'Registers of Newly Arrived Citizens'. Pious, industrious and often literate, these skilled artisans of every description made up the ranks of Calvinism and overflowed into other sects like the Mennonites and the strange and varied creeds lumped together under the Anabaptists. At Norwich and Colchester also they joined their co-religionists: the child who wrote from Norwich to his grandmother at Ypres was not untypical of the Calvinist household. '. . . we are living in great quietness and peace and the word of God is much preached among us. For half a year I learnt book binding, but it gave little profit: now I have another Trade. My eldest sister works for Pieter Bake of Ypres who has a brewery here in Norwich. My brother Willekin is learning the trade of a cutler: Father is working in a thread twist factory: my little sister spins thread.'[2] Diligent artisan households such as this were the backbone of the early Calvinist community. It is not difficult to see why some of them rose to wealth and status in a still medieval society where most things worked by rote if at all, where high days and holy days went together and the pace of man was the pace of the ox. Calvin's teaching may well have encouraged the man who brought thrift and sobriety to his task to see material success as the sign of God's favour: and since none in his heart could scrutinize the inscrutable will of God, all kept on trying. In this fairly mobile society, the workaday virtues brought their rewards: hence a growing degree of coincidence between the business

---

[1] G. M. Trevelyan, *England under the Stuarts* (London, 1904), 225-6.
[2] Huguenot Society Publications, 1887-8, ed. W. J. C. Moens.

communities of the later seventeenth and eighteenth centuries and the Protestant sects. The material success of the early, humble Calvinists and the growth in their numbers had, however, a result which would not have been so welcome to the founders. The Calvinist Church underwent a process often repeated in later forms of Protestantism and threw off its own schismatics—Arminians, for example, Independents, Baptists, Mennonites, Quakers, Unitarians. As the idea of tolerance grew amongst Protestants, the early tension between Puritan and profit-maker slackened. As piety became more and more evangelical, the consciences of the business community were more easily accommodated. But these were the phenomena of a Protestantism much adapted to social circumstances. The early reformers would have found it difficult to recognize, and impossible to accept, as their doctrine.

If Protestantism and the Protestant ethic seem to explain less of the economic phenomena than they seemed at one time to do, it also appears that there is, in the Reformation era, less to be explained. The sixteenth century witnessed important economic changes. The expansion of Europe brought on to the scene new supplies of silver, new sources of spices. The volume of trade grew, population increased, new routes and entrepôts were established as old ones declined: and these things brought important social changes in their wake as prices rose. Some incomes were adjusted to the new levels of prices, some more than adjusted, while some stayed still. Yet the economic development of Europe between the French invasions of Italy and the end of the Thirty Years War contains more of imitation and readjustment than of genuine innovation. Leadership in economic matters passed slowly from the Mediterranean to the north, and as the Italian cities declined, those of the Netherlands rose. But there was little in the way of business or industrial technique in use in the northern economies that would have been unfamiliar to a Venetian merchant or a Florentine clothier of the fifteenth century. Late medieval Italy knew all the most sophisticated techniques of banking, credit and international exchange. It was to the House of the Tedeschi at Venice that Jacob Fugger the Second went to learn the arts of trade which he later employed to expand the House of Fugger into one of the largest business enterprises of the fifteenth century. The trade and banking of Bruges were dominated by the 'nations' (colonies) of the Genoese, Venetian, Florentine, Milanese and Lucchese merchants. It is not accidental that van Eyck's portrait of the Lucchese merchant Arnolfini and his wife has come down to us as a typical portrait of a late medieval merchant. In Elizabethan London the leading bankers were Italians or Spaniards still—Cavalcanti, Giraldi, Pallavicini—and even James I was still employing Burlamachi as his private financial agent. In the Dutch Republic some physical links between the emerging mercantile economy of the north and the old tradition that derived from Italy remained in the persons of acclimatized Italians like the Vernatti family who were active as financiers in both Holland and England. Nor was there any radical change in the way the economies themselves worked. The theory and practice of the entrepôt was as important in the Dutch Republic as it had been in the Venetian, and the largest share of the wealth won by the Dutch came from the services they offered the rest of the world as middlemen. It was no accident, either, that the Dutch merchants who in the early decades of the seventeenth century were appropriating the Italian methods of deposit banking should have employed de Keyser to design for them a Bourse purely Italian in style; for not the least important items in the traffic between Italy and the north were the conceptions of architecture and planning which helped to shape the new mercantile cities of the north—conceptions such as those found in the books, maps and drawings of the works of Serlio, Palladio, Vignola and Scamozzi which were published in Holland in these years. The 'Italianate' character of drama worried not a little the Puritans of the north. The two most creative musicians of contemporary Holland and Germany, Sweelinck and Schutz, were both pupils of the Gabrielis, organists of St Mark's, Venice. Thus the rising mercantile economies of the north not only borrowed the economic ideas and techniques of Italy but reproduced as best they could the social and aesthetic context in which the Italian economy had flourished. 'Amsterdam is a young Venice in the arts of trade and every day becomes more skilled,' wrote the Stadholder of Holland in 1526. 'With its water, its situation, population and canals running by every street', wrote Guicciardini thirty years later, 'it is very like Venice.'

Inasmuch as the mercantile society of northern Europe contained an industrial element, this too resembled that found in Italy. The decay of the ancient city industries of Italy—the cloth and silk industries of Florence, Milan, Parma, Como, Lucca, Genoa and eventually Venice herself—had its analogy in the decay of the ancient cities of the southern Netherlands; and the reasons were in both cases the same: the cumbrous regulation of industrial production by the corporations. The great difference was only this: that in the Netherlands and in East Anglia the cloth industry succeeded—as the Italian industries in general failed to do —in emancipating itself from the control of the urban guilds and thereby equipped itself to organize more flexibly to meet the whims of fashion and demand. Important though they were, the technical innovations in the soap, glass and metal industries did not come near to changing the nature of sixteenth or seventeenth-century society. Throughout Europe, including Britain, 'industry' continued to mean textile manufacture, ranging from the finest and most sophisticated worsteds and silks of

Holland or England to the coarse woollens or linens of Germany or Poland. Everywhere, these industries were closely linked with farming and the countryside. To repeat: the organization of industry remained a good deal more primitive than the organization of commerce, and the largest debt of commercial technique was owed to Italy, especially in accountancy, which was basic to all other forms of business development. In all respects, the similarities between the characteristics of the highly developed economy of late medieval Italy and those of the north European economies of the early modern age are more striking than the differences. The same was true of the merchants and bankers themselves. A Medici or Datini or a Fugger would have found his modes of thought and behaviour perfectly well understood in the company of a Trip or a Pels or a Deutz of seventeenth-century Amsterdam. If problems of usurious conduct troubled the mercantile mind less and less as time went on, this was not because Calvinism succeeded in its original objects but because it had failed.

The two areas which in 1500 represented the richest and most advanced concentrations of trade, industry and wealth were the quadrilateral formed by the Italian cities Milan, Venice, Florence and Genoa; and the strip of the Netherlands that ran from Ypres north-east past Ghent and Bruges up to Antwerp. It was not merely coincidence that these were the areas where the tradesmen of the cities had been most successful in emancipating themselves from feudal interference and in keeping at bay the newer threat of more centralized political control offered by the new monarchies. In the fleeting intervals between the storms of politics and war, men here glimpsed the material advance that was possible when tradesmen were left in peace unflattered by the attentions of strategists who regarded their activities as the sinews of war. Precisely because the political and social relationships in which the merchants here lived were so relatively simple, these economic societies left behind them very little in the way of speculative literature. The precocious economic development of the cities of Italy and the Low Countries was cradled in the civic independence of those cities where merchants had achieved political power. The way in which that power was exercised varied from one city to another. At Venice the 'state' seemed to achieve a certain degree of independence of the rich patricians themselves, while it did not in Genoa. The Venetian Republic built galleys, fixed freight rates, auctioned galleys to private bidders, maintained factories and arranged routes and protection for Venetian ships. Yet neither here nor in the Netherlands did the *political* or social situation provoke merchants or statesmen into speculation about the relationship between economic and other activities. Such 'economic' literature as emerged from these urban economies was of two kinds: either ruminations, in the medieval tradition, on the moral implications and problems posed by business life, or attempts to deal with the purely technical problems of a mercantile economy—largely questions of exchange, credit and money. Far the most fertile source of semi-economic literature at Florence, Venice and Genoa in the sixteenth century was the seemingly endless controversy on the legitimacy of interest. The priestly disputants, Augustinian and Dominican, friars, theologians, lawyers, Archbishops and Cardinals continued with more vigour than result the quarrel heightened by the growth of deposit banking and of associations of lenders in what were called *monti*. Closely related to this was the equally brisk and equally sterile priestly debate over profit gained through bills of exchange. Suggestions that the public pawnshops that had sprung up all over Italy and the Netherlands between the fifteenth and sixteenth centuries should be allowed to charge interest to cover the expenses of management provoked another battle of words between Franciscan defenders and Augustinian and Dominican critics. Was begging to be prohibited—as the Government of Spain and the Netherlands proposed—or not? In Italy and Spain the Franciscans and Dominicans were again at issue and in the Netherlands the intervention of the Chancellor of the University of Bruges (Aegidius Witsius's *De Continendis et aliendis domi pauperibus*) links the medieval quarrel to the new problem of poverty and the provision of workhouses for the able-bodied poor. A much smaller volume of technical manuals, like Davanzati's *Lazione delle Moneta* (1588) and Scaruffi's *Alitinonfo* moved the debate from the moral on to the practical plane but did not succeed in making it any more interesting. The advanced urban economies did not, it seems, make for searching enquiry or radical thinking about economic problems *per se*. These were to come, not from comfort but from stress, not from satisfaction but from discontent. It was not from the rich mercantile cities of the north but from the Papal prison at Naples that there came one of the first Italian treatises addressed to the problem of how to increase the volume of trade within a state: Antonio Serra's *Brief Discourse on a Possible means of causing Gold and Silver to abound in Kingdoms where there are no mines* (1613) was a more serious work than its title might imply. Why were the Neapolitan provinces so poor and why were Venice and Genoa so rich? Like the majority of writers of the sixteenth and seventeenth centuries, Serra was convinced—and there is no certainty that he was wrong—that the distress of the kingdom of Naples could be traced not least to the scarcity of specie. He rejected utterly the opinion of contemporaries (like de Sanctis) that this was simply due to the high rate of exchange which could be regulated by checks on the outward movement of bullion, and sought the causes in the condition of trade between Naples and her neighbours. If a nation contracts debts greater than the credits it earns, no amount of regulation will prevent the export of its money. Serra therefore turns to the economic conditions which will make a nation a creditor amongst its neighbours: to do this it must rely on the fruits of its soil, the quantity of its manufactured exports; this in turn depends on the character of its population, its enterprise in breaking into foreign trade with new industries and the success with which it can intrude into world trade as a middleman. To help to achieve these objects—to develop nascent industries, stimulate exports and influence the exchanges—governments are entitled to intervene in economic affairs. All this has a familiar ring to a reader conversant with the debate that took place a few years later in England between Thomas Mun and his opponents. Earlier than Mun, Serra has some claim to be among those who first suspected the superficiality of much monetary analysis of contemporary economic distress and sought for deeper causes in the conditions of trade and industry. It hardly needs to be added that his views had not the slightest influence on his contemporaries or on the authorities in the kingdom of Naples: to all intents and purposes Serra's *Breve Trattato* with its pungent and detailed criticism of state policy lay buried for a century and a half. It would be unjust to suppose that this in any way represented special prejudice against a provincial rebel. To do it justice, the Spanish system of government oppressed its subjects pretty equally: the hand of dynast, bureaucrat and tax gatherer fell upon all without much distinction in that exhausted and ruined kingdom, which the riches of the Indies only succeeded in impoverishing. It was not for want of criticism. From the ranks of the *politicos*, recruited almost entirely from the secular clergy, there came throughout the sixteenth and seventeenth centuries a constant barrage of criticism of state policy. Mariana, Marquez, Gonzalez de Ayala, Carranza, Fajardo and many others pleaded for a sound currency, warned against the operation of Gresham's Law, and belaboured the folly of attempting to prohibit the export of treasure while at the same time incurring vast foreign debts. Moncada and Navarrete attacked the laws by which government tried to regulate the price and movement of corn, criticized the expulsion of the Moriscos and saw the glorious crusades of Spain as the root cause of the progressive and continuous decay of trade and industry. But all to no purpose. Taxation grew, monopolies multiplied; the richest treasure house in the world had to end by debasing its coins, and the ambition of every Castilian burgher became to raise his family to *hidalgo* rank and purchase exemption from taxation. In all this there was neither policy nor logic but only a kind of fiscal desperation that contradicted every kind of sense and ignored all advice. It was to remain true for a very long time: as Coleridge said of Sicily in his *Table Talk*: 'You may learn the fundamental principles of political economy in a very compendious way by taking a short tour through Sicily and simply reversing in your mind every law, custom and ordinance.'

While rationality and official policy were growing ever wider apart in Spain and her dominions, the new states that were rising in Britain and France were marked by persistent if not wholly successful attempts to draw thought and policy together more closely. This is not to say that statesmen and administrators always fashioned their legislation wisely, much less that it always succeeded in its aims, wise or unwise. But it is difficult not to see a broad *rapprochement* between what many writers and thinkers were saying, and the legislative acts of government: a *rapprochement* that contrasts markedly with the quarrel between the Spanish statesmen and the Spanish *politicos*. There have been many attempts by historians and economists to define the nature and ends of these policies of economic nationalism. Some writers have seen them as emerging from the ambitions of statesmen aiming principally at building up the power of their states. To others they represented merely the sectional ambitions of traders, a conspiracy contrived by a minority for their own private interests. 'Our merchants and manufacturers', wrote Adam Smith in the chapter of *The Wealth of Nations* entitled *The Mercantile System*, 'have been by far the principal architects.' Conducted in these terms the debate tended to attribute one of two alternative aims to the creators of 'the mercantile system': the end was either 'power' or 'plenty'. It seems doubtful whether the controversy is a very fruitful one. For it becomes plain as soon as we try to define what 'mercantilists' meant by 'power' that they were thinking of a political system which rested on an economic basis and had certain economic ends. Equally, 'plenty' was thought of in relation to politics and strategy. 'Wealth' was not merely an economic conception; it had to be of a character that would coincide with and reinforce the strength of the nation and its capacity to defend itself—perhaps even to seize victory and its spoils from weaker neighbours. 'Power' and 'Plenty', that is to say, were not mutually exclusive conceptions but complementary conceptions. The emphasis fell on the one or the other according to time, place and persons, but the two conceptions were never wholly divorced. How, indeed, in the conditions of almost constant warfare of sixteenth and seventeenth-century Europe, with Leviathan heir to the inhumanity of medieval warfare and the technology of the new science, could it be otherwise? There was as yet no room for the luxury of a strictly differentiated 'economic' version of economic science. If the 'state' needed the resources of the merchant, the merchant could ill do without the resources of the 'state'. Such at any rate was the case in the states along the western seaboard of Europe, where dynasticism saw the advantages of a marriage with trade and in saner moments came to decent terms over a settlement. Exploited and oppressed the new partner often was, by wildly fanatic or idly extravagant consorts: but there remains a striking difference between the chaos that was Castile and the generally accepted orthodoxy regarding national economic objectives and methods of achieving them found in most other national states. Adam Smith's history may not have been impeccable, but there was some truth in his contention that 'the mercantile system'—that complex of rules by which the Government intervened to promote a certain conception of trade—was the result of arguments 'addressed by merchants to Parliaments and the Counsels of Princes, to nobles and country gentlemen...'. From a 'fruitless care' to obtain and keep as much precious metal as possible for their country, the mercantilists had turned to another problem: the balance of trade. To achieve a favourable balance of trade, said Adam Smith, they had devised 'two great engines': one a set of legislative measures designed to encourage exports (or more strictly the export of *manufactured* goods) and another set designed to discourage imports (or more strictly the import of *manufactured* goods). Conversely, raw materials needed for industrial use were to be kept for home industry or imported as freely and cheaply as possible when it was necessary to obtain them abroad. Adam Smith's criticisms of the system fall to be considered elsewhere: but whether historically well-founded or not, the nature of the legislative system called 'mercantilist' is not in doubt. The 'two great engines' were real. Their origins were more debatable.

Much of the apparatus of economic control which came later to be associated with the economic or political ambitions of the modern state was in fact medieval in origin: the product of parochial or sectional demand or of simple xenophobia. Nothing was more characteristic of the 'mercantile system' than the attention given by thinkers, administrators and legislators to reserving supplies of English wool for the use of the English cloth industry. When the doctor in the *Discourse of the Common Weal of this Realm of England* (1581. Ed. Lamond, pp. 86–7) argued that the export of wool was 'not sufficient to bringe in treasure' and that England stood to gain more by keeping supplies at home for the 'clothiers, tanners, copers, and worsted makers—which, by their misteries and faculties, doe bringe in anie treasour', he was only repeating what had been government policy since the mid-fifteenth century. Trade and industrial interests combined with fiscal need to fashion a system of industrial protection—a ban on imported woollen manufactures—with prohibitions on the export of wool. The kind of industrial pressure behind such policies was occasionally revealed, as, for example, in the dispute in Henry VIII's time over York's surviving right to export Yorkshire wool. In 1529 the clothiers of the country complained that this export deprived them of wool supplies. An Act passed in that year annulled York's privilege. The comprehensive navigation policy of the Stuart period finds its origins in the medieval measures taken against Italian merchants, partly on sumptuary and partly on other grounds:

> The grete galleys of Venees and Fflorence
> Be wel ladene with thynges of complacence
> All spicerye, and of grocers ware,
> Wyth swete wynes, all manere of chaffare,
> Apes and Japes and marmasetts taylede,
> Trifles, trifles that littelle have availede
> And thynges wyth whiche they fetely blere oure eye,
> With thynges not enduryng that we bye.

But the author of the *Libelle of English Polycye*, like a dozen others, held that the offence of these foreigners was double: they brought gew-gaws and took away the 'brightest jewell'—England's wool. The scarcity of precious metals in the later Middle Ages led one state after another to interfere with their export. When Edward IV made it a felony to export bullion, the Act implied that there were two reasons for this: it was to preserve the country from being drained of its currency and to avoid the political dangers to the Government of having no treasure with which to meet emergencies. Similar instances of more or less unrelated elements of local or group interests at work to produce embryonic mercantilism may be collected from other European countries. The Italian, Hanseatic and Flemish cities all developed their own versions of a 'navigation code' restricting their merchants' use of foreign shipping. In Germany the cities regularly carried on a battle against the surrounding countryside for the control of food and industrial raw materials. In some cases a *Bannmeile* was created and within it any food or materials produced had to go to the city. No industry was allowed which might compete with the city's handicrafts. Thus the interests of urban consumers and producers were promoted in a way which finds echoes but no exact counterpart in England or France, but foreshadows later national economic exclusiveness to a remarkable degree. In France, by contrast, the consciousness of the national implications of economic policy is early and pervasive. If the silk industry of Lyons deserved encouragement, it was not because it would benefit Lyons but because it would benefit France. In his edict of 15 December 1466 Louis XI declared:

Nous avons été avertis qu'à l'occasion de la necessité où l'on est d'aller chercher et faire venir du dehors de notre royaume les draps d'or et de soye, il sort de ce royaume la somme de 4,500,000 écus d'or environ, ce qui est chose fort préjudiciable à nous–même ... c'est pourquoi, afin d'obvier à la grande sortie d'or et d'argent qui chaque année se fait de notre royaume à cause des dis draps d'or et de soye ... nous avons ordonné après mures et grandes délibérations de notre Conseil, de fair établir cet art des draps d'or et de soye pour être exercée en la ville de Lyon et pour ce motif d'y faire venir des homes et des femmes experimentées en ce métier.

Scattered through the royal edicts and the *cahiers* are hundreds of similar expressions of incipient economic nationalism. The exporters of coin and bullion were a favourite target. Jacques Coeur was condemned in 1453 for allegedly sending money out of the kingdom. The Papacy was constantly under fire for draining France of her money. 'Money', said a *cahier* of the Estates-General in 1484, 'is in the body politic what blood is in the human body: it is then necessary to examine what bleedings and purgings France has undergone,' and added that the Papacy had recently robbed France of two millions of gold. Thus bullionism was used to support Gallicanism and vice versa. The author of *Le Débat des Hérauts d'Armes de France et D'Angleterre* in the mid-fifteenth century joined the legislators in a general ode of satisfaction at the natural sources of wealth that France commanded, making her virtually independent of foreigners. And recurrently there appeared in the edicts and pamphlets the attacks on luxury—extravagance of apparel for men and women, the use of perfumes and the importation of vain trifles. Bullionism combined with the old sumptuary tradition in the ban on gold and silver thread and gilded furnishings.

The policies of economic nationalism that were adopted by the rising states of modern Europe and which came to be called 'mercantilist' had their roots in these scattered acts and thoughts of feudal and municipal authorities of the past. There was little intellectual or logical coherence about them. Moral disapproval of luxury, emotional distrust of strangers, superstitious reverence for the special merits of gold and silver, monopolists' fears for their monopolies and others' fears of monopolies—these were all jumbled together in a mixture that reflected a greater or lesser degree of human stupidity and human shrewdness. Yet from the mid-sixteenth century onwards there are increasing signs that thinkers, administrators, governments of the new states in western Europe are beginning to gather their ideas on economic policy into some kind of shape. The costs of dynasticism were rising rapidly. Courts were larger and more luxurious. Wars were longer. The yield of crown lands and spasmodic war levies did not add up to enough to support the costs of the new nationalism, even when supplemented by the sale of posts, monopolies and the like. No government could remain wholly unaware that there was a relationship between its own solvency and the economic welfare of its subjects. '. . . the wealth of the subiectes', said the doctor in the *Discourse of the Common Weal*, 'is the wealthe of the Kinge.' The results of this realization varied from state to state, and the failure of historians to agree on the merits or motives of the government intervention that followed as a natural consequence, and formed the central feature of all 'mercantilist' belief, is not surprising when contemporaries themselves were so divided in their opinions. The main fact was the increasing disposition on all sides to believe that it was the task of governments to regulate the economic life of their subjects according to certain rules. The policies adopted varied to some extent according to the economic and social structure of the state concerned. In some states policy was imposed from above: in others it sprang from consultation and co-operation with individual or group interests. Nowhere did the older moral, sumptuary antipathy to luxury entirely disappear. Everywhere empiricism rather than scientific rationality was characteristic of the movement. Agrarian states differed in their methods from those with a substantial element of maritime trade and urban industry. The timing varied from place to place, the characteristic doctrines and policies being generally soonest to appear and soonest to die amongst the maritime nations of the Atlantic seaboard, slowest to appear and slowest to die in Europe east of the Elbe, and in the peripheral states of the Iberian Peninsula and the south and east Mediterranean. The measures that were taken cannot always be directly or rationally related to local circumstances. For there was a considerable and surprisingly swift traffic in ideas from country to country. Appropriate or otherwise, there seems to be an increasing uniformity of doctrine amongst thinkers and policy-makers on general principles as the seventeenth century proceeds. Overtly or otherwise, the central principle came to be that of the balance of trade: and it first appears in a clearly defined form in England.

Round about the middle years of the sixteenth century the balance of trade in its classic form becomes the leading theme of several writers. The author of the *Discourse of the Common Weal*, writing in 1549, put it thus: '. . . we must alwaies take care that we bie no more of strangers than we sell them [for so we sholde empoverishe ourselves and enriche them]' and both he and Gresham referred to a calculation of the customs made in the time of Edward III from which (it was suggested) it could be seen that exports had then exceeded imports. Two years after the first draft of the *Discourse* was written William Lane was suggesting to Cecil that he should use the customs figures to find out whether exports exceeded imports or vice versa. Two years later, William Cholemeley, a London grocer, drew the further conclusion in a petition that exports were not large enough to pay for imports and that treasure was being drained overseas as a result. Such ideas were not wholly new. What has been called 'the balance of bargains' theory had long been implicit in legislative provisions by which successive governments had tried to regulate individual contracts between English and foreign merchants so as to make them add to the volume of bullion or coin available in the country. An English merchant selling goods in the official staple towns on the Continent was compelled to bring back a proportion of his proceeds in cash. The alien who sold goods in England was compelled by the Statutes of Employment to spend a proportion of his gains in England. The customers, who collected tariff dues, and the royal exchanger, who changed the customers' foreign coinage into English coins, supervised these regulations. What gave added force to the conception of a balance at this time was, in all probability, the arrival on the English scene of double-entry book-keeping at a time when it could combine with a growing consciousness of the corporate character of the nation state. Double entry had been in use in Italy since at least the fourteenth century —experts now despair of being more precise than that—but when the *Discourse* first appeared Pacioli's systematic treatise was little more than half a century old. The earliest double-entry accounts (of Thomas Howell, a Spanish merchant) were a quarter of a century old. Gresham himself was keeping his own accounts on the new principles, as were many others. Hugh Oldcastle's gloss on Pacioli—the first study in English—was not yet a decade old. *The Maner and Fourme* by James Peale, the first text on book-keeping of purely English origin, was to appear four years after the *Discourse* in 1553. Unquestionably, the idea of a 'balance' taken from the ledger had a powerful influence on economic writers who developed from it a theory of national equilibrium, with the rider that any disequilibrium had to be remedied by payments in cash. The phrase 'balance of trade' appears to have been first used by Misselden in *The Circle of Commerce* (1618), but the idea is inherent in the explanatory note which William Lambarde, the Kentish antiquary, added on Hales's remarks about foreign trade: 'If we send out more comodities in valeu than we bringe home, the overpluis cometh in in coyne; but if we bringe in more, then the overpluis must nedes be paid for in moneye, and this is the measure of increasinge or diminishinge the coyne, except of that little which is found within the realme.' Thus a main principle of economic thought and policy for the next two centuries was clearly enunciated.

These basic principles for measuring the national advantage were already well established when the Age of Discovery began. The urge towards discovery was itself in part a reflection of the material hopes of the pioneers and the rulers who financed them. Likewise, the potentialities of the new age were seen by contemporaries largely as a means to fulfil the demands of a national policy of economic and strategic security. The 'Capitulations' of April 1492 between Columbus and Ferdinand and Isabella bear eloquent witness to the financial hopes entertained by both parties. For Columbus set out not only with one completed introduction to the 'Grand Khan' and two blanks for any other potentates he might meet, but with a promise of 10 per cent of all gold, gems, spices or merchandise produced or obtained by trade within those domains, tax free; the right to invest in one-eighth of any ship going thither; as well as eternal lien on these rights for his heirs and successors. The attraction exercised by the hope of treasure did not lose its potency for a very long time. The charters of colonial companies paid special attention to mining rights; witness, for example, the grant to the Royal African Company in January 1663 which conferred title to 'all mines of gold and silver and the sole privilege of trade' in that order.

The good fortune of Spain in acquiring vast supplies of silver was seen by other rulers as an immediate and uncomplicated windfall to the Spanish government: its disadvantages, if there were disadvantages, were not apparent to them. Rising Bourbon and falling Habsburg worshipped at economic altars that were not markedly different, and successive English rulers continued to hope that the eastern coast of North America might prove a new Peru. The great new companies of Elizabeth's reign all bear the same mark. Russia was originally a staging post in the 'Russia' Company's quest for the wealth of the Indies and Cathay and the fabled mines of Golconda. Frobisher sought the same goal by the north-west route on his first voyage. He was lured aside on his second and third voyages by the mirage of gold ore in Newfoundland. The Company of the Mines Royal hoped for gold and silver under English soil, and joint-stock companies of privateers, with government blessing, preyed on the seaborne trade of others for long periods of the reign.[1]

It is not easy for a modern eye to bring the nature of these enterprises into focus. Half a century ago, historians debated whether they were great essays in state policy and prestige or merely treasure hunts of a private and generally deplorable character. Greater knowledge has made it difficult to subscribe wholly to the simple theses of either William Cunningham (who held the former view) or George Unwin (who held the latter). The most recent historian of the Russia Company, for example, observes that the original enterprise of 1553 involved 240 Londoners, including high officers of state as well as merchants and navigators. There was, he thinks, no single motive to explain the origin of the enterprise: state policy, national prestige, the lure of gold and silver, geographical curiosity—all were present.[2] Elizabeth, in her bargaining with the czars on behalf of the company, was resolutely

---

[1] See George Unwin, *Studies in Economic History*, Ch. v *passim* esp. p. 175.
[2] T. S. Willan, *The Early History of the Russia Company* (Manchester, 1956), 1–2.

business-like, sticking grimly to questions of trading privileges, while the other side ranged orientally over all kinds of political and dynastic affairs.

If it is less simple than it was formerly for the historian to separate off trade wars from legitimate trade in that age of violence, it is also less simple to draw the history of trade into clearly defined phases. One school of thought has suggested that the drive for colonies began with the simple search for treasure and developed later into a more sophisticated view of the general economic value of colonies; in particular, that colonies would free the mother country from dependence on foreigners for valuable materials and thereby achieve a net saving of precious metals as well as a greater degree of strategic security.[1] This consideration was certainly prominent in many minds: it is clearly set out by Hakluyt:

The Countries . . . of America whereunto we have just title . . . being answerable in climate to Barbary, Egypt, Syria, Persia, Turkey and Greece, all the islands of the Levant Sea, Italy, Spain, Portugal, France, Flanders, High Almayne, Denmark, Eastland, Poland and Muscovy, may presently or within a short space afford unto us, for little or nothing, and with much more safety, either all or a great part of the commodities which the aforesaid countries do yield us at a very dear hand and with manifold dangers.

The passage demonstrates how, at a very early stage in English colonial enterprise, men formulated the ideas which were finally carried into practice in the Navigation Code of the Commonwealth and Restoration period. Yet it is doubtful whether there is any clear progression from 'bullionist' to 'mercantilist' views, from 'state' enterprise to 'private' enterprise. The boards of the late Stuart companies— like the African or Fishery Companies—were just as odd a mixture of courtiers, hangers-on, state officials and merchants as those of Elizabeth's time. Treasure continued to be held in high esteem, probably for very good reasons. What changed perceptibly were the ideas, policies and laws which aimed at conserving and increasing the supply of treasure. One embarrassing, but ultimately educative, characteristic of some of these new colonial and peripheral trades became steadily clearer as time went by: some, notably those to the east and perhaps north too, called for large supplies of precious metals in the first instance to be used as a purchasing medium by the European traders. They could only increase the net amount of bullion or coin available to their parent countries if the commodities they produced were re-sold for bullion or coin to an amount greater than that absorbed by the original purchases abroad.

[1] See, for example, R. L. Schuyler, *The Fall of the Old Colonial System* (Oxford, 1945), 11–13.

This major fact had to be accommodated within any set of doctrines designed to prove the benefits of colonial trades.

The central features of mercantilist policy were gathered together and restated in classical form three-quarters of a century after the appearance of the *Discourse* by Thomas Mun in his *England's Treasure by Fforraign Trade*. Mun's work became the bible of later mercantilists— Adam Smith thought it was the model upon which continental mercantilism was built—but its gospel was ancient by the time it was thought worthwhile to publish it. Like most mercantilist writing it was the product of crisis—in this case the depression of the early 1620's—but its publication was delayed until its robust anti-Dutch sentiments appeared appropriate in the cold war tactics that preceded the war of 1665. It said no more and no less than the *Discourse*. 'The ordinary means to increase our wealth and treasure is by *Fforraign Trade*, wherein we must ever observe this rule; to sell more to strangers yearly than wee consume of theirs in value.' Mun illustrates his principle thus: if (he says) we export goods to the value of £2,200,000 and import goods valued at £2,000,000, we must win the difference in treasure. But if the situation is reversed we lose treasure. This principle, simple to grasp and easy to adapt to almost anybody's case, was to be elaborated and modified as the seventeenth century went on; but its obstinate longevity as the central principle of the mercantile system may be seen from Matthew Decker's *Essay on the Causes of Decline of the Foreign Trade* which went into a second edition in 1749, exactly two centuries later than the *Discourse* and probably a century and a quarter after Mun. Decker, in some respects leaning away from state regulation towards freedom of trade, can write as though it were a truism:

Therefore if the Exports of Britain exceed its Imports, Foreigners must pay the balance in Treasure and the Nation grow Rich.

But if the Imports of Britain exceed its Exports, we must pay the Foreigners the balance in Treasure and the Nation grow poor.

No wonder the free trading prophets of the Victorian Age like McCulloch were mortified by the obstinate persistence of the people in this simple heresy. This, the balance of trade fallacy as they thought it, was 'the gilded image of clay and mud' that stood, an object of slavish adoration, long after wise men like North and Hume had exploded its foundations. Before we look at those foundations it is worth noting that the apparent continuity of principle that stretches from mid-sixteenth to mid-eighteenth century conceals one important development: the problem of foreign exchange in relation to the national welfare was made to take second place to the flow of trade and the conditions which governed that flow, a change symbolized in the famous controversy of the 1620's between Gerard Malynes and his critics—especially Mun and Misselden. Malynes was in the sixteenth-century tradition. Like Sir Thomas Gresham in Henry VIII's day, Malynes believed firmly in the efficacy of monetary control and regulation. Gresham, whose official concern to raise loans for his Prince was second only to his unofficial concern to explain to his master his own success in doing so, thought that England's best policy was to keep the value of her currency in the market as high as possible because (he argued) this would bring in specie and make it cheaper for England to buy foreign goods. He ignored the reaction of such a policy on export markets. More than half a century later, Edward Misselden, deputy governor of the Merchant Adventurers and in some respects strongly inclined to Mun's view that trade dominated the exchanges, could yet argue the merits of a 'low exchange'. A high exchange did not suit the Merchant Adventurers who, as exporters, found markets difficult and lost on the exchange of their proceeds from Flemish into English money.

The quarrels of economic experts are apt to become remote from the practical issues which originally generated them. The controversies of the 1620's would have no particular claim to record if they had turned merely on abstract principles: but they did not. The outcome was in effect a victory for Mun. Chapter after chapter of *England's Treasure by Fforraign Trade* rams home the doctrine that no amount of monetary manipulation—prohibitions on bullion export, enhancing or debasing of moneys, compulsory regulations governing the proceeds of exports, the 'admirable feats of bankers'—could affect the national welfare: it was 'The Ballance of our Fforraign Trade' that was 'the Rule of our Treasure'. And these beliefs guided, or at any rate coincided with, an increasing volume of legislation from Mun's time forward, which all aimed at enlarging exports and controlling while diminishing, according to certain principles, the volume of imports. The office of the Royal Exchanger was not in the event revived and its passing after 1628 witnessed to the dwindling faith that monetary policy was a controlling factor in the economy and could be regulated without regard to physical trade movements. So did the relaxing after the Restoration of official prohibitions on the export of foreign coin and bullion. Local coin it was still illegal to send abroad.

This slackening of monetary controls, and the tightening of regulations over the import and export of commodities that found its supreme expression in the so-called Navigation Code, provoked Adam Smith to observe that the mercantilists were here merely turning away from one fruitless care to another 'much more intricate, much more embarrassing and just equally fruitless'. Home trade (said the Father of Political

Economy) was disregarded by the mercantilists. Indeed everything was disregarded by them.

No sophistry [wrote McCulloch] was ever more completely successful. . . . Agriculture, commerce and manufacturers ceased to be objects of public solicitude. The 'balance of trade' was regarded as the only source of national wealth and the only measure of its increase; and all the complex machinery of premiums and bankers on the one side, and of restrictions and prohibitions on the other, was set in motion to render it favourable.[1]

As these proved defective, McCulloch continued, diplomatic, military and naval forces were all deployed to speed on the process 'in the vain attempt to realize an imaginary advantage, to seize a mere *ignis fatuus*'. That much of the mercantilist plan misfired, that economic ambition, private and national, acted as a provocation to war is not to be doubted. But, for the rest, much of the classical argument against the mercantilists was rhetorical and inaccurate. Quite apart from judgments on the practical results of their policies, mercantilist writers almost without exception related the 'balance of trade' arguments closely to the increase of the national product from the land and from industry. As regards commerce, restrictive principles were frequently used, but always with the idea that in the longer term the volume of trade might be increased. As a French historian has remarked: 'Les préoccupations monétaires sont le point de départ des mercantilistes, le productivisme et l'industrialisme sont le moyen d'avoir un commerce extérieur prospère qui est leur but.'[2] Again without prejudging questions of the practical efficacy of the legislative programme designed to achieve the mercantilists' ends, the literature that forms the background of debate to it does not suggest that the charge of 'intellectual confusion' which (as Keynes said) the economists brought against the mercantilists, was justified. How far did they, in reality, consider wealth and money to be 'in common language . . . in every respect synonymous'?[3] The *Discourse of the Common Weal* is very clear on this point. Precious metals are light to carry in relation to their value; they do not perish; they go current everywhere; they are most easily divided into many pieces; for these reasons 'they are chosen by a common consent of all the world, that is known to be of *anie Civilitie to be instrumantes of exchange to mesure all things by, most apt to be ether caried far, or kept in store, or to receave [ for] thinges whereof we have aboundance, and to purchase by theim other thinges which we lacke, when ore wheare we have most neede*'. To this lucid good

---

[1] *Early English Tracts on Commerce*, ed. J. M. McCulloch (1856; Cambridge University Press reprint, 1954), vi–vii.
[2] J. Morini-Comby, *Mercantilisme et Protectionnisme. Essai sur les Doctrines Interventionnistes en Politique Commerciale du XVe au XIXe Siècle* (Paris, 1930).
[3] *Wealth of Nations*, bk IV, chap. 1.

sense the author adds some observations on desirable and less desirable occupations which suggest that though the debate on the primacy of commercial and monetary regulation still had three-quarters of a century to run, he himself was already aware of the basic importance of the productive factors in the national economy. There were (he says) 'Three sortes of misteryes'; those who took money out of the country; those who neither took out nor brought in but 'that which they doe get, they spend againe in the countrie'; and those who brought treasure in. The first—broadly speaking the importing interests—included 'mercers, grocers, vintners, haberdashers, mileyners'; to be reckoned 'tollorable, and yet not so necessarie in a Commonwealth but they might be but spared of all other'. Without compensating gains elsewhere they might be an expensive luxury. The second group comprised the tinker–tailor –candlestick-maker type of artisan and neither made nor lost from a national point of view. It was the third sort—'the clothiars, tannars, cappers and worsted makers'—who were to be cherished as bringing in treasure from abroad. These were the occupations which reduced England's dependence on imports, saving 'an infinite Treasour that goeth now over for so manie of the same', and supplied the exports that brought a positive access of money. Already the idea of national power is present: the realm will be replenished 'of people able to defende it, and also winne much treasour to the same'. Nor is the model for all this far to seek: it is 'the countrie of Flaunders and Germany ... wheare, through such occupations, it hath so manie and wealthie cities, that it weare uncredible in so little grounde to be'.

A reading of the *Discourse*, judicious, judicial, analytical, makes it difficult to sustain the conventional view that there was an intellectual progress in mercantilism, from the darkness of bullionism through the twilight of balance-of-trade doctrine to the dawn of *laissez-faire* and orthodox economic science. Here is no simple-minded bullionism confusing wealth and money: if there is emphasis on treasure it is for practical reasons bedded in the conditions of the day. If princes need 'greate treasure ... agaynst all eventes' it is because the author has in mind that

yf we should have warres or dearthe, as we have had, and shoulde nede either artilerie [munitions] or other aide of straungers, it is not the coine we have nowe could provide us that. And so likewise, yf we should have great scarcitie of corn within the realme, for the which we should be driven to fetche it from outewarde partes, it is not our money would purchase it.

He answers, two centuries in advance, Adam Smith's argument that necessary imports can always be paid for by commodity exports: these, even in plenteous years 'bringe in but skant enoughe of thinges necessarie'. So that 'yf bothe warre and dearthe should come together, as it hath ere this, how shoulde we doe? Surely we should be in a verie harde case and muche in danger of straungers.' If this was written in 1548 or 1549 the writer was not to have to wait long for his fears to be realized; the failure of the harvest in western Europe in 1556 strained the monetary resources of the area to the utmost by setting up a demand for Baltic grain which drained away silver and was largely responsible for the widespread financial crises of that year.[1] Other acts referred to the same fear of a haemorrhage of treasure: the Act of 1566 which aimed to encourage the home production of salt started its preamble with a reminder that provision of salt from abroad 'doth cost great soomes of money to The empoverishment of this Realme by wasting and conveying of the Treasure and Coyne of thys Realme into Forreiyn Parteis . . .'. Like these, but more systematically, Mun's *England's Treasure by Fforraign Trade* shows how dangerously facile is the argument that the mercantile system was constructed from ignorance and confusion regarding the nature of wealth and money. Its central doctrine is, as has been shown, the balance of trade: it was this, not 'Exchange' (as Malynes had argued), that was the worker of 'admirable feats'. Yet the function of the favourable balance in producing a net gain of treasure was not regarded in any abstract or superstitious way. Mun is perfectly well aware that trade *could* be carried on without the use of money, that (as he says) 'there was great trading by way of commutation or barter when there was little money stirring in the world'. Having himself worked as a merchant in Tuscany he is aware that the most advanced trading communities of his day, the Italian cities, had supplemented and replaced the use of precious metallic money by 'bills of debt' and 'Banks both publick and private, wherein they do assign their credits from one to another daily for very great sums with ease and satisfaction by writing only . . .'. He saw clearly the consequences of pushing the logic of bullionism to extremes; 'for all men do consent that plenty of money in a kingdom doth make the native commodities dearer . . .' and that though this might benefit 'some private men in their revenues' it was 'directly against the benefit of the Publique' in so far as high prices might check consumption and thereby reduce markets, trade and employment. The moral of the whole of this section of Mun's work is that the first practical function of money is to be employed in trade, not least in international trade. There is (he might have argued) no conflict between this argument and his insistence that a wise and mighty Prince will yearly 'lay up treasure' against sudden dearth and war, for some of this reserve, it appears, would be 'issued out continually' to subjects in the shape of contracts to

[1] A. Friis, 'An Inquiry into the Relations between Economic and Financial Factors in the 16th and 17th centuries', *Scandinavian Economic History Review* (1950).

build warships, buy and store corn, erect banks, and maintain the armed forces and their equipment.

It was not the habit of mercantilists to extrapolate their logic too far. For Mun the problem of national wealth was simply analogous to the problem of private wealth—'it cometh to pass in the stock of a kingdom as in the estate of a private man'. 'Sufficient unto the day' might have been their text and they would have been shocked by the scientific irresponsibility of a Hume who could, with an equanimity born of a sound faith in the laws of demand and supply, face the prospect of the over-night loss by Britain of four-fifths (why only four-fifths?) of her supply of bullion. Adam Smith's analogy between the detention of unnecessary amounts of gold and silver in a kingdom and the maintenance of surplus stocks of kitchen utensils would have seemed to Mun not so much sacrilegious as silly. So would the contradictions of the *Wealth of Nations* in the matter of bullion. For if (Mun might well have asked) it was true that one of the most remarkable economic developments of the century before he wrote was the spreading use of paper money and credit, if this had economized enormously in the use of the precious metals and effectively increased the circulation of money based on gold and silver, was this itself not a tacit admission that earlier ages suffered a dependence on gold and silver from which society had only recently been released? Some of the practical preoccupations which Mun had in mind are well known—the need, for example, for the East India Company (his own company) to export silver by means of which oriental goods were purchased for return shipment and re-export. This was not, as it was sometimes supposed, an isolated case, though it was an extreme one. To Mun there were '. . . many countreys which may yield us very profitable trade for our mony, which otherwise afford us no trade at all, because they have no use of our wares . . .'. The East Indies is first in his mind but he quotes Italy and Turkey similarly and brackets with these 'the East Countreys' as an area where a merchant with hard cash to dispose of might buy wheat, bring it back to his warehouse and re-export it to Spain or Italy at the right moment with great profit. It would be futile to argue that Mun's logic is always satisfactory or to deny that the policies he recommends would have run into serious problems. What seems clear is that his preoccupation with bullion rests on keen observation and intimate, if sometimes short-sighted, acquaintance with the techniques of domestic and international trade. Whereas later writers were frequently to fall into the error of assuming the existence of a sophisticated machinery of credit and payment, Mun assumes that it may frequently be necessary to pay foreigners in hard cash or lose the opportunity of a bargain altogether. It is true that he probably failed to understand the true nature of the bi-metallic flow of money which resulted from governmental manipulations of coinage for political ends, and that he had an inadequate appreciation of the interaction between trade movements and exchange problems. But there seems to have been a solid basis for the belief of Mun and his contemporaries that an extraordinary importance attached to the precious metals in the conduct of foreign trade.

When Mun was writing, the trades which posed the largest problems were those to the East and the Baltic. In both areas the difficulty arose first from the inability or unwillingness of the local inhabitants to buy enough goods to make reciprocal trade possible, and secondly from the absence of any stable system of multilateral payments (other than by means of corn or bullion) by which this disequilibrium could be remedied. The decision to revoke the penalties on the export of foreign coin and bullion in 1663 sprang partly from the observation that the Dutch Republic allowed freedom of movement to specie and still managed not only to retain its currency but to strengthen its position as a bullion market. Linked with this (and virtually overlooked by subsequent commentators) was the problem of what might be called the 'hard currency' areas. 'And forasmuch' (said the first words of the clause in the Act for the Encouragement of Trade which altered the law) 'as severall considerable and advantagious Trades cannot be conveniently driven and carried on without the species of Money or Bullion,' freedom to export must be allowed. The emphasis on the northern trades altered as time went on. As England's dependence on imported food lessened with the expansion of acreage and the improvement of techniques, the need to contemplate a large drain of silver was proportionately lessened. On the other hand the dependence on the Baltic area for naval stores grew greater, not less. The later attempts to develop New England as an alternative source of supply of timber and tar owed much to the belief that financially as well as strategically—and were not the two considerations one and the same?—much was to be gained by reducing dependence on the Baltic monopoly of strategic commodities. This preoccupation was still strong at the turn of the century: when the Commissioners of Trade and Plantations reported to the Lords on the state of the national economy in February 1701–2 they commented that

... we were overbalanced in our trade with Sweden and the Baltic about 200,000 l. per annum, in our trade to Denmark about 150,000 l. per annum, that ... we had for several years exported to the East Indies above 400,000 l. in bullion ... and that for some years before the late war we had been overbalanced in the French Trade about one million per annum.

But, a modern critic might ask, were these deficits not counterbalanced by the credits within Britain's international trading relationships?

With a total balance increasingly favourable, did the mechanism of cancellation through exchange not take care of the problems of individually unfavourable balances? The answer would seem to be that it did not.

The mercantilists formulated their doctrines in an age when trade had burst out of its traditional European confines within which merchants knew one another and traded along well-established lines, and had expanded into the peripheral areas of Asia, Africa, America; with this expansion had come new problems of payment and risk. These arose partly (as we have said) from lack of purchasing power, difficulties of meeting the unfamiliar tastes of consumers in tropical areas, above all from the absence of any of the means by which difficulties of payment are met in a multilateral trading system. Some of these difficulties were gradually solved as the Dutch, in particular, spread the network of trade and payment in the North and East. But many remained. 'The *East India* Company', wrote Newton's successor at the Mint, 'will always want great quantities of silver . . . all the wine, brandy, brocades, toys, lace and cambric from *France* and Flanders, and the iron and naval stores and timber from *Denmark* and *Sweden*, are paid for with gold and silver . . . .' Moreover, to add to these anxieties, no-one could feel satisfied that a calculation of the balance of payments which rested on the notoriously defective customs figures and omitted all consideration of invisible imports and exports, was in the least reliable.

The most striking testimony to the continuing role played by gold and silver in bridging the gaps in the system of international payment comes from such accounts as Henry Oxenford's *Essay towards Finding the Ballance of our Whole Trade* (1698–1719). Oxenford, the assistant inspector general of customs, was no rhetorician; his survey is dull, factual and repetitive. But it establishes beyond doubt the defective structure of the contemporary system of international payments which threw merchants and governments back on to dependence on the precious metals. Such problems were not the particular care of those states, like Britain or France, which are commonly regarded as pursuing definable 'mercantilist' policies. Perhaps the most illuminating evidence regarding the nature of trade with the Baltic area and the East comes from Dutch and Danish sources and shows that the Dutch, like the English, depended on a free flow of bullion and coin to maintain and raise the level of their foreign trade. '. . . the inhabitants of Holland', says he who was, next to Mun, the most influential economic writer of the seventeenth century,

can trade in no countries but by carrying goods thither, which having sold and turned into money, they convert it into other goods which they find there, or failing that, return their money into Holland by exchange; but if such foreign lands have little or no occasion for our goods, but afford rich commodities (to us) then is it not evident that we cannot trade with them to any purpose, unless we carry thither gold and silver in coin or in bullion ? And since by consequence everyone knows that *Norway*, the *East Country, Smyrna, Persia, India, China* &c. do afford us infinitely more merchandize than they take of us, *we cannot trade with them but by gold and silver.*[1]

Here in a nutshell is a *rationale* of the contemporary attitude to bullion. A later French analysis of the Dutch trading structure tallies with this.[2] The Dutch would be unable to trade on anything like the scale they did in the north unless they brought money or bullion with them—to Danzig, Norway, Konigsberg, and Russia. There can be little doubt, as the most recent and detailed study of the Baltic trade remarks, that the Danish Sound was the ultimate destination of much of the contents of the Silver Fleets from Spanish America. The other main stream, as the figures for Dutch and English companies show, was directed towards India. There were other, more local needs. Genoa, buying silk and grain from Sicily, found that Sicilians insisted on being paid in silver *ginovines*. On balance, there seems little reason to doubt that over long periods of time Europe exported at least as much silver as it received.

The views of those—like Mun or Child—who had a direct interest in overseas trades needing the lubrication of bullion and of those—like Downing or Coventry—who were persuaded that such trades were, for one reason or another, important for the public weal, go some way to provide a rational basis for policies aimed at increasing the nation's available supply of treasure. Side by side with such views, and to no small degree pulling against them in matters of trade and monetary policy, were those whose prime concern was with the coinage. This was probably the most fundamental reason for mercantilist anxiety over the supply of precious metals within a country. Mercantilists did not, as has been pointed out, press their logic too far. Mun was alive to the operation of what we should call quantity theory. Nor was Henry Robinson, author of *The Trades Increase* (1641), under any illusion as to the folly of a monopolistic scramble for treasure by one nation at the expense of others: '. . . it is our benefit that monies be plentifull also in countries where we carrie our commodities to sell . . . lest we fare as Alexander the Great who haveing neare conquered the whole world, wept because there was no more left for him to conquer'. The apparent disregard, by mercantilist authors, of the consequences of treasure accumulation which has puzzled later writers[3] is partially explained by a rule of thumb

---

[1] *Political Maxims of the State of Holland*, ascribed to Jan de Witt, but in reality by the Leiden clothier Pieter de la Court, published 1662.

[2] P. D. Huet, *Memoirs of the Dutch Trade* (London, 1717–19).

[3] See e.g. Heckscher, *Mercantilism*, II, chap. iv.

precept (drawn no doubt from business experience) that a profit was better than a loss, a truth which they assumed held good for nations as for individuals. Not being logicians, it seemed to them unnecessary to press the matter further. In so far as there were doubts, they were not likely long to survive consideration of the other main bogey of the times—the fear of a 'scarcity of money'. Throughout the entire period, but especially in times of trade depression in the 1620's, in 1649, the 1660's and 1690's, the lament was heard that the 'scarcity of money' was the reason why unsold stocks of goods accumulated and hands were idle. It was, after all, not altogether surprising that in countries that possessed no native resources of precious metals there should be some understandable anxiety as to the effect of foreign trade on the currency itself. The relationships between trade movements, exchange rates and such phenomena as the flow of money that resulted from bimetallic adjustments or debasements were all very imperfectly understood. The idea that the currency, upon which (short of barter) the level of trade and employment and indeed life of the people depended, should be left to the mercies of *laissez-faire*, occurred to no one. Such preoccupations cannot be dismissed as a superstition from which wiser opinion was free. The conflict between those who regarded the condition of the currency as a higher priority than the prosperity of the silver-exporting companies or merchants was not limited to England. When silver prices rose alarmingly in Holland throughout the 1680's and 1690's the authorities placed a total prohibition on the export of silver, largely at the behest of the currency authorities: this provoked a vigorous protest from the Burgomasters of Amsterdam:

... as a result of a general ban on (silver) export this country's trade not only with the East, Muscovy, Westphalia etc. but also with the East Indies, would be bound to come to a standstill or at any rate be greatly hampered, as without ready money trade is impossible. That in particular the city of Amsterdam—being the place where practically all bills of exchange payable within Europe are drawn, remitted or otherwise discounted or negotiated—will suffer tremendously and may even run the risk of losing much of the bill of exchange trade if her money changers and merchants are no longer free, in the case of places where bills are drawn or paid at a loss, to send from this country silver or specie to avoid such loss.

The Burgomasters' fears of 'the shortage of bullion and specie in this country and the anxiety felt here that they may become even scarcer' were strangely like those anxieties which were besetting their English neighbours a few years earlier, causing the Treasury to see whether the customs figures might be analysed so as 'to make a Ballance of the Trade betweene this Kingdome and any other part of the world' and to appoint an inspector general of customs to further these enquiries.

The structure and character of the Dutch economy was such that the concept of the trade balance had little or no meaning for them (see below): but there is no reason to suppose that a Dutch merchant would have differed substantially from the new and energetic secretary of the British treasury, William Lowndes, when he wrote of England's situation in 1695 that '... the Original Cause of the Scarcity of Silver in England and of the Loss by the Foreign Exchange on Remittances ...' was 'the *Ballance of Trade*'. This English habit of crystallizing the economic situation in terms of the balance was undoubtedly linked closely to the fact that English export trade was still based principally on an indigenous primary material and native manufacture: and it is no accident that the plea for a more liberal, rational and less superstitious policy towards the precious metals came from those merchants and companies who, like Mun and Child, were concerned with those *re-export* trades which were to achieve the great revolutionary changes in England's foreign trade in the seventeenth and eighteenth centuries. In short, as England's trading structure assumed some of the entrepôt characteristics which had earlier marked that of the Dutch, men's ideas on monetary policy were adjusted to fit the change—not so much, though, one should add, as to persuade them to allow the export of English coin, which remained strictly prohibited.

A central feature, then, of contemporary economic thought continued to be the very high premium placed on the precious metals. This way of thinking was not limited to those who are classically regarded as mercantilists: it was shared by the practical, sophisticated and cosmopolitan merchants of the Dutch Republic. It sprang from a number of contemporary factors. The Europe that was only in places beginning to free itself from the methods of barter in international trade was not yet fully equipped with those methods of payment and credit which some later writers seem to have assumed. Traditions of barter still existed in the Baltic ports: Glasgow's trade with Africa and the West Indies was still conducted on a barter basis in the eighteenth century. Until a more flexible mechanism of payment could be devised, the logical progress was from barter to cash payments. Before men could be induced to put their faith in paper money, and the various forms of I.O.U.'s accepted by later generations, there were certain obstacles to be overcome. One was the rigidity of the trading patterns of mercantilist Europe frequently imposed by the monolithic character of the trade between areas. When Adam Smith suggested that the mercantilists, in their obsession with treasure, ignored the alternative possibilities of meeting their obligations by paying with commodity exports, his anachronism pointed straight at a major difficulty of sixteenth and seventeenth-century international economic relations: and his comment that while the 'rude produce' of primitive ages was obviously unsuitable for such exchange, 'the finer and more improved manufactures' were admirably fitted because of their small bulk, reveals how innocent he was of the fundamental problems of the mercantilist age. The problems of payment that put a premium on treasure arose precisely because western Europe wanted more Baltic produce than could be paid for in goods acceptable to the producers. The Dutch did better than the English in these trades because they disposed of a larger variety of goods obtained by their middleman trading and especially of larger volume of specie. The same was true in the East where they succeeded to a considerable extent in creating an entrepôt system between the Middle East, the Indian mainland, the Archipelago, China and Japan, that eliminated some part of the need to rely on the export of specie from Europe. The English were less successful and continued to export enormous quantities of silver—nearly £9 millions in the first twenty years of the eighteenth century, or one-third as much again as the total silver coinage of England in 1701 —to meet that problem described by the English factors at Fort St David in 1693, but by no means to be found only in trade in India. 'The natives', they wrote, 'will not truck their pepper for goods, for if they cannot have ready [money] for their pepper, they care not to dispose of it.' Behind the declining importance of silver money—first relating to gold, then absolute—lay the fact that silver had a higher value as an international trading commodity than as a domestic coinage. The further East you traded, the higher the value of silver relative to gold and to goods.

Finally, besides these pecularities of a European economy still primitive, still much concerned with the exchange of primary commodities like corn, timber, fish, salt, wine and wool, there were problems posed by war, violence, political unrest. The prejudices and superstitions that lingered in the minds of men and seemed so foolish and irrational to the *philosophes* and economists were in part a reflection of the times. 'War', writes Sir George Clark of the seventeenth century, '. . . may be said to have been as much a normal state of European life as peace. . . .'[1] A war might cut off whole areas from trade: piracy and privateering were a continual threat to sea-borne cargoes. Even in peace time poor communications might hold up acceptances or autarkic policies isolate a country from free intercourse with all but the metropolis. Violence and threat of violence in this turbulent age may help to explain why men put more trust in treasure than in I.O.U.'s. Such were some of the considerations which caused statesmen as well as merchants to regard a favourable balance of trade (as Keynes put it) as 'a prime object of

---

[1] G. N. Clark, *The Seventeenth Century* (Oxford, 1947), 98.

practical statecraft' rather than the 'puerile obsession' that it seemed to later economists.[1]

If there was, then, some *rationale* to be found in the contemporary economy for the mercantilists' preoccupation with treasure, what of the other charges of Adam Smith, McCulloch and others that under the mercantile system 'the home trade was not regarded', that agriculture, commerce and industry were neglected in favour of the *chimaera* of the 'balance'? The objectives at which the balance-of-trade argument was aimed were neither purely economic, nor purely politically related to the strategic 'power' of the state. It cannot be denied that in the century that saw the construction of the 'system' in England—from 1620 to 1720— the residual, if not final, aim of many who thought about the problem was the winning of treasure for the national economy. Francis Brewster, writing in 1702, was no less categorical than Thomas Mun had been in the 1620's that 'the full employment of all Hands in the Nation is the surest way and means to bring BULLION into the Kingdom'. And the idea survived, as we have seen, in Decker and other writers, half a century longer. But this was not to say that the 'balance' excluded other considerations from their minds: on the contrary, the notion was to them a dynamic one. If exports were to be increased and the reliance on imports diminished—whether the end of all was to accumulate bullion, make the state more powerful, the people (or certain groups of them) more wealthy, increase England's self-sufficiency, or raise larger taxes— there must necessarily be intervention in the economic process and output must be raised in quantity and quality. The process was not smooth. Legislation came in spasms, but over a period of roughly a century it showed a steady development of the ideal of promoting exports and reducing imports. The medieval statute books were littered with Acts and fragments of Acts which appeared to aim at similar objects—to promote wool-growing or cloth-making or shipbuilding or prevent loss of bullion—but in the new phase the economic legislation acquires a theoretical coherence and an administrative persistence that was lacking in the old. The Acts pay less attention to matters of price, of quality and of manufacturing method, and concentrate on the larger issues that were conveniently crystallized in the concept of the balance of trade. The speculative abstractions of the debate over bullion are abandoned: in the new phase it was not so much what was true or right that was held to matter but what could be understood most easily and carried out most effectively.

Again, no amount of manipulation of the evidence has yet proved that the various types of government enjoyed or suffered by seventeenth-century Englishmen differed markedly in their attitude to the problems

[1] J. M. Keynes, *The General Theory of Employment, Interest and Money* (1936), 333.

of the national economy. Nothing could be more mistaken than to suppose that republican government was in its nature more responsive to the demands of private trade than royal government. The tension between the merchants of the New England colonies and the Puritan gentlemen who from the start guided their destinies, taking action when necessary in good medieval fashion against the immoral abuses of commercial behaviour, has been mentioned before. No such scruples bothered James I (who was ready to lend his ear to the proposals of those who would lend him their cash) or Charles II (who took a virtuous interest in economic affairs in his early years of office, regularly conferring with 'the most active merchants', offering to do all he could for the advancement of trade and securing appropriate representations of the royal family and their supporters in such hopeful projects as the African trading companies, the Royal Fishery and the Hudson's Bay Company). The interests of the great exporting companies were reflected in both the Navigation Acts—one passed under the Commonwealth, the other under the restored monarchy. Economic policy might be trimmed or restrained in deference to the larger issues of either Stuart dynasticism or the Cromwellian Protestant Alliance, but there is nothing to suggest that any seventeenth-century government had any quarrel with the general aims of mercantilist economics, though any government might throw its weight on the scales against imprudent violence to trade rivals, as Cromwell did from 1654–8 and Charles II did in 1664.

The new phase of thought and policy, characterized by the partnership of public and private interest, the state and the merchant, pursuing an ideal that is not only national power but a combination of national power with private and social profit, might well be taken to date from 1622 and from the Commission which in that year reported on measures to combat the economic depression that followed the so-called Cokayne project, that ill-starred piece of mercantilism *manqué*. The close of the great creative period of mercantilism was signified by that famous speech from the throne of 1721 in which Walpole announced his intention of rationalizing the existing mass of mercantile legislation with its residual confusion of tariffs and duties so as to extend the nation's commerce 'upon which the riches and grandeur of this nation chiefly depend'. 'Nothing', he went on, 'would more conduce to such an end than to make the exportation of our own manufactures, and the importation of the commodities used in the manufacturing of them, as practicable and easy as may be; by this means the balance of trade may be preserved in our favour, our navigation increased and greater numbers of our poor employed.' This did not, it should be stressed, spell the end of the idea of economic interventionism. It symbolized the fact that the classical apparatus of mercantilism was complete. Henceforth the emphasis was to be on its modification, notably in the direction of a larger and larger amount of protection for growing industries.

The Commission of 1622 came at the end of a long and deplorable story of economic mismanagement of which the Cokayne project was only a part. The ostensible purpose of Cokayne and his supporters was to elevate the making of cloth in England from the manufacture of a semi-finished article to that of a fully finished one. It appeared to many therefore to hold out possibilities of increased employment for cloth workers, especially for finishers and dyers, and to promise a larger share of the profitability of the market as between England and the Dutch Republic and in general to promote those ideas of a favourable balance of trade which were already in process of formation. Its internal politics were less creditable and reflected the real nature of Cokayne's ambition: to break the Merchant Adventurers' hold on the export of cloth. The details of the scheme need not concern us: enough to say it failed disastrously and left a trail of economic wreckage in its wake. In the process of clearing up the damage, which included massive un-employment and distress and a major quarrel with the Dutch, it became clear that a change had occurred in the dominant body of public opinion as to the causes of the crisis and remedies that might be applied. Proposals for further monetary manipulation and a renewal of existing prohibitions on bullion export, melting down of coin and the use of precious metals in manufacture were, as usual, the first resort of the harassed officials whose task it was to cope with the crisis. Even in the debates of 1621 the most favoured approach to the depression was the time-honoured lament of 'the scarcity of coin'. Yet wiser counsels were stirring within the group of royal advisers led by Sir Lionel Cranfield. A committee of 1620 established specifically to deal with the monetary problem had shied off, temporized and finally killed the proposals for dealing with matters by lightening the silver coin. The Commission of 1622 followed this up with positive recommendations, all of them re-volving round the principle, not in itself new but here expounded with a new clarity and definition, of the balance of trade. It was no accident that among the commissioners was Thomas Mun; and his presence provides the most important link between the propaganda and the economic policy of the times. The commissioners put forward six main principles upon which national economic policy should henceforward be based. They were: (1) To reserve English raw materials to the cloth industry by prohibiting the export of wool, fullers earth, pipe clay, etc. especially to Holland. (2) To injure Dutch competitors by stopping English ships and merchants from supplying them with Spanish or Turkish wool. (3) To reduce the need for imports and the drain of treasure by developing manufactures; linen would be made here and home-grown hemp and flax would make England independent of the Baltic. (4) The fisheries now exploited by the Dutch would be exploited in future by English companies and the Dutch ousted. (5) Foreign merchants and shipmasters who earned money in England by importing goods to England were to be compelled to spend the money they earned here on English manufactures. (6) Goods imported from abroad must come either in English ships or ships belonging to the country producing the goods. All these principles, except (5), were to prove a root from which elaborate later policies were to stem. Jointly, they represent a strategy of attack, in the name of economic nationalism and the balance of trade, on the profitable but vulnerable positions held by the Dutch in the European economy— as middlemen, brokers, refiners, finishers. It is not difficult to see here the work of the same hand that sketched out the principle of 'natural' and 'artificial' wealths in *Englands Treasure by Fforraign Trade*.

If we duly consider England's Largeness, Beauty, Fertility, Strength, both by sea and land, or multitude of warlike people, Horses, Ships, Ammunition, advantageous situation for Defence and Trade, number of seaports and harbours, which are of difficult access to enemies, and of easie outlet to the inhabitants, wealth by excellent fence woods, Iron, Lead, Tynn, Saffron, Corn, Victuals, Hides, Wax and other Natural Endowments; we shall find this Kingdome capable to sit as master of a Monarchy. For what greater glory and advantage can any powerful nation have, than to be thus richly and naturally possessed of as things needful for food, Rayment, War and Peace, not only for its own plentiful use, but also to supply the wants of Other Nations, in such a measure, that much money may be thereby gotten yearly, to make the happiness complete.

Unfortunately, a second look showed that not all these natural riches were made the most of. The Dutch, on the other hand, occupying a small country with no natural resources 'not fully so big as two of our best shires' had shown what could be done by *artifice*, by 'their continual industry in the trade of Merchandize'. By this they had made themselves the richest nation in the world, not least at the expense of the English. For the foundation of their trade was shipping. This in turn was founded on their herring fisheries and these lay along the coasts of England. Here within sight of the English sailed the Dutch fishing fleets for a large part of the year—'whereby many thousands of Households, Families, Handicrafts, Trades and Occupations are set on work, were maintained and prosper, especially the sailing and navigation', together with the public revenues for the state.

Jealousy, ambition and common sense were then the principal springs of the policy later called mercantilism. The prohibitions on the export of raw materials used in cloth-making were repeated and strengthened year by year through the century to survive as a principal target for the attacks of Adam Smith. For Stuarts, Parliament men and limited monarchy alike, they were a common article of faith. The difficulty of enforcing these measures and the fact that other lines of supply were open to competitors kept alive the idea of blockading alternative sources of wool. A scheme of 1651 planned to pre-empt all the wools of Segovia and Castile through a private company which would make an agreement with the king of Spain and thereby cut off four-fifths of the Dutch supply of raw wool. The idea was revived again in 1662. Whether anything came of these schemes in practice is doubtful, but it was a device always liable to be thought of in times of crisis, as 1622, 1657 and 1662 all were for the clothiers.

Plans for new industries like linen manufacture, and the growing of crops such as hemp and flax which provided industrial raw materials, were all closely tied to ideas for reducing imports and boosting exports. Rich as England was (said Mun) she might be much richer 'by laying out the waste grounds (which are infinite) . . . hereby to supply ourselves and prevent the importation of Hemp, Flax, Cordage and Tobacco and divers other things which we now fetch from strangers to our great impoverishing'. The theme that because we were 'weak in our knowledge' we were 'poor in our treasure' was repeated constantly throughout the century: but it was not until the end of it that persistent effort presented England with a cloth industry that could rival the Dutch at Leiden in their skill at all branches of technique and export a fully finished article, or a linen industry that could rival that of Haarlem. The schemes for 'the waste grounds' matured more quickly. As early as 1589 an early projector conjured up visions of the Fens round the Wash drained and converted into a land of plenty, 'a storehouse for the whole Realm, with a superabundance to save for foreign lands'. Here 200,000 people would live in laudable abundance, shipping would thrive on the grain trade and so would the blacksmith, the shipwright the seaman, the sail-maker, etc. A million acres would support 300,000 cattle and 25,000 cavalry horses. Here was 'a regal conquest, a new republic and a complete state'. In the 1620's the draining of Hatfield Chase, an impassable morass of 70,000 acres between Humber, Trent and Ouse, raised the value of land from sixpence to ten shillings an acre. From there the great Dutch engineer, Vermuyden, turned to the Fens proper—'the sink and drain of 13 counties', a land 'of great waters and a few reeds thinly scattered . . .'. By the mid-1650's Samuel Hartlib described the reclaimed land as 'growing the best Hempe in England as well as Flax, oats, wheat, Cole seed for oil, and wood'. Altogether the projectors must have reclaimed the largest part of half a million acres.

The condition of the fisheries, touched on by the Commission of

1622, was an old occasion for lamentation. From June to December the Dutch herring fleet followed the shoals down from Shetland to the Thames Estuary. English critics of this insult to national pride estimated in huge and no doubt exaggerated figures the value of the catch to their rivals. But they scarcely outdid the Dutch themselves in assessing its importance and, indeed, it was difficult to overstate the value of an industry which was as much the base of the Dutch economy as agriculture was of the English. Here, then, was a persistent source of friction in Anglo-Dutch relations and the origin of fundamental disputes over the legal basis of maritime sovereignty. For while the Dutch claim to freedom of fishing found its classical statement in Grotius's *Mare Liberum*, the English replied through John Selden's *Mare Clausum*. There was besides a series of attempts, all ill-starred, to organize English fishery companies. But just as the English appear to have lacked the skilled techniques of dressing and dyeing cloth, so they lacked the no less mysterious skill required for catching, salting, and barrelling herrings. The fishery question therefore continued to act as a provocation to those wilder spirits who thought England's best short cut to wealth and strength lay through a Dutch War. Their theories were tested in 1652 and 1665 and found wanting.

The many motives and ambitions, private and public, which churned together in men's minds in the seventeenth century to produce the complex of thought and policy known as mercantilism, had their *chef d'œuvre* in the Navigation Laws. To understand their purpose we must remember the growing importance of the new colonial territories. The original economic motive of exploration had often been the search for precious metals. This had given way in time to a popular hope that the colonies would form alternative, cheaper and safer sources of supply for those necessary commodities which England drew from foreign countries. Yet such hopes had been repeatedly thwarted by the skill of the Dutch in inserting themselves between colonial producer and English buyer. Hence, it was thought, a drain of money to pay for cargoes and freight; hence the nation was robbed of the chance to build up a fleet and a body of seamen not only for economic profit but for defence. The neat and ingenious formula of the Act of 1651 aimed at cutting out the Dutch merchants and shipmasters from all the *import* trade into England. Before there was satisfactory evidence as to its exact results it was replaced by the Acts of 1660, 1662 and 1663 which extended the scope of the earlier Act; the aims were more limited, the administration more efficient, and the most recent historian to examine their operation in detail formed a high opinion of their efficacy.[1] Under the guidance of Sir George Downing, to whom the title of architect of the mercantile

[1] L. A. Harper, *The English Navigation Laws.*

system should perhaps be awarded, the trade between England and the Colonies was henceforth enclosed, protected and canalized in English shipping. The old attempts to prohibit the export of treasure by direct ban were now largely abandoned. The emphasis had moved towards building up the volume and value of exports, reducing the volume and value of imports carried in foreign-owned shipping and winning as much in the way of income from freights in British shipping as possible. So after an interval of nearly forty years, the proposals of Mun and his colleagues came into full operative force.

Yet in all this there was more than simply the myth of the 'balance'. That the conception of the 'balance' and its relationship to the bullion issue was loose, that it became the prime economic *cliché* of the day, that it meant and could be made to mean, many different things to many different people and interests—none of these propositions can be denied. It is nevertheless quite false to see it as a stultifying, obstructive element in thought or policy. Whatever its precise effects may have been— and they can never be known—mercantilists in general saw the theory of the 'balance' as a dynamic theory the vitalizing power of which ran down into every vein of the economic body. The measures taken in relation to the cloth trade—to reserve raw materials, acquire technicians and protect markets—were regarded not merely as an aid towards a favourable balance: a favourable balance was itself a measure of national well-being, reflecting (as they believed) more employment for the poor, more wealth for the employers, more profit and power to the nation as a whole. The Navigation Acts, the other great basis for the economic system, aimed at the twin goals of strategic power and economic wealth through shipping and colonial monopoly. Yet it is worth noticing that amongst the first commodities from the colonies to be 'enumerated' were the tropical dyes used in the cloth industry. In this respect the legislators were merely extending to the new phase of colonial exploitation the principle, already centuries old, of reserving to national industry the raw materials it needed against the competition of rural industries in France and Holland. That fiscalism was an element in economic policy is certain: yet the fiscalism of English mercantilism often seemed to move in parallel with powerful private and public interests and was less evidently damaging to economic development than the fiscalism of Spain or the German princedoms that moved contrary to such interests. Granted that the best laid plans of economic policy-makers tend to be fossilized by time and rusted by jobbery, that any bureaucracy becomes unresponsive and corrupt in the end and that England was in the last analysis no exception, the *ideas* of English mercantilism in its creative century when examined free of doctrinal prejudice seem remarkably relevant and fertile.

The ideas on national policy that developed in France in the early modern period show many basic similarities to those of England, though strongly modified by economic circumstances—especially the nature of economic resources—by those political institutions that diverged so markedly from their English equivalents in these years, and by personal considerations and accidents that left their mark on the French economy. Most of all the development of economic policy and ideas was influenced by France's natural size and wealth: with her 16 million inhabitants she had already in 1600 a population more than twice that of Spain or Great Britain and Ireland, three times that of Habsburg Austria and more than eight times that of the Dutch Republic. While economic centralization was foreign to the Dutch, and was to suffer the beginning of eclipse in England during the seventeenth century, it was in France to reach its grand climax under Colbert. The resources that were to come under this central control included the agricultural output—wine and grain—of one of the richest areas in Europe, the shipping and trade of ports like Bordeaux and Marseilles which were to rise to pre-eminence in the seventeenth and eighteenth centuries. The economic union of the area was in some senses artificial, for transport was often poor or non-existent and impediments to trade—tolls and local peculiarities—persisted down to the Revolution. Yet the political unity was real and it meant that the economic doctrines that grew up from the end of the Middle Ages and were finally crystallized in Colbert's Code were imposed, for good or ill, on all trade and industry within this, the largest politically unified area of the contemporary world. The actions and ideas of French kings, statesmen and economists interacted constantly with their own physical context, ambition and lust for conquest, being in part man's response to the realization that France was inherently, but as yet only potentially, capable of European hegemony.

It is characteristic of French politico-economic thought from the mid-fifteenth century to the early seventeenth century, from the *Débat des Hérauts d'Armes* to Richelieu's *Testament Politique*, to ponder continually the potential wealth and strength of France against her actual weakness: in this respect reminding our English reader of Thomas Mun's theme of 'natural' and 'artificial' riches. The French herald boasts of the ponderable and imponderable advantages that France possesses—her fine harbours, timber, iron, salt, vineyards, mines, fisheries, her great and industrious population, not to speak of the pleasures afforded by the excellence of her hunting, the beauty of her ladies, and the spiritual comfort afforded by the profusion of holy relics. French economics were nothing if not generously humane. Yet here, as in the writings of Richelieu, there is the admission of the economico-strategic weakness of France—the absence of a strong mercantile fleet which would enable

France to maximize her wealth and form the basis of a navy that would when necessary take by force what could not be taken by trade. This specific linking of power and wealth as the twin and inseparable ends of French national policy in Richelieu's thought, and the means by which he proposed to achieve his objects—through great trading companies, through colonial exploitation, through those trades which yielded a net supply of bullion, and always based on naval strength—was not original. All his ideas can be traced back as they emerged embryonically and spasmodically in the *cahiers* and the writings of sixteenth-century economists and administrators. Throughout there grew a notion of the national advantage measured in effect (though not so clearly as in English contemporary thought) by reference to the balance of trade and frequently to the net yield of bullion to the state. Thus a *cahier* of the three States General of 1484 will lay it down that: 'Money is in the body politic what blood is in the human body: it is then necessary to examine what bleedings and purgings France has undergone. . . .' From this time on a regular stream of royal letters forbade the export of money to Rome: one of the roots of Gallicanism was bullionist. Sumptuary laws that forbade the use and importation of luxury articles except for royal persons were another result of the same line of thought.

By the second half of the sixteenth century these primitive ideas of medieval origin had already given rise to a corpus of legislation, probably most honoured in the breach, aimed at national self-sufficiency and the nourishment of national production. The theme of a *cahier* of 1576 is that money will be gained if the people can be set to work on manufacturing the raw materials in which France abounds. That such pious expressions of economic platitude took a long time to emerge in detailed and effective administrative form does not necessarily dispose of their importance. The science of economic administration on a national scale was slow to grow: that is all. Some instances of practicality there are already. Mutio, a Venetian, receives in 1557 a ten-year licence to manufacture glassware. Antoine Carras is exempted from taxes so that he may raise mulberry trees for the silk industry. De Roberval has official help to discover and develop mines to reduce the drain of treasure. The idea recurs ever more frequently that not the least merit of such schemes will be to employ the able-bodied poor—a recommendation of industrial activity that strongly appealed to Richelieu and Colbert for political as well as economic reasons. 'Les peuples', said Richelieu, 'deviennent ingouvernables avec l'aisance.' Colbert spent a considerable part of his working life haranguing his Intendants in turn on the merits of industry as the foundation of social order as well as of national welfare. Industry was still seen as a social tranquillizer; not yet as a social irritant. Hence the theme of an edict of 1572 which banned the import of foreign textiles so that the subjects of France 'can better devote themselves to the manufacture and working up of wool, flax, hemp and tow . . . and so get the profit that foreigners now make'. Such theories pointing towards *étatisme* and economic autarky are the stuff of the three most considerable economic writers of the later sixteenth and early seventeenth centuries—Bodin, de Laffemas and Monchrétien. Jean Bodin is best known as a political theorist, a defender of absolute hereditary monarchy and the most influential exponent of that explanation of the great contemporary price-rise which linked it causally with the influx of American bullion (see H. Hauser (ed.), *La Vie Chère au XVIe siècle: la réponse de Jean Bodin à M. de Malestroict.* 1568 (1932)). Yet in the history of the formation of national policy his role was not unimportant, and he pushed a stage further the process of which the legacy of medieval commonplaces—sumptuary, bullionist, chauvinist—was moulded into a theory and practice coherent within itself. He reiterated the ancient theme: 'Salt, wine and wheat are the inexhaustible mines of France.' By exporting these and other goods to Spain, she could obtain treasure. France's imports, said Bodin, were few—oils, spices and silks chiefly— but even these could be cut down if Frenchmen were energetic and resourceful enough. His conclusion was that France should tax manufactures upon import and raw materials upon export. And this was the economic programme he defended before the States in 1576—a rational programme of protection to replace the merely fiscal tariff of 1540. In France also, therefore, the 'two great engines' of policy, as Adam Smith called them, were present in embryo three-quarters of a century before the publication of Mun's classic exposition of mercantilism. The system was extended and developed during the reign of Henri Quatre when the need was especially acutely felt of a systematic attack on the problems that arose from the neglect and confusion of the time of the Wars of Religion. True, there was little that was original and much that was naïve in the work of Barthélemy de Laffemas, Henry's valet who rose to be controller general of commerce and president of the Conseil de Commerce. France's generous resources are contrasted with her miserable management of them. Bullion—'the nerves and support of kingdoms and monarchs'—is lost through idleness and ill-regulated trade. Pack mules came from Italy with unnecessary imports and returned loaded with money: so did the Italian circus performers who provided frivolous and unnecessary entertainment for France in return for treasure, while the wool of Languedoc leaked away to the benefit of the industrious Milanese. And so on. The need was for a system of royal encouragement and state regulation of industry through guilds. De Laffemas in many ways foreshadows Colbert, especially in his passionate belief in the efficacy of industrial regulation. Nor did he stop at theorizing. It was said that under his leadership the Commission de Commerce held 150 meetings in little more than two years between 1601 and 1604. Silk manufacture, horse-breeding, linen and fustian manufacture, gilt leather-work on the Spanish model, glass, tiles, tapestry, rich textiles in the south, river and canal works, shipbuilding and general inventions were only a few of the matters investigated. Over de Laffemas, as over his contemporary Antoine de Monchrétien, author of the *Traité de l'Oeconomie Politique* (1615), hangs that air of fantasy which the economists of the Janus-headed century shared with its poets and scientists, and which was the product of its unique mixture of medieval and modern elements of thought. Yet for all the crudities and oddities of Monchrétien, he reflects one novel aspect of contemporary affairs. Far more than his predecessors he emphasizes the value of the colonial trades— especially the American—as potential sources of raw materials, timber, spices, etc. which France had still to buy from foreigners, supposedly for bullion. Here Monchrétien foreshadows the great Companies of Richelieu and later Colbert, the Compagnie de la Nouvelle France and the Compagnie des Isles d'Amérique which attempted to develop trade with Canada and the West Indies. In his perception of the coming importance of colonial commodities, in his recognition that the importance of treasure was in fact symbolic, Monchrétien had moved ahead of his predecessors, and in the discussions of the States General of 1614 and the Assembly of Notables of 1626 especially, as well as in the policies of Richelieu, the influence of Laffemas and Monchrétien can be detected. Unpropitious as the preceding century had been to the peaceable growth of trade and industry, the curious work called *Le Commerce Honorable* by the Carmelite monk Saint Jean (or Jean Eon) which appeared on the eve of the Fronde throws an interesting light on the penetration of a feudal society by merchants. Where would be the *noblesse de la Robe* if it were not for the fees paid to its members by merchants engaged in litigation over trade? More than that, members of the *noblesse* often owed their offices to the fortunes brought to them by their wives, the daughters of burghers who had made their money in trade. It was not yet as clear as it was later to become that French society was to evolve very differently from English. That it was to do so was not a little due to the inhuman diligence with which Colbert sought, by one reform after another, to place industry at the service of the king and the state.

It is not only historians who have agreed to regard Colbert as the symbol and crown of *étatisme*. Contemporaries set the fashion. To Molière he was 'le grand Colbert', whose 'savants fatigués' formed the material basis of French supremacy in Europe. For Boileau, Colbert had rendered France industrious and thereby liberated her from thraldom to her neighbours. Racine, in the preface of *Bérénice*, spoke of 'l'admiration de toute la France pour cette pénétration à laquelle rien n'échappe, pour cet esprit vaste qui embrasse et qui exécute tout à la fois tant de grandes choses, pour cette âme que rien n'étonne et que rien ne fatigue'. The emphasis, be it noted, is on energy and tenacity rather than on intelligence. There is indeed a large measure of truth in the contention that Colbert's mind never rose to the level of a general idea. Here was the perfect bureaucrat whose concern was with the way the machinery ran, rather than with the function it performed. The latter was not a matter for rational analysis: it was part of the legacy of social thought handed down from earlier generations of thinkers and administrators. Colbert's task was not to examine this existing *congeries* of ideas and institutions: it was to codify the ideas and stabilize and standardize the institutions. Thus he inherited, without quibble or trepidation, the conventional view of overseas trade. World trade was essentially a static affair: the amount of bullion, shipping and trade was fixed. France's task was to conduct a 'war of money' with the rest of Europe. Commerce (he wrote) 'is a perpetual and peaceable war of wit and energy among all nations,' and by 1670 he could congratulate himself that France had 'conquered' in this economic warfare every nation except the Dutch, whose resources in the trades to the Baltic, the Far East and the Atlantic had kept them going. But the great trading companies created or renewed since the accession of the *Roi Soleil* were 'like armies', attacking them everywhere, and would soon wear them down. Nothing could be further from the truth than that view of Colbert which represents him as an earnestly pacific commercial attaché whose social ends were frustrated by a bellicose master. The logic of Colbert's inherited prejudices was conflict. To many earlier French writers the main enemy of France economically had been the Italians who had eaten their way into the vitals of France: over their heads Colbert promoted the Dutch. It was the Dutch who were the 'mortal enemies' of France. He therefore approved as a matter of course the attack on the Dutch Republic of 1672 and dreamed of incorporating its assets into the French kingdom.

Behind Colbert's views on trade lay his ideas on bullion. Impressed by the power which he believed had been brought to the Habsburgs by their control of Central American silver supplies, he made it his aim to obtain and keep supplies of silver circulating in France. Only foreign trade could attract bullion and keep it circulating and prevent it draining away. Again, one finds the conventional ideas of his predecessors cast into more precise form. Like his English and Dutch contemporaries he looked upon trade with Spain as the greatest potential bullion-winner:

trade with the East as the main potential threat. Marseilles, exporting silver to the Levant and the East, was one of his permanent anxieties. Bodin's protectionist principles, now nearly a century old, were put vigorously into force for the benefit of industry, for, more overtly than his English contemporaries, Colbert recognized manufactures to be the source not only of wealth but of social contentment. Here, again, he was only following out, as we have seen, an earlier mode of thought, but, as ever, executing it with unprecedented vigour. No *arcanum* of industrial life was left unexplored by the chain of authority which stretched from the policy-making body at the apex of Colbert's pyramid, the Conseil de Commerce, down to the enforcement officers who pursued the *règlements* in all their detail through the manufacturing process, ensuring that the fabrics of Dijon contained 1,408 threads per cloth, those of Chatillon 1,216. The trick of compelling all craftsmen to belong to a guild had been tried before by impecunious governments. Now it was tried again. So that while in England the age of mercantilism saw the *internal* regulation of industry (as distinct from the regulation of external trade) falling slowly into disuse, in France mercantilism was identified popularly most of all with the minutely detailed regulation of industry. Overtly the aims of this intervention were twofold: to ensure quality and impose a social discipline—'to drive fear into the workers' hearts' as Colbert's *instruction* of 1669 put it bluntly. The Code of Commerce, drawn up with Savary's help, regulated every aspect of industry and still forms the basis of French commercial law. To some extent, Colbert's measures resembled the earlier attempts of English theorists and legislators to promote industrial and technological progress. The introduction of foreign entrepreneurs and technicians has, as we have seen, precedents in French as well as English history in the years from the mid-sixteenth to mid-seventeenth century. Likewise the grant of a soap monopoly is reminiscent of Charles I's disastrous experiment of 1631. The minute attention to the techniques of textile dyeing in the *règlements* reminds one of the Cokayne project and the subsequent attempts to learn and propagate an art still largely a Dutch monopoly in northern Europe. All these aspects of Colbert's policy were natural phenomena in a society still basically agricultural, still ignorant and still agreeably and medievally casual about the need for methodical and accurate work. The system was not, in any theoretical way, inappropriate to the times, and there can be little doubt that it registered some successes, especially in the supply of military and naval equipment, and in the market for luxury textiles, glass, porcelain and the like. The makers of French gobelins, furnishings, laces, ribbons, mirrors, porcelains were the rivals and heirs of the Italian pioneers. Even in the more workaday world of plain cloths and linens, there was advance; and the survey of the French textile industry carried out ten years after Colbert's death shows it to be widespread and flourishing. These industries all made some contribution to French exports: all contributed towards a reduction of imports. To trace at all specifically the relationship between government intervention and industrial progress in France is impossible. Unreliable as English customs figures are, the French are worse and the interest in the 'balance of trade' was not sufficiently strong or effective to produce any figures comparable even to the English tables till 1756. We can do no more than balance probabilities: and the probability is that the defects of the Colbertian system grew with time. It was not necessarily of the first importance that the *règlements*, the guild ordinances and the rest of the apparatus of economic control and stimulus had also a fiscal aim. The system that Colbert inherited, strengthened and enforced had its own *rationale*. This was not fiscalism run amuck as in Spain or Naples. Nevertheless as time passed and the need for revenue was made more pressing by wars —not least those which, like the Franco-Dutch war of 1672-8 were the product of mercantilist logic—the aim of the 'system' became more fiscal and less economic. More and more offices were sold for profit. Colbertism became, as a French scholar has said, 'a meddling tyranny'. All bureaucracies, however honestly and intelligently conceived at the outset, tend to ossify, to drift away ever more remotely from their task as circumstances change, at worst to degenerate into a dead hand and a corruption. At Colbert's arrival into high administration his first task was to reform taxation and raise the royal revenue. The goal was never achieved: and in fact grew more remote down to the Revolution. The offices that should have been part of a reforming administration became themselves objects of sale. The system produced social parasites like Madame de Rosemain who developed a profitable trade in industrial privileges by mustering the services of a crowd of court pimps and adventuresses. At her trial she observed that if all those who carried on similar business were punished, several Bastilles would be necessary to contain them. The Paris chief of police confirmed her belief. Hardly a name at court did not figure on her lists.

The vast machinery of regulation built up by Colbert and his successors stemmed from a bureaucrat's contempt for trade and industry— for the merchants '. . . who nearly always understand merely their own little Commise and not the great forces which make commerce go'. There was an element of truth in the comment: but as an argument for an economic administration in the age of dynasticism the shrewdness was disastrously shallow. Not the least reason for the violent reaction of the eighteenth century against all forms of intervention was the simple fact that the best-laid plans of the mercantilist age had become obsolete, irrelevant and corrupt. This kind of *reductio ad absurdum* argument itself stimulated the search for any welcome signs that a freer economy, even though based on the short-term views of short-sighted men, could be justified by logic or evidence.

France, it is true, led the world in the volume of industrial production, foreign and domestic trade, down to a date late in the eighteenth century. This was probably due in large measure to the richness of her resources, the size and intelligence of her population, and the location of France in relation to labour and markets. But it would not be right to exclude the possibility that the royal interest, conveyed through Colbert, stimulated production and continued the process, begun under Louis XIII, of offering social incentives to commercial enterprise by opening the ranks of nobility to those enriched in trade. There was nothing inherently harmful in bringing the prizes of social success within the reach of the deserving rich, in ministering to the simple ambition that the fortunate ones shared with M. Jourdain to become a *mamamouchi*, preferably of local vintage. There were few doors, it has been said, which were not open to wealth in eighteenth-century France. What was dangerous was the effect that the bureaucratic tyranny and corruption engendered by the decay of Colbert's centralized regulation had on the spirit of enterprise. Eighteenth-century France was full of invention: yet the rate at which inventions passed into industrial application was far slower than in England: and it will appear on examination that many French inventions were developed and applied in England and Scotland because their authors became discouraged by official obstruction and victimization.[1] The richest and most influential sections of French bourgeois society in the post-Colbert period were not industrial entrepreneurs or ordinary merchants. The *bourgeois vivant noblement* consisted of tax-collectors, financiers and lawyers who enjoyed the rich pickings of a bureaucratized society. Talent, enterprise and capital were continually drawn off from productive industry and trade and employed in the dubious arts of a public finance that was often very private indeed in character. Thus, though the mercantilist age in England was dubbed 'Parliamentary Colbertism'[2] there was a fundamental difference between the mercantile system in England and in France: though many of the measures adopted seem alike in method and principle, in origin they are different and in purpose different at least in emphasis. Even Adam Smith had to allow that the objects of the mercantile system in England were economic, if improper: the aim was 'production' and the interests nurtured were those of the producers. Among the contrivers of the system, he thought, 'our merchants and manufacturers have been by

---

[1] See S. T. McCloy, *French Inventions of the 18th century.*
[2] W. Cunningham, *Growth of English Industry and Commerce*, II (1903 edn.), section III, p. 403.

far the principal architects'.[1] Nothing of this kind could have been said of French mercantilism. In France regulation was handed down from on high, it was 'royal Colbertism'. Colbert might consult merchants and after his death more were added to the Council of Commerce. But there was little evidence that they manipulated government policy in Colbert's time or even later. There was therefore no parallel to the situation in England where the great companies, shipowners, woollen manufacturers, iron-masters, hat-makers, sugar-planters, and many other interests, lobbied, harangued and bribed to get their own way, or something like it. Nor is there any parallel to the great literary debate on policy which went on for nearly two of the centuries of mercantilism—certainly from the early 1600's to the French Revolution. There is nothing like Mun, Child, Brewster or any of the score of mercantilist writers who dealt with thought and policy. The works of Jacques Savary and his sons form a fascinating commentary on French business and economic practice: but they do not deal with policy as their English contemporaries regularly did. The title of the *Parfait Négociant* is an adequate guide to its contents and character. It did not befit an ex-merchant to comment on policy to his master. Even the organization of trade was more a matter for authority than in England. There the companies were in general the creation of merchants with royal encouragement. In France the India Company was formed by the king and Colbert with the co-operation of the merchants. The difference of emphasis was significant. The end of policy itself often appeared to be to chasten the merchant and scourge the labourers rather than benefit them: the beneficiary was the state as personified (did not Louis himself put it thus?) in the royal office. Once that premise was accepted the slope that led from Colbertism down to purest fiscalism was slippery indeed.

In 1664, during the war of words that preceded the outbreak of the second Anglo-Dutch War in the following year, Colbert himself observed to Louis in a memorandum that the Dutch were trying to capture world trade in order to increase their strategic power.

Upon this [he wrote] they base the principal doctrine of their Government, knowing full well that if they but have the mastery of trade, their powers will continually wax upon land and sea, and will make them so mighty that they

---

[1] It should be added that in practice the merchants rarely got all they asked for. Long before the appearance of a career civil service to stand as buffer between minister and lobbyers, kings and ministers were served by councillors one of whose principal tasks was to sift the demands of, *inter alia*, the merchant interests. Thus neither the first nor later Navigation Acts represented what the trading companies or Trinity House asked; but what (respectively) Oliver St John and George Downing thought might be granted consistent with the general interest. The Board of Trade finally set up in 1696 was not the 'mercantile' Board the merchants tried to press on the government but much more the committee of 'experts' which John Locke, philosopher and economist, recommended.

will be able to set up as arbiters of peace and war in Europe and at their pleasure
set bounds to the justice and all the plans of the Princes.[1]

Similar allegations were made by English writers at the same time.
Yet without any falling into sentimentalism about Dutch policy (which
was invariably shrewd, self-interested and no less ruthless than that of
their rivals) the accusation must be rejected as misinformed. No *congeries* of political units in contemporary Europe had less sense of
sovereignty, less ambition for 'power' than the Dutch Republic. The
original rebellion against Spain sprang largely from a conservative
hatred and distrust of the new-fangled centralizing plans of Philip II,
who was trying to weld the oddly-sorted medieval collection of duchies,
counties and bishoprics into a united kingdom with Brussels as its
capital. One Dutch writer has appropriately described the early stages of
the revolt as 'The Revolt of Medievalism'.[2] And medieval, in this sense,
the republic which finally emerged continued to be. The oligarchy of
town merchants, already a powerful influence in the local states, wielded
virtual dictatorship, though a benevolent and tolerant dictatorship, in
the new state. Against any pretensions to sovereignty that might conflict with mercantile interests, whether the pretensions came from the
House of Habsburg or the House of Orange, the merchant republicans
resolutely set their face. To them the modern state, the New Monarchy,
the Roman Law, Divine Right of Kings, all pointed in one direction—
the victory of a dynasticism that owed responsibility to nobody but itself.
The welfare of a merchant republic was not compatible with the caprice
inseparable from monarchy which would subordinate trade to politics,
diplomacy, fiscalism, war. The 'state' that arose upon the traditional
political institutions and the inherited and developing economic structure
was far too atomistic and too vulnerable to harbour plans such as those
attributed to it by Colbert. Profits? yes: power? only so far as it might
be necessary to protect private trade and provide the minimum apparatus
for survival in a world of war. And that reluctantly, for even convoys
meant taxes. Equally the rulers of the merchant republic disliked the
intolerance and dangerous fanaticism of the Calvinists, whose taste for
democracy seemed inevitably to threaten Protestant crusades and whose
loyalty to the House of Orange led them to support the Stadholder
regardless of the real interests of the Republic. With a ramshackle
federal constitution, and divided horizontally by religion and class
differences as well as vertically by regional differences, the Republic of
merchants offered no threat to peace: the permanent query was
whether she offered adequate protection to the property of her

[1] Quoted in G. J. Renier, *The Dutch Nation* (1944), 133.
[2] Renier, *op. cit.*, bk. I, chap. II.

citizens whose technological prowess and resulting prosperity made them a perpetual target for less skilled, less diligent but more bellicose neighbours.

Like the economically mature city states of Italy, the merchants of the cities of the Netherlands were practitioners of the arts of commerce, rather than expounders of it. Relatively little economic literature emerged from the busy conglomerations of offices, warehouses and weigh-houses called Amsterdam, Delft, Rotterdam and the rest. The controversies between the Calvinist divines like Voetius and their opponents turned, as did the controversies in the Italian trading cities, on curiously medieval topics: still principally on usury and the legitimacy of interest. And so far as 'policy' in the larger sense was concerned, whereas in France the absence of debate was due to the political impotence of the merchant class, its relative absence in Holland was due to their very power. In this politically atomized society where *raison d'état* was generally subordinated to the private interests of trade, national policy was reduced to something residual, not positive. Reluctantly, the merchant republic might agree to be taxed, mobilized or in some way organized for military or economic warfare, but it did so only in emergency and as a matter of last resort. This was not a matter of national character. As fighting seamen, the Dutch were outclassed by none: moreover in the tropics the policies of the Dutch trading companies, freed from the prudent restraint exercised by their statesmen in Europe, often conducted their affairs with vigorous ferocity. Sir George Downing was by nature and training no friend of the Dutch and their policies, but there was a mite of truth in his jibe that while they were all for *mare liberum* in Europe, *mare clausum* ruled elsewhere. Basically the explanation was the character of the Dutch trading system and of the republic itself. Whereas the larger states by whom they were flanked had economies basically agricultural, with industries rising, so to speak, upon resources locally supplied—wool, flax, iron, timber, grain—the Dutch had developed essentially as brokers, exchangers, shippers, or at the most manipulators, finishers and refiners of goods produced elsewhere by others.

The opportunity seized by the Dutch merchants was probably, *au fond*, the growth of population in different parts of sixteenth and early seventeenth-century Europe which offered profitable markets to suppliers of grain and other basic necessities of life. Amsterdam and, to a lesser extent, the other cities were essentially entrepôts. Balance-of-trade doctrine, therefore, which was strongly attached to the idea of retaining local raw materials for profitable manufacture and export, protecting local manufactures, encouraging industrial techniques and the like, found little response from a people for whom such considerations were, in the nature of things, largely irrelevant. Technologically speaking they were already, in the industries that did concern them, ahead of their neighbours. So far as trade movement was concerned, they were not for the most part interested in subordinating the *nature* of the flow of goods to its *volume*. Their fortunes lay in their skill in buying in and re-selling—essentially a question of judging the time and the place. In any event, to have collected any usable or valid data about the balance of Dutch trade would have been an almost insuperable task, pre-supposing a centralized administration which did not exist. Shaping 'policy', even more agreeing upon measures, in such circumstances was a virtual impossibility: and though the interests of an important local industry like Leiden's woollen manufactures were not neglected, they had in the end to play second fiddle to the general concern that the flow of trade in and out of the entrepôt should not be hampered. Even Leiden's industry was dominated by merchant interests.

The classic statement of the fundamental basis of Dutch policy was contained in the work that first appeared in 1662 under the title *Het Interest van Holland* and was later translated into French and English. Popularly attributed to John de Witt, the Dutch statesman, it was for the greater part the work of the Leiden merchant Pieter de la Court. The *Maxims*, as they became known, remained for most European readers the standard account of the Dutch economy and the political and economic preoccupations which guided it. With an insouciant disregard for the passage of time, writers were still quoting as relevant its statistics of the value and volume of Dutch trade more than half a century later.[1] De la Court was primarily concerned with the conditions of welfare and prosperity for the Province of Holland: in fact, he takes these to be coincidental with the welfare of the whole federation. And if his work has a theme, it must be freedom—freedom from persecution, freedom from taxation, freedom from monopoly and regulation, freedom from dynasticism, freedom—above all—from war. Freedom from persecution he takes to be a condition of economic health and prosperity. Was it not toleration that had, in the early years of the War of Independence, brought skill and capital flocking from the rest of Europe—especially from the southern provinces of the Netherlands—and was not this the basis of Dutch success? This freedom of conscience had been betrayed by Calvinist intolerance. Meantime, taxes and duties had become a crippling burden on enterprise. Taxes, he recognizes, there must be, for trade must be protected by convoy: but taxation should fall on anybody rather than on the entrepreneur whose efforts form the basis of everybody else's property. Let public servants, foreigners, rentiers, artists be

---

[1] See, e.g., Sir Matthew Decker, *Essay on the Decline of the Foreign Trade*, 1739.

taxed but leave the trader and manufacturer free to create wealth. All those who had taken shelter behind the privileges of corporations or other monopolistic cliques must be deprived of their benefits and brought back to be judged by the yardstick of free competition. The flow of precious metals must be free of restrictions, not least because a number of countries—Norway, the Baltic lands, the Middle and Far East—'do afford us infinitely more merchandise than they take of us, we cannot trade with them but by gold or silver'.

De la Court's logic is, within its limits, irrefutable. Given that the merchant community was the dynamic factor in the economy, he was correct to suspect centralized power as the major threat to its welfare. Dynasticism is the bogey—in earlier ages Habsburg dynasticism, now (potentially anyway) Orange dynasticism. *Ab furore monarcharum, Libera nos, Domine* sums up everything that the republican merchant class felt about the perils of government in the age of dynastic ambition. This leads directly to his main fear: war. 'Above all things war, and chiefly by sea, is most prejudicial, and peace very beneficial, for Holland.' Holland's merchants had too much at stake to risk war except under extreme provocation: only 'the intolerable slavery of being governed by the will of a single person' would justify Holland's resort to war, as it had resorted against Philip II. The threats of aggression must in all other circumstances be fought with diplomacy, perhaps with economic weapons—tools and imports—but not with open war. Amongst Holland's neighbours, only England need really be feared, and even England suffered some disadvantages in a sea war with Holland—her coast was long and vulnerable and the winds favoured the Dutch. There was no case for an alliance with England, but equally no case for a war. The solution was '. . . in all our differences give them good words and gain time in hopes that in these monarchical Governments the Kings will either follow their pleasures, or through excess of luxury and court robbery, waste all their revenues and run themselves into debt or die, or perhaps fall into a foreign or intestine war'. In all of which he showed a pretty shrewd grasp of the political conditions of Holland's neighbours, as 1667 and 1678 were to show. The *Maxims* are, in fact, a curious mixture of the precocious and the antique. The distrust of sovereignty was as old as the loose easy-going feudalism of the Burgundian kingdom itself: certainly we are here listening to the recurrent echoes of that 'medievalism', that conservatism, from which the revolt against Spain in large measure sprang. Yet again, the *Maxims* were frequently to be looked upon as prophetic in their insistence on freedom as the key to national well-being. Later writers who acknowledged their debt to them, like Decker, have frequently been included amongst those who powerfully influenced Adam Smith towards doctrines of economic freedom.[1] In reality, the *Maxims* were first and foremost strictly practical, utilitarian and contemporary. Their relevance for the author (or authors) was to the immediate situation in which Holland found herself at, roughly speaking, the restoration of Charles II to the English throne, the accession of Louis XIV to the French. What sounds like economic doctrine, *laissez-faire* in embryo, was in reality not so much doctrine as what appeared to be the inescapable course that lay before a state such as Holland if it was to avoid being destroyed and absorbed by other more powerful neighbours. Yet, because Holland was a mature economy (if a vulnerable one), much of the empiricism of the *Maxims* turned out to have a wider relevance than that of its immediate context. And later economies, as they grew in skill and wealth, forsaking the path of conquest, looked back with interest on the common wisdom they contained.[2] By this time, however, by one of those ironies in which history abounds, the Dutch Republic itself had fallen victim to the burdens of taxation. It had avoided the dangers of internal dynasticism: it could not avoid the catastrophes which Bourbon dynasticism heaped upon it. The stagnation of its overseas trade after 1730 was due in large measure to the mercantilist rivalry it encountered from France and Britain. But the total collapse of its industries seems to have stemmed from the burden of internal taxation, excises in particular, which drove up wages and costs, sapping the competitive power and initiative of its industrial class. This in turn derived from the enormous burden of defence costs falling upon a small state poor in resources, territory and population.

This was in the future. For at least a century after the appearance of de la Court's work, the European nations were engaged in wars the motives of which were often in large measure economic. The first Anglo-Dutch War of 1652 sprang from a complex of problems, but economic rivalry was a very important source of trouble, if not the main one. The second Anglo-Dutch War of 1665 was the classic instance of a commercial war. Its roots were in the ambitions of a partnership between city, court and navy to bring to a successful and profitable end a war which they regarded as having been inadvisedly intermitted by Cromwell in 1654. Meanwhile Colbert's tariffs of 1664 and 1667 proved to be the preliminary to the war of 1672 in which, as we have seen, jealousy of the wealth of the Dutch Republic played a leading part. In all the verbal diplomatic and propagandist preliminaries to these wars it was made plain that the functions of the Dutch were regarded by English and French as incompatible with those notions of economic sovereignty which, however vaguely defined, have sufficient coherence to be

[1] See *D.N.B.*: Decker, Sir Matthew.
[2] For a more detailed account see C. Wilson, *Profit and Power* (1957), esp. chap. II.

recognizable as 'mercantilist'. To oust the Dutch from their middleman function in trade; to replace them as carriers of imports and exports; to deprive them of raw materials that might better be employed by local labour and made the basis of exports of greater value; to prevent them supplying luxury goods and trifles in return for precious metals or more valuable commodities—all these motives are common to English and French commentaries. Behind them all lay the conception, not always overt, of the balance of trade. It was no accident that the classic statement of this, Mun's *Treasure by Fforrayn Trade*, was published for the first time in 1664, nearly half a century after its composition, as part of the war of nerves against the Dutch. For it has not always been remarked that while one half of Mun's work is a sober and apparently generalized exposition or balance of trade doctrine, the latter half is a passionate diatribe against the Dutch and all their works. ' *The United Provinces*', he wrote, 'are like a fair bird suited with goodly borrowed plumes; but if every Fowl should take his feather, this bird would rest near naked.' In common parlance the philosophy was that of Monck in 1663: 'What matters this or that reason? What we want is more of the trade the Dutch now have.' Or of the naval contractor whom Pepys heard in the coffee house in February 1664 expounding the merits of a 'Dutch war and conquest': 'that the trade of the world is too little for us two, therefore one must down.'[1] This was the common stock of ideas of which wars were made and they were derivatives of the more technical and sophisticated versions of mercantilist doctrine. The idea of international conflict was inherent in balance-of-trade dogma: economic warfare led imperceptibly to warfare proper. For when the pace of peaceful progress proved too slow to satisfy the more impatient spirits (as it invariably did) the temptation to take a military short cut was strong. Especially when the proposed victim was as strategically vulnerable as the Dutch Republic seemed, on the face of things, to be.

There were, of course, interruptions in the process described above. The economic ambitions of the City of London might be held in check, as they were by Cromwell. The First Dutch War was wound up for political and religious reasons. Peace was maintained, though precariously, during the Protectorate because of those schemes which bulked larger in Cromwell's mind than the satisfaction of supposed economic grievances against the Dutch. In the end, Anglo-Dutch rivalry faded because of the threat of a French European hegemony, the implications of which were political and religious rather than economic. In the eighteenth century, however, economic rivalry with France continued to be a dominant motive for war. The recovery and progress of French trade became an obsession by the 1740's. A pamphleteer of 1745 could

[1] Wilson, *op. cit.*, chaps. VII–IX.

argue that '... our Commerce will, in general, flourish more under a vigorous and well managed naval war, than under any peace which should allow an open intercourse with those two nations [France and Spain]'. The Second Dutch War had seen the European conflict extended to West Africa and the West Indies in the scramble for slaves and tropical produce. The *asiento* was too meagre a prize from the Spanish Succession War. Ostensibly the *casus belli* in 1739 was Spanish interference with British smugglers. In the war of 1744 England saw an opportunity to wreck the French sugar colonies. The rewards of colonial trade—the fish, fur and timber of North America and the markets and products of the West Indies—were a prime object of Pitt and his city supporters in the Seven Years War and Pitt's 'system' embodied as clearly as any of the previous century that dual character of mercantilism which Professor Viner has identified as common to all its exponents.[1] 'Our trade depends upon a proper exertion of our maritime strength: that trade and maritime force depend upon each other.... The riches, which are the true resources of the country, depend upon commerce.'[2] Yet already before the end of the war there was evidence that the merchant interest was less confident of the virtues of war as an instrument of policy, and with the exception of Pitt himself, the statemen—Walpole, Pelham, Newcastle, Bedford—were nervous of war and reluctant to resort to its arbitrament. The peace of 1763 that restored to France much of what had been fought over reflected, temporarily, confusion as to where national policy should lead. England was not yet ready for a full-blown policy of pacific *laissez-faire*: but 1763 suggested that the days of bellicose mercantilism were coming to an end. England was beginning to have too much to lose and dubiously little to gain by war. From this point forward her situation began to approximate even more closely to that of the Dutch in the seventeenth century. Less self-sufficient for food and materials, with capital at risk in ships and stocks the world over, England begins to wear the aspect of a state whose ambitions are beginning to be balanced by her responsibilities.

It used to be widely held that the century following the Peace of the Pyrenees (1659) was one of stagnation in economic science. More recent studies have shown this to be greatly exaggerated. Although no great new concepts were established, this is the time when faith in some of those previously accepted began to burn low in western Europe. Both in England and France the expansion of overseas (and especially colonial) commerce—itself explicable by no simple formula as in some other periods—together with the growth of credit institutions, banking and

---

[1] See Jacob Viner, *Power versus Plenty*, World Politics, I, No. 1 (1948).
[2] Quoted in Admiral Sir Herbert Richmond, *Statesmen and Sea Power* (Ford Lectures, 1943), 133.

public finance led some writers to modify and some even to challenge the validity of doctrines hitherto often stated as self-evident and simple truths. If the doctrine of the balance of trade or the reverence accorded to the precious metals was to survive the changes in economic structure and institutions—such as, for example, the multiplication of trade routes, types of commodity and markets—it was only by matching these growing complexities in the real world by greater sophistication in the world of theory. In some of those who were writing in England round about the turn of the century, later economists of the classical school were rejoiced by what they interpreted as the first signs of an enlightened appreciation of the merits of economic freedom. Dudley North, a prominent man of affairs and business in late Stuart England, published in 1691 his *Discourses upon Trade*. When the Political Economy Club republished these in 1856 McCulloch, the editor, could scarcely find words adequate to praise this 'uncompromising advocate of commercial freedom'. He was 'An Achilles without a heel, he has no vulnerable points, no bounties, no prohibitions'. His system was 'sound throughout, consentaneous in its parts, and complete'. What particularly warmed the early Victorian heart was North's wisdom in equating the interest of the nation with that of the individual and his contempt for bullionist superstition embodied in regulations which he dismissed as no better than attempts to hedge in the cuckoo. No people, wrote North, 'ever yet grew rich by policies; but it is peace and industry and freedom that bring trade and wealth, and nothing else'. Praise even more extravagant was reserved for the tract entitled *Considerations on the East India Trade* (1711), with its attack on those textile manufacturers who were demanding protection against the import of oriental stuffs and its eulogies on the use of machinery and the principle of the division of labour, illustrated 'with a skill and felicity which even Smith has not surpassed but by which he most probably profited'. Mr Macaulay was no less impressed: 'The pamphlet on the East India Trade is excellent, first-rate. I have seen nothing of that age equal to it. . . .' More recent students of the history of economic thought have assigned a place higher than either of these to Bernard Mandeville, whose *Fable of the Bees* (1714–28) carried to its logical, if—to some—offensive, conclusion the idea adumbrated by North and later enshrined in Pope's couplet:

That REASON, PASSION answer one great aim;
That true SELF-LOVE and SOCIAL are the same.

Mandeville's long essay, more intelligible under its alternative title (*Private Vices, Publick Benefits*), has rightly been described as the greatest literary source of *laissez-faire*.

There can be little doubt that the greater elasticity which new economic institutions—banks, notes, bills and other instruments of credit and payment—introduced into the contemporary economic system reduced, over the long term, the general anxiety about supplies of precious metals and helped thereby to lessen the concern shown for the trade balance to the extent that the two phenomena had been connected in men's minds. The change was not immediate. Francis Brewster, writing in his *New Essays on Trade* in 1702, could still appeal directly to the old anxiety: Essay V is entitled 'That the full employment of All Hands in the Nation is the surest way and means to bring Bullion into the Kingdom'. And we have seen that Decker, nearly half a century after Brewster, is still repeating the formula in more or less the same terms as Mun had stated it. Yet in general there was an undeniable change in the attitude to economic policy. Keynes once claimed that mercantilism was primarily a policy of employment. It is very doubtful if the thesis could be substantiated for the earlier period, when the preoccupation with bullion suggests a direct and probably rational concern with its utility in contemporary conditions. From the Restoration onwards, however, a growing concern can be detected for the employment of the labouring poor.

Such concern with employment was not in itself new. Elizabethan writers had pondered the value of different types of labour to the economy as a whole, and their views had found an echo, though perhaps not a very audible one, in such Elizabethan legislation as the *Act Touching Clothworkers* of 1556 (which attempted to promote manufactured exports) and the *Act Avoiding Divers Foreign Wares made by Handicraftsmen Beyond the Seas* of 1562, which speaks for itself. Yet, in general, Elizabethan labour legislation was medieval in its aims. Its purpose was not to promote economic growth or social change, but to check it. Cecil's so-called 'industrial programme' of 1559 was a cautious and conservative document that set the tone for much of the social legislation of the reign. Morality of a workaday kind had remained its basis 'to the intent youth may be accustomed and brought up in labour and work, and thus not like to grow to be idle rogues ...', but usually morality with a social purpose: the preservation of order. And by 'order' the Elizabethans had not understood a merely negative absence of trouble. For legislators, as for Spenser, Shakespeare, Elyot, Hooker, Raleigh and many others, the social order reflected the order of the universe itself, where:

> The heavens themselves, the planets and this centre
> Observe degree, priority and place
> Insisture course proportion season form
> Office and custom, in all line of order;

The effects of interfering with or destroying nature's order were fear-some to contemplate:

> Take but degree away, untune that string,
> And hark, what discord follows.

The theme of the poet and the philosopher was also the theme of legis-lators. Their aim was to hold social change in check, prevent the en-croachment of class upon class, keep a watchful eye on technical innovations that might have social repercussions; in short, to stabilize and preserve the existing social order. These ideas were slow to die; but gradually, almost imperceptibly, in the course of the seventeenth century, they were accommodated to a growing tolerance of the notion that a man might better himself. More than that, by bettering himself, he might better others. For William Petty it appeared better to give exports away for poor returns provided it kept men in work and preserved their skill, rather than 'to let those thousand men by non-employment lose their faculty of labouring'.[1] Many other writers took up Josiah Child's theme: it was man's 'Duty to God and Nature to Provide for and Employ the Poor'. The revised version of mercantilism took therefore a more 'social' view of the economy: we are moving into the age of the Charity School Movement, the workhouse, the spinning schools, the orphanages, and the hospitals. Woefully inadequate as they often were even by contemporary standards, and horrifying by those of later ages, these institutions represented an attempt to soothe men's consciences and combine the process with economic beneficence to society. Many of these schemes had their origin—and for many their justification—in the contribution they made towards improving the country's trade balance: the great multitude of unemployed or under-employed poor seemed to many the country's largest wasted asset as well as a standing threat to public order and public health. 'I cannot for-bear repeating it', wrote Brewster, 'that the neglect of the poor seems the greatest mistake in our Government.' An economic writer like Child therefore adopted a new method of 'measuring' the progress of the national welfare. The balance-of-trade figures were too unreliable: what mattered was national production as measured by the general volume of trade and shipping and by the number of hands kept busy. Unlike some of his contemporaries Child did not believe that low wages were essential to maintain the nation's competitive strength in world markets. High wages were 'an infallible evidence of the riches of that country' while low wages were 'proof of the poverty of that place'. The very vagueness of Child's ideas is evidence of a genuine realization of the

---

[1] W. Petty, *Writings*, I, 60.

complexity of the problem: its difficulties are appreciated, but there is as yet no adequate analysis to explore them. Implicitly, he hints that an unfavourable balance *might* conceal a national gain. In the writings, varied though they are in style and purpose, of North, Mandeville, Child and Locke we are within sight of a new conception of social welfare: one aspect of it was to be summarized by Dean Tucker in the *Elements of Commerce*: 'In a world where the greater number are employed, there lies a balance, such balance, I mean, as only deserves public regard: the balance of industry, for money without industry is a hurt, not a blessing.' Place this side by side with Hume's attack on the theory of the balance of trade and we are within sight of Adam Smith's *reductio ad absurdum* of the whole structure of mercantilist thought; yet however confident economists might be of the self-regulatory nature of the economy, it took a very long time to convince administrators and even business men that regulation was otiose. Even at Manchester the large element of empiricism in free trade doctrine was much in evidence in the 1820's when imprudent doctrinaires from elsewhere raised the question of removing prohibitions on the export of textile machinery. And by the time the last vestiges of mercantilism went in the 1860's, the day was not far off when voices would begin to demand state assistance against the threat of German and American competition—itself the product of a new mercantilism.

In France, much as in England, the attack on the institutions and orthodoxy of mercantilism had two sources: one was the interest of those merchants who saw themselves penalized by the system of regulation or excluded from the privileges afforded to others; the other was the dissatisfaction of philosophers who, turning away finally from the ethics of economic behaviour to its motivation, found it difficult to reconcile their conclusions with the assumptions upon which state interference rested. Few of the merchants from the chief provincial cities who were invited to be deputies in the *Conseil de Commerce* after 1700 would have questioned the fundamental tenets of Colbert; but an increasing number plucked up courage to attack monopolies in which they had no share or tariffs which damaged the interests of their region. Yet even if this might be called dog-in-the-manger economics, important results flowed from it. The deputies of Rouen and Nantes, for example, were moved to attack the monopolistic Guinea Company because its failure to supply enough slaves to the French West Indies was said to be the cause of the high prices of West Indian goods imported into the French ports.[1] This is a precise parallel, it may be noticed, to the attacks launched in 1697 in England on the monopoly of the Royal African

---

[1] C. W. Cole, *French Mercantilism, 1683–1700*, pp. 255–8.

Company by a combination of consumers (Jamaican planters and British tradesmen) and suppliers (London and West Country clothiers) all of whom felt that their interests would be served by enlarging and opening up the trade.[1] In the same way, on the level of commercial criticism, the Deputy from Lyons made a speech in 1701 almost Cobdenite in its belief in the pacific nature of international trade. This led to a suggestion that a policy of reciprocity should be followed in regard to tariffs, a view that matches closely a remark of Josiah Child in his earlier *New Discourse of Trade*: 'If we would engage other nations to trade with us, we must receive from them the fruits and commodities of their countries as well as send them ours.'

A little later comes, from an odd source, an indication that some Frenchmen shared the feeling found in contemporary English writing that policy should be directed more consistently to social ends. Vauban, having spent his life and his genius in the service of his king, put his retirement to use in a study of the economic condition of France. His *Dixme Royale* appeared in 1707, only a short time before his death. Primarily a plea for tax reform, it adverted to the need for better conditions for the labouring poor. If they were better paid, clothed and fed, and taxed less they would 'work with more heart and vigour': and in their labour lay the great source of France's riches and power. 'No better service (Vauban concluded) can be done to monarchs than to remind them continually of this truth.' Louis did not relish Vauban's advice and the Marshal died still under royal displeasure. Others were more receptive and Vauban's views were quoted extensively by later writers in those countries (like Spain) which adopted mercantilist ideas in the course of the eighteenth century. Clearly there was in the air something in the nature of a revolt against the chauvinism and bellicosity of the earlier brands of mercantilism, though it would be wrong to take it too seriously. Even those spokesmen of the trading middle class, like Mandeville and Defoe in England and the deputies of Nantes, Rouen and Lyons in France, who seemed to be anticipating the accents of Victorian Liberals at favourable moments, were apt to revert swiftly to form at less auspicious times, repeating the old formulae of economic nationalism and abandoning incontinently their plans to develop domestic industry.

The cry of the deputy from Nantes: 'Liberty is the soul of commerce' sounds—though sounds falsely—like the accent of philosophy. With more justice, the authentically fundamental criticisms of Boisguilbert, the lawyer and landowner who attacked the whole of Colbert's schemes as synonymous with France's misfortunes, deserve to be so regarded.

[1] K. G. Davies, *The Royal African Company* 1957, 133.

Boisguilbert's views encompass most of the new opinions being expressed in England, especially on the subject of bullion. 'Gold and silver are not and never have been wealth in themselves and are of value only in relation to and only in so far as they can procure the things necessary for life, for which they serve merely as a gauge and an evaluation.' Money, which ought to be the servant of trade, had become the master, and instead of circulating in pursuance of its real purpose, was being hoarded instead of being spent, because the obstructions to trade kept prices low. Here again is an anticipation of future ideas. In embryo or more, it has been said, Boisguilbert expounds every argument against the bullionist position which the economists of the next century were to deploy.[1] Boisguilbert, like his English contemporaries, propounds the theory of the identity of self interest and social welfare. '... everything will work out fairly provided Nature is left alone. . . .' Slowly the two prongs of the attack on Colbertism became one. When Colbert had asked the merchants of Lyons what could be done to advance their trade and serve their commerce they had replied—the legend ran—'Laissez-nous faire'. It was the Marquis d'Argenson, a member of the first Economic Club—the Entresol—who turned the phrase from the market place into an economic principle. While d'Argenson dropped the 'nous', Gournay, his contemporary, who had translated Child and Culpeper into French and written (as Turgot said) voluminously on almost every aspect of trade and political economy, added the classic words 'laissez-passer'. Thus the grievances of the merchants coalesced with the scepticism of those believers in the *droit naturel* whose convictions compelled them to challenge anyone who claimed an 'integral and universal capacity of directing all commerce'. It was impossible. *Non datur scientia.*

Thus far it could be said that economic theory and economic policy in western Europe had been generated in varying degrees by traders themselves. Spontaneously in the cities of Italy and the Low Countries, rather less so in England, and in France with distinct guidance—dictation even—from above, the volume of trade had swollen, and with it and the social benefits and the political ambitions it inspired came the theories we call mercantilist—at bottom, simply the conviction that trade enriched the nation more rapidly than agriculture. Even in France, however, where economic organization was dictated from above, there was already present long before the emergence of 'Colbertism' a considerable volume of trade and a merchant community already numerous, though not sufficiently coherent as yet to influence policy against the ambitions of dynasts and nobles whose interest in trade

---

[1] C. W. Cole, *op. cit.*, 244.

was largely political, strategic and fiscal. This element of spontaneity in the economies of the western European seaboard sprang, without doubt, from the sea itself. Only by water could any considerable volume of bulky commodities be carried before the revolution in transport that came only with the eighteenth and nineteenth centuries. Canal building could extend the benefits which proximity to the sea conferred—hence Colbert's partnership with Riquet to construct the Canal of the Two Seas linking the Garonne with the Mediterranean—but even navigable rivers offered only modest returns in an age when power was lacking to move boats against the current. The pack-horse could move goods only in quantities that restricted its use largely to luxury goods. The belief that voyages were restricted to routes that hugged the coast is untrue, though probably a statistically high proportion did. Nevertheless the great trades that fertilized the economies of western Europe were those which were carried on in bulk commodities—grain, timber, salt, wine— between the Baltic, the western seaboard and the Mediterranean: and these were joined, in the seventeenth and eighteenth centuries, by the newer trades to the eastern and transatlantic trades which grew, organically, out of the earlier trade—the East Indian trades, for example, were carried on by Levant interests—and threw new bulk commodities, sugar, tobacco and cotton, on to the markets of Europe. As we have seen, some of the regions fertilized by these trades had not succeeded in achieving or had not sought to achieve that form of political organization we call the national state. Those that did—England and France—developed, adopted and matured the forms of policy we recognize as mercantilist. By the second half of the eighteenth century they were ready, intellectually if not institutionally, to jettison the apparatus of mercantilism as outmoded by the development of trade and industry. Elsewhere, however, conditions were entirely different. South of the Pyrenees, east of the Elbe, and in the medievally backward areas of southern Italy, economic and social conditions lagged far behind those of western Europe. A not unimportant phase of the eighteenth-century Enlightenment consisted of the borrowing, by the thinkers and rulers of such areas, of the ideas and institutions which western Euope had found appropriate and apparently efficacious in the previous century: in economic terms the adoption of mercantilism in theory and (erratically) in practice by the benevolent despots. As an example of the transplantation of ideas and institutions over long distances it has no equal before the twentieth-century westernizing of Russia and the East. It shares with it a certain brittle and artificial quality.

Nowhere in Europe was poverty and confusion worse than in Spain. 'Ce serait se tromper considérablement que de calculer l'Espagne d'après la France,' wrote the French Ambassador at Madrid in 1759.

Les pays de cette première monarchie sont absolument dépeuplés; il n'y a ni industrie, ni bonne foi: quasi point de police et peu de justice; les peuples sont paresseux et peu laborieux; il n'y a dans l'intérieur ni chemins, ni canots [*sic*], ni rivieres navigables, peu de voitures. En un mot, on peut dire que ce pays est en arrière de tous les autres de deux siecles au moins.[1]

For once, it seems unnecessary to suspect the antics of exaggeration. Many years later Cabarrús, the reformer and financier, exclaimed: 'How many poor have we amongst us? It might be said, without exaggeration, that virtually the whole nation is poor: it would be much easier to count those very rare persons who possess everything, than the virtual totality of the population who possess nothing.' Spaniards had not stood wholly idle before this spectacle, so rich in challenge, so empty of response. In 1724 there had appeared the first edition of Geronimo de Uztáriz's *Teórica y Práctica de Comercio y de Marina*, a purely mercantilist analysis of and prescription for Spain's economic ills. With that speed and enthusiasm which characterized Spanish government only when faced with the threat of reform, the authorities had seized and destroyed all the copies, but in 1742 it appeared once more. Nine years later it was translated into English as *The Theory and Practice of Commerce and Maritime Affairs*. The case of the argument was the trade balance. Spain suffered by having bought of foreigners 'more merchandise and fruits than we have sold them so as to make a ballance to our disadvantage of millions of dollars yearly'. From there the orthodox argument flows naturally. Most of Spain's exports consist of the raw materials which she ought to keep for her own use—the wool, raw silk, cochineal, indigo, vanilla and iron ore are the 'new weapons for our destruction'. On the other hand the fiscal system positively encourages the import of manufactures which prevent local industries getting a start in life. How stupid it all is! For is it not 'an infallible maxim' that the more our imports of foreign merchandise exceed the exports of our own, 'so much the more unavoidable will be our misery and ruin at last . . .'? Other nations—France and England in particular—have constructed systems of regulation to encourage their own manufactures and restrain imports by policy. This was the purpose, says Uztáriz, of Colbert's tariffs of 1664 and 1667: this was the purpose of the English prohibitions on the export of wool: this is why the Dutch have freed the imports of Spanish wool from all imports or restrictions. For is not the value of a manufactured cloth five times the value of the material that goes into it, the rest of the value being added by skill? The failure of Spain to follow these rules of elementary wisdom has meant the loss of gold and silver at an average

[1] Quoted from J. Sarrailh, *L'Espagne Eclairée de la Seconde moitié du XVIIIe Siècle* (Paris, 1954), 7.

rate of 20 million dollars a year to countries that supply her with goods and services. Out of the thousands of millions of dollars that Spain has received in bullion from America since 1492, only 100 millions remain. The moral was plain: Spain needed more manufactures. Uztáriz speculates on the results which would accrue from the establishment of a revived silk and woollen industry at Seville. Sixty thousand weavers might be employed and they in turn would need the services of 'shop-keepers, taylors, shoemakers, perukemakers, hatters, butchers, bakers, carpenters, bricklayers, smiths, surgeons, bankers ... and the like'. Seville would not only be self-sufficient: with her resources 'and that distinguishing blessing of a large river navigable for many leagues' she would sell to foreigners much more than she bought of them, enjoying 'riches and plenty, in lieu of that scarcity of money and other distresses they now suffer'. Similar blessings might follow in other cities— Segovia, Toledo, Cordova, Granada, Mercia, Valencia, Zaragoza, Valladolid, Medina del Campo, etc. But none of this would happen unless the 15 per cent tax on the export of manufactures and the *alcavala*, the sales tax of 15-20 per cent, were first removed. All this was pure mer-cantilism of the earlier seventeenth-century vintage. But with a hint of that 'social' concern which was beginning to characterize mercantilist writings elsewhere, Uztáriz quotes Vauban's *Dixme Royale* to show that it is 'the labour, commerce and tribute' of 'the common people' that enrich a king and his kingdom. It is they who supply the labourers and husbandmen and the soldiers and sailors for defence. But he ends again on the authentic note of the mercantilist faith: trade needs the support of naval power, and naval power needs trade as its basis. Good ships must be built 'both for war and traffick', 'so that these [trade and sea-power] are two inseparable companions and one cannot subsist without the other and it behoves us with equal zeal and vigilance to labour at the establishment and preservation of both'.

It was all eloquent, speculative, idealist, medieval and imitative. The examples were drawn, as Uztáriz says,

from France, England and Holland whose rules in this instance cannot fail of being received ... as very prudent and worthy of imitation, since it is by means of them they have found out a way to extend and preserve the com-merce, riches, plenty and splendour they now enjoy and also render themselves respectable by their land and naval armaments all over the world: while on the contrary, by our neglect and mismanagement, Spain is always oppressed and in some measure despised for its weakness.

What Uztáriz never examines is precisely how the new industries are to be established or who is to establish them. Nor did Bernardo de

Ulloa who in 1740 published in even greater detail his own recommendations for a revivified economy—a 'supplement' (as he said) to Uztáriz. In the absence of any mechanism for doing anything, the writings of Uztáriz and Ulloa lay dormant for another twenty years, the victims of the deadening apathy and inertia of Spain. Things were very different in Portugal, where the long Atlantic seaboard with the excellent ports of Lisbon and Oporto had bred a knowledge of trade and maritime affairs. Here by the 1750's Pombal was well advanced with reforms that were to change the character of Portugal, some of them reflecting the kind of proposals put forward by Uztáriz and Ulloa. Meanwhile the reformers who followed in Spain were more influenced by the growing body of rational and physiocratic thinkers and less by the English and Dutch models that had attracted their predecessors. In the writings of the reformers who gathered in high expectation round Charles III—the Frenchman Cabarrús, the Irishman Bernardo Ward, and Jovellanos, the greatest of the reformers—the influence of French philosophy is strong. There is more talk of Reason and less of the balance of trade, and a recognition that education must come before more grandiose shortcuts to social prosperity. The physiocratic ideal directed the thoughts of Ward in particular to the land, neglected and unexploited, that was Spain's largest real asset. Such plans could only take concrete form in one way—through the person of the king. Upon Charles III therefore the reformers poured out praise loyal and extravagant. Only he could spread, through institutions, the light the economists had revealed in their books.

The reforms that were attempted under the enlightened despotism of Charles III were compounded of ideas drawn equally from the older mercantilism and the new physiocracy. In Spain there was scope for reformers of both kinds: they could but try. Campomanes, the statesman who probably saw most clearly the roots of Spanish decadence, placed the emphasis on reform of industry, trade and technical education, and published addresses on such subjects as 'Fostering Popular Industry' and 'Education for Artisans'. Jovellanos was more imbued with the principles of the new thought from France. He always started with liberal ambitions, even though he tended to end on a note of conservatism. His *Report on the Liberty of Crafts* (1785) began an attack on the *gremios* (craft guilds), but ended by making membership of a universal guild compulsory for all masters, artisans and apprentices. *The Report on Agrarian Reform*, ten years later, inveighed against the waste of land, commons, entails, clerical mortmain, and the privileges of the Mesta, and advocated enclosure, irrigation and water transport. Even here he jibbed at the last moment against free trade in corn. Meanwhile Cabarrús, disciple of Rousseau, led the attack on the problem of poverty, denouncing the administration of the existing asylums, orphanages and hospitals as corrupt, inhuman and inadequate, while Ward in his *Obra Pia* called for inquiries into the way these matters were managed abroad. Thus, consistent or otherwise, mercantilist or physiocrat, the reformers stimulated their royal master to do more than his predecessors had done. For a brief spell—until the War of Independence in fact—they managed to create the illusion of an economic renascence. The *Societies of the Friends of the Country* which had begun in 1746 multiplied until by the end of the century they totalled seventy-two. Teaching centres for science and technology were set up; there were experiments in agricultural methods and in textile manufacture. The government built model factories to make glassware, cabinet work and tapestry at Madrid, and elsewhere for fabrics, hats, cottons, porcelain, brass and other wares. Ministers and diplomats put economic bargaining high on their list of duties and treaties were made with Turkey and the new United States. The problem of the social status of trade and industry was tackled in 1776 by a decree which declared that the exercise of a trade or craft 'being honest and honourable' did not disqualify the operator from the privileges of citizenship or even of nobility. Women were given the right to work in industry. New standards were established for textiles. Other industries were exempted from taxation. Foreign traders and technicians were encouraged to join the new industries with their capital and skill.

Was it for these reasons that the population began to increase again? That prosperity seemed to return to the towns of Catalonia, the Basque Provinces, Asturias, Valencia, Segovia? It is very doubtful. Looked at as a whole, Spain remained poor and inert. Little or no alleviation of the terrible poverty of the countryside can be discerned. Slavery—mostly affecting Moors and Negroes—remained legal. The skill required to work the mines at Guadalcanal or in Aragon was supplied by foreigners —English or German. The largest part of the merchandise needed by Spain's colonial dependencies came from foreign sources. Spain's contribution was a mere trickle—perhaps 8 per cent of the total. The economy of Spain had not in fact been transformed or even reformed. If Cabarrús is to be believed, it remained so 'vicious' as to be beyond repair. Spain had witnessed, as M. Sarrailh has said, a series of courageous attempts to develop individual welfare and national prosperity, conceived in a spirit of liberty and justice: but they remained attempts against hopeless odds that left later generations of reformers to renew the battle 'contre des forces inexpugnables et des abus toujours renaissants'.

What was true of Spain was true also of those parts of southern Italy which were until 1713 her possessions. Here a few fertile strips of land along the coast with groves of oranges, vines and olives, such as those round Naples or along the Tyrrhenian sea in Calabria, threw into contrast the general poverty and infertility of the mountainous districts behind them. A passionate and unstable people might rise up in fury as it did under Masaniello in 1647. But such violent outbursts were as short as they were sharp: in general the attitude to poverty and oppression was one of fatalistic resignation that derived in part from the climate, reinforced no doubt by the mixture of Arab blood that came with the invasions and raids of centuries. Not, on the face of it, a promising context for intellectual inquiry. Yet here—as, to a lesser extent, in Scotland —poverty seems to have acted as a spur to intellectual curiosity, and Naples, not particularly remarkable otherwise for intellectual prowess, produced in the second half of the eighteenth century a series of economic thinkers of a very high order. The phenomenon was not new. Serra, it will be recalled, was a Calabrian. Now a new generation arose to carry further the inquiries he had started. Ferdinando Galiani forms a link with the earlier Neapolitan economists. Like a good number of his predecessors he was a priest and later an administrator, a member of the supreme board of trade at Naples and afterwards a diplomat in Neapolitan service abroad. Galiani wrote voluminously, offending the physiocrats (as he was bound to do) by his mercantilist tendencies. Yet there was a sort of consistency in his empiricism. Every nation and every age required, thought Galiani, different laws and it was absurd to legislate according to abstract and absolute principles, for man's needs are not everywhere and at all times the same. In his best-known work, *Della Moneta*, first published anonymously in 1750, he put forward a theory of value which was nearer to that of the marginal utility of the nineteenth century than to that of contemporaries in England or France.[1] In his general outlook on trade policy Galiani was a mercantilist: hence his interest in reviving his *Della Moneta* in the forgotten *Breve Trattato* of Antonio Serra which had lain unnoticed for more than a century. So was Paolo Doria, the Genoese mathematician and friend of Vico, who seems to have spent most of his life in Naples. Galiani's contemporary, Antonio Broggia, also a Neapolitan, leaned perhaps more to physiocracy than Galiani. His *Trattato dei Tributi* and *Trattato delle Monete* established him as an authority on taxation and money with an international reputation: though no doubt his *Trattato della Sanita* was considered of equal importance by many of his contemporaries at home. The fourth, and unquestionably the most important of the early Neapolitan thinkers who revived the study of political economy, was Antonio Genovesi, for whom Bartolomeo Intieri founded the first chair of economics in Europe under the title of a chair of mechanics and commerce. Like Galiani,

---

[1] For a study of the early Italian and German economic thinkers see L. Cossa, *Guide to the Study of Political Economy* (translated by Jevons, London, 1880), and the same author's *Introduction to the Study of Political Economy* (translated by L. Dyer, London, 1893).

Genovesi was something of an empiricist. The immense learning of his *Lezioni* is unquestionable, but his more physiocratic contemporaries and successors criticized them as disjointed and without system. It is easy to see why Genovesi was a mercantilist—enlightened and moderate, but a mercantilist whose sympathies were with Child, Petty, Uztáriz rather than with Quesnay. Only a mercantilist would have thought it worth while to translate (as he did) Thomas Mun's work into Italian. For him the principal importance of economics was that it was 'la scienzia che abbraccia le regole per rendere la sottoposta nazione popolata, potente, soggia, poleta' (the science which embraces the laws which make an inferior nation populous, powerful, wise and cultured). Only a Neapolitan knew how much southern Italy needed such a science. For fifteen years Genovesi lectured with eloquence and missionary zeal to a Neapolitan audience, spreading the passion for national improvement and civil reform, and furnishing material for many other economists, Filangieri, Palmieri, Briganti and Galanti among them. If any single man was responsible for the interest in social subjects so general in Naples in the last decades of the century, it was Genovesi. Genovesi was not, it will be seen, in any way an original thinker. His creed was a variation on the orthodox mercantilist theme. For him there was 'useful commerce' (which exported manufactures and brought back raw materials in return) and 'harmful commerce' (which exported raw material and brought back manufactures in return). Intervention, on the other hand, should be directed only at the latter. 'Useful commerce' deserved liberty and flourished best under free conditions. Amongst the eclectics— Forbonnais in France, Steuart in England and the cameralists (see below) in Germany—Genovesi was probably the most influential; his works were translated into German and Spanish and widely read.[1]

Italy was in fact remarkable in these years for an outburst of intellectual curiosity on social matters. Journals on economic subjects were founded at Florence, Venice and Turin. The Venetian Government set up an agricultural academy on the *terra firma*. The second chair in economic science was founded by the Austrian Government for Beccaria at Milan in 1768 and occupied by him till 1770. Beccaria anticipated many of the principles of the *Wealth of Nations* and popularized the phrase *la massima felicita divisa nel maggior numero* twelve years before it was taken up by Bentham. Paradisi was at Modena, Sergio at Palermo, while Ortes, the Venetian monk and perhaps the most original thinker amongst the Italian economists, was brooding over what he deemed, not unreasonably, to be the insoluble economic problems of Italy. Nor is there much evidence of any immediate relationship

[1] For the most modern assessments of Genovesi, see *Studi in Onore di Antonio Genovesi* (Naples, 1956).

elsewhere in Italy between mercantilist aspirations and the practical behaviour of governments. Those who, like Beccaria in Lombardy and
Dolfin in Venice, protested against the dead hand which the guilds and
corporations laid on economic life, found little response. Pascoli's proposals for reviving the trade of the Papal Provinces on mercantilist lines
in 1733 had little visible effect. The most notable, perhaps the only
single exception to the indifference and lethargy which was the general
fate of mercantilist schemes was in Tuscany where Bandini wrote, in
1737, his celebrated essay on the reclamation of the Sienese marshes. The
*Discorso Economico* as it was entitled, was a plea to the grand-duke,
Francis, to use the marshes as a demonstration of the truth—which
Bandini derived largely from Vauban—that if taxes, officials, regulations were reduced or better still abolished, a prosperous peasantry would
see to it that abundant supplies of food were the result. This was
developed into a general plea for a more rational and freer economy and
eventually, though only after long delay, bore fruit. The area affected
was the lower part of the province of Siena comprising about two-fifths
of the whole of Tuscany. Francis, to whom the appeal was addressed,
was not impressed, but his successor Peter Leopold followed up Bandini's
proposals. This was an exceptional case. In general the effects of mercantilist aspirations in Spain and Italy were not ponderable, and for this
there were two main reasons. The first was the magnitude of the problems
where the misgovernment of centuries had been superimposed on the
handicaps of a terrain often barren, a climate often unfavourable and a
population inured to fatalism where material considerations were involved. Only the shock of a new technology—especially in transport—
could have effected any heroic advance, and this was not present. The
second reason derives from the first. The mercantilism of Spain and Italy
was purely derivative from English, French and Dutch models. Yet it
imitated only the theory and very largely ignored the social institutions
from which that theory emerged and upon which, as foundations, it
rested. In England, Holland, and even in France, there were merchant
communities skilled in ancient expertise; the opening up of colonial
trades was on their initiative and had expanded their prosperity. Corporate organization and balance of trade theory and policy was but a
rationalization of their ambitions. The largest part of English mercantilist literature was the work of practising merchants or men with
mercantile connections—Mun, Misselden, Violet, Child, North, Gee,
Defoe—and even in France the experience of the merchant class was
recorded and spread by writers like Savary and Forbonnais. In general it
was otherwise in Spain and Italy. Economic writings came mostly from
ecclesiastics or lawyers. Genovesi started his career in holy orders.
Galiani was a *monsignore*, Bandini, Ortes, Pascoli were ecclesiastics.

Galanti was a lawyer. Others, like Beccari and Verri, were nobles. Of the large number of Italian writers on economics in the eighteenth century only two names of note are those of merchants: Belloni was a Roman banker; Broggia was a Neapolitan merchant who turned to politics. The same held good of the latter-day Spanish mercantilists. Uztáriz was a civil servant: Ulloa was a Madrid magistrate. From this derives a certain unreality about their writings and proposals. The balance of trade instead of being the measure of the efforts of an existing body of merchants, is viewed as a sort of *deus ex machina* which will itself create trade, of the volume and character required to provide revenue for the Prince, employment for the people, wealth and strength for the State. The need for enterprise, application and skill is secondary, if it is present at all, in the calculations. While in Spain legislators got as far as admitting that commercial activities were not necessarily dishonourable, they fell short of taking active steps to train tradesmen and endow them with positive status. Yet this, not the large abstractions that went to make up policy, was the real nub of the matter.

In central, northern and eastern Europe, a superficial reading of the literature on economic subjects might lead a reader to conclude that conditions were similar to those in Spain and southern Italy: a backward economic region ruled by princes who, either in their own interests or those of their state, adopted the orthodox principles of mercantilism as the basis of economic policy. To some extent this is true. There was in Germany, as in Spain and Italy, a late flowering of mercantilism. Princes did adopt the methods advocated by earlier writers and administrators in England and France, and copied by German mercantilists of the late seventeenth and eighteenth centuries. Nothing could be more conventionally mercantilist than Frederick the Great's own concise if unoriginal dictum:

In order that a country may flourish it is first of all necessary that it have a favourable balance of trade; if it pays more for its importations than it gains from its exportations, it will necessarily become poorer from year to year. If a man has a purse of five score ducats and draws one out every twenty-four hours without putting anything back, in one hundred days he will have nothing left. The way to avert such a catastrophe is for a State to consume all its own raw products in home manufactures, to found other skilled industries for working over imported materials, and to make production cheap in order to obtain control of foreign markets.[1]

The analogy can be pursued. Much of Frederick's work in founding new industries and enterprises had disappeared by the time of Jena. Here

[1] From *Oeuvres de Frédéric*, IX, 206. The quotation is from the *Essai sur les formes de Gouvernement* and probably dates from 1777.

again, it is argued, is a case of hot-house growth. The mercantilist plant withered, it appears, when exposed to the air, and no longer tended by its royal gardener. In all this there is a measure of truth. The eighteenth-century mercantilism of the German states shared in some degree the artificiality of mercantilism elsewhere. Yet it differed in certain important respects, both as regards its ideas and the execution of those ideas. There is moreover some reason to suppose that the policies penetrated more deeply and had more enduring effects than has sometimes been supposed.

Large areas of Germany and the states to the east of Germany were economically backward by comparison with the West. Largely agrarian, the more eastern areas had seen their feudalism debased into a brutal system of slavery. A Germanic aristocracy had reduced a largely Slav peasantry to a condition as bad as that existing anywhere else in Europe, and the Thirty Years War had made conditions even worse. Even in 1694 a Pomeranian law could authorize lords to brand on their backs any peasants who ran away. The east German peasant could be described as 'gloomy, discontented, slavish . . . a hapless missing link between a beast of burden and a man'. To Frederick, whose 'enlightenment' included plans to lighten the burdens of the peasants on his own lands (some third part of his kingdom) the peasantry were 'a kind of vegetable as compared with the French'. In any event little was done, even by Frederick. Germany, especially towards the east, remained obstinately backward, lacking roads, let alone civility. Gentlemen on their Grand Tours did not go far eastwards and a few who did (like Burney in 1772 in search of material for his *Survey of European Music*) encountered such difficulties and endured such inconveniences, incivilities, insults and physical ill-treatment as not to encourage others to follow their example. Yet not everywhere was barbarism. Westwards, rural conditions were more like those of other Western economies, and everywhere there were signs of industry though usually of a rough kind.

Most areas made linen, and from Bavaria to East Prussia, from Westphalia to Silesia there was hardly a hamlet where there was not a loom. The Rhine had its textile industries. In the mountains, especially in central and eastern Germany where wood fuel and water power were abundant, there was mining and metallurgy. Along the north German coast were the great ports where the traditions of merchant skill remained strong, and in many towns there were skilled craftsmen and mechanics from whose ranks later entrepreneurs were to rise. Of these widespread but scattered instances of German industrialization it is possible to make too much and too little. Dispassionate observers writing as late as the 1830's were to remark on the backwardness of German industry as a whole, its unit still small. They picture an economy held back by lack of transport, by tariffs between states, by peasant conservatism in the countryside and by guild conservatism in the towns. River tolls were, throughout the period, the curse of the German economy. Shipping disappeared from the upper Rhine after the Thirty Years War. Wine and wheat, it was claimed, trebled in price between Mannheim and the Dutch frontier because of tolls. On the lower Rhine, toll restrictions confined trade to small sections of the river. On the Elbe the confusion was at least as great. A boat travelling from Dresden to Hamburg in the early eighteenth century took four weeks over the journey: out of these, three were taken up with toll formalities. Timber travelling down the river paid toll in kind. By 1685, out of a consignment of sixty planks going from Saxony to Hamburg, fifty-four went as tribute to the rulers of intervening States including Brandenburg and Luneburg. Only six reached their destination. Altogether the Elbe navigation included forty-eight separate toll barriers: thirty were territorial, ten municipal and seven were owned by feudal lords. It was the same throughout Germany and within the scores of states which composed Germany. This toll system lasted till after the French Revolution, for the German princelings were too dependent on it as a source of income to be able to abolish it. Yet until it was abolished there could be little general economic progress, save along the coast. Here, on the southern shore of the Baltic the old Hanseatic ports were still important. Amongst them Hamburg was chief, with a bank (founded in 1619) second only to the Bank of Amsterdam, a thriving trade in linens locally bleached and a wide range of refining and finishing industries. This was an exceptional case.

Throughout Germany as a whole the story was one of potentiality frustrated by politics. Yet there can be no doubt the potentiality was there. Amongst the weavers, dyers, carpenters, locksmiths, nailsmiths and miners of Germany were to be found the ancestors of later captains of German industry. In the north—Holstein in particular —the peasants themselves went into business, selling and buying grain and timber and even trading overseas to Norway and Holland in ships co-operatively owned. In Bohemia and Silesia peasants set up as traders, perhaps through connections made in their function as waggoners and carriers. It was traders of peasant origin who established the Bohemian glass industry of the eighteenth century. In the Austrian territories, but especially in Bohemia, such economic development as there was owed most to the enterprise of the nobles—Count Josef von Bolza, Count Ferdinand Harrach, Baron Neffzer and a score of others—whose estates provided the sites for industrial concerns. Count Joseph Maximilian Kinsky (1705–80), for example, had eleven different industrial enterprises on his own estates. Similar phenomena were to be found elsewhere in eastern Europe. At Urzecze, south of Minsk, then in Polish territory, the Princess Radziwill established in 1737 a glass and mirror factory on one of her estates. It worked for over a century. Such developments were not novel. They had their precedents in the work of Duke Julius von Braunschweig who, 200 years earlier, had launched into mining enterprises and salt wells on a large scale: or the even more ambitious schemes of Daniel Rantzau. But such examples now became more common, so that an industry like the Thuringian china manufacture owed its existence to aristocratic enterprise and capital. There were, nevertheless, obvious limits set by the shortage of capital to the operation of such enterprises. The most important aspect of aristocratic enterprise is therefore the experience it offered to a class of men from whom high state officials were recruited. The training and experiments of this laboratory came to fruition in the even larger enterprises of the mercantilist state. For it was characteristic of German thought and policy that it sought from the start to remedy the deficiencies of private capital and enterprise by state help. Where there was virtually no middle class from which to recruit tradesmen, salesmen, managers, clerks and the like, their place had to be taken by state officials, who were frequently of noble family: in Prussia men like Count Reden, the founder of the Silesian iron industry (1752–1814), or Friedrich Bückling, one of the earliest builders of steam-engines in Germany. In Austria Otto Ludwig von Loscani (1702–57) and Freiherr von Sorgenthal (1735–1805) were two of many who did constructive work as government officials to build up the economic life of Austria and her territories. The Saxon Count von Einsiedel (1737–1810) established, with the aid of imported workers and technical information, an iron foundry—one of a number originating in this way in Lower Saxony. Evidently much of the development of trade and industry that sprang up, apparently spontaneously, in Germany in the seventeenth and eighteenth centuries owed its origins to the nobility acting either as private entrepreneurs or as state officials. Yet it would be rash to assume that either they or their masters were moved simply by the immediate spur of financial need. As the historian of this phase of German economic development has pointed out, the need for profits for the state did not exclude the possibility that other motives, political and economic in character, might coexist with the fiscal motive.[1] The fact that (say) Spanish and Prussian governments both had fiscal aims in their economic policy is less important than the fact that the former sought its ends through a chaotic and self-defeating muddle of assorted imposts, while the latter came to be guided by principles such as those enunciated by Frederick the Great. Yet again,

---

[1] Fritz Redlich. *Entrepreneurship in the Initial Stages of Industrialisation (Germany)*, Papers of Center for Entrepreneurial Research 1954 (Cambridge, Mass.).

when the particular inquiries and recommendations of the seventeenth and eighteenth-century German and Austrian economic writers are analysed, it will be found that though they derive (like those of their Spanish and Italian contemporaries) from English and French sources and examples, they exhibit certain characteristics peculiar to themselves: characteristics, moreover, that were clearly related to the German situation. In particular, that though as a rule they share the general principles of mercantilists everywhere, they are more precise in method and aim, more concerned with economic administration than with theory. They do not disregard the differences in social and economic structure between Germany and the states they take as working models, and they are concerned to instruct their readers in the practical working of trade and industry. These features of German writers have sometimes been held to derogate from the value of their ideas: on the contrary they illuminate vividly the nature of the economy from which they derived, where politics and war had added artificial to natural obstructions hampering economic progress and where the dearth of private economic agents could only be supplied by the state. The biographies of the German mercantilists suggest that theory and practice were often closely connected. Marx could allege in *Das Kapital* that German political economy was a ready-made commodity imported from England and France and handled by German professors who remained 'no more than scholars'. There was something in the gibe so far as the period after Adam Smith was concerned. As regards the mercantilist age the charge was baseless. Germany's 'cameralists' were a distinct and significant order of thinkers. The phrase *Kameralwissenschaft* derived from the chamber (camera) in which the revenue and expenditure of the prince were administered, and strictly speaking the 'science' referred to the effects of expenditure on the fund of wealth from which revenue might be drawn. In its narrowest sense, cameralism was apt to become a string of treatises on taxation. In its wider sense it comprehended doctrines affecting the economic welfare of the state, the nature of the administration demanded to put those doctrines into effect, as well as the technical aspects of trade and industrial and agricultural production. As the territorial sovereignty of the princes came into its own after the Treaty of Westphalia, cameral science developed as a body of doctrine independent of the jurisprudence with which it had earlier been yoked. Its immediate object was—for reasons already suggested—to train a staff of competent officials to raise and manage the state revenues and foster the interests of the states ravaged by decades of war and destruction of life and resources. Here were the roots of the German conviction (that was to survive the logical sophistries (as they seemed) of more fortunate economies) that the construction of a strong and prosperous economy demanded a partnership between government and entrepreneur. Waste lands had to be re-cultivated and re-populated, war debts liquidated, industry revived with the aid of new and borrowed skills. Thus cameral science became in its varied respects a theory of agriculture, a theory of population, a theory of taxation. The school of *Kameralgelehrten* was split into two 'confessions' that corresponded to the religious dualism of the Empire: a Catholic branch grouped round the Habsburgs, a Protestant that attached ever more closely to the growing ascendancy of the Hohenzollerns.

Amongst the Austrian school the father figure was unquestionably Johann Joachim Becher (1625–85). An ex-physician, Becher moved in 1666 to Vienna where he taught at the newly-founded *Commerz-Collegium*. Two years later he published his famous *Politische Discurs von den Eigentlichen Ursachen des Auf- und Abnehmens der Reiche, Städte und Republiken*. The spirit of Becher's work is that of the mercantilists: like his English predecessors and Italian successors he preached parochialism, denouncing those merchants who imported from abroad goods that might be produced at home as 'propolists' (perpetrators of *propolium*—usurious forestalling). The practical origin of this xenophobia was the stream of French luxury goods entering Austria, which official policy had for years been trying to exclude. Those who were willing to invest in native industry were by contrast virtuous pillars of society. The final aim of territorial administration should be a '*volkreiche und nahrhafte Gemeinde*' and a prosperous agriculture to support such a population. To this extent—that he avoids any bullionist conceptions of policy—Becher has much in common with his English contemporaries and French and Italian successors like Vauban, Genovesi and Bandini. There is, that is to say, a strong 'social' element in his thought. For all that he had a streak of the charlatan in him, Becher was a lively and practical thinker whose writings remain close to reality. He was himself a member of that strange collection of cranks, impostors and near-geniuses the seventeenth century called 'the projectors', a *genus* whose social role and achievements have yet to be properly assessed. One writer has compared Becher with Leibniz in the breadth and versatility of his learning.[1] But Becher was also a bold if generally unsuccessful entrepreneur, setting up the famous Manufacturenhaus auf dem Tabor at Vienna where he was under contract to make all kinds of textiles, kitchen utensils, dyes, to refine sugar, smelt metals and separate out gold and silver. At Munich and Walpersdorf he set up silk manufactures—the latter on the estates of a feudal entrepreneur Count Sinzendorf who had other similar projects to his credit already.

Becher's ideas (and his projects) were carried on by his son-in-law

[1] Redlich, *op. cit.*, p. 14.

Philipp Wilhelm von Horneck (Hornick or Hörningk) and Wilhelm Freiherr von Schroeder. Von Horneck, an administrator in the service of the Prince-bishop of Passau, was principally concerned to show how the House of Habsburg could improve its fortunes by a rational economic policy. His ideas, mercantilist in general character, were set out in his *Oesterreich über alles, wann es nur will* (1684). Like his father-in-law he was especially anxious to hoist France with her own petard. Hence his famous dictum: 'it were better to give two thalers for a commodity and keep them in the country than to give only one which leaves the country'. All foreign manufactures, it followed logically, should be prohibited—without waiting for corresponding industries to arise at home. They would follow at once, anyway. Horneck was understandably popular and influential. Even Joseph II found much that was persuasive in him. The third of the early cameralist trio, von Schroeder, who inherited Becher's enterprise at Vienna, was a son of the chancellor of the Duke Ernest of Gotha and seems to have spent his early career in the duke's service. A passionate alchemist, he migrated to Holland and England, where he was in service to Charles II whom he presented in 1670 with a drinking vessel of red glass of his own manufacture. He then returned to succeed Becher at Vienna, and after the 'house' was burnt in the Turkish siege, to take up an administrative post in Hungary. In 1686 he completed his celebrated *Fürstliche Schatz- und Rent-Kammer*, using the writings of both Mun and de la Court. From them he derived, not (as has sometimes been assumed) an orthodox mercantilism of the balance-of-payments type, but one which made a very reasonable allowance for the 'social' demands upon policy. That is to say, 'it was not the import and export of *money* but the equilibrium of the different *trades* which causes the wealth or poverty of a country'. Of the three 'producing' classes—peasants, mechanics and merchants—it was the merchants who were the 'hands and feet' of the state because they were responsible for 'external' movement. But because they were more apt to be *cives orbis quam urbis* they were better left to their own business than installed as advisers and policy makers. Policy should be framed by reference to an inventory of home manufactures like the one used by the Duke of Gotha. Tables of imports and exports must be prepared which should act as 'the spectacles of the state'; for by then applying a suitable system of duties 'the whole clockwork of commerce and manufacture can be set to go fast or slow'.

Meanwhile, similar views were developing in the Protestant states. Veit Ludwig von Seckendorff—the 'great Seckendorff' as he was known —succeeded von Schroeder's father as chancellor to the Duke of Gotha and advised in his lifetime all the reigning princes of Saxony. His ideas were, like those of the Austrian cameralists, mercantilist, modified in the direction of population theory. The true wealth of a nation lay in 'the numbers of the subjects'. But he recognized the importance of enterprise in his taxation theory: those who can provide employment for the masses should receive corresponding privileges by tax policy. It was a characteristically German blend of mercantilism, with the emphasis on power but a shrewd attention to prosperity: neither purely imitative (as the Spanish version of mercantilism was apt to be) nor academic (like the Italian) nor dangerously original (like the French). From this point onwards the nature of German thought becomes clearer as, one after another, the cameralists concentrated on what was deemed to be specific and relevant to the rehabilitation of Germany. Von Rohr sets out the theory of rural economy in his *Compendiöse Haushaltungsbibliothek*. The economics of forestry are covered by von Carlowitz in his *Silvicultura oeconomica*. Süssmilch, taking as his text the scriptural injunction 'Be fruitful and multiply', may be regarded as the voice of his master, Frederick the Great, who saw to it that he rose from his original rank of army chaplain to the Prussian Academy of Sciences. This obsession with an indefinite expansion of population was to characterize pretty well all the cameralists, except Pufendorf. The strongly statistical character of Süssmilch's writings is a sign of the times: others—Conring, Schmeizel, Achenwall and Scheözer—were all developing the study of statistics at Jena, Halle and Göttingen, with an eye to its relevance to government administration. Even Leibniz—like Newton—remained close to the practical aspects of public administration. But none of the cameralists deals more characteristically with the 'induced birth' that was German enterprise than Jacob Marperger (1656–1730). Marperger was the earliest German economist to propose a systematic education for business. His earlier suggestions were that *professores mercatores* should be attached to existing universities. By 1723 when he published his *Trifolium mercantile aureum* this had become a proposal for a commercial academy in Saxony to teach not only commercial subjects in the narrow sense, but economics, technology, geometry, history, mechanics and languages. Finally he submitted a plan for a staff college where professors of economics, law, geography, history and the useful arts would lecture to an audience of business men and government officials. Marperger's prolix and tortuous writings ran into thousands of pages and occupied not a little of the remarkable *Cameralisten Bibliothek* of 1762 that itself filled 700 pages. Yet his writings were neither absurd nor abortive. They had issue in the commercial academy set up in Hamburg in 1767 by Johann Georg Büsch, a mathematician and amateur economist, in partnership with a local merchant. The *Hamburgische Handlungs-Akademie*, as it was called, with its fifty or so students mostly between fifteen and eighteen years of age, resembled a little in its curriculum an

English Dissenting Academy. Büsch, mercantilist by inclination, was further strengthened in his beliefs by reading the *Inquiry* of James Steuart, who as a Jacobite fled to Germany in 1746 and worked for some time in Baden and Württemburg. It has even been suggested that influences such as these help to explain why business men in general continued to think on mercantilist lines, resisting the logical blandishments of *laissez-faire* which proved so tempting to statesmen and philosophers. There were other academies elsewhere. The Duke of Württemberg set up the *Hohe Karlsschule*, and while Göttingen refused to accept commercial courses, the University of Würzburg was more accommodating. Büsch himself was invited by Maria Theresa to submit a plan for a commercial academy on the lines of his own. It was established in 1770. A commercial high school set up in Berlin in 1791 had a chequered career and collapsed in 1806. It posed a problem for the future. So far the academies had simply aimed to produce efficient merchants. The question was beginning to be asked how this aim could be reconciled with the larger demands of education in a wide sense.[1]

The later cameralists, von Justi and von Sonnenfels, collected and summarized the ideas of their predecessors: Justi leaning towards the physiocrats, von Sonnenfels strongly away from them. Yet in one important respect Justi continued the older tradition: he is best known for his dictum that a state cannot be over-peopled. For Sonnenfels a limit to population was set by the opportunities of employment. He systematized, on this account, a distinction that had already appeared in the writings of later English mercantilists. There were, he said, two ways of measuring the balance of trade—by monetary effects and by its effects on employment. And the two could work in contrary fashion. If Austria and Portugal trade together and Austria sells £2¼ million of linens in exchange for £2 million of diamonds, the transaction is, monetarily, unfavourable to Austria for she has parted with commodities of greater value for commodities of less: but the balance of advantage is in Austria's favour because the transaction is one that keeps her population employed.

The peculiar qualities of German mercantilism were, then, neither originality nor universalism. Most of the writers derived their ideas, consciously or otherwise, from earlier writers and practitioners of economic nationalism in England or France: but they adapted them conscientiously to German needs, orientating them towards the practical, the administrative, the parochial, rather than towards the larger economic generalization of universal validity. They were mainly concerned with the factors of production and trade, not omitting the entrepre-

[1] See F. Redlich, 'Academic Education for Business', *Business History Review*, xxxi, no. 1 (1957).

neur himself who, in the special conditions that afflicted Germany and retarded the development of her society, had to be sought to a great extent amongst the nobility and the state officials. The cameralist writers themselves frequently figured as entrepreneurs in action, as Becher and von Schroeder did at Vienna and as Justi did as a director of mines and superintendent of glass and steel works at Berlin. Nothing helped to stimulate the business capacities of the German nobility more than the realization of the potential value of the *Bergregal*, the monopoly rights of mining. Kings and princes commissioned aristocratic public administrators of mining and smelting: the iron mines of Silesia and Bohemia were administered in this way. Amongst the great aristocratic administrators of eighteenth-century Germany, Count Reden in Prussia, Freiherr von Heinitz in Saxony and later in Prussia, and Freiherr von Trebra of Saxony were all primarily concerned with mining. But mining was far from being the only field for enterprise. In textiles, pottery, even in wholesale trading, nobles took part. Conversely a merchant like Konrad Sorgel might turn government official and be ennobled for his work as a state entrepreneur in the metal, textile, china and glass manufactures of Austria.

By the middle of the eighteenth century, opinion in the West was no longer unanimous on the virtues of mercantilist intervention in economic affairs. Many still held by the old doctrine that the amount of international trade was a fixed quantity that would be shared by the various states according to their power to grab and hold it. The attitude to war of those who held such views would vary according to their interest. Many of them in England supported war against Spain in 1739 or against France in 1756. Like their city ancestors of the 1660's they clamoured for a 'war of trade': only it was now a French war not a Dutch war. 'Our trade', William Beckford, one of London's greatest West India merchants, declared to Parliament, 'will improve by the total extinction of theirs.' But this was no longer an unchallenged axiom of policy. In England and in France, to say nothing of Holland, the voices of philosophy were questioning many of the basic assumptions of mercantilism. The logic of David Hume was mightily persuasive to the cultivated mind, and though the new philosophy would never have been voted in by a democratically organized society, arguments such as these found many admirers in those sections of society that produced Britain's governors:

Suppose four-fifths of all the money in Great Britain to be annihilated in one night... what would be the consequence? Must not the price of all labour and commodities sink in proportion and everything be sold as cheap as they were in former days? What nation could then dispute with us in any foreign market or pretend to navigate or sell manufactures at the same price which to us would afford sufficient profit? In how little time therefore must this bring back the money which we had lost and raise us to the level of all the neighbouring nations: where, after we have arrived, we immediately lose the advantage of the cheapness of labour and commodities and the further flowing in of money is stopped by our fullness and repletion.

Another 100 years were to elapse before Britain accepted in full this demonstration of the self-regulating character of the economic mechanism: but from this time on the number of those who were persuaded—like Hume—to pray for the prosperity of Spain and even of France in the interest of British subjects grew steadily. It was otherwise in Germany, where the enlightened despots were busy breathing life into cameralist theories. The very struggle between Prussia and Austria was itself a mercantilist war, almost, one might say, of the colonial type. The attack on Silesia did not spring from purely economic motives, but the economic resources of the area were certainly a prize of the first order and Frederick was conscious of their value. Here was a region rich in industrial resources, deposits of mineral ores virtually untapped, and industrial skill. His description of it—'my new Peru'—was not an idle phrase: the seizure of Silesia was merely one episode in the busy process of German colonization eastwards. Similarly, though more peacefully, the great reclamation schemes, especially the recovery of the swamps of the Oderbruch below Frankfort. As soon as the Silesian campaign was ended, Frederick took up the plan for the Oderbruch pigeon-holed years before by Frederick William. The river channel was deepened, dykes and ditches to stop the persistent winter overflow were constructed, the shrubs cleared, the wild animals exterminated, the soil drained. None of the complaints that arose from the Stettin merchants, owners of adjoining land, or local fishermen and hunters deterred Frederick. The work was completed in 1753: Frederick could claim that he had conquered a new province without a war. Twelve hundred families, attracted by the offer of privileges and exemptions from taxation and military service, were swiftly settled here alone. Altogether it has been estimated about 300,000 immigrants were settled on Pomeranian territory. The acquisition of Silesia, the improvement in the Oder navigation, the development of Stettin harbour—all hung together. Likewise the Plauen and Finow canals that joined Breslau to Berlin and Berlin to Hamburg provided another outlet for Silesian goods, and enabled eastern Europe to obtain colonial wares and French wines and luxury foods via Hamburg.

The close attention paid, and rightly paid, to the questions of population and transport links Frederick to the true cameralist tradition. His own *credo* on trade and manufacture reveals him as a mercantilist of the old kind, preoccupied with the bullion issue and aiming already at that hoard of 18 million thalers with which he began the Seven Years War.

The basic rule to follow in connection with all trade and manufacture is to prevent money from flowing permanently out of the country; an attempt should always be made to bring it back again into Prussia. The exodus of money can best be prevented by producing in Prussia all kinds of goods which were formerly imported. All imports are to be indicated by invoices which list commodities imported into Prussia and sold here. From these lists it is easy to judge which factories can be enlarged and which should be readjusted to another type of production.

The second way to prevent an undue exodus of money from the country is to purchase necessary foreign commodities at their original source, thus taking the trade in one's own hands instead of leaving it to foreign agents. This means that goods costing a thaler in Hamburg probably cost only a gulden if they are purchased directly from Spain. The resulting decrease in commodity prices would be a distinct gain, quite apart from the direct profit to domestic Prussian traders, for it implies also a relative loss to Hamburg and Dutch merchants.

Manufacture of arms results in large quantities of money within the country. Increased production could, however, be a source of even greater wealth, because of our propinquity to Poland and Russia, for these countries are in constant need of all commodities, and are therefore forced to maintain indirectly the industry of their neighbours. All these reasons must cause the ruler of Prussia to encourage manufacture and trade, whether through direct subsidies or through tax exemptions, so that they may be in a position for large-scale production and trade.

It was this mercantilist programme of national economic development that Frederick put into vigorous practice by his *Rétablissements* after the Seven Years War. This was the most ambitious example of economic planning in European history to date. Between 1763 and 1786, 60 million thalers were disbursed from the state treasury to stimulate recovery and growth of the Prussian economy. Under administrators like von Heinitz and von Hagen the new mercantilism used private enterprise when it could find it—usually in the west. At Krefeld, for example, where the von der Leyen brothers could provide initiative, intervention was limited to granting them an industrial monopoly of silk production. In Berlin, silk manufacture became a state enterprise because there was no private enterprise to carry out the programme. Within a conventional framework of regulations aimed at preventing the export of raw materials, especially wool, and the import of foreign manufactures, at stimulating local manufactures by bounties, monopolies and privileges, at encouraging the immigration of skilled craftsmen, a remarkable growth of industry took place. There were monopolies for iron production in Westphalia, metal and mining companies in

Silesia, trading monopolies like the Levant and Russia Companies, the State Bank of 1766. But, as the historian of the German silk industry Otto Hintze pointed out, the 'centre and summit' of the programme was the plan for the fine textile manufactures. Like Colbert, whose plans his own so closely resembled, Frederick saw luxury manufactures as the money-spinners of international trade. Hence the central importance of the great public warehouses for the raw materials required by these trades—wool, cotton, silk—upon which vast sums were lavished in order to provide an inexhaustible market for the native grower and an abundant source of supply for the manufacturer. The silk magazine alone had a capital of 80,000 thalers. These and scores of other schemes were watched with the closest attention by the king in person. Nothing was too trivial for him. Clay pipes are imported: cannot they be made at home? Striegau wants a factory: why not put down a chemical plant there? Why cannot Prussia make crackle-ware? Let the envoy at Dresden find some Saxon workmen to show Prussia how to do it. Why are the peasantry no longer spinning their own flax? Let some Saxon women who like the music of the spinning-wheel and loom be settled in Brandenburg to set the local women a good example. And so on. The royal tour each year produced a crop of observations, plans and questions for the harassed bureaucracy. The lands that Frederick inherited in 1740 exported only raw products— wool, linen and timber. By the end of his reign his vigorous application had helped to create textile factories of all kinds, sugar refineries, porcelain and pottery works, iron and steel mills, paper and leather works. Some of these were industries that had declined in the previous reign and been reinvigorated by Frederick's energetic measures, but many were new.

It is not easy to assess the merits of Frederick's work. Sir James Harris, the English envoy, wrote in 1776 that Frederick could never be made to understand that the real wealth of a sovereign consisted in 'the ease and affluence of his subjects' and not in the large treasure 'dormant in his coffers'. It was not quite fair: vast sums were expended on priming the industrial pump and it was not possible for a king like Frederick to disregard military emergencies in laying his economic plans. Again, there was some truth in the charge that amongst the industries he attempted to establish were some that 'were as little likely to flourish in Prussia as the banana or the orange in Greenland'.[1] Yet in general it is to be doubted if Frederick misjudged the economic future worse than many other entrepreneurs, private and public. The reason why many of his ventures lay bankrupt and abandoned by the time of Jena is to be found in circumstances beyond his control. Like Joseph II, whose own economic plans for developing industry and relaxing guild and monopoly control

[1] H. Tuttle, *History of Prussia under Frederick the Great*, II (London, 1888), 101.

were more liberal than Frederick's, though essentially cameralistic, Frederick was not strong enough to break down the network of tariffs and tolls that hampered the internal trade of Germany and the Habsburg lands. This was one problem that had to await solution after 1815: yet the so-called decline of Prussian foreign trade from the levels of 1752 to the reduced levels of thirty years later reflected in part the larger production for the home market. In general the annual value of industrial production had risen steeply, especially in Silesia. The collapse in face of the Napoleonic armies came partly because the new state was still only a mechanical structure. There had been no time for the artificially induced commerce and industry of Prussia to transform the nature of Prussian society itself, and as late as 1842 an English observer who had travelled all round Germany could reflect that: 'The country is not commercial enough to have created such a wealthy middle class as shall be independent enough of Government. . . .'[1] The 'middle class' was still composed predominantly of government officials, mostly minor. Frederick himself never saw that social change was itself a necessary consequence of his ideas if they were to be successfully applied. Feudalism, Junkerdom and industrialization were not ultimately compatible. Prussia emerged into the nineteenth century a strange mixture, but socially she was still feudal. Organic social change began after 1815 and was registered in 1848. The new factors in the situation that distinguished it from the situation of the eighteenth century were peace and the Zollverein. Yet he would be an unjust judge who left out of account the important opportunities given to enterprise by the vigorous if unequal experiments of Frederick.

Rich resources, favourable climate and a strong monarchy did not necessarily constitute an infallible formula for mercantilist development. The so-called Age of Empire in Swedish history (1600–1720) saw the considerable resources of Sweden exploited to finance the interminable wars in which Sweden was engaged for 75 out of the 120 years of the period. 'In no other period of Swedish history', wrote Heckscher, 'has the entire economic system been so geared to political action.'[2] The drain on the population and the urgent need for foreign currency to discharge her military obligations compelled successive kings to mortgage such assets as they possessed to the foreign bidders who had the resources of capital and technology to face the risks involved. Such a one was Louis de Geer, the Amsterdam capitalist of Walloon extraction who occupied a commanding position in almost every field of economic activity in mid-seventeenth-century Sweden. The export of copper, the mining and manufacture of iron, copper, tin, wire, paper, cloth, shipbuilding,

[1] W. Howitt, *Rural and Domestic Life of Germany* (London, 1842).
[2] E. Heckscher, *An Economic History of Sweden* (Cambridge, Mass., 1954), 79.

banking, colonial and retail trade were only a few of his ventures. De Geer owned or leased vast tracts of land all over central and eastern Sweden, and his invested capital was enormous. Yet he, and many others amongst the entrepreneurs who were granted privileges by the government, remained essentially foreign.

Sweden was not immune from mercantilist influences. There was some tariff protection, some grant of privileges. A few trading companies were founded, of which only those set up to trade in tar were successful. Strategic considerations led Gustavus Adolphus to subsidize shipowners to build armed merchantmen which could be easily converted to naval use. The system survived from 1645 to the end of the century, but the growing size and complexity of warships proper rendered its utility dubious. On the whole, mercantilist policies seem to have borne little fruit, largely no doubt because the financial needs of government were too exigent to permit any consistent pursuit of the economic well-being of the state. There was apparently no widespread revolt against the system or lack of it: only one writer of any consequence, Johan Classon Risingh, appeared in the seventeenth century, and his *Tract of Commerce* (1669) was a contradictory jumble of old-fashioned bullionism and appeals to the freedom and mercantile efficiency of the Dutch. Nor did the following period down to the Napoleonic Wars add much more, in spite of a torrential downpour of economic pamphlets in the mid-1760's—on an average one every five days. Most of it was mercantilism of the cameralist type, strongly influenced by Becher and the German school and to a lesser extent by earlier English mercantilists like Mun and Child, now reaching Sweden in French translation. Most of it was, like Swedish thought of the seventeenth century, derivative and often remote from Swedish conditions. Most of those who wrote were nobles or academics or bureaucrats. Swedish mercantilism thus tended to diverge from economic reality, which often reflected a national tendency to seek freedom from control and regulation. Of the eighteenth century it has been said that 'everything was tried and nothing achieved'.[1] There was neither the upsurge of enterprise from below nor consistent pressure from above to bring about the social transformation which characterized the more vigorous mercantilist states. Sweden's day was postponed until later.

The historiography of the 'mercantile system' since the eighteenth century is characterized by a series of violent reactions. To Adam Smith, who popularized if he did not actually invent the term, it symbolized a confusion of ideas; first 'money' had been falsely identified with 'wealth'; then the 'fruitless care' for money had been replaced by an equally 'fruitless care' over the balance of trade. A needless apparatus of

[1] Heckscher, *op. cit.*, p. 207.

regulation had been built up, for the benefit of a small clique of vested interests. The system had benefited 'the rich and powerful' at the expense of 'the poor and indigent'. Consumption, the sole end and purpose of all production, had been subordinated to production and to the interests of the producers. This condemnation of the 'system' as a conspiracy of the part against the whole provoked, in due course, an opposing view elsewhere. In Germany the absence of any spontaneous commercial and industrial development after the Thirty Years War had forced rulers and thinkers to look to the state and its servants for the initiative that was voluntarily forthcoming further west and in more fortunate societies. The German school of historical economists, and Gustav Schmoller in particular, came to take a very different view of the history of state intervention, as favourable as Adam Smith's was damning. The ideas behind the 'system', wrote Schmoller, 'were nearer reality than the theory of Adam Smith ...'. There was a connection between economic life and the essential, controlling, organs of social and political life. Economic institutions depended on the action of political bodies; individual economic action could not go on in a political vacuum. This was why Germany, politically disintegrated, had lagged behind those unified states which had pursued a consistent policy of economic encouragement through tariffs, protection, bounties and the like. Frederick the Great had seen the necessity of state action: yet even to Schmoller, there was no case for making a dogma of *étatisme*. Not the least merit of Frederick's policy was that it aimed to create a healthy economy 'by state initiative and political means, and then, as quickly and completely as possible, to set it on its own feet and create thriving private businesses—and so render itself superfluous'. Frederick's policies were not, in fact, very different from those of successive English and French governments which had put the power of the state at the service of its economic interests and 'obtained thereby the lead in the struggle for riches and industrial prosperity'. Through William Cunningham, this more favourable attitude came back into English history. It was the task of historians, he wrote, to 'trace out the conscious efforts ... to develop the resources and expand the commerce of the realm: such deliberate endeavours were made through political institutions for political objects and affected our progress for good or evil'. Cunningham's advocacy provoked in turn opposition from such historians as W. A. S. Hewins and especially from George Unwin for whom state intervention in economic affairs was either sham or evil. The historian who has provided the most thorough study of mercantilism, Eli Heckscher, came to conclusions that did not differ substantially from those of earlier orthodox economists. Most mercantilist theory was misconceived and most policy misguided. Indeed, the system itself represented not so much an 'economic' apparatus in the proper sense of the word as an attempt to force economic policy into the service of state 'power' as an end in itself. Heckscher's criticisms in turn provoked Keynes to a rational defence of mercantilism on purely economic grounds which, though somewhat anachronistic, had the merit of refusing to dismiss as a mere 'puerile obsession' a concern for the balance of trade which had lasted for more than four centuries, surviving for two of those at least the logical *reductio ad absurdum* of the classical school of professional economists. It was not altogether surprising that some historians, surveying the history of the controversy, came to the conclusion that the whole concept was a source of confusion which, if it could not be abolished was at any rate best avoided.[1]

What remains at the present stage of the controversy? That from the sixteenth to the eighteenth centuries at least, in many places much longer, and throughout a considerable area of the civilized (in the material sense) world today, a number of governments, their servants and their subjects shared naturally in a belief that there was virtue in the regulation of the economic life of the community by its rulers. The community was not as yet invariably a nation state though it tended increasingly to assume that form. In Italy and the Netherlands, nevertheless, some city states still had virtually autonomous status.

The majority of those who have written of the mercantile system, though they might differ violently as to the merits of the system, did not, until comparatively recently, differ on what they meant by the system. To Adam Smith and to Schmoller, to Hewins, Cunningham and Unwin, the central feature was what Adam Smith called 'the two great engines by which the mercantile system proposes to enrich every country . . . with the ultimate object . . . of an advantageous balance of trade'. The 'engines' were twin sets of laws to regulate exports and imports designed to build up local industry by protecting it from foreign competition, by providing it with raw materials at low cost and at the same time to reduce dependence on manufactured imports. The balance of trade was not, it would appear on closer inquiry, so much 'the ultimate object' of the system as a means of measuring the efficacy of the controls adopted. There can be little question that the conception of the balance was adopted from business practice and the growing use of double-entry book-keeping, where the 'balance' served the same purpose of control. Leviathan, the argument ran, might well keep his accounts like a good merchant. Thomas Mun repeatedly compares

---

[1] For a survey of the origins of the phrase and subsequent controversies see Charles Wilson, 'Mercantilism: Some Vicissitudes of an Idea', *Economic History Review*, 2nd ser., x, no. 2 (1957). Also A. V. Judges, *The Idea of the Mercantile State* (Transactions Royal Historical Society, 1939).

'the stock of a kingdom' to 'the estate of a private man'. But what, the questioner might go on to ask, did the 'balance' show? In the early formulations of mercantilist theory, and in Mun in particular, the answer is quite simple. It showed the gain or loss to the nation by trading; the gain or loss being realized in treasure. On this depended the nation's currency and its continuing ability to conduct overseas trades in certain areas where bullion was required as a purchasing medium. In the second half of the century an important change occurs in the theory. The balance of trade continues to be the pivot upon which all turns, but its function is interpreted in a new way. Child was amongst the first of a number of mercantilists who, for one reason or another, put employment on a level with the acquisition of treasure as an aim of policy. The 'favourable balance' is now justified because it results in the employment of a larger number of hands (in Child's phrase); or, more often, a growing scale of employment is said to indicate, more surely than any of the possible (but fallible) means of calculating the balance itself, that the national economy is healthy. This was the view which was most common amongst continental mercantilists of the later phases. It found a place in the thought of the Spanish school and it was a dominant *motif* in the writings of Italians like Genovesi and Bandini. Above all it was the guiding principle of the cameralists from Becher to Sonnenfels. Nor was this a case of *post hoc* being mistaken for *propter hoc*. With the coming of university professorships of political economy (especially in Italy and Germany), the multiplication of journals and institutes devoted to the study of economic subjects of one sort or another, the doctrines of mercantilism were disseminated. Uztáriz was translated into English in 1751 (nine years after its definitive appearance in Spain), two years later—by Forbonnais—into French, and in 1793 into Italian. Ulloa's work appeared in French translation in 1753, thirteen years after its publication in Spain. Savary's *Dictionnaire*, published in France 1723–30, appeared in English in 1749. John Cory's *Essay on the State of England* (1695) was translated into French in 1755 and into Italian (by Genovesi) in 1764. With the Italian edition went an Appendix containing a translation of Mun's *England's Treasure by Fforraign Trade*. Belloni's *Del Commercio* (1750) appeared in English two years later. The Neapolitan Government ordered an Italian translation of an anonymous *Essai* on the corn trade, published in London in 1754 and in Berlin in the next year, actually the work of Herbert, a follower of Boisguilbert. De la Court's *Interest van Holland* (1662) came out in a German edition in 1672, in English in 1702 and in French in 1709. James Steuart's *Enquiry* of 1767 appeared in German in 1769 and in French in 1789. Genovesi's *Lezioni* of 1765 appeared in German in 1776 and in Spanish in 1785. Locke's *Treatises* appeared in Italian in 1751. Such examples show that the recurrence of similar mercantilist ideas in different countries was not accidental. Rightly or wrongly, the mercantilist prescription seemed not only appropriate but seductive to rulers, administrators and economists in search of an economic creed for local application.

How far the change from 'monetary' to 'social' aims was itself a product of the spread of mercantilist ideas from the western European seaboard to east and south is an open question. Here again there seems to be a difference of emphasis between English writers like Child, who begin to manifest signs of a social conscience on wages and employment that foreshadow the later humanitarians, and the cameralists, whose concern with employment is an essential part of their concern with population: this in turn reflects their own—and even more their masters'—preoccupation with the strategic aspects of economic policy. This difference itself illustrates the way in which mercantilist thought and policy moved to and fro between the twin objectives of national prosperity and national power. 'In all ages', wrote Schmoller, 'history has been wont to treat national power and national wealth as sisters; perhaps they were never so closely associated as then.'[1] Professor Viner has also elaborated and analysed the relationship (which he believes was characteristic of all mercantilism) between wealth and power as proper and reconcilable objectives of national policy. The formula for the balancing of the two varied markedly from place to place and from time to time. In Holland, where policy was apt to be the product, residual and passive, of friction between the various mercantile interests, subject only to state guidance at time of crisis, security was likely to play second fiddle to prosperity in the councils of the Republic. The predominant interests were those of the merchants who operated in the entrepôt trades. Their concern was with the free flow, in and out, of the maximum stream of goods. Abroad they were preoccupied with overcoming the opposition of monopolists (like the Spanish and Portuguese) whose privileges rested on assumptions of maritime and territorial sovereignty inimical to trade. The conception of the balance of trade meant nothing to the Dutch. Freedom of the seas, as expounded by Grotius, was far more important to them; and with it went the doctrine of 'free ships, free goods' which canonized their rights, as neutrals, to trade freely with belligerents during the more or less continuous wars that marked the century of their greatness. Their natural situation and the nature of their economic growth meant that they had a great fleet of highly vulnerable merchant ships at risk, an open target for a rival with naval power. The Dutch economic gains were not in question: but they were made at great risk in the Europe of 1648. The most astonishing feature of the strategic situation of these years is the success with which the Dutch admirals like Tromp and de Ruyter beat off

[1] G. Schmoller, *The Mercantile System* (London, 1896), 50.

the English and French attacks and even mounted their own offensive strategy against their foe. But such successes were as often the result of the incompetence of the enemy or the fortuitous intervention of the elements as of calculated tactics. By and large, the wealth of the Dutch was the result of a multiplicity of individual commercial transactions. State intervention was minimal.[1] At the other extreme came Prussia, where everything depended on the vigour with which the king and his officials could contrive and execute a policy to create trade and industry in a devastated and backward society that lacked any element of spontaneous organic growth. In Spain and Italy, though physical conditions differed widely from those of Germany, there appeared an equal need for economic stimulation, but in spite of a rich crop of writings, mercantilism remained, for reasons set out in this essay, an aspiration, since the state proved unable to evolve methods of compensating for the absence of private initiative or for combating the presence of obstacles to economic progress. Between these extremes of freedom and authority, of devolution and centrality, between the natural birth of the Dutch economy and the induced birth of the Prussian, were the two western economies whose rivalry filled the eighteenth century: England and France. It was characteristic of English mercantilism that it derived, intellectually and administratively, from a partnership of merchant and official. Most of the formative writing came from merchants like Mun and Child and bore the stamp of their mercantile training and interests. '... mercantilist writers', Heckscher wrote, 'were mostly connected with trade in one form or another.'[2] Their contribution was fundamental to the shaping of the British economy. Mr Ashley has shown how, in the evolution of the Navigation Acts (which even Adam Smith thought of as an instrument of power rather than of prosperity), the formula was influenced by the demands of the great trading companies, especially the importing interests.[3] Nevertheless the final formulae were the work of lawyers like St John and government servants like Shaw and Downing.

[1] It should perhaps be said that contemporary English observers did not always agree with the view expressed above. Sir George Downing wrote from Holland on Christmas Day 1663:

'I find that a Gardner doth not more contribute to the growing of his Herbs and trees than doth the Government of any Country to the Growth of its Trade. Holland was Holland from the beginning of the World. But never a place of trade till within these 50 or 60 yeares, that the Government did espouse that interest. And I doe evidently see in all my experience here, that it is not the People putts on the Government but the Governors by prudent orders and contrivences putt on the People to all manner of Trade. ...'

It should be remembered, of course, that he was engaged in trying to persuade his own masters at home to 'putt on the People' and allowance should be made for an element of advocacy.

[2] *Economic History Review*, 2nd ser., III (1950).

[3] M. P. Ashley, *Financial and Commercial Policy under the Protectorate* (1934), chap. XIII.

The merchants did not get the whole of their demands which were trimmed and adjusted to what seemed to less directly interested parties to be a larger conception of the national interest. The administration normally kept the merchant interest at arm's length. Their petitions and counter-petitions were listened to and their advice was asked. Mun would be asked to sit on the Commission of 1622, but the business of policy *making* remained with the Privy Council. Lionel Cranfield had made his fortune in business and his business experience was of the utmost value to James I, but it was as a privy councillor, peer of the realm and high state official that he influenced policy, not as a merchant. The creation in 1660 of a vast Council of Trade containing sixty-two members, mostly merchants, was an aberration that can be explained only by the anxiety of the new king to prove his zeal for the nation's trade, a zeal only matched by his inexperience of its affairs. Clarendon opposed it and its fate proved the wisdom of his opposition. Six years later it was extinct and thereafter only the Board of Customs amongst the commissions was strongly mercantile and it was subject to the treasury commissioners. The merchant did not, as a rule, penetrate far—*qua* merchant —into the *arcana* of government. But his influence and advice were ever present as the process of shaping policy went on. In France, also, the merchant community was consulted but, as the historian of 'Colbertism' has remarked, its influence on policy is not readily discernible.[1] Colbert, a doctrinaire and an authoritarian, himself dictated the organization of trade and industry, dismissing the views of merchants as inevitably self-interested, and myopic. The trading companies were run by the government and their course shaped by what the king and his advisers thought were the national interests. The difference between the methods of *formulating* policy in England and France was not quite so large as has sometimes been assumed, and certainly not absolute. But the difference of degree was important. The mercantile view was more carefully considered in England, largely because the king and his advisers knew that before the proposals reached their final legislative form, they would be subject to scrutiny by Parliament, pushed and pulled by a score of local and immediate interests, all capable of making a nuisance of themselves to government. Adam Smith's gibe that the mercantile system was the product of a partnership between princes, nobles and country gentlemen who did not understand trade and tradesmen who did not understand national policy was not wholly baseless: but in so far as it contained a measure of truth, it was not *originally* much more than the platitude that government can never wholly reconcile the interests of the particular and the general, that all legislation and regulation based initially on observed facts tends to become, sooner or later,

[1] C. W. Cole, *Colbert and a Century of French Mercantilism*, II, chap. XIV.

remote from the circumstances and interests which gave rise to it. It would be foolish to pretend that the policies of mercantilism were proof against the law of ossification or deny that many of them became corrupt and outmoded by change. As the Dutch obstinately continued to argue, it was never safe to trust dynasticism with power. Yet there was nothing inherently unreasonable about the economic aspirations which underlay the mercantilist scheme of things, and though foreign observers (like Catherine the Great) thought the English system subordinated greatness too clearly to trade—the English, she said, were 'first and always traders'—the evidence suggests that the claims of economic and strategic policy, of private merchant and the interest of the state, were balanced with considerable success. The results have not always been palatable to critics of later ages, who, thinking themselves more virtuous or more intelligent, have examined and found wanting the motives, logic, morals, methods and behaviour of mercantilists. It is certainly true that mercantilist policy concealed private aims that were frequently sordid, greedy and brutal. At best its object was national gain, and the welfare of the national group was held to justify the ill-treatment of those outside the group. Its logic thus led to plunder, violence and war, overt or disguised as piracy and privateering. What observers of a later age have separated out as the 'economic' elements of thought and policy are not in fact intelligible except as an organic part of the whole process of 'state-making': mercantilism (Schmoller wrote) '. . . in its innermost kernel is nothing but state-making—not state-making in a narrow sense but state-making and national-economy-making at the same time'.[1] To judge mercantilist thought by the criteria of later economic logic is wholly to misconceive its character. The concept of a separate science of wealth had not yet emerged. The use of words like 'economic', 'economy', 'economist', in their present sense is no older than the nineteenth century. In the seventeenth century they were applied only to the art of private housekeeping from which their later scientific terminology was derived in much the same way that the concept of the trade balance was borrowed from the accounting practice of private business. Mercantilists had not attained to the apparent philosophic detachment of 'economics' in its later sense. Their ends were at once more immediate and larger than those of the 'economist'. They insisted on living in the real world and not in an imaginary one, on seeing economic institutions in the political setting with which they themselves were faced. And their first principle was to take account that the age was one of violence. The pursuit of economic ends without the backing of force was not possible. 'Profit and power', wrote Child,

---

[1] *Op. cit.*, p. 50.

'ought jointly to be considered'. Child was only one of many who preached the essentially dual nature of policy. This explains why so much of the literature of English mercantilism, with its emphasis on power, was the work of private merchants who understood that in the conditions in which they lived, their interests could be protected and furthered only with the help of the state. They had inherited from the medieval world the habit of corporate association for political, economic and social ends, and they continued it in the age of the great companies and the nation state. For them the state was but the largest of the corporate bodies designed, amongst other things, for their benefit. By taxation, tariffs, subsidies and the like it could influence relations with competitors. Its ambassadors could with gifts win the favour of the Grand Turk or the Czar and secure discrimination against rivals. Down to the time of Wedgwood it was expected that an ambassador's duties would include those of acting as commercial traveller for his nation's industries abroad. Above all, the warships of the state were there to protect the sea lanes of commerce and sometimes to destroy the seaborne trade of rival nations.

To Adam Smith the ideas behind the mercantile system were misguided, its ends partial and unjust, its administration corrupt and its very existence irrelevant if not positively mischievous. But the arguments of the *Wealth of Nations* were the product of logic working upon material drawn from the observation of three relatively mature mercantile economies: those of England, France and Holland. They did not have the same appeal to those who were still concerned with the earlier stages of the transition from agrarian to mercantile economy, to whom the invisible hand seemed to manifest itself all too infrequently. Adam Smith's injunctions against the attempt 'to make at home what it will cost more to make than to buy...' likewise seemed to have little relevance to those for whom the alternative of buying abroad meant an indefinite future as a primary producer: and they included not only the mercantilists of the Old World but of the New: as Alexander Hamilton's *Reports* showed. It is indeed arguable that to base policy on the assumption that costs of production were something fixed and calculable reflected an essentially static theory designed to petrify the *status quo* and discourage economic change. For all its failures and absurdities, there was a dynamic element in mercantilist thought. Faith in the potential ability to learn, develop and expand seemed to survive continual disappointment. The mercantilists may not have been intellectually impressive by the canons of a later time, but their vitality and confidence were enormous. Opinion does not frown as severely as it used to do on the kind of measures they took, and the latest historian to examine the Navigation Laws has concluded that if they are judged in relation to the end they were designed to accomplish the Laws were successful.[1] There will not be universal agreement that this analysis of individual pieces of legislation is practicable. The matter may be viewed, however, from a much wider angle. If the Europe of 1750 is compared with the Europe of 1600 in respect of population, resources, standards of living, national incomes, both gains and losses can be recorded. In Spain and Hungary, population had dwindled. War and its aftermath had created crises and depressions in the textile industries of western Europe and some of the policies adopted look more like restrictive than expansive measures. Yet in spite of local and temporary evidence of contraction there can be no doubt that the period was generally one of expansion. Population was increasing, not spectacularly, but steadily. The volume of overseas and especially colonial trade of e.g. France and Britain grew remarkably. Yet there is in this period no single phenomenon that can be produced to 'explain' the expansion, in the way historians have used the price revolution of the sixteenth century or the inventions of the Industrial Revolution to 'explain' economic growth in those periods. If anything, the 150 years that form the central, classic age of mercantilism were times of stable or falling prices and little spectacular invention intrudes itself upon the motions of industry and trade. These seem, in fact, to represent more a multiplication of the number of units of production and exchange in operation rather than any novel socio-economic system. The methods of production and exchange of goods underwent some change, but the increased volume was due more to the *spread* of existing methods from place to place than to radical innovation. Enterprise seems to take the form of imitation, modification, repetition throughout a geographical area, and of employing a range of commodities, both enlarged and varied by exploration. Behind all this was the organized pursuit of material gain and it would be rash to dismiss the thesis that it was this which makes intelligible the more rapid material progress of the West as compared with the apathy and stagnation of, say, Asia. Perhaps the most important thing about the mercantilists was that they believed that material change was possible and desirable and supported their belief with an unprecedented concentration of organized human energy.

[1] L. A. Harper, *The English Navigation Laws* (New York, 1939), 377. Mr Davis reaches similar conclusions in his *Rise of the English Shipping Industry* (1962).

# Bibliographies

## EDITORS' NOTE

In accordance with the established practice of the Cambridge series of histories, the bibliographies printed below are selective and incomplete. Their purpose is not to list all the publications bearing directly or indirectly on the subject, but to enable the readers to study some of the topics in greater detail. As a rule, books and articles superseded by later publications have not been included, and references to general treatises indirectly relevant to the subject-matter of individual chapters have been reduced to the minimum. As most of the chapters are not new pieces of research, but summaries and interpretations of knowledge already available in secondary literature, references to original sources have either been left out altogether or have been confined to the principal and most essential classes of evidence.

Within the limits set by these general principles, the individual contributors were given the freedom of composing and arranging bibliographies as they thought best. The 'layout' of the bibliographical lists, therefore, varies from chapter to chapter. The editors did not even find it desirable to insist on a uniform method of abbreviating the references to learned periodicals, since the same learned periodicals may be referred to more frequently in some bibliographies than in others. The authors were asked to make their own decisions about abbreviations, and to explain them, if necessary, in prefatory notes to their bibliographies. The prefatory notes will also explain the other special features of the separate lists of authorities.

# CHAPTER I

## *The Population of Europe from the Black Death to the Eve of the Vital Revolution*

### I. GENERAL

BERGUES, HÉLÈNE [et al.]. *La prévention des naissances dans la famille* (Institut Nationale d'Études Démographiques: Travaux et Documents, Cahier no. 35). Paris, 1960.

BOWEN, IAN. *Population*. London, 1954.

CARR-SAUNDERS, A. M. *The Population Problem: A Study in Human Evolution*. Oxford, 1922.

—— *World Population: Past Growth and Present Trends*. New York, 1936.

COLNAT, ALBERT. *Les épidémies et l'histoire*. Paris, 1937.

DASZYNSKA, ZOFIA. 'Stoff und Methode der historischen Bevölkerungsstatistik.' *Jahrbücher für Nationalökonomie und Statistik*, LXVI, 1896.

DIEPGEN, PAUL. *Geschichte der Medizin*, I–III. Berlin, 1949–55.

DREW, JOHN. *Man, Microbe and Malady*. Harmondsworth, 1950.

DRIGALSKI, WILHELM. *Männer gegen Mikroben: Pest, Cholera, Malaria und ihre Verwandten in Geschichte und Leben*. Berlin, 1951.

DYMOND, J. R. 'Fluctuations in Animal Populations.' *Transactions of the Royal Society of Canada*, XLI, sec. V, 1947.

ELTON, CHARLES. *Voles, Mice and Lemmings*. Oxford, 1942. Part I: *Voles and Mouse Plagues*.

GONNARD, RENÉ. *Histoire des doctrines de la population*. Paris, 1923.

GREENWOOD, MAJOR. *Epidemics and Crowd Diseases. An Introduction to the Study of Epidemiology*. London, 1935.

GYÖRY, TIBERIUS VON. *Morbus hungaricus*. Jena, 1901.

HAESER, HEINRICH. *Lehrbuch der Geschichte der Medizin und der epidemischen Krankheiten*. Vol. III: *Geschichte der epidemischen Krankheiten* (3rd ed.). Jena, 1882.

HENRIPIN, JACQUES. *La population canadienne au début du XVIIIe siècle* (Institut National d'Études Démographiques: Travaux et Documents, Cahier no. 22). Paris, 1954.

HIMES, NORMAN E. *Medical History of Contraception*. Baltimore, 1936.

HIRSCH, AUGUST. *Handbook of Geographical and Historical Pathology*. 3 vols. (Transl. by Charles Creighton.) London, 1883, 1885, 1886.

HIRST, L. FABIAN. *The Conquest of Plague: A Study of the Evolution of Epidemiology*. Oxford, 1953.

KEYSER, ERICH. 'Neue deutsche Forschungen über die Geschichte der Pest.' *Vierteljahrschrift für Sozial- und Wirtschaftsgeschichte*, XLIV, 1957.

KING, LESTER S. *The Medical World of the Eighteenth Century*. Chicago, 1958.

LANDRY, ADOLPHE. *Traité de démographie* (2nd ed.). Paris, 1949.

LORIMER, FRANK [et al.]. *Culture and Human Fertility*. Unesco, 1954.

MACKENROTH, GERHARD. *Bevölkerungslehre*. Berlin, Göttingen, Heidelberg, 1953.

MALTHUS, THOMAS ROBERT. *An Essay on the Principle of Population*. 1st ed., 1798 (reprinted by the Royal Economic Society, London, 1926). 7th ed., 1872 (reprinted in Everyman's Library, London, 1933).

MOMBERT, PAUL. *Bevölkerungslehre*. (Grundrisse zum Studium der Nationalökonomie, XV). Jena, 1929.

PEARL, RAYMOND. *The Natural History of Population*. Oxford, 1939.

PEIGNOT, GABRIEL. *Essai chronologique sur les hivers les plus rigoureux, depuis 396 ans avant Jésus-Christ jusqu'en 1820 inclusivement*. Dijon, 1821.

PENTLAND, H. C. 'Feudal Europe an Economy of Labour Scarcity.' *Culture* (Quebec), XXI, 1960.

PRINZING, FRIEDRICH. *Epidemics Resulting from Wars*. Oxford, 1916.

REINHARD, MARCEL R. *Histoire de la population mondiale de 1700 à 1948*. Paris, no date (1949).

RIQUET, R. P. 'Christianisme et population.' *Population*, IV, 1949.

RUSSELL, JOSIAH COX. 'Demographic Pattern in History.' *Population Studies*, I, 1948.
SAUVY, ALFRED. 'On the Relations between Domination and the Numbers of Men.' *Diogenes: An International Review of Philosophy and Humanistic Studies*, no. 3, 1953.
—— *Richesse et Population*. Paris, 1943.
—— *Théorie générale de la population*. I, *Économie et population*. Paris, 1952.
SHORT, THOMAS. *A Comparative History of the Increase and Decrease of Mankind in England and Several Countries Abroad*. London, 1767.
STERN, BERNHARD JOSEPH. *Society and Medical Progress*. Princeton, 1941.
STICKER, GEORG. *Abhandlungen aus der Seuchengeschichte und Seuchenlehre*. Vol. I/1: *Die Geschichte der Pest*. Giessen, 1908.
THOMPSON, WARREN S. *Population Problems* (4th ed.). New York, Toronto, London, 1953.
UNITED NATIONS, Department of Social Affairs, Population Division. *The Determinants and Consequences of Population Trends* (Population Studies, No. 17). New York, 1953.
WALFORD, CORNELIUS. *The Famines of the World: Past and Present*. London, 1879.
WESTERGAARD, HARALD L. *Die Lehre von der Mortalität und Morbilität* (2nd ed.). Jena, 1901.
WINSLOW, CHARLES-EDWARD AMORY. *The Conquest of Epidemic Disease: A Chapter in the History of Ideas*. Princeton, 1943.
ZINSSER, HANS. *Rats, Lice and History*. New York, 1935.

## II. EUROPE

ABEL, WILHELM. *Agrarkrisen und Agrarkonjunktur in Mitteleuropa vom 13. bis zum 19. Jahrhundert*. Berlin, 1935.
—— 'Wachstumschwankungen mitteleuropäischer Völker seit dem Mittelalter.' *Jahrbücher für Nationalökonomie und Statistik*, CXLII, 1935.
—— *Die Wüstungen des ausgehenden Mittelalters* (2nd ed.). Stuttgart, 1955.
—— 'Wüstungen und Preisfall im spätmittelalterlichen Europa.' *Jahrbücher für National-ökonomie und Statistik*, CLXV, 1953.
ARIÈS, PHILIPPE. 'Attitudes devant la vie et devant la mort du XVIIe au XIXe siècle'. *Population*, IV, 1949.
—— *See also* VENARD, ANDRÉ.
BAEHREL, RENÉ. 'La mortalité sous l'Ancien Régime.' *Annales: Économies, Sociétés, Civilisations*, XII, 1957.
BELOCH, KARL JULIUS. 'Antike und moderne Grosstädte.' *Zeitschrift für Socialwissenschaft*, I, 1898.
—— 'Die Bevölkerung Europas im Mittelalter.' *Zeitschrift für Socialwissenschaft*, III, 1900.
—— 'Die Bevölkerung Europas zur Zeit der Renaissance.' *Zeitschrift für Socialwissenschaft*, III, 1900.
—— 'Die Entwicklung der Grosstädte in Europa.' *Huitième Congrès International d'Hygiène et de Démographie, Budapest, 1.–9. Sept., 1894. Comptes-Rendues et Mémoires* (ed. Sigismond de Gerlóczy), VII, Budapest, 1896.
BEVERIDGE, SIR WILLIAM H. 'Weather and Harvest Cycles.' *Economic Journal*, XXXI, 1921.
BRAUDEL, FERNAND. *La Méditerranée et le Monde méditerranéen à l'époque de Philippe II*. Paris, 1949.
BRITTON, C. E. *A Meteorological Chronology to A.D. 1450* (Geophysical Memoirs No. 70). London, 1937.
CARPENTIER, ÉLISABETH. 'La peste noire: Famines et épidémies au XIVe siècle.' *Annales: Économies, Sociétés, Civilisations*, XVII, 1962.
CIPOLLA, CARLO, DHONDT, JEAN, POSTAN, M. M., and WOLFF, PHILIPPE. 'Rapport Collectif.' *IXe Congrès international des sciences historiques. Paris, 28 août–3 septembre 1950*. Rapports I, Paris, 1950.
COULTON, GEORGE GORDON. *The Black Death*. London, 1929.
CURSCHMANN, FRITZ. *Hungersnöte im Mittelalter*. Leipzig, 1900.
DHONDT, JEAN. *See* CIPOLLA, CARLO.
DIETERICI, K. F. W. 'Über die Vermehrung der Bevölkerung in Europa seit dem Ende oder der Mitte des siebenzehnten Jahrhunderts.' *Philologische und historische Abhand-lungen der Königlichen Akademie der Wissenschaften zu Berlin aus dem Jahr 1850*. Berlin, 1852.

FOURASTIÉ, JEAN. 'De la vie traditionelle à la vie "tertiaire".' *Population*, XIV, 1959.

GANSHOF, F.-L. *Étude sur le développement des villes entre Loire et Rhin au Moyen Age.* Paris and Brussels, 1943.

GRAUS, FRANTIŠEK. 'Autour de la peste au XIVe siècle.' *Annales: Économics, Sociétés, Civilisations*, XVIII, 1963.

HÄPKE, RUDOLF. *See* INAMA-STERNEGG, KARL THEODOR VON.

HAZNAL, Z. 'European Marriage Patterns in Perspective.' *Population in History*. Ed. D. V. Glass and D. E. C. Eversley. London, 1965.

HECKER, J. F. C. *The Epidemics of the Middle Ages*. Transl. by B. G. Babington. London, 1844.

HELLEINER, KARL F. 'Europas Bevölkerung und Wirtschaft im späteren Mittelalter.' *Mitteilungen des Instituts für österreichische Geschichtsforschung*, LXII, 1954.

—— 'New Light on the History of Urban Populations.' *Journal of Economic History*, XVIII, 1958.

—— 'Population Movement and Agrarian Depression in the Later Middle Ages.' *Canadian Journal of Economics and Political Science*, XV, 1949.

—— 'The Vital Revolution Reconsidered.' *Canadian Journal of Economics and Political Science*, XXIII, 1957.

HOBSBAWM, E. J. 'The General Crisis of the European Economy in the 17th Century.' *Past and Present*, nos. 5 and 6, 1954.

HOPKINS, SHEILA V. *See* PHELPS BROWN, E. H.

INAMA-STERNEGG, KARL THEODOR VON, and HÄPKE, RUDOLF. 'Die Bevölkerung des Mittelalters und der neueren Zeit bis Ende des 18. Jahrhunderts in Europa': Article 'Bevölkerungswesen'. *Handwörterbuch der Staatswissenschaften* (4th ed.). II. Jena, 1924.

KAWAN, LEONE. *Gli esodi e le carestie in Europa attraverso il tempo* (R. Accademia Nazionale dei Lincei, Pubblicazioni della Commissione Italiana per lo Studio delle grandi Calamità, III). Rome, 1932.

KRAUSE, JOHN T. 'Some Implications of Recent Work in Historical Demography.' *Comparative Studies in Society and History*, I, 1959.

LADURIE, EMMANUEL LE ROY. 'Histoire et climat.' *Annales: Économies, Sociétés, Civilisations*, XIV, 1959.

LANGER, WILLIAM L. 'Europe's Initial Population Explosion.' *The American Historical Review*, LXIX, 1963.

LEVY, CLAUDE. 'Quelques exemples de "birth control" aux XVIe, XVIIe et XVIIIe siècles.' *Le Concours Medical*, LXXIX, 1957.

LOPEZ, R. S. and MISKIMIN, H. A. 'The Economic Depression of the Renaissance.' *The Economic History Review*, 2nd ser., XIV, 1962.

LUCAS, HENRY S. 'The Great European Famine of 1315, 1316, and 1317.' *Speculum*, V, 1930.

LÜTGE, FRIEDRICH. 'Das 14./15. Jahrhundert in der Sozial- und Wirtschaftsgeschichte.' *Jahrbücher für Nationalökonomie und Statistik*, CLXII, 1950.

MISKIMIN, H. A. *See* LOPEZ, R. S.

MOLS, ROGER. *Introduction à la démographie historique des villes d'Europe du XIVe au XVIIIe siècle* (Université de Louvain: Recueil de Travaux d'Histoire et de Philologie, 4th ser., fasc. 1–3). Vols. I–III, Louvain, 1954–6.

MOMBERT, PAUL. 'Die Anschauungen des 17. und 18. Jahrhunderts über die Abnahme der Bevölkerung.' *Jahrbücher für Nationalökonomie und Statistik*, CXXXV, 1931.

MOUSNIER, ROLAND. 'La démographie européene aux XVIIe et XVIIIe siècles.' *Problèmes de Population: Conférences de la Quinzaine Universitaire Européenne, 7–19 mai 1951*. Strasbourg, 1951.

OLBRICHT, KONRAD. 'Die Vergrosstädterung des Abendlandes zu Beginn des Dreissigjährigen Krieges.' *Petermanns Geographische Mitteilungen*, LXXXV, 1939.

PELLER, SIGISMUND. 'Mortality, Past and Future.' *Population Studies*, I, 1948.

—— 'Studies on Mortality since the Renaissance.' *Bulletin of the History of Medicine*, XIII, 1943; XVI, 1944; XXI, 1947.

PERROY, ÉDOUARD. 'À l'origine d'une économie contractée: Les crises du XIVe siècle.' *Annales: Économies, Sociétés, Civilisations*, IV, 1949.

PHELPS BROWN, E. H. and HOPKINS, SHEILA V. 'Builders' Wage-rates, Prices and Population: Some Further Evidence.' *Economica*, new series, XXVI, 1959.

—— —— 'Wage-rates and Prices: Evidence for Population Pressure in the Sixteenth Century.' *Economica*, new ser., XXIV, 1957.

POSTAN, M. M. 'Revisions in Economic History: The Fifteenth Century.' *Economic History Review*, IX, 1939.

—— 'Note.' *Economic History Review*, 2nd ser., XII, 1959.

—— 'Some Economic Evidence of Declining Population in the Later Middle Ages.' *Economic History Review*, 2nd ser., II, 1950.

—— 'Die wirtschaftlichen Grundlagen der mittelalterlichen Gesellschaft.' *Jahrbücher für Nationalökonomie und Statistik*, CLXVI, 1954.

—— See also CIPOLLA, CARLO.

RENOUARD, YVES. 'Conséquences et intérêt démographiques de la Peste noire de 1348.' *Population*, III, 1948.

ROBINSON, W. C. 'Money, Population and Economic Change in Late Medieval Europe.' *Economic History Review*, 2nd ser., XII, 1959.

RÖRIG, FRITZ. 'Die europäische Stadt.' *Propyläen-Weltgeschichte*, IV, 1932.

RUSSELL, JOSIAH COX. *Late Ancient and Medieval Population* (Transactions of the American Philosophical Society, new ser., XLVIII, part 3). Philadelphia, 1958.

—— 'Late Mediaeval Population Patterns.' *Speculum*, XX, 1945.

SALAMAN, R. N. *History and Social Influence of the Potato*. Cambridge, 1949.

STANGELAND, CHARLES EMIL. *Pre-Malthusian Doctrines of Population: A Study in the History of Economic Theory* (Columbia University Studies in History, Political Science and Public Law, XXI, part 3). New York, 1904.

UTTERSTRÖM, GUSTAF. 'Climatic Fluctuations and Population Problems in Early Modern History.' *Scandinavian Economic History Review*, III, 1955.

VENARD, ANDRÉ and ARIÈS, PHILIPPE. 'Deux contributions à l'histoire des pratiques contraceptives.' *Population*, IX, 1954.

WEBER, WILHELM and MAYER-MALY, THEO. 'Studie zur spätmittelalterlichen Arbeitsmarkt- und Wirtschaftsordnung.' *Jahrbücher für Nationalökonomie und Statistik*, CLXVI, 1954.

WEIKINN, CURT. *Quellentexte zur Witterungsgeschichte Europas von der Zeitwende bis zum Jahre 1850* (Quellensammlung zur Hydrographie und Meteorologie, I). Vols. I₁–I₄. Berlin, 1958–63.

WOLFF, PHILIPPE. See CIPOLLA, CARLO.

## III. THE BRITISH ISLES

ATSATT, MARJORY. *Population Estimates for England and Wales from the Eleventh to the Nineteenth Centuries*. Mimeogr. American Documentation Institute, Washington, D.C., No. 1459 [1940].

AYDELOTTE, FRANK. *Elizabethan Rogues and Vagabonds* (Oxford Historical and Literary Studies, I). Oxford, 1913.

BEAN, J. M. W. 'Plague, Population and Economic Decline in England in the Later Middle Ages.' *Economic History Review*, 2nd ser., XV, 1963.

BELL, WALTER GEORGE. *The Great Plague in London in 1665*. London, 1924.

BERESFORD, MAURICE. *The Lost Villages of England*. London, 1954.

BEVERIDGE, SIR WILLIAM H. *Prices and Wages in England from the Twelfth to the Nineteenth Century*. Vol. I. London, 1939.

BRETT-JAMES, NORMAN G. *The Growth of Stuart London*. London, 1935.

BROWN, R. G. See McKEOWN, THOMAS.

BROWNLEE, JOHN. 'The Health of London in the Eighteenth Century.' *Proceedings of the Royal Society of Medicine*, XVIII (Epidemiology), 1925.

—— 'The History of the Birth and Death Rates in England and Wales Taken as a Whole, from 1570 to the Present Time.' *Public Health*, XXIX, 1916.

BUCKATZSCH, E. J. 'The Constancy of Local Populations and Migration in England before 1800.' *Population Studies*, V, 1951.

BUER, MABEL C. *Health, Wealth, and Population in the Early Days of the Industrial Revolution*. London, 1926.

—— 'The Historical Setting of the Malthusian Controversy.' *London Essays in Economics: In Honour of Edwin Cannan*. London, 1927.

CHAMBERS, J. D. *The Vale of Trent 1670–1800*. (Economic History Review Supplements, III.) London, New York [1957].

COLEMAN, D. C. 'Labour in the English Economy of the Seventeenth Century.' *Economic History Review*, 2nd ser., VIII, 1956.

*A Collection of the Yearly Bills of Mortality from 1657 to 1758 Inclusive*. London, 1759.

CONNELL, K. H. 'Land and Population in Ireland.' *Economic History Review*, 2nd ser., II, 1950.

—— *The Population of Ireland, 1750–1845*. Oxford, 1950.

CREIGHTON, CHARLES. *A History of Epidemics in Britain*. 2 vols. Cambridge, 1891, 1894.

DARIVAS, BASIL. 'Étude sur la crise économique de 1593–1597 en Angleterre et la Loi des Pauvres.' *Revue d'histoire économique et sociale*, XXX, 1952.

DRAKE, MICHAEL. 'An Elementary Exercise in Parish Register Demography.' *Economic History Review*, 2nd ser., XIV, 1962.

—— 'Marriage and Population Growth in Ireland, 1750–1845.' *Economic History Review*, 2nd ser., XVI, 1963.

DRUMMOND, J. C. and WILBRAHAM, ANNE. *The Englishman's Food: A History of Five Centuries of English Diet*. London, 1939.

EVERSLEY, D. E. C. 'A Survey of Population in an Area of Worcestershire from 1660–1850 on the Basis of Parish Records.' *Population Studies*, X, 1956–7.

—— 'Population and Economic Growth in England before the "Take-off".' *First International Conference of Economic History, Stockholm, 1960: Contributions [and] Communications*. Paris, 1960.

GEORGE, M. DOROTHY. *London Life in the XVIIIth Century*. London, 1930.

GLASS, DAVID V. 'Gregory King's Estimate of the Population of England and Wales, 1695.' *Population Studies*, III, 1949–50.

—— 'The Population Controversy in Eighteenth-Century England. Part I: The Background.' *Population Studies*, VI, 1952.

GONNER, E. C. K. 'The Population of England in the Eighteenth Century.' *Journal of the Royal Statistical Society*, LXXVI, 1913.

GRAS, N. S. B. *The Evolution of the English Corn Market* (Harvard Economic Studies, XIII), Cambridge, Mass., 1915.

GRAUNT, JOHN. *Natural and Political Observations made upon the Bills of Mortality*. Ed. Walter F. Wilcox, Baltimore, 1939.

GREENWOOD, MAJOR. *Medical Statistics from Graunt to Farr*. Cambridge, 1948.

GRIFFITH, G. TALBOT. *Population Problems of the Age of Malthus*. Cambridge, 1926.

—— 'Rickman's Second Series of Eighteenth-Century Population Figures.' *Journal of the Royal Statistical Society*, XCII, 1929.

HABAKKUK, H. J. 'English Population in the Eighteenth Century.' *Economic History Review*, 2nd ser., VI, 1953.

HOLLINGSWORTH, T. H. 'A Demographic Study of the British Ducal Families.' *Population Studies*, XI, 1957.

—— *The Demography of the English Peerage* (Supplement to *Population Studies*, XVIII 2). London, 1964.

JONES, P. E. and JUDGES, A. V. 'London Population in the Late Seventeenth Century.' *Economic History Review*, VI, 1935.

JUDGES, A. V. *See* JONES, P. E.

KNORR, KLAUS E. *British Colonial Theories*. Toronto, 1944.

KRAUSE, J. T. 'Changes in English Fertility and Mortality, 1781–1850.' *Economic History Review*, 2nd ser., XI, 1958.

—— 'The Medieval Household: Large or Small?' *Economic History Review*, 2nd ser., IX, 1957.

—— 'Some Neglected Factors in the English Industrial Revolution.' *Journal of Economic History*, XIX, 1959.

KUCZYNSKI, R. R. 'British Demographers' Opinions on Fertility, 1660 to 1760.' *Political Arithmetic: A Symposium on Population Studies*. Ed. Lancelot Hogben. London, 1938.

LEVETT, A. ELIZABETH. *The Black Death on the Estates of the See of Winchester* (Oxford Studies in Social and Legal History, V), Oxford, 1916.

LONGDON, J. 'Statistical Notes on Winchester Heriots.' *Economic History Review*, 2nd ser., XI, 1959.

MCKEOWN, THOMAS and BROWN, R. G. 'Medical Evidence Related to English Population Changes in the Eighteenth Century.' *Population Studies*, IX, 1955.

MARSHALL, T. H. 'The Population Problem during the Industrial Revolution.' *Economic History: A Supplement of the Economic Journal* I/4, 1929.

MORRELL, C. CONYERS. 'Tudor Marriages and Infantile Mortality.' *Journal of State Medicine*, XLIII, 1935.

MULLETT, Charles F. *The Bubonic Plague and England*. Lexington, 1956.

OGLE, WILLIAM. 'An Inquiry into the Trustworthiness of the Old Bills of Mortality.' *Journal of the Royal Statistical Society*, LV, 1892.

PICKARD, RANSOM. *The Population and Epidemics of Exeter in pre-Census Times*. Exeter, 1947.

POSTAN, M. M. and TITOW, J. 'Heriots and Prices on Winchester Manors.' *Economic History Review*, 2nd ser., XI, 1959.

RICH, E. E. 'The Population of Elizabethan England.' *Economic History Review*, 2nd ser., II, 1950.

RICKMAN, J. 'Estimated Population of England and Wales.' *Great Britain: Population Enumeration Abstract*, XXII, 1843.

ROGERS, JAMES E. THOROLD. *A History of Agriculture and Prices in England*. Vols. I–VII, Oxford, 1866–1902.

—— *Six Centuries of Work and Wages*, 10th ed. London, 1909.

*Royal Commission on Population. Report Presented to Parliament . . . June 1949*. Cmd. 7695. London, 1949.

RUSSELL, JOSIAH COX. *British Medieval Population*. Albuquerque, 1948.

SALTMARSH, JOHN. 'Plague and Economic Decline in England in the Later Middle Ages.' *Cambridge Historical Journal*, VII, 1941.

SCHREINER, JOHAN. 'Wages and Prices in England in the Later Middle Ages.' *Scandinavian Economic History Review*, II/2, 1954.

SHORT, THOMAS. *New Observations, Natural, Moral, Civil, Political, and Medical, on City, Town, and Country Bills of Mortality*. London, 1750.

TITOW, J. *See* POSTAN, M. M.

TUCKER, G. S. L. 'English Pre-Industrial Population Trends.' *Economic History Review*, 2nd ser., XVI, 1963.

USHER, ABBOTT PAYSON. 'Prices of Wheat and Commodity Price Indexes for England, 1259–1930.' *Review of Economic Statistics*, XIII, 1931.

WILBRAHAM, ANNE. *See* DRUMMOND, J. C.

WILLIAMS, DAVID. 'A Note on the Population of Wales.' *Bulletin of the Board of Celtic Studies*, VIII/4, 1937.

WILSON, FRANK PERCY. *The Plague in Shakespeare's London*. Oxford, 1927.

## IV. FRANCE

ARIÈS, PHILIPPE. *Histoire des populations françaises et de leurs attitudes devant la vie depuis le XVIIIe siècle*. Paris, 1948.

—— 'Sur les origines de la contraception en France.' *Population*, VIII, 1953.

BAULANT, MICHELINE and MEUVRET, JEAN. *Prix des céréales extraits de la mercuriale de Paris (1520–1698)*. 2 vols. Paris, 1960, 1962.

BLACKER, J. G. C. 'Social Ambitions of the Bourgeoisie in 18th Century France, and their Relation to Family Limitation.' *Population Studies*, XI, 1957.

BLOCH, MARC. *Les caractères originaux de l'histoire rurale française*. Oslo, 1931.

BOISLISLE, ARTHUR M. DE. *Le Grand Hiver et la disette de 1709*. Paris, 1903.

BON, HENRI. *Essai historique sur les épidémies en Bourgogne*. Dijon, no date.

BONDOIS, PAUL-M. 'La misère sous Louis XIV. La disette de 1662.' *Revue d'histoire économique et sociale*, XII, 1924.

BOUCHARD, GEORGES. 'Dijon au XVIIIe siècle: Les dénombrements d'habitants.' *Annales de Bourgogne*, XXV, 1953.

BOUDET, MARCELLIN and GRAND, ROGER. *Étude historique sur les épidémies de peste en Haute-Auvergne*. Paris, 1902.

BOURGEOIS-PICHAT, JEAN. 'Évolution générale de la population française depuis le XVIIIe siècle.' *Population*, VI, 1951.

BOUTRUCHE, R. *La crise d'une société. Seigneurs et paysans du Bordelais pendant la Guerre de Cent Ans* (Publications de la Faculté des Lettres de l'Université de Strasbourg, fasc. 110). Paris, 1947.

BRIDGE, JOHN S. C. *A History of France from the Death of Louis XI. IV: France in 1515*. Oxford, 1936.

CANARD, J. 'Les mouvements de population à Saint-Romains d'Urfé de 1612 à 1946.' *Bulletin de la Diana*, XXIX/4, 1945.

CHATELAIN, ABEL. 'Notes sur la population d'un village bugiste, Belmont, XVIIe–XIXe siècles.' *Revue de Géographie de Lyon*, XXVIII, 1953.

CLÉMENT, L. *Essai d'histoire locale: Routot des origines à la Révolution*. Fécamp, 1950.

DAINVILLE, FRANÇOIS DE. 'Un dénombrement inédit au XVIIIe siècle: L'enquête du Contrôleur générale Orry—1745.' *Population*, VII, 1952.

DELATOUCHE, R. 'Agriculture médiévale et population.' *Les Études Sociales*, II, 1955.

DES CILLEULS, ALFRED. *La population de la France avant 1789*. Paris, 1885.

DOLLINGER, PH. 'Le chiffre de population de Paris au XIVe siècle.' *Revue historique*, CCXVI, 1956.

DUBLED, HENRI. 'Conséquences économiques et sociales des "mortalités" du XIVe siècle, essentiellement en Alsace.' *Revue d'histoire économique et sociale*, XXXVII, 1959.

DURANTY, MARQUIS DE. *See* GAFFAREL, PAUL.

FAGE, ANITA. 'Les doctrines de population des Encyclopédistes.' *Population*, VI, 1951.

—— 'Économie et population: les doctrines françaises avant 1800.' *Population*, IX, 1954.

FEILLET, ALPHONSE. *La misère au temps de la Fronde et Saint Vincent de Paul*. 5th ed. Paris, 1886.

FOURQUIN, GUY. 'La population de la région parisienne aux environs de 1329.' *Le Moyen Age*, LXII, 1956.

GAFFAREL, PAUL and DURANTY, MARQUIS DE. *La peste de 1720 à Marseille et en France*. Paris, 1911.

GAUTIER, ÉTIENNE and HENRY, LOUIS. *La population de Crulai, paroisse normande*. Paris, 1958.

GOUBERT, PIERRE. *Beauvais et le Bauvaisis de 1600 à 1730*. 2 vols. Paris, 1960.

—— 'En Beauvaisis. Problèmes démographiques de XVIIe siècle.' *Annales: Économies, Sociétés, Civilisations*, VII, 1952.

—— 'Une richesse historique en cours d'exploitation: Les registres paroissiaux.' *Annales: Économies Sociétés, Civilisations*, IX, 1954.

GRAND, ROGER. *See* BOUDET, MARCELLIN.

GRAS, P. 'Le registre paroissial de Givry (1334–57) et la Peste noire en Bourgogne.' *Bibliothèque de l'École des Chartes*, C, 1939.

GREER, DONALD. *The Incidence of the Emigration during the French Revolution* (Harvard Historical Monographs, XXIV). Cambridge, Mass., 1951.

HADSEL, L. 'Huguenot Immigration to England after the Revocation of the Edict of Nantes.' *Transactions of the Huguenot Society of South Carolina*, XLVI, No. 46, 1941.

HAUSER, HENRI. *Recherches et Documents sur l'Histoire des Prix en France de 1500 à 1800*. Paris, 1936.

HENRY, LOUIS. 'Une richesse démographique en friche: Les registres paroissiaux.' *Population*, VII, 1953.

—— *See also* GAUTIER, ÉTIENNE.

HIGOUNET, CHARLES. 'Mouvements de population dans le midi de la France du XIe au XVe siècle.' *Annales: Économies, Sociétés, Civilisations*, VIII, 1953.

LABROUSSE, H. 'Le prix du blé en France au XVIIIe siècle.' *Revue d'histoire économique et sociale*, XIX, 1931.

LARENAUDIE, MARIE-JOSÈPHE. 'Les famines en Languedoc aux XIVe et XVe siècles.' *Annales du Midi*, LXIV, 1952.

LATOUCHE, R. 'Le prix du blé à Grenoble du XVe au XVIIIe siècle.' *Revue d'histoire économique et sociale*, XX, 1932.

LEVASSEUR, E. *La population française.* 3 vols. Paris, 1889, 1891, 1892.

LOT, FERDINAND. 'L'état des paroisses et des feux de 1328.' *Bibliothèque de l'École des Chartes*, XC, 1929.

—— 'Recherches sur la population et la superficie des cités remontant à la période gallo-romaine.' *Bibliothèque de l'École des Hautes Études. Sciences historiques et philologiques*, fasc. 287, 296, 301. Paris, 1945, 1950, 1953.

MARION, MARCEL. 'Une famine en Guyenne, 1747–48.' *Revue historique*, XLVI, 1891.

McCLOY, SHELBY T. *Government Assistance in Eighteenth-Century France.* Durham, N.C., 1946.

MEUVRET, JEAN. 'Les crises de subsistances et la démographie de la France d'Ancien Régime.' *Population*, I, 1946.

—— *See also* BAULANT, MICHELINE.

MOHEAU (pseud. for Baron de Montyon). *Recherches et considérations sur la population de la France 1778.* Ed. René Gonnard. Paris, 1912.

MOURS, S. 'Essai d'évaluation de la population protestante française aux XVIIe et XVIIIe siècles.' *Bulletin protestant français*, CIV, 1958.

MOUSNIER, ROLAND. 'Études sur la population de la France au XVIIe siècle.' *XVIIe Siècle: Bulletin de la Société d'Étude du XVIIe Siècle*, II/16, 1952.

PERROY, EDOUARD. 'La crise économique de XIVe siècle d'après les terriers Foréziens.' *Bulletin de la Diana*, XXIX, 1945.

PRAT, GENEVIÈVE. 'Albi et la Peste noire.' *Annales du Midi*, LXIV, 1952.

REINHARD, MARCEL. 'La population française au XVIIe siècle.' *Population*, XIII, 1958.

—— 'La Révolution française et le problème de la population.' *Population*, I, 1946.

RIGAULT, JEAN. 'La population de Metz au XVIIe siècle: Quelques problèmes de démo-graphie.' *Annales de l'Est*, 5th ser., 2nd year, 1951.

ROUPNEL, GASTON. *La ville et la campagne au XVIIe siècle: Étude sur les populations du Pays dijonnais.* Paris, 1955.

SAMSON, RENÉ. *Un village de l'Oise au XVIIe siècle* (Bibliothèque de Travail, no. 187–188). Cannes, 1952.

SAUVY, ALFRED. 'Some Lesser Known French Demographers of the Eighteenth Century.' *Population Studies*, V, 1951.

SCHÖNE, LUCIEN. *Histoire de la population française.* Paris, 1893.

SCOVILLE, WARREN C. 'The Huguenots and the Diffusion of Technology.' *Journal of Political Economy*, LX, 1952.

SÉE, HENRI. 'The Intendants' *Mémoires* of 1698 and their Value for Economic History.' *Economic History Review*, I, 1928.

—— 'Peut-on évaluer la population de l'ancienne France?' *Revue d'Économie Politique*, XXXVIII, 1924.

SPENGLER, JOSEPH J. *Économie et population. Les doctrines françaises avant 1800.* Paris, 1954.

—— *France Faces Depopulation.* Durham, N.C., 1938.

—— *French Predecessors of Malthus: a Study in Eighteenth-Century Wage and Population Theory.* Durham, N.C., 1942.

USHER, ABBOTT PAYSON. 'The General Course of Wheat Prices in France, 1350–1788.' *Review of Economic Statistics*, XII, 1930.

—— *The History of the Grain Trade in France, 1400–1710* (Harvard Economic Studies, IX). Cambridge, Mass., 1913.

VINCENT, FRANÇOIS. *Histoire des famines à Paris.* Paris, 1946.

VICENT, PAUL E. 'French Demography in the Eighteenth Century.' *Population Studies*, I, 1947.

WOLFF, PHILIPPE. *Commerces et marchands de Toulouse (vers 1350–vers 1450).* Paris, 1954.

## V. THE LOW COUNTRIES

ARNOULD, MAURICE-A. 'Ath et Avesnes en 1594. État démographique de deux villes hennuyères à la fin du XVIe siècle.' *Annales du Cercle Royal Archéologique d'Ath*, XXVII, 1941.

—— 'Aux sources de notre démographie historique: Les registres paroissiaux en Belgique.' *Bulletin de Statistique*, XXXIV, 1948.

—— *Les dénombrements de foyers dans le comté de Hainaut (XIVe–XVIe siècle)*. Brussels, 1956.

BLOCKMANS, FRANS. 'De bevolkingscijfers te Antwerpen in de XVIIIde eeuw.' *Antwerpen in de XVIIIde Eeuw*. Antwerp, 1952.

BONENFANT, PAUL. *Le problème du paupérisme en Belgique à la fin de l'ancien régime*. (Académie royale de Belgique, Classe des lettres et sciences morales et politiques. Mémoirs, 2nd ser., XXXV, 1934.)

BOUMANS, R. 'De demografische evolutie van Antwerpen (XVe–XVIIIe eeuw).' *Statistisch Bulletin*, XXXIV, 1948.

—— 'Le dépeuplement d'Anvers dans le dernier quart du XVIe siècle.' *Revue du Nord*, XXI, 1947.

COSEMANS, ALEXANDER. *De bevolking van Brabant in de XVIIe en XVIIIe eeuw*. Brussels, 1939.

CUVELIER, JOSEPH. *Les Dénombrements de Foyers en Brabant (XIVe–XVIe siècle)*. Brussels, 1912.

—— 'Les fouages dans le Quartier de Bois-le-Duc au XVe siècle.' *Bulletin de la Commission Royale d'Histoire*, LXXXII, 1913.

—— 'La population de Louvain aux XVIe et XVIIe siècles.' *Annales de la Société d'Archéologie de Bruxelles*, XXII, 1908.

DALLE, D. 'De Volkstellingen te Veurne en in Veurne-Ambacht op het einde van de zeventiende eeuw.' *Bulletin de la Commission Royale d'Histoire*, CXX, 1955.

DE BROUWERE, J. 'Les dénombrements de la Châtellenie d'Audenarde (1469–1801).' *Bulletin de la Commission Royale d'Histoire*, CIII, 1938.

DEMEY, J. 'Proeve tot raming van de bevolking en de weefgetouwen to Ieper van de XIIIe tot de XVIIe eeuw.' *Revue Belge de Philologie et d'Histoire*, XXVIII, 1950.

*Les Dénombrements de Foyers en Brabant. See* CUVELIER, J.

*Dénombrements des Feux des Duché de Luxembourg et Comté de Chiny*, ed. Jacques Grob. Vol. I, Brussels, 1921.

DE SMET, JOSEPH. 'Le dénombrement des foyers en Flandre en 1469.' *Bulletin de la Commission Royale d'Histoire* XCIX, 1935.

—— 'Les dénombrements de la population dans la Châtellenie d'Ypres (1610 et 1615 à 1620).' *Bulletin de la Commission Royale d'Histoire*, XCVI, 1932.

DE VOOYS, A. C. 'De Bevolkingsspreiding op het Hollandse Platteland in 1622 en 1795.' *Tijdschrift van het Koninklijk Nederlandsch Aardrijkskundig Genootschap*, LXX, 1953.

*Documents pour Servir à l'Étude des Maladies Pestilentielles dans le Marquisat d'Anvers Jusqu' à la Chute de l'Ancien Régime*. Ed. A.-F.-C. Van Schevensteen. 2 vols. Brussels, 1931–2.

DONY, ÉMILE. 'Le dénombrement des habitants de la Principauté de Chimay en 1616.' *Bulletin de la Commission Royale d'Histoire*. LXXVI 1907.

*Enqueste ende Informatie upt stuck van der Reductie ende Reformatie van den Schiltaelen . . . over de Landen van Holland ende Vrieslant Gedaen in den Jaere MCCCCXCIIII*. Ed. Robert Fruin. Leiden, 1876.

FRIIS, ASTRID. 'An Inquiry into the Relations between Economic and Financial Factors in the Sixteenth and Seventeenth Centuries. I: The Two Crises in the Netherlands in 1557.' *Scandinavian Economic History Review*, I/2, 1953.

GROB, JACQUES. *See* DÉNOMBREMENTS DES FEUX.

IJZERMAN, A. W. *De 80-jarige oorlog*. Leiden [no date].

—— *Nederland als grote mogenheid*. Amsterdam [no date].

*Informacie up den Staet, Faculteyt ende Gelegentheyt van de Steden ende Dorpen van Hollant ende Vrieslant om daernae te Reguleren de Nyeuwe Schiltaele, Gedaen in den Jaere MDXIV*. Ed. Robert Fruin. Leiden, 1866.

MOLS, ROGER. 'Beschouwingen over de Bevolkingsgeschiedenis in de Nederlanden (XVe en XVIe eeuwe).' *Tijdschrift voor Geschiedenis*, LXVI, 1953.

—— 'Die Bevölkerungsgeschichte Belgiens im Lichte der heutigen Forschung.' *Vierteljahrschrift für Sozial- und Wirtschaftsgeschichte*, XLVI, 1959.

—— 'Une source d'histoire démographique. Les anciens registres paroissiaux de Theux.' *Miscellanea historica Alberti de Meyer*. Louvain, 1946.

Pirenne, Henri. 'Les dénombrements de la population d'Ypres au XVe siècle (1412–1506).' *Vierteljahrschrift für Social- und Wirtschaftsgeschichte*, I, 1903.

Posthumus, N. W. *Inquiry into the History of Prices in Holland*. Vol. I, Leiden, 1946.

Rogghé, P. 'De zwarte Dood in de zuidelijke Nederlanden.' *Belgisch Tijdschrift voor Philologie en Geschiedenis*, xxx, 1952.

Ruwet, J. 'Crises démographiques: Problèmes économiques ou crises morales? Le pays de Liège sous l'Ancien Régime.' *Population*, IX, 1954.

Torfs, Louis. *Fastes des calamités publiques survenues dans les Pays-Bas et particulièrement en Belgique: Épidémies, famines, inondations*. Paris and Tournai, 1859.

Van Dillen, J. G. 'Summiere staat van de in 1622 in de provincie Holland gehouden volkstelling.' *Economisch-Historisch Jaarboek*, xxi, 1940.

Vannérus, Jules. 'Les anciens dénombrements du Luxembourg.' *Compte Rendu des Séances de la Commission Royale ou Recueil des ses Bulletins*, lxx (5th ser., xi), 1901.

—— 'Dénombrements luxembourgeois du quinzième siècle (1472–1482).' *Bulletin de la Commission Royale d'Histoire*, cvi, 1941.

Van Nierop, Leonie. *De bevolkingsbeweging der Nederlandsche stad*. Amsterdam, 1905.

Van Schevensteen, A.-F.-C. See *Documents pour Servir à l'Étude des Maladies Pestilentielles*.

Van Werveke, Hans. 'Het bevolkingscijfer van de stad Gent in de veertiende eeuw.' *Miscellanea L. van der Essen*. Brussels, 1947.

—— 'De Curve van het Gentse Bevolkingscijfer in de 17e en de 18e eeuw.' *Verhandelingen van de Koninklijke Vlaamse Academie voor Wetenschappen, Letteren en Schone Kunsten van België*, Klasse der Letteren, x, no. 8, 1948.

—— 'Demografische problemen in de zuidelijke Nederlanden (17e en 18e eeuw).' *Mededelingen van de Koninklijke Vlaamse Academie voor Wetenschappen, Letteren en Schone Kunsten van België*, Klasse der Letteren, xvii, no. 1, 1955.

—— 'La famine de l'an 1316 en Flandre et dans les régions voisines.' *Revue du Nord*, clxi, 1959.

—— 'De zwarte Dood in de zuidelijke Nederlanden (1349–1351).' *Mededelingen van de Koninklijke Vlaamse Academie voor Wetenschappen, Letteren en Schone Kunsten van België*, Klasse der Letteren, xii, 1950.

Verbeemen, J. 'De werking van economische factoren op de stedelijke demografie der XVIIe en der XVIIIe eeuw in de Zuidelijke Nederlanden.' *Revue Belge de Philologie et d'Histoire*, xxxiv, 1956.

Wyffels, A. 'De omvang en de evolutie van het Brugse bevolkingscijfer in de 17de en de 18de eeuw.' *Revue Belge de Philologie et d'Histoire*, xxxvi/2, 1958.

## VI. Germany and Austria

Abel, Wilhelm. 'Verdorfung und Gutsbildung in Deutschland zu Beginn der Neuzeit.' *Geografiska Annaler*, xliii, 1961.

—— 'Wandlungen des Fleischverbrauchs und der Fleischversorgung in Deutschland seit dem ausgehenden Mittelalter.' *Berichte über Landwirtschaft: Zeitschrift für Agrarpolitik und Landwirtschaft*, xxii/3, 1937.

Arndt, Carl. *Die Einwohnerzahlen der niederdeutschen Städte von 1550 bis 1816*. Philos. Dissertation, Univ. Hamburg, 1946 (typescript).

Bücher, Carl. *Die Bevölkerung von Frankfurt am Main im XIV. und XV. Jahrhundert*. Tübingen, 1886.

Bücher, Karl. *Die Frauenfrage im Mittelalter* (2nd ed.). Tübingen, 1910.

Crum, Frederick S. 'The Statistical Work of Süssmilch.' *Publications of the American Statistical Association*, vii, 1901.

Deutsches Städtebuch. Ed. Erich Keyser. Vols. I–III. Stuttgart, 1939–56.

Dreyfus, François G. 'Prix et population à Trèves et à Mayence au XVIIIe siècle.' *Revue d'histoire économique et sociale*, xxxiv, 1956.

Eheberg, K. Th. 'Strassburg's Bevölkerungszahl seit Ende des fünfzehnten Jahrhunderts bis zur Gegenwart.' *Jahrbücher für Nationalökonomie und Statistik*, xli, 1883.

ELSAS, M. J. Umriss einer Geschichte der Preise und Löhne in Deutschland. Vols. I–II. Leiden 1936–49.

FRANZ, GÜNTHER. *Der Dreissigjährige Krieg und das deutsche Volk* (2nd ed.). Jena, 1943.

GOEHLERT, V. 'Die Ergebnisse der in Österreich im vorigen Jahrhundert ausgeführten Volkszählungen im Vergleiche mit jenen der neueren Zeit.' *Sitzungsberichte der Wiener Akademie der Wissenschaften.* Phil.-hist.Klasse, XIV, 1854.

GROSSMANN, H. 'Die Anfänge und geschichtliche Entwicklung der amtlichen Statistik in Österreich.' *Österreichische Statistische Monatsschrift*, New Ser., XXI, 1916.

GÜRTLER, ALFRED. *Die Volkszählungen Maria Theresias und Josefs II, 1753–1790.* Innsbruck, 1909.

HÖMBERG, ALBERT. *Siedlungsgeschichte des oberen Sauerlandes* (Geschichtliche Arbeiten zur westfälischen Landesforschung, III). Münster, 1938.

JASTROW, J. *Die Volkszahl deutscher Städte zu Ende des Mittelalters und zu Beginn der Neuzeit* (Historische Untersuchungen, ed. J. Jastrow, I). Berlin, 1886.

JOLLES, OSKAR. 'Die Ansichten der deutschen nationalökonomischen Schriftsteller des sechszehnten und siebzehnten Jahrhunderts über Bevölkerungswesen.' *Jahrbücher für Nationalökonomie und Statistik*, New Ser., XIII, 1886.

KELTER, ERNST. 'Das deutsche Wirtschaftsleben des 14. und 15. Jahrhunderts im Schatten der Pestepidemien.' *Jahrbücher für Nationalökonomie und Statistik*, CLXV, 1953.

KEYSER, ERICH. 'Die Ausbreitung der Pest in den deutschen Städten.' *Ergebnisse und Probleme moderner geographischer Forschung: Hans Mortensen zu seinem 60. Geburtstag* (Abhandlungen der Akademie für Raumforschung und Landesplanung, XVIII). Bremen, 1954.

—— 'Die Bevölkerung der deutschen Städte.' *Städtewesen und Bürgertum als geschichtliche Kräfte. Gedächtnisschrift für Fritz Rörig.* Lübeck, 1953.

—— *Bevölkerungsgeschichte Deutschlands* (3rd ed.). Leipzig, 1943.

KISSKALT, KARL. 'Epidemiologisch-statistische Untersuchungen über die Sterblichkeit von 1600–1800.' *Archiv für Hygiene und Bakteriologie*, CXXXVII, 1953.

—— 'Die Sterblichkeit im 18. Jahrhundert.' *Zeitschrift für Hygiene und Infektionskrankheiten*, XCIII, 1921.

KLEIN, HERBERT. 'Das Grosse Sterben von 1348/49 und seine Auswirkung auf die Besiedlung der Ostalpenländer.' *Mitteilungen der Gesellschaft für Salzburger Landeskunde*, C, 1960.

KOERNER, FRITZ. 'Die Bevölkerungszahl und -dichte in Mitteleuropa zum Beginn der Neuzeit.' *Forschungen und Fortschritte*, XXXIII, 1959.

KOLLNIG, KARL. *Wandlungen im Bevölkerungsbild des pfälzischen Oberrheingebietes.* Heidelberg, 1952.

KORTH, SIEGFRIED. 'Die Entstehung und Entwicklung des ostdeutschen Grossgrundbesitzes.' *Jahrbuch der Albertus-Universität zu Königsberg/Preussen*, III, 1953.

KRAUSSE, JOHANNES. 'Unterschiedliche Fortpflanzung im 17. und 18. Jahrhundert.' *Archiv für Bevölkerungswissenschaft und Bevölkerungspolitik*, X, 1940.

KUHN, WALTER. *Geschichte der deutschen Ostsiedlung in der Neuzeit.* Vols. I, II, Cologne-Graz, 1955, 1957.

LAMMERT, GOTTFRIED. *Geschichte der Seuchen, Hungers- und Kriegsnoth zur Zeit des Dreissigjährigen Krieges.* Wiesbaden, 1890.

LESKY, E. 'Die österreichische Pestfront an der k.k.Militärgrenze.' *Saeculum*, VIII, 1957.

*Materialien zur Geschichte der Preise und Löhne in Österreich.* Ed. Alfred Francis Pribram. Vol. I. Vienna, 1938.

MEYER, A. O. 'Ein italienisches Urteil über Deutschland und Frankreich um 1660.' *Quellen und Forschungen aus italienischen Archiven*, IX, 1906.

POHLENDT, HEINZ. *Die Verbreitung der mittelalterlichen Wüstungen in Deutschland* (Göttinger Geographische Abhandlungen, Heft 3). Göttingen, 1950.

PRIBRAM, ALFRED FRANCIS. *See Materialien.*

REINCKE, HEINRICH. 'Bevölkerungsprobleme der Hansestädte.' *Hansische Geschichtsblätter*, LXX, 1951.

—— 'Bevölkerungsverluste der Hansestädte durch den Schwarzen Tod 1349–50.' *Hansische Geschichtsblätter*, LXXII, 1954.

RICHTER, GERTRAUD. 'Klimaschwankungen und Wüstungsvorgänge im Mittelalter.' *Petermanns geographische Mitteilungen*, XCVI, 1952.

RIEMANN, F. 'Preise und Löhne in der deutschen Landwirtschaft während des 17. und 18. Jahrhunderts.' *Landwirtschaftliches Jahrbuch für Bayern*, XXX, 1953.

RUNDSTEDT, HANS-GERD VON. *Die Regelung des Getreidehandels in den Städten Südwestdeutschlands und der deutschen Schweiz im späteren Mittelalter und im Beginn der Neuzeit.* Stuttgart, 1930.

SCHMÖLZ, FRANZ and THERESE. 'Die Sterblichkeit in Landsberg am Lech von 1585–1875.' *Archiv für Hygiene und Bakteriologie*, CXXXVI, 1952.

SCHMOLLER, GUSTAV. 'Die historische Entwicklung des Fleischkonsums sowie der Vieh- und Fleischpreise in Deutschland.' *Zeitschrift für die gesamte Staatswissenschaft*, XXVII, 1871.

SCHÜNEMANN, KONRAD. *Österreichs Bevölkerungspolitik unter Maria Theresia.* Berlin, 1935.

SCHUUR, KURT. *Kinderzahl und Kindersterblichkeit früherer Jahrhunderte.* Cottbus, 1936.

SÜSSMILCH, JOHANN PETER. *Die göttliche Ordnung in den Veränderungen des menschlichen. Geschlechts aus der Geburt, dem Tode und der Fortpflanzung desselben erwiesen* (4th edn.). Berlin, 1788.

WOEHLKENS, ERICH. *Pest und Ruhr im 16. und 17. Jahrhundert* (Schriften des Niedersächsichen Heimatbundes E.V., New Ser., XXVI). Hanover, 1954.

WOPFNER, HERMANN. 'Güterteilung und Übervölkerung tirolischer Landbezirke im 16., 17., und 18. Jahrhundert.' *Südostdeutsche Forschungen*, III, 1938.

ZUR MÜHLEN, HEINZ VON. 'Die Entstehung der Gutsherrschaft in Oberschlesien.' *Vierteljahrschrift für Sozial- und Wirtschaftsgeschichte*, XXXVIII [no date].

## VII. SWITZERLAND

AMMANN, HEKTOR. 'Die Bevölkerung der Westschweiz im ausgehenden Mittelalter.' *Festschrift Friedrich Emil Welti.* Aarau, 1937.

—— 'Die Bevölkerung von Stadt und Landschaft Basel am Ausgang des Mittelalters.' *Basler Zeitschrift für Geschichte und Altertumskunde*, XLIX, 1950.

BICKEL, WILHELM. *Bevölkerungsgeschichte und Bevölkerungspolitik der Schweiz seit dem Ausgang des Mittelalters.* Zürich, 1947.

—— 'Early Swiss Mortality Tables.' *Schweizerische Zeitschrift für Volkswirtschaft und Statistik*, LXXXV, 1949.

BUOMBERGER, FERDINAND. 'Bevölkerungs- und Vermögensstatistik in der Stadt und Landschaft Freiburg um die Mitte des XV. Jahrhunderts.' *Freiburger Geschichtsblätter*, VI–VIII, 1900.

BURCKHARDT, ALBRECHT. *Demographie und Epidemiologie der Stadt Basel während der letzten drei Jahrhunderte, 1601–1900.* Basel, 1908.

DASZYNSKA, ZOFIA. *Zürichs Bevölkerung im XVII. Jahrhundert. Ein Beitrag zur historischen Städtestatistik.* Berne, 1889.

DENZLER, ALICE. *Die Bevölkerungsbewegung der Stadt Winterthur von der Mitte des 16. bis zum Ende des 18. Jahrhunderts.* Winterthur, 1940.

HENRY, LOUIS. *Anciennes familles genevoises. Étude démographique: XVIe–XXe siècle.* (Institut National d'Études Démographiques, Travaux et Documents, Cahier no. 26.) Paris, 1956.

MAYER, KURT B. *The Population of Switzerland.* New York, 1952.

SCHNYDER, WERNER. *Die Bevölkerung der Stadt und Landschaft Zürich vom 14.–17. Jahrhundert* (Schweizer Studien zur Geschichtswissenschaft, XIV/1). Zürich, 1925.

## VIII. ITALY

ALEATI, GIUSEPPE. *La popolazione di Pavia durante il dominio Spagnolo.* Milan, 1957.

—— and CIPOLLA, CARLO M. 'Il trend economico nello Stato di Milano durante i secoli XVI e XVII.' *Bollettino della Società Pavese di Storia Patria*, XLVIII–L, 1950.

BATTARA, PIETRO. 'La popolazione di Firenze dal XIV al XVI secolo.' *Economia: Revista di Economia Comparativa e di Scienze sociali*, XVIII, 1935.

BELOCH, KARL JULIUS. 'Bevölkerungsgeschichte der Republik Venedig.' *Jahrbücher für Nationalökonomie und Statistik*, 3. Folge, XVIII, 1899.

—— *Bevölkerungsgeschichte Italiens*. Vol. I, Berlin and Leipzig, 1937. Vol. II, Berlin and Leipzig, 1939. Vol. III, Berlin, 1961.

BELTRAMI, DANIELE. *Storia della popolazione di Venezia dalla fine del secolo XVI alla caduta della repubblica*. Padua, 1954.

BESTA, BEATRICE. 'La popolazione di Milano nel periodo della dominazione Spagnola.' *Atti del Congresso Internazionale per gli Studi sulla Popolazione, Roma, 7–11 Settembre 1931* (ed. Corrado Gini). Vol. I. Rome, 1933.

BESTA, ENRICO. 'I censimenti Milanesi di Francesco II Sforza e di Carlo V.' *Atti del Congresso Internazionale per gli Studi sulla Popolazione, Roma, 7–11 Settembre 1931* (ed. Corrado Gini). Vol. I, Rome, 1933.

CARPENTIER, ÉLISABETH. *Une ville devant la peste. Orvieto et la Peste Noire de 1348*. Paris, 1962.

CIPOLLA, CARLO M. 'The Decline of Italy.' *Economic History Review*, 2nd ser., V, 1952.

—— *Mouvements monétaires dans l'État de Milan (1580–1700)*. Paris, 1952.

—— 'Per la storia della popolazione lombarda nel secolo XVI. *Studi in Onore di Gino Luzzatto*, II. Milan, 1950.

—— 'Profilo di storia demografica della città di Pavia.' *Bollettino Storico Pavese*, VI, 1943.

—— 'Revisions in Economic History: The Trends in Italian Economic History in the Later Middle Ages.' *Economic History Review*, 2nd ser., II, 1949.

—— *See also* ALEATI, GIUSEPPE.

CONIGLIO, GIUSEPPE. *Il Regno di Napoli al tempo di Carlo V*. Naples, 1951.

CORRADI, ALFONSO. *Annali delle epidemie occorse in Italia dalle prime memorie fino al 1850*. 3 parts, Bologna, 1865, 1867, 1870.

CORRIDORE, FRANCESCO. *Storia documentata della popolazione di Sardegna (1479–1901)* (2nd ed.). Turin, 1902.

COSTA, ANTONIO. 'La peste in Genova negli anni 1656–57.' *Atti del Congresso Internazionale per gli Studi sulla Popolazione, Roma, 7–11 Settembre 1931* (ed. Corrado Gini). Vol. I. Rome, 1933.

DONAZZOLO, PIETRO and SAIBANTE, MARIO. 'Lo sviluppo demografico di Verona e della sua provincia dalla fine del secolo XV ai giorni nostri.' *Metron*, VI, 1926.

FELLONI, GIUSEPPE. 'Per la storia della popolazione di Genova nel secoli XVI e XVII.' *Archivio Storico Italiano*, CX, 1952.

FIUMI, ENRICO. 'La demografia fiorentina nelle pagine di Giovanni Villani.' *Archivio Storico Italiano*, CVIII, 1950.

FORTUNATI, PAOLO. 'La popolazione Friulana dal secolo XVI ai giorni nostri.' *Atti del Congresso Internazionale per gli Studi sulla Popolazione, Roma, 7–11 Settembre 1931* (ed. Corrado Gini). Vol. I, Rome, 1933.

GIGLI, FERNANDA. 'La densità di popolazione in Toscana nei secoli XVI e XVIII.' *Rivista Geografica Italiana*, LXI, 1954.

HEERS, JACQUES. *Gênes au XVe siècle. Activité économique et problèmes sociaux*. Paris, 1961.

PARDI, G. 'Disegno della storia demografica di Firenze.' *Archivio Storico Italiano*, LXXIV/1, 1916.

PARENTI, GIUSEPPE. 'Fonti per lo studio della demografia Fiorentina: I libri dei morti.' *Genus*, VI–VIII, 1943–9.

—— *Prezzi e mercato del grano a Siena (1546–1765)*. Florence, 1942.

—— *Prime ricerche sulla rivoluzione dei prezzi in Firenze*. Florence, 1939.

PETINO, ANTONIO. 'Primi assaggi sulla »Rivoluzione dei prezzi« in Sicilia: I prezzi del grano, dell'orzo . . . a Catania dal 1512 al 1630.' *Studi in Onore di Gino Luzzatto*, II. Milan, 1950.

REYNAUD, PIERRE. *La théorie de la population en Italie du XVIe au XVIIIe siècle*. Lyon and Paris, 1904.

RODENWALDT, ERNST. 'Pest in Venedig 1575–1577. Ein Beitrag zur Frage der Infektkette bei den Pestepidemien West-Europas.' *Sitzungsberichte der Heidelberger Akademie der Wissenschaften*, Mathematisch-naturwissenschaftliche Klasse, Jahrgang 1952, 2. Abhandlung.

SAIBANTE, MARIO. *See* DONAZZOLO, PIETRO.

ZERBI, LUIGI. 'La peste di San Carlo in Monza.' *Archivio Storico Lombardo*, 2nd ser., fasc. XXX, 1891.


IX. SPAIN AND PORTUGAL

AMMANN, HEKTOR. 'Vom Städtewesen Spaniens und Westfrankreichs im Mittelalter.' *Studien zu den Anfängen des europäischen Städtewesens* (Vorträge und Forschungen, herausgegeben vom Institut für geschichtliche Landesforschung des Bodenseegebietes, vol. IV), Lindau and Constance, n.d. (1958).

EDGE, P. GRANVILLE. 'Pre-census Population Records of Spain.' *Journal of the American Statistical Association*, XXVI, 1931.

ELLIOTT, JOHN. 'The Decline of Spain.' *Past and Present*, no. 20, November 1961.

FUENTES MARTIÁÑEZ, MARIANO. *Despoblación y repoblación de España (1482–1920)*. Madrid, 1929.

GIRALT, E. *See* NADAL, J.

GIRÃO, AMORIM. *See* VELHO, FERNANDA.

GIRARD, ALBERT. 'Le chiffre de la population de l'Espagne dans les temps modernes.' *Revue d'histoire moderne*, III, 1928 and IV, 1929.

—— 'La répartition de la population en Espagne dans les temps modernes.' *Revue d'Histoire économique et sociale*, XVII, 1929.

GONZÁLEZ, TOMÁS. *Censo de población de las provincias y partidos de la Corona de Castilla en el siglo XVI*. Madrid, 1829.

HAMILTON, EARL J. *American Treasure and the Price Revolution in Spain, 1501–1650* (Harvard Economic Studies, XLIII). Cambridge, Mass., 1934.

—— *Money, Prices and Wages in Valencia, Aragon, and Navarre, 1351–1500* (Harvard Economic Studies, LI). Cambridge, Mass., 1936.

—— 'Revisions in Economic History: The Decline of Spain.' *Economic History Review*, VIII, 1938.

—— *War and Prices in Spain, 1651–1800* (Harvard Economic Studies, LXXXI). Cambridge, Mass., 1947.

LAPEYRE, HENRI. *Géographie de l'Espagne morisque*. Paris, 1959.

MACHADO, MONTALVÃO, J. T. 'A população portuguesa através da História.' *Jornal do Médico*, XVI, 1950.

NADAL, J. and GIRALT, E. *La population catalane de 1553 à 1717*. Paris, 1960.

*Relaciones Historico-Geografico-Estadisticas de los Pueblos de España Hechos por Iniciativa de Felipe II*. Ed. Carmelo Viñas y Mey and Ramón Paz. Vol. I: *Provincia de Madrid*; Vol. II: *Reino de Toledo*. Madrid, 1949, 1951.

RUIZ ALMANSA, JAVIER. *La población de Galicia, 1500–1945, segun los documentos estadisticos y descriptivos de cada época*. (Publicaciones del laboratorio de demografia retrospectiva Española, Vol. I). Madrid, 1948.

SMITH, ROBERT S. 'Barcelona "Bills of Mortality" and Population, 1457–1590.' *Journal of Political Economy*, XLIV, 1936.

—— 'Fourteenth-Century Population Records of Catalonia.' *Speculum*, XIX, 1944.

—— 'Spanish Population Thought before Malthus.' *Teachers of History: Essays in Honor of Laurence Bradford Packard*. Ed. H. Stuart Hughes, *et al.* Ithaca, N.Y., 1954.

VANDELLOS, J. A. 'La evolución demográfica de España.' *Bulletin de l'Institut international de statistique* (Netherlands), XXVII, 1934.

VELHO, FERNANDA and GIRÃO, AMORIM. 'O mais antigo Censo da População de Portugal (1527).' *Boletim do Centro de Estudos Geográficos* (Coimbra) No. 8–9, 1954.

VERLINDEN, CHARLES. 'La grande peste de 1348 en Espagne.' *Revue Belge de Philologie et d'Histoire*, XVII/1, 1938.


X. THE SCANDINAVIAN COUNTRIES

BOËTHIUS, BERTIL. 'New Light on Eighteenth Century Sweden.' *The Scandinavian Economic History Review*, I/2, 1953.

GILLE, H. 'The Demographic History of the Northern European Countries in the Eighteenth Century.' *Population Studies*, III, 1949–50.

HAMMARSTRÖM, INGRID. 'The "Price Revolution" of the Sixteenth Century: Some Swedish Evidence.' *Scandinavian Economic History Review*, V, 1957.

HECKSCHER, ELI F. (transl. by Göran Ohlin). *An Economic History of Sweden* (Harvard Economic Studies, XCV), Cambridge, Mass., 1954.

—— 'Swedish Population Trends before the Industrial Revolution.' *Economic History Review*, 2nd ser., II, 1950.

HYRENIUS, HANNES. 'Reproduction and Replacement: A Methodological Study of Swedish Population Changes during 20 Years.' *Population Studies*, IV/1, 1951.

JUTIKKALA, EINO. *Die Bevölkerung Finnlands in den Jahren 1721–49* (Annales Academiae Scientiarum Fennicae, B LV/4). Helsinki, 1945.

—— 'Can the Population of Finland in the 17th Century Be Calculated?' *Scandinavian Economic History Review*, V, 1957.

—— 'The Great Finnish Famine in 1696–97.' *Scandinavian Economic History Review*, III, 1955.

SCHREINER, JOHAN. Pest og Prisfall i Senmiddelalderen (*Avhandlinger utgitt av det Norske Videnskaps-Akademi i Oslo*, Hist.-Filos. Klasse, 1948, no. 1). Oslo, 1948.

SUNDBÄRG, GUSTAV. *Bevölkerungsstatistik Schwedens, 1750–1900*. Stockholm, 1907.

SUNDQUIST, S. *Sveriges folkmängd på Gustaf II Adolfs tid*. Lund, 1938.

SWEDEN, Statistika Centralbyrån. *Historisk Statistik för Sverige*. I. Befolkning, 1720–1950. Stockholm, 1955.

THOMAS, DOROTHY SWAINE. *Social and Economic Aspects of Swedish Population Movements, 1750–1933*. New York, 1941.

UTTERSTRÖM, GUSTAF. 'Population and Agriculture in Sweden, circa 1700–1830.' *Scandinavian Economic History Review*, IX, 1961.

—— 'Some Population Problems in Pre-Industrial Sweden.' *Scandinavian Economic History Review*, II/2, 1954.

WARGENTIN, PER WILHELM. *Tables of Mortality Based upon the Swedish Population, Prepared and Presented in 1766*. Stockholm, 1930.

## XI. THE BALKAN COUNTRIES AND EASTERN EUROPE

BARKAN, ÖMER LÛTFI. 'Les déportations comme méthode de peuplement et de colonisation dans l'Empire Ottoman.' *Revue de la Faculté des Sciences Économiques de l'Université d'Istanbul*, XI, 1953.

—— 'Essai sur les données statistiques des registres de recensement dans l'Empire Ottoman aux XVe et XVIe siècles.' *Journal of the Economic and Social History of the Orient*, I/1, 1957.

—— '»La Méditerranée« de Fernand Braudel vue d'Istamboul.' *Annales: Économies, Sociétés, Civilisations*, IX, 1954.

BELOCH, KARL JULIUS. 'Bevölkerungsgeschichte der Republik Venedig.' *Jahrbücher für Nationalökonomie und Statistik*, III. Folge, XVIII, 1899.

HOSZOWSKI, STANISŁAW. 'Dynamika rozwoju zaludnienia Polski w epoce feudalnej, X–XVIII w.' *Roczniki Dziejów Społecznych i Gospodarczych*, XIII, 1951.

—— *Les prix à Lwow (XVIe–XVIIe siècles)*. Paris, 1954.

JABŁONOWSKI, ALEKSANDER. *Polska XVI wieku pod względem geograficzno-statystycznym*, VI–XI. Warsaw, 1894–1910.

KULA, WITWOLD. 'Stan i potrzeby badań nad demografią historyczną dawnej Polski, do początków XIX wieku.' *Roczniki Dziejów Społecznych i Gospodarczych*, XII, 1951.

LADENBERGER, TADEUSZ. *Zaludnienie Polski na początku panowia Kazimierza Wielkiego*. Lwów, 1930.

MITKOWSKI, JOZEF. 'Uwagi o zaludnieniu Polski na początku panowia Kazimierza Wielkiego.' *Roczniki Dziejów Społecznych i Gospodarczych*, X, 1948.

PAWIŃSKI, ADOLF. *Polska XVI wieku pod względem geograficzno-statystycznym*, I–V. Warsaw, 1883, 1886, 1895.

RUTKOWSKI, JAN. *Histoire économique de la Pologne avant les partages*. Paris, 1927.

STOIANOVICH, TRAIAN. 'Land Tenure and Related Sectors of the Balkan Economy, 1600–1800.' *Journal of Economic History*, XIII, 1953.
VIELROSE, EGON. 'Ludność Polski od X do XVIII wieku.' *Kwartalnik Historii Kultury Materialnej*, V, 1957.

## CHAPTER II

## Scientific Method and the Progress of Techniques

The following short bibliography is intended to serve as a general guide to further study, and not as an exhaustive enumeration of relevant publications. It omits all reference to articles in periodicals, to contemporary and modern editions of scientific writings, and to biographies. Much further bibliographical information may be found in the works listed below, especially in those under the heading 'General'.

### I. GENERAL

BURTT, E. A. *Metaphysical Foundations of Modern Physical Science*. London, 1932.
BUTTERFIELD, H. *The Origins of Modern Science* (2nd ed.). London, 1957.
CASTIGLIONI, A. *History of Medicine* (2nd ed.). New York, 1947.
DRUMMOND, J. C. and WILBRAHAM, A. *The Englishman's Food*. London, 1939.
GRAS, N. S. B. *A History of Agriculture in Europe and America*. New York, 1925.
HALL, A. RUPERT. *The Scientific Revolution, 1500–1800* (2nd ed.). London, 1962.
HANSON, N. R. *Patterns of Discovery*. Cambridge, 1958.
MUMFORD, L. *Technics and Civilization*. New York, 1934.
NEF, J. U. *Cultural Foundations of Industrial Civilization*. Cambridge, 1958.
SALAMAN, R. N. *The History and Social Influence of the Potato*. Cambridge, 1949.
SINGER, CHARLES, HOLMYARD, E. J., HALL, A. R. and WILLIAMS, T. I. *A History of Technology*, III. Oxford, 1957.
TATON, R. (ed.). *Histoire Générale des Sciences*, II. Paris, 1958.
UCCELLI, A. *Storia della Tecnica dal Medio Evo ai Nostri Giorni*. Milan, 1945.
USHER, A. P. *A History of Mechanical Inventions* (2nd ed.). Cambridge, Mass., 1954.
WOLF, A. *A History of Science, Technology and Philosophy in the 16th and 17th Centuries*, (2nd ed.). London, 1950.

### II. SCIENCE

ARBER, AGNES. *Herbals* (2nd ed.). Cambridge, 1953.
BALL, W. W. R. *An Essay on Newton's Principia*. London, 1893.
BOAS, MARIE. *The Scientific Renaissance, 1450–1630*. London, 1962.
—— 'The Establishment of the Mechanical Philosophy.' *Osiris*, X, 1952.
—— *Robert Boyle and 17th Century Chemistry*. Cambridge, 1958.
BROWN, HARCOURT. *Scientific Organisations in 17th Century France*. Baltimore, 1934.
COHEN, I. B. *Franklin and Newton*. Philadelphia, 1956.
COLE, F. J. *A History of Comparative Anatomy*. London, 1949.
CLARK, G. N. *Science and Social Welfare in the Age of Newton*. Oxford, 1937.
CROMBIE, A. C. *Medieval and Early Modern Science*, II. New York, 1959.
DIJKSTERHUIS, E. J. *The Mechanization of the World Picture*. Oxford, 1961.
DRAKE, S. *Discoveries and Opinions of Galileo*. New York, 1957.
DUGAS, R. *History of Mechanics*, trans. J. R. Maddox. London, 1955.
—— *La Mécanique au XVIIIe Siècle*. Paris, 1954.
HALL, A. RUPERT. *Ballistics in the Seventeenth Century*. Cambridge, 1952.
—— *From Galileo to Newton, 1630–1720*. London, 1963.
HALL, A. R. and M. B. *Unpublished Papers of Isaac Newton*. Cambridge, 1962.

JOHNSON, F. R. *Astronomical Thought in Renaissance England*. Baltimore, 1937.
KOYRÉ, A. *Etudes Galiléennes* (*Actualités Scientifiques et Industrielles*, nos. 852–4). Paris, 1939.
—— *From the Closed World to the Infinite Universe*. Baltimore, 1957.
—— *La Revolution Astronomique*. Paris, 1961.
KREMERS, E. and URDANG, G. *History of Pharmacy*. Philadelphia, 1940.
KUHN, T. S. *The Copernican Revolution*. Cambridge, Mass., 1956.
LEICESTER, H. M. *The Historical Background of Chemistry*. London and New York, 1958.
LENOBLE, R. *Mersenne, ou la Naissance du Mécanisme*. Paris, 1943.
LYONS, SIR H. *The Royal Society, 1660–1940*. Cambridge, 1944.
MERTON, R. K. 'Science, technology and society in 17th century England.' *Osiris*, IV, 1938.
METZGER, HÉLÈNE. *Les Doctrines Chimiques en France du début du XVIIe à la fin du XVIIIe siècle*, I (all published). Paris, 1923.
MOUY, P. *Le Développement de la Physique Cartésienne*. Paris, 1934.
ORNSTEIN, M. *The Role of Scientific Societies in the 17th Century*. Chicago, 1928.
RONCHI, V. *Histoire de la Lumière*, trans. J. Taton. Paris, 1956.
TAYLOR, E. G. R. *The Mathematical Practitioners of Tudor and Stuart England*. Cambridge, 1954.

### III. TECHNOLOGY

CLOW, A. and N. *The Chemical Revolution*. London, 1952.
DAUMAS, M. *Les Instruments Scientifiques au XVIIe et XVIIIe Siècles*. Paris, 1953.
DONALD, M. B. *Elizabethan Copper*. London, 1955.
FORBES, R. J. *Short History of the Art of Distillation*. Leiden, 1948.
HART, I. B. *The Mechanical Inventions of Leonardo da Vinci*. London, 1925.
HOOVER, H. C. and L. H. (trans.) G. Agricola, *De re metallica* (2nd ed.). New York, 1950.
NEF, J. U. *The Rise of the British Coal Industry*. London, 1932.
PARSONS, W. B. *Engineers and Engineering in the Renaaissance*. Baltimore, 1939.
SMITH, C. S. *A History of Metallography*. Chicago, 1960.
SMITH, C. S. and GNUDI, M. *The Pirotechnia of Vannoccio Biringuccio* (2nd ed.). New York, 1959.
SMITH, C. S. and SISCO, A. *The Treatise on Ores and Assaying of Lazarus Ercker*. Chicago, 1951.
STRAUB, H. *A History of Civil Engineering. An Outline from Ancient to Modern Times*, trans. E. Rockwell. London, 1952.
TREUE, W. *Kulturgeschichte der Schraube*. Munich, 1955.
WAILES, R. *The English Windmill*. London, 1954.

# CHAPTER III

## *Transport and Trade Routes*

ALBION, R. G. *Forests and Sea Power*. Cambridge, Mass., 1926.
ANDERSON, ROMOLA and R. C. *The Sailing Ship*. London, 1947.
BARBOUR, V. 'Dutch and English merchant shipping in the seventeenth century.' *Economic History Review*, II (1930), 2.
BIANCHINI, L. *Storia economica-sociale de Sicilia*. Naples, 1841.
BONREPOS, R. de. *Histoire du canal de Languedoc*. Paris, 1805.
BORAH, W. W. *Early Colonial Trade and Navigation between Mexico and Peru* (Ibero-Americana no. 38). Berkeley, California, 1954.
BRAUDEL, F. *La Mediterranée et le monde mediterranéen a l'époque de Philippe II*. Paris, 1949.
BRAUDEL, F. and ROMANO, R. *Navires et marchandises à l'entrée du port de Livourne, 1547–1611*. Paris, 1951.

CANABRAVA, A. P. *O comércio português no Rio da Prata, 1580–1640.* São Paulo, 1944.

CARANDE, R. *Carlos V y sus banqueros.* 2 vols. Madrid, 1943–9.

CHAUNU, H. and CHAUNU, P. *Séville et l'Atlantique.* 11 vols. Paris, 1955–9.

CHAUNU, P. *Les Philippines et le Pacifique des Ibériques.* Paris, 1960.

CHILD, Sir J. *The New Discourse of Trade.* London, 1669.

DAENELL, E. *Die Blütezeit der deutschen Hanse.* 2 vols. Berlin, 1905–6.

DAVIS, R. *Rise of the English Shipping Industry.* London, 1962.

VAN DRIEL, A. *Tonnage Measurement, a Historical and Critical Essay.* The Hague, 1925.

EDMUNDSON, G. *Anglo-Dutch Rivalry during the first Half of the Seventeenth Century.* Oxford, 1911.

EHRENBERG, R. *Das Zeitalter der Fugger.* 2 vols. Jena, 1922.

ELLINGER BANG, N. *Tabeller over skibsfart og varetransport gennen Øresund 1497–1660.* 2 vols. Copenhagen, 1906–22.

FARIA E SOUSA, M. DE. *Asia portuguesa.* Oporto, 1945.

FAYLE, C. E. *A Short History of the World's Shipping Industry.* London, 1933.

FERNÁNDEZ DURO, C. *Disquisiciones náuticas.* 6 vols. Madrid, 1876–81.

FORBES, R. J. *Notes on the History of Ancient Roads and their construction.* Amsterdam, 1934.

GAUTIER, H. *Traité de la construction des chemins.* Paris, 1716.

GOMES DE BRITO, B. (ed.). *Historia trágico—maritima em que se escreven chronologicamente os naufragios que tiverão as naos de Portugal, depois que se poz em exercicio a navegação da India.* 2 vols. Lisbon, 1735–6.

GOTHEIN, E. 'Zur Geschichte der Rheinschiffahrt.' *Westdeutsche Zeitschrift fur Geschichte und Kunst XIV,* (1895), 254.

HAGEDORN, B. *Die Entwicklung der wichtigsten Schiffstypen bis ins 19 Jahrhundert.* Berlin, 1914.

HARING, C. H. *Trade and Navigation between Spain and the Indies.* Cambridge, Mass., 1918.

HEYD, W. *Histoire du commerce du Levant au moyen-âge.* Leipzig, 1885–6.

HUNTER, Sir W. W. *History of British India 1500–1700.* 2 vols. London, 1899–1900.

JAL, A. *Archéologie navale.* 2 vols. Paris, 1840.

JENKINS, J. T. *The Herring and the Herring Fisheries.* London, 1927.

—— *A History of the Whale Fisheries.* London, 1921.

JONGE, J. C. DE. *Geschiednis van het Nederlandsche Zeewesen.* 5 vols. Zwolle, 1869.

KLERK DE REUS, G. C. *Geschichtlicher Überblick der Niederländisch-Ostindischen Compagnie.* Batavia, 1894.

LALANDE, J. J. LE F. DE. *Des canaux de navigation.* Paris, 1778.

LANE, F. C. *Venetian Ships and Ship-builders of the Renaissance.* Baltimore, 1934.

—— 'Tonnages, Medieval and Modern', *Economic History Review,* Second Series, XVII (1964), 213–33.

LECCHI, A. *Trattato de' canali navigabili.* Milan, 1824.

LINDSAY, W. S. *History of Merchant Shipping and Ancient Commerce.* 4 vols. London, 1874–6.

LEFEBRE DES NOËTTES, R. *La force motrice animal à travers les ages.* Paris, 1924.

MACPHERSON, D. *Annals of Commerce.* 4 vols. London, 1805.

MAGE, A. *De la navigation intérieure en France.* Paris, 1840.

MAURO, F. *Le Portugal et l'Atlantique au XVIIe siècle.* Paris, 1960.

MILLER, L. R. 'New evidence on the shipping and imports of London, 1601–1602.' *Quarterly Journal of Economics,* 41, p. 740.

MOLLAT, M. *Le navire et l'économie maritime du XVe au XVIIIe siècle.* Paris, 1959.

OPPENHEIM, M. *History of the Administration of the Royal Navy.* 2 vols. London, 1896.

PARENTI, G. *Prime ricerche nella rivoluzione dei prezzi in Firenze.* Florence, 1939.

PARSONS, W. B. *Engineers and Engineering in the Renaissance.* Baltimore, 1939.

POMMEUSE, H. DE. *Des canaux navigables . . . avec des recherches comparatives sur la navigation intérieure de la France et celle de l'Angleterre.* Paris, 1822.

POUJADE, J. *La route des Indes et ses navires.* Paris, 1946.

QUIRINO DA FONSECA, H. *Os Portugueses no mar.* Lisbon, 1926.

RAMÉE, D. *La locomotion: histoire des chars, carrosses, omnibus et voitures de tous genres.* Paris, 1856.

RIVE, B. L. DE. *Précis historique et statistique des canaux et rivières navigables de la Belgique.* Brussels, 1835.

SCHAUBE, A. *Geschichte des mittelalterlichen Handels und Verkehrs zwischen Westdeutschland und Italien*. 2 vols. Leipzig, 1900.

SCHAUBE, A. 'Die Anfänge der venezianischen Galeerenfahrten nach der Nordsee.' *Historisches Zeitschrift*, CI (1908), 37.

SLUITER, E. 'Dutch-Spanish rivalry in the Caribbean area, 1594–1609.' *Hispanic American Historical Review*, XXVIII (1948), 179.

SOMBART, W. *Der moderne Kapitalismus*. Leipzig, 1916–17.

TEUBERT, O. *Die Binnenschiffahrt*. Leipzig, 1912.

TROCMÉ, E. and DELAFOSSE, M. *Le commerce rochelais de la fin du XVe siècle au début du XVIIe siècle*. Paris, 1953.

USHER, A. P. 'Spanish ships and shipping in the sixteenth and seventeenth centuries.' *Facts and Factors in Economic History*. Cambridge, Mass., 1932.

USHER, A. P. 'The growth of English shipping, 1572–1922.' *Quarterly Journal of Economics*, XLII (1927–8), 467.

VIGNON, E. J. M. *Etudes historiques sur l'administration des voies publiques en France*. 4 vols. Paris, 1862.

VOGEL, W. 'Zur grosse der Europäischen Handelsflotten im 15, 16 und 17 Jahrhundert.' *Forschungen und Versuche zur Geschichte des Mittelalters und der Neuzeit*. Jena, 1915.

WIEL A. *The Navy of Venice*. London, 1910.

WILLAN T. S. *River Navigation in England, 1600–1750*. Oxford, 1936.

WITSEN N. *Aeloude en Hendendaegsche Scheeps-Bouw en Bestier*. Amsterdam, 1671.

## CHAPTER IV

## European Economic Institutions and the New World; The Chartered Companies

### I. GENERAL

BLAKE, J. W. *European Beginnings in West Africa, 1454–1578*. London, 1937.
—— *Europeans in West Africa, 1450–1560*. London, Hakluyt Society, 1942.

BONNASSIEUX, P. *Les Grandes Compagnies de Commerce*. Paris, 1892.

CHAUVIN, P. *Histoire de l'Amérique latine*. Paris, 1949.

HARDY, O. and DUNKE, G. S. *A History of the Pacific Area in Modern Times*. Boston, 1949.

LLOYD, C. *Pacific Horizons*. London, 1946.

MAJUNDAR, R. C., RAYCHAUDHURI, H. C. and KALININKAR, D. *An Advanced History of India*. London, 1946.

MEILE, P. *Histoire de l'Inde*. Paris, 1951.

MORELAND, W. J. and CHATTERJEE, A. C. *A Short History of India*. New York, 1953.

PANIKKAR, K. M. *A Survey of Indian History*. Bombay, 1954.

PENROSE, B. *Travel and Discovery in the Renaissance, 1420–1620*. Cambridge, Mass., 1952.

POWELL-PRICE, J. C. *A History of India*. London, 1955.

PRATT, SIR J. *The Expansion of Europe in the Far East*. London, 1947.

RAWLINSON, H. G. *A Concise History of the Indian People*. London, 1946.

SAINTOYANT, J. *La colonisation européenne du XVème siècle*. Paris, 1948.

SCHRAUM, P. E. *Deutschland und Ubersee*. Kiel, 1950.

WILBUR, M. E. *The East India Company and the British Empire in the Far East*. New York, 1945.

### II. BELGIUM

ANCIAUX, L. *La participation des Belges à l'oeuvre coloniale des Hollandais aux Indes Orientales*. Brussels, 1955.

CUVELIER, MSGR (ed.). *Relation sur le Congo du Père Laurent de Lucques, 1700–1717*. Brussels, 1953.

PRIMS, F. *Voor de geschiedenis van de Oostendse Compagnie*. Brussels, Meded. van de Academië van Marine van België, 1953.


## III. ENGLAND

ANDREWS, C. M. *The Colonial Period of American History*. 4 vols. New York, 1912.

ASHTON, T. S. (ed.). *The Letters of a West African Trader, Edward Grace, 1767–1770*. London, Council for Preservation of Business Archives, 1950.

BHATTACHARYA, SUKUMAR. *The East India Company and the Economy of Bengal, 1704 to 1740*. London, 1950.

BOYD, J. P. 'The Susquehannah Company, 1753–1803.' *Journal of Economic and Business History*. 1931–2.

CRAVEN, W. F. *The Southern Colonies in the Seventeenth Century, 1607–1689*. Louisiana, 1949.

COTTON, SIR E. *East Indiamen, the East India Company's Maritime Service*. London, 1949.

DAVIES, K. G. *The Royal African Company*. London, 1957.

DONNAN, E. 'The early days of the South Sea Company.' *Journal of Economic and Business History*, 1929–30.

FAWCETT, SIR C. *The English Factories in India*, vol. IV, *The Eastern Coast and Bay of Bengal*. Oxford, 1955.

FINLAY, J. *James Finlay and Company Ltd., manufacturers and East India Merchants, 1750–1950*. Ed. Colm Brogan. Glasgow, 1951.

*Fort William—India House Correspondence and other contemporary papers relating thereto, 1748–1800*. Ed. K. K. Datta, N. K. Simba and others. 21 vols. Delhi, 1949–.

FURBER, HOLDEN. *John Company at Work*. Harvard, 1948.

—— 'The United Company of Merchants of England trading to the East Indies, 1783–96.' *Economic History Review*, 1940.

McGRATH, P. *Merchants and Merchandise in Seventeenth-century Bristol*. Bristol, Bristol Record Society, 1955.

—— *Records relating to the Society of Merchant Venturers of the City of Bristol in the Seventeenth Century*. Bristol, Bristol Record Society, 1951.

McKANN, F. T. *The English Discovery of America to 1585*. New York, 1952.

MINCHINTON, W. E. *The Trade of Bristol in the Eighteenth Century*. Bristol, Bristol Record Society, 1957.

PARKINSON, C. N. *Trade in the Eastern Seas, 1793–1813*. Cambridge, 1937.

PHILIPS, C. H. DE. *Correspondence of David Scott, director and chairman of the East India Company, 1787–1805*. 2 vols. London, Camden Society, 1951.

RICH, E. E. (ed.). *Copy-book of Letters Outward of the Hudson's Bay Company, 1680–1687*. London, Hudson's Bay Record Society, 1948.

—— *The History of the Hudson's Bay Company, 1670–1870*. 2 vols. London, 1958–9.

—— (ed.). *Hudson's Bay Copy Booke of Letters Commissions Instructions Outward 1688–1696*. London, Hudson's Bay Record Society, 1957.

—— (ed.). *Minutes of the Hudson's Bay Company, 1679–84*. 2 vols. London, Hudson's Bay Record Society, 1945, 1946.

SUTHERLAND, L. S. 'The East India Company in eighteenth-century politics', *Economic History Review*, 1947.

THORNTON, A. P. *West India Policy under the Restoration*, Oxford, 1955.

WILLIAMSON, J. A. *Voyages of the Cabots and the English Discovery of North America under Henry VII and Henry VIII*, London, 1929.


## IV. FRANCE

BIGGAR, H. P. *The early Trading Companies of New France*. Toronto, 1901.

BLET, H. *France d'Outre-Mer*. Grenoble, 1950.

—— *Histoire de la colonisation française, des origines à 1815*. Grenoble, 1946.

BONNAULT, C. DE. *Histoire du Canada français*. Paris, 1950.

BRUNSCHWIG, H. *La colonisation française*. Paris, 1949.

COLE, C. WOOLSEY. *Colbert and a Century of French Mercantilism.* 2 vols. New York, 1939.
—— *French Mercantilism, 1683–1700.* New York, 1943.
CONAN, J. 'La dernière Compagnie française des Indes.' *Revue d'histoire économique et sociale.* 1939.
DEBIEN, G. *L'émigration poitevine vers l'Amérique au XVIIème siècle.* Paris, 1952.
—— *Une plantation à Saint-Domingue.* Cairo, 1941.
—— *Le peuplement des Antilles françaises au XVIIème siècle.* Cairo, 1942.
—— *La société coloniale aux XVIIème et XVIIIème siècles.* Paris, 1953.
DELCOURT, A. *La France et les établissements français au Sénégal entre 1713 et 1763.* Dakar, 1952.
DESCHAMPS, H. *Méthodes et doctrines coloniales de la France.* Paris, 1953.
DIAGON, G. (ed.). *Arrêts du Conseil Supérieur de Pondichéry, 1735–1820.* 8 vols. Pondicherry, 1935–41.
ESQUER, G. *L'anticolonialisme au XVIIIème siècle.* Paris, 1951.
GIRAUD, M. *Histoire de la Louisiane française.* 2 vols. Paris, 1953, 1958.
GROUX, L. 'Colonisation au Canada sous Talon.' *Rev. d'hist. de l'Amérique française.* Montreal, IV, 1950.
—— *L'Histoire du Canada français.* Montreal, 1952.
HARDY, G. *Histoire de la colonisation française.* Paris, 1937.
HARSIN, P. 'La création de la Compagnie d'Occident.' *Revue d'histoire économique et sociale.* 1956.
JULIEN, CH. A. *Les Français en Amérique de 1713 à 1783.* Paris, 1951.
—— *Histoire de l'expansion et de la colonisation françaises.* Paris, 1948.
LE BLANT, R. 'La Compagnie de la Nouvelle France et la restitution de l'Acadie, 1627–1636.' *Revue de l'histoire des colonies.* 1955.
LOKKE, C. L. *France and the Colonial Question.* New York, 1952.
LONGNON, A. *Correspondance du Conseil Supérieur de Bourbon et de la Compagnie des Indes, 1732–1736.* Saint-Denis de la Réunion, 1933.
LOUIS-JARAY, G. *L'empire français d'Amérique.* Paris, 1937.
MARTIN, G. *La doctrine coloniale de la France en 1789.* Paris, 1934.
SCHAPPER, B. 'À propos de la doctrine et de la politique coloniales de Richelieu.' *Revue d'histoire des colonies.* 1954.
SURINDRA, NATH SEN. *The French in India.* London, 1947.
—— *Travels of the Abbé Carré in India and the Near East, 1672–1674.* 2 vols. London, Hakluyt Society, 1947–.
VIGNOLS. L. 'Early French Colonial Policy.' *Journal of Economic and Business History.* 1929.
WARD, C. *The Dutch and Swedes on the Delaware, 1609–64.* Philadelphia, 1930.
WEBER, H. *La Compagnie française des Indes.* Paris, 1904.

## V. HOLLAND

BASTIN, J. *Raffle's Ideas on the Land Rent System in Java.* The Hague, 1954.
BLONK, A. *Cornelis de Houtman en het begin onzer zeevaert of Indië, 1565–1599.* Ryswick, 1937.
BOXER, C. R. *Jan Compagnie in Japan, 1600–1817.* The Hague, 1950.
COLENBRANDER, H. T. *Jan Pieterszen Coen.* The Hague, 1934.
COOLHAAS, W. P. *Jan Pieterszen Coen.* The Hague, 1952.
DE GRAAF, H. J. *Geschiedenis van Indonesië.* The Hague, 1949.
DE JONGH, B. *Het Krijgtwezen onder de Oostindische Compagnie.* The Hague, 1950.
DE LAET, J. *Jaerlyck Verhael van de Verrichtingen der Geoctroeerde West Indische Compagnie in den thien Boeken uitgegeven.* 4 vols. The Hague, 1937.
DEN HAAN, J. C. and VAN WINTER, P. J. *Nederlandersover de Zeën.* Utrecht, 1940.
FURNIVALL, J. S. *Netherlands India.* Cambridge, 1944.
HOEGEWERFF, G. J. (ed.). *Journalem van de gendenckwaerdige zeystem van W.1. Bontekoe, 1618–25.* The Hague, 1952.
HOOGENBECK, N. H. *De rechtsvoorschriften voor de Compagnie of Oost Indie, 1595–1620.* Utrecht, 1940.

KENNING, J. *De Tweede Schipvaart der Nederlanders naar Oost-Indië onder Jacob Cornelitz van Neck en Wybrant.* 2 vols. The Hague, 1938–40.

MENKMAN, W. R. *De Nederlanders in het Caraïbische zeegebiet.* Amsterdam, 1942.

MOLLEMA, J. C. *De reis om de wereld van Olivier van Noort, 1598–1601.* Amsterdam, 1937.

PELZER, A. N. *Jan van Riebeeck, 1618–1677.* Pretoria, 1944.

PHILLIPS, J. D. *Pepper and Pirates: Adventures in the Sumatra Pepper Trade of Salem.* Boston, 1949.

STAPEL, F. W. *Corpus diplomaticorum Neerlands-Indiennis.* Amsterdam, 1943.

—— *Geschiedenis van Nederlandsch Indië.* Amsterdam, 1938–40.

—— *De Oost Indische Compagnie en Australië.* Amsterdam, 1937.

STAPEL, F. W., MARTIN, H. and HOOGENBECK, H. *Indië schrijft zyn eygen geschiedenis.* Amsterdam, 1943.

UNGER, W. S. *Het archiev der Middelburgse Commercie Compagnie.* The Hague, 1952.

—— 'Die resolutiën der Compagnie of Oost-Indië te Middelburg.' *Economisch-Historisch Jaarboek.* Amsterdam, 1947.

—— 'Het inschrijvingkregister van de Kamer Zeeland der Vereenigde Oost-Indische Compagnie.' *Economisch-Historisch Jaarboek.* Amsterdam, 1950.

VAN DAM, P. *Beschryving van de Oostindische Compagnie.* The Hague, 1943.

VAN KLAVEREN, J. J. *The Dutch Colonial System in the East Indies.* The Hague, 1953.

VOGEL, J. P. *Journal van Katelaers hofreis naar dem Groot Mogol te Lahore.* The Hague, 1937.

WARNSINCK, J. M. C. *Itinerario, voyage ofte sheepvaart van Jan Huygen van Linschoten naar Oost ofte Portugals Indien, 1579–1592.* The Hague, 1939.

## VI. PORTUGAL

GODINHO, V. M. 'A economia das Canarias nos seculos XIVe XV mos.' *Rev. de Hist.* São Paulo, 1952.

—— *Historia economica e sociale da expansao portugueza.* Vol. 1. Lisbon, 1947.

DA SILVA, J. G. *Alegaçao a favor de Companhia Portugueza da India Oriental.* Lisbon, 1950.

DE FREITAS, G. 'A Companhia Geral de Comercio do Brazil, 1649–1720.' *Rev. de Hist.* São Paulo, 1951.

DE LANNOY, C. and VAN DER LINDEN, H. *Histoire de l'expansion coloniale des peuples européens.* Vol. 1. *Spain and Portugal.* Brussels, 1907.

DIEGUES, J. M. 'As Companias Privilegiadas no comercio colonial.' *Rev. de Hist.* São Paulo, 1950.

KIEMEN, M. C. *The Indian Policy of Portugal in the Amazon region, 1614–1693.* Washington, 1954.

LAUDE, ABBÉ NORBERT. *La Compagnie d'Ostende et son activité coloniale au Bengale.* Brussels, 1944.

LIVERMORE, H. V. and ENTWISTLE, J. *Portugal and Brazil.* Oxford, 1953.

RICARD, R. *Le commerce de Berbérie et l'Organization économique de l'Empire portugais aux XVème et XVIème siècles.* Paris, Annales de l'Institut d'Études Orientales, 1936.

WELCH, S. *South Africa under King Sebastian and the Cardinal, 1557–1580.* Cape Town, 1950.

—— *Portuguese and Dutch in South Africa.* Cape Town, 1951.

## VII. SPAIN

BAGUÉ, S. *Economia de la sociedad colonial.* Buenos Aires, 1949.

BORAH, W. *Early Colonial Trade and Navigation between Mexico and Peru.* Berkeley, 1954.

BENAVENTI, M. *Relaciones de la Nueva España.* Mexico, 1956.

CHAUNU, H. and CHAUNU, P. *Séville et l'Atlantique, 1504–1650.* 3 vols. Paris, 1956.

CHEVALIER, F. *La formation des grands domaines au Mexique.* Paris, 1952.

DE AYALA, P. 'El régimen comercial de Canarias en las Indias en los siglos XVI, XVII, y XVIII.' *Revista da historia.* Madrid, 1951.

DE LUZ, F. M. *O conselho da India.* Lisbon, 1952.

FARIAS, E. A. 'La politica española sobre poblacion indigena.' *Revista nacional cultura.* Caracas, 1955.

FOLMER, H. *Franco-Spanish Rivalry in North America, 1542–1763*. Glendale, 1953.

HANKE, L. and AUGUSTIN, M. C. *Cuerpo de documentos del sigle XVI sobre el derecho de España en las Indias y las Filipinas*. Mexico, 1943.

HANKE, L. *Bartolomé de las Casas*. The Hague, 1951.

—— *The Spanish Struggle for justice in the conquest of America*. University of Pennsylvania Press, 1949.

—— *La Villa Imperial de Potosi*. Sucre, Bolivia, 1954.

HARING, C. H. *The Spanish Empire in America*. Oxford, 1947.

HOWE, W. *The Mining Guild of New Spain and its Tribunal General, 1770–1821*. Cambridge, Mass., 1949.

KONETZKE, R. *Coleccion de documentos para la historia de la formacion social de Hispano-america*. 1. *1493–1592*. Madrid, 1953.

—— *La migracion española al Rio de la Plata durante el siglo XVI*. Madrid, 1952.

—— *Das Spanische Weltreich, Grundlagen und Entstehung*. Munich, 1943.

LAVALA, S. *La encomienda indiana*. Madrid, 1935.

—— *Estudios Indianos*. Mexico, 1949.

—— *Institutiones juridicas en la conquista de America*. Madrid, 1935.

LAVALA, S. and CASTELO, N. *Fuentes para la historia del Trabajo en Nueva España, 1575–1805*. 8 vols. Mexico, 1939–46.

MADARIAGA, SALVADOR DE. *The Rise of the Spanish Empire*. London, 1948.

MERRIMAN, R. B. *The Rise of the Spanish Empire*. 3 vols. London, 1918–25.

MORALES, FR. PATRON. *Jamaica española*. Seville, 1952.

PARRY, J. H. *The Audiencia of New Galicia in the Sixteenth Century*. Cambridge, 1948.

—— *The Spanish Theory of Empire in the Sixteenth Century*. Cambridge, 1940.

PEREZ, R. D. *Historia de la colonizacion española en America*. Madrid, 1947.

—— *Recopilacion de Leyes de los Regnas de las Indias, 1680–*. 3 vols. New edition, Madrid, Consejo de la Hispanidad, 1943.

SCHÄFER, E. *Der Königlich Spanische oberste Indienrat, Consejo Real y supremo de las Indias*. Hamburg, 1936.

SCHURZ, W. L. *The Manila Galleon*. New York, 1939.

SIMÕES DE PAULA, E. 'Inventario de documentos ineditos de interêsse para a historia de São Paulo.' *Revista de Historia*. São Paulo, 1952.

SIMPSON, L. B. *The Encomienda in New Spain*. Berkeley, 1950.

SMITH, R. S. *The Spanish Guild Merchant*. Durham, N.C., 1940.

VASCONCELOS, J. *El sistemo de gobierno en la Colonia*. Mexico, 1952.

VILLENA, G. L. *Las minas de Huancavelica en los siglos XVI y XVII*. Seville, 1949.

WILGUS, C. A. *The Development of Hispanic America*. New York, 1947.

WILLIAMS, E. 'The Negro slave trade in Anglo-Spanish relations.' *Caribbean Historical Review*. Trinidad, 1950.

# CHAPTER V

## *Crops and Livestock*

ARBER, A. *Herbals*. Cambridge, 1912.

BEER, G. L. *The Old Colonial System 1660–1754*, Part I. 2 vols. New York, 1912.

BURTON, W. G. *The Potato*. London, 1948.

CARRIER, L. *The Beginnings of Agriculture in America*. New York, 1925.

CHATT, E. M. *Cocoa*. New York and London, 1953.

CHEESMAN, E. E. 'The history of introduction of some well-known West Indian Staples.' *Tropical Agriculture*. Vol. 16, p. 101, 1939.

CHEVALIER, A. and EMMANUEL, H.-F. *Le Tabac*. Paris, 1948.

CHEVALIER, A. *Le Café*. Paris, 1949.

COLLINS, J. L. *The Pineapple*. London and New York, 1960.

CROFTON, R. H. *A Pageant of the Spice Islands*. London, 1936.
CURSON, H. H. and THORNTON, R. W. 'A contribution to the study of African native
cattle.' *Onderstepoort Journal of Veterinary Science*. Vol. 7, p. 613, 1936.
DEERR, N. *The History of Sugar*. 2 vols. London, 1949–50.
FAIRHOLT, F. W. *Tobacco: Its History and Associations*. London, 1876.
FURNIVALL, J. S. *Netherlands India*. Cambridge, 1944.
GOSSE, P. *St. Helena 1502–1938*. London, 1938.
HAARER, A. E. *Modern Coffee Production*. London, 1956.
VAN HALL, C. J. J. *Cocoa*. London, 1914.
HARLER, C. R. *The Culture and Marketing of Tea* (2nd ed.). London, 1956.
HOWELL, C. E. *Tea*. London, 1951.
JONES, W. O. *Manioc in Africa*. Stanford, 1959.
KIRKPATRICK, F. A. *The Spanish Conquistadores* (2nd ed.). London, 1946.
LYDEKKER, R. *The Ox and Its Kindred*. London, 1912.
MASEFIELD, G. B. *A Short History of Agriculture in the British Colonies*. Oxford, 1950.
MCINTOSH, T. P. *The Potato: Its History, Varieties, Culture and Diseases*. Edinburgh, 1927.
MITRANY, D. *The Land and the Peasant in Rumania*. London, 1930.
PARKER, H. H. *The Hop Industry*. London, 1934.
PITMAN, F. W. *The Development of the British West Indies, 1700–1763*. New Haven and
London, 1917.
PRESTAGE, E. *The Portuguese Pioneers*. London, 1933.
PURSEGLOVE, J. W. 'History and functions of botanic gardens with special reference to
Singapore.' *Tropical Agriculture*. Vol. 34, p. 165, 1957.
RIBEIRO, O. *Geografía de España y Portugal*. Vol. V. Barcelona, 1955.
RIDLEY, H. N. *Spices*. London, 1912.
SALAMAN, R. N. *The History and Social Influence of the Potato*. Cambridge, 1949.
SHEPHARD, C. Y. 'British West Indian economic history in Imperial perspective.'
*Tropical Agriculture*. Vol. 16, p. 151, 1939.
SPRAGUE, G. F. *Corn and Corn Improvement*. New York, 1955.
U.S. Bureau of the Census. *Historical Statistics of the United States, Colonial Times to 1957*.
Washington, 1960.
VLEKKE, B. H. M. *Nusantara: A History of the East Indian Archipelago*. Cambridge, Mass.,
1943.
WADHAM, S. M. and WOOD, G. L. *Land Utilization in Australia* (2nd ed.). Melbourne,
1950.
WILLIAMSON, J. A. *A Short History of British Expansion*. London, 1927.
YOUATT, W. *The Pig*. London, 1860.

## CHAPTER VI

## *Colonial Settlement and Its Labour Problems*

### I. UNPUBLISHED DOCUMENTS

London, Public Record Office, Series CO. I.

### II. PUBLISHED WORKS

ALBUQUERQUE, AFFONSO. *See* BIRCH, W. DE G.
ANDREWS, C. M. *British Committees, Commissions and Councils of Trade and Plantations*.
Baltimore, 1908.
—— *The Colonial Period of American History*. 4 vols. New Haven, 1934–8.
ANDREWS, K. R. (ed.). *English Privateering Voyages to the West Indies, 1588–1595*. London,
Hakluyt Society, 1959.
ARBER, E. (ed.). *The Travels and Works of Captain John Smith*. 2 vols. Edinburgh, 1910.
BARBOUR, V. *Capitalism in Amsterdam in the Seventeenth Century*. Baltimore, 1950.

BARROS, R. DE. *The Origins of the British Colonial System, 1578–1660.* New York, 1908.

BEER, G. L. *The Old Colonial System.* 2 vols. New York, 1933.

BIRCH, W. DE. G. (ed.). *The Commentaries of the great Afonzo Dalboquerque.* 4 vols. London, Hakluyt Society, 1875–83.

BLAKE, J. W. *European beginnings in West Africa, 1554–1578.* London, 1937.

BONNASSIEUX, P. *Les Grandes Compagnies de Commerce.* Paris, 1892.

BORAH, W. and COOK, S. F. *The population of Central Mexico, 1531–1601.* Berkeley, 1960.

BOURNE, E. G. *Spain in America, 1450–1580.* New York, 1904.

BOXER, C. R. *The Dutch in Brazil, 1624–1654.* Oxford, 1957.

—— *Salvador de Sã and the struggle for Brazil and Angola, 1602–1686.* London, 1952.

BRAKEL, S. van. *De Hollandsche Handelscompagneen der zeventiende Eewe.* The Hague, 1908.

BURN, W. L. *The British West Indies.* London, 1951.

—— *Emancipation and Apprenticeship in the British West Indies.* London, 1937.

CASAS, BARTOLOMEO DE LAS. *Apologética historia de las Indias.* Ed. M. Serrano y Sanz. Madrid, 1909.

—— *Historia de las Indias.* 3 vols. Ed. G. de Reparaz. Madrid, 1929.

CHEMIN-DUPONTÈS, P. *Les Compagnies de Colonisation en Afrique Occidentale sous Colbert.* Paris, 1903.

CORBETT, J. S. *Drake and the Tudor Navy.* 2 vols. London, 1917.

CRAVEN, W. F. *The Southern Colonies in the Seventeenth Century, 1607–1689.* Louisiana, 1949.

CROUSE, NELLIS M. *The French Struggle for the West Indies, 1665–1713.* New York, 1943.

DAVENPORT, F. G. (ed.). *European Treaties bearing on the History of the United States.* 4 vols. Washington, 1917–37.

DAVIES, K. G. *The Royal African Company,* London, 1957.

DONNAN, E. *Documents illustrative of the History of the Slave Trade to America.* Washington, 1930–5.

DRAKE, T. E. *Quakers and Slavery in America.* New Haven, 1950.

EDMUNDSON, G. *Anglo-Dutch Rivalry during the first half of the Seventeenth Century.* Oxford, 1911.

—— 'The Dutch power in Brazil.' *English Historical Review,* XI, 1896.

FAGE, J. D. *An introduction to the history of West Africa.* Cambridge, 1955.

FISKE, J. *The Dutch and Quaker Colonies in America.* 2 vols. Boston, 1899.

FOSTER, SIR Wm. (ed.). *The Voyages of Sir James Lancaster to Brazil and the East Indies, 1591–1603.* London, Hakluyt Society, 1940.

FREYRE, GILBERTO. *The Masters and the Slaves.* New York, 1946.

—— *The Portuguese and the Tropics.* Lisbon, 1961.

FURNIVALL, J. S. *Netherlands India.* Cambridge, 1944.

GASTON-MARTIN, DR. *L'ère des négriers, Nantes au xviiie siècle.* Paris, 1931.

—— *Histoire de l'esclavage dans les colonies françaises.* Paris, 1948.

GIRAUD, M. *Histoire de la Louisiane française.* 2 vols. Paris, 1953–8.

—— *Le métis canadien.* Paris, 1945.

HANKE, L. *The First Social Experiments in America.* Cambridge, Mass., 1935.

HARDING, N. DERMOTT. *Bristol and America, a Record of the First Settlers, 1654–1685.* London [no date].

HARDY, G. *Histoire de la colonisation française* (5th ed.). Paris, 1947.

HARING, C. H. *The Spanish Empire in America.* New York, 1947.

—— *Trade and Navigation between Spain and the Indies in the time of the Hapsburgs.* Cambridge, Mass., 1918.

HARLOW, V. T. *A History of Barbados, 1625–1685.* Oxford, 1926.

HAUSSER, H. *La Pensée at l'Action Économiques du Cardinal de Richelieu.* Paris, 1944.

HIGHAM, C. S. S. *The development of the Leeward Islands under the Restoration.* Cambridge, 1921.

HOTTEN, J. C. *The original Lists of Persons of Quality . . . and others who went from Great Britain to the American Plantations.* Reprinted New York, 1931.

JACKSON, M. V. *European Powers and South-east Africa.* London, Royal Empire Society, 1942.

JENKINSON, H. *Records of the English African Companies*. Transactions of the Royal Historical Society, VI, 1912.

JOBSON, R. *The Golden Trade*. London, 1623; reprinted Teignmouth, 1904.

KELLER, A. G. *Colonisation. A Study of the founding of New Societies*. Boston, 1908.

KIRKPATRICK, F. A. *Latin America*. Cambridge, 1938.

—— *The Spanish Conquistadores*. London, 1934.

LANNOY, C. DE and VAN DER LINDEN, H. *L'Expansion coloniale des peuples Européens, Portugal et Espagne*. Brussels, 1907.

LATOURETTE, K. S. *History of the Expansion of Christianity*. 7 vols. New York, 1943–7.

LEROY-BEAULIEU, P. *De la colonisation chez les peuples modernes*. 2 vols. (6th ed.). Paris, 1908.

LIGON, R. *A true and exact history of the island of Barbados*. London, 1657.

McLACHLAN, J. O. *Trade and Peace with old Spain, 1667–1750*. Cambridge, 1940.

MACLEOD, W. C. *Contacts of Europe with the American Aborigines; European Civilization, its Origin and Development*. Ed. E. Eyre. Vol. VII. Oxford, 1939.

MADARIAGA, SALVADOR DE. *The Rise of the Spanish Empire*. London, 1947.

MARGRY, P. *Mémoires et documents pour servir à l'histoire des origines françaises des pays d'outre-mer*. 6 vols. Paris, 1879–87.

MATHIESON, W. L. *British Slavery and its Abolition*. London, 1926.

MIMS, S. L. *Colbert's West India Policy*. New Haven, 1912.

MONTCHRÉTIEN, A. DE. *Traicté de l'oeconomie politique*. Ed. Th. Funck-Brentano. Paris, 1925.

MOSES, B. *The Spanish Dependencies in South America*. 2 vols. London, 1914.

NATHAN, SIR M. 'The Gold Coast at the end of the seventeenth century under the Danes and Dutch.' *Journal of the African Society*, IV. London.

NEWTON, A. P. *The Colonising Activities of the English Puritans*. New Haven, 1914.

—— *The European Nations in the West Indies, 1493–1688*. London, 1933.

PARES, R. *War and Trade in the West Indies*. Oxford, 1936.

—— *A West India Fortune*. London, 1949.

PARRY, J. H. *Europe and a Wider World*. London, 1949.

—— *The Spanish Theory of Empire in the Sixteenth Century*. Cambridge, 1940.

PARRY, J. H. and SHERLOCK, P. M. *A Short History of the West Indies*. London, 1956.

PITMAN, F. W. *The Development of the British West Indies*. New Haven, 1917.

PRESTAGE, E. *The Portuguese Pioneers*. London, 1933.

PRICE, A. GRENFELL. 'Pioneer reactions to a poor tropical environment.' *American Geographical Review*. New York, July 1933.

—— 'White settlers in the Tropics.' *American Geographical Society*. New York, 1939.

PYM, SIR ALAN. *Colonial Agricultural Production*. London, 1946.

QUINN, D. B. (ed.). *The Roanoake Voyages*. 2 vols. London, Hakluyt Society, 1955.

RAGATZ, L. J. *The Fall of the Planter Class in the British Caribbean*. New York, 1928.

RICH, E. E. 'The population of Elizabethan England.' *Economic History Review*, 1950.

—— *The First Earl of Shaftesbury's Colonial Policy*. Transactions of Royal Historical Society, 5th ser., vol. 7, 1957.

SACO, J. A. *Historia de la esclavitud de la raza africana en el Nuevo Mundo*. 2 vols. Barcelona, 1879–93; reprinted Havana, 1938.

SAINTOYANT, J. *La colonisation Européenne du xve au xix Siècle*. 3 vols. Paris, 1938–40.

—— *La colonisation française sous l'Ancien Régime*. 2 vols. Paris, 1929.

SCOTT, W. R. *The Constitution and Finance of English, Scottish and Irish Joint-Stock Companies to 1720*. 3 vols. Cambridge, 1911–12.

SCELLE, G. *La traite négrière aux Indes de Castille*. 2 vols. Paris, 1906.

SCHOELCHER, V. (ed. A. CÉSAIRE). *Esclavage et Colonisation*. Paris, 1948.

SÉE, H. 'Commerce française à Cadix et dans l'Amerique Espagnole au xviii siècle.' *Revue d'histoire moderne*, 1928.

SHERLOCK, P. M. *See under* PARRY, J. A.

SIMPSON, L. B. *The Emancipation of the Indian Slaves and the Resettlement of the Freedmen, 1548–1555*. Berkeley, 1940.

—— *The encomienda in New Spain, 1492–1550*. Berkeley, 1929.

—— *The Repartimiento System of Native Labor in New Spain and Guatemala*. Berkeley, 1938.

SLUITER, E. 'Dutch-Spanish rivalry in the Caribbean area.' *Hispanic American Historical Review*, 1948.

SMITH, A. E. *Colonists in Bondage*. Chapel Hill, N.C., 1947.

SMITH, CAPT. JOHN. *Travels and Works*. Ed. E. Arber. 2 vols. Edinburgh, 1910.

THOMAS, DALBY. *Historical account of the Rise and Growth of the West India Colonies*. London, 1690.

VAN DER LINDEN, H. *See under* LANNOY, C. DE.

VIGNOLS, L. 'L'institution des Engagés, 1626–1774.' *Revue d'histoire économique et sociale*. Paris, 1928.

VLEKKE, B. H. M. *Nusantara, a History of the East Indian Archipelago*. Cambridge, Mass., 1943.

WEGG, J. *Antwerp, 1447–1559*. London, 1916.

WHEELER, J. *A Treatise of Commerce*. Ed. G. B. Hotchkiss, New York, Facsimile Text Society, 1931.

WHITEWAY, R. S. *The Rise of the Portuguese Power in India, 1497–1550*. London, 1899.

WILLIAMS, E. *Capitalism and Slavery*. Chapel Hill, N.C., 1944.

WILLIAMSON, J. A. *The Caribee Islands under the Proprietary Patents*. Oxford, 1926.

—— *Hawkins of Plymouth*. London, 1949.

WRIGHT, I. A. (ed.). *Documents concerning English Voyages to the Spanish Main, 1569–80*. London, Hakluyt Society, 1932.

—— *Further Documents concerning English Voyages to the Spanish Main, 1580–1603*. London, Hakluyt Society, 1951.

—— *Spanish Documents concerning English Voyages to the Caribbean, 1527–68*. London, Hakluyt Society, 1929.

WRONG, G. M. *The Rise and Fall of New France*. 3 vols. Toronto, 1928.

WYNDHAM, HON. H. A. *The Atlantic and Slavery*. Oxford, 1935.

—— *The Atlantic and Emancipation*. Oxford, 1937.

ZAVALA, S. *La encomienda indiana*. Madrid, 1935.

—— *New Viewpoints on the Spanish Colonisation of America*. Philadelphia, 1943; translation of *Ensayos sobre la colonización española en América*. Buenos Aires, 1944.

ZAVALA, S. and ZAVALA, M. C. (eds.). *Fuentes para la historia del trabajo en Nueva España*. Mexico, 1939–45.

ZOOK, G. F. *Company of Royal Adventurers Trading to Africa*. Lancaster, Pennsylvania, 1919.

# CHAPTER VII

## *Prices in Europe from 1450 to 1750*

The bibliography of the history of prices is vast and far exceeds the space allotted to this chapter. The books and articles listed here are intended to represent the published data, the classic studies and the discussions which constitute the subject.

ABEL, W. *Agrarkrisen und Agrarkonjunktur in Mitteleuropa vom 13 bis zum 19 Jahrhundert*, Berlin, 1935.

—— 'Bevölkerungsgang und Landwirtschaft im ausgehenden Mittelalter im Lichte der Preis- und Lohnbewegung.' *Schmollers Jahrbuch*, 1934.

—— *Die Wüstungen des ausgehenden Mittelalters*. Jena, 1943.

—— 'Wüstungen und Preisfall im spätmittelalterlichen Europa.' *Jahrbücher für Nationalökonomie und Statistik*. 1953.

ACHILLES, W. 'Getreidepreise und Getreidehandelsbeziehungen europäischer Räume im 16 und 17 Jahrhundert.' *Zeitschrift für Agrargeschichte und Agrarsoziologie*, 1959.

ADAMCZYK, W. *Ceny w Lublinie od XVI do końca XVIII wieku*. Lwow, 1935.

—— *Ceny w Warszawie w XVI i XVII wieku*, Lwow, 1938.

ALIVIA, G. 'Di un indice che misura l'impiego monetario dell'oro relativamente a quello dell'argento e le sue variazioni dal 1520 ad oggi.' *Giornale degli Economisti*, 1911.

ANDERSSEN, W. 'Materialien zum ragusanischen Mass- und Geldwesen.' *Vierteljahrschrift für Sozial- und Wirtschaftsgeschichte*, 1935.

ANZANO, T. DE. *Reflexiones Económico-Politicas sobre las causas de la Alteración de Precios.* Saragossa, 1768.

ARENS, F. 'Analekten zur Geschichte des spätmittelalterlichen Geldhandels in Dauphiné.' *Vierteljahrschrift für Sozial- und Wirtschaftsgeschichte*, 1928.

D'AVENEL, VICOMTE G. *Histoire économique de la propriété, des salaires, des denrées et de tous les prix en général, depuis l'an 1200 jusqu'à l'an 1800.* 7 vols. Paris, 1894–1926.

—— *Histoire de la fortune française: la fortune privée à travers sept siècles.* Paris, 1927.

BAEHREL, R. 'Economie et histoire: à propos des prix.' *Hommage à Lucien Febvre.* 2 vols. Paris, 1954.

—— 'L'exemple d'un exemple: histoire statistique et prix italiens.' *Annales: Economies, Sociétiés, Civilisations*, 1954.

—— 'Pitié pour elle et pour eux.' *Annales: Economies, Sociétiés, Civilisations*, 1955.

—— 'Prix, superficies, statistique, croissances.' *Annales: Economies, Sociétiés, Civilisations*, 1961.

—— *Une croissance: la Basse-Provence rurale depuis la fin du XVIe siècle jusqu'à la veille de la Révolution.* 1 vol. + graphs. Paris, 1961.

BANG, N. E. *Tabeller over Skibsfart og Varetransport gennem Øresund 1497–1660.* 2 parts in 3 vols. Copenhagen, 1906–22.

—— and KORST, K. *Tabeller over Skibsfart og Varetransport gennem Øresund 1661–1783 og gennem Storebaelt 1701–1748.* 2 parts in 3 vols. Copenhagen, 1930–45.

BARBIERI, G. 'Un'azienda agricola parmense ed i prezzi dei cereali intorno alla metà del secolo XVI.' *Saggi di storia economica italiana.* Bari, 1948.

BARKAN, O. L. 'Le chantier d'une grande mosquée à Istanbul au XVIe siècle.' *Annales: Economies, Sociétiés, Civilisations*, 1962.

BARTOLINI, D. 'Contribuzioni alla storia e statistica dei prezzi e salari la metida del frumento, vino ed oglio dal 1670 al 1685.' *Annali di Statistica*, 1879.

—— *Contribuzione per una storia dei prezzi e salari*, Rome, 1881.

—— 'La metida del frumento, vino ed oglio dal 1670 al 1685 nel commune di Portogruaro.' *Annali di Statistica*, 1879.

—— 'Prezzi e salari nel commune di Portogruaro durante il secolo XVI.' *Annali di Statistica*, 1878.

BATH, B. H. SLICHER VAN. *De agrarische Geschiedenis van West-Europa (500–1850).* Utrecht, 1960. (and English translation, London, 1963).

BAULANT, M. and MEUVRET, J. *Prix des céréales extraits de la mercuriale de Paris (1520–1698).* 2 vols. Paris 1960–2.

BEELE, SLOET VAN DE. 'Diagramme représentant les prix moyens des céréales au marché d'Arnhem entre le 11 novembre et le 22 février des années 1544 à 1869 dressé d'après des données officielles.' *Bijdragen tot de Statistiek van Nederland, Nieuwe Volgreeks XXVI.* The Hague, 1903.

BENNETT, M. K. 'British wheat yield per acre for seven centuries.' *Economic Journal Supplement*, III, 1934–7.

BERNARDINO, A. 'Contributo alla storia dei prezzi in Sardegna tra la fine del secolo XVIII e il principio del secolo XIX.' *Giornale degli Economisti.* 1931.

BERRY, T. S. *Western Prices before 1861.* Cambridge, Mass., 1943.

BEVERIDGE, LORD. *Prices and Wages in England from the Twelfth to the Nineteenth Century.* Vol. 1. London, 1939.

—— 'A statistical crime of the seventeenth century.' *Journal of Economic and Business History.* 1928–9.

—— 'The trade cycle in Britain before 1850.' *Oxford Economic Papers.* 1940.

—— 'Wages in the Winchester Manors.' *Economic History Review.* 1936–7.

—— 'Weather and harvest cycles.' *Economic Journal.* 1921.

—— 'Wheat measures in the Winchester Rolls.' *Economic Journal Supplement*, II, 1930–3.

—— 'Wheat prices and rainfall in western Europe.' *Journal of the Royal Statistical Society.* 1922.

—— 'The yield and price of corn in the Middle Ages.' *Economic Journal Supplement*, I, 1926–9.

BEZANSON, A., GRAY, R. D. and HUSSEY, M. *Prices in Colonial Pennsylvania 1770–1790*. Philadelphia, 1935.
—— *Wholesale Prices in Philadelphia 1784–1861*. 2 vols. Philadelphia, 1936–7.
BEZANSON, A., DALEY, B., DENISON, M., and HUSSEY, M. *Prices and Inflation during the American Revolution, Pennsylvania 1770–1790*. Philadelphia, 1951.
BEZARD, Y. *La vie rurale dans le sud de la région parisienne de 1450 à 1560*. Paris, 1929.
BLOCH, M. 'L'histoire des prix: remarques critiques.' *Annales d'histoire économique et sociale.* 1939.
—— 'La monnaie de compte.' *Annales d'histoire économique et sociale.* 1935.
—— 'Les mutations monétaires et les dettes.' *Annales d'histoire économique et sociale.* 1934.
—— 'Prix, monnaies, courbes.' *Annales: Economies, Sociétés, Civilisations.* 1946.
—— 'Le problème de la monnaie de compte.' *Annales d'histoire économique et sociale.* 1938.
—— 'Le problème de l'or au moyen âge.' *Annales d'histoire économique et sociale.* 1933.
—— 'Le salaire et les fluctuations économiques à longue période.' *Revue historique.* 1934.
BODIN, J. *La Réponse de Maistre Jean Bodin, Avocat en la Cour, au Paradoxe de Monsieur de Malestroit touchant l'enchérissement de toutes choses et le moyen d'y remédier*. Paris, 1568. Ed. E. Coornaert. Paris, 1932.
BOLDRINI, M. 'L'organizzazione annonaria di Matelica nel secolo XVII.' *Giornale degli Economisti.* 1921.
—— 'Il prezzo del pane in Matelica nel secolo XVII.' *Giornale degli Economisti.* 1921.
BORAH, W. and COOK, S. F. *Price trends of some basic commodities in Central Mexico 1531–1570*. Berkeley, 1958.
BRAUDEL, F. 'Histoire et sciences sociales: la longue durée.' *Annales: Economies, Sociétés, Civilisations.* 1958.
—— *La Méditerranée et le monde méditerranéen à l'époque de Philippe II*. Paris, 1949.
—— 'En relisant Earl J. Hamilton: de l'histoire de l'Espagne à l'histoire des prix.' *Annales: Economies, Sociétés, Civilisations.* 1951.
—— and SPOONER, F. *Les métaux monétaires et l'économie du XVIe siècle. Rapport au Congrès International des Sciences Historiques.* Rome, 1955.
BRENNER, Y. S. 'The inflation of prices in early sixteenth century England.' *Economic History Review.* 1961.
BRESCIANI-TURRONI, C. 'Movimenti di lungha durata dello sconto et dei prezzi.' *Giornale degli Economisti.* 1917.
PHELPS BROWN, E. H. and HOPKINS, S. 'Builders' wage-rates, prices and population: some further evidence.' *Economica.* 1959.
—— 'Seven centuries of building wages.' *Economica.* 1955.
—— 'Seven centuries of the prices of consumables, compared with builders' wage-rates.' *Economica,* 1956.
—— 'Seven centuries of wages and prices: some earlier estimates.' *Economica.* 1961.
—— 'Wage-rates and prices: evidence for population pressure in the sixteenth century.' *Economica.* 1957.
CAGNAZZI, L. DE SAMUELE. *Notizie dei prezzi di alcune derrate di alimento per più di due secoli. Atti della Accademia Pontaniana.* 1810.
CALÒ, G. *Indagine sulla dinamica dei prezzi in Genova durante il secolo XVII*. Vol. I, Università degli Studi di Genova, Anno Academico, 1957–8.
CASTILLO, A. 'Dette flottante et dette consolidée en Espagne de 1557 à 1600.' *Annales: Economics, Sociétés, Civilisations.* 1963.
CHABANEAU, C. 'Cartulaire du Consulat de Limoges.' *Revue de Langues Romaines.* 1895.
CHABERT, A. 'Encore la révolution des prix au XVIe siècle. *Annales: Economies, Sociétés, Civilisations.* 1957.
CHABOD, F. *Note e documenti per la storia economico-finanziaria dell'Impero di Carlo V.* Padua, 1937.
CHAUNU, H. and P. *Séville et l'Atlantique 1504 à 1650.* 11 vols. Paris, 1955–60.
CIPOLLA, C. M. *Mouvements monétaires dans l'Etat de Milan (1500–1700)*. Paris, 1952.
—— 'La prétendue "révolution des prix": réflexions sur l'expérience italienne.' *Annales: Economies, Sociétés, Civilisations.* 1955.
—— 'Storia dei prezzi e storia della moneta.' *L'Industria.* 1950.

CLARK, G. N. 'The occasion of Fleetwood's "Chronicon Preciosum".' *English Historical Review*. 1936.

COLE, A. H. *Wholesale Commodity Prices in the United States 1700–1861.* 2 vols. Cambridge, Mass., 1938.

CONIGLIO, G. *Annona e calmieri a Napoli durante la dominazione spagnuola. Archivio storico per le provincie napoletane.* 1940.

—— *Note sulla storia della politica annonaria dei Vicere spagnuoli a Napoli. Archivio storico per le provincie napoletane.* 1941.

—— *La rivoluzione dei prezzi nella città di Napoli nei secoli XVI e XVII.* Spoleto, 1952.

COORNAERT, E. *La draperie-sayetterie d'Hondschoote (XIVe–XVIIe siècles).* Paris, 1930.

CRAEYBECKX, J. 'Brood en levensstandard. Kritische nota betreffende de prijs van het brood te Antwerpen en te Brussel in de XVII en de XVIII eeuw.' *Bijdragen tot de Prijzengeschiedenis.* 1958.

DAUPHIN, V. 'Recherches pour servir à l'histoire des prix des céréales et du vin en Anjou sous l'Ancien Régime, XIe siècle à 1789.' *Revue de l'Intendance.* 1934.

DELATTE, I. 'Prix et salaires en Hainaut au XVIe siècle.' *Annales du Cercle Archéologique de Mons.* 1937–8.

DELUMEAU, J. *Vie économique et sociale de Rome dans la seconde moitié du XVIe siècle.* 2 vols. Paris, 1957–9.

DENIS, H. 'Les index numbers au XVIe siècle en Flandre.' *Annales de l'Institut des Sciences Sociales.* 1900.

DESMAREZ, G. 'Notice critique pour servir à l'histoire des prix.' *Revue de l'Université de Bruxelles.* 1901–2.

DEWEY, E. R. and DAKIN, E. F. *Cycles: the Science of Prediction.* New York, 1950.

DIECK, A. 'Lebensmittelpreise in Mitteleuropa und im Vorderen Orient vom 12 bis 17 Jahrhundert.' *Zeitschrift für Agrargeschichte und Agrarsoziologie.* 1955.

DITTMANN, O. 'Die Getreidepreise in der Stadt Leipzig im XVII, XVIII und XIX Jahrhundert.' *Mitteilungen des Statistische Amtes der Stadt Leipzig.* 1891.

DREYFUS, F.-G. 'Beitrag zu den Preisbewegungen im Oberrheingebiet im 18 Jahrhundert.' *Vierteljahrschrift für Sozial- und Wirtschaftsgeschichte.* 1960.

—— 'Prix et population à Trèves et à Mayenne au XVIIIe siècle.' *Revue d'histoire économique et sociale.* 1956.

DUPRÉ DE SAINT-MAUR, N. F. *Essai sur les monnaies, ou réflexions sur le rapport entre l'argent et les denrées.* Paris, 1746.

—— *Recherches sur la valeur des monnaies et sur les prix des grains, avant et après le Concile de Francfort.* Paris, 1762.

EINAUDI, L. (ed.). 'Dei criteri informatori della storia dei prezzi.' *Rivista storia economica.* 1940.

—— *Paradoxes inédits du seigneur de Malestroit touchant les monnoyes avec la réponse du Président de la Tourette.* Turin, 1937.

ELSAS, M. J. 'Price data from Munich 1500–1700.' *Economic Journal Supplement*, III, 1934–7.

—— *Umriss einer Geschichte der Preise und Löhne in Deutschland vom ausgehenden Mittelalter bis zum Beginn des neunzehnten Jahrhunderts.* 2 vols. in 3 parts Leiden, 1936–49.

ESPEJO, C. *Carestiá de la Vida en el Siglo XVI, Revista de Archivos, Bibliotecas y Museos,* 3ª Época, xxv.

FALKE, J. 'Geschichtliche Statistik der Preise im Königreich Sachsen.' *Jahrbücher für Nationalökonomie und Statistik.* 1869–70.

FANFANI, A. 'Un effetto economico della scoperta dell'America.' *Rivista internazionale di Scienze Sociale.* 1937.

—— *Indagine sulla rivoluzione dei prezzi.* Milan, 1940.

—— 'La rivoluzione dei prezzi a Milano nel XVI e XVII secolo.' *Giornale degli Economisti.* 1932.

FARAGLIA, N. F. 'Storia dei prezzi in Napoli dal 1131 al 1860.' *Atti del Reale Istituto di Incoraggiamento.* 1878.

FEBVRE, L. 'L'afflux de métaux d'Amérique et les prix à Séville.' *Annales d'histoire économique et sociale.* 1930.

—— 'Le problème historique des prix.' *Annales d'histoire économique et sociale.* 1930.

FEBVRE L. 'Or d'Amérique et capitalisme.' *Annales d'histoire économique et sociale.* 1931.

FELIX, D. 'Profit inflation and industrial growth: the historic record and contemporary analogies.' *Quarterly Journal of Economics,* 1956.

FETTEL, J. *Die Getreide- und Brotversorgung der freien Reichstadt Esslingen, 1350–1802.* Stuttgart, 1930.

FISHER, F. J. 'Commercial trends and policies in the sixteenth century.' *Economic History Review.* 1940.

FLEETWOOD, W. *Chronicon Preciosum: or, an account of English money, the price of corn and other commodities for the last 600 years in a letter to a Student in the University of Oxford.* London, 1707.

FOURASTIÉ, J. 'Quelques réflexions sur le mouvement des prix et le pouvoir d'achat des salaires en France depuis le XVIIIe siècle.' *Bulletin de la Société d'Histoire Moderne.* 1953.

FRANCHINI, V. *Contributo alla storia dei prezzi in Italia.* Rome, 1928.

FRIEDENBERG, P. 'Die schlesischen Getreidepreise vor 1740.' *Zeitschrift des Vereins für Geschichte Schlesiens.* 1906.

FRIEDMAN, M. (ed.). *Studies in the Quantity Theory of Money.* Chicago, 1956.

FRIIS, A. 'An inquiry into the relations between economic and financial factors in the sixteenth and seventeenth centuries.' *Scandinavian Economic History Review.* 1953.

—— and GLAMANN, K. *A History of Prices and Wages in Denmark, 1660–1800.* Copenhagen, 1958.

FURTAK, T. *Ceny w Gdańsku w latach 1701–1815.* Lwow, 1935.

GILBOY, E. W. *Wages in Eighteenth Century England.* Cambridge, Mass., 1934.

GIOIA, M. *Su commercio de'commestibili e caro prezzo del vitto.* Avignon, 1830.

GIRALT RAVENTÓS, E. 'En torno al precio del trigo en Barcelona durante el siglo XVI.' *Hispania,* 1958.

GIRARD, A. 'La guerre des monnaies.' *Revue de Synthèse.* 1940–5.

GODARD, J. 'Contribution à l'étude de l'histoire du commerce des grains à Douai du XIVe au XVIIe siècle.' *Revue du Nord.* 1944.

GODINHO, V. M. *Prix et monnaies au Portugal.* Paris, 1955.

GOUBERT, P. *Beauvais et le Beauvaisis de 1600 à 1730: contribution à l'histoire sociale de la France du XVIIe siècle.* Paris, 1960.

GRIZIOTTI-KRETSCHMANN, J. *Il problema del trend secolare nelle fluttuazioni dei prezzi.* Pavia, 1935.

GUITTON, H. *Essai sur la loi de King.* Bordeaux, 1938.

HABAKKUK, H. J. 'The long term rate of interest and the price of land in the seventeenth century.' *Economic History Review.* 1952–3.

HAMILTON, E. J. 'American treasure and Andalusian prices 1503–1660.' *Journal of Economic and Business History.* 1928.

—— *American Treasure and the Price Revolution in Spain 1501–1650.* Cambridge, Mass., 1934.

—— 'American treasure and the rise of capitalism (1500–1700).' *Economica.* 1929.

—— 'The decline of Spain.' *Economic History Review.* 1937–8.

—— 'The History of Prices before 1750.' *XIe Congrès International des Sciences Historiques, Rapports I.* Stockholm, 1960.

—— 'The mercantilism of Geronimo de Uztáriz: a re-examination 1670–1732.' *Economics, Sociology and the Modern World.* 1935.

—— 'Monetary problems in Spain and Spanish America 1751–1800.' *Journal of Economic History.* 1944.

—— *Money, Prices and Wages in Valencia, Aragon and Navarre, 1351–1500.* Cambridge, Mass., 1936.

—— 'Prices and wages at Paris under John Law's system.' *Quarterly Journal of Economics.* 1936–7.

—— 'Prices and wages in Southern France under John Law's system.' *Economic Journal Supplement,* III, 1934–7.

—— 'Prices as a factor in business growth: prices and progress.' *Journal of Economic History,* 1952.

HAMILTON E. J. 'Profit inflation and the Industrial Revolution, 1751–1800.' *Quarterly Journal of Economics*. 1941–2.
—— 'Spanish mercantilism before 1700.' *Facts and Factors in Economic History*. Cambridge, Mass., 1932.
—— 'The use and misuse of Price History.' *Journal of Economic History*. 1944 (Supplement).
—— 'Wages and subsistence on Spanish treasure ships 1503–1660.' *Journal of Political Economy*. 1929.
—— *War and Prices in Spain, 1651–1800*. Cambridge, Mass., 1947.
HAMMARSTRÖM, I. 'The "Price Revolution" of the sixteenth century: some Swedish evidence.' *Scandinavian Economic History Review*. 1957.
HANAUER, A. *Etudes économiques sur l'Alsace ancienne et moderne*. 2 vols. Paris and Strasbourg, 1876–8.
HARING, C. H. 'American gold and silver production in the first half of the sixteenth century.' *Quarterly Journal of Economics*. 1914–15.
HARSIN, P. *Les doctrines monétaires et financières en France du XVIe au XVIIIe siècle*. Paris, 1928.
HAUSER, H. 'Un comité international d'enquête sur l'histoire des prix.' *Annales d'histoire économique et sociale*. 1930.
—— 'La question des prix et des monnaies en Bourgogne dans la seconde moitié du XVIe siècle.' *Annales de Bourgogne*. 1932.
—— *Recherches et documents sur l'histoire des prix en France, 1500–1800*. Paris, 1936.
HECKSCHER, E. *Sveriges ekonomiska historia från Gustav Vasa*. 2 vols. Stockholm, 1935–6.
HELFERICH, J. A. *Von den periodischen Schwankungen im Wert der edele Metalle von der Entdeckung Amerikas bis zum Jahr 1830*. Nürnberg, 1843.
—— 'Württembergische Getreide- und Weinpreise von 1456 bis 1628; ein Beitrag zur Geschichte der Geldentwertung nach der Entdeckung von Amerika.' *Zeitschrift für die gesammte Staatswissenschaft*. 1858.
HELLEINER, K. F. 'The vital revolution reconsidered.' *Canadian Journal of Economics and Political Science*. 1957.
HOLTROP, M. W. 'Theories of the velocity of circulation of money in earlier economic literature.' *Economic Journal Supplement*, I, 1926–9.
HON-FIRNBERG, H. *Lohnarbeiter und freie Lohnarbeit im Mittelalter und zu Beginn der Neuzeit*. Baden b. Wien, 1935.
HOSZOWSKI, S. 'L'Europe centrale devant la révolution des prix.' *Annales: Economies, Sociétés, Civilisations*. 1961.
—— *Ceny we Lwowie w latach 1701–1914*. Lwow, 1934.
—— *Ceny we Lwowie w XVI i XVII wieku*. Lwow, 1928 (and French translation, Paris, 1954).
HOUTTE, H. VAN. *Documents pour servir à l'histoire des prix de 1381 à 1794*. Académie Royale de Belgique, Commission Royale d'Histoire. Brussels, 1902.
HOUTTE, J. A. VAN. *Het economisch Verval van het Zuiden, Algemeene Geschiedenis der Nederlanden*. Vol. v. 1952.
HUMBOLDT, F. H. A. VON. 'Uber die Schwankungen der Gold produktion mit Rücksicht auf staatswirtschaftliche Probleme.' *Deutsche Vierteljahrschrift*. 1838.
HUTCHINS, B. L. 'Notes towards the history of London wages.' *Economic Journal*. (IX) 1899 and (X) 1900.
IMBERT, G. *Des mouvements de longue durée Kondratieff*. Aix-en-Provence. 1959.
INAMA-STERNEGG, K. TH. VON. 'Quellen der historischen Preisstatistik.' *Statistischen Monatsschrift*. 1886.
JACOB, W. *An Historical Inquiry into the Production and Consumption of Precious Metals*. 2 vols. London, 1831.
JANAČEK, J. *Rudofinské drahotni řády, příspěvek k dějinám cenové revoluce v Čechách*. Prague, 1957.
JOUANNE, 'Les monographies normandes et l'histoire des prix.' *Normania*. 1931.
JUDGES, A. V. 'Scopi e metodi della storia dei prezzi.' *Rivista Storia Italiana*. 1951.
KELLER, L. 'Zur Geschichte der Preisbewegung in Deutschland während der Jahre 1466–1525.' *Jahrbücher für Nationalökonomie und Statistik*. 1879.

KELSALL, R. K. 'Wages of northern farm labourers in mid-eighteenth century.' *Economic History Review*. 1937–8.

KELTER, E. *Geschichte der obrigkeitlichen Preisregelung*. Jena, 1935.

KERHUEL, M. *Les mouvements de longue durée des prix*. Rennes, 1935.

KERRIDGE, E. 'The movement of rent, 1540–1640.' *Economic History Review*. 1953–4.

KIRKLAND, J. *Three Centuries of Prices of Wheat, Flour and Bread*. London, 1917.

KNOOP, D. and JONES, G. P. 'Masons' wages in medieval England.' *Economic Journal Supplement*, II, 1930–3.

KONDRATIEFF, N. D. 'Die langen Wellen der Konjunktur.' *Archiv für Sozialwissenschaft und Sozialpolitik*. 1926.

KOENIGSBERGER, H. G. 'Property and the price revolution.' *Economic History Review*. 1956.

KOPPE, W. 'Zur Preisrevolution des 16 Jahrhunderts in Holstein.' *Zeitschrift der Gesellschaft für Schleswig-Holsteinische Geschichte*. 1955.

KUZNETS, S. *Secular Movements in Production and Prices*. Boston, 1930.

—— 'Statistical trends and historical changes.' *Economic History Review*. 1950–1.

LABROUSSE, C. E. *Esquisse du mouvement des prix et des revenues en France au XVIIIe siècle*. 2 vols. Paris, 1933.

—— 'Observations complémentaires sur les sources et la méthodologie pratique de l'histoire des prix et des salaires au XVIIIe siècle.' *Revue d'histoire économique et sociale*. 1938.

—— 'Le prix du blé en France au XVIIIe siècle.' *Revue d'histoire économique et sociale*. 1931.

—— *La crise de l'économie française à la fin de l'Ancien Régime et au début de la Révolution*. Vol. I. Paris, 1944.

—— 'Le prix du blé en France dans la seconde moitié du 18e siècle d'après les états statistiques du Contrôle Général.' *Revue d'histoire économique et sociale*. 1930.

—— 'Quelques observations sur la lecture des courbes économiques.' *Annales historiques de la Révolution Française*. 1937.

—— Un siècle et demi de hausse des prix agricoles (1726–1873). *Revue Historique*. 1940.

LATOUCHE, R. 'Le mouvement des prix en Dauphiné sous l'Ancien Régime.' *Annales de l'Université de Grenoble*. 1935.

—— 'Le prix du blé à Grenoble du XVe au XVIIIe siècle.' *Revue d'histoire économique et sociale*. 1932.

LEBER, J. M. C. *Mémoires sur l'appréciation de la fortune privée au Moyen Age relativement aux variations des valeurs monétaires et du pouvoir commercial de l'argent*. Paris, 1844.

LE BRANCHU, J.-Y. *Ecrits notables sur la monnaie, XVIe siècle, de Copernic à Davanzati*. 2 vols. Paris, 1934.

—— 'La théorie quantitative de la monnaie au XVIe siècle.' *Revue d'économie politique*. 1934.

LEHR, J. *Beiträge zur Statistik der Preise insbesondere des Geldes und des Holzes*. Frankfurt a. M., 1885.

LEFEBVRE, G. 'Le mouvement des prix et les origines de la Révolution française.' *Annales d'histoire économique et sociale*. 1937.

LENNARD, R. 'Statistics of corn yield in medieval England.' *Economic Journal Supplement*, III, 1934–7.

LESCURE, J. *Hausses et baisses de prix de longue durée*. Paris, 1933.

LEVASSEUR, E. 'Une méthode pour mesurer la valeur de l'argent: des variations de la valeur de l'argent au seizième siècle.' *Journal des Economistes*. 1856.

—— 'Les prix, aperçu de l'histoire économique de la valeur et du revenu de la terre du commencement du XIIIe à la fin du XVIIIe siècle, avec un appendice sur le prix du froment et sur les disettes, depuis l'an 1200 jusqu'à l'an 1891.' *Mémoires de la Société Nationale d'Agriculture de France*. 1896.

—— *Rapport sur deux concours pour le prix Rossi*. Paris, 1894.

—— 'Tableaux des prix de céréales à Paris.' *Séances et Travaux de l'Académie des Sciences Morales et Politiques*. 1912.

LEWIS, G. R. *The Stannaries*. Cambridge, Mass., 1924.

LEXIS, W. 'Beiträge zur Statistik der Edelmetalle.' *Jahrbücher für Nationalökonomie und Statistik*. 1879.

LIAUTEY, A. *La hausse des prix et la lutte contre la vie chère en France au 16e siècle*. Paris, 1921.

Livet, G. *L'Intendance d'Alsace sous Louis XIV, 1648–1715*. Strasbourg, 1956.

Lloyd, W. F. *Prices of Corn in Oxford in the beginning of the Fourteenth Century; also from the year 1583 to the Present Time*. Oxford, 1830.

Lonardo, P. *Contributo alla storia dei prezzi nelle provincie napoletane*. Naples, 1904.

Maas, W. 'Zur Geschichte der Preise in Polen, Österreich und Oberdeutschland.' *Vierteljahrschrift für Sozial- und Wirtschaftsgeschichte*. 1938.

McArthur, E. A. 'A fifteenth-century assessment of wages.' *English Historical Review*. 1898.

Maddalena, A. de. *Prezzi e aspetti di mercato in Milano durante il secolo XVII*. Milan, 1950.

Magoldi, V. and Fabris, R. 'Notizie sui salaie e sui prezzi di alcune derrate alimentari e prodotti industriali nelle citte di Milano, Venezia, Genova e Firenze nei secoli XIII al XVIII.' *Annali di Statistica*. 1878.

Mandich, G. 'Formule monetarie veneziane del periodo 1619–1650.' *Il Risparmio*. 1957.

Mankov, A. G. *Le mouvement des prix dans l'Etat Russe du XVIe siècle* (French translation). Paris, 1957.

Mantellier, P. *Mémoire sur la valeur des principales denrées et et marchandises qui se vendaient ou se consommaient en la ville d'Orléans au cours des XIVe, XVe, XVIe, XVIIe, et XVIIIe siècles, Mémoires de la Société Archéologique de l'Orléanais*. Vol. v, 1862.

Massa, C. *Il prezzo del grano e dell'orzo in terra di Bari (1419–1727). Atti dell'Accademia Pontaniana*. 1908.

—— *I salari agricoli in terra di Bari (1447–1733). Atti dell'Accademia Pontaniana*. 1911.

Mazières, L. de. 'Note sur les prix en France.' *La Science Historique*. 1922.

Mensi, F. 'Zur Geschichte der Preise und Löhne in Steiermark.' *Zeitschrift des Historischen Vereines für Steiermark*. 1935.

Messance, F. *Réflexions sur la valeur du blé tant en France qu'en Angleterre, depuis 1674 jusqu'en 1764* (printed as an appendix to *Recherches sur la Population*). Paris, 1766.

Meuvret, J. 'Conjoncture et crise au XVIIe siècle: l'exemple des prix milanais.' *Annales: Economies, Sociétés, Civilisations*. 1953.

—— *La géographie des prix des céréales et les anciennes économies européennes, prix méditerranéens, prix continentaux, prix atlantiques à la fin du XVIIe siècle. Revista da Economia*, vol. IX.

—— *L'histoire des prix des céréales en France dans la seconde moitié du XVIIe siècle, sources et publication, Mélanges d'Histoire Sociale*. 1955.

—— *Les mouvements des prix de 1661 à 1715 et leurs répercussions, Communication faite à la Société de Statistique de Paris*. 1944.

—— 'Simple mise au point.' *Annales: Economics, Sociétés, Civilisations*. 1955.

Mira, G. *Contributo per una storia sui prezzi in alcune provincie delle Puglie. Atti della Società Italiana di Statistica*. 1942.

—— *Un episodio di politica annonaria: importazione di grani a Como nel 1628. Aspetti dell'economia comasca*. Como, 1939.

—— 'I prezzi dei cereali a Como dal 1612 al 1658.' *Rivista Internazionale di Scienze Sociale*. 1941.

Moreyra y Paz Soldan, M. *En torno a dos valiosos documentos sobre Potosi*. Lima, 1953.

Nadal Oller, J. 'La revolución de los precios españoles en el siglo XVI. *Hispania*. 1959.

Naudé, W. *Die Getreidehandelspolitik der Europäischen Staaten vom bis zum 18 Jahrhundert, I—Die Getreidehandelspolitik, Acta Borussica, 1896; II—Die Getreidehandelspolitik und Kriegsmagazinverwaltung Brandenburg-Preussens bis 1740* (W. Naudé and G. Schmoller), *Acta Borussica*, 1901; *III—1740–1756* (G. Schmoller, W. Naudé and A. Skalweit), *Acta Borussica*, 1910; *IV—1756–1806* (A. Skalweit), *Acta Borussica*, 1931.

Nef, J. U. 'A comparison of industrial growth in France and England from 1540 to 1640.' *Journal of Political Economy*. 1936.

—— 'The Industrial Revolution reconsidered.' *Economic History Review*. 1943.

—— 'Prices and industrial capitalism in France and England (1540–1640).' *Economic History Review*. 1937.

—— 'Silver production in Central Europe 1450–1618.' *Journal of Political Economy*. 1941.

NIELSEN, A. 'Dänische Preise 1650–1750.' *Jahrbücher für Nationalökonomie und Statistik.* 1906.

NOTTIN, L. *Recherches sur les variations des prix dans le Gâtinais du XVIe au XIXe siècle.* Paris, 1935.

PARENTI, G. *Prezzi e mercato del grano a Siena (1546–1765).* Florence, 1942.

—— *Prime ricerche sulla rivoluzione dei prezzi in Firenze.* Florence, 1939.

PELC, J. *Ceny w Gdańsku w XVI i XVII wieku.* Lwow, 1937.

—— *Ceny w Krakowie w latach 1369–1600.* Lwow, 1935.

PESÁK, V. *Polské prace a methody pře studi u historie cen, Věstnik Československé Akademie Zemědělska.* 1935.

PETINO, A. *I prezzi del grano, dell'orzo, dell'olio, del vino, del cacio a Catania dal 1512 al 1630.* Milan, 1949.

—— *La questione del commercio dei grani in Sicilia nel Settecento.* Catania, 1946.

PHINNEY, J. T. 'Gold production and the price level: the Cassel three per cent.' *Quarterly Journal of Economics.* 1933.

POPELKA, F. 'Die Bewegung der Fleischpreise in Österreich im 16 Jahrhundert.' *Zeitschrift des Historischen Vereines für Steiermark.* 1935.

—— 'Die Lebensmittelpreise und Löhne in Graz vom 16 bis zum 18 Jahrhundert.' *Vierteljahrschrift für Sozial- und Wirtschaftsgeschichte.* 1930.

POSTHUMUS, N. W. *De Geschiedenis van de Leidsche Lakenindustrie.* 3 vols. The Hague, 1908–39

—— *Inquiry into the History of Prices in Holland.* 2 vols. Leiden, 1946–65.

PRIBRAM, A. F. *Materialien zur Geschichte der Preise und Löhne in Österreich.* Vol. 1. Vienna, 1938.

QUENEDEY, R. *Les prix des matériaux et de la maind'oeuvre à Rouen du XIVe au XVIIIe siècle.* Rouen, 1927.

QUIRING, H. *Die Geschichte des Goldes.* Stuttgart, 1948.

RAVEAU, P. *L'agriculture et les classes paysannes.* Paris, 1926.

—— 'La crise des prix au XVIe siècle en Poitou.' *Revue Historique.* 1929.

—— *Essai sur la situation économique et l'état social en Poitou au XVIe siècle.* Paris, 1931.

—— *La vie économique en Poitou au XVIe siècle.* Poitiers, 1917.

ROBINSON, W. C. 'Money, population and economic change in late medieval Europe. *Economic History Review.* 1959, and Note by M. M. Postan, *ibidem.*

ROGERS, J. E. THOROLD. *A History of Agriculture and Prices in England From the Year after the Oxford Parliament (1259) to the Commencement of the Continental War (1793).* 7 vols. Oxford, 1866–1902.

—— *Six Centuries of Work and wages.* 2 vols. London, 1884.

ROMANO, R. *Commerce et prix du blé à Marseille au XVIIIe siècle.* Paris, 1956.

—— 'Une économie coloniale: le Chili au XVIIIe siècle.' *Annales: Economies, Sociétés, Civilisations.* 1960.

—— 'Tra XVI e XVII secolo. Una crisi economica: 1619–1622.' *Rivista Storica Italiana.* 1962.

ROSCHER, W. *Über Kornhandel und Theuerungspolitik.* Stuttgart, 1852.

ROSSI, E. and ARCARI, P. 'I prezzi a Genova dal XII al XV secolo.' *La Vita Economica Italiana.* 1933.

SACHS, W. 'Agricultural conditions in the Northern Colonies before the Revolution.' *Journal of Economic History.* 1953.

SCHMOLLER, G. 'Die historische Entwicklung des Fleischconsums sowie der Vieh- und Fleischpreise in Deutschland, I, Die Zeit bis zum 30 jährigen Kriege.' *Zeitschrift für die gessamte Staatswissenschaft.* 1871.

—— *Die historischer Lohnbewegung von 1300–1900 und ihren Ursachen.* Berlin, 1902.

SCHOLLIERS, E. 'De levensstandaard der arbeiders op het einde der XVIe eeuw te Antwerpen.' *Tijdschrift voor Geschiedenis.* 1955.

SCHUMPETER, E. B. 'English prices and public finance, 1660–1822.' *Review of Economic Statistics.* 1938.

SELLA, D. 'Les mouvements longs de l'industrie lainière.' *Annales: Economies, Sociétés, Civilisations.* 1957.

SIEGEL, S. *Ceny w Warszawie w latach 1701–1815.* Lwow, 1936.

SILLEM, J. A. *Tabellen van marktprijzen van graanen te Utrecht in de jaaren 1393 tot 1644, Verhandelingen der Koninklijke Akademie van Wetenschappen te Amsterdam.* Amsterdam, 1901.

SHAW, W. *The History of the Currency, 1252–1894.* London, 1895.

SIMIAND, F. *Les fluctuations économiques à longue période et la crise mondiale.* Paris, 1932.

—— 'La monnaie, réalité sociale.' *Annales sociologiques.* 1934.

—— *Recherches anciennes et nouvelles sur le mouvement général des prix du XVIe au XIXe siècle.* Paris, 1932.

SOETBEER, A. *Edelmetall-Produktion und Wertverhaltniss zwischen Gold und Silber zeit der Entdeckung Amerikas bis zur Gegenwart.* Gotha, 1879.

—— *Materialen zur Erläuterung und Beurteilungen der wirtschaftlichen Edelmetallverhältnisse und der Währungsfrage.* Gotha, 1881 and 1886.

SPOONER, F. C. *L'économie mondiale et les frappes monétaires en France 1493–1680.* Paris, 1956.

—— *Secular Price Movements and Problems in Capital Formation, Report to the Congress on Economic History, Aix-en-Provence.* 1962.

STEFFEN, G. *Studien zur Geschichte der englischen Lohnarbeiter* (German translation). 3 vols. Stuttgart, 1901–1905.

TENENTI, A. and VIVANTI, C. 'Le film d'un grand système de navigation: les galères vénitiennes XIVe–XVIe siècles.' *Annales: Economies, Sociétés, Civilisations.* 1961.

TOMASZEWSKI, E. *Ceny w Krakowie w latach 1601–1795.* Lwow, 1934.

TOOKE, T. and NEWMARCH, W. *A History of Prices and of the State of the Circulation.* 6 vols. London, 1838–57.

USHER, A.P. 'The general course of wheat prices in France 1350–1788.' *Review of Economic Statistics.* 1930.

—— 'Prices of wheat and commodity price indexes for England 1259–1930.' *Review of Economic Statistics.* 1931.

VERHAEGEN, A. 'Note sur le travail et les salaires en Belgique au XVIIIe siècle.' *Bulletin de l'Institut de Recherches Economiques et Sociales de l'Université de Louvain.* 1953.

VERLINDEN, C., CRAEYBECKX, J., and SCHOLLIERS, E. 'Mouvements des prix et des salaires en Belgiques au XVIe siècle.' *Annales: Economies, Sociétés, Civilisations.* 1955.

VERLINDEN, C. (director), edited by J. Craeybeckx. *Dokumenten voor de Geschiedenis van Prijzen en Lonen in Vlaanderen en Brabant XVe–XVIIIe eeuw.* Bruges, 1959.

VETTIGER, M. *Die agrare Preispolitik des Kantons Basel im 18 Jahrhundert.* Weinfelden, 1941.

VIGNOLS, L. 'Salaires des ouvriers et prix des matériaux employés aux travaux publics à Saint-Malo 1737–1744 et 1755–1762.' *Annales de Bretagne,* 1931.

VILAR, P. 'Elan urbain et mouvement des salaires: le cas de Barcelone au XVIIIe siècle.' *Revue d'histoire économique et sociale.* 1950.

—— 'Histoire des prix, histoire générale.' *Annales: Economies, Sociétés, Civilisations.* 1949.

—— 'Problems of the formation of capitalism.' *Past and Present.* 1956.

—— 'Remarques sur l'histoire des prix.' *Annales: Economies, Sociétés, Civilisations.* 1961.

WÄCHTER, H. H. *Ostpreussiche Domänenvorwerke im 16 und 17 Jahrhundert.* Würzburg, 1958.

WAILLY, N. DE. *Mémoire sur les variations de la livre tournois depuis le règne de Saint Louis jusqu'à l'établissement de la monnaie décimale.* Paris, 1857.

WALTHER, A. 'Geldwert in der Geschichte.' *Vierteljahrschrift für Sozial- und Wirtschaftsgeschichte.* 1912.

WARREN, G. F. and PEARSON, A. F. *Wholesale Prices for 213 years, 1720 to 1932, Memoir No. 142, Agricultural Experiment Station, Cornell University.* Ithaca, 1932.

WASCHINSKI, E. *Währung, Preisenwicklung und Kaufkraft des Gelds in Schleswig Holstein von 1226–1864.* 2 vols. Neumünster, 1952–9.

WERWECKE, H. VAN. 'Monnaie de compte et monnaie réelle.' *Revue Belge de Philologie et Histoire.* 1934.

WIEBE, G. *Zur Geschichte der Preisrevolution des XVI und XVII Jahrhunderts.* Leipzig, 1895.

YOUNG, A. *An Inquiry into the Progressive Value of Money in England.* London, 1812.

—— *An Enquiry into the Rise of Prices in Europe.* London, 1815.

Zöpfl, G. 'Eine ältere Getreidepreisstatistik.' *Jahrbücher für Nationalökonomie und Statistik.* 1895.

Zolla, D. 'Les variations du revenu et du prix des terres en France au XVIIe et XVIIIe siècles.' *Annales de l'Ecole libre des Sciences Politiques.* 1893–4.

# CHAPTER VIII

## Trade, Society and the State

*Algemene Geschiedenis der Nederlanden* (1954). Vols. VII and VIII. (Chapters by J. G. van Dillen and J. de Vries.)

Aström, S. E. *From Cloth to Iron. The Anglo-Baltic Trade in the late Seventeenth Century.* 1963.

Andrews, C. M. *The Colonial Period.* 1912.

Ashley, M. P. *Commercial Policy under the Cromwellian Proctetorate.* 1934.

Bailyn, B. *The New England Merchants in the Seventeenth Century.* 1955.

Baasch, E. *Holländische Wirtschaftsgeschichte.* 1927.

Beer, G. L. *The Old Colonial System.* 2 vols. 1912.

Boissonnade, P. *Colbert.* 1932.

Braudel, F. *La Mediterranée.* 1949.

Christensen, A. E. *Dutch Trade to the Baltic about 1600.* 1941.

Cipolla, C. 'The decline of Italy.' *Economic History Review.* 1952.

Clark, G. N. *A Guide to English Commercial Statistics, 1696–1782.* 1938.

Coleman, D. C. 'Eli Heckscher and the Idea of Mercantilism.' *Scandinavian Economic History Review.* 1957.

Cole, C. W. *French Mercantilist Doctrines before Colbert.* 1931.

—— *Colbert and a Century of French Mercantilism.* 2 vols. 1939.

—— *French Mercantilism, 1683–1700.* 1943.

—— and Clough, S. B. *Economic History of Europe.* 1941.

Cossa, L. *Guide to the Study of Political Economy* (trans. W. Jevons). 1880.

—— *Guide to the Study of Political Economy* (trans. L. Dyer). 1893.

Cory, J. *An Essay on the State of England.* 1695.

Davies, K. G. *The Royal African Company.* 1936.

Davis, R. *The Rise of the English Shipping Industry in the Seventeenth and Eighteenth Centuries.* 1962.

De Witt, J. *The True Interest and Political Maxims of the Republic.* 1702.

Decker, M. *An Essay on the Causes of the Decline of the Foreign Trade.* 1739.

De Roover, R. *Gresham on Foreign Exchange.* 1949.

Dorn, W. L. *Competition for Empire, 1740–1763.* 1940.

Elliott, J. H. 'The decline of Spain.' *Past and Present.* 1961.

Freudenberger, H. *The Waldstein Woollen Mill. Noble Entrepreneurship in Eighteenth Century Bohemia.* 1962.

Friis, A. *Alderman Cockayne's Project and the Cloth Trade.* 1927.

Genovesi, A. *Studi in Onore di.* 1956.

Gray, A. *Development of Economic Doctrine.* 1948.

Hammerström, I. 'The price revolution in the sixteenth century.' *Scandinavian Economic History Review.* 1957.

Heaton, H. *Economic History of Europe.* Revised ed., 1948.

Heckscher, E. *Economic History of Sweden.* Trans. G. Ohlin, 1954.

—— *Mercantilism.* 2 vols. Revised ed., 1955.

Harper, L. A. *The English Navigation Laws.* 1939.

Hauser, H. 'The characteristic features of French economic history.' *Economic History Review.* 1933.

Henderson. W. O. *The State and the Industrial Revolution in Prussia* (1958).

HOUTTE, J. A. VAN. 'Anvers aux XVe et XVIe siècles.' *Annales*. 1961.
HUME, D. *Works*. 4 vols. Ed. by T. H. Green and T. H. Grose, 1874.
JUDGES, A. V. 'The idea of the mercantile state.' *Trans. Royal Historical Society*. 1939.
KÜLISCHER, J. *Allgemeine Wirtschaftsgeschichte*. Vol. II. 1929.
LANE, F. and RIEMERSMA, J. C. *Enterprise and Secular Change*. 1953.
LETWIN, W. *Sir Josiah Child, Merchant Economist*. 1959.
LÜTGE, F. *Deutsche Sozial- und Wirtschaftsgeschichte*. 1960.
LUZZATO, G. *An Economic History of Italy*. Trans. P. Jones. 1961.
MANDEVILLE, B. *The Fable of the Bees or Private Vices, Publick Benefits*. 1924
MACGREGOR, D. H. *Economic Thought and Policy*. 1949.
McCLOY, S. T. *French Inventions of the Eighteenth Century*. 1952.
MEOLI, U. *Il Pensiero Economico del Condillac*. 1961.
MORINI-COMBY, J. *Mercantilisme et Protectionnisme*. 1930.
PARIS, R. *Histoire du Commerce de Marseille de 1660 à 1789*. 1957.
PETTY, SIR W. *Writings*. 2 vols. Ed. C. H. Hull. 1899.
REDLICH, F. 'Entrepreneurship in the initial stages of industrialisation.' *Explorations in Entrepreneurial History*. 1954.
—— 'Academic education for business.' *Business History Review*. 1957.
SAMUELSSON, K. *Religion and Economic Action*. Trans. G. French. Ed. D. C. Coleman. 1961.
SARRAILH, J. *L'Espagne Eclairée de la Seconde Moitié du XVIIIe siècle*. 1954.
SAVARY, J. *Le Parfait Négociant*. 1675.
SCHMOLLER, G. *The Mercantile System*. 1896.
SCOVILLE, W. C. *The Persecution of the Huguenots and French Economic Development, 1680–1720*. 1960.
SEE, H. *La France Economique et Sociale au XVIIIe siècle*. 1925.
SELLA, D. *Commerci e Industrie a Venezia nel secolo XVII*. 1961.
SMITH, A. *The Wealth of Nations*. 2 vols. Ed. E. Cannan. 1904.
STRAUSS, E. *Sir William Petty*. 1954.
SUPPLE, B. E. *Commercial Crisis and Change in England, 1600–1642*. 1959.
TAWNEY, R. H. *Religion and the Rise of Capitalism*. 1926.
—— *Lionel Cranfield: Business and Politics under James I*. 1958.
THORNTON, A. P. *West India Policy under the Restoration*. 1956.
TUCCI, U. *Lettres d'un Marchand Venitien Andrea Berengo, 1553–1556*. 1957.
TUTTLE, H. *History of Prussia under Frederick the Great*. 2 vols. 1888.
ULLOA, B. *Rétablissement des Manufactures et du Commerce d'Espagne*. 1753.
UZTÁRIZ, G. DE. *The Theory and Practice of Commerce and Maritime Affairs*. Trans. J. Kippax. 1751.
VAUBAN, S. DE. *Le Dixme Royal*. 1707.
VINER, J. 'Power versus plenty.' *World Politics*. 1948.
VRIES, J. DE. *De Economische Achteruitgang der Republiek in de Achttiende Eeuw*. 1959.
WILSON, C. 'Mercantilism: some vicissitudes of an idea.' *Economic History Review*. 1957.
—— *Profit and Power*. 1957.
—— 'Treasure and trade balances.' *Economic History Review*. 1949.

## FOR REFERENCE

*The New Cambridge Modern History* (especially vols. V and VII).
*Encyclopedia of the Social Sciences*. 1930.
*Essays in Economic History*. Ed. E. M. Carus-Wilson. Vol. I. 1954; Vols. II and III. 1962.
*Stockholm, 1960* (Communications and Contributions to the First International Conference on Economic History).

# INDEX

Abel, Wilhelm, 69 n. 374, 394, 406, 414, 425, 428, 452
Académie Royale des Sciences, Paris, 118, 120, 121, 152
Acadie, Compagnie de l', 228
Accademia del Cimento, 118
Achenwall, German statistician, 559
Achilles, Walter, 396 n., 398 n.
Act for Encouragement of Trade, 509
Acts of Trade, 206; *see also* Navigation Acts
Aden, 163, 165, 166
Adriatic as trade artery, 155
Africa
  East Africa: trade, 164; in gold and ivory, 192
  introduction of crops to, 285–6
  North Africa: grain imports, 157; leather exports, 161; war against Christian commerce, 185–6
  South Africa: Dutch in, 198; Portuguese in, 164, 195
  West Africa: slaves from, 203, 204, 205, 308–11; *see also* Slave Coast; trade with Spanish America, 199
  *see also* colonization
Agricola, Georg, 101, 423
agriculture, 142–4
  arable land, cereal production, 414, 419; harvest failures, 75–6, 507
  changing husbandry, 68–9
  crop dispersal: economic effects of, 286–8; overseas, 276, 279–82; intertropical movements, 282–6; into Europe, 276–9
  crop rotation, 143
  crops: cassava, 275, 285; cocoa, 275, 284, 295; coffee, 197, 275, 296–7; fruits, 278, 286; maize, 275, 276–7, 285; potatoes, 275, 278, 286, 292, 299–300; rice, 275, 286, 287; sweet potatoes, 275, 277, 286; sugar—*see* sugar; tea, 284, 297–9; tobacco, 204, 205, 275, 277, 283, 287, 293–5; turnips, 299–300; yams, 285
  fertilizers, 144
  implements, machinery, 143, 292
  livestock: cattle, 281, 282; dogs, 275; goats, 280; guinea-pigs, 279; horses, 279, 282; pigs, 279, 280, 281, 299; rabbits, 280; sheep, 281, 301; turkeys, 279
  livestock movements: intertropical movements, 286; introduced to

agriculture (*cont.*)
  America, 280–2; introduced to Australia, 301; introduced to Europe, 279
  stockraising, 414, 415
  Venetian academy of, 550
Aix-la-Chapelle, Treaty of, 56, 354
Albuquerque, Affonso d', 304–5
Alembert, Jean le Rond d', 121
Alexander VI, 248
Alsace, 43
alum, 161–2
Alva, Duke of, 36
Amboyna, 197, 288, 289, 365, 367–72 *passim*
America
  livestock introduced to, 280–2
  timber supplies, 180
  *see also* New England
American Independence, War of, 273, 294, 298
Amsterdam
  as entrepot, 532; for grain trade, 171, 189
  money market at, 387, 388, 461, 462, 509, 510, 512
Anabaptists, 489
anatomy, 106
Anderssen, Walter, 386
Anglo-Spanish treaty, 1604, 189
Angola, 205, 235, 307, 330, 336, 354
  Company of (French), 354
animals, wild, trade in, 193
Annobon, island of, 291, 336
Antigua, 348
Antilles,
  French in, 228, 250
  Spanish in, 235
  sugar production in, 268
  tobacco production, 205
Antwerp
  as international port, 376
  money in, 448
  population of, 17, 36, 82
  prosperity in sixteenth century, 169
  sack of, 293
Apian, Peter, 110
apprenticeship, 240
Apulia, grain supplies from, 157, 158
Arabs
  as coffee-drinkers, 296
  as traders, 163, 164, 165, 191, 197
  rising against Turks, 166
  North African aggression, 185–6
  and slave trade, 308, 328
Aragon, population, 22, 28, 48

## DATE DUE

| 12/15/89 | | | |
|---|---|---|---|
| | | | |
| | | | |
| | | | |
| | | | |
| | | | |
| | | | |
| | | | |
| | | | |
| | | | |
| | | | |
| | | | |
| | | | |
| | | | |
| | | | |
| GAYLORD | | | PRINTED IN U.S.A. |